EXTENDING PSYCHOLOGICAL FRONTIERS

Selected Works of Leon Festinger

Leon Festinger

EXTENDING PSYCHOLOGICAL FRONTIERS

Selected Works of Leon Festinger

STANLEY SCHACHTER
MICHAEL GAZZANIGA
EDITORS
WITH AN INTRODUCTION BY
HENRI ZUKIER

Russell Sage Foundation   New York

The Russell Sage Foundation

The Russell Sage Foundation, one of the oldest of America's general purpose foundations, was established in 1907 by Mrs. Margaret Olivia Sage for "the improvement of social and living conditions in the United States." The Foundation seeks to fulfill this mandate by fostering the development and dissemination of knowledge about the political, social, and economic problems of America. It conducts research in the social sciences and public policy and publishes books and pamphlets that derive from this research.

The Board of Trustees is responsible for oversight and the general policies of the Foundation, while administrative direction of the program and staff is vested in the President, assisted by the officers and staff. The President bears final responsibility for the decision to publish a manuscript as a Russell Sage Foundation book. In reaching a judgment on the competence, accuracy, and objectivity of each study, the President is advised by the staff and selected expert readers. The conclusions and interpretations in Russell Sage Foundation publications are those of the authors and not of the Foundation, its Trustees, or its staff. Publication by the Foundation, therefore, does not imply endorsement of the contents of the study.

Library of Congress Cataloging-in-Publication Data

Festinger, Leon, 1919–
    Extending psychological frontiers: selected works of Leon Festinger/Stanley Schachter and Michael Gazzaniga, editors; with an introduction by Henri Zukier.
        p.   cm.
    "H. Festinger's bibliography: p.
    Includes bibliographical references (p.   )
    ISBN 0-87154-275-7
    1. Social psychology.   I. Schachter, Stanley, 1922–
II. Gazzaniga, Michael S.   III. Title.
HM251.F39   1989
302—dc20   89-24204
                                                                              CIP

10 9 8 7 6 5 4 3 2 1

Preface

Attempting to pick and choose among Leon Festinger's theoretical writings and research papers for what could be called a Festingerschrift, has been no simple task. Festinger's interests shifted so dramatically and so often during his life that probably no one person is sufficiently expert to be able to select *the* crucial papers during all phases of his career. To make these selections, we have, therefore, relied heavily on the judgment of his colleagues and students at the various stages of his research career.

Schachter was Festinger's student and research assistant during his social communication-social comparison period and takes responsibility for the selection of papers representative of this stage of his career. Dorwin Cartwright, Festinger's colleague at Iowa, M.I.T., and Michigan, was an indispensable kibitzer on the early work with Lewin in the pregroup dynamics days. Elliot Aronson, also a Festinger Ph.D., selected work from the dissonance period. Arien Mack and Mike Gazzaniga are largely responsible for the selection of papers representing Festinger's work in perception. Henri Zukier, a colleague at the New School, contributed an overview and appreciation of Festinger's intellectual and research career. Finally, we are particularly grateful to Nicholas Christenfeld and Barry Rodstein who took on much of the editorial labor of adapting individual papers and chapters to "collection" format.

The rather large section called "Miscellany" is simply an assemblage of everyone's favorite Festinger experiment. Unlike most of his work, these particular experiments are not part of a well-developed theoretical or research structure. Though almost all of these experiments did stimulate a considerable body of research, it wasn't research in which Festinger was involved—mostly, we suspect, because he'd had a new idea which interested him more.

There is one conspicuous omission in this volume. Festinger was a statistician and methodologist who published important work in nonparametric statistics and scaling. We decided not to reprint any of his methodological contributions except for an article on laboratory experimentation (an approach to research in social psychology which he refined to a rigorous art form). We did so partially because of space limitations, but chiefly out of the conviction that Festinger's importance lies in his theories and substantive discoveries. His methodological papers, however, are listed in the complete Festinger bibliography at the end of this volume.

Stanley Schachter
Michael Gazzaniga

Contents

PART C
COGNITIVE DISSONANCE
THEORY AND RESEARCH

PART D
PERCEPTUAL PROCESSES

PART E
THE HUMAN LEGACY

PART F
A MISCELLANY

PART G
BIOGRAPHICAL NOTES

PART H
BIBLIOGRAPHY

Introduction

The decades after the Second World War were an era of uncommon imaginativeness and insight in social psychology, which produced new ways of understanding the social nature of human behavior and transformed social-psychological inquiry into a rigorous intellectual and experimental discipline. Leon Festinger's work includes many landmarks in the history of this transformation and defines the broad contours of the field. Edward Jones, a statesman in social psychology working outside the Festingerian tradition, has articulated the common view: Festinger has been "the dominant figure in social psychology" since Kurt Lewin (Jones, 1985), and "whatever the future holds, the dissonance research 'movement' has been the most important development in social psychology to date" (Jones, 1976). Rarely has the growth of a scientific field been so entwined with the work of one individual.

Festinger pursued his scrutiny of human conduct in a variety of research programs which fundamentally transformed psychological thinking over a period of forty years. This collection encompasses Festinger's classic contributions of enduring influence in social psychology, as well as papers which mark important junctures in the development of his work. Because of the variety of the work, even within a particular period, the collection is not organized in strict chronological order. The thematic arrangement of the writings is more apt to bring forth, across the diversity of subject matters, the tightly and finely wrought mesh of problems and ideas, the new conception of social science inquiry, and the richly imaginative intellectual style, which contribute to the vast import and impact of Festinger's work.

The research in this volume transcends the traditional bounds of the discipline. General problems are pursued in a great variety of particular contexts, as Festinger constantly pushed back the frontiers of the field. In the following pages, one encounters many topics: maze running in rats; the voting behavior of Catholics and Jews in mixed groups; coalition formation in competitive bargaining; the effects of unethical behavior on the people who engage in it; a mathematical model of decision-making; the meaning of minute eye-movements (as recorded by high-technology optical apparatus and computer) for a theory of the conscious experience of perception; the social-psychological implications of the stones and bones found at Near Eastern campsites some 18,000 years old; housing satisfaction at an MIT residential project; and the proselytizing behavior of a cultist group.

The writings in this volume also have permeated the general cultural and scientific sphere—far more than any other line of research in experimental social psychology. The work has been influential in literary theory of fiction; in ethnological studies of modern industry and of percussive noise in ritual; in demographic studies of fertility, marketing research, and philosophical works on justificationism and free will; in histories of ancient Rome, of the American involvement in Vietnam, of Madison's trade negotiations with France in 1811, and of China's cultural revolution; in studies of Karl Marx's social theories, discussions of Supreme Court decisions, economic theories of income redistribution, and the editorial columns of major newspapers.

Although Festinger's ideas eventually captured the educated imagination, many of them initially aroused intense controversy (e.g. Chapanis and Chapanis, 1964; Mowrer, 1963). If the texts now appear prescient, it is because they have come to shape the field. Originally, they oftentimes violated prevailing conventions of thought and technique with propositions such as the following: social influence could best be achieved by changing behavior, rather than attitudes; smaller, rather than larger, rewards or punishment were more effective in persuasion, contrary to common reinforcement principles; the greater the effort the higher the enjoyment of the activity; after a choice or commitment is made, it will typically trigger a reevaluation of the available alternatives; systematic principles of human cognition and behavior also could be derived from rat studies or historical data. The studies in this volume constantly shake old certainties and habits of thought, the many fixtures of the mind noticed only when one stumbles over them while following Festinger's line of argument. The writings arouse the reader from any "dogmatic slumber." Festinger's seemingly counterintuitive but ultimately persuasive propositions afford fresh insights into traditional problems. The insights frequently make our world look strange again, and restore our sense of wonderment, as the familiar reality is reconstructed from novel principles. Van Gogh, in bold strokes, forced us to look at the world in different ways, and led us to discern the flame within the tree. Festinger's work also casts habitual phenomena in a new light. The penetrating originality of the work asserts itself throughout, and in re-reading it one experiences anew, at many turns of the argument, the sense of the unexpected.

At the heart of Festinger's research programs there always are an important idea and a question, which are pursued in their full complexity. In the beginning there is, typically, a riddle, which maps domains of conceptual ignorance. The theory of cognitive dissonance evolved out of Festinger's puzzlement over the rumors that swept neighboring villages following a local earthquake in India. *The Human Legacy* begins with a set of important questions: What were the origins of human societies that today face so many problems? What were the beginnings of our present way of life? Throughout Festinger's work, there is a persistent refusal to understand the seemingly obvious, and a conviction that uncovering the question may indeed be harder than solving it. The opening of *The Human Legacy* (Chapter 18) expresses the spirit of the entire work: "Let us take a look at this curious animal, the modern human being, to ask if we really know much about him or are we simply accustomed to, and adapted to, his peculiarities." (p. IX) Festinger's writings expand at once both our knowledge and our ignorance.

In Festinger's work, questions trigger systematic inquiry and the answers that emerge rarely fail to intrigue in their own right and to pose new problems along the way. The theoretical paper on "Informal Social Communication" (Chapter 5) originates in an applied study of architectural and ecological factors affecting housing satisfaction in two new MIT housing projects (Festinger, Schachter, and Back, 1950). The study employed interviews, sociometric tests, and other standard measures. Festinger and his colleagues, however, became puzzled by a finding in one of the housing projects, which indicated a strong correlation between the degree of friendship in a group of residents and the homogeneity of opinions in the group. This finding, wholly incidental to the purpose of the investigation, converted a prosaic housing study into an initial exploration of social influence processes and led, eventually, to two major theories in social psychology, the theory on pressures toward uniformity in a group and the social comparison theory (Chapter 6).

In the pursuit of the problem, Festinger evolved a new way of theorizing and doing research on complex social phenomena. Kurt Lewin, Festinger's mentor, had emphasized that an understanding of causal relationships could be derived only from the psychological representation of reality in individual consciousness. Such understanding, Lewin argued, required consideration of the interrelatedness of the person and the environment, epitomized in the concept of the "life space." Lewin also developed dynamic concepts which led to important empirical work on issues such as the psychological effects of task interruption, leadership climate, or level of aspiration. Seminal though it was, Lewin's field-theoretical approach remained largely a set of formal abstractions of considerable suggestive value.

Festinger transformed this metatheoretical view of psychology into an experimental approach with a unique combination of methodological rigor, creative power, and critical insight. Although there had been earlier experimental studies in social psychology, Festinger converted the experiment into a powerful scientific instrument with a central role in the search for knowledge. His approach became the major paradigm of the field. In Festinger's use, the psychological experiment was designed not only for testing or verification, it was also a method of discovery. It was science through thinking and imagining, not just through the collection of data. The experiment served as a means of understanding and clarifying conceptual issues and scrutinizing reality.

The experiment thus required the cultivation, in the laboratory, of important real-life situations linked to theory. The studies in this volume all attest to Festinger's talent in bringing "powerful social situations that made big differences" into the laboratory. Experimentation was an art form that required considerable stagecraft. There are many ingenious sets and scripts in the following pages—from the study of "overheard" persuasive communications (Chapter 23) to the central principle of dissonance studies.

Dissonance experiments required a fine balance of experimental influence hardly discernible behind deceptively simple procedures. The experimenter must apply the kinds of pressure that induce participants in the studies to behave in ways they would not ordinarily do and yet to believe they do so of their own volition. A little less pressure, and people might not oblige; a little more, and they might feel obliged, and experience no dissonance. The procedural ingenuity and the conceptual richness of Festinger's experiments have remained unmatched in the history of social psychology. His writings are both the manifesto of experimental social psychology and its most distinguished case-book. The studies have the sustaining force of demonstration: Experimentation in the laboratory can reveal significant aspects of human behavior and can yield new insights into important processes, by systematically interfering with them or manipulating them.

Festinger's pursuit of the problem in its full complexity and the consequent fecundity of his experimental approach stand out against much work that preceded and followed. Scientific psychology has often aimed for conceptual and methodological simplification to meet standards of experimental rigor. Behaviorism, which dominated psychology from the 1930s to the 1950s, insisted that psychology examine only observable phenomena and study the associations between measurable stimuli and overt behavioral responses. This positivistic approach excluded from the purview of psychology any consideration of "mentalistic" concepts—cognitive or affective processes not readily in sight. Behaviorist research thus focused on the effects of reinforcements, which afforded precise experimental manipulations and measurements. The stimulus-response language considerably limited the usefulness of the experimental framework for the description of complex human conduct. From the early studies on level of aspiration and the experiment on differential appetite in the rat, Festinger's work reintroduced the concern with inner experience and with motivational and cognitive dynamics into social psychology. The internal events are explored, not phenomenologically, but through systematic experimentation. The individual is not viewed as a passive processor of stimuli or of information. Needs and aspirations, thinking and behavior of necessity are intertwined; they may, however, not be coordinated to each other, leading to states of tension and conflict. Motivational forces are treated as an integral part of the process: affect does not simply overwhelm or disrupt the "ordinary" course of behavior or thinking, but organizes and redirects behavioral dynamics in predictable ways. The conceptual complexity of the approach also is reflected experimentally. In all the studies, the inner experiences of cognition and affect are linked to action, and the claims of the work are invariably staked on actual behavioral outcomes. Participants in Festinger's studies *are* involved. The arousal of cognitive dissonance, in the experiments, is linked to a behavioral commitment, which carries significant pleasant or unpleasant implications for the individual. More dramatically, the cultists in *When Prophecy Fails* (Chapter 13) gave up their jobs and possessions for a central belief, shortly before it was incontrovertibly discredited.

The insistence on a comprehensive understanding of human conduct is exemplified in the many uses of imprecision in the work. On the one hand, the work is characterized by impressive precision. In the early paper offering a mathematical model of decision-making; in the formal, hypothetico-deductive presentation of the theories of informal social communication and of social comparison processes, reminiscent of the rigorous formulations of behavioristic frameworks; in Festinger's important statistical and methodological contributions, which are not included in this collection (except for Chapter 25). These formalist talents were coupled, however, with creative thinking and with a cultivation of imagination and imprecision in the quest for new discoveries. The theory of cognitive dissonance is presented in a few sentences and in simple, succinct, and sweeping terms. There are hardly any specific definitions or operational principles. This deliberate conceptual vagueness initially provoked considerable criticism. It also produced, it soon became apparent, more important ideas and experimentation than any other theory in social psychology.

Festinger, indeed, had warned repeatedly of "the trap of premature precision." Precision of design and measurement could obscure or kill the basic phenomenon. Exacting methodology could acquire functional autonomy and become its own raison d'être. In the name of cumulative research, available paradigms and means of measurement might dictate the argument and lead it towards unrelieved triviality and tedium. Unlike much behaviorist research, Festinger's work is not driven by a single overarching theory, which seeks different contexts for the exemplification of its basic argument. Nor is the research driven by the available techniques or observations. The initial vagueness of ideas is in deference to the preeminence of the problem, leaving room for conceptual growth. In Festinger's studies, the experimenter and the reader never lose sight of the phenomenon, and only rarely can they anticipate the outcome of the experiment. One usually learns something from a Festinger study, something no one knew before he had done the study.

The conception of the research, at its most serious, springs from considerable intellectual playfulness, even bravura. Often the execution of a study required similar qualities. In its early stages, the theory of cognitive dissonance is put to test by infiltrating, with two colleagues, a close-knit cult communicating with spacemen in flying saucers and preparing for the imminent end of the world. The chapter in this volume (Chapter 13) depicts the charged atmosphere in the cult. The book itself (Festinger, 1957; and see Festinger, 1987) also evokes the lot of the investigators: how they kept a continuous vigil at the home of the leader during the final days; how they would dash off to the toilet to take notes in private, or to a nearby hotel room to dictate observations; or how they were practicing standard evacuation procedures to board the saucer that would rescue the group of elects.

In building his arguments on the interaction between the laboratory and wider natural contexts, Festinger constantly expanded the range of acceptable evidence. He brought into the laboratory many phenomena which did not seem amenable to experimental analysis; conversely, he never hesitated to leave the safety of the laboratory or the familiarity of previous research when other, unconventional contexts appeared theoretically promising for the understanding of functional relationships or push the problem a bit further. In one research program, Festinger explored the minute processes of visual perception. Then, in *The Human Legacy* and related work (Chapters 18, 19), paleontological and archaeological data are brought to bear on the same fundamental questions about human nature and social organization that animate the experimental work. The analysis of the prehistoric record is made to yield evidence, more sparse and limited, but no less telling than data from an M.I.T. housing project, a cultist group, or a vision experiment. The many implications of the work for current psychological theory readily impose themselves on the reader. The prehistoric work demonstrates in yet another way that systematic psychology is not the sole province of the laboratory, nor is it spontaneously generated by the experimental design. Psychology, rather, entails an insistent scrutiny of reality, contemporary or historical, and a consequentiality of thought, which yielded, in Festinger's work, cumulative insights and a global view of human conduct unrivaled in the history of social psychology. The work is a striking realizatin of the scientific ideal set forth by Kant (1766/1968, Part 2, Chapter 3): "To pursue every inclination of our curiosity and to set no other limits to our passion for knowledge than the limits of our ability indeed befits scholarship. But it requires true wisdom to choose, among the countless problems which present themselves, those whose solution is important to humanity."

A common theme underlies many of Festinger's research programs. The inquiry into the dynamics of human behavior focuses on the individual change that follows conflict or social influence. The studies are experiments in calculated tension between alternatives or contrary forces, which impel a change in thinking, feeling, or behavior in foreseeable ways. The tension may arise from facing competing alternatives: in the early theory of decision-making, the individual is confronting such choice, and so are the animals in the study on differential appetite in the rat. In subsequent research, the tension was heightened and its source was located within the individual. In the theories on level of aspiration, informal social communication, or social comparison, the tension develops from the divergence between personal characteristics and external stipulations; between an individual's aspiration level for performance and the known performance of other individuals; between an individual's opinions or abilities and the standards of significant others. Finally, in dissonance theory, the tension is wholly internal: the individual holds simultaneously two beliefs which are psychologically inconsistent.

The 1942 study on differential appetite in the rat (Chapter 20), Festinger's M.A. thesis at the University of Iowa, already contained the seeds of the cognitive perspective of his work. Festinger's entire research challenged, then marked the end of the preeminence of reinforcement theory in social psychology. Dissonance theory, for instance, demonstrated that small reinforcements were more effective, in certain circumstances, than large reinforcements, in promoting behavioral change, and that the effects reflected cognitive processes. Festinger's animal studies pressed the critique of S-R theory in behaviorism's own traditional domain and with its distinctive methodology. The differential appetite study suggested that the rats' behavior was linked to subjective considerations and to standards rooted in the animals' prior personal history. The study anticipated the concept of "relative deprivation," which would subsequently gain wide sociological currency (e.g. Stouffer et al., 1949; Merton and Kitt, 1950; Runciman, 1966). Stouffer and his colleagues described a number of cases in which the soldiers' satisfaction with army life did not reflect their objective well-being in the service; individual satisfaction was contingent, instead, on subjective standards on the comparison of one's condition with the lot of other pertinent groups of soldiers. The animal learning studies with Lawrence presented in ·this volume (Chapter 11) extend the reversal of behaviorist theory and techniques and propose that rats have cognitions, and indeed may reduce dissonance the way humans do. The studies challenged classic behavioral concepts by offering dissonance accounts for the maintenance of behavior patterns and resistance to extinction.

The studies on level of aspiration in this volume (Chapters 1, 2, 3), which also antedate "The American Soldier," further explore the inherent relativity of judgments. The theory proposes that an individual's sense of success or failure on a task is not simply influenced by absolute performance but by the relation of performance to level of aspiration. The goals which the individual seeks to attain are set, in turn, as a function of their desirability and of the subjective probability of success. Individual performance thus is influenced by the person's own goals and by the expectations or performance of other pertinent people. Classic sociological theory had focused on the influences of groups upon their members, until reference group theory drew attention, in the sixties, to the influence of groups to which the individual does not actually belong (see Merton, 1968). The chapter in this volume with K. Lewin and other colleagues (Chapter 3) anticipates such concerns and considers, analytically and empirically, the determinants of the selection of various groups of reference, including nonmembership groups.

The theory of informal social communication (Chapter 5) offered an analysis of pressures towards uniformity in a group, which has remained the prevalent perspective on processes of conformity. The theory conceptualizes both individuals and small groups as systems in tension. Differences of opinion *between* individual members of a group threaten the equilibrium of the group and generate pressures to make members conform in ideas or behavior. The theory identifies two major sources of pressure. One class of reasons for conformity are "group locomotion" reasons—the desire for appreciation by the group or for gratifications associated with the group, or the need to work jointly toward the achievement of some group goal. Alternatively, conformity may spring from "social reality" reasons. Individuals are motivated to assess the correctness of their opinions, and when physical, objective means of validation are not available, they rely on the consensus of other people for confirmation of their beliefs. The distinction between the two kinds of motives for conformity recurs, in different guises, in most studies of social influence. Other studies of conformity had demonstrated the existence of the one or another kind of pressure toward conformity, but did not provide a theoretical understanding of the dynamics involved. For instance, Sherif's (1936) studies of the autokinetic effect illustrated the informational conformity of individual judgments in a highly ambiguous context. In contrast, Asch (1951) studied "group acceptance" motives for conformity, when unambiguous individual perceptions were called into question by a discrepant social consensus. It was Festinger, however, who developed the classic theoretical analysis of the processes of social influence evident in these and other studies of conformity.

Pressures towards uniformity often entail a change in patterns of group communication with the individual who holds a discrepant opinion. This process is at the center of another major research tradition in social psychology, concerned with attitude change through persuasive communication. The studies on this topic which are included in this volume (Chapters 22, 23, 24) reflect this approach to social influence, in which attempts at attitude change are based on a direct confrontation with the discrepant attitude or behavior.

The theory of social comparison processes (Chapter 6), published in 1954, developed the earlier ideas about "social reality" and self-evaluation into a seminal framework which is still influential today (e.g. Darley and Goethals, 1980; Rofe, 1984; Suls and Miller, 1977). The framework combined the notion of judgmental relativity developed in the studies of level of aspiration, with the processes of social influence and communication into a general theory of self-other comparisons in the assessment of one's opinions and abilities. Social theorists such as Cooley (1902) and Mead (1934) had previously emphasized the social influences on the self-concept. Social comparison theory for the first time explicated the dynamics of such influence, which were rooted in the inevitable discrepancies between the individual's own opinions and abilities and those of other people chosen for comparison. The theory specifies the antecedents of comparison; the criteria for the choice of others for reference; and the consequences of comparison, and of resultant discrepancies in a group with respect to opinions or abilities. The detailed arguments have found echoes in the subsequent elaborations of reference group theory. Within psychology, the idea of social evaluation exercised considerable influence. Schachter's (1959) classic work on the psychology of affiliation drew on the theories of social comparison and of pressures towards uniformity, in exploring the motives for social affiliation and, particularly, the relationship between anxiety and affiliation. Schachter's theory of emotion (Schachter, 1964) demonstrated the implication of social comparison processes in emotional experience and in the identification of one's emotional states. Festinger's theory of social comparison and Schachter's theory of emotional experience were, in turn, combined with Heider's (1958) writings about person perception in an influential paper by Kelley (1967), which marked the beginning of the attributional perspective in social psychology.

Social comparison also played a role in work on equity theory (e.g. Austin, 1977), on social interaction (e.g. Thibaut and Kelley, 1959), on modeling (e.g. Berger, 1977), and on many other issues.

Social comparison examined how the individual incorporated and adapted to the standards of actual or imagined others. In contrast, cognitive dissonance theory considers pressures from within, as the individual confronts conflicts pitting, at times, his actual self against his imagined self. The theory of cognitive dissonance, first advanced in 1957, integrates experimental work, field observations, and formal arguments across many different subject matters. The simple and elegant propositions mark a profound and lasting departure from many commonplaces in psychology.

Traditional accounts of decision-making depict a deliberative process, in which the careful consideration and weighing of the reasons for and against available alternatives leads to an informed choice. Behavior directly executes individual intentions and goals, and the weight ultimately assigned to the various options can be inferred from the chosen course of action. Indeed, rationality is typically construed as purposive behavior oriented toward the alternative that emerged from the deliberations with the greatest weight attached to it. In consequence, all attempts at attitude or behavior change are directed at the deliberative process, prior to the actual decision. Such a conception also underlies, for example, the research on persuasive communication. Dissonance theory argued that a decision does not simply reveal the prior role of various considerations; instead, decision-making is a self-constructing process, in which the choice of a particular alternative alters prospectively the relative influence of the competing considerations. A decision or choice reinforces the appeal of the selected alternative, which becomes, after the choice, the individual's strongest preference, even if it did not carry such determining weight at the time of the decision. A process of self-justification changes the individual's preferences after the choice, and then influences future decisions. Dissonance theory thus starts where other theories left off: after the decision or the commitment have been made.

Dissonance also reverses the traditional relationship between attitude and behavior: in dissonance studies influence never is directed at the early, deliberative stages of the unfolding behavior, nor is it openly oriented to the behavior itself. Dissonance interventions modify the behavior in subtle ways, and thereby bring about a change in the antecedent attitude. This counterintuitive argument soon demonstrated its considerable power: dissonance studies, such as the ones represented in this volume (see Chapters 11, 12, 13, 14), were alone able to bring about profound and lasting behavioral change. Conceptually and experimentally, dissonance theory has been social psychology's most notable achievement.

The research program in visual perception marks Festinger's intellectual turn to a very different perspective in his exploration of basic psychological processes. Few others, such as Francis Crick, the biophysicist who helped unravel the molecular structure of DNA, ever undertook such a radical move into an entirely new and highly technical field. The visual system, Festinger argued, could provide insights into the workings of the central nervous system and into the nature of consciousness. Indeed, according to the efferent model of perception, which Festinger explores, visual experience is not at all a simple and straightforward process. The visual system is an unusual system in that it does not obtain information about eye position or eye movements from feedback from the extraocular muscles that move the eyes (inflow information). Instead, the visual system only gets knowledge about the position of the eye by monitoring the efferent (outflow) commands of the central nervous system to the eye muscles, which tell the eye where to go. This output information, disentangled from any sensory input, could afford a glimpse of the nature of consciousness. The efferent readiness theory presented in this collection (Chapter 15) extends earlier arguments of Wundt and J. G. Taylor. The theory suggests that perception is learned and consists of sets of acquired responses (such as eye movements) to visual input. The incoming stimulation arouses a learned program that controls a pattern of eye movements. Perception does not require that the eye movements *actually* be executed, and the activation of the preprogramed readiness to respond is sufficient to determine the conscious experience of perception.

Visual experience thus depends on several kinds of knowledge, which are not always all available or coordinated. Veridical perception of a moving target also requires the correct combination of accurate outflow information with inflow information about the movement of the target on the retina. Festinger's approach to vision, like his earlier work, takes advantage, in some studies, of the lack of coordination or incompatibility of available information, to gain important psychological insights. In the paper with Burnham and others (Chapter 15), the theory of efferent readiness is tested by asking subjects to wear prism spectacles which cause straight lines to appear curved, and to make arm movements corresponding to the objective contour of the lines while viewing them through the prisms. The study with Easton (Chapter 16) explores a perceptual distortion, the Fujii illusion, which is attributed to a divergence between the oculomotor commands issued to the eyes and the actual behavior of the eyes. A target that actually moves with uniform speed in a square path will be perceived, instead, to follow a pincushion-like path. The illusion is linked to the fact that the eye is physically unable to suddenly turn at the corners of the square, in spite of instructions to do so by the central nervous system. Thus, the retinal information about the motion of the target differs from the reported visual perception, and the actual directions of the eye movements probably differ from what the eye was instructed to do.

The research on visual perception used sophisticated computations of minute phenomena to explore individual processes. In the historical investigations, Festinger again boldly shifts field and focus, to examine large-scale phenomena and an elementary data base. In *The Human Legacy* and related work (Chapters 18, 19), Festinger uses bones, tools, and other archaeological evidence with the virtuosity of an expert sleuth to reconstruct patterns of prehistoric life. As in the experimental work, Festinger focuses on the dynamics of change. He examines the transition to modern human society, through issues such as the origins of the sedentary way of life, the beginnings of religious belief systems, of war and slavery, and the emergence of large and stratified societies. Festinger's last, unfinished work carried the exploration forward into the Middle Ages. In this work, the contrasts between the Byzantine and Western societies and the profound technological and social changes in the West afforded the riddle and the road toward the understanding of people and society.

This collection of writings thus offers a privileged window onto an extraordinarily varied and enriching intellectual exploration. One can delight, in the following pages, in the many small gems or in the sweep of the larger canvas. The selection underscores Festinger's place as a towering figure in contemporary social science and as one of its foremost adventurers of the mind. The work has transformed, forever, the ways of doing social science and of thinking about people. It expands, immeasurably and enduringly, the scope of our understanding and experience.

Henri Zukier

Author's Note: I am grateful to Stanley Schachter for generous criticisms and comments.

References

ASCH, S. E. (1951) Effects of group pressure upon the modification and distortion of judgment. In H. Gerskow (Ed) *Groups, leadership and men.* Pittsburgh: Carnegie Press, 177–190.

AUSTIN, W. (1977) Equity theory and social comparison processes. In J. M. Suls and R. L. Miller (Eds) *Social comparison processes.* Washington: Hemisphere Publishing.

BERGER, S. M. (1977) Social comparison, modeling and perseverance. In J. M. Suls and R. L. Miller (Eds) *Social comparison processes.* Washington: Hemisphere Publishing.

CHAPANIS, N. P. and CHAPANIS, A. (1964) Cognitive dissonance. *Psychological Bulletin* 61, 1–22.

COOLEY, C. H. (1902) *Human nature and social order.* New York: Scribner.

DARLEY, J. M. and GOETHALS, G. R. (1980) A naive psychological analysis of the causes of ability-linked performances. In L. Berkowitz (Ed) *Advances in experimental social psychology.* Vol. 13. New York: Academic Press.

FESTINGER, L., SCHACHTER, S., and BACK, K. (1950) *Social pressures in informal groups: A study of human factors in housing.* New York: Harper.

FESTINGER, L. (1987) A personal memory. In N. E. Grunberg, R. E. Nisbett, J. Rodin, and J. E. Singer (Eds) *A distinctive approach to psychological research. The influence of Stanley Schachter.* Hillsdale, New Jersey: Erlbaum.

HEIDER, F. (1958) *The psychology of interpersonal relations.* New York: Wiley.

JONES, E. E. (1976) Preface. In J. W. Brehm, and A. R. Cohen (Eds) *Explorations in cognitive dissonance.* New York: Wiley.

———. (1985) Major developments in social psychology during the past five decades. In G. Lindzey and E. Aronson (Eds) *Handbook of social psychology.* New York: Random House.

KANT I. (1766/1968) Träume eines Geistersehers. In Kants Werke. (Ausgabe der Preussischen. Akademie der Wissenschaften.), Band II, Berlin: Walter de Gruyer & Co.

KELLEY, H. H. (1967) Attribution theory in social psychology. In D. Levine (Ed) *Nebraska symposium on motivation.* Lincoln: University of Nebraska Press.

MEAD, G. H. (1934) *Mind, self and society.* Chicago: University of Chicago Press.

MERTON, R. K. and KITT, A. S. (1950) Contributions to the theory of reference group behavior. In R. K. Merton and P. F. Lazarsfeld (Eds) *Continuities in social research.* Glencoe, Illinois: Free Press.

MERTON, R. K. (1968) *Social theory and social structure.* Glencoe, Illinois: Free Press.

MOWRER, O. H. (1963) Cognitive dissonance or counterconditioning? A reappraisal of certain behavior "paradoxes." *Psychological Record* 13, 197–211.

ROFE, Y. (1984) Stress and affiliation: activity theory. *Psychological Review* 91, 235–250.

RUNCIMAN, W. G. (1966) *Relative deprivation and social justice: A study of attitudes to social inequality in twentieth century England.* Berkeley: University of California Press.

SCHACHTER, S. (1959) *The psychology of affiliation.* Stanford, California: Stanford University Press.

————. (1964) The interaction of cognitive and physiological determinants of emotional state. In L. Berkowitz (Ed) *Advances in experimental social psychology.* Vol. 1. New York: Academic Press.

SHERIF, M. (1936) *The psychology of social norms.* New York: Harper.

STOUFFER, S. A., SUCHMAN, E. A., DEVINNEY, L. C., STAR, S. A., and WILLIAMS, R. M., Jr. (1949) *The American soldier (Vol. 1): Adjustments during army life;* STOUFFER, S. A., LUMSDAINE, A. A., LUMSDAINE, M. H., WILLIAMS, R. M., Jr., SMITH, M. B., JANIS, I. L., STAR, S. A., and COTTRELL, L. S., Jr. (1949). *The American soldier (Vol. 2): Combat and its aftermath.* Princeton, New Jersey: Princeton University Press.

SULS, J. M. and MILLER, R. L. (Eds) (1977) *Social comparison processes: Theoretical and empirical perspectives.* Washington, D.C.: Hemisphere Publishing.

THIBAUT, J. W. and KELLEY, H. H. (1959) *The social psychology of groups.* New York: Wiley.

PART
A
INDIVIDUAL PSYCHOLOGY

1

Wish, Expectation, and Group Standards as Factors Influencing Level of Aspiration

Previous experiments have demonstrated that the level of aspiration is determined by a manifold of factors. Some of these factors are: effects of success and failure (Gardner, 3; Sears, 7); certain personality variables (Escalona, 2; Gould and Kaplan, 4); and previous successes of the individual (Sears, 7). There are also factors in the social environment of the individual which affect his level of aspiration. Evidence of this has been found by Chapman and Volkmann (1) and by Hertzman and Festinger (5). From these studies we find that in a social situation the performance of others in the group exerts a strong influence on the level of aspiration.

Problem

The present experiment is oriented toward the problem of inducing changes in the aspiration level by making known to the subjects the performance of other individuals. The problem is specifically, first, how will the level of aspiration be affected if the individual knows that he is scoring above or below others, and, secondly, will the status of these other individuals be important in influencing his level of aspiration?

SOURCE: Festinger, L. *J. abnorm. soc. Psychol.*, 1942, 37, 184–200.

Procedure

Two experiments were conducted, for each of which 40 subjects, all undergraduates of the University of Iowa, were used. Eighty-six per cent of the subjects were sophomores and juniors. The mean age of the subjects was 20.6 years.

Materials

Two tasks were used in each experiment: (a) synonym tests, 15 lists of 24 words each for which the subjects were to supply synonyms beginning with the letter A or B or C, in which one and one-half minutes were allowed for the completion of each list; and (b) information tests, 17 lists of 22 questions each, in which most of the questions required a one-word answer, and two minutes were allowed for the completion of each list. Both tasks are identical with the ones used and described by Hertzman and Festinger (5). One synonym list and one information list were used as practice lists. Each other list was treated as a separate trial.

Conduct of the Experiment

Both experiments were divided into two sessions. In the first session the practice and the first eight information lists were given the subject to be followed by the practice and the first seven synonym lists. The second session took place about a week after the first one. In the second session the subject was retested with the last eight information tests and the last seven synonym tests. In both sessions, after each list, with the exception of the practice list, the subject was told his score and, in Experiment I, was asked, "What do you think you will get next time, that is, what score do you expect to get on the next test?" In Experiment II they were asked, "What score would you like to get next time, that is, what do you intend to get on the next test?" This was the only difference between the two experiments.

Experimental Variables

The experimental variables were introduced in the second session. In addition to being told his score after each trial, the subject was also told the average performance and average estimate of a fictitious group of 50 subjects before making his own estimate for the subsequent trial. The information concerning the group scores was adapted to each individual.

Fifteen subjects were made to score below the fictitious group. Fifteen others were made to score above it. The difference between the individual's performance and the performance of the fictitious group was always about two points for each subject. When the individual was made to score below the group, the level of aspiration of the group was reported to have been about two points higher than their performance level. When the individual was told he was scoring above the group, the group estimates were reported to be about two points below their performance level.

The nature of the group to which the subjects were compared was also varied. Ten subjects were told that the group was made up of high-school students, ten subjects were told that the group consisted of college students in their own year, and the remaining ten were told that the group was made up of graduate students. In each of these comparisons, five subjects were made to score above the group and five to score below it. Ten subjects were given no more information in the second session than in the first session; that is, the experimental variables were omitted on this group. These served as a control group.

Scores Obtained

For each subject the average performance, average aspiration, and average discrepancy score were obtained for the synonym and information tests in both sessions. The average discrepancy score was the average difference between the performance and the estimate for the next trial. In addition, the difference between the average discrepancy score in the first session and the average discrepancy score in the second session for the same subject was calculated for each test. This measure was called the change score. It was given a positive sign if the change was in the upward direction and was given a negative sign if the change was in the downward direction.

Interview

At the end of the second session an interview lasting about an hour was given to each subject. This interview attempted to cover most of the relevant points influencing the subjects' estimates and the changes in the estimates when these occurred.

Experiment I

Results

The changes in the discrepancy score from session I (non-social situation) to session II (social situation) for each group in the experiment are shown in Table 1.1. The second and third columns give the mean discrepancy score for each group in the first and second sessions. The fourth column gives the change scores, i.e., the changes in descrepancy scores from the first to the second session. The fifth and sixth columns give the value of "*t*" for these changes and the level of significance for these "*t*" tests respectively. Throughout the table the hypothesis being tested by the "*t*" test is that the change score is not significantly greater than zero.

The results presented in this table may be summarized as follows: When the individuals are placed above a group, the discrepancy score changes downward; if the subjects are placed below a group, the discrepancy score changes upward. This holds for all the comparison groups. These changes are significant at the 1-per-cent level in four out of six cases.

It may be noticed from column two that the "above" groups have

Table 1.1 Change in Discrepancy Score from Session I to Session II (Experiment I)

Comparison Groups	Mean Perf. in Sess. I*	Mean Disc. Score Sess. I	Mean Disc. Score Sess. II	Mean Change Score	Value of "*t*"	Level of Sig. (Percentage)
Above H.S.	6.08	27	−.06	−.33	1.78	11
Below H.S.	6.57	−.53	1.23	1.77	5.07	1
Above coll.	7.68	.04	−1.34	−1.38	6.67	1
Below coll.	6.75	−.24	.77	1.01	4.53	1
Above grad.	6.52	1.19	−.83	−2.02	6.28	1
Below grad.	7.45	−1.65	−1.01	.64	1.31	25
Control high	6.48	.57	.24	−.33	1.85	10
Control low	6.97	−.46	−.27	.19	.98	45

All "*t*" tests beyond the 1-per-cent level of significance are simply marked 1 per cent. All the "*t*" tests in the above table are for 9 degrees of freedom, and a value of 3.25 is necessary for significance at the 1-per-cent level. All those which do not reach the 5-per-cent level are not regarded as significant.
*The performance in session II was experimentally kept at approximately the same level as in session I.

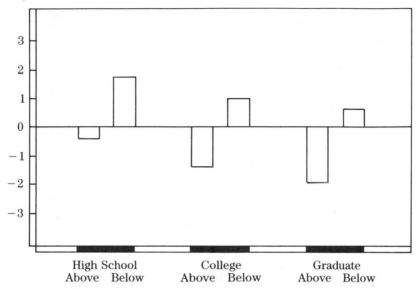

Figure 1.1   Changes in discrepancy scores in Experiment I.

higher mean discrepancy scores in session I than do the "below" groups. The question arises as to whether this is an important factor in observed changes in discrepancy score. To help answer this question the control group was split into a high group (high in terms of the discrepancy score in the first session) and a low group. Neither of the control groups shows any significant change in its discrepancy scores. Consequently, the original height of the discrepancy does not in itself determine the change or nature of the change.

In Figure 1.1 the change scores for these experimental groups have been graphically represented. The control group has been omitted from this figure because their changes are consistently insignificant. Several trends and comparisons which are not readily discenible in Table 1.1 become apparent as we examine the bar graph. A relationshop exists between the magnitude of the change scores and the status of the group with which the subjects were compared. The magnitude of the average change score, when the shifts are downward, increases as we go from a high-school group comparison to a graduate group comparison. For the upward changes there is an equally consistent trend. Here the magnitude of the changes decreases as we go from a high-school group comparison to a graduate-student group comparison.

Table 1.2   Analysis of Variance of Groups by Positions on Absolute Changes in Discrepancy Scores (Experiment I)

	H.S.	Coll.	Grad.	Total	Mean
Above	.33	1.37	2.02	37.23	1.24
Below	1.76	1.01	.64	34.13	1.14
Total	20.92	23.85	26.59	GT = 71.36	
Mean	1.05	1.19	1.33	GM = 1.19	

GT × GM = 84.92

	SS	df	V
Between positions	.20	1	.20
Between groups	.83	2	.41
Remainders	20.26	2	10.13
Between cells	21.28	5	
Within cells	52.84	54	.98
Total	74.12	59	

$$\frac{\text{Remainder variance}}{\text{Within-cells variance}} = \frac{10.13}{.98} = 10.34, \text{ for 2 and 54 degrees of freedom,} \\ \text{significant at 1-per-cent level}$$

The between-positions variance and the between-groups variance are not significant.

The significance of the comparisons observed in Figure 1.1 may be tested by the method of analysis of variance (Lindquist, 6). In Table 1.2 an analysis of variance on these data is presented. The between-position variance is not significant, which means that the amount of change is the same whether the subjects are placed above or below a group. The between-groups variance is not significant, which means that the amount of change is the same for each comparison group if we lump the "above" and "below" categories. The remainder or interaction variance, however, is significant. This means that the above and below categories act differentially on the different comparison groups. The interaction variance is clearly due to the increasing and decreasing trends which we noticed in Figure 1.1. Since the interaction variance is significant we may conclude that these are significant trends. The higher the status of the group the more influence it has if one is scoring above it and the less its influence if one is scoring below it . This generalization can, of course, be made only within the limits of the range of status in the experiment. It may very well be that beyond this range, that is, comparison with a group "too far" above or "too far" below the individual, different results will appear.

Interview Data

The interviews were analyzed in three ways; first, the original meaning of the estimate and how it changed in the second session; secondly, the reaction of the subject to the scores and estimates of the group and to his position in relation to the group; and, thirdly, feelings of success and failure in the first and second sessions.

The Meaning of the Estimate

The first analysis tells us whether the observed change in discrepancy score represented changes in the meaning of the estimate. Of the five subjects in the "above high-school" group, four of the subjects did not report any change in the meaning of the estimate. An example is:

> (First session) My estimate was made on the basis of what I had scored before. I tried to hit an average and tried to make it an impartial estimate. (Placed above high-school group.) I thought I should do a bit better than the high-school group and so I estimated one or two points above their performance. The estimate meant about the same as it did last week.

The one subject who did not follow this pattern did actually change his estimate downward and reported:

> (First session) The estimate was what I wanted to get on the next test. The estimate represented my idea of what a good score would be. (Placed above high-school group.) The estimate today was what I thought I would get. There was less striving today than last week because I felt a certain measure of satisfaction in being above the high-school group.

In the "below high-school" group all five of the subjects reported a change of the following type in the meaning of the estimate:

> (First session) My estimate was what I thought I ought to be able to get. (Placed below high-school group.) Today I was determined to do better, and I think my estimates went up a little because I was trying harder today. The estimates today were a more definite goal.

In the "above college" group all of the subjects reported shifts in the meaning of their estimates to their being less of a goal in the second session than they had been in the first. Examples are:

(First session) I kept my estimates above my scores. The estimate was a goal to reach. (Placed above college group.) Today my own scores didn't enter into my estimates. I didn't try to do better than last week. My goal today was simply to stay above the group.

(First session) I based the estimates on my previous scores and tried to keep them a little above the average. (Placed above college group.) My estimates today were a minimum and I actually expected to do better than my estimates.

For the "below college" group three subjects reported such shifts in the meaning of their estimates as would be expected to lead to a higher discrepancy score, while two reported no change in meaning. One of these latter two did actually shift his discrepancy score appreciably upward. No more examples of these changes in meaning are given since those already presented are quite representative.

For the "above graduate-student" group all the subjects reported changes in the meaning of the estimates which indicated a downward direction.

For the "below graduate-student" group all the subjects retained essentially the same meaning in their estimates from the first to the second situation.

From this we can see that the observed shifts in discrepancy scores were accompanied by real changes in the meaning of the situation for the subject.

The Reaction of the Subject to His Position Relative to the Group

The second item in the interview analysis is a determination of the factors in the situation which influenced the subjects most. All the subjects who reported that the group to which they were compared did influence them reported that the main influence was the group scores and the relation between these and their own scores. Very few individuals admitted being influenced by the estimates of the group, but when such influence was reported it was in the nature of a tendency to conform to the group way of estimating.

The amount of influence which the group had upon the individual as reported in the interviews would probably have much to do with the magnitude of the change in discrepancy score. Statements of each subject from the interviews were rated separately by three persons on a scale from 0 to 10, where 0 represented no influence of the group at all, and 10 represented a maximum amount of influence. Examples of statements getting a rating of 10 are:

> I thought I should be able to do about two better than the group. My own performance didn't enter into my estimates at all. I felt bad or good about my scores only in relation to the scores of the group. The low estimates of the group helped me to lower my estimates.

> The fact that I was below the group made me raise my estimates up between my own performance and the scores of the group. I wanted to reach the group. The group overestimation made it easy for me to raise my estimates. The fact that the group never reached their estimates rather justifies my overestimation.

Some examples of statements receiving a rating of 0 are:

> The scores and estimates of the group had nothing to do with my estimates because the group didn't mean a thing to me.

> The estimates meant absolutely nothing to me today, and the group had no influence on them. My estimates were completely divorced from everything but my own scores.

Some examples of statements lying between these extremes are:

> I didn't think I was scoring as much above the high-school students as I should be, and so I put my estimates two or three points above their scores. The underestimation of the group didn't influence me.

> I based my estimates partly on my own scores and partly on the group averages. I felt pretty good about being above the group. The fact that the group estimated pretty low didn't mean much to me.

Intercorrelations between the ratings of the three different raters were calculated for the purposes of estimating reliability. The three correlations are: .81, .92, and .83. The ratings of the three persons on each subject were averaged to the nearest whole number to get the final rating.

The correlation between these ratings of the extent of group influence and the amount of change in discrepancy score from the first to the second situation is .76. The amount of group pressure felt by the subject seems to have an appreciable relation to the degree to which his discrepancy score changes.

Feelings of Success and Failure
The third item of analysis involves feelings of success and failure in the first and second sessions. The changes in these feelings from the first to the second session might also have some relation to the amount of change in the discrepancy score. The total interviews were rated for success and failure feelings in session I and then again for session II by the same three persons. The ratings for both sessions were done on a scale from 5 (representing an extreme amount of success feelings) to −5 (representing an extreme amount of failure feelings); 0 represented rather neutral feelings. The intercorrelations for the three raters on session I are: .93, .94, and .94. For session II these correlations are: .93, .89, and .86. The three ratings were again averaged to give the final rating for each subject. The absolute difference between the ratings in session I and session II for each subject was then calculated. These differences were correlated with the absolute change in discrepancy score. The correlation is .17, indicating that in this specific setting there is little or no relationship between amount of change in feelings of success and failure and amount of change in discrepancy score.

Experiment II

Results

We now turn to Experiment II, where the subjects were asked to state what score they would like to get, as contrasted with the first experiment where they were asked what they expected to get.

Table 1.3 shows the discrepancy scores of the various groups and the changes from the first to the second session. The fourth column gives these change scores (the difference between column two and column three). The fifth and sixth columns give the values of "*t*" and their levels of significance respectively. The hypothesis being tested in each case is that the change is not significantly greater than zero. The results of this table may be summarized thus: When the subject is placed above a group the discrepancy score changes downward; when he is placed below a group the discrepancy score changes upward, with the exception of the placement below a graduate group, which results in a downward change of the discrepancy score. In five of the six cases the changes are significant at the 1-per-cent level.

As in Part I and for the same reason, the control group has been split into a high and a low group on the basis of its discrepancy scores in the

Table 1.3   Change in Discrepancy Score from Session I to Session II (Experiment II)

Comparison Groups	Mean Perf. in Sess. I	Mean Disc. Score Sess. I	Mean Disc. Score Sess. II	Mean Change Score	Value of "*t*"	Level of Sig. (Percentage)
Above H.S.	6.84	3.03	.35	− 2.67	3.66	1
Below H.S.	5.54	.48	1.01	.53	2.01	9
Above coll.	7.53	2.32	− .81	− 3.13	9.36	1
Below coll.	6.34	− .06	1.08	1.15	4.16	1
Above grad.	6.95	3.18	− .43	− 3.60	4.77	1
Below grad.	6.33	2.63	1.12	− 1.46	3.59	1
Control high	6.73	4.12	3.61	− .51	2.06	9
Control low	7.23	1.86	1.78	.07	.32	75

All "*t*" tests beyond the 1-per-cent level of significance are simply marked 1 per cent. All the "*t*" tests in the above table are for 9 degrees of freedom, and a value of 3.25 is necessary for significance at the 1-per-cent level. All those which do not reach the 5-per-cent level are not regarded as significant.

first session. Again neither of the control groups shows any significant change in the discrepancy score.

In Figure 1.2 the change scores from Table 1.3 have been graphically represented. The control groups have been omitted from this figure since they do not change significantly. The most striking thing about the graph is that the changes which occur in a downward direction are of much greater magnitude than those in an upward direction. It also seems that the changes in discrepancy score for both the above and below groups increase in magnitude as we go from the high-school to the graduate-student group comparison.

In Table 1.4 an analysis of variance testing the significance of these observations is presented. The between-positions variance is significant beyond the 1-per-cent level, which means that those individuals placed above a group changed their discrepancy scores to a significantly greater extent than did those who were placed below a group. The between-groups variance is significant at the 20-per-cent level of confidence. This test, although not significant, suggests that there may be a relationship between the status of the comparison group and the extent of the change in the discrepancy score induced by it, the high-school group, with the lowest status, inducing the least change and the graduate-student group, with the highest status, inducing the most change. The interaction variance is not significant.

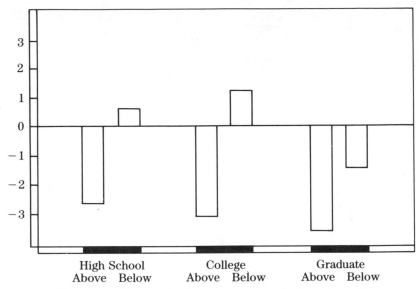

Figure 1.2 *Changes in discrepancy scores in Experiment II.*

Interview Data

The interviews were analyzed in the same manner as in Experiment I.

The Meaning of the Estimate

Four of the five subjects who were placed above a high-school group reported that their estimates changed from representing a goal in the first session to a rather neutral estimate in the second session. The following report is typical:

> (First session) The estimate was what I thought I ought to get and I was trying hard to reach the estimate I set for myself. (Placed above a high-school group.) The estimates today were just a method of competing with the high-school group. I wasn't trying for a high goal today at all.

The subject who did not follow this pattern reported his estimate as meaning the same in both sessions. This subject's discrepancy score did not change appreciably.

Three of the five subjects who were placed below a high-school group reported no change in the meaning of their estimates. Two of the

Table 1.4   Analysis of Variance of Groups by Positions on Absolute Changes in Discrepancy Score (Experiment II)

	H.S.	Coll.	Grad.	Total	Mean
Above	2.67	3.13	3.60	94.08	3.14
Below	.33	1.15	1.46	31.31	1.04
Total	32.02	42.81	50.56	GT = 125.39	
Mean	1.60	2.14	2.52	GM = 2.09	

$$GT \times GM = 262.07$$

	SS	df	V
Between positions	65.68	1	65.68
Between groups	8.69	2	4.35
Remainder	.06	2	.03
Between cells	74.43	5	
Within cells	136.26	54	2.52
Total	210.69	59	

$\dfrac{\text{Between-positions variance}}{\text{Within-cells variance}} = \dfrac{65.68}{2.52} = 26.07$ for 1 and 54 degrees of freedom, significant beyond 1-per-cent level

$\dfrac{\text{Between-groups variance}}{\text{Within-cells variance}} = \dfrac{4.35}{2.52} = 1.72$ for 2 and 54 degrees of freedom, significant at 20-per-cent level

The interaction (remainder) variance is not significant.
The within-cells variance is used throughout as the error variance, since it is larger than the remainder variance.

subjects reported changes of which the following is a representative example:

> (First session) My estimate was what I thought I ought to be able to get. (Placed below high-school group.) Today I was determined to do better and I think my estimates went up a little because I was trying harder today. The estimates today were a more definite goal.

All of the subjects placed above a college group reported changes in the meaning of their estimates from being a goal in the first session to the absence of such goal strivings in the second session. These reports are similar to those already given.

Four of the five subjects placed below a college group reported that their estimates changed from representing an average or a low goal to representing a high goal. One subject reported no change in the meaning of the estimate. These verbal reports correspond to the observed changes in the discrepancy score.

All the subjects placed above the graduate-student group reported changes in the meaning of their estimate which indicated a downward direction.

All five subjects placed below the graduate-student group likewise reported changes indicating a downward direction. The type of change here is not similar to any of those already presented. An example is:

> (First session) My estimates in the information tests fluctuated between an ideal impractical goal and what I thought I could get. In the synonyms the estimates remained a high ideal goal which I knew I would not reach. (Placed below graduate-student group.) Today the estimates took the position of a goal only slightly above my own scores. I was satisfied with scoring below the graduate students.

Thus, as in Experiment I, we find that the observed shifts in the discrepancy scores were indicative of real changes in the meaning of the estimates.

The Amount of Group Influence
The ratings were made on Experiments I and II simultaneously and so the examples and reliabilities presented for this item of analysis for Experiment I hold for this experiment also. The correlation between the ratings of the amount of influence which the group had upon the subject and the absolute change in discrepancy score from the first to the second session was .58.

Changes in Feelings of Success and Failure
The third item of analysis was treated as in Experiment I. The ratings were done together, and the reliabilities presented for these ratings in Experiment I hold here too. The correlation between the absolute difference of the ratings of success and failure from session I to session II and the absolute change in discrepancy score is equal to .46. Thus, for this experiment we find a relationship between the change in the amount of success or failure which the subject felt and the extent of the change in his discrepancy score.

Comparison Between Experiments I and II

Rather large differences are found between the results of the two experiments and these seem to be due to the different form of the experimental question used to elicit the estimate, since this was the only difference between the two experiments. The question as asked in Experiment I forces the subject to be realistic in his estimate. We shall hereafter refer to the subjects of Experiment I as the "expect" group. The question asked in Experiment II permits the subject to be more wishful or unreal in his estimate. The subjects of Experiment II will hereafter be referred to as the "like" group.

In the first session the expect group had a mean discrepancy score of $-.102$, while the like group had a mean discrepancy score of 2.19. The "t" test between these two means yields a value of 9.60, which is significant far beyond the 1-per-cent level. Those in the like group then keep their level of aspiration generally higher above their performance than do those in the expect group, which is plausible if they are being more wishful in their estimates.

The like group is also significantly more variable in its discrepancy scores in the first session than is the expect group. The variance of the discrepancy scores for the like group is 3.57, and for the expect group it is 1.26. The F test is significant beyond the 1-per-cent level of confidence. This result is also plausible since the expect group was forced to be realistic by the nature of the question asked, while some subjects in the like group might be realistic and others might be more unrealistic.

A similar comparison for the change score yields differences of the same type between the like and expect groups. The like group changes its discrepancy scores to a greater degree than does the expect group. The mean absolute change score for the former is 2.09 and for the latter, 1.19. The "t" is 3.18 and is significant at the 1-per-cent level. Also, the like group is again more variable than the expect group. The variance of the change scores for the former is 3.57 and for the latter, 1.26. The F test is significant at the 1-per-cent level. In short, the discrepany score changes to a greater extent as a result of group comparison when one is more wishful.

If this interpretation of the above differences is correct, there should be a positive relationship between the height of the discrepancy score in the first session (taken as a measure of how wishful the subject is) and the absolute amount of the change in discrepancy score from the first to the second session. The correlation between these two variables is .67 for the like group and .42 for the expect group, confirming the expectation. The smaller correlation for the expect group is natural since this group constitutes a more homogeneous one with respect to reality-unreality than does the like group.

A comparison of Figures 1.1 and 1.2 shows differences in the responses of the like and expect groups to the various group comparisons. Whereas the like group shows greater shifts when placed above a comparison group than when placed below, the expect group shifts equally for both positions.

While the realistic person cannot avoid the feeling of failure, the more wishful person can do so to a certain extent and therefore not respond to a failure situation. Therefore, if we are correct in assuming that the upward shift in the discrepancy score when the subjects are placed below a group is a reaction to failure, the like group should shift less under these circumstances. Our results bear out this conclusion. Some additional corroboration of this explanation is to be found in the correlations already reported between change in success-failure feelings and absolute change score. For the expect group this correlation is .17, while for the like group it is .46. If the amount of shift in a failure situation is dependent upon the extent to which the subject is unable to avoid feeling such failure (is forced to feel the failure), then one should expect some such moderate correlation as is found for the like group, since the latter group is more heterogeneous in this respect than the former. Also in support of this is the fact that in the "below high-school" group, where it is easier to avoid the failure situation, that is, where one can more easily refuse to be judged by the same standards by which a group of lower status is judged than when one is a member of the group, the like group does not change its discrepancy score significantly while the expect group does.

Table 1.5 shows that the changes in discrepancy score are accompanied by changes in the feelings of success and failure. The average success-failure ratings (interview data analysis number three) are presented for each group. The change in success-failure ratings uniformly follows the direction of the change in discrepancy score for every group.

We also see that the like group tends to shift its discrepancy scores to a greater extent the higher the status of the comparison group; the expect group does this only when it is above the group, but shows an opposite trend when placed below the comparison group. (See Figure 1.1.) It seems here that the expect group is behaving realistically toward the situation in terms of where they should be in relation to the other group, while the like group responds more to the general status of the comparison group.

In short, one might say that the expect group behaves realistically and the like group reacts in a wishful manner.

Table 1.5   Changes in Success-Failure Ratings

	Rating in Sess. I	Rating in Sess. II	Change in Rating	Corresponding Change Score
Expect				
Above H.S.	−2.6	0	2.6	−.33
Below H.S.	−2.0	−3.2	−1.2	1.77
Above coll.	1.4	4.2	2.8	−1.38
Below coll.	−2.2	−3.6	−1.4	1.01
Above grad.	−.2	3.8	4.0	−2.02
Below grad.	−2.6	−.6	−2.0	.64
Like				
Above H.S.	−3.0	1.4	4.4	−2.67
Below H.S.	−1.2	−3.8	−2.6	.53
Above coll.	−3.2	2.4	5.6	−3.13
Below coll.	−1.6	−3.4	−1.8	1.15
Above grad.	.4	3.8	3.4	−3.60
Below grad.	−2.6	.4	3.0	−1.46

Summary

To observe the effects which knowledge of group standards would have on the level of aspiration of the individual, a test-retest situation was used, the two test sessions being separated by about a week. In the second session different individuals were told the scores made on the tests he was taking by either a group of graduate students, a group of college students, or a group of high-school students. The scores reported for the groups were fictitious so that for each comparison half the subjects scored above the group and the other half scored below. Since the subjects themselves were college students, the comparisons may be regarded as being, with respect to one's own group, a group of lower standing, or a group of higher standing. The change in discrepancy score from the first to the second session was the principal measure used.

Those subjects who behaved realistically in the experimental situation uniformly raised their discrepancy score when scoring below a group, the magnitude of this change being greatest for the high-school group comparison and least for the graduate group comparison. They uniformly lowered their discrepancy score when scoring above a group, the magnitude of the change being greatest for the graduate group comparison and least for the high-school group comparison.

Those subjects who behaved unrealistically uniformly lowered their discrepancy score when scoring above a group, but also lowered their discrepancy score when placed below the graduate group. They raised their discrepancy score for the other two comparisons.

Whereas for the realistic group the changes up and down were of about equal magnitude on the average, for the unrealistic group the downward shifts were significantly larger than the upward shifts. The unrealistic group had a higher initial discrepancy score and a greater average shift in discrepancy score than the realistic group.

Analysis of the data gathered in interviews with the subjects showed that the observed changes represented psychological changes in the meaning of the situation.

===

At the time of this article, Leon Festinger was at the Iowa Child Welfare Research Station, University of Iowa. He expressed indebtedness to Dr. Kurt Lewin, under whose direction this experiment was done.

References

CHAPMAN, D. W., & VOLKMANN, J. A social determinant of the level of aspiration. *J. abnorm. soc. Psychol.*, 1939, **34**, 225–238.

ESCALONA, S. K. The effect of success and failure upon the level of aspiration and behavior in manic-depressive psychoses. In Lewin, K., Lippitt, R., & Escalona, S. K. Studies in Topological and Vector Psychology: I. *Univ. Ia. Stud. Child Welf.*, 1940, 16, No. 3, 199–307.

GARDNER, J. W. Aspiration level in response to a prearranged sequence of scores. *J. exp. Psychol.*, 1939, **25**, 601–621.

GOULD, R., & KAPLAN, N. The relationship of level of aspiration to academic and personality factors. *J. soc. Psychol.*, 1940, **II**, 31–40.

HERTZMAN, M., & FESTINGER, L. Change in explicit goals in a level of aspiration experiment. *J. exp. Psychol.*, 1940, **27**, 439–452.

LINDQUIST, E. F. *Statistical analysis in educational research.* Boston: Houghton Mifflin, 1940.

SEARS, P. S. Level of aspiration in academically successful and unsuccesful children. *J. abnorm. soc. Psychol.*, 1940, **35**, 498–536.

2

A Theoretical
Interpretation of Shifts
in Level of Aspiration

Summary of Experimental Procedure
and Results

In experiments aimed to discover the factors influencing the level of
aspiration two sessions, separated by about a week, were held with each
subject. The subjects were all college students mostly in their sophomore year. In each session a measure of the level of aspiration of the
subject was obtained. The measure obtained was expressed in terms of
the difference between the subject's performance and his estimate of
future performance. This measure has been called the discrepancy
score. Three experimental variables were introduced: (a) Reality-Irreal-
ity variable.—In order to elicit the estimate of performance for the next
trial half of the subjects were asked, "What score do you expect to get
next time?" The others were asked, "What score would you like to get
next time?" These have been called the "expect" (reality) and "like" (irreality) groups respectively. (b) Group variable.—This variable was introduced during the second experimental session. One third of the subjects were compared to a high school group, one third to a college group
and one third to a graduate student group. (c) Position variable.—This
variable was also introduced during the second session. Half of the subjects were told that they were scoring above the average of the compar-

SOURCE: Festinger, L. *Psychol. Rev.*, 1942, **49**, 235–250. [MS. received September 19, 1941]

ison group. The other half were told that they were scoring below the average of this other group.

The three variables cut across one another so as to form twelve distinct experimental groups of equal size. What these twelve groups are can be seen by the headings along the abscissa in Figure 2.1. (Expect, above high school; like, above high school; expect, above college; etc.)

Figure 2.1 presents most of the results necessary for an understanding of the relevance of the explanation which forms the main body of this paper. The white bars show the changes in discrepancy score from the first to the second session for all the "like" groups. The shaded bars give the corresponding data for all the "expect" groups.

In the expect experiment all the above groups shift their discrepancy score downward, while all the below groups shift their discrepancy score upward. The trend in the magnitude of shift for the above groups is the inverse of the trend for the below groups going from high school to graduate student comparisons.

In the like experiment the direction of the shift is the same as for the expect experiment except for the below graduate student group. This is the only below group that shift their discrepancy score downward. In extent of the shift, unlike the expect group, the like group shows an

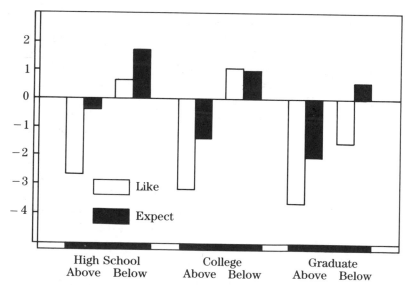

Figure 2.1   Changes in discrepancy score from first to second session.

increasing magnitude of shift with increasing status of the comparison group for the above and below groups alike.

The expect and like groups differ in certain other respects. The discrepancy score for the like group in session I is significantly higher and more variable than for the expect group. The changes in discrepancy score from the first to the second session are also higher and more variable for the like than for the expect group.

We shall now attempt to explain these results by first developing a theory of level of aspiration and then seeing if the implications of our theory are consistent with the results of this experiment.

Theoretical Discussion

Let us consider the case of a hypothetical subject "A" who has been scoring about 8 on the average in a series of tests. His level of aspiration has hovered about the value 9. While actually scoring 8 he has this goal of 9 which he expects to reach. When he gets a score of 9 he feels a certain measure of success in having reached what he is aiming at.

"A" is now told that on this test where he scored 8 a group of other college students scored only 6. He is scoring above the average of this group. Up to this point he has considered a score of 8 as only fair, and a score of 7 was rather bad. Now he finds out that a score of 7 is good, in fact a score of 6 is an average score with which he might very well be satisfied. There is no longer any point in striving for a score of 9 when a score of 7 is a good one to get. It may possibly seem even a bit foolish to keep on trying to get 9. As a result, "A" lowers his level of aspiration to 8. He now merely wants to maintain his present position.

However, suppose that "A" had been told that the average score for the college students was 10. The situation would be quite different. A score of 8 is definitely a bad score. Even a score of 9 which he had previously looked forward to is a bad score. "A" wants at least to do as well as the group. He therefore sets himself a new goal of 10.

"A" changed his behavior in different ways as a result of different changes in his situation. The essence of these situation changes was that "A's" idea of what constituted a good score and what a bad score was changed. When told what others had scored on these tests the attractiveness and unattractiveness of various levels of achievement are changed for him. In short, the change in the situation produced a change in the valence of regions of performance.

We can state then that the level of aspiration is a function of how desirable it would be to succeed at a certain level of performance: a function of the positive valence of success.

It seems to "A" that a score of 10 is more desirable than a score of 8. It is certainly more desirable to get 12 than to get 10. The positive valence of success, then, seems to increase with the level of difficulty.

"A" does not, however, set his goal at 12 or 14 although success at these levels would undoubtedly be more desirable than success at 10. It will be disagreeable to try for something and not get it. We can then state that the level of aspiration is also a function of how disagreeable failure would be at the different levels of performance: a function of the negative valence of failure.

It is more disagreeable to "A" to try to get 10 and fail than to try for 12 and fail. It is even more disagreeable to fail while trying for 8. The negative valence of failure therefore decreases as the level of difficulty increases.

If this analysis is true we would expect "A" to choose the highest possible level of performance as his goal since here the positive valence of success is highest and the negative valence of failure is lowest. "A" does not do this. Escalona (2) suggests the following explanation. It is doubtful whether the desirability of success and the undesirability of failure at a given level of performance are both present in the life space of "A" with equal effectiveness at all times. The desirability of success is uppermost in his mind if success is most probable, while the undesirability of failure is uppermost in his mind if failure is most probable. It is then the subject's expectancy of success and failure at a given level of performance which will define the relative potency of the valences of success and failure at that level. At easy levels the probability of success is very high and so the potency of the positive valence of success will be great and the potency of the negative valence of failure correspondingly small. The opposite will hold for the difficult levels of performance. We now see why "A" does not place his level of aspiration at the highest possible point.

We have distinguished four factors which influence the choice of a goal: the positive valence of success (Va_s), the negative valence of failure (Va_f), the potency of success (Po_s), and the potency of failure (Po_f). The choice of goal region (L), that is to say, the level of aspiration, will be determined by the resultant force toward L, the strength of which depends on these four factors. This resultant force (f^*) for a given level of difficulty may be determined by the equation:

$$f^*_{p,L} = Po_{s,L}\,(Va_{s,L}) - Po_{f,L}\,(Va_{f,L}) \tag{1}$$

That region (L) toward which f^* is greatest will be chosen as the goal region.

$$\text{Level of aspiration} = L \text{ at which } f^*_{p,L} = \text{maximum} \qquad (2)$$

In a task which presents a range of difficulty, these four factors may have values at each point in the range. Each of these factors may then be represented by a curve extending through that part of the difficulty range for which that factor has a value. We shall now more adequately define these four factors:

1. Valence of success (Va_s) is defined as the positive valence of future success as it appears to the subject when setting his goal. This valence would be very low, or perhaps zero at the very easy levels and would rise to a maximum at the difficult levels of performance. It is probably an S shaped curve because the areas of too difficult and too easy performance seem only slightly differentiated with regard to valence.
2. Valence of failure (Va_f) is similarly defined as the negative valence of future failure as it appears to the subject when setting his goal. This curve would be high at the easy levels and low at the difficult levels.
3. Expectancy of success (Po_s) is defined as the judgment of the individual at the time when he sets his goal as to the probability of reaching a given level of performance. This curve would be high at the easy levels (the individual would feel sure he could score at least that much) and would be very low at the difficult levels (the individual would be sure he could not score that much). The maximum value of this curve (practical certainty) is unity.
4. Expectancy of failure is correspondingly defined as the subjective probability of failure at the time of setting the goal. Mathematically the $Po_f = 1 - Po_s$. Psychologically this is not necessarily so although on the whole it is approximately correct: the expectation of failure decreases as the expectation of success increases.

The curve of the resultant forces which will determine the choice of goal region may be derived by formula (1). The region at which this curve reaches its maximum will be the level of aspiration.

Figure 2.2 is an illustrative example of the derivation of such a resultant curve from the curves of the four factors above presented. The ab-

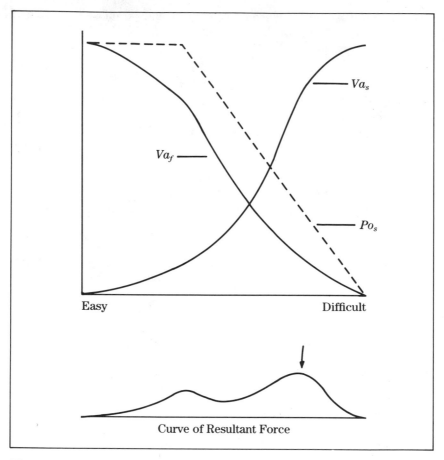

Figure 2.2   Derivation of the resultant force (f*$_{P,L}$) *from a set of valence and potency curves of given value.*

scissa represents different regions of difficulty and along the ordinate are arbitrary units in which the valences are measured. The curve for the potency, of course, has different units along the ordinate, but the two have been superimposed. The curve for the potency of failure has not been represented since all along it is merely 1 minus the potency of success curve. The point at which the resultant curve reaches its maximum (indicated by the arrow) is the point at which the level of aspiration is set.

Let us now discuss this curve analytically with a view to understanding the way in which it depends on the four factors. In this curve should be distinguished: (a) the maximum point; (b) the gradient away from this maximum and the amount of difference within the curve; (c) the height of the curve above the zero point.

The height of the Va_s and the Va_f curves will depend upon how intensely the individual in question feels about future success and failure respectively. For an individual who feels success very strongly and failure rather weakly, the former curve will be high and the latter low. The reverse situation may also be the case. This lowering and raising of the heights of these curves does not affect the point at which the resultant force will reach its maximum *as long as the slope of the curve is not altered.* It does, however, affect the height of the resultant curve. The higher the Va_s curve, the higher will be the resultant curve; the higher the Va_f curve, the lower will be the resultant curve. The height of the resultant curve at a given point shows the strength of the force toward this difficulty level (L). This resultant force will be positive if the failure factors ($Va_f \cdot Po_f$) are less than the success factors ($Va_s \cdot Po_s$), since $f^*_{P,L} > 0$. In the reverse case, $f^*_{P,L} < 0$, or $f^*_{P,-L} > 0$: there is a tendency for the subject away from L.

Changes in the position of the valence curves along the abscissa and changes in the slope will affect the point at which the resultant curve reaches its maximum. The more toward the easy level the Va_s curve rises, the more will the resultant's maximum be pushed toward the easy level. The more toward the difficult level the Va_f curve falls, the more will the resultant's maximum be pushed toward the easy level.

Such changes in the positions and magnitudes of the various curves can and do take place during a succession of trials, e.g., by learning, better acquaintance, etc. Such changes can also be induced by arbitrarily setting the positions of the valence curves for the individual by making him compare himself with other individuals.

Derivation of Results
for the "Expect" Experiment

Our results may, to a certain extent, be explained on the basis of the above theory as follows:[1]

If the individuals are told that they are scoring above a college group (the individuals being college students) certain valence changes occur.

---

1. In the following derivation it will be assumed that the individual's judgment of his own ability (the probability curves) remains the same and that the Va_f curve likewise remains unchanged.

The easier levels, which have now been pronounced to be good scores, will get a higher positive valence than they had had, i.e., the Va_s curve will start to rise at a lower level of difficulty than it did previously. This results in a shift to the left of the point at which the resultant force reaches its maximum; the level of aspiration goes down.

If the individuals are told that they are scoring below a college group the opposite effect is obtained. Scores which were previously considered good are no longer attractive. The curve shifts to the right and the level of aspiration goes up.

If these induced standards are not of one's own group, the status of the other group with respect to the individual will be important. If the other group occupies a lower status (e.g., a high school group), being above them produces little change in the curve's position. The subject feels that his own standards should be higher than those of the high school group. Being below a group of lower status should produce a change of even greater magnitude than a similar position with respect to one's own group. In this case similar to the situation of scoring below one's own group, levels of difficulty which were previously satisfactory are no longer attractive. The fact that they are not even good for a lower group should make their valence drop even more sharply. The curve then shifts considerably to the right. The level of aspiration should rise accordingly.

If the induced standards are those of a group with higher status than one's own (e.g., a graduate student group) the effects should be opposite. Being below this higher group should produce no change. Being above this higher group should produce a very great shift in the rise of the Va_s curve toward the easy level. The level of aspiration should again behave accordingly.

The results coincide with these derivations. Figure 2.1 shows (1) the downward changes (above group) increase with increasing status of the comparison groups, and, (2) the upward changes (below group) decrease. In addition, (3) the upward is greater than the downward change for the high school group, and (4) the reverse is true for the graduate student group.

Derivation of Results
for the "Like" Experiment

The main difference between the like and expect experiments is that the subjects of the former behave on a more irrealistic level because of the emphasis on wish rather than expectation in the instructions. The chief differences between the levels of reality and irreality (5) are that the level of irreality presents a more fluid medium. Locomotion through barriers is easier than on the level of reality. Because of fewer restraining forces on the level of irreality, the response to equal driving forces would be greater on the irreality level than on the reality level. On the level of irreality then, the individual can structure his life space in accordance with his wishes. If this is true, then the like category is less bound by considerations of reality in achieving success and avoiding failure than the expect category which behaves realistically.

This theory points to the following conclusions: (1) The discrepancy between level of aspiration and performance should be greater for the like group than for the expect group. (2) The amount of change in discrepancy score after comparison with other groups should be greater for the like group. (3) The like group should show more latitude in accepting or rejecting the standards of other types of groups. (4) The like group should show more freedom in accepting or rejecting the same group standards under different conditions in line with their wishes.

Conclusions (1) and (2) are found to be true. The like group does have a higher mean discrepancy score and a higher mean change in discrepancy score than the expect group. Conclusions (3) and (4) will be discussed below.

We have seen that the choice of a goal level was largely guided by the negative valence of failure and the positive valence of success. This tendency to avoid failure and achieve success is present throughout and may lead, for example, to rationalization after the action (blaming the tool). This tendency has been reported frequently by other experimenters and is one of the basic facts in a level of aspiration situation.

Another way to avoid failure or achieve success in our experimental setting lies in accepting or rejecting the standards of the comparison group. For example, a child in school who continually gets grades far below the group might accept his position as low and reject the group's standards as binding for himself.

Such rejection of the standards of one's own group seems to be rather difficult. A person has more latitude, however, in accepting or rejecting standards of some group other than his own. An adult will usually refuse to see his actions judged according to the standards of preschool children, both in a positive and negative sense. Experiments have clearly shown that the areas of "too easy" and "too difficult" lie outside the region in which success and failure are felt.

In the light of the above elaboration of our theory, the results of the like group become compatible with those of the expect group. The acceptance of a position below a high school group means admitting failure which the like group can avoid by refusing to compare themselves with the high school group. Thus the Va_s curve remains relatively unchanged.

In the same wishful manner the like group accepts the standards of the high school group when placed above it, since such acceptance means success. The level of aspiration accordingly shifts downward. The more realistic expect group cannot do this.

It is difficult to refuse to compare oneself to one's own group. Therefore the shifts in level of aspiration resulting from comparison with the college group are similar for the like and the expect category.

When placed above graduate students the like group consistently shift their level of aspiration downward to a very great degree, but when placed below graduate students they also shift downward. The former is in line with the theory but no ready explanation of the latter finding is available. Perhaps the position below a group of high status forces them to become more realistic in their behavior.

Our last conclusion (4), derived from the greater fluidity of the ir-reality level, is related to the amount of shift in the like as compared to the expect group. Our hypothesis is that the like group more easily than the expect group avoid failure by refusing to accept group standards and more easily create for themselves a feeling of success by accepting group standards. This is substantiated by the fact that for the like group the shifts occurring on being placed above a group are of much greater magnitude than those occurring when they are placed below a group. The magnitudes are very nearly the same in the case of the expect group.

Acceptance of Group Standards and Feelings of Success and Failure

Our theory states that the acceptance of group standards depends upon whether such acceptance means success or failure. If this is correct, then we should expect that with acceptance of a "favorable group standard" the general feeling of being "successful" should increase. With the acceptance of an "unfavorable" group comparison the general feeling of being unsuccessful should increase.

As previously reported (3) the interviews held with the subjects after the experiment were rated according to the degree of the subject's feeling of success and failure in each session as a whole. The analysis (3, Table V) shows that in every case where the discrepancy score shifted downward a change in the success-failure ratings occurred. These changes indicate more feeling of success or less feeling of failure, both of which imply the same direction of change. In every case of an upward shift in discrepancy score the opposite direction is indicated in the success-failure ratings. This relation holds for all groups including the below graduate student group. These results strongly support our theory.

The Effect of the Relative Weight of the Group Standards on Shift in Discrepancy Score

Gould and Lewin (4) show that a variety of problems related to level of aspiration can be dealt with by distinguishing different frames of reference existing simultaneously for the person. Each of these frames of reference contributes a specific amount of positive or negative valence to a certain difficulty level. One of these frames of reference is one's own past performance which gives to higher achievements a positive valence and to lower achievements usually a negative valence.

One might regard the introduction of the comparison group scores into the life space of the subject as the introduction of a new frame of reference which will in part determine the positions of our hypothetical curves. One can assume that the only frame of reference which existed previously was the individual's own performance. The extent to which the individual accepts this new frame of reference should determine the extent to which his level of aspiration will shift in the direction expected from our theory.[2]

When the individual is told what others have scored, he is placed in an overlapping situation. He has two sets of standards before him: his own, which up to this time he has been using, and those of the group. The more potent (relative weight) the group standards are, the greater should be the magnitude of the shifts.

The construct "potency" is conceptually relatively simple (6), but much difficulty has been encountered in its operational definition. One successful attempt at such a definition has been made by Barker, Dembo and Lewin (1) in determining potency of a background of frustration for an immediate situation.

As reported in our previous paper (3) the interviews were rated on the amount of attention which the individual paid to the standards of the group to which he was compared. This rating was done on a ten-point scale and forms a convenient operational definition of the potency

2. We have seen that the like group was able to reject completely this new frame of reference when they were placed below high school students.

of that frame of reference relative to the other frames of reference which determine the level of aspiration.

To get reliable means the subjects were arranged in three groups: those for whom the group had a potency of 1, 2, or 3, those for whom the potency of the group was 4, 5, or 6, and those for whom these values were 7, 8, or 9. In no case was the potency rated as 10.

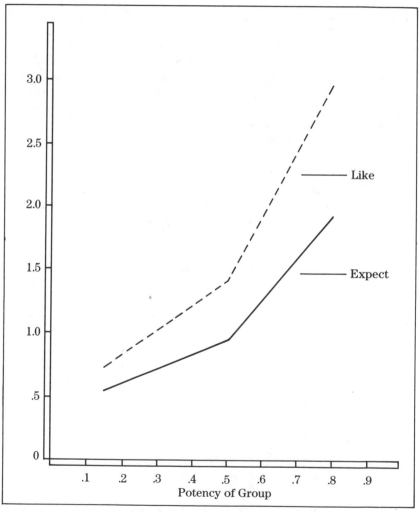

Figure 2.3   *Magnitude of change in discrepancy score as a function of the potency of the comparison group.*

The curves of the potency of the group plotted against the amount of change in discrepancy score are presented in Figure 2.3. The greater the potency of the group standards as a frame of reference, the more does the discrepancy score change from its previous position. This holds for both like and expect groups.

The curve for the like group consistently lies above the curve of the expect group. This is additional proof of the greater fluidity of the more irreal behavior of the like group.

Summary

This paper deals with the theoretical questions concerning the effect which the knowledge of group standards has on the level of aspiration of the individual. It also deals with the difference between wishes (like group) and expectations (expect group) in this respect. The experimental data on which our theory is based have been summarized. These data consist of responses of college students who were placed in positions above and below high school, college, and graduate student groups.

The experimental results become understandable if one analyzes (a) the strength and direction of the driving forces, (b) the strength of the restraining forces and (c) the potency (relative weight) of certain frames of reference.

The following derivations were made and are corroborated by the experimental data:

1. The direction of shift in discrepancy was derived from the changes in valence resulting from the introduction of a new frame of reference.

2. The magnitude of shift was greater, the greater the potency of the new frame of reference.

3. The magnitude of shift was greater, the smaller the restraining forces. This means (a) that the discrepancy score is greater for the like group than for the expect group, and (b) that the shifts in discrepancy score are greater for the like than for the expect group.

4. The relative weakness of restraining forces on the level of irreality enables easier structuring according to one's wishes. It follows from this that: (a) in accepting or refusing to accept the standards of a group as a frame of reference for one's own level of aspiration, the like group is guided more by their wishes than the expect group. The like group refuses acceptance if acceptance would

mean failure and accepts if acceptance means success; (b) this differential acceptance can be applied less to the standards of one's own group than to groups above or below one's own status.

It was possible to provide an operational definition of the potency of a frame of reference.

When this article was written, Leon Festinger was at the State University of Iowa. This was the second of two articles reporting an experiment done as a thesis for the degree of Master of Arts. The first article (3) presented the results in full. Indebtedness for aid and advice was again expressed to Dr. Kurt Lewin.

References

1. BARKER, R., DEMBO, T., & LEWIN, K. Frustration and regression: An experiment with young children. Studies in Topological and Vector Psychology II. *Univ. Ia. Stud., Stud. Child Welf.*, 1941, **18**, No. 1, pp. 314.

2. ESCALONA, S. K. The effect of success and failure upon the level of aspiration and behavior in manic-depressive psychoses. In Lewin, K., Lippitt, R., & Escalona, S. K. Studies in Topological and Vector Psychology I. *Univ. Ia. Stud., Stud. Child Welfare*, 1939, **16,** No. 3, pp. 307.

3. FESTINGER, L. Wish, expectation and group standards as factors influencing the level of aspiration. *J. abn. soc. Psychol.*, 1942, **37**, 184–200.

4. GOULD, R., & LEWIN, K. Toward a theory of level of aspiration. (To be published.)

5. LEWIN, K. *Principles of topological psychology*. New York: McGraw-Hill, 1936, pp. 231.

6. _____. The conceptual representation and the measurement of psychological forces. *Duke Univ. Series, Contrib. to Psychol. Theory*, 1938, 1, No. 4, pp. 247.

3

Level of Aspiration

Almost any set of psychological problems, especially those in the fields of motivation and personality, inevitably involves goals and goal-directed behavior. The importance of setting up goals for behavior is especially accentuated in a culture with as strong a competitive emphasis as ours. Until recently, however, little formal attempt has been made to study goals as phenomena in themselves and the effects of attainment or non-attainment of goals on the behavior of the individual.

The concept of "level of aspiration," introduced by Dembo (published in 1931), made explicit the possibility of observing goal levels occurring in the course of a relatively specific activity, designating some of the factors associated with fluctuation of such goals and linking the experimentally observed manifestations of goal-striving to the individual's behavior in other situations. The experimental results stemming from her observations and those of Hoppe (1930), who performed the first experiment directed toward analysis of the aspiration phenomena, have mounted until at the present time there is a considerable body of data bearing on the problems of that goal-striving behavior which occurs within a range of difficulty, i.e., *level of aspiration*. Gradually also seem to be emerging the common factors which establish the level of aspiration phenomena with reference to other fields and problems of psychology, notably to social standards and forces, conflict and decision, personality characteristics, value phenomena, success and failure, developmental aspects of personality. This is, then, an appropriate time to look backward at the trends of the last decade and forward to the future directions in which research may profitably be directed. A review of the

SOURCE: Lewin, K., Dembo, T., Festinger, L., & Sears, P. In Hunt, J. McV. (ed.). *Personality and the behavior disorders*. New York: Ronald, 1944, pp. 333–378.

relevant literature up to 1941 may be found in Frank (1941), and Rotter (1942) has examined critically the material which seeks to evaluate the methodological aspects of level of aspiration.

What Is the Level of Aspiration?

A Typical Sequence of Events

In discussing the many problems and aspects of the level of aspiration, it may be helpful to consider a sequence of events which is typical for the situations concerned. A person has scored 6 in shooting at a target with ring 10 at the center. He decides the next time to try for 8. He attains 5, is much disappointed, and decides to try the next time to reach 6 once more.

Within such a sequence we can distinguish the following main points (Figure 3.1):

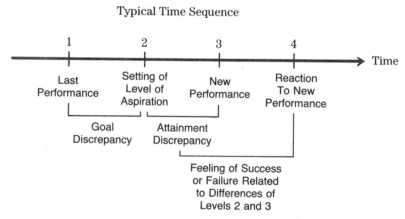

Typical Time Sequence

Figure 3.1   Four main points are distinguished in a typical sequence of events in a level of aspiration situation: last performance, setting of level of aspiration for the next performance, new performance, and the psychological reaction to the new performance. The difference between the level of the last performance and the level of the new goal is called goal discrepancy; the difference between the goal level and that of the new performance is called attainment discrepancy. This difference is one of the bases of the reaction at the point 4.

1. The (last) past performance (in our example: "has scored 6").
2. The setting of the level of aspiration, e.g., deciding how high to set the goal for the next performance ("try for 8").
3. The execution of action, e.g., the new performance ("attains 5").
4. The reaction to the level of attainment, such as feeling of success or failure ("disappointment"), leaving the activity altogether, or continuing with the new level of aspiration ("try again for 6").

Each of these four points can be discussed in relation to one another. In case an individual begins a new activity, no past performance would appear within the sequence, although he might have had experience with similar activities.

Each point within the time sequence represents a situation that has characteristic problems. For the dynamics of the level of aspiration, point 2 (setting of the level of aspiration) and point 4 (reaction to achievement) are particularly significant. Two problems arise immediately, then, out of consideration of this sequence: (a) What determines a level of aspiration? (b) What are the reactions to achieving or not achieving the level of aspiration?

Description of Terms Involved in the Sequence

Some of the terms and factors involved may well be identified before proceeding to discussion of the experimental data.

ACTION GOAL—IDEAL GOAL; INNER DISCREPANCY; CONFIDENCE LEVEL. We have mentioned before that the level of aspiration presupposes a goal which has an inner structure. In our example the individual will not merely shoot, but tries to hit the target and even a certain area of the target. What he would really like to do is hit center. This is his "ideal goal." Knowing that this is "too difficult" for him, at least at the present, he sets his goal at 8 for the next action. This we will call his "action goal." It is the level of the action goal which is usually taken as the criterion for the level of aspiration for an individual at a given time. Frank, one of the early investigators in this field, defines the level of aspiration as "the level of future performance in a familiar task which an individual, knowing his level of past performance in that task, explicitly undertakes to reach" (1935a, p. 119).

Setting the action goal at point 2 of the time sequence (Figure 3.1) does not mean that the individual has given up his ideal goal. In order to understand this behavior, we must consider the action goal as within the whole goal structure of the individual. This may include quite a number of more or less realistic goal levels. Goal levels within one goal structure may include a high dream goal, a somewhat more realistic wish goal, the level which the person expects to reach when he tries to judge the situation objectively, and a low level he might hit if luck were against him. Somewhere on that scale will be what can be described as the action goal, e.g., what the person "tries for" at that time; somewhere his ideal goal will be located. Sometimes the individual comes closer to his ideal goal, sometimes the distance between the ideal goal and the action goal becomes wider. This is called "inner discrepancy."

Another characteristic of the goal structure is the discrepancy between the level of the action goal and the level of the expected performance. This difference might be characterized directly as the "goal-expectation discrepancy." This discrepancy will depend in part on the "subjective degree of probability" which the individual holds with reference to his chances of reaching his action goal. One expression of the subjective probability is the confidence level.

PAST PERFORMANCE—GOAL; GOAL DISCREPANCY.   One can compare the level of aspiration, e.g., the level of the action goal at point 2 in our time sequence (Figure 3.1), with the level of the past performance (point 1 of our time sequence). The difference between the two levels has been called "discrepancy score." Since there are other discrepancies important for the level of aspiration, we will call this one "goal discrepancy." The goal discrepancy is said to be positive if the level of the goal lies above that of the past performance; otherwise, it is called a negative goal discrepancy.

LEVEL OF ASPIRATION AND ATTAINMENT; ATTAINMENT SCORE; SUCCESS, FAILURE.   The individual has set his level of aspiration and then has acted with this goal in mind (point 3 of the time sequence, Figure 3.1). The level of this performance can be called "attainment or performance score." The difference between the level of aspiration and the attainment score may be called "attainment discrepancy." It is said to be positive if the attainment is higher than the level of aspiration. It is called negative if the attainment falls short of the level of aspiration.

The direction and size of the attainment discrepancy are two of the major factors for the feeling of success or failure. The term "success" or "failure" will be used to indicate the psychological factor of feeling success or failure and not as indicating the difference between the level of aspiration and the achievement. Everyday language speaks of success and failure in both meanings, sometimes referring to the difference between points 2 (level of aspiration) and 3 (new performance) of our time sequence, sometimes referring to point 4. The difference between points 2 and 3 is called "attainment discrepancy." The success and failure indicate a reaction to this discrepancy (point 4 of the time sequence).

OPERATIONAL DEFINITIONS: VERBAL GOAL AND TRUE GOAL. How the different goal levels and performance levels can be measured or defined operationally is a technical question which frequently has to be answered differently in different experimental settings. To observe or measure the level of performances (points 1 and 3 of the time sequence) is frequently not difficult if one uses proper activities.

More difficult is a direct measurement of the level of aspiration or other points of the psychological goal structure, such as the ideal goal or the level of expectation. Once the laws of the level of aspiration are known it will be possible to use a number of reactions for an indirect determination. Today one of the best methods of determining the level of aspiration, the ideal goal or the level of expectation is, as a rule, the direct expression of the subject. Of course, there is the danger that the verbal or written statement of the individual may actually not reveal his "true" action goal, his "true" ideal goal, or "true" expectation. It would not be a safe procedure to ask an individual after the performance, e.g., at point 4 of our time sequence, what his level of aspiration had been at point 2, because after failure his verbal expression might easily be a rationalization. It is important to have the verbal expression given during that situation to which it refers. In case the social atmosphere is sufficiently free, the direct expression of the individual is at present for many settings the best approximation and, therefore, the best operational definition of the various goal levels. For the action goal, the actual behavior of the individual in a choice among tasks on various levels of difficulties can be used as a behavioral measure.

The problem of the determination of true and/or verbal level of aspiration has proved a difficult one for many of the earlier investigators in this field. Hoppe (1930) employed various lines of evidence in inferring a given subject's momentary level. Since later investigators have preferred to use more definite behavior for the inference of aspiration level, the breadth of the operations studied has been to a certain extent restricted in the interests of methodological precision. Gardner (1940b) has clarified the theoretical situation resulting from the attempts to improve on Hoppe's methods of measurement without making entirely specific the consequences of the methodological changes.

SIZE OF GOAL UNITS.   An individual may throw a ring over a stake. He may or may not reach his goal. In another case his goal might be to throw a series of five rings over a stake. How good his achievement is (nothing missed, three missed) can be stated in this case only after all five rings are thrown. His reaction to this achievement with the feeling of success or failure will be related to the achievement as a whole rather than to each ring separately.

The size of the units of activity to which a goal refers is an important point to be considered in the discussion of the level of aspiration. The maximum size and the complication of units to which a goal might refer are important characteristics of certain maturity levels in children. To avoid misunderstandings one will always have to keep in mind the size and character of the activity unit to which the goal refers.

What Determines the Level of Aspiration?

Reference Scales

Experimental work on the level of aspiration has brought out the variety of influences which are present for a single decision as to action goal. Some of these influences are probably rather stable and permanent in their effects; i.e., their value will be much the same for all individuals of a given culture in a variety of competitive situations. It has been found, for example, that nearly all individuals of western culture, when first exposed to a level of aspiration situation, give initially a level of aspiration which is above the previous performance score, and under most conditions tend to keep the goal discrepancy positive. The effects of cultural pressures toward improvement in performance, and the value which positive discrepancies have for many individuals in stimulating them to greater endeavor, have been brought out by a number of investigators in this field (e.g., Gould, 1939). Such influences may be conceived of as frames, involving a scale of values, within which the individual makes his decision as to a goal. The relative dominance or potency of each scale of reference is a function (a) of more temporary situational factors and (b) of general cultural factors. For either of these the momentary level of aspiration can be regarded as determined (a) by the individual's perception of his position on each reference scale which is relevant to his present situation, and (b) by the forces which act upon him in these positions. This point of view will be developed more extensively in the summary. Here will be considered the experimental data relevant to understanding the various phenomena.

Temporary Situational Factors

Success and Failure Within a Series
The statement can be made that generally the level of aspiration will be raised and lowered respectively as the performance (attainment) reaches or does not reach the level of aspiration. In speaking of shifts in the level of aspiration which rigidly adhere to the above principle, Jucknat (1937) has introduced the term "typical" cases. The existence of "atypical" cases will be discussed later. This experimenter used two series of ten mazes in a range of difficulty, one series in which the mazes were solvable and one in which they were not. With thirty children as subjects, the following results were obtained: In the solvable series the level of aspiration rose from a beginning level of 5.6 to an end level of 7.5. Of the observed shifts in level of aspiration, 76% were upward and 24% downward. In the nonsolvable series the level of aspiration fell from a beginning level of 6.5 to an end level of 3.6. Of the observed shifts, 84% were downward and 16% upward. Thus, under one condition 76% and under the other 84% of the shifts were "typical" ones, and the general trend followed the "typical" pattern.

Festinger (1942a), analyzing data specifically for this purpose, obtained the following results. After attainment of the level of aspiration there were 51% raisings, 41% staying on the same level, and 8% lowerings of the level of aspiration. After nonattainment of the level of aspiration these figures are 7%, 29%, and 64%, respectively. There were 219 shifts after attainment and 156 shifts after nonattainment.

Jucknat has carried this type of analysis one step further with a rating of the *reaction* to the attainment or nonattainment, i.e., the strength of success or failure judged to be experienced by the subject. Table 3.1 gives these results.

From this it appears that the stronger the success the greater will be the percentage of raising the level of aspiration, and the stronger the failure the greater the percent of lowering the level of aspiration.

Thus we find that there is a high degree of agreement not only as to the direction which the shift in level of aspiration will take after success and failure, but even as to the percentage of such changes which will occur.

Transfer
Jucknat (1937) continued her work by investigating the effects of success or failure in one task on the level of aspiration for a subsequent task. Using the same two series of pencil and paper mazes, on one of which the subjects always get success and the other on which they always get failure, she finds that the reactions to the series given first affect the

Table 3.1   Frequency of Raising or Lowering of the Level of Aspiration After Different Intensities of Success and Failure

	Shifts After Success				Shifts After Failure		
	S!!	S!	S	DS	F	F!	F!!
Number of cases	24	45	29	34	36	41	17
Percentage raising	96	80	55	56	22	19.5	12
Percentage lowering	4	20	45	44	78	80.5	88

(Taken from Tables 3a and 3b, Jucknat, 1937, p. 99)

S!!	Very good success	F	Weak failure without evidence of se-
S!	Good success		rious feelings
S	Just successful solution without evi-	F!	Strong failure
	dence of distinct success	F!!	Very strong failure
DS	Solution with considerable effort		

level of aspiration behavior in the other series of tasks, the extent of the effect depending upon the extent to which the second series is regarded as a continuation of the first series. When the success series follows the failure series, the beginning level of aspiration for the second is lower than it was for the first series. When the failure series follows the success series, the reverse is true. If the success and failure series are made to look more different than previously, the effects are less marked although in the same direction as described above.

This indicates that less transfer of reactions to attainment of the level of aspiration occurs when the two series do not appear to constitute a single task. Thus the beginning level of aspiration for the second series is always put somewhere between the beginning and end levels of the first series. When the two series appear contiguous, the beginning level of the second series is nearer the end level, but when the two series appear different, the beginning level of aspiration for the second is nearer to the beginning level of aspiration of the first. The effect of one series on the other is then a partial one, the amount depending upon the similarity between the tasks.

Frank (1935b) finds that the level of aspiration on a "normal" task differs according to whether it followed an easy activity or a hard one. The average height of the beginning level of aspiration is higher when the normal task follows the easy activity than when it follows a hard one.

Range of Level of Aspiration

It is important to answer various further questions: within what absolute levels of difficulty will the person set his goal level; within what ranges of performance will feelings of success and failure be experienced; and when will the person cease setting up aspiration levels for a given task?

There are some indications. An adult usually does not set any level of aspiration in connection with buttoning his overcoat nor does he set one in connection with physically impossible accomplishments. When faced with a difficulty continuum, the individual will set up goals near the boundaries of his ability. Experimental verification of this may be found in Hoppe (1930). Using a task which was ordinarily performed in about 88 seconds by the subjects, Hoppe found it impossible to produce feelings of success by setting a goal of 120 seconds or more nor could he produce failure by imposing a goal of 60 seconds or less. Under these circumstances the individual set up his own goals. Success and failure were experienced only when the goals ranged from 65 to 110 seconds.[1]

This tendency against setting up levels of aspiration in regions of activity which are either "too" easy or "too" difficult is also reflected on those occasions of stopping activity after a series of trials. Data on such cessation of activity is reported by Hoppe (1930) and Jucknat (1937). Hoppe (p. 20) reports that out of 42 cases of spontaneous stopping, ten stopped after a complete success "when raising the level of aspiration seems impossible either because the limits of personal ability have been reached or because the nature of the task or the instructions hinders such raising." Twenty-three cases stopped after complete failure "when the last possibility of getting a success is exhausted." Eight cases stopped after a single success following a series of failures when the previous failures had demonstrated the unlikeliness of a success with a higher level of aspiration. One case stopped after a single failure. Jucknat (p. 103) reports that of those subjects stopping after successes, 42% stopped on reaching the maximum possible achievement, 50% stopped after insufficient success, and 8% stopped before the maximum in spite of good successes.

From the above reported data it seems that in general there is a tendency to stop when the possibilities of achieving further success are not good. R. R. Sears (1942) found, furthermore, that subjects under failure conditions needed significantly more reminding than did subjects working under a success condition in order to have them state the level of aspiration. Here no stopping was permitted, but the failure subjects

1. There are two cases out of 124 which did feel success when a goal of 150 seconds was imposed. The rest fall within the limits mentioned.

were able to a certain extent to withdraw themselves from the situation by not making the verbal statement of their goals.

General Cultural Factors

Standards of One's Own Group

The level of aspiration situation may involve certain clearly defined reference scales, i.e., the individual's performance is judged on a reference scale of another individual or the group to which he belongs. Anderson and Brandt's (1939) experiment illustrates the effects of this procedure. Their subjects (fifth-grade children) were given a series of six cancellation tests spaced a half-week apart. The relative performance scores of the subjects were posted on a graph so that each subject could see how he stood in relation to the group but could not identify the position of any other child. Before each succeeding test the subjects were asked to write down privately the score they thought they could make on the succeeding trial. The graphs showing the relative standing were kept up to date throughout the experiment. Grouping the subjects according to performance quartiles gives clear-cut trends showing the effectiveness of the knowledge of group standing. For the upper quartile (those scoring highest in the group) the level of aspiration was, on the average, 5.8 points below the performance level. For the second quartile the level of aspiration was, on the average, 1.9 points above the performance level. For the third quartile the level of aspiration was 2.1 points above the performance level. For the fourth, or lowest, quartile the level of aspiration was 13.6 points above the performance level. In short, we find a consistent trend in which those subjects who find themselves above the average of the group tend to have a negative discrepancy score, those finding themselves close to the average of the group tend to have a slightly positive discrepancy score, while those finding themselves below the mean of the group tend to have a very large positive discrepancy score. The correlation between discrepancy score and position of performance with respect to the group mean, taking positive and negative discrepancies into account, was $-.46$, i.e., the lower the performance relative to that of the group, the larger the discrepancy. The same result was found for college students, working in small groups, by Hilgard, Sait, and Magaret (1940). Here public announcement of the performance scores was made, while the levels of aspiration were recorded privately. These workers also performed a second experiment (1940) in which the ranking of the subjects in the group was experimentally controlled by giving some of the subjects hard problems, others problems of medium difficulty, and others easy problems. These three groups form the low, medium, and high performance groups. In this experiment the effect of the position in the group on the level of aspiration is more marked than when the natural performance was allowed to have its effect. Whereas all three groups start off with approximately the same amount of positive discrepancy score, by the last four trials the group that had easy materials has a discrepancy score of -3.4; the group that had medium materials has a discrepancy score of $+1.0$; and the group that had the difficult problems has a discrepancy score of $+4.2$. These experiments give reason to assume the existence of a frame of reference in which the individual's performance is placed on the scale formed *by the performances of his group*. Gardner's (1939) technique of reporting performance scores in terms of prearranged percentile values has the effect, similarly, of placing the subject's score with reference to that of others, and his finding that the goal discrepancies were higher at the lower portions of the performance curve than vice versa is consistent with the other findings.

Standards of Other Groups

The fact that the level of aspiration is subject to regular and consistent influence by the subject's knowledge of his own standing relative to that of his group suggests the possibility that knowledge of performances of other groups, identifiable as more or less prestigeful or superior than the subject's own, may have a similar effect. The scale of values defined by the "own group" may, in effect, be extended upward and downward with knowledge about other groups. Chapman and Volkman (1939) made the first attack on this problem. By giving groups of college students comparison scores of (a) literary critics, (b) students, (c) WPA workers, for a test of "literary ability," they were able to manipulate the level of aspiration in a clear-cut way. The comparison scores were actually all equal but this fact was not known to the subjects. The heights of the aspiration levels for the various groups followed this order, from lowest to highest: (a) comparison with experts (critics), (b) no comparison, (c) comparison with own group (students), (d) comparison with inferiors (WPA). The subjects giving these results had not taken the test and they were therefore ignorant of their own performance scores, although they knew the maximum possible score and the score obtainable by chance. Gould and Lewis (1940) and Festinger (1942a) followed this experiment with others which offer corroborative evidence for the influence of group standards of varying prestigefulness. The latter investigator used as the chief experimental measure the *change* in goal discrepancy score from a condition in which the subject had no scores but his own previous ones with which to compare his present performance, to an experimental condition in which his score was made to appear either above or below one of three groups: (a) high school, (b) college, and (c) graduate students. The subjects, themselves, were college students. The trends which the results show are illustrated in Figure 3.2, which gives the change in size and direction of goal discrepancy scores when the subjects believed that their performances were either inferior to (below) or superior to (above) those of one of the comparison groups. Here we have a reference scale with a gradient of positive valence related to the prestige of the comparison group. This scale of values is analogous to that reported in the previous section in which the individual was placed with reference to his own group, but in the present case the individual is placed with reference to other groups which are conceptualized in a definitely valuative way. This frame of reference will be identified as that embodying comparisons with *other groups* of varying prestige.

Aspirations of Group
The individual may orient himself with respect to others' aspirations as well as to their performances. Hertzman and Festinger (1940) have explored this problem. After the average discrepancy scores for the sub-

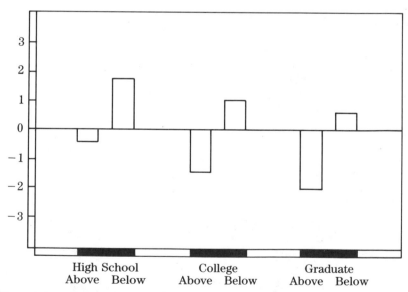

Figure 3.2 *Changes in discrepancy score for college students compared to groups of low, medium, or high prestige.*

jects in a first experimental session had been determined, the subjects were given a second experimental session a week later at which they were told the average score and average level of aspiration of a group of other people of their own scholastic standing. The scores attributed to the group were arranged so that the individual's performance was equal, on the average, to the performance of the group. The positive or negative sign of the group goal discrepancy, however, was reported as opposite to that of the subject. The results showed that the level of aspiration changed significantly from the first to the second session in the direction of conforming to the group, i.e., the changes observed in level of aspiration were changes in the direction of the group level of aspiration. Changes from the first to the second session were statistically significant. Interviews with the subjects indicated that the conscious effect of such conforming to the group was very slight, or even nonexistent. The subjects' main conscious set was toward the scores (performances) of the group rather than toward the levels of aspiration. This would make one tend to suspect that although such conforming to group atmospheres exists, its effect in most cases is weak as compared to the effect of the performance of the group. It is, however, a frame of reference which may exert considerable influence under some conditions.

Psychological Effects of Socio-Economic Background
A study by Gould (1941) gives evidence that goal discrepancies are related to various factors in the background of the subjects. Those individuals giving relatively low (negative or low positive) discrepancy scores, when compared to those giving predominantly high positive scores, are found to be also in a relatively more favorable social and economic position. Indices as: more college training and income of the subjects' fathers, extent to which the students are not required to work their way through school, birth of the parents in this country, and expectancy of larger salaries in the future are found on the side of those subjects showing lower discrepancy scores. This reference scale and the one to be discussed in the next section represent attitudes toward endeavor and aspiration which have been determined before the subject comes to the experiment. Their effects are apparently similar to those in which an external standard is set by the experimenter on the foundation of internalized attitudes and values.

Habitual Success and Failure
Jucknat (1937) has evidence of the effect of another background factor on level of aspiration. When her experimental group of 500 children is divided into those who have been consistently good, medium, or poor

students in their school work, differences in the height of the first level of aspiration are found between the groups. Faced with mazes placed in an ascending order of difficulty from 1 to 10, the group of good students set an initial level of aspiration rather high in the scale, between 7 and 10. The medium students' average was in the middle ranges, between 5 and 6. The poor students tended to set the aspiration level either low or high, between 1 and 4 on the one hand or between 7 and 10 on the other.

P. S. Sears (1940) selected small groups of children who had had clearly different school experience over a period of time with respect to success and failure. Those of the past failure group showed a higher goal discrepancy on the average than those of the past success group. More pronounced, however, was the wide variability among subjects of the failure group, such that the range of discrepancies was from very high positive to negative scores. The variability among subjects of the success group was much less, with discrepancies almost entirely within the small positive range.

Reality Levels

When a subject is asked to state his goal verbally he may interpret this question in many different ways and the stated goal will differ according to the particular interpretation made. Gould (1939) showed this to be the case when she asked her subjects the question "What will you do next time?" Some subjects took the question to mean what they thought they really would get. Others interpreted the question as meaning what they hoped to get and responded accordingly. Gould distinguished three general groups in regard to interpretation of the experimental question: (a) those who set their level of aspiration at a minimum which the individual undertakes to overreach; (b) those who set it at a maximum which represents a mark they hope to come close to (actually being prepared not to reach it); (c) those who set their stated level of aspiration at about the average of their performance.

Thus a variety of attitudes on the part of the subjects will influence the nature of the results obtained through statements of aspiration levels. The stated action goal may represent, as Gould says, an incentive in one case and in another a protection against possible failure. The desire to come as close as possible to the level of aspiration, or to "guess accurately," may be a factor in some cases. Frank (1936) used comparison questions for eliciting the level of aspiration and finds that subjects who were asked "What do you think you will do?" were more likely to adopt a goal of trying to come close to their "guesses" than subjects who were asked "What do you intend to do?"

Festinger (1942a) found that subjects who were asked "What score would you like to get next time?" had a significantly higher discrepancy score (2.19) than subjects who were asked "What score do you expect to get next time?" (−.10). The former group was also significantly more variable than the latter in its goal discrepancy score. This result is completely corroborated in a study by Irwin and Mintzer (1942). Different attitudes, such as those occasioned by the two questions used by Festinger, may be interpreted as possessing different degrees of reality. The subject who tells what he expects to get seems to be realistic and keeps his level of aspiration close to his performance. The subject who tells what he hopes or what he likes seems to become wishful and unrealistic and raises his goal far above his performance level.

There is some evidence favoring this type of interpretation. Frank (1935c), reasoning that a play situation is less bound to reality than a serious situation, finds that the discrepancy scores for a task like quoit-throwing which has a playful character are greater than for tasks of more serious nature such as printing. Sears (1940) finds that the subjects with a low positive discrepancy score (realistic subjects) show more flexibility in the level of aspiration than those with a high positive discrepancy score (irrealistic subjects), i.e., they are more sensitive to changes in the performance. Corroborating this is the finding by Irwin and Mintzer (1942) that their "realistic" group showed a significantly greater number of changes of the level of aspiration than did the other group. Festinger (1942a) found that when compared to the performance of other groups, the unrealistic subjects behaved so as to avoid failure to a greater extent than did the realistic subjects by refusing to be influenced by an unpleasant external standard.

We may summarize these experimental findings as follows: The realistic attitude will produce a small discrepancy score with a level of aspiration that is flexible and responsive to changes in performance. The unrealistic attitude will produce a large discrepancy score with level of aspiration which is unresponsive to reality influence, and may reflect a wishful attitude toward the attainment of the action or stated goal.

In an attempt to control more adequately the attitude of the subject, Preston and Bayton (1941) asked their subjects to state three levels of aspiration; namely, the least they expected to do, the most they hoped to do, and what they actually thought they would do. Their results show that while the least estimates are unrelated to either of the other two estimates, there is a high correlation between the actual and the maximum estimates. In addition, the actual estimates are always closer to the maximum than to the least estimates. This suggests that even a statement involving a supposedly objective ("actual") estimate will, in the absence of external factors designed to control the subjects' attitudes, tend in the upward rather than the downward direction. The actual as well as the maximum estimate thus appears to be more influenced by wishful considerations than does the least estimate. The latter may be regarded by the subject as a performance which he *might* (but hopes he will not) sink to if conditions are especially adverse.

Individual Differences

Previous sections have shown that numerous factors tend to influence the level of aspiration in certain rather consistent ways. Application of the principles resulting from the previous discussion to the prediction of a specific individual's behavior involves an additional problem, viz., to what extent are the experimentally observed behavior patterns samples of behavior which may occur in more than one goal-striving situation? This is the problem of generality of the behavior pattern, whether the generality be that involved in setting levels of aspiration for two motor tasks or that involved in estimating one's score on a golf game and on an important examination. The generality is measured by the correlation of the behavior in two different situations. Whether the operations measured in these situations are the subject's own verbal statements involving explicit goals or are nonverbal behaviors interpreted by another person, the relations obtained are representative of the extent to which the same reference scales and other dynamic factors are involved in both. Viewed in this way, the problem of generality is one of determining within what limits the same factors will be found playing a significant role in different situations.

Closely allied to the study of generality by correlation of specific aspiration level scores is the analysis of the relation between experimentally obtained scores and other personality variables. Not all of these variables are conceptually relevant to goal-setting, but because most of them have been first observed clinically in the goal-setting situation, the majority are closely related to that aspect of behavior. Both generality and the establishment of relationships with other variables involve comparison of individuals in two or more situations.

A third problem is that of the variability of behavior within a single situation. Instead of asking whether one individual maintains, in different situations and on various measures, the same relative position with respect to other members of the group, we may inquire as to the extent of difference between individuals on a single measure under specified conditions. For example, one might ask whether there is greater variability in a highly structured situation than in one in which various individual interpretations are possible, and if so, what the conditions are for structuralization of goal situations. This problem has so far received little attention in the literature, but there is evidence that, in a gross way, the heterogeneity of behavior is important for understanding the behavior in such situations. Once the factors determining the individual's behavior in one experimental situation have been established, the analysis may be continued, as described above, in terms of the generality of his position on various tasks and operations which may be significant for generalizing about his behavior.

The literature in this field falls naturally into several groups. First, the most experimental work has been directed toward ascertaining the extent of generality of the *goal discrepancy score* in various tasks, and this will be first discussed. Second, many workers have felt the inadequacy of thus depending on a single measure culled from the wealth of material which the level of aspiration situation yields, and have attempted to utilize measures other than the goal discrepancy. Two types of study have appeared so far: (a) those of the statistical generality of the secondary measures, and (b) those attempting an analysis of the "course of events" or patterning of the level of aspiration behavior. Third, the relationship of aspiration responses to factors beyond the confines of the experimental level of aspiration situation has been investigated. Although this problem is commonly referred to as that of correlated "personality traits," it is, as has been shown, that of more broadly conceived generality of goal behavior combined with exploration of relations to other, possibly independent, variables. Fourth, there is the examination of variability within a group of persons put under various experimental conditions.

Generality of the Goal Discrepancy Score

Hoppe (1930) was aware of the broad problem of generality and devoted some time to demonstrating the consistency of the behavior of different individuals. The first specific study of generality of the discrepancy was performed by Frank (1935a). Correlating the discrepancy scores for two different sessions on the same task he finds correlations ranging from .57 to .75 for two of his tasks. For the third task the correlations are .26 and .63. From these data he concludes that the level of aspiration behavior is consistent and explains the low correlation for the third task (quoits) by the fact that it was more of a play (irreal) situation, and therefore the individual's reactions to it are less bound by realistic factors which tend to stabilize the behavior in the other situation. Correlations within the same session of the discrepancy scores between his first two tasks, printing and spatial relations, also yield fairly large coefficients, ranging from .50 to .65. Correlations involving the quoits were mostly either zero or slightly positive. Gould (1939), using six different tasks, three given in one session and three in another, finds intercorrelations among the tasks on the discrepancy score ranging from .44 to .04 with a median inter-correlation of .29. When the correlations were calculated separately for those tasks given in the same session and for those given in different sessions, the median intercorrelation for the discrepancy score on tasks given in the same session goes up to .46 while the median intercorrelation for discrepancy score on tasks given in different sessions stays at .30. Gould's correlations, although lower than those obtained by Frank, still indicate some tendency toward consistency. The fact that the correlations were higher for tasks in the same session leads Gould to make the interpretation that the individuals respond more to the situation than to the task itself.

The difference between the results of Gould and Frank is perhaps due to the greater diversity of tasks used by Gould and the lesser amount of control over the subjects' attitudes in the Gould experiment.[2] Gardner (1939), more adequately controlling the latter factor, obtains generality correlations close to Frank's. Gardner's technique involves arranging the situation so that all subjects have the same scores. The series of scores present in one place a rising curve of performance (successful experience), in another place a falling curve (failure experience), with occasional reversals in order. Four tasks were used and generality correlation coefficients were calculated for the discrepancy scores at different places along the performance curve. The mean correlation for the beginning level of aspiration was .37. A mean correlation of .37 was also obtained for the average of three consecutive discrepancy scores in that part of the curve where the performance remained on the same level. In the middle portion of the curve the performance rapidly increases for three trials and then after a single reversal increases for another two trials. The mean correlation coefficient for the average of the discrepancy scores for the five increasing performances was .55. After this rising portion, the performance curve slowly but regularly falls for five performances. The mean intercorrelation for the average discrepancy scores of these five trials was .61. The intercorrelations of the average discrepancy

2. The two tasks for which Frank obtained relatively high correlations were rather similar in nature, and it will be remembered, for the quoits, which were quite different from his other tasks, the correlations were lower. In addition, the question used by Gould, "What will you do next time?" probably allows more fluctuation of attitude than the question of "What do you intend to do?" used by Frank. Gardner asked the subject where he "expected to stand" in relation to a group of students.

scores over the whole series of performances with the exception of the first two and last two trials yields a mean of .57.

Conflicting results on the question of generality are to a large extent reconciled in the results obtained by Heathers (1942). With the idea that the amount of generality observed will depend to a large extent on the similarities of the different situations, Heathers varied three factors of the objective situation to determine their influence on the degree of generality: the scale or units in which the performance scores were presented to the subject, the shape of the curve which the series of performance scores followed, and the motivation of the subjects. Prearranged performance scores were used and the subject was asked to tell what score he was "going to try to make on the next trial," or what his goal was.

When the scale of units in which the scores were reported to the subjects and the shape of the performance curve are both the same in two tasks, the correlation of the discrepancy scores for these tasks is .87. When the curves are the same but the scale in which the scores are reported is different for the two tasks, this correlation drops to .67. The difference between these two correlations is statistically significant, indicating that the difference in scale is enough of a difference in similarity between the two situations to reduce significantly the degree of generality. No significant differences were found between correlations for the group having both scale and curve constant and the group for which the scale was constant but the curve was varied. Generality in both instances is very high, with correlations ranging from .74 to .86. There is evidence that variation in shape of curve will produce differences in generality if, as the author concludes, "the contours of the curve are different enough to provide the subject with different interpretations concerning the amount and rate of his improvement" (p. 403). In the present case the average amount of increase for all the curves was about the same from beginning to end, and therefore the total success and failure experience is presumably roughly equivalent. Reliable differences in generality are obtained when the curves are split so that amounts of improvement, with consequent changes in amount of success stimulation, are varied. These results indicate how important it is to distinguish in detail the specific success and failure conditions for any measure of generality.

When both the shape of the curve and the scale are varied, the results are significantly different from the case where they were both held constant. For the latter group the correlations range from .93 to .79 while for the former group they vary from .35 to .74.

In another group of subjects the motivation to perform well on the tasks was varied by making the task an intelligence test and offering prizes for good performances for one group. The generality correlation coefficient for the group that was highly motivated to do well was .93 for the two tasks in the first experimental session. The comparable correlation for the group which was not highly motivated to do well was .84. This difference is significant statistically. Significant differences do not appear, however, in the correlations obtained from a second session at which it appeared that the high level of motivation arranged for the experimental group had considerably declined.

It is interesting to note that the average intercorrelation for tasks during the same experimental session is .81 while the average intercorrelation for tasks in different experimental sessions is .62. This latter value of .62 agrees rather well with the average intercorrelation of .57 reported by Gardner (1940). The relatively greater constancy of the subjects' attitudes and moods within the same experimental session undoubtedly makes for a greater similarity between tasks on the same day as compared with tasks on different days.

One can also look at the question of generality by investigating the extent to which experience of success or failure in one situation will affect the level of aspiration in another situation. This might be called a "transfer effect." Jucknat's and Frank's findings on this problem have been reported already. The transfer effect of success and failure is greatest when the subject finds the two tasks to be similar or two parts of one larger activity.

Generality of Other Measures Related to the Level of Aspiration

Rotter (1942b), calculating test-retest generality after a period of one month, found the following correlations on a motor performance task in a situation where the subject was rewarded for correct estimates and penalized for incorrect. For the number of times the subject reached or exceeded his estimate, the coefficient is .46; for the shifts up and down, respectively, following such "success" or "failure" to reach the estimate, .56; frequency of shifts, .70. All the coefficients are statistically significant and indicate a certain stability of measures of aspiration behavior other than discrepancy.

Patterning of discrepancy scores and other measures related to level of aspiration has been observed by many investigators and rough attempts at formulation of such patterns are described by Sears (1940), working with school children, and Rotter (unpublished) for adults.

In the case of neither investigation is it found that patterns are rigidly marked off from one another; rather, these combinations of factors are described as rough approximations of constellations which may prove to have psychological significance.

Both workers find that there is a pattern represented by (a) the "low positive discrepancy score," utilized in a realistic way with adequate adjustment to both success and failure. Responsiveness of the level of aspiration up or down following changes of similar direction in performance score is rather high; flexibility (shifts) of the level of aspiration is average, (b) the "low negative discrepancy score" pattern is chiefly characterized by a protectively low action goal, which is ordinarily kept below the level of performance. Slightly less responsiveness and flexibility are found to be associated with this kind of response than with the preceding.

Sears gives data on two more patterns, the "high positive discrepancy" pattern, with very low flexibility and responsiveness, and the "mixed" pattern in which responses are irregular and highly variable throughout the successive trials of one task. Rotter distinguishes seven more types of pattern: the "medium high positive discrepancy" associated with responsiveness to success and failure and a realistic attitude; the pattern of "achievement following" in which the level of aspiration is constantly changed to conform as exactly as possible to the level of the previous performance; the "step" pattern, characterized by shifts in an upward direction only; the "very high positive" pattern, with responses largely of a phantasy nature; the "high negative" pattern; the "rigid" pattern, showing an absence of shifts regardless of achievement, and the "confused" or "breakdown" pattern.

Hilgard and Sait (1941) asked subjects to estimate their past as well as their future performance, and thus obtained two discrepancies in addition to the usual goal discrepancy: (a) estimate of past performance minus (true) past performance, and (b) estimate of future performance minus (true) future performance. The third difference used was the familiar goal discrepancy. Odd-even reliabilities for all three discrepancies are satisfactory, and generality coefficients between two motor tasks fairly high. The authors conclude that subjective distortion enters into estimates made of both past and future performance, i.e., goal strivings are not only oriented toward the future, but also influence an individual's perception of his past. These influences are not consistent in direction for different individuals, but do show considerable generality, i.e., for the same individual, the direction of the distortion appears rather consistent from task to task.

Preston and Bayton (1941) further vary the standard technique in asking subjects (a) what they actually expect to get, (b) the least they would be likely to get, and (c) the most they would hope to get. Generality of these estimates from task to task is rather high. In a second paper (1942), correlations between the various estimates are presented. Those between the least and the actual estimates and between least and maximum are all negligible, while correlations between the actual and the maximum estimates are appreciable (range from .45 to .84).

Personality Characteristics

All workers in this field are agreed that the level of aspiration situation is a favorable milieu in which to observe individual traits relating to the competitive and goal behavior of the subject. So far, however, objective demonstration of relationships has proceeded but slowly.

The problem basic for personality characteristics as determinants of the level of aspiration behavior is the evaluation of relative weights which different reference scales have for a given individual. For example, social standards may play a relatively greater role for one subject than for another in the same objective situation; failure may be more decisive than success and a wishful attitude may be more characteristic of a given subject in a certain situation than is a more realistic attitude.

Hoppe (1930), Jucknat (1937), and Frank (1935c) describe types of personality traits which are deduced from the level of aspiration situation and which are regarded as influential in determining the behavior in that situation, e.g., ambition, prudence, courage to face reality. Independent measures of the personality factors were not obtained by these investigators.

Gould and Kaplan (1940) and Gardner (1940) have made correlational studies relating certain broad personality variables to goal discrepancy scores. The former investigators found only insignificant relationships between discrepancy scores and scores (a) for dominance-feeling (Maslow inventory) and (b) extraversion-introversion (Guilford). Gardner obtained ratings for his subjects on a number of broad traits culled from the observations of Hoppe, Jucknat, and Frank. These also show low correlations with discrepancy scores, although in each case the findings were in the same direction as the hypotheses of the previous investigators would suggest.

Frank (1938) reports correlations obtained in connection with Murray's personality studies. Size of goal discrepancy is positively correlated (.20 or higher) with personality variables involving, according to Frank's analysis, the following factors: "(1) the wish to do well (often unaccompanied by the will to do well), (2) a subjective attitude, and (3) the ability to dismiss failures." Evidently some slight relationships make their appearance through such correlational techniques, but the evidence is far too slim to provide a solid basis for future thinking in this area. The variables so far investigated are probably too broad and generalized to be usefully isolated as correlatives or determinants of specific level of aspiration scores such as the goal discrepancy.

More fruitful than correlational studies has been analysis of factors associated with "high," "medium," and "low," or "negative" discrepancy scores. Results showing differences in security of socio-economic and academic status between groups of subjects which show chiefly one of these types of scores have been discussed in a previous section. Gardner's "high" and "low" discrepancy groups give results which are confirmatory though based on small numbers of subjects and statistically not highly significant. In his experiment, the ten subjects having the highest average (positive) discrepancy scores were also rated highest on (a) *dissatisfaction with status* and (b) *importance attached to intellectual achievement.* The ten subjects having the lowest discrepancy scores were rated lowest on (a) *subjective achievement level,* (b) *general sense of security,* (c) *tendency to face failure frankly,* (d) *realism,* and (e) *motivation,* and were rated highest on *fear of failure.* These ratings were made outside of the experimental situation by raters who were thoroughly acquainted with the subjects.

Sears (1941) has made clinical studies of selected small groups of children who were highly motivated for good school work and had been either (a) highly successful or (b) unsuccessful at obtaining good school status over a period of several years. When these subjects were divided according to size of discrepancy scores for experimental school type tasks, certain related factors emerged as also differentiating these groups. Children using predominantly a "high" discrepancy pattern are poorer in school achievement than the other groups and are rated as showing an attitude of low self-confidence accompanied by rather free admission of their incompetence. Here is an example of a specific relationship between goal setting for success and self-confidence. The correlation holds between behavior in the experimental level of aspiration (for school tasks) area and the aspirations (also for school tasks) observed in the schoolroom and clinical situations. Those children showing characteristically the "low positive" discrepancy ("realistic") reaction are, on the other hand, rated as highly confident, successful and comfortable in their achievement. Behavior problems and unfavorable personality traits (rated by the teacher) appear less frequently in them than in the other groups. A third group, called in this study the "negative discrepancy" group, is equivalent to Gould's and Gardner's "low" groups. These children fall in between the other two in confidence and academic success, but are differentiated from both others in terms of high ratings for self-consciousness, socially rather than self-oriented motivation, defensiveness and self-protection in their attitudes toward failure. It is of some interest with respect to generality of aspiration that when in this study the subjects rated themselves on a paper and pencil questionnaire with reference to a number of diverse life activities, their averages for the ratings "how good I am at" and "how good I wish I were at" followed the course to be predicted on the basis of the aspiration level classification if the "how good I am at" rating is conceived as analogous to a performance score and the "how good I wish I were at" rating analogous to a level of aspiration score. The high positive discrepancy group showed the greatest difference between perceived and wished-for skills, the low positive group the next difference, and the negative discrepancy group the least difference.

Similar findings are reported by Rotter (unpublished) who has amplified and elaborated the discrepancy patterns as previously described. Three patterns of response, the low positive, low (slightly) negative, and medium high discrepancy score patterns are designated arbitrarily as "socially acceptable" methods of solution for the self-evaluation problem presented in the level of aspiration situation.[3] Six other patterns, including the very high positive and high negative discrepancies, step, rigid, confused, and achievement-following patterns, are designated as "socially unacceptable." Prison inmates were classified, in terms of past history and present behavior in situations involving self-evaluation, into (a) a "normal" group, in which goals had in actual behavior been held fairly close to the experiences of achievement, (b) a "defeated" group, whose behavior was characterized by lack of confidence, strong fear of failure, and protection against failure by setting very low explicit goals, (c) a "conflict-tension" group characterized by inability to reach a decision in problem situations. The "normal" group of prisoners showed in the level of aspiration situation a preponderance of the "socially acceptable" patterns over the "unacceptable," while acceptable and unacceptable were approximately evenly balanced in the "defeated" and "conflict-tension" groups. Of the other subjects employed, college cripples as compared to college normals had a relatively high percentage in the protective high negative discrepancy score pattern. College students showed higher percentages of "achievement-following" and "step patterns" than did the hospital employees, but were not up to them or to

---

3. In this case a premium was put on exact estimation of performance by specially designed instructions similar to those of Hausmann (1933).

the "normal" prison group in terms of percentage of acceptable patterns used.

Yacorzynski (1942) has studied the relation between degree of effort expended on a task and the direction of the aspiration level. An inverse relation appears between these two variables; i.e., an increasing degree of effort is associated with a decreasing number of predictions that the scores will improve. *Confidence* in one's own ability, he feels, may increase predictions of improved scores on successive trials and also decrease the amount of effort shown.

Variability Within a Group

A given attitude permits according to its nature greater or smaller individual differences. Thus as we have seen before, the realistic attitude binding the subject to his performance will not permit so much deviation from this point as appears in the wide range of irreality or wishful thinking. The distribution of individual scores according to these attitudes can be measured by the variability of the group.

Festinger (1942) finds that a group forced to a realistic attitude is less variable than one for which the instructions permitted various degrees of realism. McGehee (1940) devised an experiment in which the future of performance was estimated by an observer while the person performing set a level of aspiration. The levels of aspiration were regularly more variable than the estimates of the other person, though in this case the differences do not reach complete reliability.

Sears (1940) found reliable differences in spread of scores (group variability) between groups whose past school experience of the task had been either successful or unsuccessful. The success subjects showed on the average lower discrepancies than did the failure subjects and appeared more realistically oriented to their levels of aspiration, but the most marked differences between groups were those of the variability of the scores. The failure group showed a spread of discrepancies varying from negative to high positive, while the success group scores were concentrated within the low positive range. Further, those subjects of the failure group who utilize the high positive discrepancy maintain their discrepancies rigidly, without the responsiveness to performance and attention to the performance scores which seem to be related to a realistic attitude.

Another kind of variability is that shown by the individual subject in the generality of his behavior on different tasks. Gould (1939) finds a correlation of .33 between variability of this kind and height of discrepancy. That is, there is a tendency for those having low or negative discrepancies to respond more to the situation as a whole than to the specific task, while those with high discrepancy scores on some tasks tend to vary more in their responses from task to task.

The Development of the Level of Aspiration

The age level at which a level of aspiration can be said to exist depends upon a number of considerations. Observational evidence suggests the existence of a "rudimentary" level of aspiration in very young children. Repeated efforts toward a difficult accomplishment are observed in the very young child, e.g., in his attempts to walk independently, to pull off an article of clothing, or to sit down upon a chair. However, before these behaviors can be regarded as precursors of the level of aspiration phenomena previously discussed, it is necessary to postulate the development of the child's thought processes to a level which permits cognition, comparison, and choice of psychological values in general and specifically of that value continuum or scale called "overcoming of difficulties."

Steps Preceding the Fully Developed Level of Aspiration

Fales (1937) considered the child's wanting to do something by himself rather than with someone's help as a stage preceding the full development of the level of aspiration. This type of behavior may be called "rudimentary aspiration." The level of aspiration differs from "rudimentary aspiration" by being the stage at which achievement *levels* can be distinguished.

The strivings for "independence" as a rule occur only in a situation where moderate difficulties exist. Thus the child tries to become independent in his marginal areas of ability.

Fales studied two- and three-year-old children in a nursery school performing the activity of putting on and taking off wraps. The percentage of refusal of help was taken as a measure of "rudimentary aspiration." This was found to exist already at the two-year-old level.

Fales next trained one group of children in taking off their wraps and compared this group before and after training with a group which was not trained. The comparison observations were made in putting on the wraps. The group which received the training, that is, the group which became more skilful and more secure in its performance, increased considerably in percents of refusal of help as compared with the group which did not receive training.

In another experiment Fales praised one group of children for their endeavors. They were compared with a group which was not praised. The praised group increased in "independence" considerably more than the control group and even exceeded the trained group mentioned above. It may be concluded that training the child to become more skilful and rewarding the independent behavior by praise promotes "rudimentary aspiration."

Anderson (1940) used a ring-throwing task with three groups of children averaging about three years, five and a half years, and eight years of age, respectively. This investigator distinguishes four aspects of behavior, each of which shows different developmental steps. They are: (1) *Manner of throwing*, i.e., the child can get the rings on by actually placing them, by dropping them, or by throwing the rings from a distance. The developmental steps follow this order. (2) *Rethrowing of rings*. Rings which were missed may or may not be rethrown by the child. The latter indicates a higher developmental stage. When rings are rethrown they may be rethrown immediately or after a whole series has been thrown. The latter is again a higher developmental step. (3) *Size of unit*. Of those subjects who threw the rings, some regarded each ring as a unit while others regarded the series of five rings as a unit. The latter is considered a higher developmental step. (4) *Amount of failure*. The willingness of the subject to risk missing rings was also taken as an indication of a higher development of level of aspiration behavior.

Taking the above described factors into consideration, Anderson attempted to determine the "maturity" of the level of aspiration. The highest possible maturity score is 9. The mean maturity scores for the oldest, middle, and youngest groups are 8.54, 6.34, and 2.13, respectively. The differences among all these groups are statistically significant. The maturity scores for the groups on each of the separate factors making up the total score follow the same pattern. Thus we find the maturity of the level of aspiration, in terms of adult standards, increased with age.

Anderson's experiments show that in his experimental set-up all components of the level of aspiration observed in adults in a similar situation can be found in the eight-year-olds. Jucknat's (1937) findings are consistent with these results. She finds no differences in the level of aspiration behavior in regard to beginning and end levels in a group of children between the ages of 11 and 12 and a group of adults. The tasks she used were solvable and unsolvable mazes.

There are conditions under which the level of aspiration behavior of the child can appear less mature than it actually is under optimal conditions. Such a condition exists when the "means to a goal" character of the task is emphasized. Anderson reduced the emphasis on performance *per se* by giving a reward for getting many rings on the stick. The mean maturity scores for the oldest, middle, and youngest groups were reduced to 7.34, 5.03, and 1.03, respectively. The differences between the reward and nonreward situations are significant for each group, the maturity score being uniformly lower in the reward situation.

A regression to a lower developmental level with respect to the maturity of the level of aspiration probably could be produced in children in a frustration situation. This can be expected because frustration experiments in adults (Dembo) showed that subjects, performing the ring-throwing task, would start to rethrow rings and, instead of throwing them from the distance, place them on the stick when severely frustrated.

For further research it would be important to investigate the development in respect to different reference scales (see pp. 40 to 59, and pp. 73 to 78) of the level of aspiration.

Summary and Theoretical Considerations

The studies of the level of aspiration have grown from empirical findings and have been influenced by various considerations. Some studies have tried to determine the factors which influence the raising and lowering of the level of aspiration and to understand the conditions of success and failure; others concern themselves with the question of the degree to which personality traits play a role. A theoretical survey and summary may help to clarify a situation which is at present a bit chaotic, and to give orientation to further experimentation. No attempt will be made in this summary to take in all the results. Essentially we will follow the "resultant valence theory" which has been presented by Escalona (1940) and elaborated by Festinger (1942b). Gould and Lewin (unpublished manuscript) have brought this theory into a wider setting by linking it to various "frames of reference."

Level of Aspiration as a Choice Situation; Valences and Probability

A basic problem of the level of aspiration can be formulated as an apparent discrepancy between the tendency to set up higher and higher goals (that is, a willingness to enter difficult undertakings) and the customary notion that life is governed by the tendency to avoid unnecessary effort (parsimony). Have we to assume an innate tendency to "strive for higher things" to explain the fact that the individual prefers the difficult task or prefers doing certain activities himself rather than using the easy way of being helped by someone else (page 60)?

According to Escalona this problem can be solved if one considers the psychological situation as it exists at the time when the individual makes up his mind about the next goal; that is, the point 2 of our sequence (page 36).

The psychological situation at that moment can be characterized as a choice situation (Figure 3.3). The person has to decide whether he will

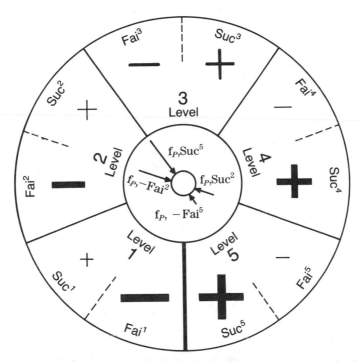

Figure 3.3   The difference in the attractiveness of the various difficulty levels 1 to 5 of the activity is determined by the valence of future success (SUC) and failure (FAI) at that level. The valence of success increases, that of failure decreases with increasing difficulty level. Correspondingly the force toward success, for instance, $f_{P,Suc}^5$ is greater than the force $f_{P,Suc}^2$ on level 2. The force away from failure $f_{P,-Fai}^5$ is smaller than $f_{P,-Fai}^2$. Therefore, the total valence of the more difficult level is higher than the easier level.

choose a more difficult, an equally difficult, or an easier level; for instance, whether he will try to finish the job on hand in 10 minutes, or only in 12 or 15 minutes. (Actually, he could also "stop" entirely, which means a change to a different activity. We will consider this aspect of the choice later.)

One can state analytically for this as for any other choice situation that that action is chosen as a goal for which the sum of attractiveness (position valence) minus the sum of disagreeableness (negative valence) is a maximum. To determine this maximum one should know the factors which bring about the positive or negative valences of these different actions. We will discuss some of these factors in a step-by-step order, going from the general to the specific.

The choice in the case of the level of aspiration involves the relative valences of variations in the *same* activity; in dealing with a choice between different tasks, e.g., target shooting, multiplying two-place numbers, and solving puzzles, a great many factors enter into the valences or attractiveness. Prediction is more difficult in this case since wide individual differences result. In level of aspiration situations analysis of the choice is somewhat simplified by the fact that the general character of the activity is constant. The choice is determined by the different valences which different degrees of difficulties within the same activity have for the person.

The individual faces the possibility of succeeding or failing and the positive or negative valence of such a future success or failure on the various levels is one of the basic elements for the decision. To determine the valence (Va) of each level (n) of activity $[Va(A^n)]$ we have to consider the negative valence that future failure has on that level $[Va(Fai_A{}^n)]$ and the positive valence of success on that level $[Va(Suc_A{}^n)]$.

$$Va(A^n) = Va(Suc_A{}^n) + Va(Fai_A{}^n).\text{[4]} \tag{1}$$

The valences of future success and failure on various levels may be illustrated by the example of doing twenty simple additions in a given time. To the adult subject, achievement on a very easy level, such as finishing the twenty simple additions in one hour, would not bring any appreciable feeling of success. This is "child's play." The valence of success on this level 1 (Table 3.2, columns 2 and 3) is approximately zero. The valence of success on levels of greater difficulty, such as finishing

---

4. As the valence of failure is usually negative (neg Va) and the valence of success is usually positive (pos Va) formula (1) means that usually the former is subtracted from the latter: $Va(A^n) = $ pos $Va(Suc_A{}^n) - $ neg $Va (Fai_A{}^n)$.

these additions in 50 minutes, 40 minutes, and so on, continues to be zero until the tasks cease to be altogether "too easy." Then the valence of achievement starts to be perceptibly positive although at first very small. In our example (Table 3.2) we assume that at the difficulty level 4, the valence of success will equal 1.

With increased difficulty the valence of success also increases. Finally, we reach the level of difficulty that taxes the person's ability to capacity. There the valence is likely to be at a maximum (arbitrarily indicated by 10). Still more difficult levels beyond the boundary zone of ability will probably have the same high positive valence.

Higher on the scale there are degrees of difficulty which seem "entirely out of reach of the individual," for instance, solving the twenty additions in 20 seconds (level 14), and levels above this which are "humanly impossible," for instance, finishing the task in 5 seconds. Such levels are usually not even considered and one might leave these values blank on the scales. The greater the degree of difficulty, therefore, the higher the valence of success, within the boundary zone of ability.

The absolute value of the negative valence of failure usually changes in the opposite direction. On levels of extreme difficulty the negative valence of failure would be negligible. Even on the level of very difficult performance, failure might have no negative valence. The negative valence increases until it reaches a maximum in the area of relatively easy tasks. There it remains close to a maximum and finally drops out of consideration somewhere in the area of "too easy" tasks.

Within the crucial range of difficulty we can say that:

$$\text{pos } Va(Suc_A^{high}) > \text{pos } Va(Suc_A^{low}) \tag{2}$$
$$\text{neg } Va(Fai_A^{high}) < \text{neg } Va(Fai_A^{low}) \tag{3}$$

The total valence of the level according to formula (1) is the algebraic sum of these valences. As the positive valence of success increases with difficulty and the negative valence of failure decreases we can conclude, from formulae (2) and (3), that the total valence on the high level should always be greater than the total valence on the lower level because

$$Va(A^{high}) = Va(Suc_A^{high}) + Va(Fai_A^{high}) > Va(Suc_A^{low}) + \tag{4}$$
$$Va(Fai_A^{low}) = Va(A^{low})$$

The analytical considerations lead therefore to the conclusion that, given the valence of success and failure which is predominant in our culture, there is nothing paradoxical in the fact that people reach out for difficult tasks. We rather have now to explain why it is not always the most difficult task which is chosen.

Probability of Future Success; the Basic Theoretical Assumption

The answer is that we have to deal here with a *future* success and failure. The individual is, therefore, not only influenced by the attractiveness of such an event but also by the probability of its occurrence as this is seen by him (Figure 3.4).

Columns 4 and 5 (Tables 3.2 and 3.3) give values for subjective probability of succeeding or failing. The probability of success increases from zero to 100% with decreasing difficulty and the probability of failure changes in the opposite direction.

Escalona sets forth the "resultant valence theory" according to which the choice is determined, not by the valence of future success or failure as such, but rather by these valences modified by the probability of the occurrence of these events. The most simple assumption is that this "weighted" valence of success $[°Va(Suc_A{}^n)]$ is the product of the valence and of the probability of success.

$$°Va(Suc_A{}^n) = Va(Suc_A{}^n) \cdot \text{Prob.}(Suc_A{}^n) \tag{5a}$$

The corresponding formula for failure is:

$$°Va(Fai_A{}^n) = Va(Fai_A{}^n) \cdot \text{Prob.}(Fai_A{}^n) \tag{5b}$$

Columns 6 and 7 in Tables 3.2 and 3.3 give the values of the weighted valences of future success and failure. The sum of these valences will be called "resultant weighted valence" $[°Va(A^n)]$.

$$\text{Level of aspiration} = n \text{ if } °Va(A^n) = \text{maximum} \tag{6}$$

Column 8 gives the values for these "resultant weighted valences." In Table 3.2 the maximum of the resultant weighted valence lies on level 8 of the scale of possible objectives. It means that under the given conditions the individual will choose the objective 8 as his goal. We can represent that by indicating a "goal line" across the diagram. The curve of resultant weighted valence shows a decrease from the level of maximum toward both the levels of greater and of smaller difficulties.

Mathematically the 50–50 level of probability of failure and success is identical with the "most probable achievement." That level of achievement which is subjectively the most probable is usually meant when one speaks of one's expectation. In other words, the level of expectation is identical with the subjective 50–50 probability of failure and success.

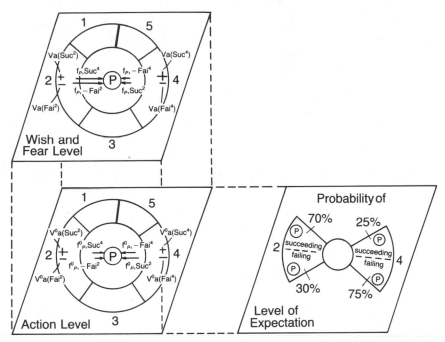

Figure 3.4 *Figure 3.3 takes into account the valences of success and failure but not the probability of the succeeding or failing at the various degrees of difficulty. Such a situation corresponds psychologically to a constellation which may exist on the "wish and fear level." The constellation of forces on the "action level" depends, in addition, on the individual's perception of the future, that is, the structure of the "level of expectation." Notice the difference in the direction of the resultant forces on the wish and on the action level.*

1, 2, . . , 5 *tasks of increasing degrees of difficulty;*
$Va(Suc^2)$ *valence of success in task 2* ⎫
$Va(Fai^2)$ *valence of failure in task 2* ⎬ *on wish and fear level.*
　　　　　　　　　　　　　　　　　　　　⎭

$V°a(Suc^2)$ *weighted valence of success in task 2* ⎫
$V°a(Fai^2)$ *weighted valence of failure in task 2* ⎬ *on action level.*
　　　　　　　　　　　　　　　　　　　　　　⎭

$f_{P,Suc}{}^2$ *force toward success in task 2.*
$f_{P,-Fai}{}^2$ *force away from failure in task 2.*
$f°_{P,Suc}{}^2$ *weighted force toward success in task 2.*

Table 3.3 shows the same distribution of valences of success and failure, but in this example we assume that the individual expects to show a better performance next time. This rise of his expectation from level 7 to level 8 raises the position of the maximum resultant valence from level 8 to level 10.

Table 3.2 Example of Reference Scales Underlying a Level of Aspiration*   Table 3.2a†

	1	2	3	4	5	6	7	8	
	Levels of Possible Objective	Valences of		Subjective Probability		Weighted Valence of		Resultant Weighted Valence	Resultant Weighted Valence When Group Standard Has Potency = .3
		Fut. Suc.	Fut. Fai.	Succeeding	Failing	Fut. Suc.	Fut. Fai.		
↑ Too difficult	15	10	0	0	100	0	0	0	0
	14	10	0	0	100	0	0	0	0
	13	10	0	0	100	0	0	0	0
	12	10	0	0	100	0	0	0	0
	11	10	0	5	95	50	0	50	47
	10	9	0	10	90	90	0	90	63 Level of
	9	7	−1	25	75	175	−75	100 Level of	−35
	8	6	−2	40	60	240	−120	120 ↑	−24 g ds = 3
								aspiration g ds = 1	aspiration
	7	5	−3	50	50	250	−150	100	−50
	6	3	−5	60	40	180	−200	−20	−98
	5	2	−7	75	25	150	−175	−25	−93
	4	1	−9	90	10	90	−90	0	−30
	3	0	−10	95	5	0	−50	−50	−50
Too easy ↓	2	0	−10	100	0	0	0	0	0
	1	0	−10	100	0	0	0	0	0

Level of past performance and of expectation

68

*Column 1 indicates the possible objectives. The "too difficult" and "too easy" levels correspond to the areas where the subjective probability of failing (column 5) and of succeeding (column 4) are 100% or close to 100%. Columns 2 and 3 give valences of future success and failure on each level; they vary between 0 and 10. Columns 6 and 7 represent the weighted valences, e.g., valence times probability, according to formulae (5a) and (5b). Column 8 gives the resultant valence according to formula (6) (see p. 66).

In this schematic example the level of past performance is assumed to have been on the level 7. The individual expects his next performance to lie on the same level, perhaps because he has found it difficult to reach that level. This "level of expectation" corresponds to the 50–50 level of subjective probability. The level of aspiration according to formula (6) is determined by the maximum value of the resultant weighted valence, that is, in our example the value of 120 corresponding to difficulty level 8. The goal discrepancy score (g ds), that is, the level of aspiration minus the level of past performance, equals 1.

†Table 3.2a represents the resultant weighted valence in a case where the valences of future success and failure are based on two reference scales: the one is the scale related to group standards as expressed in columns 2 and 3 of Table 3.5; the other scale of reference might have the same distribution of values as that in columns 2 and 3 of Table 3.2. This distribution of values might be an expression, for instance, of the valences based on one's own past performance.

The relative weight or "potency" of these two frames of references might be 3 (group standard) to 7. In such cases the valence of future success or failure would be determined by the sum of the corresponding values on the two frames of reference multiplied by that fraction which represents the relative potency of that scale. For instance, the valence of future success on the level 7 would be 5 × .7 + 2 × .3; that of future failure would be − 3 × .7 − 10 × .3. These values would have to be weighted by the subjective probability of success and failure as usual.

Our example shows that the poor student in our case would set his level of aspiration less high if he is not exclusively influenced by the reference scale of the group standard: the goal discrepancy equals 3 instead of 4 as in Table 3.5.

Table 3.3 Example of Reference Scales Underlying a Level of Aspiration*

1	2	3	4	5	6	7	8	
	Valences of		Subjective Probability		Weighted Valence of		Resultant Weighted Valence	
Possible Objective	Fut. Suc.	Fut. Fai.	Succeeding	Failing	Fut. Suc.	Fut. Fai.		
15	10	0	0	100	0	0	0	
14	10	0	0	100	0	0	0	
13	10	0	0	100	0	0	0	
12	10	0	5	95	50	0	50	
11	10	0	10	90	100	0	100	
10	9	0	25	75	225	0	225	Level of Aspiration
9	7	− 1	40	60	280	− 60	220	$att\ ds = -2$
8	6	− 2	50	50	300	− 100	200	$g\ ds = 3$ — Level of New Performance
7	5	− 3	60	40	300	− 120	150	Level of Past Performance
6	3	− 5	75	25	300	− 125	175	"Post-Factum Goal Line"
5	2	− 7	90	10	180	− 70	110	
4	1	− 9	95	5	95	− 45	50	
3	0	− 10	100	0	0	0	0	
2	0	− 10	100	0	0	0	0	
1	0	− 10	100	0	0	0	0	

*Table 3.3 shows the same level of past performance and the same distribution of valences of success and failure as Table 3.2. However, the 50–50 level of subjective probability, corresponding to the expectation for the next performance, lies one level higher. As a result, the maximum resultant weighted valence is raised so that the goal discrepancy score ($g\ ds$) is now 3.

The level of new performance is 8. The attainment discrepancy ($att\ ds$) is, therefore, − 2 and would usually lead to the feeling of failure. In our case the individual consoles himself by setting up a "post-factum" goal line on the level of his past performance, in this way creating a "satisfactory" post-factum attainment score of + 1.

In case of realistic judgment the individual will place his expectation somewhere within the boundary zone of his ability. Given a distribution of valences like that in Table 3.2 or 3.3, the goal line will tend to lie relatively close to the subjective 50–50 level of probability. It can be concluded, therefore, that the level of aspiration should tend to lie close to the boundary zone of ability of the person at that time. Indeed, the experiments show that, on the whole, the probability scale has sufficient weight to keep the level of aspiration close to that zone. A young child will not generally try to lift a weight as heavy as his father can, although he might try to reach the level of aspiration of his older sibling. The factors which tend to move the goal line outside the boundary zone of ability will be discussed presently.

The theory thus far explains several groups of experimentally established facts:

1. The tendency to seek a relatively high level of aspiration.
2. The tendency of the level of aspiration to go up only to certain limits.
3. The tendency of the level of aspiration to stay out of an area too difficult and too easy.

It is probably safe to assume that the subjective *probability* of success is, for the same person, more or less inverse to the probability of failure, that is, probability of success plus the probability of failure equals 100. However, it would be incorrect to assume that the *valence* of success and the valence of failure are always inverse. Great differences exist among people in regard to the degree to which they are ruled by the tendency to avoid failure or by the tendency to seek success. Some people appear very much afraid of failure and to them the possibility of failure is uppermost in their minds. These people would show high negative valences on column 3 (see Table 3.4). In general this lowers the level on which the maximum weighted valence lies. That this derivation is well in line with the experimental findings relative to the effect of fear of failure on the discrepancy score (page 37) will become clearer if we consider in more detail the factors which determine the distribution of values on the scales of valences and on the scales of subjective probability.

We are now going to discuss factors underlying the distribution of values in columns 2, 3, 4, and 5, Tables 3.2 to 3.4.

Table 3.4 Example of Reference Scales Underlying a Level of Aspiration*

1	2	3	4	5	6	7	8
	Valences of		Subjective Probability		Weighted Valence of		Resultant Weighted Valence
Possible Objective	Fut. Suc.	Fut. Fai.	Succeeding	Failing	Fut. Suc.	Fut. Fai.	
15	10	0	0	100	0	0	0
14	10	0	0	100	0	0	0
13	10	0	0	100	0	0	0
12	10	0	0	100	0	0	0
11	10	0	5	95	50	0	50
10	9	0	10	90	90	0	90
9	7	− 2	25	75	175	− 150	25
8	6	− 4	40	60	240	− 240	0 ← $g\ ds = 3$
7	5	− 6	50	50	250	− 300	− 50
6	3	− 10	60	40	180	− 400	− 220
5	2	− 14	75	25	150	− 350	− 200
4	1	− 18	90	10	90	− 180	− 90
3	0	− 20	95	5	0	− 100	− 100
2	0	− 20	100	0	0	0	0
1	0	− 20	100	0	0	0	0

*The values on the scale of valence of future success and on the scales of subjective probability are the same as in Table 3.2. The negative valences on the failure scale are doubled, expressing the great weight which failure has for the individual. It is obvious that, as a rule, the greater negative values on column 3 would tend to lower the position of the resultant weighted valence. In our example the greater fear for failure actually raises the level of the resultant valence in an atypical way from the level 8 to the level 10. Such atypical cases where fear of failure leads to a high level of aspiration and a high goal discrepancy score (equals 3) are frequently observed. They are one of the reasons why a group of individuals who fail show a great scattering of discrepancy scores.

Scales of Reference

Factors Determining the Values on the Scale of Probability

PAST EXPERIENCE. A main factor which determines the subjective probability of future success and failure is the past experience of the individual in regard to his ability to reach certain objectives.

In case an individual has had *much experience* in this particular activity, he will know pretty well what level he can expect to reach or not to reach. That means that his 50 – 50 level of probability of succeeding or failing will be well defined and the gradient of values on the probability scale will be steep; the steepness will be the greater the less the performance of the individual in this particular task fluctuates. Thus, the experiments about transfer (page 41) show that success or failure in one area influence the level of aspiration in a second area less if the person is well at home in the second area than if this area is new to him.

At the other extreme are cases where the subjective probability is practically undetermined. Here the observations are also in line with the theory. In fields of activity which a person *tries* for the first time in his life and where he is unable to judge his probable performance, the individual frequently does not spontaneously set himself a definite level of aspiration. Instead he goes into the action without definite goal level; in popular terms he merely "tries it out."

It is not only the average past performance which determines the subjective probability. If, for instance, the *sequence* of achievements follows an order such that the later trial is better than the previous one, the individual will feel that he "is steadily improving." He is then likely to expect that he has not yet reached the end of the learning process and will place the 50 – 50 level of probability higher than his last achievement. This will tend to lead to a rise in the level of aspiration (Table 3.3).

One would expect that the *last* success and failure will have a particularly great influence on the subject's expectation of the future achievement level because of the greater psychological weight of the more recent experience. The fact that all the experiments find that much of lowering and raising is dependent upon the quality of the last performance proves in general the correctness of this statement.

However, it would be erroneous to treat the effect of past experiences only as a result of their recency. A given sequence of achievements will set up certain "*subjective* hypotheses" which the subject uses to predict his achievement. In the case of a nonachievement which is linked, for instance, to outside disturbances, the subject is not likely to lower his level of aspiration in the way he would if he believed that the nonachievement represented a genuine decrement in his performance ability. Each trial may be regarded by the subject as an additional datum to be added to what he already knows about the activity and may change his ideas about probability of achievement. Therefore, if the previous performance has been accompanied by feelings of success, the level of aspiration should tend to rise in most cases if the previous performance has by its less good quality engendered failure reactions, the level of aspiration should tend to go down. It is well in line with this derivation that after "barely reached successes" as well as after "weak failures" the level of aspiration tends to remain unchanged.

In studying individual differences we have become more and more aware that individual constancies (for instance, in regard to the discrepancy score) are much less if the sequence pattern is not kept constant. Future investigations will do well to be still more careful on this point.

GOOD STRUCTURE OF ACTIVITY.   Aside from past experience, certain cognitive settings influence the expectation of future success and failure. If, for instance, the series of levels to be chosen from has a definite upper and lower limit, the probability of reaching what is in that setting "top performance" may appear less probable. The tendency to make higher and higher records in some sports seems to be related to a goal structure which appears to have no upper limit. The effect of using large or small numbers when the experimenter indicates success or failure seems to be based on similar factors.

WISH, FEAR, AND EXPECTATION.   The judgment of the probability of success or failure on a given level is not only determined by past experience and "realistic" considerations, but also by wishes and fears, i.e., by the valence of future success and failure. This is proved by the fact, for instance, that knowledge of group standards influences our level of expectation. In other words, the various parts of the life space are an interdependent field: the realistic expectancy is based mainly on past experiences. The structure of the psychological past affects the structure of the psychological future. However, the expectancy or reality level of the psychological future is also affected by the wish and fear (irreality) level of the psychological future.

Scales of Reference
Underlying the Valences of Future Success and Failure

The numerical values for the valences along the scale of future success or failure follow the general observation that the valence of success, within limits, is an increasing function of the difficulty of the objective, and the valence of failure a decreasing function of difficulty. This is usually correct in our culture, but only as a first approximation. It is the result of a composite picture, some of the constituents of which we will discuss briefly.

GROUP STANDARDS.   Individuals belonging to a certain group are usually deeply affected by the "standards" of this group. In matters of level of aspiration, such a standard means that a frame of reference exists on which the standard level is particularly significant.

In some cases, for instance, in case of the ideology underlying the college term "Gentleman *C*," the group standard is equivalent to the maximum valence on the scale of success: to be either above or below this standard is considered less desirable than the standard (Table 3.5). The fashion, particularly in democratic countries, frequently follows a similar pattern of an optimum rather than a maximum of elegance as the most desirable level.

In other cases, the group standard merely indicates a level at which the valence gradient is particularly steep: there is little success valence and much negative valence of failure immediately below the group standard, and much success and little failure valence directly above group standard.

For Table 3.5, which is an example of the first type, the resultant valences are figured for an individual who has his achievement score (50 – 50 probability) definitely below the group standard, for one whose achievement lies at the group level, and for one individual above that level. One can see that, independent of the level of probable achievement, the maximum resultant valence (and therefore the goal line) should lie close to the group standard. The experimental results (page 000) show that this is true. They also show, as one would expect, that these phenomena are the more striking the greater the relative weight of such a frame of reference. (Compare Table 3.5 and Table 3.2a.)

In extreme cases of regard for such standards the most able person should tend to keep his level of aspiration low and may even show a negative discrepancy score; the least able person should keep up a high level of aspiration even at the price of a great positive discrepancy score. It is obvious that such a constellation might lead to a level of aspiration

Table 3.5 Example of the Effect of a Group Standard. Comparison of an Individual with Low, Medium, and High Performance Level*

Possible Objective	Valence		Subj. Prob. of Success for a Person with			Resultant Weighted Valence for a Person with		
	Suc.	Fai.	Low Perf.	Medium Perf.	High Perf.	Low Perf.	Medium Perf.	High Perf.
15	6	0	0	0	10	0	0	60
14	6	0	0	0	25	0	0	150
13	6	0	0	5	40	0	30	240
12	6	0	0	10	50 Last	0	60	300
11	8	0	5	25	60	40	200	400
10	9	− 1	10	40	75	0	300	650
9	10	− 8	25	50	90 Last	− 350	100	820
8	6	− 10	40	60	95	− 360	− 40	520
7	2	− 10	50	75	100 Last	− 400	− 100	200
6	0	− 10	60	90	100	− 400	− 100	0
5	0	− 10	75	95	100	− 250	− 50	0
4	0	− 10	90	100	100	− 100	0	0
3	0	− 10	95	100	100	− 50	0	0
2	0	− 10	100	100	100	0	0	0
1	0	− 10	100	100	100	0	0	0

Group standard

$g\,ds = 4$ $g\,ds = 1$ $g\,ds = -3$

performance

*In this example the group standard lies on the position of the maximum valence of success and on a steep gradient of the valence scale of failure. Columns 3, 4, and 5 indicate the subjective probability of success for three individuals whose performance is below the group standard, on the group standard and above the group standards, for instance, a poor, medium, and good student in a class. To condense the table we are not presenting the scale of probable failure which is the converse of that of success. It is assumed in our example that our three individuals are rather realistic and that their level of expectation, that is, the 50 – 50 level of probable success, lies on the level of their past performance.

If the group standards were the only scale determining the valence of success and failure, the level of aspiration of all three individuals would lie on or above the group standard; this would mean that the poor student would have a high positive goal discrepancy score ($g\ ds = 4$); the best students, a negative discrepancy score ($g\ ds = -3$). In our example the level of aspiration of the poor students would be even higher than that of the good ones.

This example illustrates why the level of aspiration might be kept above or below one's own ability.

As a rule, of course, the scale related to the group standards is only one of several reference scales underlying the valence of future success and failure. Table 3.2a gives the result of a combination with another reference scale.

well above or below the "boundary zone of ability." This is illustrated by experimental data previously cited.

Standards set from outside do not need to come from a definitely structured group, such as the school class or an age group. Frequently they are related to another individual, for instance, the father, the friends, the wife, or they are based on certain requirements of law or society. As a rule, there are, coexisting, quite a number of such scales of reference which include certain standards.

Past Achievements; the Space of Free Movement

Certain standards may result from the fact that the individual "competes with himself." In this case his "past achievements" not only determine the probability of future achievements; they also provide certain standards for future goals (Table 3.2a).

One factor which seems to be important for the striving toward the more difficult is the desire to reach beyond the area which has been accessible until then to the person. The totality of accessible areas of activities is called "space of free movement." A person's space of free movement is limited partly by the rules of society and the power of other persons, partly by his own ability or what is called the nature of things. The growth of the space of free movement is a fundamental factor of development, and the reaching out for the yet unreached is a powerful desire of the child and of many adults in many fields of activity. One can view the tendency to raise the level of aspiration as due partly to these desires.

In summing up we might state: a multitude of coexistent frames of reference may underlie the probability scale and the scale of valences of future success and failure. They can technically be recombined to these main scales if one attributes to each of the underlying frames of reference scales (uRS) the relative weight or potency with which it influences the individual; for instance, we would have three reference scales indicated by uRS^1, uRS^2, and uRS^3, underlying the valence of success. If uRS^1 were twice as influential as a motive for this individual as the reference scales uRS^2 and uRS^3, the value of the valence of success and failure on a given level would be calculated by referring to the corresponding levels on the underlying reference scale according to the formula $uRS^1 \times .5 - uRS^2 \times .25 - uRS^3 \times .25$. Table 3.2a presents an example. *Differences of "culture" as well as differences of "personality" might then be represented as a number of frames of reference and a pattern of relative weight.*

The Discrepancy Score and the Relative Potency of the Various Frames of Reference

The recent studies of the level of aspiration have expressed their results frequently in terms of goal discrepancy score, that is, of the difference between level of aspiration and past achievement. Although the discrepancy score in itself is an important aspect of the problems of the level of aspiration, most workers in the field agree that it has been somewhat overstressed. It is recognized that the discrepancy score is a resultant of many factors and that it is important to find out what are the particular factors behind a certain discrepancy score in a given case.

DISCREPANCY SCORE, LEVEL OF EXPECTATION, AND THE DISCREPANCY BETWEEN EXPECTATION AND PAST PERFORMANCE.   If a person were entirely realistic, his expectation would on the average coincide roughly with his future performance. That means that the discrepancy score between past performance and expectation should be the same as the difference between his past and his new performance. As a rule, it would be zero or slightly positive.

Actually our "expectation" is not entirely independent of our wishes and fears. However, this dependency is less close than that between these wishes and fears and the level of aspiration. From this follows that the discrepancy between the level of expectation and past performance should be less than the discrepancy between level of aspiration and past performance (discrepancy score). Experiments show the correctness of this conclusion.

They also show that the variability of the discrepancy is less in regard to expectation than in regard to the level of aspiration. This follows theoretically from the fact that the variability of the level of aspiration depends not only on the variability of the values on the probability scale but in addition on the variability of values on the valence scales.

THE EFFECT OF THE STRUCTURE OF THE REFERENCE SCALES AND OF THEIR RELATIVE POTENCY.   The example of discrepancy scores in Tables 3.2 to 3.5 may suffice to show that the size and direction of the discrepancy score depend upon the level of the last achievement, upon the distribution of values along each of the reference scales, and upon the relative potency of each reference scale. It is, therefore, impossible to predict a discrepancy score accurately without knowing these data for the particular case. It is, however, possible to make certain general statements about the effect on the discrepancy score of a change in the relative potency of various reference scales, if the numerical values along these scales are kept constant and if we refer to situations where the learning improvement is not important.

Realism

Realism in matters of the level of aspiration refers to one or both of two factors: (1) it refers to the probability scale and means closeness of expectation and "reality"; that is, closeness of the 50–50 level of "subjective" and of the "objective" probability. Such a correctness of judgment about one's own future action may be measured by the discrepancy between expectation and new performance. (2) Realism refers to a tendency to keep the maximum resultant weighted valence close to the 50–50 level of subjective probability. This implies that the individual chooses a distribution of values on the valence scales in such a way that this closeness of expectation and action goal results. We have previously spoken about the fact that the subjective probability scale is not entirely independent of the valence scale. Realism implies that, inversely, the distribution of the valence scale is not entirely independent of the probability scale.

It follows from this consideration that the absolute size of the goal discrepancy score would be the smaller the more realistic the person is. This is borne out by a number of findings:

1. Realism is obviously greater in case the subject is asked what he "expects" than what he would "like to get." Indeed, the discrepancy score is smaller in the first case.
2. The "realistic" attitude is greater in work than in play situations or activities. Correspondingly, the discrepancy score is smaller in the former.
3. Realism should be greater for "realistic" than for "irrealistic" persons. The experiments bear out the derivations.
4. Success, if not given in too strong doses, should make for a less tense emotional situation than failure, particularly in cases of repeated failure. Emotionality makes for an irrealistic attitude. We should expect, therefore, the absolute size of the discrepancy score to be greater in case of a chronic failure situation than in continued success. This derivation is again borne out by several experiments.

The Values on the Success Valence Scale Relative to the Values on the Failure Valence Scale

The discrepancy score should be the more positive the higher the values on the success scales are, relative to the absolute values of the failure scale on the same level, provided that the gradient on each scale is not changed. This is borne out by a number of findings.

The Readiness to Take Risks

Lowering the values of the failure scale means psychologically being less afraid of failure. This would tend to move the resultant valence and therefore the goal line up relative to the achievement, resulting in high positive discrepancy scores. In other words, the relative weight of the success and failure scale determines what is usually called the readiness of the individual "to take risks" or to be cautious.

The findings about individual differences are in line with this conclusion.

Being Inside or Outside the Failure Region

The tendency to avoid future failure, or the force on the person away from failure ($f_{P,-Fai}$) is a function of the present position of the person, particularly whether he sees himself at present in the region of "being successful" or "failing." It seems that the force $f_{P,-Fai}$ is usually greater and, therefore, the values on the failure scale higher if the person is at present in the region of failing (Fai) than if he is in a region of not failing ($NFai$). This holds at least as long as the person does not "accept" being a failure. Accepting failure frequently creates a "don't care" attitude which is equivalent to the diminishing of the valence of failure. Usually, however, it holds:

$$f_{Fai,-Fai} > f_{NFai,-Fai} \tag{7}$$

From this assumption we can derive a number of conclusions which are all borne out by experiments.

1. A recent failure should tend to lower the level of aspiration. This is one of the major findings in the field. The "atypical" cases of raising the level of aspiration after failure (occurring in from 10% to 20% of the cases) would follow from a decrease in the realism of the situation or from acceptance of "being a failure."

2. The level of aspiration should decrease more after strong failure than after a weak failure. It should, of course, increase after success.

3. Due to the cumulative effects of the above mentioned factors the person who fails habitually should have a lower discrepancy score than the person who usually succeeds. Atypical cases of high positive discrepancy score after habitual failure would again be understandable as a result of the factors mentioned in paragraph 1.

4. There should be a tendency to avoid finishing a series of trials with a failure since this means letting oneself remain relatively permanently in the area of failure.

The Variability of Discrepancy Score
and the Ease of Changing the Level of Aspiration

The ease with which the level of aspiration can be changed, that is, the width of change by a small additional force, depends on the flatness of the curve of the resultant weighted valence near its maximum. Obviously, the same factor would determine the variability of the discrepancy score.

The gradient toward the more easy task in Table 3.3, column 8, for instance, is less steep than in Table 3.2, column 8. The steepness of the resultant valence curve depends on the steepness of the gradient on the various reference scales, their relative position to each other, and their potency.

For instance, if group standards play a great role and if the distribution of values along that scale shows as steep a gradient as in columns 2 and 3, Table 3.5, a lowering of the potency of that scale and an increase of the potency of other reference scales (which have the distribution, for instance, of columns 2 and 3, Table 3.2), would flatten out the curve of the resultant valences and make the individual more ready to change. Table 3.2a is an example of such a combination resulting in a small gradient on the resultant valence curve.

In cases where the probable achievement is quite precisely known and where the individual is realistic the gradient should be relatively steep.

Reaction to Achieving or Not Achieving the Level of Aspiration

After the person has set his level of aspiration and then acted, he reacts to his achieving or not achieving his goals (point 4 in Figure 3.1). The main types of reactions are the following:

Feeling of Success and Failure

The experiments show that the feeling of success and failure does not depend on an absolute level of achievement. What for one person means success means failure for another person, and even for the same person the same achievement will lead sometimes to the feeling of failure and sometimes to the feeling of success.

What counts is the level of achievement relative to certain standards, in particular to the level of aspiration (goal line): if the achievement lies on or above the goal line, the subject will probably have a feeling of success; if it lies below the goal line he will probably feel failure, depending on the size of this difference and the ease with which the achievement has been reached.

Rationalization, Avoidance of Feeling of Failure

The forces $f_{P,Suc}$ and $f_{P,-Fai}$, that is, tendencies to seek success and avoid failure, are one of the bases for the level of aspiration. They also influence strongly the events at the point 4 of our sequence. The tendency to stay out of the failure region can lead to what is called rationalization.

There are two ways in which an individual after failing to achieve his level of aspiration still may avoid the feeling of failure.

1. He might change his goal line *post factum*, for instance, after a person has tried for level 10 (Table 3.3) but reached only 8 he might then say, "Well, that is still better than any previous achievement" (or better than the average of previous achievement, or better than another person). In other words, he might switch his standard in a way which amounts to a sufficient lowering of his goal line afterwards (see notes on Table 3.3).

2. Severing the relation between achievement and the individual himself as a "responsible" person is another means of avoiding failure. Only if the result of the action is "attributed" to the person as actor and not attributed to other persons or to "nature" can we speak psychologically of an "achievement" of this person. There is a tendency after failure to link the poor result to a faulty instrument, to sickness, or to any event "outside the power" of the individual involved (see Gould and Hoppe). The fact that such severing of the link between the result and the individual is more frequent after poor than after good achievement shows that it can be due to the force of avoiding failure.

Continuing the Activity with a New Trial or Stopping

As a result of his achievement, the individual might decide to attempt a new trial in the same activity or to stop.

Whether a person will continue or stop depends on a great number of factors, such as, the hope of doing better, his being on the whole successful or unsuccessful, his involvement in the particular activity, the alternative he would have in regard to other activities, and so on. Finally, however, the stopping or not stopping depends upon whether for the force $f_{P,A}$ is smaller or greater than zero (where A means the activity on hand).

$$\text{Stopping occurs if } f_{P,A} < 0 \qquad (8)$$

In case no outside pressure is exerted on the individual to continue, the individual will stop if the maximum value on the resultant valence curve is still negative, or more correctly if this value is smaller than the valences of an alternative activity. In line with this theory, Escalona (1940) found that patients in a mental hospital who disliked going back to the ward were less ready to stop than those who wanted mainly to be left alone.

One factor which tends to lower the values of the resultant weighted valence curves is a general decrease of the probability of success. This explains why and when after a series of failures the person will stop.

The values for the person with low, medium, and high performance in Table 3.5 are an example of how the decrease in the probability of success leads to a higher negative resultant valence. Whereas for the successful person all values on the scale of resultant valences are positive, indicating an attractiveness of the activity as a whole, most of the values for the unsuccessful person are strongly negative. This indicates a negative valence for the task as a whole and the individual should stop if the only remaining positive value on the level 11 should disappear.

In case of pressure, the individual will continue as long as the force away from the activity $f_{P,-A}$ is smaller than the pressure exerted.

In case the individual chooses to continue with the same activity, his level of aspiration will be determined by the factors we have discussed.

General Conclusion

These theoretical considerations show that most of the qualitative and quantitative results related to the level of aspiration can be linked with three factors, namely, the seeking of success ($f_{P,Suc}$), the avoiding of failure ($f_{P,-Fai}$), and the cognitive factor of a probability judgment. These forces operate in a setting which has to be characterized as a choice for a future objective. The strength of these forces and the values corresponding to the subjective probability depend on many aspects of the life space of the individual at that time, particularly on the way he sees his past experience and on the scales of reference which are characteristic for his culture and his personality.

On the whole, the study of the level of aspiration has reached a point where the nature of the problems and their relations to other fields is sufficiently clear to be useful as a guide for future research. Within the field of "goal behavior" one can distinguish problems of "goal striving" and problems of "goal setting." Goal striving is a "directed" behavior toward existing goals and is closely related to problems of locomotion toward a goal, of frustration, reaching a goal and consummatory behavior. Goal setting is related to the question of what goal will emerge or become dominant after another goal has been reached or not reached. Within this field lie, for instance, the problems of psychological satiation and a major part of the problems of level of aspiration. The latter, however, are closely interwoven with all aspects of goal behavior.

Future research can, it appears, be conducted along two general lines.

1. One can try to understand more fully the general laws of the level of aspiration. The analysis is far enough along at present to encourage an attempt to determine quantitatively the values on the various scales of reference. Such an attempt would give insight, for instance, into the factors which determine our probability judgment about our future, and would be of considerable value for the general theory of cognitive processes and perception. It would permit a quantitative approach to such divergent questions as a theory of choice and compromise; the effect of past experience and group belonging on certain aspects of cultural values, e.g., their distribution, interdependence, and rigidity; the factors determining the "ability to take it"; and problems of development and regression in regard to complying to rules.

2. It is possible to use level of aspiration techniques as an instrument to compare different cultures and to characterize their systems of values in a quantitative way. Similarly, these techniques may become progressively more useful for measuring individual differences of value systems and of other major characteristics of the normal and abnormal personality.

References

ANDERSON, C. (1940) The development of a level of aspiration in young children. Iowa City: Dissertation, University Ia.

ANDERSON, H. H., & BRANDT, H. F. (1939) Study of motivation involving self-announced goals of fifth grade children and the concept of level of aspiration. *J. soc. Psychol.*, **10**, 209–232.

CHAPMAN, D. W., & VOLKMANN, J. (1939) A social determinant of the level of aspiration. *J. abnorm. soc. Psychol.*, **34**, 225–238.

DEMBO, T. (1931) Der Ärger als dynamisches Problem. (Untersuchungen zur Handlungs- und Affektpsychologie. X. Ed. by Kurt Lewin.) *Psychol. Forsch.*, **15**, 1–144.

ESCALONA, S. K. (1940) The effect of success and failure upon the level of aspiration and behavior in manic-depressive psychoses. *Univ. Ia Stud. Child Welf.*, **16**, No. 3, 199–302.

FALES, E. (1937) Genesis of level of aspiration in children from one and one-half to three years of age. (Reported in Anderson, C., 1940)

FESTINGER, L. (1942a) Wish, expectation, and group standards as factors influencing level of aspiration. *J. abnorm. soc. Psychol.*, **37**, 184–200.

———— (1942b) A theoretical interpretation of shifts in level of aspiration. *Psychol. Rev.*, **49**, 235–250.

FRANK, J. D. (1935a) Individual differences in certain aspects of the level of aspiration. *Amer. J. Psychol.*, **47**, 119–128.

———— (1935b) The influence of the level of performance in one task on the level of aspiration in another. *J. exp. Psychol.*, **18**, 159–171.

———— (1935c) Some psychological determinants of the level of aspiration. *Amer. J. Psychol.*, **47**, 285–293.

———— (1936) A comparison between certain properties of the level of aspiration and random guessing. *J. Psychol.*, **3**, 43–62.

———— (1938) Level of aspiration test. In Murray, H. A., et al. *Explorations in personality*. New York: Oxford University Press, pp. 461–471.

———— (1941) Recent studies of the level of aspiration. *Psychol. Bull.*, **38**, 218–225.

GARDNER, J. W. (1939) Level of aspiration in response to a prearranged sequence of scores. *J. exp. Psychol.*, **25**, 601–621.

———— (1940a) The relation of certain personality variables to level of aspiration. *J. Psychol.*, **9**, 191–206.

———— (1940b) The use of the term "level of aspiration." *Psychol. Rev.*, **47**, 59–68.

GOULD, R. (1938) Factors underlying expressed "level of aspiration." *J. Psychol.*, **6**, 265–279.

———— (1939) An experimental analysis of "level of aspiration." *Genet. Psychol. Monogr.*, **21**, 1–116.

———— (1941) Some sociological determinants of goal strivings. *J. soc. Psychol.*, **13**, 461–473.

GOULD, R., & KAPLAN, N. (1940) The relationship of "level of aspiration" to academic and personality factors. *J. soc. Psychol.*, **11**, 31–40.

GOULD, R., & LEWIS, H. B. (1940) An experimental investigation of changes in the meaning of level of aspiration. *J. exp. Psychol.*, **27**, 422–438.

HAUSMANN, M. F. (1933) A test to evaluate some personality traits. *J. gen. Psychol.*, **9**, 179–189.

HEATHERS, L. B. (1942) Factors producing generality in the level of aspiration. *J. exp. Psychol.*, **30**, 392–406.

HERTZMAN, M., & FESTINGER, L. (1940) Shifts in explicit goals in a level of aspiration experiment. *J. exp. Psychol.*, **27**, 439–452.

HILGARD, E. R., & SAIT, E. M. (1941) Estimates of past and of future performances as measures of aspiration. *Amer. J. Psychol.*, **54**, 102–108.

HILGARD, E. R., SAIT, E. M., & MAGARET, G. A. (1940) Level of aspiration as affected by relative standing in an experimental social group. *J. exp. Psychol.*, **27**, 411–421.

HOPPE, F. (1930) Erfolg und Misserfolg. (Untersuchungen zur Handlungs- und Affectpsychologie: IX. Ed. by Kurt Lewin.) *Psychol. Forsch.*, **14**, 1–62.

IRWIN, F. W., & MINTZER, M. G. (1942) Effect of differences in instructions and motivation upon measures of the level of aspiration. *Amer. J. Psychol.*, **55**, 400–406.

JUCKNAT, M. (1937) Leistung, Anschpruchsniveau und Selbstbewusstsein. (Untersuchungen zur Handlungs- und Affectpsychologie: XX. Ed. by Kurt Lewin.) *Psychol. Forsch.*, **22**, 89–179.

LURIE, W. A. (1939) Estimating the level of vocational aspiration. *J. soc. Psychol.*, **10**, 467–473.

MCGEHEE, W. (1940) Judgment and level of aspiration. *J. gen. Psychol.*, **22**, 3–15.

PRESTON, M. G. (1942) Use of the coefficient of correlation in the study of the D-score for the level of aspiration. *Amer. J. Psychol.*, **55**, 442–446.

PRESTON, M. G., & BAYTON, J. A. (1941) Differential effect of a social variable upon three levels of aspiration. *J. exp. Psychol.*, **29**, 351–369.

———— (1942) Correlations between levels of aspiration. *J. Psychol.*, **13**, 369–373.

ROTTER, J. B. (1942a) Level of aspiration as a method of studying personality: I. A critical review of methodology. *Psychol. Rev.*, **49**, 463–474.

———— (1942b) Level of aspiration as a method of studying personality: II. Development and evaluation of a controlled method. *J. exp. Psychol.*, **31**, 410–422.

———— (1944) Level of aspiration as a controlled method of personality study using selected groups. (Unpublished)

SEARS, P. S. (1940) Levels of aspiration in academically successful and unsuccessful children. *J. abnorm. soc. Psychol.*, **35**, 498–536.

———— (1941) Level of aspiration in relation to some variables of personality: clinical studies. *J. soc. Psychol.*, **14**, 311–336.

SEARS, R. R. (1942) Success and failure: a study of motility. In McNemar, Q., & Merrill, M. A. *Studies in personality*. New York: McGraw-Hill, pp. 235 – 258.

YACORZYNSKI, G. K. (1942) Degree of effort: III. Relationship to the level of aspiration. *J. exp. Psychol.*, **30**, 407 – 413.

4

A Quantitative Theory
of Decision

Introduction

The mark of maturity of a science is the extent to which it can state its laws and functional relationships in precise mathematical terminology. Statistical techniques, especially those employing the theories of probability, have found wide application in psychology. Some geometrical concepts, particularly those of topology, have also been used although somewhat less widely. Rarely, if ever, however, has there been a thorough application of both types of mathematical means in psychological theory.

Recently in psychophysics an attempt has been made by Cartwright (5) to utilize geometrical concepts in the construction of a theory which brings psychophysics and "motivation psychology" closer together. We shall here attempt to bring statistical and geometrical concepts together in a quantitative theory of decision.

Cartwright presented a theory of decision-time in topological and vectorial terms which leads to the gross prediction that decision time approaches a maximum as the relative frequency of a given response approaches 50 per cent. This theory makes congruent otherwise unrelated and apparently inconsistent psychophysical data. In the present paper we shall make a refinement and further quantification of the theory so that the absolute values of *both* decision-time and relative frequency may be predicted for specified conditions.

The discussion of these refinements will be facilitated by a summary of the earlier statement of the theory. Cartwright assumed that the

SOURCE: Cartwright, D., & Festinger, L. *Psychol. Rev.*, 1943, **50**, 595 – 621.

forces determining judgment time in a psychophyical experiment operate in essentially the same way as those determining any sort of decision. A topological representation of a simple decision situation and the
forces which determine its outcome are reproduced in Figure 4.1. In
this hypothetical case only two alternatives (A and B) are possible, and,
assuming that they are both attractive, two forces ($f_{P,A}$ and $f_{P,B}$) act
upon the person in the direction of these alternatives.

From the definition of the concept of force it follows that the person
will choose the alternative toward which the stronger force is directed,
and moreover, that *he can choose neither alternative as long as the two
forces are of equal magnitude.* Assuming that time is required for an
initial balance of forces to become upset, we can conclude that whenever a balance of forces arises, decision-time will be lengthened.

When a subject is asked to make a judgment about the nature of a
stimulus, the goal of a cooperative subject is "to be right." If the stimulus is clearly longer, the region, "saying 'longer,' " L, is contained in
the region, "being right," R, since "saying 'longer' " and "being right"
are viewed as equivalent. Since the region "being right" has a positive
valence, and since L is included in R, the force correlated to the valence
has the direction toward the region L ($f_{P,L}$). Similarly, the region "being
wrong," W, has a negative valence and contains the region "saying
'shorter,' " S. The force related to the negative valence will, therefore,
be directed away from S ($f_{P,-S}$). Since the forces $f_{P,L}$ and $f_{P,-S}$ are
equivalent in direction, the sum of these may be considered as coordinated to the positive valence. The force acting upon P is clearly in the
direction of the region L, and the subject will, therefore, respond
"longer" without hesitation.

Similarly, when the variable stimulus is clearly perceived as shorter
than the standard, the force on P is directed toward S and the subject
will respond "shorter" without hesitation.

When the stimulus falls upon the boundary between the regions in

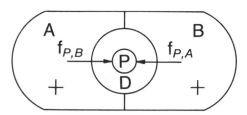

Figure 4.1 *A topological representation of a decision involving two alternatives. Region P represents the person, region D represents the activity of deciding, and A and B stand for the two alternatives.*

the phenomenal field it is equally probable that either judgment will be correct. The region "saying 'longer,' " L, is thus contained in two overlapping regions: "being right," R, and "being wrong," W. The region S, also is contained in the two regions R and W. In other words, both situations discussed above are functioning simultaneously. The presence of these two overlapping situations places the person between conflicting forces.

The strength of each of the forces acting on the person will depend upon how much weight or potency each situation has for the subject. Stated formalistically, in overlapping situations, the strength of the effective force acting on a person $(^{o}f_{P,G})$ *is equal to* the strength which that force would have if there were only one situation, *multiplied by* the potency of the situation to which it belongs (18):

$$^{o}f_{P,G} = f_{P,G} \cdot Po(S). \tag{1}$$

The potency of each overlapping situation is determined by the subject's feeling of probability that his judgment is correct. For example, if the subject feels both situations to be equally probable, the potency of each situation is equal to 0.5. (The sum of the potencies is arbitrarily set equal to 1.) The person is located, therefore, between opposite forces of equal magnitude and, as in Figure 4.1, cannot change his psychological position (*i.e.*, make a judgment) until the situation changes. Time will be consumed before this change can occur and we may, therefore, expect judgment-time to be lengthened when the stimulus falls on a boundary in the phenomenal field. Assuming further that the balance of forces will be upset in each direction equally often, repeated presentations of this situation will not only give a lengthened average judgment-time but also a relative frequency of judgment of longer (or shorter) of 50 per cent.

In another article, Cartwright (4) presented data which strongly support the theory by showing that the decision time curve reaches a peak when the stimulus approaches the boundary between two categories of response. The average distance between the 50 per cent point of relative frequency and maximum decision time was 0.6 units of the stimulus scale.

Mathematical Statement of the Theory of Decision

Aside from its inability to lead to more than gross quantitative predictions, the theory presented above is deficient in one other important respect. As it stands, any imbalance of forces, no matter how slight, is said to lead to a decision. Actually, a person usually will not announce his judgment before a given magnitude of difference between driving forces is reached. In any situation which can be set up in an experiment, restraining forces are also present which prevent the subject from going off "half-cocked." The person wishes to be reasonably certain that he is correct. In other words, the resultant of the driving forces ($f_{P,L}$ and $f_{P,S}$) must have a greater magnitude than the restraining force opposite to leaving D, ($f_{\overline{D,-D}}$). Only when this state of affairs is reached can a decision occur. In short, decision time may be lengthened even when the conflicting driving forces are not exactly equal.

A quantification may now be accomplished by making certain assumptions about the way in which the driving forces and the restraining forces fluctuate in time. Here, as in any other case, one can observe only the effect of the resultant force not its single components.

It is a common procedure to start with certain assumptions concerning the single forces. From them certain statements concerning the nature of the resultant force can be derived synthetically. Mathematically, this constitutes a procedure of defining the original distributions of forces and of deriving the resultant distribution. The conclusions may then be tested empirically. We will proceed in this order.

Fluctuation of Potency

For any given physical setting in which a decision or judgment is to be made, we assume that the potency of each situation fluctuates in time and distributes itself normally about a given mean value, with variance equal to σ_{Po}^2. More precisely, the distribution of potency in time, for an infinite length of time may be defined by the distribution function:

$$f(Po) = \frac{1}{\sigma_{Po}\sqrt{2\pi}} e^{-\frac{(Po - M_{Po})^2}{2\sigma_{Po}^2}}. \tag{2}$$

Fluctuation of Force

As seen above, fluctuations of potency cause the forces toward making a decision to fluctuate according to the potency fluctuation. In a setting where a judgment of longer or shorter must be made, the force toward saying longer ($f_{P,L}$) will fluctuate normally in time about a given mean value and the force toward saying shorter ($f_{P,S}$) will also fluctuate about its mean value. The equations of these two distribution functions are written in exactly the same form as that for potency except for the substitution of the correct values of the mean and variance which characterize these distributions.

The relative potency of one situation is, by definition, one minus the potency of the other situation. Therefore, the variance of the potency distribution functions for both situations are equal. Accordingly, since the fluctuation in force is due to this fluctuation in potency, the variance of the distribution of forces toward "saying 'longer' " will be equal to the variance of the distribution of forces toward "saying 'shorter' " $(\sigma_{f_{P,L}} = \sigma_{f_{P,S}})$.

Fluctuation of Differences Between Forces

At any time t there occurs a pairing of randomly selected forces,[1] one toward "saying 'longer' " and one toward "saying 'shorter.' " Let us call the distribution of the differences between these opposite forces the z function. This function, for an infinite number of pairings can be defined from the two force distributions. The z function distributes itself normally about its mean, which *is equal to* the mean of the distribution of forces toward "saying 'longer' " *minus* the mean of the distribution of forces toward "saying 'shorter.' " (Positive is the direction of longer and negative the direction of shorter.) The variance of the z distribution is equal to the variance of the $f_{P,L}$ distribution plus the variance of the $f_{P,S}$ distribution, plus two times the product of the two sigmas ($\sigma_z^2 = \sigma_{f_{P,L}}^2 + \sigma_{f_{P,S}}^2 + 2\sigma_{f_{P,L}}\sigma_{f_{P,S}}$). The last term is added because the pairings from the two force distributions will have a perfect negative correlation, since their respective potencies are perfectly negatively correlated. Since $\sigma_{f_{P,L}} = \sigma_{f_{P,S}}$ the variance of the z distribution will be four times as great as the variance of either of the force distributions. This z distribution is the distribution of the resultant force toward making a decision. It may be written as follows:

$$f(z) = \frac{1}{2\sigma_{f_{P,L}}\sqrt{2\pi}} e^{-\frac{[z - (M_{f_{P,L}} - M_{f_{P,S}})]^2}{8\sigma_{f_{P,L}}^2}} \tag{3}$$

1. The following questions arise concerning the nature of these fluctuations. If at t_1 a given potency exists, then at the immediately following t_2 can any other potency, within the range of fluctuation, exist, or must the fluctuations be continuous? It may be seen, however, that the choice between an assumption of continuous or discontinuous fluctuation does not affect our analysis or the derivations. In either case the distribution functions and the probabilities of obtaining given pairings are the same, and in either case, the initial potency at the time of presentation of the stimuli is a matter of random occurrence.

Fluctuation of Restraining Forces

We now make specific our assumption regarding the distribution of the restraining force ($rf_{\overline{D, -D}}$) which has the direction opposite to leaving the region of decision. This restraining force distributes itself normally about a constant mean value with given sigma. It may be written as follows:[2]

$$f(rf) = \frac{1}{\sigma_{rf}\sqrt{2\pi}}\, e^{-\frac{(rf - M_{rf})^2}{2\sigma_{rf}^2}}. \tag{4}$$

Fluctuation of Resultant Force

Let us now consider the distribution function resulting from random pairings of z values with rf values. We shall call this the z' distribution. It is the distribution of the final resultant forces away from the area of decision.

Obviously the pairing which occurs here is a pairing of values of rf with absolute values of z. Any pairing in which the absolute z is greater than the rf will yield a z' value which is greater than zero. Treated in this way a final resultant force greater than zero towards "saying 'longer' " is confused with a final resultant force greater than zero towards "saying 'shorter.' " There is, however, another method which keeps these two separate and which is mathematically equivalent to it. In this method the algebraic signs of the z values are maintained in the pairings. (In our z distribution we have defined positive as being the direction of "saying 'longer' " and negative the direction of "saying 'shorter.' ") The function obtained by this method of pairing can be defined in terms of the already defined z distribution and the rf distribution. The z' function will distribute itself normally about its mean, which is equal to the mean of z minus the mean of rf. The variance of the z' distribution is equal to the sum of the variances of the z and rf distributions. We may write the equation as follows:

$$f(z') = \frac{1}{\sqrt{4\sigma_{f_{P.L.}}^2 + \sigma_{rf}^2}\,\sqrt{2\pi}}\, e^{-\frac{[z' - (M_z - M_{rf})]^2}{2(4\sigma^2 {f_{P.L.}} + \sigma_{rf}{}^2)}}. \tag{5}$$

2. This formula is probably not fully correct. The mean of the distribution of restraining forces should also be expressed as a decreasing function of time since there is good reason to suppose that the longer the individual stays in the decision region, the weaker are the restraining forces against leaving it. We are, however, not prepared at present to make any more specific assumption as to the exact nature of this function. As long as we deal with decisions of relatively short duration, the error involved because of this omission is probably small.

The probability that a value picked at random from the z' distribution will be greater than zero in the direction of saying longer is the integral of the z' distribution from zero to infinity, since this area includes all such cases:

$$\text{Prob. of Longer} = \int_0^\infty f(z')\, dz'. \tag{6}$$

The z' function is a distribution of $(f_{P,L} - f_{P,S} - rf)$. Now let us define a similar z'' function which equals $(f_{P,S} - f_{P,L} - rf)$. As in the z' distribution the probability that a value picked at random from the z'' distribution will be greater than zero in the direction of saying shorter is the integral of the z'' function from zero to infinity:

$$\int_0^\infty f(z'')\, dz''.$$

This area includes all those cases where the final resultant force would be in the direction of saying shorter.

Since the variance of z' and z'' are equal $(\sigma_{z'}^2 = \sigma_{z''}^2)$,

$$\int_0^\infty f(z'')dz'' = \int_{-\infty}^{-2rf} f(z')dz'. \tag{7}$$

We may therefore go ahead using the z' distribution only.

With the aid of the preceding formulations, the theoretical values of relative frequency of judgment and decision-time may now be defined.

The expected frequency with which judgments of longer will occur is equal to the integral of the z' distribution from zero to infinity (6). The expected frequency with which judgments of shorter will occur is equal to the integral of the z' distribution from $- 2rf$ to minus infinity (7). Integral (6) plus integral (7) are the total number of decisions which will occur. The area under the z' function between $- 2rf$ and 0 is equal to the probability of not obtaining a decision.

Theorem: The relative frequency of judgments of longer is equal to Integral (6) divided by the sum of Integrals (6) and (7). The relative frequency of judgments of shorter is equal to Integral (7) divided by the sum of Integrals (6) and (7).

As was stated above, values of z' between 0 and $-2rf$ will not yield any decision. The probability that a randomly selected z' value will not give a decision is, then, the integral of the z' function from $- 2rf$ to 0:

$$\text{Prob. (No-Decision)} = \int_{-2rf}^0 f(z')dz'. \tag{8}$$

The area defined by this integral may be called the area of no-decision. Since the subject must make a decision he must wait until a z' value occurs which is outside this area. Obviously then this area of no-decision is related to decision time. The larger the area of no-decision, the longer on the average will the subject take before he makes his decision. We then state that decision time is linearly proportional to Integral (8). To convert this into units of seconds this integral must be multiplied by some constant k. One more constant must be added to the equation since even an "immediate" decision will not be immediate but will depend on the reaction time of the subject.

Theorem: Decision Time is equal to a constant times Integral (8) plus a base value:

$$\text{D.T.} = K \int_{-2rf}^{0} f(z')dz' + B. \tag{9}$$

Since Integral (8) is one minus the sum of Integrals (6) and (7) this may also be written:

$$\text{D.T.} = K(1 - [\text{Prob. Longer} + \text{Prob. Shorter}]) + B. \tag{9A}$$

On the basis of the above theorems we may now proceed to plot our theoretical functions of decision time and relative frequency. The theorems show that two factors influence both relative frequency and decision time, namely, the magnitude of the restraining force and the mean of the z distribution. The latter, it will be remembered, expresses the difference between the force toward saying longer and the force toward saying shorter (the resultant of the driving forces). As the difference between the stimuli increases the mean of this z distribution will also increase. It seems most convenient, then, to plot our theoretical curves along an abscissa indicating magnitude of the mean of the z distribution. When plotted in this way, a separate function will, of course, exist for each mean restraining force.

In order to work with these functions, numerical values must be assigned to the constants in the equations. We have done this in the following way: The variance of the z' distribution has arbitrarily been assigned the value of unity. This value affords us a convenient scale according to which we may assign numerical values to our variables. Thus, the means of the z distribution have been expressed in terms of the variance of the z' distribution, and this scale constitutes our abscissæ for plotting the functions. That is to say, a mean of the z distribution which is equal to the variance of the z' distribution has a value of 1. A mean of the z distribution twice this size has a numerical value of 2. We shall hereafter refer to this scale of mean values as the z *scale*.

From our theorem of relative frequency and of the z scale we now have a set of coordinate axes on which to plot curves of relative frequency. From the theorem of decision time (dropping out the constants since these do not affect the shape of the curves) and the z scale we have a matrix for plotting decision time. These curves will show us exactly how relative frequency and decision time vary with the z scale for given values of the mean restraining force. Figures 4.2 and 4.3 show families of theorctical relative frequency curves and theoretical decision-time curves respectively for the indicated values of the restraining forces. (The numerical values assigned to the mean of the restraining force distributions are again in terms of the z scale, namely, the mean restraining force divided by the variance of the z' distribution.) The relative frequency curves form normal ogives. Only one-half of each curve

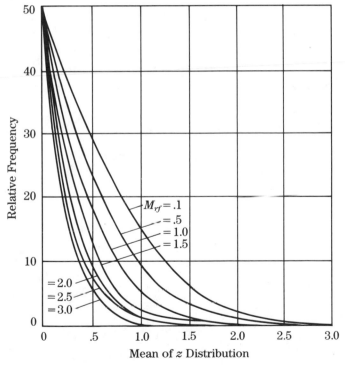

Figure 4.2   Theoretical relative frequency curves for indicated mean values of restraining force ($M_{r,f}$).

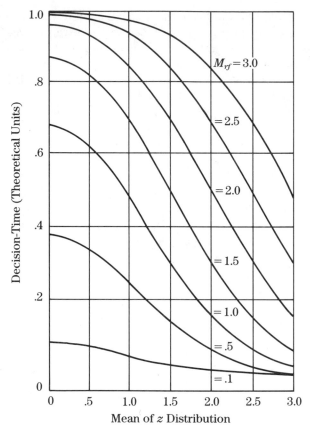

Figure 4.3   Theoretical decision-time curves for indicated mean values of re-straining force ($M_{r,f}$).

is plotted since the other half of the curve is merely the plotted half rotated 180 degrees. Similarly only one-half of each of the decision time curves is presented since the complete curves are symmetrical about the y axis.

Derivations

To test empirically the correctness of these curves it is necessary to relate the unit of the z scale of forces to the unit of the range of stimuli. Once a precise relation between these units has been established, exact predictions follow for both decision-time (Figure 4.3) and relative frequency (Figure 4.2). If it is not possible to state this relation in quantitative terms, however, certain more general assumptions permit some predictions which can be tested.

It can be safely assumed that with increasing difference between the standard and the variable stimuli, the difference in relative potency, and, thus, the difference between the driving forces becomes greater. In other words, values of the z scale may be assumed to vary monotonically with the values of stimulus differences.[3]

Derivation 1[4]

As a relative frequency approaches 50 per cent, decision-time approaches a maximum. (Confirmed by Kellogg, 16; Johnson, 15; Cartwright, 4.)

Derivation 1a

The average decision-time for all judgments taken together will be greater in experiments employing three categories of response than in those using only two categories, ceteris paribus. (Confirmed by Kellogg, 16; Cartwright, 4.)

Derivation 1b

The relation between the degree of similarity of the stimuli compared and the length of judgment-time depends upon the location of the 50 per cent points of the curve of relative frequency. (Confirmed by Kellogg, 16; Cartwright, 4.)

Derivation 2

The decision-time curve leaves its base farther away from the 50 per cent point than the relative frequency curves leaves 0 per cent. (Decision-time is a more sensitive measure of conflict than relative frequency.) This derivation follows from the possibility that a situation may occur where, although a difference of forces almost never arises which is large enough to give a judgment of, for example, "shorter," the initial

---

3. Essentially the same assumption is made in the theory by Cartwright (5).
4. Those derivations which have already been stated by Cartwright (5) will be restated briefly with the references to confirmatory experimental evidence.

pairing might result in a z' value falling in the "no-decision area." This fact can be clearly seen by comparing the curves of decision-time and relative frequency in Figures 4.2 and 4.3.

Derivation 2a

The distance from the point where the decision-time curve leaves its base to the point where the relative frequency curve leaves zero is a direct function of the magnitude of the main restraining force. As the restraining force increases in magnitude the relative frequency curve rises closer to the 50 per cent point while the decision-time curve rises farther away from the 50 per cent point. (Compare Figures 4.2 and 4.3.)

Derivation 3

The maximal decision time is a direct function of the magnitude of the restraining force. The precise form of the curve can be seen in Figure 4.4.

Derivation 3a

The steepness of the decision-time curve is a direct function of the magnitude of the restraining force (Figure 4.3).

If the assumption is made (1) that in a psychophysical judgment experiment instructions emphasizing speed reduce the restraining force below that of the usual instructions, and (2) that instructions emphasizing accuracy increase the restraining force above that of the usual instructions, then we may take data from Johnson (15) for immediate verification of the predictions in Derivation 3 that the maximal decision-time would be greatest for the accuracy instructions, next for the usual instructions and lowest for the speed instructions. The data for the three subjects reported by Johnson corroborate the prediction:

| Subject | Maximal Time for | | |
	Acc.	Usual	Speed
K	8.5	6.0	1.8
V	6.0	3.5	.68
Z	2.0	1.7	.52

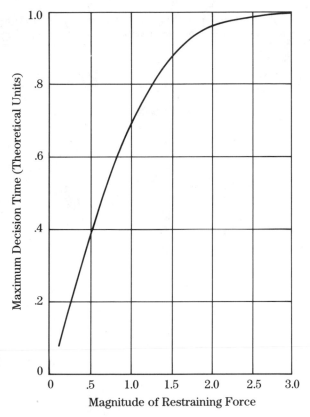

Figure 4.4 Maximal decision-time as a function of mean restraining force.

Casual inspection of Johnson's data shows Derivation *3a* to be corroborated. This can also be inferred from the maximal decision-times given,
since for all three conditions the base values of the decision-time curve
were approximately equal.

Derivation 4

The precision of the relative frequency ogive increases as the restraining
force increases (Figure 4.2). Table 4.1 and Figure 4.5 show this relationship more precisely. Since the precision of the relative frequency ogive
is used as a measure of sensitivity in some psychophysical experiments,
sensitivity as thus measured is affected by certain attitudes on the part
of the subject.

**Table 4.1   Standard Deviation and Precision of the Relative Frequency
Ogive as a Function of the Magnitude of the Mean Restraining Force**

M_{rf}	Standard Deviation	Precision (h)
.1	.935	.756
.2	.875	.808
.3	.820	.862
.4	.770	.918
.5	.722	.979
.6	.680	1.040
.7	.643	1.100
.8	.606	1.167
.9	.574	1.232
1.0	.545	1.297
1.1	.518	1.365
1.2	.493	1.434
1.3	.470	1.504
1.4	.450	1.571
1.5	.430	1.644
2.0	.351	2.014
2.5	.296	2.389
3.0	.255	2.773

Derivation 5

The above derivations have assumed that the restraining forces are equal
in both directions (*e.g.*, the restraining force against "saying 'longer' " is
equal to the restraining force against "saying 'shorter' "). When the restraining forces are of different magnitudes, the maximal decision time,
the steepness of the decision time curve and the precision of the relative
frequency ogive assume values which are obtained when the restraining
forces are the same in both directions, and of a magnitude equal to the
average of the unequal restraining forces.

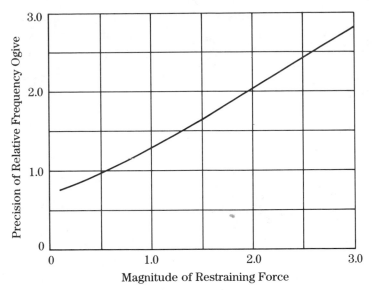

Figure 4.5   Precision of relative frequency ogive as a function of mean restraining force.

Derivation 5a

Under the conditions described in Derivation 5, the 50 per cent point is shifted towards the side of the greater restraining force by a distance along the abscissa equal to one-half the difference between the restraining forces.

Assuming that in a three category psychophysical experiment (judgment of equal allowed) instructions which create an attitude against giving judgments of equal increase the restraining force against "saying 'equal,'" the following statements can be made:

Under conditions where an attitude against giving a judgment of equal is created:

1. The maximal decision-time on each side of the equal category will be increased.
2. The steepness of the decision-time curve will be increased.
3. The precision of the relative frequency curves for longer and shorter judgments will be increased.
4. Both 50 per cent points will shift toward equality, making the distance between them smaller.

5. The average decision-time for judgments of equal will be increased.

The last two statements have been confirmed by a series of studies from the University of Pennsylvania (3, 7, 8, 9). No data seem to be available for the other three statements.

Fitting to Empirical Data

The theory as it has been elaborated up to this point still confronts the problem of precise application to empirical data. Specifically, the problems which must be faced and answered are as follows:

1. In the plotting of the theoretical functions of relative frequency and decision-time we have used a scale of arbitrary units in stating the magnitude of the mean of the z distribution. Theoretically these units are linearly related to differences in the potency of situations in which longer or shorter is correct. In order to convert our theoretical abscissa into an empirical one, some quantitative, operational definition of potency must be made. To meet this need the following operational definition is put forward: The confidence with which the subject makes his judgment may be taken as a measure of the difference in potency between the two overlapping situations. The confidence reflects the subjective probability that the judgment is correct. For example, if the subject gives a judgment of longer, but has absolutely no confidence in the correctness of his judgment, then the difference in potency is zero: "longer being correct," has a potency of .5 and "shorter being correct" has a potency of .5.[5] If the subject gives a judgment of longer and is absolutely confident that his judgment is correct, then the difference in potency is equal to 1; the situation in which longer is correct has a potency of 1; and the situation in which shorter is correct has a potency of 0. We further state, to make the definition complete, that confidence is a linear function of difference in potency.

Thus, if in the process of gathering data we also get judgments of confidence on some arbitrary linear scale, then these judgments, multiplied by some constant, may be converted to our theoretical z abscissa.

2. Our theoretical units with which we have plotted our decision-

5. At first glance it may seem impossible to obtain any judgment at a time when the confidence equals zero. Theoretically, of course, this is correct. It is here assumed, however, that the subject can give a confidence rating which will reflect the average potency for the duration of the decision.

time functions are not in units of seconds. We have stated above that we have made our units relate to seconds in a linear manner as defined by the equation for decision-time.

The problem of determining the constants in this equation remains. The base constant (reaction time of the subject) may vary from situation to situation. The method of determining this base constant is defined as follows. That value of decision time which is obtained when the potency of one response's being correct is 1, and the other, 0, is taken as the base constant for our conversion into seconds. The rationale for the above procedure consists in the fact that when the difference in potency is 1, then there is no conflict of forces and we obtain the equivalent of an "immediate" decision.[6]

3.   The constant of conversion into units of seconds must of course be determined empirically by orthodox methods of curve fitting. The following restriction must, however, be observed in regard to the constant of conversion into seconds and the constant of conversion of the confidence scale into the z scale. Once such a constant is determined for a given subject under some condition, this constant must also hold for that subject under all other conditions. This restriction is meaningful for if these constants do not remain the same for the same individual under different conditions, then these constants would cease to have any theoretical meaning but would become merely the finding of a number which will make a curve fit. If our definition of psychological time is related to physical time units, then the same constant should be used in converting it to time units, at least for the same subject. And if our confidence scale really measures differences in potency, then the same difference in the confidence scale should refer to the same potency differences for the same individuals.[7]

4.   The last problem which must be faced is the determination of the value of restraining force which is present for any set of empirical data. This determination is largely a matter of trial and error. It is not, how-

6. In instances of extremely high restraining forces, this statement is not absolutely correct. In such cases even decisions at a potency difference of 1 will be slightly delayed beyond the reaction time. The amount of this delay, however, is very small and may either be ignored or taken into account by subtracting an empirically determined value from the actual decision-time.

7. For the same subject the psychological unit of time might change drastically because of some change in the meaning of the situation for the subject. Also, since the constant of conversion of the confidence scale into the z scale depends upon the meaning which the subject gives to his confidence scale, it is easy to imagine a situation where the confidence scale changes markedly in meaning necessitating a change of the constant. We do not, however, consider such marked changes to occur very frequently.

ever, a value which may be juggled around independently of the other values involved. To illustrate this procedure let us follow through a hypothetical case of determining the restraining force value for a given set of data. There are two empirical functions whose exact shape will be determined by the restraining force magnitude, namely, decision-time and relative frequency plotted against a scale of confidence. It will be remembered that all of the relative frequency curves are normal ogives theoretically, but that the precision of the ogives decrease with a decrease in the magnitude of the restraining force. And we know exactly what the value of the standard deviation in z scale units is for every value of restraining force (Figure 4.5). Therefore, if we determine the standard deviation of our empirical relative frequeny curve, the choice of any value for the restraining force immediately fixes the constant of conversion of the confidence scale into the z scale along the abscissæ. Then, with this conversion already determined, the decision-time curve must also fit. Figure 4.3 shows that the steepness of the decision-time curve increases with an increase in the magnitude of the restraining force. Therefore, in the fitting of the data, a choice of restraining force value which is too low will yield a theoretical decision-time curve which is less steep than the empirical one. The choice of a too high restraining force value will yield a theoretical decision-time curve which is steeper than the empirical one. The correct value of the restraining force, then, lies somewhere in between and must be found by trial and error. Then the correct constant of conversion of theoretical decision-time units into units of seconds may be determined. Now, for all other conditions of the same subject there are no more constants to be determined. Everything has already been set: the time conversion constant, the conversion constant along the abscissa, and the value of the restraining force for any other condition (for now the standard deviation of the empirical relative frequency curve defines the standard deviation of the theoretical ogive which in turn defines the magnitude of restraining force).

Thus, the empirical tests of the derivations made from the theory become very rigid, quantitative tests.

Review of Data Pertinent to the Theory

Some additional data, already existing in the literature, can be examined from the point of view of a tentative evaluation of the theory presented above.

Johnson (15), in a typical psychophysical experiment, dealt with the usual two categories of judgments. Measures of both relative frequency and decision time were obtained. In addition, ratings were obtained of the confidence with which the decisions had been made. These confidence ratings were made on a linear scale from zero to one hundred. Three sets of instructions were employed: The subjects made judgments under the usual set of instructions, under instructions emphasizing accuracy, and under instructions emphasizing speed.

The confidence ratings obtained in this way are identical with our operational definition of differences in potency. The accuracy and speed instructions are factors which we may assume will respectively increase and decrease the magnitude of the restraining force from what it was under the usual instructions. Thus, the experiment forms a convenient vehicle for a tentative test of our theory.

Unfortunately, however, there were only ten judgments for each stimulus value. The results are therefore somewhat unreliable relative to the precision of the theoretical predictions. Further, and more serious, is the fact that the data for relative frequency are presented only for the condition of usual instructions, and then not in a form convenient for our purposes. Without the relative frequency data, fewer checks on our theoretical derivations are available.

Figure 4.6 gives the theoretical curves drawn to the empirical data for decision time for one of Johnson's subjects under the three conditions described above. The conversion of confidence to the z scale along the abscissa is constant under all three conditions. The equation for this conversion is $C = 32z$. The constant for the conversion of the theoretical decision-time curves into units of seconds is also the same for all three conditions. This constant is 11.3. The base constant is different for the three conditions as should be expected if the change in attitude affects reaction time. It is interesting to note, however, that the base constants are about the same for the accuracy and usual instructions.

While for the usual instructions the restraining force is .40, under conditions emphasizing accuracy it goes up to .88 and with instructions emphasizing speed it drops to .10. How well the theoretical curves fit the empirical data may be judged by the reader for himself.

There are also data showing that the relationships derived from the theory hold in areas outside of psychophysical judgments. Dashiell (6) in an experiment on affective judgments found results consistent with the theory. A number of colors were compared with each other and the rank order of preference established on the basis of the number of times each color was chosen. When the judgment times are arranged according to the number of steps of separation in the preference series between the two colors presented, the data in Figure 4.7(b) are obtained. Although we do not know the relationship between the abscissa on this graph and the abscissa of our theoretical curves, it is clear that the same

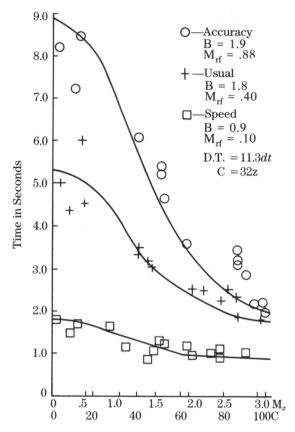

Figure 4.6   Theoretical decision-time curves fitted to data from one subject under three conditions of judgment. (Recalculated from Johnson, 15.)

type of function obtains. (Since the smallest separation could be one there is no value for zero preference scale separation. According to the theoretical function, this curve should level out somewhat between 0 and 1.)

There are also relevant data available from experiments involving conflict between different goals. Wells (19) conducted an experiment in which subjects chose between liquids ranging in taste from desirable to undesirable. Although the data are not presented in a form convenient for the present comparison, the results are in line with our theory in that the average decision time for choices between similar tastes is greater than for dissimilar tastes, similarity again being defined in terms of similarity in degree of preference.

Barker (1) reports a study of similar nature. Seven liquids were paired with each other and the preference rankings determined in a manner similar to that used by Dashiell (6). Two variations were employed: In the "real" choice situation the subjects actually had to drink some of the liquid they chose; in the "hypothetical" choice situation they were required to choose the liquid they would prefer to drink if required to do so. It is clear that the restraining forces against making a decision are stronger in the "real" choice situation than in the "hypothetical" choice situation. The data for these two groups are produced in Figure 4.7(a). As in the case of the graph of Figure 4.7(b), the relation between this empirical abscissa and our theoretical abscissa is unknown. Again, however, it is obvious that the curves obtained are of the same general type as the theoretical curves. In addition, in line with the theory, the curve of the "hypothetical" choice situation shows a lower maximal decision time and less steep slope than the curve for the "real" choice situation.

Relevance to Measurement of Forces

How far the present type of analysis has gone toward measuring forces is still a matter for consideration. To accomplish a measurement of forces in a constellation such as is under consideration, we are faced with two problems:

1. Measuring the difference between two driving forces.
2. Measuring the magnitude of the restraining force.

Both 1 and 2 involve the measurement of the mean of the normal distribution, and, in addition, measurement of the variance of these distributions. What has been done in this direction?

We have constructed a scale called the z scale which has the usual arithmetic properties. A value of 2 along this scale is twice as great as a value of 1. Using this scale we can say that one restraining force distribution, for example, has a mean value of .9 and another has a mean value of .5; that one z distribution has a value of 1.5 and another a value of .8.

But these numbers on the proposed scale are not measures which can be compared from individual to individual. The numbers, when assigned, refer to a ratio of the magnitude of the mean of a distribution divided by the variance of another distribution. This fact implies that a mean of a z distribution which is twice as great as the mean of a second z distribution is assigned the same number on the scale if the variance

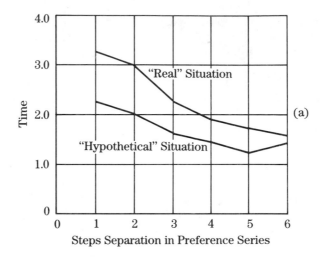

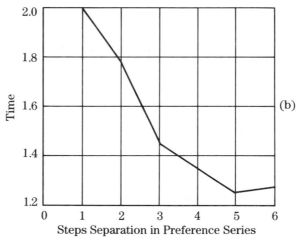

Figure 4.7   (a) Time elapsing during the resolution of conflict between alternatives separated by different "distances" in the preference series. (From Barker, 1.) (b) Time elapsing for esthetic judgments between alternatives separated by different "distances" in the preference series. (From Dashiell, 6.)

of the z' distribution corresponding to the latter is twice as great as the variance of the z' distribution corresponding to the former.

For the purposes of the present theory, and for the purposes of the present derivations, the above constitutes a correct procedure. The empirical effects of these two situations would be identical. From the point of view of measurement of magnitude of forces, however, this procedure is inadequate. For the same individual in two different situations it does constitute a real scaling of magnitudes of forces if we assume that the variance of the z' distribution (our unit of measurement) stays the same for that individual in the two situations. For a comparison between different individuals between whom the variance of the z' distribution is not equal, however, we must know the relative size of the variances in order to say anything about the relative magnitudes of the forces.

The possibilities of further progress in the direction of measurement of forces seems to hinge on the question of being able to separate the measure of magnitude from the measure of variability. If this separation can be made, the problem is largely solved.

Summary and Conclusions

The successful, mathematical quantification of a scientific theory constitutes to some degree in itself a test of that theory. If the logical prerequisite of inner consistency contained in such a test is met, an important step forward is made. In the development of science this has repeatedly shown itself to be true. Theories, which when vaguely formulated appear to be adequate, are frequently shown to be self contradictory and inadequate when subjected to an attempted quantification. Even as far back as the seventeenth century the Cartesian alternative to the Newtonian theory of gravitation was discarded because Newton himself showed that a quantification of the Cartesian theory was self-contradictory.

Except for some rare instances, theories in psychology have been stated in relatively vague, nonquantitative terms. When more rigid quantification of these theories is attempted, many of them will undoubtedly be found inadequate.

In the preceding pages a theory of decision situations has been stated precisely and quantitatively. The theory has been developed to that point where quantitative derivations from the theory are capable of being subjected to direct, quantitative empirical test.

We may summarize as follows:

1. A theory of decision which combines a topological analysis with a vectorial analysis of a decision situation has been elaborated mathematically.
2. Through this mathematical elaboration a successful quantification of this theory was accomplished in a form amenable to empirical testing.

3. The type of theoretical analysis used has methodological significance. Irrespective of the school of thought, or of the theoretical
constructs involved, this type of approach can be used to measure
the dynamic factors in a psychological situation. From measures of
frequency and decision time we may infer the magnitudes of the
forces operating. This type of analysis is applicable to a wide variety of psychological problems.

Experiments specifically oriented toward testing the quantitative predictions from the theory presented in this paper are reported elsewhere
by Festinger (10, 11).

When this chapter was written, Dorwin Cartwright was with the Department of Agriculture in Washington and Leon Festinger was at the
State University of Iowa.

References

1. BARKER, R. B. An experimental study of the resolution of conflict by children. In *Studies in personality, contributed in honor of Lewis M. Terman.*
New York: McGraw-Hill, 1942.
2. BORING, E. G. The psychophysics of color tolerance. *Amer. J. Psychol.*,
1939, **52**, 384–393.
3. CARLSON, W. R., DRIVER, R. C., & PRESTON, M. G. Judgment times for
the method of constant stimuli. *J. exp. Psychol.*, 1934, **17**, 113–118.
4. CARTWRIGHT, D. The relation of decision-time to the categories of response.
Amer. J. Psychol., 1941, **54**, 174–196.
5. _____. Decision time in relation to the differentiation of the phenomenal
field. *Psychol. Rev.*, 1941, **48**, 425–442.
6. DASHIELL, J. F. Affective value distance as a determinant of esthetic judgment times. *Amer. J. Psychol.*, 1937, **50**, 57–67.
7. FERNBERGER, S. W. The effect of the attitude of the subject upon the measure of sensitivity. *Amer. J. Psychol.*, 1914, **25**, 538–543.
8. _____, GLASS, E., HOFFMAN, I., & WILLIG, M. Judgment times of different psychophysical categories. *J. exp. Psychol.*, 1934, **17**, 286–293.
9. _____, & IRWIN, F. W. Time relations for different categories in judgment
in the "absolute method" in psychophysics. *Amer. J. Psychol.*, 1932, **44**,
505–525.

10. FESTINGER, L. Studies of decision: I. Decision-time, relative frequency of judgment and subjective confidence as related to physical stimulus difference. *J. exp. Psychol.*, 1943, **32**, 291–306.

11. _____. Studies of decision: II. An empirical test of a quantitative theory of decision. *J. exp. Psychol.*, 1943, **32**, 411–423.

12. GEORGE, S. S. Attitude in relation to psychophysical judgment. *Amer. J. Psychol.*, 1917, **28**, 1–37.

13. HENMON, V. A. C. The time of perception as a measure of difference in sensations. *Arch. Phil., Psychol., & Sci. Methods*, 1906, No. 8, 1–25.

14. _____. The relation of time of a judgment to its accuracy. *Psychol. Rev.*, 1911, **18**, 186–201.

15. JOHNSON, D. M. Confidence and speed in the two-category judgment. *Arch. Psychol.*, 1939, **241**, 1–52.

16. KELLOGG, W. M. The time of judgment in psychometric measures. *Amer. J. Psychol.*, 1931, **42**, 65–86.

17. LEWIN, K. *Dynamic theory of personality.* New York: McGraw-Hill, 1935.

18. _____. The conceptual representation and the measurement of psychological forces. *Contr. psychol. Theory.*, 1938, **1**, No. 4, 1–247.

19. WELLS, H. M. The phenomenology of acts of choice; an analysis of volitional consciousness. *Brit. J. Psychol., Monogr. Suppl.*, 1927, **4**, No. II.

PART
B
SOCIAL COMPARISON THEORY AND RESEARCH

5

Informal Social Communication

The importance of strict theory in developing and guiding programs of research is becoming more and more recognized today. Yet there is considerable disagreement about exactly how strict and precise a theoretical formulation must be at various stages in the development of a body of knowledge. Certainly there are many who feel that some "theorizing" is too vague and indefinite to be of much use. It is also argued that such vague and broad "theorizing" may actually hinder the empirical development of an area of knowledge.

On the other hand there are many who express dissatisfaction with instances of very precise theories which do exist here and there, for somehow or other a precise and specific theory seems to them to leave out the "real" psychological problem. These persons seem to be more concerned with those aspects of the problem which the precise theory has not yet touched. From this point of view it is argued that too precise and too strict theorizing may also hinder the empirical development of an area of knowledge.

It is probably correct that if a theory becomes too precise too early it can have tendencies to become sterile. It is also probably correct that if a theory stays too vague and ambiguous for too long it can be harmful in that nothing can be done to disprove or change it. This probably means that theories, when vague, should at least be stated in a form which makes the adding of precision possible as knowledge increases. It also probably means that theory should run ahead, but not too far ahead, of the data so that the trap of premature precision can be avoided. It

SOURCE: Festinger, L. *Psychol. Rev.*, 1950, **57**, 271–282. [MS. received March 6, 1950]

117

certainly means that theories, whether vague or precise, must be in such a form that empirical data can influence them.

This article is a statement of the theoretical formulations which have been developed in the process of conducting a program of empirical and experimental research in informal social communication. It has grown out of our findings thus far and is in turn guiding the future course of the research program. This program of research concerns itself with finding and explaining the facts concerning informal, spontaneous communication among persons and the consequences of the process of communication. It would seem that a better understanding of the dynamics of such communication would in turn lead to a better understanding of various kinds of group functioning. The theories and hypotheses presented below vary considerably in precision, specificity and the degree to which corroborating data exist. Whatever the state of precision, however, the theories are empirically oriented and capable of being tested.

Since we are concerned with the spontaneous process of communication which goes on during the functioning of groups we must first differentiate the variety of types of communication which occur according to the theoretical conditions which give rise to tendencies to communicate. It is plausible to assume that separating the sources of origins of pressures to communicate that may act on a member of a group will give us fruitful areas to study. This type of differentiation or classification is, of course, adequate only if it leads to the separation of conceptually clear areas of investigation within which communication can be organized into statable theoretical and empirical laws.

We shall here deal with those few of the many possible sources of pressures to communicate in which we have thus far been able to make theoretical and empirical progress. We shall elaborate on the theory for regarding them as giving rise to pressures to communicate and on specific hypotheses concerning the laws of communication which stem from these sources.

Pressures Toward Uniformity in a Group

One major source of forces to communicate is the pressure toward uniformity which may exist within a group. These are pressures which, for one reason or another, act toward making members of a group agree concerning some issue or conform with respect to some behavior pattern. It is stating the obvious, of course, to say that these pressures must be exerted by means of a process of communication among the members of the group. One must also specify the conditions under which such pressures toward uniformity arise, both on a conceptual and an operational level so that in any specific situation it is possible to say whether or not such pressures exist. We shall, in the following discussion, elaborate on two major sources of pressures toward uniformity among people, namely, social reality and group locomotion.

Social Reality

Opinions, attitudes, and beliefs which people hold must have some basis upon which they rest for their validity. Let us as a start abstract from the many kinds of bases for the subjective validity of such opinions, attitudes, and beliefs one continuum along which they may be said to lie. This continuum we may call a scale of degree of physical reality. At one end of this continuum, namely, complete dependence upon physical reality, we might have an example such as this: A person looking at a surface might think that the surface is fragile or he might think that the surface is unbreakable. He can very easily take a hammer, hit the surface, and quickly be convinced as to whether the opinion he holds is correct or incorrect. After he has broken the surface with a hammer it will probably make little dent upon his opinion if another person should tell him that the surface is unbreakable. It would thus seem that where there is a high degree of dependence upon physical reality for the subjective validity of one's beliefs or opinions the dependence upon other people for the confidence one has in these opinions or beliefs is very low.

At the other end of the continuum where the dependence upon physical reality is low or zero, we might have an example such as this: A person looking at the results of a national election feels that if the loser had won, things would be in some ways much better than they are. Upon what does the subjective validity of this belief depend? It depends to a large degree on whether or not other people share his opinion and feel the same way he does. If there are other people around him who believe the same thing, then his opinion is, to him, valid. If there are not others who believe the same thing, then his opinion is, in the same sense, not valid. Thus where the dependence upon physical reality is low the dependence upon social reality is correspondingly high. An opinion, a belief, an attitude is "correct," "valid," and "proper" to the extent that it is anchored in a group of people with similar beliefs, opinions, and attitudes.

This statement, however, cannot be generalized completely. It is clearly not necessary for the validity of someone's opinion that everyone else in the world think the way he does. It is only necessary that the members of that group to which he refers this opinion or attitude think the way he does. It is not necessary for a Ku Klux Klanner that some northern liberal agree with him in his attitude toward Negroes, but it is eminently necessary that there be other people who also are Ku Klux Klanners and who do agree with him. The person who does not agree with him is seen as different from him and not an adequate referent for his opinion. The problem of independently defining which groups are and which groups are not appropriate reference groups for a particular individual and for a particular opinion or attitude is a difficult one. It is to some extent inherently circular since an appropriate reference group tends to be a group which does share a person's opinions and attitudes, and people tend to locomote *into* such groups and *out of* groups which do not agree with them.

From the preceding discussion it would seem that if a discrepancy in opinion, attitude, or belief exists among persons who are members of an appropriate reference group, forces to communicate will arise. It also follows that the less "physical reality" there is to validate the opinion or belief, the greater will be the importance of the social referent, the group, and the greater will be the forces to communicate.

Group Locomotion

Pressures toward uniformity among members of a group may arise because such uniformity is desirable or necessary in order for the group to move toward some goal. Under such circumstances there are a number of things one can say about the magnitude of pressures toward uniformity.

1. They will be greater to the extent that the members perceive that group movement would be facilitated by uniformity.
2. The pressures toward uniformity will also be greater, the more dependent the various members are on the group in order to reach their goals. The degree to which other groups are substitutable as a means toward individual or group goals would be one of the determinants of the dependence of the member on the group.

We have elaborated on two sources of pressure toward uniformity among members of groups. The same empirical laws should apply to communications which result from pressures toward uniformity irrespective of the particular reasons for the existence of the pressures. We shall now proceed to enumerate a set of hypotheses concerning communication which results from pressures toward uniformity.

Hypotheses About Communication Resulting from Pressures Toward Uniformity

Communications which arise from pressures toward uniformity in a group may be seen as "instrumental" communications. That is, the communication is not an end in itself but rather is a means by which the communicator hopes to influence the person he addresses in such a way as to reduce the discrepancy that exists between them. Thus we should examine the determinants of: (1) when a member communicates, (2) to whom he communicates and (3) the reactions of the recipient of the communications.

Determinants of the Magnitude of Pressure to Communicate

HYPOTHESIS 1A.   *The pressure on members to communicate to others in the group concerning "item x" increases monotonically with increase in the perceived discrepancy in opinion concerning "item x" among members of the group.*

Remembering that we are considering only communication that results from pressures toward uniformity, it is clear that if there are no discrepancies in opinion, that is, uniformity already exists in the group, there will be no forces to communicate. It would be plausible to expect the force to communicate to increase rapidly from zero as the state of affairs departs from uniformity.

HYPOTHESIS 1B.   *The pressure on a member to communicate to others in the group concerning "item x" increases monotonically with increase in the degree of relevance of "item x" to the functioning of the group.*

If "item x" is unimportant to the group in the sense of not being associated with any of the values or activities which are the basis for the existence of the group, or if it is more or less inconsequential for group locomotion, then there should be few or no forces to communicate even when there are perceived discrepancies in opinion. As "item x" becomes more important for the group (more relevant), the forces to communicate when any given magnitude of perceived discrepancy exists should increase.

Corroborative evidence for this hypothesis is found in an experiment by Schachter (8) where discussion of the same issue was experimentally made relevant for some groups and largely irrelevant for others. It is clear from the data that where the discussion was relevant to the functioning of the group there existed stronger forces to communicate and to influence the other members. Where the issue is a relevant one the members make longer individual contributions to the discussion and there are many fewer prolonged pauses in the discussion.

HYPOTHESIS 1C.   *The pressure on members to communicate to others in the group concerning "item x" increases monotonically with increase in the cohesiveness of the group.*

Cohesiveness of a group is here defined as the resultant of all the forces acting on the members to remain in the group. These forces may depend on the attractiveness or unattractiveness of either the prestige of the group, members in the group, or the activities in which the group engages. If the total attraction toward the group is zero, no forces to communicate should arise; the members may as easily leave the group as stay in it. As the forces to remain in the group increase (given perceived discrepancies in opinion and given a certain relevance of the item to the functioning of the group), the pressures to communicate will increase.

Data from an experiment by Back (1) support this hypothesis. In this experiment groups of high and low cohesiveness were experimentally created using three different sources of attraction to the group, namely, liking the members, prestige attached to belonging, and possibility of getting a reward for performance in the group activity. For each of the three types of attraction to the group the more cohesive groups were rated as proceeding at a more intense rate in the discussion than the corresponding less cohesive groups. In addition, except for the groups where the attraction was the possibility of reward (perhaps due to wanting to finish and get the reward) there was more total amount of attempted exertion of influence in the highly cohesive groups than in the less cohesive groups. In short, highly cohesive groups, having stronger pressures to communicate, discussed the issue at a more rapid pace and attempted to exert more influence.

Determinants of Choice of Recipient for Communications

HYPOTHESIS 2A.   *The force to communicate about "item x" to* A PARTICULAR MEMBER *of the group will increase as the discrepancy in opinion between that member and the communicator increases.*

We have already stated in Hypothesis 1a that the pressure to communicate in general will increase as the perceived non-uniformity in the group increases. In addition the force to communicate will be strongest toward those whose opinions are most different from one's own and will, of course, be zero towards those in the group who at the time hold the same opinion as the communicator. In other words, people will tend to communicate to those within the group whose opinions are most different from their own.

There is a clear corroboration of this hypothesis from a number of studies. In the previously mentioned experiment by Schachter (8) the distribution of opinions expressed in the group was always as follows: Most of the members' opinions clustered within a narrow range of each other while one member, the deviate, held and maintained an extremely divergent point of view. About five times as many communications were addressed to the holder of the divergent point of view as were addressed to the others.

In an experiment by Festinger and Thibaut (5) the discussion situation was set up so that members' opinions on the issue spread over a considerable range. Invariably 70 to 90 per cent of the communications were addressed to those who held opinions at the extremes of the distribution. The curve of number of communications received falls off very rapidly as the opinion of the recipient moves away from the extreme of the distribution. The hypothesis would seem to be well substantiated.

HYPOTHESIS 2B.   *The force to communicate about "item x" to* A PARTICULAR PERSON *will decrease to the extent that he is perceived as not a member of the group or to the extent that he is not wanted as a member of the group.*

From the previous hypothesis it follows that communications will tend to be addressed mainly toward those with extreme opinions within the group. This does not hold, however, for any arbitrarily defined group. The present hypothesis, in effect, states that such relationships will apply only within *psychological* groups, that is, collections of people that exist as groups psychologically for the members. Communications will tend not to be addressed towards those who are not members of the group.

The study by Schachter (8) and the study by Festinger and Thibaut (5) both substantiate this hypothesis. In Schachter's experiment those group members who do not want the person holding the extremely divergent point of view to remain in the group tend to stop communicating to him toward the end of the discussion. In the experiment by Festinger and Thibaut, when the subjects have the perception that the persons present include different kinds of people with a great variety of interests, there tends to be less communication toward the extremes in the last half of the discussion after the rejection process has had time to develop. In short, communication toward those with different opinions decreases if they are seen as not members of the *psychological* group.

HYPOTHESIS 2C.   *The force to communicate "item x" to a particular member will increase the more it is perceived that the communication will change that member's opinion in the desired direction.*

A communication which arises because of the existence of pressures toward uniformity is made in order to exert a force on the recipient in a particular direction, that is, to push him to change his opinion so that he will agree more closely with the communicator. If a member is perceived as very resistant to changing his opinion, the force to communicate to him decreases. If it seems that a particular member will be changed as the result of a communication so as to increase the discrepancy between him and the communicator, there will exist a force not to communicate to him. Thus under such conditions there will be tendencies *not* to communicate this particular item to that member.

There is some corroboration for this hypothesis. In a face to face verbal discussion where a range of opinion exists, the factors which this hypothesis points to would be particularly important for those members whose opinions were near the middle of the range. A communication which might influence the member at one extreme to come closer to the middle might at the same time influence the member at the other extreme to move farther away from the middle. We might then expect from this hypothesis that those holding opinions in the middle of the existing range would communicate less (because of the conflict) and would address fewer communications to the whole group (attempting to influence only one person at a time).

A number of observations were conducted to check these derivations. Existing groups of clinical psychologists who were engaging in discussions to reconcile their differences in ratings of applicants were observed. Altogether, 147 such discussions were observed in which at least one member's opinion was in the middle of the existing range. While those with extreme opinions made an average of 3.16 units of communication (number of communications weighted by length of the communication), those with middle opinions made an average of only 2.6 units of communication. While those with extreme opinions addressed 38 per cent of their communications to the whole group, those with middle opinions addressed only 29 per cent of their communications to everyone.

Determinants of Change in the Recipient of a Communication

HYPOTHESIS 3A.   *The amount of change in opinion resulting from receiving a communication will increase as the pressure toward uniformity in the group increases.*

There are two separate factors which contribute to the effect stated in the hypothesis. The greater the pressure toward uniformity, the greater will be the amount of influence exerted by the communications and, consequently, the greater the magnitude of change that may be expected. But the existence of pressures toward uniformity will not only show itself in increased attempts to change the opinions of others. Pressures toward uniformity will also produce greater readiness to change in the members of the group. In other words, uniformity may be achieved by changing the opinions of others and/or by changing one's own opinions. Thus we may expect that with increasing pressure toward uniformity there will be less resistance to change on the part of the members. Both of these factors will contribute to produce greater change in opinion when the pressure toward uniformity is greater.

There is evidence corroborating this hypothesis from the experiment by Festinger and Thibaut (5). In this experiment three degrees of pressure toward uniformity were experimentally induced in different groups. Irrespective of which of two problems were discussed by the group and irrespective of whether they perceived the group to be homogeneously or heterogeneously composed, the results consistently show that high pressure groups change most, medium pressure groups change next most, and low pressure groups change. least in the direction of uniformity. While the two factors which contribute to this effect cannot be separated in the data, their joint effect is clear and unmistakable.

HYPOTHESIS 3B.   *The amount of change in opinion resulting from receiving a communication will increase as the strength of the resultant force to remain in the group increases for the recipient.*

To the extent that a member wishes to remain in the group, the group has power over that member. By power we mean here the ability to produce real change in opinions and attitudes and not simply change in overt behavior which can also be produced by means of overt threat. If a person is unable to leave a group because of restraints from the outside, the group can then use threats to change overt behavior. Covert changes in opinions and attitudes, however, can only be produced by a group by virtue of forces acting on the member to remain in the group. Clearly the maximum force which the group can successfully induce on a member counter to his own forces can not be greater than the sum of the forces acting on that member to remain in the group. The greater the resultant force to remain in the group, the more effective will be the attempts to influence the member.

This hypothesis is corroborated by two separate studies. Festinger, Schachter and Back (4) investigated the relationship between the cohesiveness of social groups in a housing project (how attractive the group was for its members) and how effectively a group standard relevant to the functioning of the group was maintained. A correlation of .72 was obtained between these two variables. In other words, the greater the attractiveness of the group for the members, the greater was the amount of influence which the group could successfully exert on its members with the result that there existed greater conformity in attitudes and behavior in the more cohesive groups.

Back (1) did a laboratory experiment specifically designed to test this hypothesis. By means of plausible instructions to the subjects he experimentally created groups of high and low cohesiveness, that is, conditions in which the members were strongly attracted to the group and those in which the attraction to the group was relatively weak. The subjects, starting with different interpretations of the same material, were given an opportunity to discuss the matter. Irrespective of the source of the attraction to the group (Back used three different types of attraction in both high and low cohesive conditions) the subjects in the high cohesive groups influenced each other's opinions more than the subjects in the low cohesive groups. In short, the greater the degree of attraction to the group, the greater the amount of influence actually accomplished.

HYPOTHESIS 3C. *The amount of change in opinion resulting from receiving a communication concerning "item x" will decrease with increase in the degree to which the opinions and attitudes involved are anchored in other group memberships or serve important need satisfying functions for the person.*

If the opinion that a person has formed on some issue is supported in some other group than the one which is at present attempting to influence him, he will be more resistant to the attempted influence. Other sources of resistance to being influenced undoubtedly come from personality factors, ego needs and the like.

Specific evidence supporting this hypothesis is rather fragmentary. In the study of social groups in a housing project by Festinger, Schachter and Back (4), the residents were asked whether their social life was mainly outside the project or not. Of those who conformed to the standards of their social groups within the project about 85 per cent reported that their social life was centered mainly within the project. Less than 50 per cent of those who did not conform to the standards of the project social group, however, reported that their social life was centered mainly in the project. It is likely that they were able to resist the influences from within the project when their opinions and attitudes were supported in outside groups.

The experiments by Schachter (8) and by Festinger and Thibaut (5) used the same discussion problem in slightly different situations. In the former experiment subjects identified themselves and verbally supported their opinions in face-to-face discussion. In the latter experiment the subjects were anonymous, communicating only by written messages on which the sender of the message was not identified. Under these latter conditions many more changes in opinion were observed than under the open verbal discussion situation even though less time was spent in discussion when they wrote notes. This difference in amount of change in opinion is probably due to the ego defensive reactions aroused by openly committing oneself and supporting one's opinions in a face-to-face group.

Determinants of Change in Relationship Among Members

HYPOTHESIS 4A.   *The tendency to change the composition of the psychological group (pushing members out of the group) increases as the perceived discrepancy in opinion increases.*

We have already discussed two of the responses which members of groups make to pressures toward uniformity, namely, attempting to influence others and being more ready to be influenced. There is still a third response which serves to move toward uniformity. By rejecting those whose opinions diverge from the group and thus redefining who is and who is not in the psychological group, uniformity can be accomplished. The greater the discrepancy between a person's opinion and the opinion of another, the stronger are the tendencies to exclude the other person from the psychological group.

There is evidence that members of groups do tend to reject those whose opinions are divergent. In the study of social groups within a housing project Festinger, Schachter and Back (4) found that those who did not conform to the standards of their social group were underchosen on a sociometric test, that is, they mentioned more persons as friends of theirs than they received in return. Schachter (8) did an experiment specifically to test whether or not members of groups would be rejected simply for disagreeing on an issue. Paid participants in the groups voiced divergent or agreeing opinions as instructed. In all groups the paid participant who voiced divergent opinion on an issue was rejected on a postmeeting questionnaire concerning whom they wanted to have remain in the group. The same paid participants, when voicing conforming opinions in other groups, were not rejected.

HYPOTHESIS 4B.   *When non-conformity exists, the tendency to change the composition of the psychological group increases as the cohesiveness of the group increases and as the relevance of the issue to the group increases.*

We have previously discussed the increase in forces to communicate with increase in cohesiveness and relevance of issue. Similarly, these two variables affect the tendency to reject persons from the group for non-conformity. Theoretically we should expect any variable which affected the force to communicate (which stems from pressures toward uniformity) to affect also the tendency to reject non-conformers in a similar manner. In other words, increases in the force to communicate concerning an item will go along with increased tendency to reject persons who disagree concerning that item.

The previously mentioned experiment by Schachter (8) was designed to test this hypothesis by experimentally varying cohesiveness and relevance in club groups. In this experiment the more cohesive groups do reject the non-conformer more than the less cohesive groups and the groups where the issue is relevant reject the non-conformer more than groups where the issue is not very relevant to the group functioning. Those groups where cohesiveness was low and the issue was not very relevant show little, if any, tendency to reject the deviate.

Forces to Change One's Position in a Group

Another important source of forces to communicate are the forces which act on members of groups to locomote (change their position) in the group, or to move from one group to another. Such forces to locomote may stem from the attractiveness of the activities associated with the different position in the group or from the status of that position or the like. Thus a new member of a group may wish to become more central in the group, a member of an organization may wish to rise in the status hierarchy, a member of a business firm may want to be promoted or a member of a minority group may desire acceptance by the majority group. These are all instances of forces to locomote in a social structure.

It is plausible that the existence of a force acting on a person in a specific direction produces behavior in that direction. Where locomotion in the desired direction is not possible, at least temporarily, there will exist a force to communicate in that direction. The existence of a force in a specific direction will produce behavior in that direction. One such kind of behavior is communication. This hypothesis is not very different from the hypothesis advanced by Lewin (6) to account for the superior recall of interrupted activities.

An experiment by Thibaut (9) tends to corroborate this theoretical analysis. In his experiment he created two groups, one of high status and privileged, the other of low status and underprivileged. These two groups, equated in other respects, functioned together so that the members of the high status group could play an attractive game. The low status group functioned merely as servants. It was clear that forces were acting on the members of the low status group to move into the other group. As the privilege position of the high status group became clearer and clearer the amount of communication from the low status team to the high status group increased. The number of communications from members of the high status group to the low status group correspondingly decreased. When, in some groups, the status and privilege relationship between the two teams was reversed toward the end of the experimental session, thus reducing the forces to locomote into the other group, the number of communications to that other group correspondingly decreased.

Further corroboration is found in a preliminary experiment, mainly methodologically oriented, conducted by Back et al. (2). In this experiment new items of information were planted with persons at various levels in the hierarchy of a functioning organization. Data on transmission of each of the items of information were obtained through cooperators within the organization who were chosen so as to give adequate coverage of all levels and all sections within it. These cooperators recorded all instances of communication that came to their attention. Of seventeen acts of communication recorded in this manner, eleven were directed upwards in the hierarchy, four toward someone on the same level and only two were directed downwards. The existence of forces to move upward in such a hierarchical organization may be taken for granted. The great bulk of the communications recorded went in the same direction as these forces to locomote.

In considering communication among members of differentiated social structures it is important also to take into account restraints against communication.

Infrequent contact in the ordinary course of events tends to erect restraints against communication. It is undoubtedly easier to communicate a given item to a person whom one sees frequently or to a person to whom one has communicated similar items in the past. The structuring of groups into hierarchies, social clusters, or the like, undoubtedly tends to restrict the amount and type of contact between members of certain different parts or levels of the group and also undoubtedly restricts the content of the communication that goes on between such levels in the ordinary course of events. These restrictions erect restraints against certain types of communication.

There are some data which tend to specify some of the restraints against communication which exist. In the study of the communication of a spontaneous rumor in a community by Festinger, Cartwright, et al. (3), it was found that intimacy of friendship tended to increase ease of communication. Persons with more friends in the project heard the rumor more often than those with only acquaintances. Those who had few friends or acquaintances heard the rumor least often. At the same time this factor of intimacy of friendship was not related to how frequently they relayed the rumor to others. In other words, it was not related to forces to communicate but seemed to function only as a restraint against communicating where friendship did not exist.

There is also some evidence that the mere perception of the existence of a hierarchy sets up restraints against communication between levels. Kelley (7) experimentally created a two-level hierarchy engaging in a problem-solving task during which they could and did communicate within levels and between levels. Control groups were also run with the same task situation but with no status differential involved between the two subgroups. There was more communication between subgroups under these control conditions than where there was a status differential involved.

It seems that, in a hierarchy, there are also restraints against communicating hostility upward when the hostility is about those on upper levels. In the same experiment by Kelley there was much criticism of the *other group* expressed by both high status and low status members. The proportion of these critical expressions which are directed upward by the low status group is much less, however, than the proportion directed downward by the high status groups.

Emotional Expression

An important variety of communications undoubtedly results from the existence of an emotional state in the communicator. The existence of joy, anger, hostility and the like seems to produce forces to communicate. It seems that communications resulting from the existence of an emotional state are consummatory rather than instrumental.

By an instrumental communication we mean one in which the reduction of the force to communicate depends upon the effect of the communication on the recipient. Thus in communication resulting from pressures toward uniformity in a group, the mere fact that a communication is made does not affect the force to communicate. If the effect has been to change the recipient so that he now agrees more closely with the communicator, the force to communicate will be reduced. If the recipient changes in the opposite direction, the force to communicate to him will be increased.

By a consummatory communication we mean one in which the reduction of the force to communicate occurs as a result of the expression and does not depend upon the effect it has on the recipient. Certainly in the case of such communications the reaction of the recipient may introduce new elements into the situation which will affect the force to communicate, but the essence of a consummatory communication is that the simple expression does reduce the force.

Specifically with regard to the communication of hostility and aggression, much has been said regarding its consummatory nature. The psychoanalytic theories of catharsis, in particular, develop the notion that the expression of hostility reduces the emotional state of the person. There has, however, been very little experimental work done on the problem. The previously mentioned experiment by Thibaut in which he created a "privileged-underprivileged" relationship between two equated groups has some data on the point. There is evidence that those members of the "underprivileged" groups who expressed their hostility toward the "privileged" groups showed less residual hostility toward them in post-experimental questionnaires. There is, however, no control over the reactions of the recipients of the hostile communications nor over the perceptions of the communicators of what these reactions were. An experiment is now in progress which will attempt to clarify some of these relationships with both negative and positive emotional states.

Summary

A series of interrelated hypotheses has been presented to account for data on informal social communication collected in the course of a number of studies. The data come from field studies and from laboratory experiments specifically designed to test the hypotheses.

Three sources of pressures to communicate have been considered:

1. Communication arising from pressures toward uniformity in a group. Here we considered determinants of magnitude of the force to communicate, choice of recipient for the communication, magnitude of change in recipient and magnitude of tendencies to reject nonconforme·s.
2. Communications arising from forces to locomote in a social structure. Here we considered communications in the direction of a blocked locomotion and restraints against communication arising in differentiated social structures.
3. Communications arising from the existence of emotional states. In this area data are almost completely lacking. Some theoretical distinctions were made and an experiment which is now in progress in this area was outlined.

At the time of this article, Leon Festinger was at the Research Center for Group Dynamics, University of Michigan.

The research program described in this article consisted of a number of coordinated and integrated studies, in both the laboratory and the field. It was carried out by the Research Center for Group Dynamics under contract N6onr–23212 NR 151–698 with the Office of Naval Research.

References

1. BACK, K. The exertion of influence through social communication. *J. abnorm. soc. Psychol.*, 1950 (in press).
2. ——, FESTINGER, L., HYMOVITCH, B., KELLEY, H. H., SCHACHTER, S., & THIBAUT, J. The methodological problems of studying rumor transmission. *Hum. Relat.*, 1950 (in press).
3. FESTINGER, L., CARTWRIGHT, D., et al. A study of a rumor: its origin and spread. *Hum. Relat.*, 1948, 1, 464–486.
4. ——, SCHACHTER, S., & BACK, K. *Social pressures in informal groups: a study of a housing project.* New York: Harper, 1950.
5. ——, & THIBAUT, J. Interpersonal communication in small groups. *J. abnorm. soc. Psychol.* (in press).

6. LEWIN, K. Formalization and progress in psychology. In *Studies in Topological and Vector Psychology I.*, *Univ. Ia. Stud. Child Welf.*, 1940, 16, No. 3.

7. KELLEY, H. H. Communication in experimentally created hierarchies. *Hum. Relat.* (in press.)

8. SCHACHTER, S. Deviation, rejection, and communication *J. abnorm. soc. Psychol.* (in press).

9. THIBAUT, J. An experimental study of the cohesiveness of underprivileged groups. *Hum. Relat.*, 1950, 3.

6

A Theory of Social Comparison Processes

In this paper we shall present a further development of a previously published theory concerning opinion influence processes in social groups (7). This further development has enabled us to extend the theory to deal with other areas, in addition to opinion formation, in which social comparison is important. Specifically, we shall develop below how the theory applies to the appraisal and evaluation of abilities as well as opinions.

Such theories and hypotheses in the area of social psychology are frequently viewed in terms of how "plausible" they seem. "Plausibility" usually means whether or not the theory or hypothesis fits one's intuition or one's common sense. In this meaning much of the theory which is to be presented here is not "plausible." The theory does, however, explain a considerable amount of data and leads to testable derivations. Three experiments, specifically designed to test predictions from this extension of the theory, have now been completed (5, 12, 19). They all provide good corroboration. We will in the following pages develop the theory and present the relevant data.

HYPOTHESIS I.   *There exists, in the human organism, a drive to evaluate his opinions and his abilities.*

While opinions and abilities may, at first glance, seem to be quite different things, there is a close functional tie between them. They act together in the manner in which they affect behavior. A person's cogni-

SOURCE: Festinger, L., *Hum. Relat.*, 1954, **7**, 117–140.

tion (his opinions and beliefs) about the situation in which he exists and his appraisals of what he is capable of doing (his evaluation of his abilities) will together have bearing on his behavior. The holding of incorrect opinions and/or inaccurate appraisals of one's abilities can be punishing or even fatal in many situations.

It is necessary, before we proceed, to clarify the distinction between opinions and evaluations of abilities since at first glance it may seem that one's evaluation of one's own ability is an opinion about it. Abilities are of course manifested only through performance which is assumed to depend upon the particular ability. The clarity of the manifestation or performance can vary from instances where there is no clear ordering criterion of the ability to instances where the performance which reflects the ability can be clearly ordered. In the former case, the evaluation of the ability does function like other opinions which are not directly testable in "objective reality." For example, a person's evaluation of his ability to write poetry will depend to a large extent on the opinions which others have of his ability to write poetry. In cases where the criterion is unambiguous and can be clearly ordered, this furnishes an objective reality for the evaluation of one's ability so that it depends less on the opinions of other persons and depends more on actual comparison of one's performance with the performance of others. Thus, if a person evaluates his running ability, he will do so by comparing his time to run some distance with the times that other persons have taken.

In the following pages, when we talk about evaluating an ability, we shall mean specifically the evaluation of that ability in situations where the performance is unambiguous and is known. Most situations in real life will, of course, present situations which are a mixture of opinion and ability evaluation.

In a previous article (7) the author posited the existence of a drive to determine whether or not one's opinions were "correct." We are here stating that this same drive also produces behavior in people oriented toward obtaining an accurate appraisal of their abilities.

The behavioral implication of the existence of such a drive is that we would expect to observe behavior on the part of persons which enables them to ascertain whether or not their opinions are correct and also behavior which enables them accurately to evaluate their abilities. It is consequently necessary to answer the question as to how persons go about evaluating their opinions and their abilities.

HYPOTHESIS II.   *To the extent that objective, non-social means are not available, people evaluate their opinions and abilities by comparison respectively with the opinions and abilities of others.*

In many instances, perhaps most, whether or not an opinion is correct cannot be immediately determined by reference to the physical world. Similarly it is frequently not possible to assess accurately one's ability by reference to the physical world. One could, of course, test the opinion that an object was fragile by hitting it with a hammer, but how is one to test the opinion that a certain political candidate is better than another, or that war is inevitable? Even when there is a possible immediate physical referent for an opinion, it is frequently not likely to be employed. The belief, for example, that tomatoes are poisonous to humans (which was widely held at one time) is unlikely to be tested. The situation is similar with respect to the evaluation of one's abilities. If the only use to which, say, jumping ability was put was to jump across a particular brook, it would be simple to obtain an accurate evaluation of one's ability in this respect. However, the unavailability of the opportunity for such clear testing and the vague and multipurpose use of various abilities generally make such a clear objective test not feasible or not useful. For example, how does one decide how intelligent one is? Also, one might find out how many seconds it takes a person to run a certain distance, but what does this mean with respect to his ability—is it adequate or not? For both opinions and abilities, to the extent that objective physical bases for evaluation are not available, subjective judgments of correct or incorrect opinion and subjectively accurate assessments of one's ability depend upon how one compares with other persons.

COROLLARY II A. *In the absence of both a physical and a social comparison, subjective evaluations of opinions and abilities are unstable.*

There exists evidence from studies on "level of aspiration" which shows clearly the instability of evaluations of abilities in the absence of comparison with other persons (13, 15, 20, 21, 23). The typical situation in an experiment designed to study "level of aspiration" is as follows: a person is given a task to perform which is serial in nature. This may be a series of trials of throwing darts at a target or a series of information tests or a series of puzzles or the like. After each trial the person is told what he scored (how many points he made or how many correct answers or how long it took) and is asked to state what score he expects to get or will try for on the next trial. These experiments have previously been interpreted in terms of goal directed behavior. If we examine the situation closely, however, it is apparent that the individual's stated "level of aspiration" is actually a statement of what he considers a good performance to be. In other words, it is his evaluation, at the time, of what score he should get, that is, his evaluation of his ability. The data show clearly that if the person scores as well as he said he expected to do, he feels he has done well (experiences success) and if he scores less than his "aspirations" he feels he has done poorly (experiences failure) (17).

Let us examine, then, the stability of these evaluations in a situation where the person performing the task has no opportunity for comparison with others. The data from these studies show that the "level of aspiration" fluctuates markedly as performance fluctuates. If the person makes a score better than his previous one, then what was formerly considered a good performance is no longer good and his "level of aspiration" goes up. If his performance drops, his "level of aspiration" drops. Even after a person has had a good deal of experience at a task, the evaluation of what is good performance continues to fluctuate.

Similar instability is found in the case of opinions. When, using the autokinetic effect, persons are asked to make judgments of how far the point of light moves, these judgments continue to fluctuate before there are any comparison persons.[1]

To the extent, then, that there are relevant data available, they tend to confirm Corollary IIA concerning the instability of evaluations in the absence of comparisons.

COROLLARY II B.   *When an objective, non-social basis for the evaluation of one's ability or opinion is readily available persons will not evaluate their opinions or abilities by comparison with others.*

Hochbaum (18) reports an experiment concerning the effect of knowledge of others' opinions on one's own opinion which corroborates Corollary II B. Half of the subjects in this experiment were persuaded by the experimenter that they were extremely good at being able to make correct judgments concerning things like the issue they were to discuss. The other half of the subjects were made to feel that they were extremely poor in making such judgments. They were then asked to write their opinions down and were handed back a slip of paper presumably reporting to them the opinions of each other person in the group. In this way the subjects were made to feel that most of the others in the group disagreed with them. Those subjects who were given an objective basis for feeling that their opinion was likely to be correct did not change their opinions very often in spite of the disagreement with others in the group. Those who had an objective basis for feeling their judg-

1. Although published material on the autokinetic effect does not present the data in this form, it is clearly shown in special analysis of data from an experiment by Brehm, J. W., "A quantitative approach to the measurement of social influence." Honors thesis, Harvard University, 1952.

ments were likely to be poor changed their opinion very frequently upon discovering that others disagreed with them.

HYPOTHESIS III.   *The tendency to compare oneself with some other specific person decreases as the difference between his opinion or ability and one's own increases.*

A person does not tend to evaluate his opinions or his abilities by comparison with others who are too divergent from himself. If some other person's ability is too far from his own, either above or below, it is not possible to evaluate his own ability *accurately* by comparison with this other person. There is then a tendency not to make comparison. Thus, a college student, for example, does not compare himself to inmates of an institution for the feeble minded to evaluate his own intelligence. Nor does a person who is just beginning to learn the game of chess compare himself to the recognized masters of the game.

The situation is identical with respect to the evaluation of opinions. One does not evaluate the correctness or incorrectness of an opinion by comparison with others whose opinions are extremely divergent from one's own. Thus, a person who believes that Negroes are the intellectual equals of whites does not evaluate his opinion by comparison with the opinion of a person who belongs to some very anti-Negro group. In other words, there is a self-imposed restriction in the range of opinion or ability with which a person compares himself.

COROLLARY III A.   *Given a range of possible persons for comparison, someone close to one's own ability or opinion will be chosen for comparison.*

There is some evidence relevant to this corollary from an experiment by Whittemore (24). The purpose of the study was to examine the relation between performance and competition. Subjects were seated around a table and given tasks to work on. There was ample opportunity to observe how the others were progressing. After the experimental session, in introspective reports, the subjects stated that they had almost always spontaneously selected someone whose performance was close to their own to compete against.

COROLLARY III B.   *If the only comparison available is a very divergent one, the person will not be able to make a subjectively precise evaluation of his opinion or ability.*

There is evidence supporting this corollary with respect to abilities but no relevant evidence in connection with opinions has been found.

Hoppe (20) in his experiment on level of aspiration reports that when subjects made a score very far above or very far below their level of aspiration they did not experience success or failure respectively. In other words, this extremely divergent score presented no grounds for self evaluation. Dreyer (5) performed an experiment in which high school children were made to score either: very far above the reported average for boys like themselves; at the reported average; or very far below the reported average. After a series of trials they were asked, "How well do you feel you did on the test?" There were five possible categories of response. The top two were good or very good; the bottom two were poor or very poor. In the middle was a noncommittal response of fair. Both those who scored very far below and those who scored very far above the reported group average gave the response "fair" significantly more often than did those who scored at the reported group average. Also, on the average, the persons who had scored at the reported average felt they had done better than did those scoring far above the group. Again the data support the hypothesis.

We may then conclude that there is selectivity in comparison on abilities and opinions and that one major factor governing the selectivity is simply the discrepancy between the person's own opinion or ability and that of another person. Phenomenologically, the appearance of this process is different for opinions and for abilities but conceptually it is exactly the same process. In dealing with opinions one feels that those with whom one does not compare oneself are different kinds of people or members of different groups or people with different backgrounds. Frequently this allegation of difference, to support the non-comparability, is made together with some derogation. In the case of abilities, the phenomenal process is that of designation of status inferior or superior to those persons who are noncomparable to oneself. We will elaborate on this later.

DERIVATION A (FROM I, II, III).   *Subjective evaluations of opinions or of abilities are stable when comparison is available with others who are judged to be close to one's opinions or abilities.*

DERIVATION B (FROM I, II, III).   *The availability of comparison with others whose opinions or abilities are somewhat different from one's own will produce tendencies to change one's evaluation of the opinion or ability in question.*

There are also data to show the effect which knowledge of group opinions or group abilities have on the person's evaluations which were initially formed privately. If the evaluation of an opinion or an ability formed in the absence of the possibility of comparison with others is indeed unstable, as we have presumed, then we would expect that, given an opportunity to make a comparison with others, the opportunity would be taken and the comparison would have a considerable impact on the self evaluation. This is found to be true for both abilities and opinions. "Level of aspiration" experiments have been performed where, after a series of trials in which the person is unable to compare his performance with others, there occurs a series of trials in which the person has available to him the knowledge of how others *like himself* performed on each trial (1, 4, 6, 17). When the "others like himself" have scores different from his own, his stated "level of aspiration" (his statement of what he considers is good performance) almost always moves close to the level of the performance of others. It is also found that under these conditions the level of aspiration changes less with fluctuations in performance, in other words, is more stable. When the reported performance of others is about equal to his own score, the stability of his evaluation of his ability is increased and, thus, his level of aspiration shows very little variability. Dreyer, in an experiment specifically designed to test part of this theory (5), showed clearly that the variance of the level of aspiration was smaller when the subject scored close to the group than when he scored far above or far below them. In short, comparison with the performance of others specifies what his ability should be and gives stability to the evaluation.

Festinger, Gerard, et al. (10) find a similar situation with respect to opinions. When a person is asked to form an opinion privately and then has made available to him the consensus of opinion in the group of which he is a member, those who discover that most others in the group disagree with them become relatively less confident that their opinion is correct and a goodly proportion change their opinion. Those who discover that most others in the group agree with them become highly confident in their opinion and it is extremely rare to find one of them changing his opinion. Again, comparison with others has tended to define what is a correct opinion and has given stability to the evaluation. This result is also obtained by Hochbaum (18).

We may then conclude that Derivations A and B tend to be supported by the available data.

DERIVATION C (FROM I, III B). *A person will be less attracted to situations where others are very divergent from him than to situations where others are close to him for both abilities and opinions.*

This follows from a consideration of Hypothesis I and Corollary III B. If there is a drive toward evaluation of abilities and opinions, and if this evaluation is possible only with others who are close enough, then there should be some attraction to groups where others are relatively close with respect to opinions and/or abilities. There are data confirming this for both opinions and abilities.

Festinger, Gerard, et al. (10) report an experiment in which after each person had written down his opinion on an issue he was handed back a slip of paper presumably containing a tabulation of the opinions in the group. Some in each group were thus given the impression that most of the others in the group held opinions close to their own. The rest were given the impression that most others in the group held opinions quite different from their own. After the experiment they were each asked how well they liked the others in the group. In each of the eight different experimental conditions those who thought that the others held divergent opinions were less attracted to the group.[2]

The previously mentioned experiment by Dreyer (5) has as one of its main purposes the testing of this derivation in connection with abilities. He used a "level of aspiration" situation and falsified the scores he reported to the subject so that some thought they were scoring very far above the group, some thought they were scoring very far below the group, while others thought they were scoring about at the same level as the average of others like them. After each trial they were asked whether they wanted to continue for another trial or whether they would prefer to stop. The reasoning was that if those scoring well above or well below the group average were not able to evaluate their ability accurately, the situation would be less attractive to them and they would stop sooner. On the average, those scoring very much above the group stop after the fifth trial, while those scoring below or at the average of the group stop after the ninth trial.[3] There is no difference between those scoring at and those scoring well below the average of the group. The derivation in the case of abilities seems confirmed for deviation from the group in one direction then but not in the other. This is probably due to the presence of another pressure which we shall discuss in detail later, namely, the value placed in our culture on being better and

2. This result is not reported in the article cited. It was obtained by analyzing the data for this particular purpose.

3. It is interesting to note that on this point, the usual theory of level of aspiration (21) would lead to a quite different prediction, namely, that those scoring consistently below the group would stop earliest.

better with the result that the subjects scoring below the group wanted to, and felt that they might, improve and achieve comparability with the group average.

This result from the experiment by Dreyer (5) is also corroborated in the previously mentioned experiment by Hochbaum (18). It will be recalled that half the subjects were made to feel that their ability in judging situations of the kind they were to discuss was extremely good and very superior to the abilities of the others in the group. The other half of the subjects were made to feel that their ability was poor and considerably worse than the ability of the others in the group. At the end of the experiment all the subjects were asked whether, if they returned for another session, they would like to be in the same group or a different group. Of those who felt they were very much above the others in the group, only 38 per cent wanted to return to the same group. Of those who felt that they were considerably inferior to the others, 65 per cent wanted to return to the same group.

With the qualification concerning the asymmetry with regard to abilities the derivation may be regarded as confirmed. We will discuss the unidirectional drive upwards for abilities, which produces the asymmetry, in more detail later.

DERIVATION D (FROM I, II, III).   *The existence of a discrepancy in a group with respect to opinions or abilities will lead to action on the part of members of that group to reduce the discrepancy.*

We have stated in Hypotheses I, II, and III and in the corollaries to these hypotheses that there is a drive to evaluate accurately one's opinions and abilities, that this evaluation is frequently only possible by comparison with others and that the comparison tends to be made with others who are close to oneself on the particular ability or opinion in question. This implies that the drive to evaluate one's ability or opinion will lead to behavior which will produce for the person a situation where those with whom he compares himself are reasonably close to him, in other words, there will be action to reduce discrepancies which exist between himself and others with whom he compares himself.

Before we can discuss the data relevant to this derivation it is necessary to point out two important differences between opinions and abilities which affect the behavioral manifestations of the action to reduce discrepancies. We will state these differences in the form of hypotheses.

HYPOTHESIS IV.   *There is a unidirectional drive upward in the case of abilities which is largely absent in opinions.*

With respect to abilities, different performances have intrinsically different values. In Western culture, at any rate, there is a value set on doing better and better which means that the higher the score on performance, the more desirable it is. Whether or not this is culturally determined, and hence culturally variable, is an important question but one with which we will not occupy ourselves here.[4]

With respect to most opinions, on the other hand, in the absence of comparison there is no inherent, intrinsic basis for preferring one opinion over another. If we thought of opinions on some specific issue as ranging along a continuum, then no opinion in and of itself has any greater value than any other opinion. The value comes from the subjective feeling that the opinion is correct and valid.

HYPOTHESIS V.   *There are non-social restraints which make it difficult or even impossible to change one's ability. These non-social restraints are largely absent for opinions.*

If a person changes his mind about something, deserts one belief in favor of another, there is no further difficulty in the way of consummating the change. It is true that there are sometimes considerable difficulties in getting someone to change his mind concerning an opinion or belief. Such resistance may arise because of consistency with other opinions and beliefs, personality characteristics that make a person lean in one direction or another and the like. But the point to be stressed here is that once these resistances are overcome, there is no further restraint which would make it difficult for the change to become effective.

There are generally strong non-social restraints, however, against changing one's ability, or changing one's performance which reflects this ability. Even if a person is convinced that he should be able to run faster or should be more intelligent, and even if he is highly motivated to improve his ability in this respect, there are great difficulties in the way of consummating the change.

We may now examine the implications of Derivation D. Considering Hypothesis IV it is clear that the action to reduce the discrepancy which exists is, in the case of opinions, a relatively uncomplicated pressure toward uniformity. When and if uniformity of opinion is achieved there is a state of social quiescence. In the case of abilities, however, the action to reduce discrepancies interacts with the unidirectional push to do better and better. The resolution of these two pressures, which act

4. There is some evidence, for example, that among the Hopi Indians this preference for better performance is absent (2).

simultaneously, is a state of affairs where all the members are relatively close together with respect to some specific ability, but not completely uniform. The pressures cease acting on a person if he is just slightly better than the others. It is obvious that not everyone in a group can be slightly better than everyone else. The implication is that, with respect to the evaluation of abilities, a state of social quiescence is never reached.

Competitive behavior, action to protect one's superiority, and even some kinds of behavior that might be called cooperative, are manifestations in the social process of these pressure which do not reach quiescence. We shall now elaborate this further in considering the specific nature of the social action arising from pressures toward uniformity. There are three major manifestations of pressure toward uniformity which we shall list below together with the relevant data.

DERIVATION D_1.   *When a discrepancy exists with respect to opinions or abilities there will be tendencies to change one's own position so as to move closer to others in the group.*

DERIVATION D_2.   *When a discrepancy exists with respect to opinions or abilities there will be tendencies to change others in the group to bring them closer to oneself.*

Considering Hypothesis V in relation to the above two subderivations we can see that a difference is implied between the resulting process for opinions and for abilities. Since opinions are relatively free to change, the process of changing the positions of members of a group relative to one another is expressed in action which is predominantly socially oriented. When differences of opinion exist, and pressures toward uniformity arise, these pressures are manifested in an influence process. Members attempt to influence one another, existing opinions become less stable and change occurs. This process of social influence, as we have mentioned before, ceases if and when uniformity of opinion exists in the group.

When pressures toward uniformity exist with respect to abilities, these pressures are manifested less in a social process and more in action against the environment which restrains movement. Thus, a person who runs more slowly than others with whom he compares himself, and for whom this ability is important, many spend considerable time practicing running. In a similar situation where the ability in question is intelligence, the person may study harder. But, needless to say, movement toward uniformity may or may not occur. Even if it occurs, it will take much, much longer than in the case of opinions.

This process would, of course, not be competitive if it were not for the simultaneous operation of the unidirectional push upward which is stated in Hypothesis IV. Because of this unidirectional push and the pressure toward uniformity, the individual is oriented toward some point on the ability continuum slightly better than his own performance or the performance of those with whom he is comparing himself. If uniformity concerning an ability were reached this would not lead to a cessation of competition as long as the unidirectional push upward is operating.

There are data which corroborate the two derivations with regard to both abilities and opinions. Back (3), Festinger and Thibaut (9), Festinger, Gerard, et al. (10) and Gerard (14) have shown clearly that the presence of disagreement in a group concerning some opinion leads to attempts to influence others who disagree with them and also to tendencies to change own opinion to agree more with the others in the group. The effect of this process is to have a group move closer and closer to agreement. In groups where uniformity concerning some issue is reached the influence process on that issue ceases.

In the case of abilities the evidence is less direct for a number of reasons. First, there have been fewer studies conducted relevant to this point. Second, since the process resulting from pressure to reduce discrepancies concerning abilities is not clearly shown in a social process, and since it is complicated by the drive to do better and better, it is harder to identify. Some evidence is available from the literature on level of aspiration (21). It has been shown that in most situations, an individual's level of aspiration is placed slightly above his performance. When told the average performance of others like himself, the level of aspiration is generally set slightly above this reported group average. These results are what we would expect if the resolution of the simultaneous unidirectional drive upward and the pressure toward uniformity is indeed a drive to be slightly better than the others with whom one compares oneself. These data can then be viewed as an indication of the desire to change one's position relative to others.

An experiment by Hoffman, Festinger, and Lawrence (19) specifically designed to test parts of the present theory, shows this competitive process clearly. In a performance situation where one of three persons is scoring considerably above the other two, these two can and do act so as to prevent the high scorer from getting additional points. Thus, when the situation is arranged such that the performance of each person is controllable by the others in the group, action is taken to change the position of the members to reduce the discrepancies which exist.

Let us also examine what we would expect of the behavior of someone whose performance is considerably higher than the other members of the group and who has no other possible comparison group to turn to for his evaluation of this ability. Since the others are considerably poorer, they will not effectively serve as a comparison for his own evaluation. The pressure acting on him toward comparability can manifest itself in two ways. It is possible that under these conditions his performance will actually deteriorate slightly over a period of time. It is also possible that he will devote considerable time and effort to trying to improve the performance of the others in the group to a point where at least some of them are close to, but not equal to, him. This could take the form of helping them practice, coaching them, motivating them to improve and the like. Once comparability has been achieved, however, the process should change to the familiar competitive one.

There is some indirect corroboration of this from experimental evidence. Greenberg (16) reports a study in competition in which pairs of children, seated together at a table, were to construct things out of "stones" (blocks) which were initially all in one common pile. Grabbing blocks from the pile was one of the indications of competition while giving blocks to the others was taken as one indication of lack of competition. The author reports the case of two friends, E. K. and H. At a time when E. K.'s construction was clearly superior to that of H., H. asked for "stones" and was freely given such by E. K. Subsequently E. K. asked H. whether or not she wanted more "stones." At the end of the session, although privately the experimenter judged both constructions to be nearly equal, when the children asked "whose is better?" E. K. said "mine" and H., after a moment, agreed.

From many such pairs the author summarizes as follows: "Sometimes when a child gave another a 'stone,' it was not at all an act of disinterested generosity, but a display of friendly competition and superior skill."

DERIVATION D$_3$.   *When a discrepancy exists with respect to opinions or abilities there will be tendencies to cease comparing oneself with those in the group who are very different from oneself.*

Just as comparability can be achieved by changing the position of the members with respect to one another, so can it also be achieved by changing the composition of the comparison group. Thus, for example, if pressures toward uniformity exist in a group concerning some opinion on which there is a relatively wide discrepancy, there is a tendency to redefine the comparison group so as to exclude those members whose opinions are most divergent from one's own. In other words, one merely ceases to compare oneself with those persons.

Here again we would expect the behavioral manifestation of the tendency to stop comparing oneself with those who are very divergent to be different for opinions and for abilities. This difference arises because of the nature of the evaluation of opinions and abilities and because of the asymmetry introduced by the unidirectional push upward for abilities. We will consider these in order.

It will be recalled that opinions are evaluated in terms of whether or not subjectively they are correct while abilities are evaluated in terms of how good they seem. In other words, the existence of someone whose ability is very divergent from one's own, while it does not help to evaluate one's ability, does not make, in itself, for discomfort or unpleasantness. In the case of opinions, however, the existence of a discrepant opinion threatens one's own opinion since it implies the possibility that one's own opinion may not be correct. Hypothesis VI, which we will state below, leads us then to expect that the process of making other incomparable (ceasing to compare oneself with others) will be accompanied by hostility or derogation in the case of opinions but will not, generally, in the case of abilities.

HYPOTHESIS VI.   *The cessation of comparison with others is accompanied by hostility or derogation to the extent that continued comparison with those persons implies unpleasant consequences.*

Thus, in the case of opinions we expect the process of making others incomparable to be associated with rejection from the group. In the case of abilities, this may or may not be the case. It would be plausible to expect that there would rarely be derogation in making those below oneself incomparable. When making those above oneself incomparable, the presence of unidirectional push upward might lead to derogation in some instances.

The asymmetry introduced in the case of abilities is another difference we may expect to find. While in the case of opinions, deviation on either side of one's own opinion would lead to the same consequences, in the case of abilities there is a difference. The process of making others incomparable results in a "status stratification" where some are clearly inferior and others are clearly superior.

COROLLARY VI A.   *Cessation of comparison with others will be accompanied by hostility or derogation in the case of opinions. In the case of abilities this will not generally be true.*

Festinger, Schachter, and Back (8) and Schachter (22) have shown that when there is a range of opinion in a group there is a tendency to reject those members of the group whose opinions are very divergent from one's own. This rejection tends to be accompanied by a relative cessation of communication to those who are rejected. This is undoubtedly another evidence of the cessation of comparison with those persons.

There are data relevant to this point in connection with abilities from the experiment of Hoffman, Festinger, and Lawrence (19). In this experiment, one out of a group of three persons were made to score very much higher than the other two on a test of intelligence. When the nature of the situation allowed, the two low scoring subjects ceased to compete against the high scorer and began to compete against each other. When they did this they also rated the intelligence of the high scorer as considerably higher than their own, thus acknowledging his superiority. In those conditions where they continued to compete against the high scorer they did not rate his intelligence as higher than their own. In other words, when the situation allowed it they stopped comparing their scores with the score of someone considerably higher than themselves. This cessation of comparison was accompanied by an acknowledgment of the others' superiority. A number of sociometric questions showed no hostility toward or derogation of the higher scorer.

Having discussed the manifestations of the "pressure toward uniformity" which arises from the drive to evaluate opinions and abilities, we will now raise the question as to the factors which determine the strength of these pressures.

DERIVATION E (FROM I, II, AND III).   *Any factors which increase the strength of the drive to evaluate some particular ability or opinion will increase the "pressure toward uniformity" concerning that ability or opinion.*

HYPOTHESIS VII.   *Any factors which increase the importance of some particular group as a comparison group for some particular opinion or ability will increase the pressure toward uniformity concerning that ability or opinion within that group.*

To make the above statements relevant to empirical data we must of course specify the factors involved. The corollaries stated below will specify some of these factors. We will then present the data relevant to these corollaries.

COROLLARY TO DERIVATION E.   *An increase in the importance of an ability or an opinion, or an increase in its relevance to immediate be-*

*havior, will increase the pressure toward reducing discrepancies con-
cerning that opinion or ability.*

If an opinion or ability is of no importance to a person there will be
no drive to evaluate that ability or opinion. In general, the more important the opinion or ability is to the person, the more related to behavior,
social behavior in particular, and the more immediate the behavior is,
the greater will be the drive for evaluation. Thus, in an election year,
influence processes concerning political opinions are much more current
than in other years. Likewise, a person's drive to evaluate his intellectual ability will be stronger when he must decide between going to graduate school or taking a job.

The previously mentioned experiment by Hoffman, Festinger, and
Lawrence (19) corroborates the Corollary to Derivation E with respect
to abilities. It will be recalled that this experiment involved groups of
three persons who took an "intelligence test." The situation was arranged so that one of the subjects (a paid participant) started out with a
higher score than the other two. From then on the two subjects could
completely control how many points the paid participant scored. The
degree to which they prevented him from scoring points was taken as a
measure of the extent to which they were competing against him and
hence as an indication of the strength of the pressure toward uniformity
acting on them. Half of the groups were told that this test which they
were to take was an extremely valid test and hence a good measure of
intelligence, an ability which these subjects considered important. The
other half of the groups were told that it was a very poor test and the
research was being done to demonstrate conclusively that the test was
no good. For these subjects their performance was consequently not
important. The results showed that the competition with the high scorer
was significantly greater for the high importance than for the low importance condition.

Unfortunately there are no relevant data from experiments concerning opinions. The Corollary to Derivation E applies to opinions also,
however, and is testable.

The data which we have presented refer to changing the position of
members in the group. As the pressure toward uniformity increases
there should also be observed an increase in the tendency to cease comparison with those who are too different from oneself. Specifically, this
would mean that the range within which appreciable comparison with
others is made should contract as the pressure toward uniformity increases. This leads to an interesting prediction concerning abilities
which can be tested. The more important an ability is to a person and,
hence, the stronger the pressures toward uniformity concerning this

ability, the stronger will be the competition about it and also the greater the readiness with which the individuals involved will recognize and acknowledge that someone else is clearly superior to them. And just as in influence processes, where, once rejection has taken place there tends to be a cessation of communication and influence attempts toward those who have been made incomparable (10, 22), so we may expect that once inferior or superior status has been conferred, there will be a cessation of competition with respect to those who have been thus rendered incomparable.

Thus, for example, let us imagine two individuals who are identical with respect to some particular ability but differ markedly in how important this ability is to them personally. The prediction from the above theory would say that the person for whom the ability is more important would be more competitive about it than the other; would be more ready to allocate "inferior status" to those considerably less good than he; and would be more ready to allocate "superior status" to those considerably better than he. In other words, he would be more competitive within a narrower range.

COROLLARY VII A. *The stronger the attraction to the group the stronger will be the pressure toward uniformity concerning abilities and opinions within that group.*

The more attractive a group is to a member, the more important that group will be as a comparison group for him. Thus the pressure to reduce discrepancies which operate on him when differences of ability or opinion exist will be stronger. We would expect these stronger pressures toward uniformity to show themselves in all three ways: increased tendency to change own position, increased effort to change the position of others and greater restriction of the range within which appreciable comparison is made.

There are a number of studies which corroborate Corollary VII A with regard to opinions. Back (3) showed that in groups to which the members were highly attracted there were more attempts to influence others than in groups to which the members were less attracted. This greater exertion of influence was accompanied by more change of opinion in the highly attractive groups. Festinger, Gerard, et al. (10) showed a tendency for members of highly attractive groups to change their opinions more frequently than members of less attractive groups upon discovering that most others in the group disagreed with them. This change of opinion was before any influence had actually been exerted on them by other members of the group. They also found that there was more communication attempting to influence others in the high than in the low attractive groups.

Schachter (22) showed that this same factor, attraction to the group, also increased the tendency to cease comparison with those who differed too much. Members of his highly attractive groups rejected the deviate significantly more than did members of the less attractive groups.

Festinger, Torrey, and Willerman (12) report an experiment specifically designed to test Corollary VII A with respect to abilities. If, given a range of performance reflecting some ability, the comparison, and hence the competition, in highly attractive groups would be stronger than in less attractive groups, then this should be reflected in the feelings of having done well or poorly after taking the tests. If Corollary VII A is correct we would expect those scoring slightly below others to feel more inadequate in the high than in the low attractive groups. Similarly we would expect those scoring equal to or better than most others to feel more adequate in the high than in the low attractive groups. Groups of four persons were given a series of tests supposed to measure an ability that these persons considered important. One of the subjects was caused to score consistently slightly below the others. The other three were made to score equally well. Those members who were highly attracted to the group, and scored below the others, felt they had done worse than similar persons who were not attracted to the group. Those who were attracted to the group and had scored equal to the others felt that they had done better than did similar persons who were not attracted to the group. Thus the results of the experiment corroborate the corollary for abilities.

COROLLARY VII B. *The greater the relevance of the opinion or ability to the group, the stronger will be the pressure toward uniformity concerning that opinion or ability.*

The conceptual definition of relevance of an opinion or an ability to a group is not completely clear. There are, however, some things one can state. Where the opinion or ability involved is necessary or important for the life of the *group* or for the attainment of the satisfactions that push the members into the group, the need for evaluation in that group will be strong. Groups will thus differ on what one may call their "realm of relevance." A group of men who meet every Friday night to play poker, and do only this together, will probably have a narrow "realm of relevance." The abilities and opinions for which this group serves as a comparison will be very restricted. The members of a college fraternity, on the other hand, where the group satisfies a wider variety of the members' needs will have a wider "realm of relevance."

In spite of the conceptual unclarity which is involved it is possible to create differences in relevance of an issue to a group which are clear and unambiguous. Thus Schachter (22) created high and low relevance conditions in the following manner. Groups which were to discuss an issue relevant to the group were recruited specifically for that purpose. Other groups were recruited ostensibly for very different kinds of things and on a pretext were asked to discuss the particular issue in question. They were promised this would never happen again in the life of the group thus making this issue of low relevance to that particular group. Schachter found, confirming Corollary VII B, that the tendency to reject deviates was stronger in the high relevance condition than in the low relevance condition.

No other evidence bearing on Corollary VII B has been located.

Thus far we have discussed only factors which, in affecting the pressure toward uniformity, affect all three manifestations of this pressure in the same direction. There are also factors which affect the manifestations of pressure toward uniformity differentially. We will discuss two such factors.

HYPOTHESIS VIII.   *If persons who are very divergent from one's own opinion or ability are perceived as different from oneself on attributes consistent with the divergence, the tendency to narrow the range of comparability becomes stronger.*

There is evidence supporting this hypothesis with respect to both abilities and opinions. In the previously mentioned experiment by Hoffman, Festinger, and Lawrence (19) half the groups were told that the three persons in the group had been selected to take the test together because, as far as could be determined, they were about equal in intelligence. The other groups were told that one of the three was very superior to the others. This was reported in a manner which made it impossible for either of the subjects to suppose that he himself was the superior one. In the "homogeneous" condition the subjects continued to compete against the paid participant who was scoring considerably above them. In the condition where they thought one of the others was clearly superior they competed considerably less with the paid participant and tended to compete with each other. In other words, when there was the perception of a difference consistent with the fact that the paid participant was scoring above them, they ceased comparison with him.

There is additional evidence on this point from level of aspiration experiments. Festinger (6) reports an experiment where, on an intellectual task, subjects (college students) were told they were scoring considerably above another group which they ordinarily considered inferior to themselves (high school students) or were told they were scoring considerably below a group which they considered superior to themselves (graduate students). In these circumstances there is practically no effect on the level of aspiration. Thus, the knowledge of this other group's being divergent in a direction consistent with the label of the group had no effect on their evaluation. It is interesting to note in this same experiment that if the reported direction of difference is inconsistent with the level of the group this destroys the incomparability and the effect on the level of aspiration is very great.

The evidence concerning opinions relating to Hypothesis VIII comes from experiments reported by Gerard (14) and Festinger and Thibaut (9). In both of these experiments discussions were carried on in a group of persons with a considerable range of opinion on the issue in question. In each experiment, half of the groups were given the impression that the group was homogeneous. All the members of the group had about equal interest in and knowledge about the issue. The other half of the groups were given the impression that they were heterogeneously composed. There was considerable variation among them in interest in and knowledge about the problem. In both experiments there was less communication directed toward those holding extremely divergent opinions in the heterogeneous than in the homogeneous condition. In other words, the perception of heterogeneity on matters related to the issue enabled the members of the groups to narrow their range within which they actively compared themselves with others.

It is interesting, at this point, to look at the data from these two experiments in relation to Hypothesis III which stated that the tendency to compare oneself with others decreased as the divergence in opinion or ability increased. In both the Gerard experiment (14) and the Festinger and Thibaut experiment (9) it was found that most communication was directed toward those whose opinions were most different from the others. Since we have just interpreted a reduction in communication to indicate a reduction in comparison with others, it is necessary to explain the over-all tendency to communicate most with those holding divergent opinions in the light of Hypothesis III.

From Hypothesis III we would expect comparison to be made mainly with those closest to oneself. This is indeed true. The support one gets for one's opinion is derived from those close to one's own. However, it will be recalled that, in the case of opinions, comparison with others who are divergent represents a threat to one's own opinion. It is for this reason that communication is directed mainly toward those most divergent but still within the limits where comparison is made. This communication represents attempts to influence them. Reduction in communication to these extreme opinions indicates that the existence of these extreme opinions is less of a threat to one's own opinion. In other words, one is comparing oneself less with them. In the case of abilities we would not expect to find any such orientation toward very divergent persons. Comparison behavior in the case of abilities would follow very closely the simple relation stated in Hypothesis III.

HYPOTHESIS IX.   *When there is a range of opinion or ability in a group, the relative strength of the three manifestations of pressures toward uniformity will be different for those who are close to the mode of the group than for those who are distant from the mode. Specifically, those close to the mode of the group will have stronger tendencies to change the positions of others, relatively weaker tendencies to narrow the range of comparison and much weaker tendencies to change their own position compared to those who are distant from the mode of the group.*

Some data are available to support this hypothesis, with reference to opinions, from experiments by Festinger, Gerard, et al. (10) and by Hochbaum (18). In both of these experiments some persons in each group were given the impression that the rest of the group disagreed with them while others were given the impression that most of the group agreed with them. In both experiments there was considerably more change of opinion among the "deviates" than among the conformers. In both experiments there were considerably more attempt to influence others made by the conformers than by the deviates. While there exist no adequate data relevant to the tendency to narrow the range of comparison, corroboration is suggested in the experiment by Festinger, Gerard, et al. (10). In this experiment it was found that the deviates actually communicated less to those holding most divergent opinions than to those somewhat closer to their own position. The conformers showed the more familiar pattern of communicating most to those with extremely divergent opinions in the group.

The question may also be raised as to the determinants of the extent to which the group actually does move closer toward uniformity when pressures in this direction exist. In part, the degree of such movement toward uniformity will be dependent upon the strength of the pressures. In part they will be dependent upon other things. In the case of opinions it will be dependent upon the resistances to changing opinions, and upon the power of the group to successfully influence its members. The theory concerning the determinants of the power of the group to influence its members is set forth elsewhere (7). We will not repeat it here since the power of the group to influence its members is relatively unimportant with regard to abilities. The social process itself, no matter how much power the group has, cannot achieve movement toward uniformity on abilities. The power of the group successfully to influence its members will be effective only insofar as changing members' values concerning a given ability and increasing motivations can be effective. With respect to values and motivations concerning the ability the situation is identical with the social process that goes on concerning opinions.

Implications for Group Formation and Societal Structure

The drive for self evaluation concerning one's opinions and abilities has implications not only for the behavior of persons in groups but also for the processes of formation of groups and changing membership of groups. To the extent that self evaluation can only be accomplished by means of comparison with other persons, the drive for self evaluation is a force acting on persons to belong to groups, to associate with others. And the subjective feelings of correctness in one's opinions and the subjective evaluation of adequacy of one's performance on important abilities are some of the satisfactions that persons attain in the course of these associations with other people. How strong the drives and satisfactions stemming from these sources are compared to the other needs which people satisfy in groups is impossible to say, but it seems clear that the drive for self evaluation is an important factor contributing to making the human being "gregarious."

People, then, tend to move into groups which, in their judgment, hold opinions which agree with their own and whose abilities are near their own. And they tend to move out of groups in which they are unable to satisfy their drive for self evaluation. Such movement in and out of groups is, of course, not a completely fluid affair. The attractiveness to a group may be strong enough for other reasons so that a person cannot move out of it. Or there may be restraints, for one or another reason, against leaving. In both of these circumstances, mobility from one group to another is hindered. We will elaborate in the next section on the effects of so hindering movement into and out of groups.

These selective tendencies to join some and leave other associations, together with the influence process and competitive activity which arise when there is discrepancy in a group, will guarantee that we will find relative similarity in opinions and abilities among persons who associate with one another (at least on those opinions and abilities which are relevant to that association). Among different groups, we may well expect to find relative dissimilarity. It may very well be that the segmentation into groups is what allows a society to maintain a variety of opinions within it and to accommodate persons with a wide range of abilities. A society or town which was not large enough or flexible enough to permit such segmentation might not be able to accommodate the same variety.

The segmentation into groups which are relatively alike with respect to abilities also gives rise to status in a society. And it seems clear that when such status distinctions are firmly maintained, it is not only members of the higher status who maintain them. It is also important to the members of the lower status to maintain them for it is in this way that they can relatively ignore the differences and compare themselves with their own group. Comparisons with members of a different status group, either higher or lower, may sometimes be made on a phantasy level, but very rarely in reality.

It is also important to consider whether or not the incomparability consequent upon group segmentation is a relatively complete affair. The conferring of status in the case of abilities or the allegation of "different kind of people" in the case of opinions may markedly lower the comparability but may not completely eliminate it. The latter is probably the more accurate statement. People are certainly aware, to some extent, of the opinions of those in incomparable groups. To the extent that perfect incomparability is not achieved, this has important bearing on differences in behavior to be expected from members of minority groups. Members of minority groups, if they are unable to achieve complete incomparability with other groups, should be somewhat less secure in their self evaluations. One might expect from this that within a minority group, the pressures toward uniformity would be correspondingly stronger than in a majority group. The minority group would seek stronger support within itself and be less well able to tolerate differences of opinion or ability which were relevant to that group.

In connection with opinion formation, there is experimental evidence that this is the case (14). Subgroups which were in the minority within larger experimental groups showed evidence of stronger pressures toward uniformity within the subgroup than did the majority subgroups. In minority groups where particular abilities were relevant, we would, by the same line of reasoning, also expect stronger pressures toward uniformity and hence fiercer competition with respect to that ability than in majority groups.

We may recall that stronger pressure toward uniformity also implies the existence of stronger tendencies to regard as incomparable those who deviate markedly. Since others are made incomparable with respect to opinions by means of rejection from the group, this gives us a possible explanation of the persistent splitting into smaller and smaller factions which is frequently found to occur in minority groups which are under strong pressure from the majority segments of the population.

Consequences of Preventing Incomparability

There are predominantly two kinds of situations in which comparability is forced despite the usual tendencies not to compare oneself with those who deviate markedly. One such situation occurs when the attraction of the group is so strong, for other reasons, that the member continues to wish to remain in the group in spite of the fact that he differs markedly from the group on some opinion or ability. If, together with this state of affairs, he has no other comparison group for this opinion or ability, or if the opinion or ability is highly relevant to that group, then comparability is forced to a great extent. The psychological tendencies to make incomparable those who differ most will still be present but would not be as effective as they might otherwise be.

Under these circumstances where the attraction to the group remains high, the group has power to influence the member effectively and, in the case of opinion difference, we would expect an influence process to ensue which would be effective enough to eliminate the difference of opinion. In short, there would be movement toward uniformity. But what happens in the case of an ability? Here, while the group will probably succeed in motivating the member concerning this ability it is quite likely that the ability itself may not be changeable. We have then created a situation where a person's values and strivings are quite out of line with his performance and we would expect, if he is below others, deep experiences of failure and feelings of inadequacy with respect to this ability. This is certainly not an unusual condition to find.

The other major situation in which comparability is forced upon a person is one in which he is prevented from leaving the group. The theory concerning the effect of this situation on opinion formation is spelt out elsewhere (11). We will touch on the main points here in order to extend the theory to ability evaluation. In circumstances where a person is restrained from leaving a group either physically or psychologically, but otherwise his attraction to the group is zero or even negative, the group does not have the power to influence him effectively. Uniformity can, however, be forced, in a sense, if the group exerts threats or punishment for non-compliance. In the case of opinions, we may here expect to find overt compliance or overt conformity without any private acceptance on the part of the member. Thus a boy who is forced to play with some children whom he does not particularly like would, in such circumstances, where threat was employed, agree with the other children publicly while privately maintaining his disagreement.

Again, when we consider abilities, we find a difference which arises because abilities may be difficulty if not impossible to change on short notice. Here the deviating member who is restrained from leaving the group may simply have to suffer punishment. If he deviates toward the higher end of the ability scale, he can again publicly conform without privately accepting the evaluations of the group. If he deviates toward the lower end of the ability scale this may be impossible. Provided he has other comparison groups for self evaluation on this ability he may remain personally and privately quite unaffected by this group situation. While publicly he may strive to perform better, privately his evaluations of his ability may remain unchanged.

Summary

If the foregoing theoretical development is correct, then social influence processes and some kinds of competitive behavior are both manifestations of the same socio-psychological process and can be viewed identically on a conceptual level. Both stem directly from the drive for self evaluation and the necessity for such evaluation being based on comparison with other persons. The differences between the processes with respect to opinions and abilities lie in the unidirectional push upward in the case of abilities, which is absent when considering opinions and in the relative ease of changing one's opinion as compared to changing one's performance.

The theory is tentatively supported by a variety of data and is readily amenable to further empirical testing. One great advantage, assuming the correctness of the theory, is that one can work back and forth between opinions and ability evaluations. Some aspects of the theory may be more easily tested in one context, some in the other. Discoveries in the context of opinions should also hold true, when appropriately operationally defined, in the context of ability evaluation.

The development of the theory described in this article was aided by a grant from the Behavioral Sciences Division of the Ford Foundation. It was part of the research program of the Laboratory for Research in Social Relations.

References

1. ANDERSON, H. H., & BRANDT, H. F. Study of motivation involving self-announced goals of fifth grade children and the concept of level of aspiration. *J. soc. Psychol.*, 1939, **10**, 209–232.

2. ASCH, S. E. Personality developments of Hopi children. Unpublished manuscript referred to in Murphy, Murphy and Newcomb, *Experimental social psychology*. New York and London: Harper, 1931, 1937 (rev. ed.).

3. BACK, K. The exertion of influence through social communication. *J. abnorm. soc. Psychol.*, 1951, **46**, 9–24.

4. CHAPMAN, D. W., & VOLKMANN, J. A. A social determinant of the level of aspiration. *J. abnorm. soc. Psychol.*, 1939, **34**, 225–238.

5. DREYER, A. Behavior in a level of aspiration situation as affected by group comparison. Ph.D. thesis, 1953, University of Minnesota.

6. FESTINGER, L. Wish, expectation and group standards as factors influencing level of aspiration. *J. abnorm. soc. Psychol.*, 1942, **37**, 184–200.

7. ———. Informal social communication. *Psychol. Rev.*, 1950, **57**, 271–282.

8. FESTINGER, L., SCHACHTER, S., & BACK, K. *Social pressures in informal groups.* New York: Harper, 1950.

9. FESTINGER, L., & THIBAUT, J. Interpersonal communications in small groups. *J. abnorm. soc. Psychol.*, 1951, **46**, 92–100.

10. FESTINGER, L., GERARD, H., et al. The influence process in the presence of extreme deviates. *Hum. Relat.*, 1952, **5**, 327–346.

11. FESTINGER, L. An analysis of compliant behavior. In Sherif, M. (ed.). *Group relations at the crossroads.* New York: Harper, 1953.

12. FESTINGER, L., TORREY, J., & WILLERMAN, B. Self-evaluation as a function of attraction to the group. *Hum. Relat.*, 1954, **7**, 2.

13. GARDNER, J. W. Level of aspiration in response to a prearranged sequence of scores. *J. exp. Psychol.*, 1939, **25**, 601–621.

14. GERARD, H. The effect of different dimensions of disagreement on the communication process in small groups. *Hum. Relat.*, 1953, **6**, 249–272.

15. GOULD, R. An experimental analysis of "level of aspiration." *Gen. Psychol. Monogr.*, 1939, **21**, 1–116.

16. GREENBERG, P. J. Competition in children: An experimental study. *Amer. J. Psychol.*, 1932, **44**, 221–248.

17. HILGARD, E. R., SAIT, E. M., & MAGARET, G. A. Level of aspiration as affected by relative standing in an experimental social group. *J. exp. Psychol.*, 1940, **27**, 411–421.

18. HOCHBAUM, G. M. Certain personality aspects and pressures to uniformity in social group. Ph.D. thesis, 1953, University of Minnesota.

19. HOFFMAN, P. J., FESTINGER, L., & LAWRENCE, D. H. Tendencies toward comparability in competitive bargaining. *Hum. Relat.*, 1954, **7**, 2.

20. HOPPE, F. Erfolg und Misserfolg. *Psychol. Forsch*, 1930, **14**, 1–62.

21. LEWIN, K., DEMBO, T., FESTINGER, L., & SEARS, P. S. Level of aspiration. In *Personality and the Behavior Disorders*. New York: Ronald, 1944, Vol. 1, pp. 333–378.

22. SCHACHTER, S. Deviation, rejection and communication. *J. abnorm. soc. Psychol.*, 1951, **46**, 190–208.

23. SEARS, P. S. Levels of aspiration in academically successful and unsuccessful children. *J. abnorm. soc. Psychol.*, 1940, **35**, 498–536.

24. WHITTEMORE, I. C. The influence of competition on performance. *J. Abnorm. Soc. Psychol.*, 1925, **20**, 17–33.

7

Interpersonal Communication in Small Groups

Small face-to-face groups, or as they have sometimes been called, primary groups, play an important part in influencing attitudes and opinions of their members. This important fact about social behavior has been assumed for many years. In the past decade experimental facts have accumulated to substantiate this fact and to specify the relationships involved.

In summary, the following is a list of some major conclusions which may be drawn from experimental work:

1. Belonging to the same group tends to produce changes in opinions and attitudes in the direction of establishing uniformity within the group (5, 6).

2. The amount of change toward uniformity which the group is able to accomplish is a direct function of how attractive belonging to the group is for its members (1, 2).

3. Members who do not conform to the prevailing patterns of opinion and behavior are rejected by others in the group. The degree of rejection is a direct function of how attractive belonging to the group is for its members and of the importance for the group of the issue on which the member does not conform (2, 7).

SOURCE: Festinger, L., & Thibaut, J. *J. abnorm. soc. Psychol.*, 1951, 46, 92–99. [Received January 23, 1950]

These facts leave unclarified the means by which such social influence is accomplished. The continual process of informal communication among members of face-to-face groups in part represents the attempts to influence members by others in the group. To understand completely the social influences which groups exert we must, then, also understand the determinants of what does and does not get communicated in social groups, and who are the recipients of communications. There are some data available. These may be summarized as follows:

1. Persons whose social behavior is changed by hearing something tend to relay this information to others who are seen as likely to be affected by it (2, 3).
2. Persons who do not conform to the group pattern tend to have fewer communications addressed to them if they are rejected but tend to have more communication addressed to them if they are not rejected (7).

A more detailed understanding of this process of communication and its relation to the process of influence is the major purpose of the theories and experiments reported in this paper.

Theoretical Orientation

The fact that groups do exert pressures on their members toward uniformity is beyond dispute. For our immediate purposes we need not concern ourselves with the sources of these pressures or the reasons for their existence. We will look only at the effects of these pressures toward uniformity on the communication and influence process that actually takes place in a group. A group may be looked upon as composed of a number of parts with each part characterized by a given state[1] with respect to a certain dimension. If the group has the property of tending toward uniformity of state, then any discrepancy among the different parts of the group will give rise to forces which will be exerted on parts of the group to change their state in such as way as to re-establish uniformity. The strength of these forces will be a function of the magnitude of the tendency toward uniformity which the group possesses.

1. In the experiments to be described later an individual person is coordinated to a part of a group and an opinion concerning a certain issue to the state of the parts of the group. Cliques of people, levels in an organization, or work groups may also be looked on as parts of a group.

The force to change exerted on any particular part of the group is also a direct function of the discrepancies in state between this part and all other parts of the group. The larger the discrepancy between part A and part B, the larger will be the force exerted on A by B and on B by A, since the disequilibrium is greater, the greater this discrepancy.

The preceding hypotheses concerning tendencies toward uniformity within a group do not, of course, hold for any arbitrarily defined collection of individuals or parts. When discrepancies exist among a collection of persons, uniformity of any group that exists within this collection can be achieved either by the exertion of forces to change various parts of the group or, alternatively, by forming the group in such a way that uniformity already exists. Redefinition of the boundaries of the psychological group (changing the membership composition) can, then, also be a response which the group makes to pressures toward uniformity.

In a group where the tendencies toward uniformity concern an opinion about some issue, the exertion of pressures on persons to change their opinion must of course make themselves felt through a process of communication among them. What can we infer about this process of communication from the hypotheses we have presented?

1. Within a psychological group communications should be directed mainly toward those members whose opinions are extreme as compared to the opinions of the others. This would follow from our hypothesis that the strength of the force applied on any part of the group is a direct function of the discrepancy between the state of that part and the states of the other parts of the group.

2. If it is possible for a group to subdivide or exclude members then, as the discrepancies in state become clear, there will be tendencies to cease communicating to the extremes. This would follow from a number of considerations that have been stated or implied above.

a. If it is impossible for the group to redefine its boundaries, then uniformity can only be achieved through changing others and being receptive to change.

b. If it is possible to redefine the boundaries of the group then uniformity can also be achieved by omitting the persons with extreme opinions from the group.

c. The perception that it is possible to redefine the boundaries of the group should, then, have two consequences. There should be greater resistance to change on the part of the members, and there should be less communication to those who may be excluded from the group, namely, those with extreme opinions.

3. The less the pressure towards uniformity in a group and/or the greater the possibility for the group to subdivide, the less will be the actual accomplishment of influence. Since both of the factors here mentioned will affect the readiness of members to change in response to influence which is exerted on them, and since possible group subdivision will also prevent the exertion of influence on the most deviant members, it follows that the end result of the process of communication will be less uniformity in the group if subdivision is seen as possible or if the tendencies toward uniformity are weaker.

The experiments which are described below were specifically designed to test these hypotheses. In the description of the procedure we will elaborate further on the operational definitions of the theoretical concepts.

Experimental Procedure

Subjects

The subjects used in these experiments were college undergraduates recruited from the various sections of the elementary psychology course and the elementary course in educational psychology at the University of Michigan. All subjects were volunteers.

General Characteristics of the Groups Formed

Sixty-one groups were studied of which 24 were composed entirely of women, 37 of men. The size of groups ranged from 6 to 14 members. Each group assembled in the experimental room, and each member was assigned one of a series of small tables arranged in a circle. Each member was identified by a letter which was printed on a 5 by 8 inch card placed in front of him so that all others could see it.

General Setup for All Groups

Each group was given one problem to consider. The problem was such that opinions concerning it could be placed on a prescribed seven-point continuum. Each member was given seven 5 by 8 inch cards with numbers corresponding to those on the seven-point scale of opinion. The members were instructed to consider the problem and then, all simultaneously, to place in front of them that card which represented their tentative opinion on the matter at issue. The experimenter then proceeded to call attention to each person's decision in order both to verify it and to insure that all were fully aware of it.

Smaller slips of paper bearing some additional information relevant to the problem were then distributed at random among the subjects. It was announced that each member of the group was receiving a different item of information. The purpose of this part of the procedure was to maximize the initial force to communicate by causing each member to believe that he had some unique information relevant to the problem-solving activity. Actually, however, only two items of information were distributed. One item was intended to push the member toward the upper end of the scale, the other toward the lower end. This device was essential to get adequate dispersion along the scale.

After the subjects had read the new information, each recorded directly on his information slip his identifying letter and the scale number representing his current opinion. These were collected by the experimenter and read aloud in order to make public the new opinions. Any member whose opinion had changed was asked to make the appropriate change in the numbered card in front of him.

With this preliminary procedure finished, the experimenter described the manner in which the problem was to be discussed. Stapled pads of paper were distributed to the subjects. For each pad the staple was placed in a slightly different position on the page. These differences were undetectable to the subjects, but they allowed the experimenter subsquently to match each pad with the member to whom it had been given. The subjects were informed that discussion about the problem had to be restricted to writing notes to one another. The subjects were left free to include anything they liked in the notes. However, a member could write a note to only one person at a time, and each note must bear only the letter of the person to whom it was directed; no reference to the sender's identity was permitted. This rule was adopted to minimize the chances that any member, in the act of deciding to whom to direct a note, would be affected by a knowledge of what people had sent notes to him. On completing a note, a sender was to raise his hand, whereupon the experimenter or his assistant would deliver it to the recipient. It was emphasized that if and when any member decided to change his opinion, he should change the numbered card in front of him.

At a signal from the experimenter the subjects then began to write notes. As each note was finished, the messenger (experimenter or assistant) took the note, recorded on it the time in minutes and seconds from the starting signal, and dispatched it. A record was also kept of the exact time of each change of opinion, that is, of each change in the numbered card in front of a subject. The note-writing continued for 20 minutes.

The Discussion Problems

Two problems were used in the course of experimentation. A problem in football strategy was assigned to 31 of the groups, and a problem in evaluating a case study of a delinquent boy was assigned to the remaining 30 groups.

The problem in football was concerned with making a decision about the best strategy for an imaginary anonymous team which has the ball on the 50-yard line, first down, 5 minutes of play remaining, with the score 18–18. Seven alternative types of strategies are outlined to the subjects. These range from extremely conservative power plays (at point 1) to extremely reckless pass plays (at point 7). The two items of additional information distributed among the subjects are that "our star running back has just been injured . . ." (intended to push the recipient upward on the scale) and that "the opposing team has tightened up its pass defense and has caught on to our spectacular plays" (intended to push the recipient downward on the scale).

The case study was a brief fictitious account of the history of a boy who had caused trouble all through his life and who had ended in jail. The history of the boy was deliberately made to be as ambiguous as possible in order to encourage dispersion on the scale of opinion about the best possible way of treating the case. The subjects were told that by prior decision of the social workers assigned to the case, the boy was to be put into a foster home; the assignment for the subjects was to determine the best type of home for this boy. The scale of opinion consisted of seven alternative types of foster homes, ranging from one in which love and kindness were exclusively emphasized (point 1) to a home in which discipline and punishment were exclusively used (point 7). The two items of additional information received by the subjects were: (1) that for a period of a year his mother, acting on the advice of a social worker, had tried to make the boy's home life warm but that it did no good, since his criminal activity increased (intended to push the recipient upward on the scale) and, (2) that the boy's oldest brother had returned home for a while and had given the boy stern but fatherly discipline but the boy's delinquency only worsened (intended to push the recipient downward on the scale).

The selection of these two problems was guided by our need to create discussion situations in which there would be markedly different amounts of resistance to change of opinion. In the case study problem, it was felt that subjects would bring into the experimental situation fairly strong predispositions toward certain of the scaled opinions. These predispositions could be expected to be quite resistant to change.

In the football problem, on the other hand, there was no expectation that strong prejudgments would be imported into the situation. Relative to subjects working on the case study problem, the subjects ought more readily to accept the present experimental group as a relevant reference group for their opinions and hence ought to be relatively less resistant to change.

Experimental Variations

Six experimental variations were applied to each of the two problems. These variations were created by further instructions over and above the general instructions already described. Five groups (three male and two female) were assigned to each of the experimental variations in each of the problems, except for variation V in the football problem, which had six groups, four male and two female.

Instructions to Create the Homogeneity-Heterogeneity Variable

In the first three variations, the intention of the additional instructions was to create a perception that there was no basis for group subdivision among them. To achieve this perception the homogeneity of the group was emphasized as follows: "You people in this group have been deliberately selected to make up the kind of group we are interested in observing. You have been selected in such a way that we believe you all will have about an equal interest in this problem and about equal knowledge about it. . . ."

In the second three variations it was intended that the subjects perceive the possibility of group subdivision as having a basis in fact. The heterogeneity of the group was emphasized by telling the members that they had been selected to be as different as possible both in their interest in the problem and in their knowledge about it.

Instructions to Create the Pressure-Toward-Uniformity Variable

Variation I: High Pressure-Homogeneity (abbreviated H-Hom)
In this variation we were interested in creating very strong pressures toward uniformity of opinion. The group was told that the experimenter's interest was in observing how a group went about coming to a

unanimous decision. Thus, whatever intrinsic pressures toward uniformity might exist in the group were strengthened by externally induced pressures.

Variation II: Medium Pressure-Homogeneity (abbreviated M-Hom)
This variation was designed to produce pressure toward uniformity of a conditional nature. The instructions were that a body of experts (the coaching staff of the University of Michigan football team, for the football problem, and some members of the Law School faculty for the case study problem) had considered the problem and had unanimously decided that one of the seven scale points represented the "correct solution." The group was told that it would receive a score for its performance, which would be the proportion of members who at the conclusion of the experiment were recommending the "correct solution."

Variation III: Low Pressure-Homogeneity (abbreviated L-Hom)
No external pressure toward uniformity was applied in this variation. The group was merely informed that the experimenter was interested in observing the way a group went about discussing such a problem. In this case, it was supposed that if any pressure toward uniformity developed it would be attributable to a need for "social reality" within the group (2, 4). According to this principle, there is a force on the group member to achieve support for his point of view; and to the extent that this point of view is untestable by demonstration, the member is increasingly required to accept the criterion of social agreement with a relevant reference group.

Variation IV: High Pressure-Heterogeneity (abbreviated H-Het)
In this variation we were intent on establishing high pressure toward uniformity while at the same time permitting the formation of subgroups. The variation includes instructions that the group is composed of heterogeneous members. Otherwise it is largely a counterpart of Variation I (H-Hom). This time, however, instead of asking for a unanimous decision, the experimenter informed the group that a plurality would be sufficient. The group would be taken as recommending the decision which the greatest number of members accepted. In addition, the subjects were told that in such heterogeneous groups as this, one usually did not find more than twenty per cent of the members agreeing on any one alternative. These last two instructions were made somewhat different from the instructions in the homogeneity conditions in order to allow sub-group formation to take place.

Variation V: Medium Pressure-Heterogeneity (abbreviated M-Het)
This variation was also expected to permit subgroup formation. The instructions to these groups were substantially the same as for Variation II (M-Hom) except for the emphasis on heterogeneity of the members and an additional instruction that it was not customarily possible for more than twenty per cent of the group to hit upon the "correct solution."

Variation VI: Low Pressure-Heterogeneity (abbreviated L-Het)
Except for the pretense that the group was heterogeneously composed, this variation was precisely the same as Variation III (L-Hom).

The following tabulation is presented to help clarify the relations among the six experimental conditions:

Pressure Toward Uniformity

	High	Medium	Low
Homogeneous group	I	II	III
Heterogeneous group	IV	V	VI

Experimental Results

Hypothesis I

The volume of communication between two persons is a function of the magnitude of the discrepancy between their opinions. Since extreme opinions are most discrepant from all the other opinions, we would therefore predict that most communications should be directed toward members who hold extreme points of view.

Figure 7.1 summarizes the experimental findings relevant to this prediction in terms of the weighted number of communications. The distribution of opinions within the group could affect the pattern of communication. Thus, for example, if six members held extreme opinions and only three members maintained "middle" opinions, we would obtain a preponderance of communication to the extremes even if members were addressed at random. To correct for this, each message was weighted by the inverse in the number of persons in the group in the same relationship to the communicator as the recipient of that particular message. Thus, a communication directed toward a person at an extreme was divided by the number of persons in the group (excluding the sender of

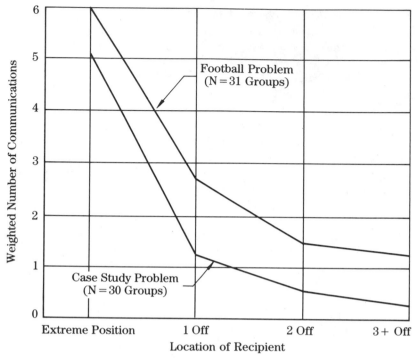

Figure 7.1 Patterns of communication (first 10 min.).

the message) who held extreme opinions at the time. When the weighted number of communications initiated during the first ten minutes[2] of each session is plotted against the location of the recipient (in terms of being at an extreme position, one point away from the extreme position, etc.), the curve falls off rapidly. This relationship seems to hold about equally for groups discussing the football problem and for groups discussing the case study problem. Out hypothesis is confirmed—the volume of communication directed toward a group member is a function of his nearness to the extreme of a range of opinions.

Hypothesis II

Since communication tends to be directed toward the extremes of a *psychological* group, it is predicted that where the formation of subgroups

2. Exactly the same type of curve is found for the second ten minutes of discussion. The curve is so consistent that only two are shown as examples.

(redefinition of the boundaries of the group) is possible there will be less communication directed toward the extremes of the *experimental* (arbitrarily defined) group. Since the heterogeneity condition provided more basis for subgroup formation than did the homogeneity condition, we may expect greater decreases in communication toward the extremes in the former as subgroups are given time to develop.

This hypothesis was tested in the following way. For each experimental group the mean value of the frequency curve showing the distribution of weighted number of communications according to the location of the recipient (as in Figure 7.1) was computed. For example, the mean of the distribution for the football problem in Figure 7.1 is .84 units away from the extreme opinion. This mean value is taken as an index of the tendency to communicate to the extremes. Low values of the index indicate a high proportion of communication to the extremes.

Table 7.1 presents these indices separately for the first and second 10 minutes of discussion for each experimental variation on the football problem. Table 7.2 gives the same data for the case study problem. In order to examine these data from the point of view of hypothesis II we will compare the indices of the first 10 minutes with the indices of the last 10 minutes in each variation. If our hypothesis is correct we would expect to find the indices increase for the heterogeneity conditions more than for the homogeneity conditions.

Examining the homogeneity conditions first we find no tendency toward any change from the first to the second 10 minutes. For the high pressure condition there is an extremely slight and insignificant increase for both discussion problems. For the medium pressure condition there is a tendency for the index to decrease, which again does not approach significance. For the low pressure condition the index stays virtually the same for the football problem and increases insignificantly for the case study problem.

In the heterogeneity conditions a quite different picture presents itself. In the high pressure condition there is no change in the index, but

Table 7.1 Mean Communication Indices for Football Problem Discussions

	First Ten Minutes				Second Ten Minutes		
	High	Medium	Low		High	Medium	Low
Hom	.68	.85	.88	Hom	.74	.63	.86
Het	.83	.83	.86	Het	.75	1.30	.99

Table 7.2   Mean Communication Indices for Case Study Problem Discussion

	First Ten Minutes				Second Ten Minutes		
	High	Medium	Low		High	Medium	Low
Hom	.27	.62	.48	Hom	.35	.56	.74
Het	.31	.50	.31	Het	.30	.72	.78

in the medium and low pressure conditions there are consistent increases in the index from the first to the second 10 minutes. Two of these four increases, the medium condition for the football problem and the low condition for the case study problem, are significant at the 5 per cent level of confidence. Taken together the changes in the medium and low pressure conditions are significant at the 1 per cent level of confidence.

There results seem to substantiate but qualify hypothesis II. While the homogeneity conditions show no increase in the index, the heterogeneity conditions show such an increase only where the pressure toward uniformity is sufficiently low to permit subgroup formation. In the high pressure conditions where strong pressures toward uniformity are exerted by the experimenter on the total group, subgroup formation does not occur. Where the pressure toward uniformity is weaker, subgroup formation does occur when a basis for it (perception of heterogeneity) exists.

It is also apparent from Tables 7.1 and 7.2 that in both the homogeneity and heterogeneity conditions, increasing the magnitude of pressure toward uniformity produces more communication toward the extremes. If we compare the indices for the high pressure and low pressure conditions we find that in the eight possible comparisons, the index for low pressure is greater in seven instances and tied in one instance. The index for medium pressure is higher than for high pressure in six of eight possible comparisons and tied in one instance. There is no consistency in the comparison between the medium and low pressure conditions.

In view of the consistency of the result we may conclude with a high degree of confidence that high pressure toward uniformity results in increased communication to the extremes. This result probably depends upon the degree to which tendencies to communicate arising from other sources can compete with communications resulting from pressures toward uniformity. When pressures toward uniformity become very high, these other forces in the situation may become less effective in comparison.

Hypothesis III

As pressure toward uniformity increases, both pressure to communicate and readiness to change also increase. Since both of these factors are conducive to change, there should be increasing change toward uniformity of opinion as the pressure toward uniformity increases.

In order to test this hypothesis a measure of the amount of change toward uniformity was calculated for each experimental group. The index used was the quotient of the standard deviation of opinions within the group by the end of the 20-minute discussion, divided by the standard deviation within the group at the beginning. The lower the index, the greater has been the change toward uniformity of opinion. Thus, for example, an index of 1.0 represents no change at all, and this value may be regarded as a base line in the figure.

Figure 7.2 presents these indices for each of the experimental variations and for each of the discussion problems. It can be seen that in each instance, as the pressure toward uniformity is decreased, the amount of change toward uniformity is decreased. The trends may be regarded as significant well beyond the 1 per cent level of confidence, since the probability of obtaining this predicted order of three points in four independent comparisons would be by chance about one in a thousand. The data fully support hypothesis III.

Hypothesis IV

If subgroup formation is seen as possible, the readiness to change when influence is exerted should be less than where no subgroup formation is possible. In addition, in the former case there is less actual exertion of influence on the extreme opinions in the group. Both of these factors should combine to produce less change toward uniformity in the heterogeneity than in the homogeneity conditions.

Figure 7.2 shows the data relevant to this hypothesis. The difference between the amount of change in the heterogeneity and homogeneity conditions is highly significant (beyond the 1 per cent level by analysis of variance) when the football problem is discussed. There is, however, little or no difference between these two conditions when the case study problem is discussed.

It will be recalled that the case study problem was selected in the belief that subjects would bring them fairly strong predispositions to-

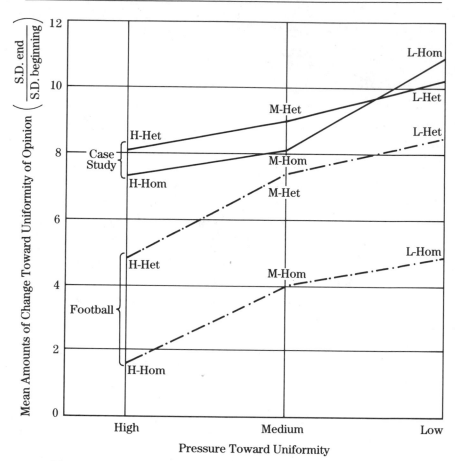

Figure 7.2   Mean amounts of change toward uniformity of opinion.

ward certain of the opinions, which would be relatively more resistant to change. The football problem was selected in the belief that subjects would not bring such predispositions into the experimental situation. This difference between the two discussion problems is clearly reflected in the much lower degree of change toward uniformity in the case study problem. It is also probable that this relatively high resistance to change in the case study problem made the added effect of the heterogeneity-homogeneity difference relatively negligible.

We may conclude that, where strong predispositions do not exist and where, consequently, the group has power to change opinions, the perception of heterogeneity will increase resistance to change. Hypothesis IV, thus amended, may be considered to be substantiated.

Summary

The variables of (1) amount of pressure toward uniformity existing in a group and (2) the degree to which the members perceived the group as homogeneously composed were manipulated experimentally in a laboratory setting of a discussion group to test certain hypotheses concerning the pattern of communication within the group and the amount of change in opinion which occurs. The results strongly support the theoretical hypotheses and may be summarized as follows:

1. When there is a range of opinion in the group, communications tend to be directed towards those members whose opinions are at the extremes of the range.
2. The greater the pressure toward uniformity and the greater the perception of homogeneous group-composition, the greater is the tendency to communicate to these extreme opinions.
3. The greater the pressure toward uniformity and the greater the perception of homogeneous group-composition, the greater is the actual change toward uniformity which takes place.

═══════════

At the time of this article, Leon Festinger and John Thibaut were at the Research Center for Group Dynamics, University of Michigan.

This study was conducted under contract with the Office of Naval Research (N6onr-23212 NR 151-698). It was part of a larger program of research on social communication and influence conducted at the Research Center for Group Dynamics at the University of Michigan.

References

1. BACK, K. The exertion of influence through social communication. *J. abnorm. soc. Psychol.*, 1951, **46**, 9–23.
2. FESTINGER, L., SCHACHTER, S., & BACK, K. *Social pressures in informal groups: A study of a housing project.* New York: Harper, 1950.
3. FESTINGER., L., CARTWRIGHT, D., et al. A study of a rumor: Its origin and spread. *Hum. Relat.*, 1948, **1**, 464–486.
4. FESTINGER, L. Informal social communication. *Psychol. Rev.*, 1950, **57**, 271–282.
5. NEWCOMB, T. *Personality and social change.* New York: Dryden Press, 1943.
6. SHERIF, M. *Psychology of social norms.* New York: Harper, 1936.
7. SCHACHTER, S. Deviation, rejection and communication. *J. abnorm. soc. Psychol.*, 1951, **46**. In press.

8

Tendencies Toward Group Comparability in Competitive Bargaining

Introduction

The present study is concerned with some of the socio-psychological factors that determine behavior in a situation where some ability is being revealed or measured. In such a situation, in order to evaluate their ability, persons frequently tend to compare their own performance with the performance of others whom they accept as comparable to themselves. As a consequence, the individual's behavior is determined more by his performance relative to those others than by the absolute level of his performance. If the situation in which the particular ability is measured is a bargaining situation where coalitions can form, it is possible to predict both the type and strength of the coalitions that form, and the relative stability of these when the composition of the group and the importance of the task for the participants is varied.

A motivational analysis of this type has implications, not only for social psychological theory but also for the theory of games (3). This is seen most clearly when "rational" bargaining behavior in the typical game situation is analyzed under the assumption that the only motivation present is a tendency on the part of each player to maximize the

SOURCE: Hoffman, P. J., Festinger, L., & Lawrence, D. H. *Hum. Relat.*, 1954, **7**, 141–160.

total number of points he obtains. Imagine a game involving three players where a fixed amount of money, points, or some commodity is to be divided among them. The rules of the game are such that no one individual can obtain the total amount by his own efforts. If any two of them agree to cooperate, they can share the amount on any basis satisfactory to the two of them. In addition the following conditions are assumed: (1) that all individuals are equally and singly motivated to obtain as large a share of the points as possible, and (2) that they are all equal in bargaining skill.

Two things should be noted about this game. First of all, while it is mandatory for two of the three players to form a coalition in order to obtain points, a given player has no rational basis for selecting between the other two members in attempting to form the initial partnership. Hence, in the long run, each of the three possible coalitions in this group will be formed equally often. The second point to note is that there is no logical termination to the bargaining process. Each player can break up any coalition formed in opposition to him by offering one player more points than he is getting from his present coalition. Hence an endless process of bargaining would develop and be maintained.

This result, however, is contrary to everyday experience. It is to be expected that coalitions will form between particular pairs of players more frequently than between others and that these will be of a relatively stable and permanent nature. The difference between the "rational" prediction illustrated above and common psychological expectation centers about the nature and variety of the motivations operating in the bargaining situation.

When the sole motivation present is the desire to obtain a maximum number of points and when the players have equal bargaining skill, all coalitions between members are equivalent and equally likely to occur. Predictable and stable coalitions can form, however, when there is a variety of motives operating and their strengths are unequally distributed among the players. Then even though two players make identical offers to a third in terms of the absolute number of points involved, these offers are not equivalent in value for that player in terms of the other satisfactions they can provide. This results in the possibility that a particular individual may find himself in an advantageous position relative to the others. HIs offers may carry both the potentiality of points and the potentiality of other satisfactions. To the extent that a second individual requires both of these types of satisfaction, there is a high probability that he will accept offers from the first player. Moreover, the player left out of such a coalition will be relatively impotent in his attempts to break it up as long as the desire for points is subordinate to the other motivations of the coalition members. From this point of view, it is obvious that coalitions may in fact become predictable and stable.

The hypotheses underlying the present experiment are first, that these additional motivations in a bargaining situation arise in part from each individual's concern about his comparability to other members of the group on the ability that is shown in the bargaining. This results in pressures to achieve uniformity in the group. In our culture, at least, there are also motivations to strive to be better than others which operate simultaneously with the pressures toward uniformity. The contrast between these types of motivation and the motivation to obtain a maximum share of the points is seen most clearly in situations where the points involved are ratings, prestige objects or other symbolic representations of relative.status. The individual's concern about them arises not because of their absolute or intrinsic value, but because in this activity they are indicative of his status relative to others. In a competitive society, such concern about the status significance indicated by the symbols tends to operate even where money or other commodities of direct utilitarian value are involved.

The influence of the concern about relative status on the formation of coalitions can be shown by referring to the previously described game. Assume that one of the individuals obtains an early initial advantage of a number of points while the others at this stage have few or none. These points function as symbols indicating to the others that this person is superior to the other two in that activity. The result is an increase in the motivation of the other two individuals of the group to draw close to him. Consequently they will be strongly motivated to form a coalition against him insofar as this aids in overcoming his lead. Furthermore, they will resist any attempt on his part to disrupt this coalition even though by accepting his offers either one of them might gain more points than he is able to obtain by remaining in the coalition. This happens because a conflict has developed between their desire to acquire the maximum number of points possible, and their desire to reduce the discrepancy between themselves and others. The refusal of offers from a person with a large initial advantage in points indicates that the conflict has been resolved in favor of the desire to reduce the discrepancy.

This analysis is based on the hypothesis that a major motivation of each individual is to compare himself with and to draw close to or surpass the others in the group. The reference individuals with whom each compares himself, however, are not selected indiscriminately. The amateur golfer does not compare himself with the professional, nor is the occasional bridge player concerned with his status relative to the expert. The conditions determining which individuals are selected as a reference group are not clearly defined as yet, but in general an individual is concerned about his status relative to others whom he considers of approximately equal ability. He tends to exclude from his comparisons individuals who appear definitely superior or inferior to him in this activity. This is identical to the process of "rejection" when pressures toward uniformity arise concerning opinions. There the individual does not evaluate his opinions by comparison with others who are too divergent. Similarly, individuals do not evaluate their abilities by comparison with those who are too divergent.

Conditions in which all members of a group regard themselves as comparable are known as "peer" conditions. Conditions in which one or more individuals are regarded by the others as non-comparable, i.e., as definitely superior or inferior, are known as "non-peer" conditions. In terms of the previous analysis, it is expected that in peer conditions predictable and stable coalitions will form in opposition to the individual who has an initial advantage. In non-peer conditions, however, this tendency will be reduced because the other members of the group are motivated to surpass each other and are less concerned with the status of the non-comparable individual. Even though the tendency to compete with the non-comparable individual is reduced, it does not disappear because the condition of non-comparability is relative and continuous, rather than all or none.

There is a second important determinant of decisions involving the formation of coalitions. It is obvious that the desire to achieve and maintain relative status will vary depending upon whether or not the individual regards his status on that task as important. The golfer or bridge player will be concerned about status differentials which develop in the play of these games but not on a wide variety of other. Similarly, performance on an activity which requires the use of intellectual abilities will result in a motivation to achieve status in direct proportion to the degree to which this type of activity is considered important by the individuals involved. Increasing the importance of a task in effect increases the individual's concern about any status differences that may develop with the result that he becomes even more motivated to equal or surpass the others. Consequently, he becomes even less willing to cooperate with anyone having an initial advantage. Thus under conditions of high task importance the coalitions become highly stable. In contrast, conditions of low task importance may result in a situation in which incidental motivations are as strong as the concern about relative status. In this case the stability of the coalitions is reduced.

In summary, it is postulated that an important motivation in a bargaining situation is the individual's concern about his status in the activity relative to other members of the group and his desire to equal or surpass them. The accumulation of points is significant for him because these represent the degree of comparability among the participating individuals. Consequently, predictable and stable coalitions in opposition to an individual having an initial advantage will occur more frequently when that individual is a peer member of the group than when he is a non-peer member. Similarly, increases in the value placed on the points as a result of making the task important to the individual increases his concern over comparability and indirectly his tendency to form stable coalitions in opposition to an individual who obtains an initial advantage. These predictions are tested by the following experiment.

Subjects and Procedure

Twenty-eight groups of subjects participated in the original experiment which was performed at Stanford University. The entire experiment was then replicated with twenty-eight groups at the City College of San Francisco. Subjects were undergraduates, drawn from the introductory psychology courses. The two groups were alike with respect to age, but the Stanford subjects were of a higher socio-economic level and probably of higher average intelligence because of the differences in entrance requirements at the two schools. Stanford subjects also appeared to be somewhat more mature and less naive than the San Francisco students, most of whom had had no previous experience as subjects in psychological experiments. Only male students were used.

The twenty-eight groups in each replication were randomly but equally distributed between the four experimental conditions: (1) high task importance and peer relations; (2) high task importance and non-peer relations; (3) low task importance and peer relations; (4) low task importance and non-peer relations. Of the three individuals in each group, two were subjects and the third was a paid-participant trained beforehand in the role he was to play. Two paid-participants were selected from Stanford for use in the Stanford experiment, and three from San Francisco City College for participation with those groups. These were male seniors who were unknown to the subjects. When the two subjects and the paid-participant arrived for the experiment, a check was made to see that the two subjects had no more than a passing acquaintance with each other and that neither knew the paid-participant. In cases where this was not true, the group was discarded. The three group members were seated around a table with the positions clearly labelled as A, B, and C. The paid-participant invariably was seated at A.

Each group was informed that the purpose of the experiment was to collect standardization and validation data on a new type intelligence test consisting of three parts. Subjects were told that the first part of the test was similar to the usual type of paper and pencil intelligence test, the second measured the ability to interact with others, and the third was designed to measure insight into one's own behavior and the behavior of others. In actuality the first was a paper and pencil intelligence test included to lend credibility to the situation, the second was the bargaining situation or test proper, and the third was a questionnaire to provide independent evidence that the experimental manipulations had changed the individuals' attitudes and perceptions. The low versus high task importance and the peer versus non-peer conditions were established in the following ways:

Task Importance

The importance of the task to the subjects was manipulated in two ways: (1) by the instructions given them concerning the validity of the test purported to be measuring intelligence, and (2) by the content of the paper and pencil test. In the high importance groups, the instructions given them just prior to beginning the experiment were as follows:

> We have asked you to come here today to take a new intelligence test which has recently been devised and which has shown itself to be highly superior to the usual kind of intelligence test. We have scheduled three of you together because, although some parts of the test are taken individually, other parts of the test require interaction among three persons. The test is separated into a number of parts and we will explain each part to you when we come to it.
>
> Let me explain to you why we are asking you to take this test. Recent research in psychology has produced new knowledge about intelligence and intelligent behavior in people which has enabled psychologists to construct this new test. It has been tried out with many different kinds of people and in every case has been shown to be greatly superior and more valid in measuring the intelligence of individuals than the older type test. Needless to say, when such an important development occurs it is extremely valuable to accumulate as much data using the test as possible. As the test has not yet been used with people on the West Coast, we are especially interested in the data we will collect here.
>
> After we measure your I.Q. with this test we will compare it with other records we can get on you and with scores you have made on

the older kinds of tests. There will be some of you for whom we do not have sufficient records. If that turns out to be the case we may have to ask you to take some other tests sometime within the next month. The results so far with this new test indicate that now, for perhaps the first time, we can really measure how intelligent a person is with an extremely high degree of accuracy. We shall of course be glad to inform each of you about your I.Q. after we have scored the test.

This emphasis on the validity of the test was underscored by the content of the items given the high importance groups during the pencil and paper part of the experiment. The printed booklet given these groups contained 24 synonym-antonym items and 20 verbal analogy items drawn from the Terman Concept Mastery test, a section from the paragraph comprehension section of the Ohio State Psychological Examination, and 10 items from the Minnesota Paper Form Board. A ten minute time limit was imposed on this test.

The instructions for the low importance groups were designed to belittle the validity of the test. After the same introductory paragraph as used for the high importance group, the instructions were as follows:

Let me explain some things to you about why we are asking you to take this test. The psychologist who published the test claimed that it was useful in measuring intelligence. Other people, trying the test out, have disputed this claim and have shown by their results that it has nothing to do with intelligence. In fact their results seem to show that it has nothing to do with anything. We have decided in the department here to do some very careful research to settle once and for all whether or not the test is any good. We have already given the test to large numbers of people, and, comparing their scores on this test with scores on other tests, with grades, and with many other measures, we are quite convinced that the present test which you will take is pretty meaningless. Nevertheless we want more data so that when we publish our results there will be absolutely no question about it.

This lack of validity was underscored by the content of the printed booklet given the low importance groups during the pencil and paper part of the test. The improvised items were of the following types: (1) general information of an extremely low difficulty level, (2) items requiring value judgments on moralistic questions, (3) items requiring judgments of occupation from facial expression, (4) items requiring judgments of emotion from facial expression, and (5) jokes to be rated in terms of their humor.

Peer versus Non-peer

The peer condition, in which each subject was to regard the other subject and the paid-participant as comparable to himself in intellectual ability, was established in part by instructions and in part by the behavior of the paid-participant. These instructions were given just after the completion of the pencil and paper test and just prior to the bargaining situation. For the peer conditions they were as follows:

> Before we start the next part of the test, I would like you to know some of the reasons for scheduling you particular three persons together in the same group. This next part of the test requires that in each of our groups the three persons should be approximately equal in intelligence and mental ability insofar as this can be roughly determined in advance. We consequently have taken the liberty of looking up your grades, your various achievement and aptitude test results, and as much else as we could get about you. We are reasonably certain that you three are very close together in intelligence as measured by those tests.
>
> In this next part of the test you will see why it is necessary to have the three of you matched so closely in intelligence. The next part requires that each of you deals with the other members in the group and consequently it is necessary that all three of you be as equal in intelligence as we could manage.

The paid-participant emphasized his equality with the others by pacing himself during the pencil and paper test at the same rate as the two subjects in the group.

In the non-peer groups, where the two subjects were to regard the paid-participant as definitely superior to themselves in intellectual ability and therefore as non-comparable, the instructions were as follows:

> Before we actually start taking the second part of the test, I would like you to know some of the reasons for scheduling you particular three persons together in the same group. We wanted to be sure that in each of our groups that take this test, there was at least one person of very superior intelligence. Now one of you here has taken an intensive battery of tests earlier in the quarter, and we asked specifically

that he sign up for this hour. The person in this group who took this intensive battery of tests earlier is the one of extremely superior intelligence.

In this part of the test, part "B," you will see the reason we were so careful to be sure that there was at least one person in the group of extremely high intelligence. The next part of the test involves dealing with others in the group and in the way the test is standardized, it is necessary that such discrepancies in intelligence among you exist.

As neither of the two subjects in the group had taken an intensive battery of tests, it was assumed that each would conclude that either the other subject or the paid-participant must be the one of extremely superior intelligence. This speculation was then directed at the paid-participant as the result of his subsequent behavior. During the paper and pencil test, he worked through the booklet easily and quickly, turning it in well before the expiration of the time limit.

Following these instructions, the next part of the test was the bargaining situation. Each of the three members of a group was given a set of triangular pieces cut out of masonite, the sets differing from each other only in colour. By assembling these pieces correctly it was possible for each member of the group to form an individual square requiring six of the seven pieces provided him. The seventh piece was a large right-angled isosceles triangle. Any combination of two players could form a "group" square by combining their large triangles. This group square had a larger area than did the individual square.

The bargaining was governed by a set of rules read to the subjects in advance of the trials. These rules emphasized that the objective of the players was to earn points, since these points were to be added to the scores on the paper and pencil test to determine the I.Q. There were to be a series of five trials, each of four minute duration, and on each of which it was possible to earn as many as eight points. These could be earned in one of two ways. If a person assembled his individual square and no other squares were formed on that trial, the square was worth eight points. If two persons combined pieces to form a group square, this square was also worth eight points, provided that the two partners agreed on how they would divide these eight points between themselves. It was permissible for either of the two persons in an agreement of this sort to break it at any time during the trial and to enter into a new agreement with the third person in the group. In the event that more than one square was formed in a given trial, only the largest square would win. In case two squares of the same size were formed, no one would get any points. There was one exception to these rules. If any person succeeded in forming the individual square on the first trial, he automatically won that trial and in addition received a bonus of twelve points which he could divide among the three players in any way he wished.

These rules achieved the following results. On the first trial while the situation was still somewhat unstructured for the subjects, each of them attempted to form an individual square because of the bonus of twelve points offered. The problem was so difficult, however, that only the paid-participant was able to do it. He always decided to keep the points for himself, thereby obtaining an initial lead of 20 points over the other two members. Because of his manipulation of the pieces, it was always clear to the other two subjects by the end of the first trial how they should go about constructing their individual squares. But since the assembly of an individual square by either of the remaining group members would result in a tie, with no points awarded, this solution became functionally useless for the remaining four trials. The only possibility remaining was for two players to form a group square from the large isosceles triangles. The paid-participant emphasized this point at the beginning of the second trial by first forming such a square with individual B and then with C as though he were just exploring the possibilities in the situation. As this group square was obviously larger than the individual square, it would always win the points when formed.

The bargaining behavior of the paid-participant during the second through the fifth trial was predetermined. At the beginning of the trial he offered to make the group square with B and to give him four of the eight points. From this point on his behavior was governed by the following rules:

1. If B said "yes," A rested until something else happened. If B said "no," A waited for a moment until some agreement between B and C had been reached.

2. If B and C did not reach an agreement, A offered B five points. If the offer was refused, he offered six. If this was refused, he offered seven. After any acceptance, he rested until something else occurred. If the offer of seven was refused, he began directing offers to C in the same sequence.

3. If the person left out made A an offer, A accepted if it gave him more points. He did not take the initiative as long as he was in a coalition.

4. If the BC coalition formed on an even split, A proceeded as in 2.
5. If the BC coalition formed on an uneven split, A made an offer of
   four to that player who was getting the least. If the answer was
   "yes," he rested. If "no," he proceeded as in 2, continuing to direct his offers to the same person until an offer was accepted or
   until an offer of seven points was refused. In this latter case he
   began directing his offers to the other coalition member.

The purpose of these rules was in part to make the bargaining behavior of the paid-participant appear natural, but at the same time to ensure
that when forced he would always offer up to seven points. In this way
the strength of the coalitions against him could be measured. As each
offer was made, it was recorded sequentially by the experimenter in
such a manner as to indicate the size of the offer, by whom it was made,
toward whom it was directed, and whether it was accepted, ignored, or
rejected. In the Stanford experiment, the subjects were given a warning
30 seconds before the end of each trial. This was eliminated in the San
Francisco replication since its effect was to materially reduce the amount
of bidding within the period prior to the warning.

Results

The results of this experiment are described under three headings. First
the data from the questionnaire are analyzed to determine the extent to
which differences in task importance and in peer relations were actually
established between the various groups. Following this, the results
bearing on the choice behavior during the last four trials of bargaining
are presented under two headings. The first of these covers terminal
coalitions, i.e., the agreements which existed at the end of a trial and
thereby determined the distribution of points. The second presents the
results pertaining to temporary coalitions, i.e., those tentative agreements existing prior to the formation of the terminal coalition.

The Success of the Experimental Manipulations

One item of the questionnaire given as the final part of the test had each
subject rate his own I.Q. and that of the paid-participant on the assumption that discrepancies in these ratings would be indicative of the extent
to which a given subject regarded A, the paid-participant, as comparable
to himself. The mean discrepancies in I.Q. ratings (rating of paid-participant minus self-rating) are evaluated in the analysis of Table 8.1. The

Table 8.1   Analysis of Discrepancies Between Subject's Rating
of Paid-Participant and Rating of Self on I.Q.

Source	d.f.	Variance Est.	P
Importance	1	11.16	
Peer vs. non-peer	1	5,304.02	<.001
Schools	1	75.45	
Interactions	4	211.66	
Error	48	92.70	

subject's rating of A in the peer conditions averages 3.27 I.Q. points more than the subject's rating of himself, but in the non-peer condition it averages 13.00 points more. This difference is significant (P<.001). Discrepancies are not significantly different for comparisons involving task importance, schools, or interactions. The assertion can therefore be made with a high degree of certainty that perceived differences in comparability were in fact established between the peer and the non-peer conditions, such differences being based upon assessment of intellectual status.

A second item in the questionnaire had the subject evaluate the bargaining situation as to the degree of validity they believed it to have as a measure of intellegence. It is possible to infer from these ratings the degree to which subjects considered their performance in the bargaining situation as important, and thus the extent to which they were thereby motivated. The obtained ratings on this item are evaluated in the analysis of Table 8.2. Subjects assigned to conditions of high task importance tend to rate the bargaining procedure as a more valid measure of intelligence than do subjects assigned to conditions of low importance

Table 8.2   Rated Validity of Bargaining Situation
as a Measure of Intelligence

Source	d.f	Variance Est.	P
Importance	1	46.29	<.001
Peer vs. non-peer	1	0.57	
Schools	1	7.00	<.01
Interactions	4	0.14	
Error	104	0.76	

(P<.001). In addition the difference attributable to the replication of the experiment is significant (P<.01), with the San Francisco subjects rating the bargaining situation as more valid than do subjects of the Stanford experiment. Since the San Francisco subjects represented a somewhat less select group in terms of college aptitude, it is reasonable to expect that they would be more concerned over their intellectual status and would consequently ascribe a higher importance to the task.

The Formation of Coalitions

Assuming that the groups were differentiated with respect to the importance of the task and the degree of comparability between members of the group, the major question is the influence of these variables on the formation of coalitions. A relatively direct measure of the extent to which coalitions were formed in opposition to the paid-participant is the discrepancy between the number of points he was able to obtain on each trial and the number he would be expected to obtain if the coalitions were formed on the basis of chance. On a chance basis the paid-participant, hereafter referred to as A, would be expected to receive on the average a third of the eight points available for division, or 2.67 points per trial, as would each of the two subjects, B and C. In the event that A receives significantly less than the average of the other members of the group, he is being discriminated against by them as far as their willingness to form coalitions with him is concerned.

The average number of points per trial earned by A in the last four trials under the various conditions of the experiment is shown in Table 8.3, along with the statistical analysis of the sums on which the averages are based.

It is apparent from Table 8.3 that A is generally unable to obtain a chance number of points under the various conditions. The one exception is the condition of low importance and non-peer relations at Stanford, in which A receives significantly more points than would be expected. Under each of the two replications of the experiment the pattern of results is essentially the same. A obtains more points under low importance than when task importance is high (P<.02), and more under the non-peer conditions than under peer conditions (P<.01). These differences are in the direction predicted by the theoretical assumptions underlying the experiment. It should be noted that in each experimental condition A receives fewer points in the San Francisco replication than at Stanford (P<.01). This consistent discrepancy becomes more meaningful when it is recalled that the questionnaire data gave evidence of higher importance being ascribed to the task in the

Table 8.3a   Average Points per Trial Earned by A

Impor.	School	Peer	Non-Peer	Avg.
High	S.F.	1.29	1.75	1.52
	Stan.	1.57	2.39	1.98
	(Avg.)	(1.43)	(2.07)	(1.75)
Low	S.F.	1.32	2.54	1.93
	Stan.	2.50	4.36	3.43
	(Avg.)	(1.91)	(3.45)	(2.68)
(S.F. avg.)		1.30	2.15	1.72
(Stan avg.)		2.04	3.37	2.71
(Avg.)		(1.67)	(2.76)	(2.21)

San Francisco groups than at Stanford. The experiment might therefore be interpreted as including three different levels of task importance instead of two. This interpretation would reconcile the differences between the two replications.

The failure of A to secure the number of points expected by chance is due to two factors: (1) he was unable to form a fair share (two-thirds) of terminal coalitions even though he was willing to offer as many as seven points, and (2) even in those coalitions of which he was a member he was unable to obtain a fair division (4 out of 8) of the points. The influence of the first factor is demonstrated in Table 8.4 where the average number of terminal coalitions including A during the four trials is tabulated. The pattern of results is the same as that involving point totals for A. For all conditions combined, A is able to form fewer terminal coalitions than would be expected on the basis of chance ($P < .01$), and therefore fewer than the average of the two subjects. Differences for

Table 8.3b   Analysis of Average Points per Trial for A

Source	d.f.	Variance	P
Importance	1	200.65	<.02
Peer vs. non-peer	1	274.57	<.01
Schools	1	208.28	<.01
Interactions	4	39.25	
Error	48	24.89	

Table 8.4a　Average Per Cent of Terminal Coalitions Having A as a Member

Impor.	School	Peer	Non-Peer	Avg.
High	S.F.	36	46	41
	Stan.	57	64	60
	(Avg.)	(46)	(55)	(50)
Low	S.F.	43	64	54
	Stan.	61	86	74
	(Avg.)	(52)	(75)	(64)
(S.F. avg.)		40	55	48
(Stan. avg.)		59	75	67
(Avg.)		(50)	(65)	(58)

each of the experimental conditions are significant at the five per cent level and are in the expected direction.

The influence of the second factor is shown in Table 8.5 where the average number of points per coalition obtained by A when A is in a coalition is tabulated. This analysis shows whether or not A is able to obtain a fair share of the points when he is one of the partners in a coalition. It is apparent from the table that the differences between means are once more in the anticipated directions. The differences between the peer and non-peer conditions and between the high and low importance conditions are only significant at the ten per cent level of confidence.[1]

Table 8.4b　Analysis of Average Number of Coalitions
　　　　　Having A as a Member

Source	d.f.	Variance	P
Importance	1	4.57	$<.05$
Peer cond.	1	5.78	$<.05$
Schools	1	5.78	$<.05$
Interactions	4	0.18	
Error	48	1.01	

1. An analysis of co-variance on average points per trial earned by A adjusted for differences in number of coalitions of which A was a member yields the same conclusions.

Table 8.5   Average Points per Coalition Earned by A

Motiv.	School	Peer	Non-Peer	Avg.
High	S.F.	3.60*	3.58†	3.59
	Stan.	3.19	3.77	3.48
	Avg.	(3.36)	(3.68)	(3.53)
Low	S.F.	3.12*	4.00	3.63
	Stan.	4.15†	5.16	4.69
	Avg.	(3.68)	(4.57)	(4.18)
S.F.	Avg.	3.36	3.81	3.61
Stan.	Avg.	3.63	4.46	4.06
		(3.51)	(4.15)	(3.86)

*Mean based on 5 groups.
†Mean based on 6 groups.
Those groups in which A never succeeded in entering a coalition had to be omitted from the analysis.

The results of these three analyses are consistent in indicating that coalitions tend to form in opposition to the player who obtains an initial advantage. The strength of this tendency is greatest when the task is of high importance to the members of the group and when they perceive each other as peers or equals. As a result of this tendency, the paid participant is unable to form his fair share of terminal coalitions and must pay more than a fair share of the points in order to form such coalitions.

One additional analysis of the terminal coalition data was made to check on the validity of a deduction which was made from the theoretical formulation of this experiment. We would expect that in the peer situation B and C would be competing primarily with A and not with each other. We should then find coalitions between B and C took the form of an even division of the points. Conversely, under non-peer conditions, B and C would be competing primarily with each other, since A would be regarded as non-comparable by both of them. As a result, terminal coalitions involving B and C would tend to take the form of an uneven division of the points. An analysis of the types of terminal coalitions involving B and C supports this deduction. Under peer conditions 63 per cent of such coalitions involved an equal split, but under non-peer conditions only 34 per cent of them did so, a difference significant beyond the .05 level. Thus, comparability of A to the other members in

Table 8.6a   Average Discrepancy Paid to Break B-C Coalition

Impor.	School	Peer	Non-Peer	Total
High	S.F.	2.2	2.0	2.1
	Stan.	3.4	2.2	2.8
	(Avg.)	(2.8)	(2.1)	(2.5)
Low	S.F.	2.4	1.8	2.1
	Stan.	1.6	1.2	1.4
	(Avg.)	(2.0)	(1.5)	(1.8)
(S.F. avg.)		2.3	1.9	2.1
(Stan. avg.)		2.5	1.7	2.1
(Avg.)		(2.4)	(1.8)	(2.1)

the group, induced by the peer conditions, makes a coalition involving an even split a desirable and stable outcome for the two subjects. Conversely, when A is incomparable, the competition between B and C makes the desirable outcome, for either one, an agreement which gives him more than the opposing subject.

Another indication of the opposition to A is shown by an analysis of the temporary coalitions, that is, those coalitions tentatively agreed to during the bargaining process. One measure of these is the number of excess points A must pay in order to break up an existing coalition between B and C. A discrepancy score was computed for all temporary coalitions in which A was not a member. This score is the difference between what the coalition subject was receiving in the coalition and what he accepted from A in breaking up the coalition. If the subject refused all offers from A then the discrepancy was calculated as if the

Table 8.6b   Analysis of Discrepancy Paid to Break B-C Coalition

Source	d.f	Variance	Est.P
Impor.	1	841.1	$<.05$
Peer cond.	1	841.1	$<.05$
Schools	1	1.4	
Impor. schools	1	970.9	$<.05$
Inter.	3	14.1	
Error	48	164.1	

subject had accepted an offer of 9 points, one more than the total number available. The average of these for each experimental condition is shown in Table 8.6. The results follow the expected pattern. A must offer more points when the task is of high importance than when it is of low importance, and must offer more under peer conditions than under non-peer. The significant interaction between Importance and Schools is due to the fact that in the San Francisco data there are no differences between the High and Low Importance conditions while in the Stanford data these differences are large.

Discussion

The theory which forms the basis for this experiment hypothesizes that competition arises because individuals, in situations where they are evaluating some ability, are strongly motivated by a concern about their comparability to other members of the group with respect to the ability which they are evaluating. This concern over comparability leads to attempts to assess the abilities of others in relation to themselves. But an individual is not concerned over the comparability of all individuals. Rather, he tends to exclude those who are perceived as definitely superior or inferior to himself in this activity and to concentrate on those who are perceived as being within the same general range of ability.

To the extent that concern over comparability is present, discrepancies in points or other symbols come to have relative rather than absolute value. They tend to be interpreted primarily as indicators of the individual's status with respect to the other members rather than as something of direct utilitarian value. This is especially true when the points grained represent intellectual, athletic, or social ability, but it is also probably true to a large extent when they represent money or commodities. As a result, whenever the task is made more important to an individual, the value of these points increases. This, in turn, adds to his concern over comparability to others and also to his motivation to surpass them on the task.

It follows from these assumptions that in a bargaining situation where all group members regard one another as comparable, stable coalitions will form in opposition to any member of the group who gains an advantage. The point advantage held by this member of the group is interpreted by the other group members as a loss in status to them, and they are consequently motivated to overcome it. Coalitions between them satisfy the motivations of both to retain comparability with each other while at the same time reducing the discrepancy between them and the individual with the initial advantage. The individual with the advantage in points cannot offer this type of satisfaction. He will be compelled to offer excessive points commensurate with the status differential which exists in order to form a coalition. On the other hand, if this advantage is held by an individual regarded by the other two as non-comparable, coalitions in opposition to him will have less tendency to form, for his point advantage represents a smaller loss of status. Non-peer conditions would therefore be expected to be more favorable for a person with an initial advantage than would peer conditions.

It similarly would be predicted that the formation of stable coalitions will be even more prominent as the importance of the task is increased. This follows from the assumption that any increase in the importance of the symbols involved strengthens the motivation to achieve comparability in the group. Thus, conditions of high task importance will be less favorable to the person with an initial advantage than will conditions of low importance.

The results of the experiment strongly support this general formulation of the motivations involved in bargaining behavior. This is shown clearly in the evidence that a group member receiving an initial advantage in points is generally discriminated against throughout the remaining trials. It is reflected in the inability of the paid-participant to enter into the expected number of terminal coalitions, in the relatively high price he is required to pay in order to enter such coalitions, and in discriminatory bargaining in opposition to him as shown in the within-trials analyses.

The evidence indicates that the strength of this opposition is a direct function of task importance and of the degree of comparability between the group members. Such an interpretation is strengthened by evidence from the questionnaire that the conditions of the experiment were successfully manipulated.

Differences between the two conditions of importance in the experiment are reliable and consistent in the analyses involving terminal coalitions, and in the intra-trial analysis of the excess of points required to break up a coalition between the two subjects. In each of these cases the bargaining was shown to be more favorable to the paid-participant under conditions of low importance than when importance was high.

The effects of the peer and non-peer conditions are similarly in substantial accord with the predictions. Under peer conditions the paid-participant is less able to obtain points, less successful in entering into terminal coalitions, and he is required to pay a higher price in order to do so than under non-peer conditions. This influence of peer relations is shown also by the excess of points which A is forced to pay in order to break up an existing coalition.

It appears then that a large initial advantage in points results in an intensification of competition against the paid-participant when that individual is regarded as comparable in ability. If the individual involved is regarded as non-comparable, the competition persists among the remaining group members, but the discrepant individual gains additional advantage by becoming the medium by which changes in status can be accomplished between the others. Support for this latter statement comes from two sources: (1) examination of the relative frequencies of occurrence of even and uneven point distributions in terminal coalitions involving B and C show that these tend to be formed with equal division of the points under peer conditions, but that under non-peer conditions such coalitions involve mainly inequitable distributions, and (2) an examination of the low importance, non-peer condition indicates that the paid-participant was able to obtain a significantly larger number of points than the average of the two subjects (Table 8.3).

Insofar as the findings in this experiment have generality, they have implications for two fields of inquiry, that of game theory and that of motivational theory, especially as each applies to social situations. Game theory specifies that the choices between alternative strategies or courses of action should be chosen in such a way as to maximize utility.

The present study suggests that the nature of the utility function for individuals is not necessarily invariant, but is subject to modification from the effects of situational variables which may differ greatly from one context to the next. Consequently, these results indicate that motivational factors such as those suggested in the present experiment need to be included in formulations relating utility to external or behavioral reference points.

The findings are more directly relevant to theories of social motivation and perception, especially as these pertain to behavior in groups. The suggestion is that an important determinant of behavior in group situations where all members are engaged in a common activity is the concern of each member about his status relative to others on that activity. This is especially true in activities where there is no clear cut criterion available for individuals evaluating the adequacy of their performance. Consequently when a discrepancy between their own standing and that of others is perceived, individuals are motivated to reduce that discrepancy. This motivation will manifest itself in a variety of ways, one of which is to form coalitions in opposition to any other member having a higher status on this task.

Assuming that this formulation has generality, it gives rise to two important theoretical problems. The results of this experiment have shown that the strength of the motivational factors involved depends in part upon the importance of the task to the individuals involved and in part on the degree of comparability between the group members. Consequently, it becomes necessary to formulate the conditions that determine whether or not a given task will be accepted as important by a given individual, and the factors controlling his acceptance or rejection of other individuals as a standard against which to evaluate his own performance. These factors undoubtedly include cultural and social variables as well as those unique to the past history of the given individual.

Summary

The present experiment on competitive bargaining behavior in a group situation utilized 56 groups, each composed of two subjects and a paid-participant. The experimental variables were: (1) the importance of the task for the individuals involved, and (2) the degree of comparability between group members (peer versus non-peer conditions). Subjects were assigned to one of four experimental conditions as follows: (1) high task importance, peer relations; (2) high task importance, non-peer relations; (3) low task importance, peer relations; and (4) low task importance, non-peer relations.

The experiment was designed so that the three group members were competing among themselves for points, but the formation of a coalition between two of them was necessary in order for points to be earned. The procedures used ensured that the paid-participant always obtained a large initial advantage. The rules governing the formation of coalitions specified that any agreements could be broken by either member of the coalition if he desired to enter a coalition with the third member. This made possible a continuous sequence of bargaining between the three members until the conclusion of the trial.

The results of the experiment were as follows:

1. The group member receiving a large initial advantage in points received significantly fewer opportunities to form coalitions than did the other group members, and was required to pay a relatively higher price in order to do so.
2. The reduction in opportunity to form coalitions and the commensurate increase in price demanded of the person receiving a large initial advantage in points were more pronounced under

conditions of high task importance than under conditions of low importance.

3. The reduction in opportunity to form coalitions and the corresponding increase in price demanded of the person receiving a large initial advantage in points were more evident under peer conditions than under non-peer conditions.

4. The results summarized in the three preceding paragraphs were reflected not only in the formation of terminal coalitions and the distribution of points therein, but also in the pattern of bargaining which occurred within trials.

When this article was written, Paul Hoffman was an instructor in psychology at the State College of Washington, Pullman, Washington; Douglas Lawrence was an associate professor of psychology at Stanford University.

The study reported here was conducted under contract Nonr 225(01) between the Office of Naval Research and Stanford University, and in cooperation with the Laboratory for Research in Social Relations of the University of Michigan. The theoretical formulations on which the study was based were developed by Dr. Leon Festinger (2).

References

1. FESTINGER, L. Informal social communication. *Psychol. Rev.*, 1950, **57**, 271–282.

2. ———. A theory of social comparison processes. *Hum. Relat.*, 1957, **7**, 2.

3. VON NEUMANN, J., & MORGENSTERN, O. *Theory of games and economic behavior*. Princeton: Princeton Univer. Press, 1944 (2nd ed., 1947).

PART
C

COGNITIVE DISSONANCE— THEORY AND RESEARCH

9

A Theory
of Cognitive
Dissonance

FOREWORD

This Foreword contains primarily a bit of the history of how the ideas
which form the core of this book arose. This chronological form is the
best way to acknowledge properly the assistance received from others—
assistance which was considerable and crucial—and at the same time
to explain how this book relates to the purposes which originally motivated it.

In the late fall of 1951 the writer was asked by Bernard Berelson, the
Director of the Behavioral Sciences Division of the Ford Foundation,
whether he would be interested in undertaking a "propositional inventory" of the substantive area of "communication and social influence." A
large body of research literature exists in this area that has never been
integrated at a theoretical level. It ranges all the way from studies on
the effects of the mass media to studies on interpersonal communication.
If a set of conceptual propositions could be adduced that tied together
many of the known facts in the area, and from which additional derivations could be made, this would be of obvious value.

The notion of attempting such a theoretical integration is always in-
tellectually attractive and challenging, although it seemed clear to everyone concerned at the time that even if successfully accomplished, it
could not hope to cover the whole of the designated area. A plan that

SOURCE: Festinger, L. *A theory of cognitive dissonance*. New York: Row, Peterson, 1957.

seemed to promise some useful results was to start out with some narrowly defined problem within the general area of "communication and social influence" and attempt to formulate a specific set of hypotheses or propositions that would adequately account for the data. If this worked out, then another narrowly defined problem could be considered, and the theory extended and modified. Admittedly, one would be confronted again and again with bodies of data with which no progress could be made theoretically. It was to be hoped that one would quickly recognize the dead end and move on to other data.

Funds provided by the Behavioral Sciences Division of the Ford Foundation made possible the collaboration of May Brodbeck, Don Martindale, Jack Brehm, and Alvin Boderman. Together we began the job by selecting the spreading of rumors as our first narrowly defined problem to work on.

The chores of collecting an exhaustive bibliography of research literature on rumor spreading, of reading the material, and of sifting fact from supposition and conjecture were comparatively easy. More difficult were the problems of integrating the material and of getting some theoretical hunches that would begin to handle the data in a satisfactory way. It was easy enough to restate empirical findings in a slightly more general form, but this kind of intellectual exercise does not lead to much progress.

The first hunch that generated any amount of enthusiasm among us came from trying to understand some data, reported by Prasad, concerning rumors subsequent to the Indian earthquake of 1934. This study is described in detail in Chapter Ten.* The fact reported by Prasad which puzzled us was that following the earthquake, the vast majority of the rumors that were widely circulated predicted even worse disasters to come in the very near future. Certainly the belief that horrible disasters were about to occur is not a very pleasant belief, and we may ask why rumors that were "anxiety provoking" arose and were so widely accepted. Finally a possible answer to this question occurred to us—an answer that held promise of having rather general application: perhaps these rumors predicting even worse disasters to come were not "anxiety provoking" at all but were rather "anxiety justifying." That is, as a result of the earthquake these people were already frightened, and the rumors served the function of giving them something to be frightened about. Perhaps these rumors provided people with information that fit with the way they already felt.

*See SOURCE.

From this start, and with the help of many discussions in which we attempted to pin the idea down and to formalize it somewhat, we arrived at the concept of dissonance and the hypotheses concerning dissonance reduction. Once the formulation in terms of dissonance and the reduction of dissonance was made, numerous implications became obvious. Following these implications through soon became the major activity of the project. For a while we continued to pursue the original notion of the "propositional inventory" and to explore the implications of the notion of dissonance; but the extraordinary difficulty of the former, together with our excitement concerning the latter, served more and more to focus our efforts.

The development of the theory did not, of course, proceed in the order in which it is presented in this book. Here the material is arranged so that the first chapters deal with relatively simple situations and later chapters become more and more concerned with complicated problems.* Actually, the first implications of the theory of dissonance that we explored were those involving problems of voluntary and involuntary exposure to information. These occurred to us first, of course, because they were related to the area of communication with which we were basically concerned. These implications also were suggested by the rumor study itself. If people sought information that would fit with how they were already reacting, certainly this process would not be confined to rumors but would also extend generally to information-seeking processes. The implications from the theory that suggested themselves, however, soon extended beyond the bounds of "communication and social influence." Nevertheless, we felt it was more fruitful to follow the leads of what now seemed to be a promising theory than to adhere rigidly to a prior plan and a designated content area.

Fortunately for the development of the theory of dissonance, we were not restricted to finding relevant data in the existing research literature, but were able to conduct our own studies specifically designed to test derivations from the theory. With funds and assistance provided by the Laboratory for Research in Social Relations of the University of Minnesota, and with some funds available from a personal grant-in-aid from the Ford Foundation, we were able to collect our own data. All the people who assisted in these studies will not be named here, since they are acknowledged in the pages of the book itself where these studies are described.

*See SOURCE.

According to some points of view, the writer should have waited another four or five years before writing this book. By that time many more studies of relevance to the theory would have been made and many unclarities would have been eliminated. But piecemeal journal publication seemed a poor way to present the theory and the variety of data relevant to it. One of the important aspects of the theory of dissonance is its ability to integrate data from seemingly different areas, and this aspect would be largely lost if it were not published in one unitary volume. Also, the writer feels that there are sufficient data now relevant to the theory to warrant communicating it to others, and sufficient corroboration of the theory to hope that others will also pursue it.

One final word of thanks is due those who in various ways helped in writing and rewriting the chapters of this book, notably, Judson Mills, Robert R. Sears, Ernest R. Hilgard, Herbert McClosky, Daniel Miller, James Coleman, Martin Lipset, Raymond Bauer, Jack Brehm, and May Brodbeck. Assistance from many of these people was possible because they and I were resident fellows at the Center for Advanced Study in the Behavioral Sciences while most of the writing on this book was done.

AN INTRODUCTION
TO THE THEORY OF DISSONANCE

It has frequently been implied, and sometimes even pointed out, that the individual strives toward consistency within himself. His opinions and attitudes, for example, tend to exist in clusters that are internally consistent. Certainly one may find exceptions. A person may think Negroes are just as good as whites but would not want any living in his neighborhood; or someone may think little children should be quiet and unobtrusive and yet may be quite proud when his child aggressively captures the attention of his adult guests. When such inconsistencies are found to exist, they may be quite dramatic, but they capture our interest primarily because they stand out in sharp contrast against a background of consistency. It is still overwhelmingly true that related opinions or attitudes are consistent with one another. Study after study reports such consistency among one person's political attitudes, social attitudes, and many others.

There is the same kind of consistency between what a person knows or believes and what he does. A person who believes a college education is a good thing will very likely encourage his children to go to college; a child who knows he will be severely punished for some misdemeanor will not commit it or at least will try not to be caught doing it. This is not surprising, of course; it is so much the rule that we take it for granted. Again what captures our attention are the exceptions to otherwise consistent behavior. A person may know that smoking is bad for him and yet continue to smoke; many persons commit crimes even though they know the high probability of being caught and the punishment that awaits them.

Granting that consistency is the usual thing, perhaps overwhelmingly so, what about these exceptions which come to mind so readily? Only rarely, if ever, are they accepted psychologically *as inconsistencies* by the person involved. Usually more or less successful attempts are made to rationalize them. Thus, the person who continues to smoke, knowing that it is bad for his health, may also feel (a) he enjoys smoking so much it is worth it; (b) the chances of his health suffering are not as serious as some would make out; (c) he can't always avoid every possible dangerous contingency and still live; and (d) perhaps even if he stopped smoking he would put on weight, which is equally bad for his health. So, continuing to smoke is, after all, consistent with his ideas about smoking.

But persons are not always successful in explaining away or in rationalizing inconsistencies to themselves. For one reason or another, attempts to achieve consistency may fail. The inconsistency then simply continues to exist. Under such circumstances—that is, in the presence of an inconsistency—there is psychological discomfort.

The basic hypotheses, the ramifications and implications of which will be explored in the remainder of this book,* can now be stated. First, I will replace the word "inconsistency" with a term which has less of a logical connotation, namely, *dissonance*. I will likewise replace the word "consistency" with a more neutral term, namely, *consonance*. A more formal definition of these terms will be given shortly; for the moment, let us try to get along with the implicit meaning they have acquired as a result of the preceding discussion.

The basic hypotheses I wish to state are as follows:

1. The existence of dissonance, being psychologically uncomfortable, will motivate the person to try to reduce the dissonance and achieve consonance.

2. When dissonance is present, in addition to trying to reduce it, the person will actively avoid situations and information which would likely increase the dissonance.

*See SOURCE.

Before proceeding to develop this theory of dissonance and the pressures to reduce it, it would be well to clarify the nature of dissonance, what kind of a concept it is, and where the theory concerning it will lead. The two hypotheses stated above provide a good starting point for this clarification. While they refer here specifically to dissonance, they are in fact very general hypotheses. In place of "dissonance" one can substitute other notions similar in nature, such as "hunger," "frustration," or "disequilibrium," and the hypotheses would still make perfectly good sense.

In short, I am proposing that dissonance, that is, the existence of nonfitting relations among cognitions, is a motivating factor in its own right. By the term *cognition*, here and in the remainder of the book,* I mean any knowledge, opinion, or belief about the environment, about oneself, or about one's behavior. Cognitive dissonance can be seen as an antecedent condition which leads to activity oriented toward dissonance reduction just as hunger leads to activity oriented toward hunger reduction. It is a very different motivation from what psychologists are used to dealing with but, as we shall see, nonetheless powerful.

And now a word about the remainder of the book.* It explores, in a wide variety of contexts, the consequences of the existence of cognitive dissonance and the attempts on the part of humans to reduce it. If someone cared to write a certain kind of book about the hunger drive in human beings, it would turn out to be similar in nature to the present volume. There might be chapters exploring the consequences of attempts to reduce hunger in a variety of contexts, ranging from a child in a highchair to an adult group at a formal banquet. In a similar way, this book* explores contexts ranging from individual decision situations to mass phenomena. Since reduction of dissonance is a basic process in humans, it is not surprising that its manifestations may be observed in such a wide variety of contexts.

The Occurrence and Persistence of Dissonance

Why and how does dissonance ever arise? How does it happen that persons sometimes find themselves doing things that do not fit with what they know, or having opinions that do not fit with other opinions they hold? An answer to this question may be found in discussing two of the more common situations in which dissonance may occur.

*See SOURCE.

1. New events may happen or new information may become known to a person, creating at least a momentary dissonance with existing knowledge, opinion, or cognition concerning behavior. Since a person does not have complete and perfect control over the information that reaches him and over events that can happen in his environment, such dissonances may easily arise. Thus, for example, a person may plan to go on a picnic with complete confidence that the weather will be warm and sunny. Nevertheless, just before he is due to start, it may begin to rain. The knowledge that it is now raining is dissonant with his confidence in a sunny day and with his planning to go to a picnic. Or, as another example, a person who is quite certain in his knowledge that automatic transmissions on automobiles are inefficient may accidentally come across an article praising automatic transmissions. Again, at least a momentary dissonance is created.

2. Even in the absence of new, unforeseen events or information, the existence of dissonance is undoubtedly an everyday condition. Very few things are all black or all white; very few situations are clear-cut enough so that opinions or behaviors are not to some extent a mixture of contradictions. Thus, a midwestern farmer who is a Republican may be opposed to his party's position on farm price supports; a person buying a new car may prefer the economy of one model but the design of another; a person deciding on how to invest his money may know that the outcome of his investment depends upon economic conditions beyond his control. Where an opinion must be formed or a decision taken, some dissonance is almost unavoidably created between the cognition of the action taken and those opinions or knowledges which tend to point to a different action.

There is, then, a fairly wide variety of situations in which dissonance is nearly unavoidable. But it remains for us to examine the circumstances under which dissonance, once arisen, persists. That is, under what conditions is dissonance not simply a momentary affair? If the hypotheses stated above are correct, then as soon as dissonance occurs there will be pressures to reduce it. To answer this question it is necessary first to have a brief look at the possible ways in which dissonance may be reduced.

Since there will be a more formal discussion of this point later on in this chapter, let us now examine how dissonance may be reduced, using as an illustration the example of the habitual cigarette smoker who has learned that smoking is bad for his health. He may have acquired this information from a newspaper or magazine, from friends, or even from some physician. This knowledge is certainly dissonant with cognition that he continues to smoke. If the hypothesis that there will be pressures to reduce this dissonance is correct, what would the person involved be expected to do?

1. He might simply change his cognition about his behavior by changing his actions; that is, he might stop smoking. If he no longer smokes, then his cognition of what he does will be consonant with the knowledge that smoking is bad for his health.

2. He might change his "knowledge" about the effects of smoking. This sounds like a peculiar way to put it, but it expresses well what must happen. He might simply end up believing that smoking does not have any deleterious effects, or he might acquire so much "knowledge" pointing to the good effects it has that the harmful aspects become negligible. If he can manage to change his knowledge in either of these ways, he will have reduced, or even eliminated, the dissonance between what he does and what he knows.

But in the above illustration it seems clear that the person may encounter difficulties in trying to change either his behavior or his knowledge. And this, of course, is precisely the reason that dissonance, once created, may persist. There is no guarantee that the person will be able to reduce or remove the dissonance. The hypothetical smoker may find that the process of giving up smoking is too painful for him to endure. He might try to find facts and opinions of others to support the view that smoking is not harmful, but these attempts might fail. He might then remain in the situation where he continues to smoke and continues to know that smoking is harmful. If this turns out to be the case, however, his efforts to reduce the dissonance will not cease.

Indeed, there are some areas of cognition where the existence of major dissonance is customary. This may occur when two or more established beliefs or values, all relevant to the area of cognition in question, are inconsistent. That is, no opinion can be held, and no behavior engaged in, that will not be dissonant with at least one of these established beliefs. Myrdal, in the appendix to his classic book, states this quite well in connection with attitudes and behavior toward Negroes. In discussing the simultaneous existence of opinions and values concerning human beings in general, Negroes in general, specific groups of Negroes, and so on, Myrdal states:

> A need will be felt by the person or group, whose inconsistencies in valuations are publicly exposed, to find a means of reconciling the inconsistencies. . . . The feeling of need for logical consistency within the hierarchy of moral valuations . . . is, in its modern intensity, a rather new

phenomenon. With less mobility, less intellectual communication, and less public discussion, there was in previous generations less exposure of one another's valuation conflicts [pp. 1029, 1030].

While I find myself in disagreement with Myrdal in the importance he places on the public exposure of the dissonance, I feel it is a good statement of some of the reasons why strong dissonance exists in this area.

The notions introduced thus far are not entirely new; many similar ones have been suggested. It may be of value to mention two whose formulation is closest to my own. Heider, in an as yet unpublished manuscript, discusses the relationships among people and among sentiments. He states that:

> Summarizing this preliminary discussion of balanced, or harmonious, states, we can say that they are states characterized by two or more relations which fit together. If no balanced state exists, then forces toward the [balanced] state will arise. Either there will be a tendency to change the sentiments involved, or the unit relations will be changed through action or cognitive reorganization. If a change is not possible, the state of imbalance will produce tension, and the balanced states will be preferred over the states of imbalance [Part II].

If one replaces the word "balanced" with "consonant" and "imbalance" with "dissonance," this statement by Heider can be seen to indicate the same process with which our discussion up to now has dealt.

Osgood and Tannenbaum recently published a paper in which they also formulated and documented a similar idea with respect to changes in opinions and attitudes. In discussing the "principle of congruity," as they call it, they state: "Changes in evaluation are always in the direction of increased congruity with the existing frame of reference [p. 43]." The particular kind of "incongruity" or cognitive dissonance with which they deal in their study is produced by the knowledge that a person or other source of information which a subject regards positively (or negatively) supports an opinion which the subject regards negatively (or positively). They proceed to show that under such circumstances there is a marked tendency to change either the evaluation of the opinion involved or the evaluation of the source in a direction which would reduce the dissonance. Thus, if the source were positively evaluated and the opinion negatively evaluated, the person might end up reacting less positively to the source or more positively to the issue. It is also clear from their data that the particular outcome depends on whether the evaluation of the source or of the issue is initially more firmly rooted in the person's cognition. If his attitude toward the source is highly "polarized," then the opinion is more likely to change, and vice versa. Indeed, by careful initial measurement of the attitudes toward the sources and toward the opinions before the dissonance is introduced, and by careful measurement of how resistant each of these is to change, the authors are able to predict quite nicely the direction, and in some instances the amount, of change in evaluation.

The important point to remember is that there is pressure to produce consonant relations among cognitions and to avoid and reduce dissonance. Many other writers have recognized this, although few have stated it as concretely and as succinctly as the authors we have mentioned. The task which we are attempting in this book is to formulate the theory of dissonance in a precise yet generally applicable form, to draw out its implications to a variety of contexts, and to present data relevant to the theory.

Definitions of Dissonance and Consonance

Most of the remainder of this chapter will deal with a more formal exposition of the theory of dissonance. I will attempt to state the theory in as precise and unambiguous terms as possible. But since the ideas which constitute this theory are by no means yet in a completely precise form, some vagueness is unavoidable.

The terms "dissonance" and "consonance" refer to relations which exist between pairs of "elements." It is consequently necessary, before proceeding to define these relations, to define the elements themselves as well as we can.

These elements refer to what has been called cognition, that is, the things a person knows about himself, about his behavior, and about his surroundings. These elements, then, are "knowledges," if I may coin the plural form of the word. Some of these elements represent knowledge about oneself: what one does, what one feels, what one wants or desires, what one is, and the like. Other elements of knowledge concern the world in which one lives: what is where, what leads to what, what things are satisfying or painful or inconsequential or important, etc.

It is clear that the term "knowledge" has been used to include things to which the word does not ordinarily refer—for example, opinions. A person does not hold an opinion unless he thinks it is correct, and so, psychologically, it is not different from a "knowledge." The same is true of beliefs, values, or attitudes, which function as "knowledges" for our purposes. This is not to imply that there are no important distinctions to be made among these various terms. Indeed, some such distinctions will be made later on. But for the definitions here, these are all "elements of cognition," and relations of consonance and dissonance can hold between pairs of these elements.

There are further questions of definition one would like to be able to answer. For example, when is an "element of cognition" *one* element, or a group of elements? Is the knowledge, "the winter in Minneapolis is very cold" an element, or should this be considered a cluster of elements made up of more specific knowledge? This is, at present, an unanswerable question. Indeed, it may be a question which does not need answering. As will be seen in those chapters where data are presented and discussed, this unanswered question does not present a problem in connection with measurement.

Another important question concerning these elements is, how are they formed and what determines their content? At this point we want to emphasize the single most important determinant of the content of these elements, namely, *reality*. These elements of cognition are responsive to reality. By and large they mirror, or map, reality. This reality may be physical or social or psychological, but in any case the cognition more or less maps it. This is, of course, not surprising. It would be unlikely that an organism could live and survive if the elements of cognition were not to a large extent a veridical map of reality. Indeed, when someone is "out of touch with reality," it becomes very noticeable.

In other words, elements of cognition correspond for the most part with what the person actually does or feels or with what actually exists in the environment. In the case of opinions, beliefs, and values, the reality may be what others think or do; in other instances the reality may be what is encountered experientially or what others have told him.

But let us here object and say that persons frequently have cognitive elements which deviate markedly from reality, at least as we see it. Consequently, the major point to be made is that *the reality which impinges on a person will exert pressures in the direction of bringing the appropriate cognitive elements into correspondence with that reality.* This does not mean that the existing cognitive elements will *always* correspond. Indeed, one of the important consequences of the theory of dissonance is that it will help us understand some circumstances where the cognitive elements do not correspond with reality. But it does mean that if the cognitive elements do not correspond with a certain reality which impinges, certain pressures must exist. We should therefore be able to observe some manifestations of these pressures. This hypothesized relation between the cognitive elements and reality is important in enabling measurement of dissonance, and we will refer to it again in considering data.

It is now possible to proceed to a discussion of the relations which may exist between pairs of elements. There are three such relations, namely irrelevance, dissonance, and consonance. They will be discussed in that order.

Irrelevant Relations

Two elements may simply have nothing to do with one another. That is, under such circumstances where one cognitive element implies nothing at all concerning some other element, these two elements are irrelevant to one another. For example, let us imagine a person who knows that it sometimes takes as long as two weeks for a letter to go from New York to Paris by regular boat mail and who also knows that a dry, hot July is good for the corn crop in Iowa. These two elements of cognition have nothing to do with one another; they exist in an irrelevant relation to each other. There is not, of course, much to say about such irrelevant relations except to point to their existence. Of primary concern will be those pairs of elements between which relations of consonance or dissonance can exist.

In many instances, however, it becomes quite a problem to decide a priori whether or not two elements are irrelevant. It is often impossible to decide this without reference to other cognitions of the person involved. Sometimes situations will exist where, because of the behavior of the person involved, previously irrelevant elements become relevant to one another. This could even be the case in the example of irrelevant cognitive elements which we gave above. If a person living in Paris was speculating on the corn crop in the United States, he would want information concerning weather predictions for Iowa but would not depend upon boat mail for getting his information.

Before proceeding to the definitions and discussion of the relations of consonance and dissonance which exist if the elements are relevant, it may be well to stress again the special nature certain cognitive elements have—usually those cognitive elements which correspond to behavior. Such a "behavioral" element, by being relevant to each of two irrelevant cognitive elements, may make them in fact relevant to each other.

Relevant Relations: Dissonance and Consonance

We have already acquired some intuitive notion of the meaning of dissonance. Two elements are dissonant if, for one reason or another, they do not fit together. They may be inconsistent or contradictory, culture or group standards may dictate that they do not fit, and so on. It is appropriate now to attempt a more formal conceptual definition.

Let us consider two elements which exist in a person's cognition and which are relevant to one another. The definition of dissonance will disregard the existence of all the other cognitive elements that are relevant to either or both of the two under consideration and simply deal with these two alone. *These two elements are in a dissonant relation if, considering these two alone, the obverse of one element would follow from the other.* To state it a bit more formally, x and y are dissonant if not-x follows from y. Thus, for example, if a person knew there were only friends in his vicinity and also felt afraid, there would be a dissonant relation between these two cognitive elements. Or, for another example, if a person were already in debt and also purchased a new car, the corresponding cognitive elements would be dissonant with one another. The dissonance might exist because of what the person has learned or come to expect, because of what is considered appropriate or usual, or for any of a number of other reasons.

Motivations and desired consequences may also be factors in determining whether or not two elements are dissonant. For example, a person in a card game might continue playing and losing money while knowing that the others in the game are professional gamblers. This latter knowledge would be dissonant with his cognition about his behavior, namely, continuing to play. But it should be clear that to specify the relation as dissonant is to assume (plausibly enough) that the person involved wants to win. If for some strange reason this person wants to lose, this relation would be consonant.

It may be helpful to give a series of examples where dissonance between two cognitive elements stems from different sources, that is, where the two elements are dissonant because of different meanings of the phrase "follow from" in the definition of dissonance given above.

1. Dissonance could arise from logical inconsistency. If a person believed that man will reach the moon in the near future and also believed that man will not be able to build a device that can leave the atmosphere of the earth, these two cognitions are dissonant with one another. The obverse of one follows from the other on logical grounds in the person's own thinking processes.

2. Dissonance could arise because of cultural mores. If a person at a formal dinner uses his hands to pick up a recalcitrant chicken bone, the knowledge of what he is doing is dissonant with the knowledge of formal dinner etiquette. The dissonance exists simply because the culture defines what is consonant and what is not. In some other culture these two cognitions might not be dissonant at all.

3. Dissonance may arise because one specific opinion is sometimes included, by definition, in a more general opinion. Thus, if a person is a Democrat but in a given election prefers the Republican candidate,

the cognitive elements corresponding to these two sets of opinions are dissonant with each other because "being a Democrat" includes, as part of the concept, favoring Democratic candidates.

4. Dissonance may arise because of past experience. If a person were standing in the rain and yet could see no evidence that he was getting wet, these two cognitions would be dissonant with one another because he knows from experience that getting wet follows from being out in the rain. If one can imagine a person who had never had any experience with rain, these two cognitions would probably not be dissonant.

These various examples are probably sufficient to illustrate how the conceptual definition of dissonance, together with some specific meaning of the phrase "follow from," would be used empirically to decide whether two cognitive elements are dissonant or consonant. It is clear, of course, that in any of these situations, there might exist many other elements of cognition that are consonant with either of the two elements under consideration. Nevertheless, the relation between the two elements is dissonant if, disregarding the others, the one does not, or would not be expected to, follow from the other.

While we have been defining and discussing dissonance, the relations of consonance and irrelevance have, of course, also been defined by implication. If, considering a pair of elements, either one *does* follow from the other, then the relation between them is consonant. If neither the existing element nor its obverse follows from the other element of the pair, then the relation between them is irrelevant.

The conceptual definitions of dissonance and consonance present some serious measurement difficulties. If the theory of dissonance is to have relevance for empirical data, one must be able to identify dissonances and consonances unequivocally. But it is clearly hopeless to attempt to obtain a complete listing of cognitive elements, and even were such a listing available, in some cases it would be difficult or impossible to say, a priori, which of the three relationships holds. In many cases, however, the a priori determination of dissonance is clear and easy. (Remember also that two cognitive elements may be dissonant for a person living in one culture and not for a person living in another, or for a person with one set of experiences and not for a person with another.) Needless to say, it will be necessary to cope with this problem of measurement in detail in those chapters where empirical data are presented and discussed.

The Magnitude of Dissonance

All dissonant relations, of course, are not of equal magnitude. It is necessary to distinguish degrees of dissonance and to specify what determines how strong a given dissonant relation is. We will briefly discuss some determinants of the magnitude of dissonance between two elements and then turn to a consideration of the total amount of dissonance which may exist between two clusters of elements.

One obvious determinant of the magnitude of dissonance lies in the characteristics of the elements between which the relation of dissonance holds. *If two elements are dissonant with one another, the magnitude of the dissonance will be a function of the importance of the elements.* The more these elements are important to, or valued by, the person, the greater will be the magnitude of a dissonant relation between them. Thus, for example, if a person gives ten cents to a beggar, knowing full well that the beggar is not really in need, the dissonance which exists between these two elements is rather weak. Neither of the two cognitive elements involved is very important or very consequential to the person. A much greater dissonance is involved, for example, if a student does not study for a very important examination, knowing that his present fund of information is probably inadequate for the examination. In this case the elements that are dissonant with each other are more important to the person, and the magnitude of dissonance will be correspondingly greater.

It is probably safe to assume that it is rare for no dissonance at all to exist within any cluster of cognitive elements. For almost any action a person might take, for almost any feeling he might have, there will most likely be at least one cognitive element dissonant with this "behavioral" element. Even perfectly trivial cognitions like knowing one is taking a walk on a Sunday afternoon would likely have some elements dissonant with it. The person who is out for a walk might also know that there are things around the house requiring his attention, or he might know that rain was likely, and so on. In short, there are generally so many other cognitive elements relevant to any given element that some dissonance is the usual state of affairs.

Let us consider now the total context of dissonances and consonances in relation to one particular element. Assuming momentarily, for the sake of definition, that all the elements relevant to the one in question are equally important, *the total amount of dissonance between this element and the remainder of the person's cognition will depend on the proportion of relevant elements that are dissonant with the one in question.* Thus, if the overwhelming majority of relevant elements are consonant with, say, a behavioral element, then the dissonance with this behavioral element is slight. If in relation to the number of elements consonant with the behavioral element the number of dissonant elements is large, the total dissonance will be of appreciable magnitude. Of course, the magnitude of the total dissonance will also depend on the importance or value of those relevant elements which exist in consonant or dissonant relations with the one being considered.

The above statement can of course be easily generalized to deal with the magnitude of dissonance which exists between two clusters of cognitive elements. This magnitude would depend on the proportion of the relevant relations between elements in the two clusters that were dissonant and, of course, on the importance of the elements.

Since the magnitude of dissonance is an important variable in determining the pressure to reduce dissonance, and since we will deal with measures of the magnitude of dissonance repeatedly in considering data, it may be well to summarize our discussion concerning the magnitude of dissonance.

1. If two cognitive elements are relevant, the relation between them is either dissonant or consonant.

2. The magnitude of the dissonance (or consonance) increases as the importance or value of the elements increases.

3. The total amount of dissonance that exists between two clusters of cognitive elements is a function of the weighted proportion of all relevant relations between the two clusters that are dissonant. The term "weighted proportion" is used because each relevant relation would be weighted according to the importance of the elements involved in that relation.

The Reduction of Dissonance

The presence of dissonance gives rise to pressures to reduce or eliminate the dissonance. The strength of the pressures to reduce the dissonance is a function of the magnitude of the dissonance. In other words, dissonance acts in the same way as a state of drive or need or tension. The presence of dissonance leads to action to reduce it just as, for example, the presence of hunger leads to action to reduce the hunger. Also, similar to the action of a drive, the greater the dissonance, the greater will be the intensity of the action to reduce the dissonance and the greater the avoidance of situations that would increase the dissonance.

In order to be specific about how the pressure to reduce dissonance would manifest itself, it is necessary to examine the possible ways in which existing dissonance can be reduced or eliminated. In general, if dissonance exists between two elements, this dissonance can be eliminated by changing one of those elements. The important thing is how these changes may be brought about. There are various possible ways in which this can be accomplished, depending upon the type of cognitive elements involved and upon the total cognitive context.

Changing a Behavioral Cognitive Element

When the dissonance under consideration is between an element corresponding to some knowledge concerning environment (environmental element) and a behavioral element, the dissonance can, of course, be eliminated by changing the behavioral cognitive element in such a way that it is consonant with the environmental element. The simplest and easiest way in which this may be accomplished is to change the action or feeling which the behavioral element represents. Given that a cognition is responsive to "reality" (as we have seen), if the behavior of the organism changes, the cognitive element or elements corresponding to this behavior will likewise change. This method of reducing or eliminating dissonance is a very frequent occurrence. Our behavior and feelings are frequently modified in accordance with new information. If a person starts out on a picnic and notices that it has begun to rain, he may very well turn around and go home. There are many persons who do stop smoking if and when they discover it is bad for their health.

It may not always be possible, however, to eliminate dissonance or even to reduce it materially by changing one's action or feeling. The difficulty of changing the behavior may be too great, or the change, while eliminating some dissonances, may create a whole host of new ones. These questions will be discussed in more detail below.

Changing an Environmental Cognitive Element

Just as it is possible to change a behavioral cognitive element by changing the behavior which this element mirrors, it is sometimes possible to change an *environmental* cognitive element by changing the situation to which that element corresponds. This, of course, is much more difficult than changing one's behavior, for one must have a sufficient degree of control over one's environment—a relatively rare occurrence.

Changing the environment itself in order to reduce dissonance is more feasible when the social environment is in question than when the physical environment is involved. In order to illustrate rather dramatically the kind of thing that would be involved, I will give a rather facetious hypothetical example. Let us imagine a person who is given to pacing up and down in his living room at home. Let us further imagine that for some unknown reason he always jumps over one particular spot on the floor. The cognitive element corresponding to his jumping over that spot is undoubtedly dissonant with his knowledge that the floor at that spot is level, strong, and in no way different from any other part of the floor. If, some evening when his wife is away from home, he breaks a hole in the floor at that exact spot, he would completely eliminate the dissonance. The cognition that there is a hole in the floor would be quite consonant with the knowledge that he jumps over the place where the hole exists. In short, he would have changed a cognitive element by actually changing the environment, thus eliminating a dissonance.

Whenever there is sufficient control over the environment, this method of reducing dissonance may be employed. For example, a person who is habitually very hostile toward other people may surround himself with persons who provoke hostility. His cognitions about the persons with whom he associates are then consonant with the cognitions corresponding to his hostile behavior. The possibilities of manipulating the environment are limited, however, and most endeavors to change a cognitive element will follow other lines.

If a cognitive element that is responsive to reality is to be changed without changing the corresponding reality, some means of ignoring or counteracting the real situation must be used. This is sometimes well-nigh impossible, except in extreme cases which might be called psychotic. If a person is standing in the rain and rapidly getting soaked, he will almost certainly continue to have the cognition that it is raining no matter how strong the psychological pressures are to eliminate that cognition. In other instances it is relatively easy to change a cognitive element although the reality remains the same. For example, a person might be able to change his opinion about a political officeholder even though the behavior of that officeholder, and the political situation generally, remain unchanged. Usually, for this to occur, the person would have to be able to find others who would agree with and support his new opinion. In general, establishing a social reality by gaining the agreement and support of other people is one of the major ways in which a cognition can be changed when the pressures to change it are present. It can readily be seen that where such social support is necessary, the presence of dissonance and the consequent pressures to change some cognitive element will lead to a variety of social processes. This will be developed in detail in Chapters Eight, Nine, and Ten,* which consider the social manifestations of pressures to reduce dissonance.

Adding New Cognitive Elements

It is clear that in order to eliminate a dissonance completely, some cognitive element must be changed. It is also clear that this is not always possible. But even if it is impossible to eliminate a dissonance, it is possible to reduce the total magnitude of dissonance by adding new cog-

*See SOURCE.

nitive elements. Thus, for example, if dissonance existed between some cognitive elements concerning the effects of smoking and cognition concerning the behavior of continuing to smoke, the total dissonance could be reduced by adding new cognitive elements that are consonant with the fact of smoking. In the presence of such dissonance, then, a person might be expected to actively seek new information that would reduce the total dissonance and, at the same time, to avoid new information that might increase the existing dissonance. Thus, to pursue the example, the person might seek out and avidly read any material critical of the research which purported to show that smoking was bad for one's health. At the same time he would avoid reading material that praised this research. (If he unavoidably came in contact with the latter type of material, his reading would be critical indeed.)

Actually, the possibilities for adding new elements which would reduce the existing dissonances are broad. Our smoker, for example, could find out all about accidents and death rates in automobiles. Having then added the cognition that the danger from smoking is negligible compared to the danger he runs driving a car, his dissonance would also have been somewhat reduced. Here the total dissonance is reduced by reducing the *importance* of the existing dissonance.

The above discussion has pointed to the possibility of reducing the total dissonance with some element by reducing the proportion of dissonant as compared with consonant relations involving that element. It is also possible to add a new cognitive element which, in a sense, "reconciles" two elements that are dissonant. Let us consider an example from the literature to illustrate this. Spiro gives an account of certain aspects of the belief system of the Ifaluk, a nonliterate society. The relevant points for our purposes here are as follows:

1. In this culture there is a firm belief that people are *good*. This belief is not only that they should be good but that they *are* good.
2. For one reason or another, young children in this culture go through a period of particularly strong overt aggression, hostility, and destructiveness.

It seems clear that the belief about the nature of people is dissonant with the knowledge of the behavior of the children in this culture. It would have been possible to reduce this dissonance in any number of ways. They might have changed their belief about the nature of people or have modified it so that people are wholly good only at maturity. Or they might have changed their ideas about what is and what is not "good" so that overt aggression in young children would be considered good. Actually, the manner of reducing the dissonance was different. A third belief was added which effectively reduced the dissonance by "reconciliation." Specifically, they also believe in the existence of malevolent ghosts which enter into persons and cause them to do bad things.

As a result of this third belief, the knowledge of the aggressive behavior of children is no longer dissonant with the belief that people are good. It is not the children who behave aggressively—it's the malevolent ghosts. Psychologically, this is a highly satisfactory means of reducing the dissonance, as one might expect when such beliefs are institutionalized at a cultural level. Unsatisfactory solutions would not be as successful in becoming widely accepted.

Before moving on, it is worth while to emphasize again that the presence of pressures to reduce dissonance, or even activity directed toward such reduction, does not guarantee that the dissonance will be reduced. A person may not be able to find the social support needed to change a cognitive element, or he may not be able to find new elements which reduce the total dissonance. In fact, it is quite conceivable that in the process of trying to reduce dissonance, it might even be increased. This will depend upon what the person encounters while attempting to reduce the dissonance. The important point to be made so far is that in the presence of a dissonance, one will be able to observe the *attempts* to reduce it. If attempts to reduce dissonance fail, one should be able to observe symptoms of psychological discomfort, provided the dissonance is appreciable enough so that the discomfort is clearly and overtly manifested.

Resistance to Reduction of Dissonance

If dissonance is to be reduced or eliminated by changing one or more cognitive elements, it is necessary to consider how resistant these cognitive elements are to change. Whether or not any of them change, and if so, which ones, will certainly be determined in part by the magnitude of resistance to change which they possess. It is, of course, clear that if the various cognitive elements involved had no resistance to change whatsoever, there would never be any lasting dissonances. Momentary dissonance might occur, but if the cognitive elements involved had no resistance to change, the dissonance would immediately be eliminated. Let us, then, look at the major sources of resistance to change of a cognitive element.

Just as the reduction of dissonance presented somewhat different problems depending upon whether the element to be changed was a

behavioral or an environmental one, so the major sources of resistance
to change are different for these two classes of cognitive elements.

Resistance to Change of Behavioral Cognitive Elements

The first and foremost source of resistance to change for *any* cognitive
element is the responsiveness of such elements to reality. If one sees
that the grass is green, it is very difficult to think it is not so. If a person
is walking down the street, it is difficult for his cognition not to contain
an element corresponding to this. Given this strong and sometimes
overwhelming responsiveness to reality, the problem of changing a behavioral cognitive element becomes the problem of changing the behavior which is being mapped by the element. Consequently, the resistance
to change of the cognitive element is identical with the resistance to
change of the behavior reflected by that element, assuming that the
person maintains contact with reality.

Certainly much behavior has little or no resistance to change. We
continually modify many of our actions and feelings in accordance with
changes in the situation. If a street which we ordinarily use when we
drive to work is being repaired, there is usually little difficulty in alter-
ing our behavior and using a different route. What, then, are the circumstances that make it difficult for the person to change his actions?

1. The change may be painful or involve loss. A person may, for
example, have spent a lot of money to purchase a house. If for any
reason he now wants to change, that is, live in a different house or
different neighborhood, he must endure the discomforts of moving and
the possible financial loss involved in selling the house. A person who
might desire to give up smoking must endure the discomfort and pain
of the cessation in order to accomplish the change. Clearly, in such circumstances there will be a certain resistance to change. The magnitude
of this resistance to change will be determined by the extent of pain or
loss which must be endured.

2. The present behavior may be otherwise satisfying. A person might
continue to have lunch at a certain restaurant even though they served
poor food if, for example, his friends always ate there. Or a person who
is very domineering and harsh toward his children might not easily be
able to give up the satisfactions of being able to boss someone, even if
on various grounds he desired to change. In such instances, of course,
the resistance to change would be a function of the satisfaction obtained
from the present behavior.

3. Making the change may simply not be possible. It would be a
mistake to imagine that a person could consummate any change in his
behavior if he wanted to badly enough. It may not be possible to change

for a variety of reasons. Some behavior, especially emotional reactions, may not be under the voluntary control of the person. For example, a person might have a strong reaction of fear which he can do nothing about. Also, it might not be possible to consummate a change simply because the new behavior may not be in the behavior repertory of the person. A father might not be able to change the way he behaves toward his children simply because he doesn't know any other way to behave. A third circumstance which could make it impossible to change is the irrevocable nature of certain actions. If, for example, a person has sold his house and then decides he wants it back, there is nothing that can be done if the new owner refuses to sell it. The action has been taken and is not reversible. But under circumstances where the behavior simply cannot change at all, it is not correct to say that the resistance to change of the corresponding cognitive element is infinite. The resistance to change which the cognitive element possesses can, of course, not be greater than the pressure to respond to reality.

Resistance to Change of Environmental Cognitive Elements

Here again, as with behavioral cognitive elements, the major source of resistance to change lies in the responsiveness of these elements to reality. The result of this, as far as behavioral elements go, is to tie the resistance to change of the cognitive element to the resistance to change of the reality, namely, the behavior itself. The situation is somewhat different with regard to environmental elements. When there is a clear and unequivocal reality corresponding to some cognitive element, the possibilities of change are almost nil. If one desired, for example, to change one's cognition about the location of some building which one saw every day, this would indeed be difficult to accomplish.

In many instances, however, the reality corresponding to the cognitive element is by no means so clear and unambiguous. When the reality is basically a social one, that is, when it is established by agreement with other people, the resistance to change would be determined by the difficulty of finding persons to support the new cognition.

There is another source of resistance to change of both behavioral and environmental cognitive elements. We have postponed discussion of it until now, however, because it is a more important source of resistance to change for environmental elements than for others. This source of resistance to change lies in the fact that an element is in relationship with a number of other elements. To the extent that the element is consonant with a large number of other elements and to the extent that changing it would replace these consonances by dissonances, the element will be resistant to change.

The above discussion is not meant to be an exhaustive analysis of resistance to change or a listing of conceptually different sources. Rather, it is a discussion which attempts to make distinctions that will help operationally rather than conceptually. In considering any dissonance and the resistance to change of the elements involved, the important factor in the attempt to eliminate the dissonance by changing an element is the total amount of resistance to change; the source of the resistance is immaterial.

Limits of the Magnitude of Dissonance

The maximum dissonance that can possibly exist between any two elements is equal to the total resistance to change of the less resistant element. The magnitude of dissonance cannot exceed this amount because, at this point of maximum possible dissonance, the less resistant element would change, thus eliminating the dissonance.

This does not mean that the magnitude of dissonance will frequently even approach this maximum possible value. When there exists a strong dissonance that is less than the resistance to change of any of the elements involved, this dissonance can perhaps still be reduced for the total cognitive system by adding new cognitive elements. In this way, even in the presence of very strong resistances to change, the total dissonance in the system could be kept at rather low levels.

Let us consider an example of a person who spends what for him is a very large sum of money for a new car of an expensive type. Let us also imagine that after purchasing it he finds that some things go wrong with it and that repairs are very expensive. It is also more expensive to operate than other cars, and what is more, he finds that his friends think the car is ugly. If the dissonance becomes great enough, that is, equal to the resistance to change of the less resistant element, which in this situation would probably be the behavioral element, he might sell the car and suffer whatever inconvenience and financial loss is involved. Thus the dissonance could not exceed the resistance the person has to changing his behavior, that is, selling the car.

Now let us consider the situation where the dissonance for the person who bought a new car was appreciable but less than the maximum possible dissonance, that is, less than the resistance to change of the less resistant cognitive element. None of the existing cognitive elements would then be changed, but he could keep the total dissonance low by adding more and more cognitions that are consonant with his ownership of the car. He begins to feel that power and riding qualities are more important than economy and looks. He begins to drive faster than he used to and becomes quite convinced that it is important for a car to be able to travel at high speed. With these cognitions and others, he might succeed in rendering the dissonance negligible.

It is also possible, however, that his attempts to add new consonant cognitive elements would prove unsuccessful and that his financial situation is such that he could not sell the car. It would still be possible to reduce the dissonance by what also amounts to adding a new cognitive element, but of a different kind. He can admit to himself, and to others, that he was wrong to purchase the car and that if he had it to do over again, he would buy a different kind. This process of divorcing himself psychologically from the action can and does materially reduce the dissonance. Sometimes, however, the resistances against this are quite strong. The maximum dissonance which could exist would, in such circumstances, be determined by the resistance to admitting that he had been wrong or foolish.

Avoidance of Dissonance

The discussion thus far has focused on the tendencies to reduce or eliminate dissonance and the problems involved in achieving such reduction. Under certain circumstances there are also strong and important tendencies to avoid increases of dissonance or to avoid the occurrence of dissonance altogether. Let us now turn our attention to a consideration of these circumstances and the manifestations of the avoidance tendencies which we might expect to observe.

The avoidance of an increase in dissonance comes about, of course, as a result of the existence of dissonance. This avoidance is especially important where, in the process of attempting to reduce dissonance, support is sought for a new cognitive element to replace an existing one or where new cognitive elements are to be added. In both these circumstances, the seeking of support and the seeking of new information must be done in a highly selective manner. A person would initiate discussion with someone he thought would agree with the new cognitive element but would avoid discussion with someone who might agree with the element that he was trying to change. A person would expose himself to sources of information which he expected would add new elements which would increase consonance but would certainly avoid sources which would increase dissonance.

If there is little or no dissonance existing, we would not expect the same kind of selectivity in exposure to sources of support or sources of information. In fact, where no dissonance exists there should be a relative absence of motivation to seek support or new information at all. This will be true in general, but there are important exceptions. Past experience may lead a person to fear, and hence to avoid, the initial occurrence of dissonance. Where this is true, one might expect circumspect behavior with regard to new information even when little or no dissonance is present to start with.

The operation of fear of dissonance may also lead to a reluctance to commit oneself behaviorally. There is a large class of actions that, once taken, are difficult to change. Hence, it is possible for dissonances to arise and to mount in intensity. A fear of dissonance would lead to a reluctance to take action—a reluctance to commit oneself. Where decision and action cannot be indefinitely delayed, the taking of action may be accompanied by a cognitive negation of the action. Thus, for example, a person who buys a new car and is very afraid of dissonance may, immediately following the purchase, announce his conviction that he did the wrong thing. Such strong fear of dissonance is probably relatively rare, but it does occur. Personality differences with respect to fear of dissonance and the effectiveness with which one is able to reduce dissonance are undoubtedly important in determining whether or not such avoidance of dissonance is likely to happen. The operational problem would be to independently identify situations and persons where this kind of a priori self-protective behavior occurs.

Summary

The core of the theory of dissonance which we have stated is rather simple. It holds that:

1. There may exist dissonant or "nonfitting" relations among cognitive elements.
2. The existence of dissonance gives rise to pressures to reduce the dissonance and to avoid increases in dissonance.
3. Manifestations of the operation of these pressures include behavior changes, changes of cognition, and circumspect exposure to new information and new opinions.

Although the core of the theory is simple, it has rather wide implications and applications to a variety of situations which on the surface look very different. The remainder of the book will spell out these specific implications of the theory and will examine data relevant to them.

THE CONSEQUENCES OF DECISIONS: THEORY

Although psychologists have paid a great deal of attention to the decision-making process, there has only been occasional recognition of the problems that ensue when a decision has been made. One of the major consequences of having made a decision is the existence of dissonance. But before going into this in detail, let us take a look at some of the statements that have recognized the problems of postdecision processes.

Discussing the problem of deciding between two mutually exclusive alternatives, both of which are attractive, Adams states:

> But mere decision is not the whole story. The unsatisfied appetite, the undischarged tension of the rejected alternative is still there unless a further process, which may be called "conflict resolution," takes place [p. 554].

In other words, Adams points out that after a decision is made, something must still be done to handle the unpleasantness of having rejected something which is, after all, attractive. He also suggests that this requires some "restructuring" or "revaluation" of the alternatives which were involved in the decision.

That this is not always easy or even possible, and that these discomforts or dissonances can build up and accumulate, is also recognized by Adams:

> It can be said, however, that the person is fortunate in whom these revaluations or restructurings or insights occur as the conflicts arise rather than letting the latter accumulate until they precipitate a more or less violent, wholesale, and uncritical revaluation of valued objects [p. 555].

When Adams speaks of "conflict resolution" and the "accumulation of conflict," he is talking about "dissonance reduction" and "accumulation of dissonance." The broadness with which the term "conflict" has come to be used seems to me to include dissonance within it. I will later suggest a more restricted use of the term "conflict."

The fact that a decision, once having been made, gives rise to processes that tend to stabilize the decision has also been recognized, particularly by Kurt Lewin. For example, Lewin [1952], in discussing the results of experiments on the effectiveness of group decisions, states:

> In the experiment on hand we are dealing with a group decision after discussion. The decision itself takes but a minute or two. (It was done through raising of hands as an answer to the question: Who would like to

serve kidneys, sweetbreads, beef hearts next week?) The act of decision, however, should be viewed as a very important process of giving domi- nance to one of the alternatives, serving or not serving. It has an effect of freezing this motivational constellation for action [p. 465].

And again in another article discussing similar material, Lewin [1951] states:

This seems to be, at least in part, the explanation for the otherwise para- doxical fact that a process like decision which takes only a few minutes is able to affect conduct for many months to come. The decision links moti- vation to action and, at the same time, seems to have a "freezing" effect which is partly due to the individual's tendency to "stick to his decision" . . . [p. 233].

This so-called "freezing effect" of decision would indeed result from the process of establishing cognitive elements consonant with the deci- sion and eliminating dissonant elements. The end result would be that having made the decision, and having taken the consequent action, one would begin to alter the cognition so that alternatives which had previ- ously been nearly equally attractive ceased to be so. The alternative which had been chosen would seem much more attractive, and the al- ternative which had been rejected would begin to seem less attractive than it had been. The result of the process would be to stabilize or "freeze" the decision.

Decisions Resulting in Dissonance

To understand why and when dissonance follows from a decision, let us first attempt to analyze one type of decision situation, namely, one where a choice is to be made between two positive alternatives. This discussion can easily be generalized to include other decision situations. Imagine a person having to choose between two alternatives, each of which is quite attractive to him. Before the decision is made he consid- ers the features of each of the alternatives and, in some manner, com- pares them. Thus, for example, a person might have to make a choice between two very desirable jobs. Before the decision is made he would probably acquaint himself thoroughly with the details of each offer. We would then have a situation where, in his cognition, there were a num- ber of elements that, *considered alone*, would lead him to choose job A and also a number of elements that, *considered by themselves*, would lead him to choose job B.

Eventually the person makes a decision—he chooses one of the two alternatives and, simultaneously, rejects the other. Let us examine the relations which then exist between the cognitive elements corresponding to this action and the cognitive elements that accumulated during the process of coming to a decision. Let us proceed as if the person in question chose job A and rejected job B. All of those cognitive elements that, considered alone, would lead him to choose job A are now consonant with the cognitive elements corresponding to the action he took. But there also exist a number of elements that, considered by themselves, would lead him to choose job B. All of these elements are now dissonant with the cognition about the action he took. The existence of this dissonance follows from the definitions in the previous chapter. Dissonance then will be a result of the simple act of having made a decision. Consequently, one may expect to see manifestations of pressures to reduce dissonance after a choice has been made.

Before proceeding to a discussion of the specific determinants of the magnitude of the dissonance which follows a decision and of the specific manifestations of the pressure to reduce it, a brief discussion expanding this analysis to include other types of decision situations is in order.

There have already been stated some excellent analyses of decision or conflict situations by Lewin [1935] and by Hovland and Sears. I will not attempt to repeat them here, but will briefly summarize only what is pertinent to our purpose.

1. *Decision between completely negative alternatives.* While this is a theoretically possible condition, it probably rarely occurs. The mere presence of two negative alternatives does not put the person in a decision situation unless there are some other factors that force him to choose between them. If this occurs, the same consequences concerning dissonance will exist after the choice has been made. There will be some cognitive elements favoring the choice of one alternative and some cognitive elements favoring the choice of the other alternative. No matter which is chosen, there will then be a number of cognitive elements dissonant with the cognition about this action.

2. *Decision between two alternatives, each having both positive and negative aspects.* This is probably the most usual type of decision situation. It is certainly clear from our previous discussion that, here too, dissonance will result when action is taken. There will be some cognitive elements corresponding to the positive aspects of the unchosen alternative and some elements corresponding to the negative aspects of the chosen alternative which will be dissonant with the cognition of having chosen one particular alternative.

3. *Decision involving more than two alternatives.* Certainly many, if not most, decisions involve more than two alternatives. Many possibilities may be present initially, or the person in the decision situation may invent compromises, new modes of action, and the like. This added complexity makes the analysis of the decision process difficult but, happily, adds very little complexity to the analysis of the dissonances which exist after the decision is made. Once more, *all those elements that, considered alone, would lead to action other than the one taken are dissonant with the cognitive elements corresponding to the action taken.*

One may, then, offer the generalization that dissonance is an almost inevitable consequence of a decision, and proceed to an examination of the factors that affect the magnitude of this dissonance.

The Magnitude of Dissonance
Following Decisions

How strong the dissonance is will depend, of course, upon the general determinants which we have stated in the previous chapter. The task here is to spell out the specific nature of these determinant as they exist in postdecision situations.

The *importance* of the decision will affect the magnitude of the dissonance that exists after the decision has been made. Other things being equal, the more important the decision, the stronger will be the dissonance. Thus, a decision to buy one automobile rather than another will result in more dissonance than a decision to buy one brand of soap rather than another; a decision to take one job rather than another will produce a greater magnitude of dissonance than a decision to go to a movie rather than a concert. In future chapters we shall refer to the variable of importance again and again since it is a general determinant of the magnitude of dissonance. Let us now move on to those considerations which are peculiar to postdecision situations.

Another major determinant of the magnitude of postdecision dissonance is the *relative attractiveness of the unchosen alternative.* This, of course, follows directly from our analysis of the postdecision situation and the reasons that dissonance exists at all. The dissonance exists because, following the decision, the person continues to have in his cognition elements that, if considered alone, would lead to an action other than the one he has taken or is engaged in. These elements reflect the desirable characteristics of the unchosen alternatives and the undesirable characteristics of the chosen alternatives. Consequently, the greater the relative attractiveness of the unchosen alternatives to the chosen alternative, the greater will be the proportion of relevant elements that are dissonant with the cognition corresponding to the action.

Figure 9.1 shows the relations we would expect between the magnitude of postdecision dissonance and the relative attractiveness of the unchosen alternative, holding constant the importance and the attractiveness of the chosen alternative. For any given relative attractiveness of the unchosen alternative, the more important the decision or the greater the attractiveness of the chosen alternative, the greater would be the resulting dissonance. As the relative attractiveness of the unchosen alternative decreases, the resulting dissonance also decreases. The pressure to reduce dissonance, it will be recalled, varies directly with the magnitude of dissonance. The discussion later on will focus on how the pressure to reduce dissonance will show itself in such situations.

First, however, it would be well to clarify a few points. Figure 9.1 is certainly not meant to imply that these relationships are linear. The exact form which these relationships would exhibit would, of course,

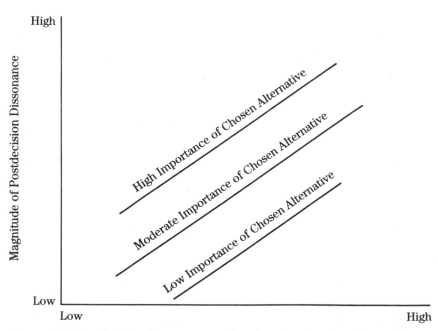

Figure 9.1 *Postdecision dissonance as a function of properties of the unchosen alternative.*

depend upon the exact nature of the metric by means of which dissonance, importance, and relative attractiveness were measured. Since as
of now there is no precise metric, it is not meaningful to talk about
the exact form of the relationship. What can be stated, however, and all
the figure is intended to convey, is the existence of steadily increasing
functions.

It is best, before going on, to also discuss the distinction between
conflict and dissonance, because they are dynamically different in their
effects. The person is in a conflict situation before making the decision.
After having made the decision he is no longer in conflict; he has made
his choice; he has, so to speak, resolved the conflict. He is no longer
being pushed in two or more directions simultaneously. He is now committed to the chosen course of action. It is only here that dissonance
exists, and the pressure to reduce this dissonance is *not* pushing the
person in two directions simultaneously.

Making this distinction necessitates specific usage of both terms. The
term "conflict" has, unfortunately, come to be used very broadly by
many persons. For example, in a recent article by Smock on intolerance
of ambiguity, one finds this statement:

> Incongruity, by definition, indicates a stimulus configuration composed of
> elements that *conflict with the "expectancies" of the individual in the sense
> he seldom, if ever, is presented with such a stimulus configuration in a
> "real-life" situation* [p. 354, italics ours].

This statement has been chosen because it tries to specify the sense
in which the word "conflict" is used. When persons speak of conflict
between opinions or values, it is frequently difficult to know just what
is meant. In Smock's use of the term, there is perhaps little distinction
between it and dissonance. But the sense is clearly different from that
use of the term that means an opposition of forces acting on the person.

Let us examine a predecision and postdecision situation to clarify the
distinction. Imagine a person who has two job offers. All the cognitive
elements corresponding to favorable characteristics of job A and unfavorable characteristics of job B (call this cognitive cluster A) steer him
in the direction of taking job A. Cognitive cluster B, elements corresponding to favorable characteristics of job B and unfavorable characteristics of job A, steer him in the direction of taking job B. Since job A
and B are mutually exclusive, he cannot have both; he is in conflict.

But it is necessary to specify further where the conflict lies. It is not
between cognitive cluster A and cognitive cluster B. That is, there is no
conflict between knowing that job A is good and also knowing that job

B is good. On a cognitive level this could simply add up to a nice, rosy picture of the world. There is no opposition between liking one thing and also liking another thing. The conflict arises because one must choose between the two possible courses of action. The person is pushed in two opposite directions at once.

Sooner or later the person makes the decision and chooses job A. Now he is no longer pushed in two opposite directions; he has chosen one of the alternatives and is no longer in conflict. But now cognitive cluster B is dissonant with his knowledge of the direction in which he is moving. This dissonance exists on a cognitive level. There is still no necessary relation between the two cognitive clusters; but while cognitive cluster A is consonant with the decision, cluster B is dissonant with it. The person now moves in one direction and attempts to reduce the cognitive dissonance.

A third variable affecting the magnitude of postdecision dissonance may be termed the degree of *cognitive overlap* of the alternatives which are involved in the decision. The degree of overlap is high if many of the elements in the cluster corresponding to one alternative are identical with elements of the cluster corresponding to the other alternative. High cognitive overlap is generally loosely implied when we speak of two things being "similar." Low degree of cognitive overlap is generally implied when we speak of two things being "qualitatively different." There is no overlap between the clusters of cognitive elements corresponding to two alternatives if none of the cognitive elements in one cluster is identical with any of the elements in the other cluster.

How, then, does the degree of cognitive overlap affect the magnitude of dissonance which results from a decision? It seems clear that the greater the cognitive overlap between the two alternatives, that is, the less the qualitative dstinction between them, the smaller the dissonance that exists after the choice has been made. This follows from consideration of the reasons for the existence of dissonance. The dissonance, it will be recalled, exists between the cognitive elements corresponding to the action that has been taken and those cognitive elements that correspond to desirable features of the unchosen alternative and to undesirable features of the chosen alternative. But let us consider that subset of the elements that identically corresponds to desirable features of both the unchosen and the chosen alternatives. Clearly, these elements are not dissonant with cognition about the action which has been taken since, considered alone, they would lead to the action taken just as cogently as they would lead to the rejected action. Exactly the same state of affairs exists with respect to those elements that correspond to identical undesirable aspects of both the chosen and unchosen alternatives.

Therefore, if the cognitive overlap is complete, that is, if *every* element in the cluster corresponding to one alternative also exists identically in the cognitive cluster corresponding to the other alternative, no dissonance at all will result as a mere consequence of the decision.

For example, if a person were offered a choice between $5.00 and $4.99, he would undoubtedly choose the first alternative. There would be no dissonance resulting from this decision even though the attractiveness of the unchosen alternative is very high relative to the attractiveness of the chosen alternative. The same absence of dissonance following the decision would hold irrespective of the absolute magnitude of the attractiveness of the alternatives. There is, of course, complete cognitive overlap. Every element corresponding to desirable properties of the unchosen alternative is identical with some element in the cluster corresponding to desirable properties of the chosen alternative. Similarly, we would expect the dissonance resulting from a choice between, say, two books to be less than the dissonance resulting from the choice between a book and a ticket to a concert. In the former instance, the cognitive overlap is undoubtedly greater.

Manifestations of Pressure to Reduce Postdecision Dissonance

As has been stated many times, the existence of dissonance will give rise to pressures to reduce it. Let us, consequently, examine the ways in which postdecision dissonance can be reduced. There are three main ways in which this might be accomplished, namely, (a) changing or revoking the decision, (b) changing the attractiveness of the alternatives involved in the choice, and (c) establishing cognitive overlap among the alternatives involved in the choice. The discussion will deal with them in that order.

Changing or Revoking the Decision

It should be emphasized that this analysis concerns itself with the state of affairs that exists immediately after the decision has been made and before further experience accumulates concerning the results and consequences of the action which has been taken. It must be recognized that at this point the existing dissonance cannot be overwhelming. Indeed, assuming that the individual chose the most favorable alternative, the weighted sum of the dissonances (each dissonant relation somehow weighted for its importance) would not exceed the weighted sum of the consonances. Consequently, reversing the decision, assuming this is possible for the moment, is not an adequate way of reducing dissonance since it would simply reverse which cognitive elements were dissonant or consonant with the cognition about the action. There may exist occasional temptations to reverse the decision since the person may be more troubled by the dissonance which exists than comforted by the consonances. But it would not constitute a reduction in dissonance. It would actually, in most cases, increase the dissonance and hence will not usually occur. It may happen that after additional information and experience has been acquired, the dissonance may have increased to a point where the person would desire to reverse the decision. It is probably correct, though, that the dissonance would have to become nearly overwhelming, that is, more than half of the cognitive elements would have to be dissonant with the cognition about the action taken, before reversal of the action would be a feasible means of coping with dissonance. This will be dealt with in later chapters.*

It is possible, however, to reduce or even eliminate the dissonance by revoking the decision psychologically. This would consist of admitting to having made the wrong choice or insisting that really no choice had been made for which the person had any responsibility. Thus, a person who has just accepted a new job might immediately feel he had done the wrong thing and, if he had it to do over again, might do something different. Or he might persuade himself that the choice had not been his; circumstances and his boss conspired to force the action on him. These are probably not usual types of solutions to the existence of dissonance. In essence they put the person back in conflict, that is, in the choice-making situation, although the choice need not, or perhaps cannot, be remade; or else it puts the person in a situation where he does not accept responsibility for what he does. These last two factors probably account in large measure for the rarity of this mode of eliminating dissonance.

Changing Cognition About the Alternatives

This is the most direct and probably most usual manner of reducing postdecision dissonance. Since the dissonance exists in the first place because there were cognitive elements corresponding to favorable characteristics of the unchosen alternative and also cognitive elements corresponding to unfavorable characteristics of the chosen alternative, it

*See SOURCE.

can be materially reduced by eliminating some of these elements or by adding new ones that are consonant with the knowledge of the action taken. The net effect of this would be to increase the proportion of relevant cognitive elements that are consonant with the action taken and hence to lessen the total dissonance that exists.

Whether or not a person is successful in reducing dissonance in this manner will depend in part on his mental agility and in part on the availability of support of one kind or another for the changes he wishes to make in his cognition. He may now be able to magnify the importance of the good points associated with the chosen alternative and to think of new advantages that he hadn't thought of before. He may be able to discover new information that favors the decision he took or to get others to agree with his action. Let us consider a hypothetical example to elucidate the process.

Imagine a person who has had to make a choice between going to a concert and accepting a friend's invitation to dinner, both being desirable activities for him. Further imagine that he accepts the dinner invitation, thus giving up the possibility of hearing the concert. He may now attempt to think of every bad thing he can about the concert. He may be very familiar with the works to be played which lessens the advantage of going to the concert. Or he may not be at all familiar with some of the things to be played, and he knows well from past experience that he doesn't get much out of hearing something for the first time. He might even reread a review of the last performance which happens to have been highly critical. In like manner he may try to think of attractive things about the evening he will spend in good social company.

Of course, the attempt to reduce dissonance might not be successful. The concert program might give no scope to his ingenious mind. The review he recalled as critical and reread might re-emphasize for him many favorable factors. And when he gets to his dinner party he might get into a conversation with someone else who wishes he had been able to go to the concert. Whether or not he gets support will determine, in part, the efficacy of these attempts.

Establishing Cognitive Overlap

As may be recalled from our previous discussion, the more the cognitive elements corresponding to the different alternatives involved in a decision are alike, the less is the resulting dissonance. Postdecision dissonance can consequently be reduced by establishing or inventing cognitive overlap. This type of reduction of dissonance is also stressed by Adams in the previously cited article. In discussing a boy who has made a decision between playing ball and going to the circus, for example, he states:

> . . . our boy restructures the situation (and hence the sentiments in-volved) and experiences an insight such that the conflicting consummatory values are seen as alternative instruments or means to a single one. . . . Thus our boy may perceive for the first time that ball game and circus are both means to recreation in general . . . [p. 554].

In other words, one way of establishing cognitive overlap is to take elements corresponding to each of the alternatives and to put them in a context where they lead to the same end result. If this is accomplished, some cognitive elements are identical in this larger context, and dissonance is reduced.

It is also possible to establish cognitive overlap in a more direct fashion. Let us briefly revert to our example of the person who accepted the dinner party invitation. Following the decision, he may remind himself that his friend has a very good collection of records. Indeed, once there he might even suggest that some music be played. Or if he had alternatively chosen to go to the concert, he might consider that he would probably meet many of his friends at the concert and that afterward they would undoubtedly spend some time together socially. In other words, cognitive overlap may be established by discovering or creating elements corresponding to the chosen alternative that are identical with favorable elements that already exist for the corresponding unchosen alternative.

Detailed discussion of the possible reduction of dissonance by lowering the importance of the whole matter has been omitted, but it must be remembered that it can and does occur. Our hunch is that it is not a major manifestation of the pressure to reduce postdecision dissonance.

Summary

Dissonance has been shown to be an inevitable consequence of a decision. The magnitude of the postdecision dissonance has been hypothesized to depend upon the following factors:

1. The importance of the decision.
2. The relative attractiveness of the unchosen alternative to the chosen one.

3. The degree of overlap of cognitive elements corresponding to the alternatives.

Once dissonance exists following a decision, the pressure to reduce it will manifest itself in attempts to increase the relative attractiveness of the chosen alternative, to decrease the relative attractiveness of the unchosen alternative, to establish cognitive overlap, or possibly to revoke the decision psychologically.

The operational problems of testing this theory will be dealt with in the next chapter* where data relevant to postdecision dissonance will be considered.

References

ADAMS, D. K. Conflict and integration. *J. Personality*, 1954, **22**, 548–56.

HEIDER, F. The psychology of interpersonal relations. Unpublished manuscript.

HOVLAND, C., & SEARS, R. R. Experiments on motor conflict. I. Types of conflict and modes of resolution. *J. exp. Psychol.*, 1938, **23**, 477–93.

LEWIN, K. *A dynamic theory of personality.* New York: McGraw-Hill, 1935.

_____. *Field theory in social science.* New York: Harper, 1951.

_____. Group decision and social change. In Swanson, G., Newcomb, T., & Hartley, E. (eds.). *Readings in social psychology.* New York: Henry Holt, 1952.

MYRDAL, G. *An American dilemma.* New York: Harper, 1944.

OSGOOD, C. E., & TANNENBAUM, P. The principle of congruity and the prediction of attitude change. *Psychol. Rev.*, 1955, **62**, 42–55.

SMOCK, C. D. The influence of stress on the perception of incongruity. *J. abnorm. soc. Psychol.*, 1955, **50**, 354–62.

SPIRO, M. Ghosts: An anthropological inquiry into learning and perception. *J. abnorm. soc. Psychol.*, 1953, **48**, 376–82.

*See SOURCE.

10

The Arousal
and Reduction
of Dissonance
in Social Contexts

The theory of dissonance is a theory concerning psychological processes which go on, somehow, inside of the individual organism. The core notions of the theory are extremely simple. These notions are that the simultaneous existence of cognitions which in one way or another do not fit together (dissonance) leads to effort on the part of the person to somehow make them fit better (dissonance reduction).

Of course, in order to make these notions amenable to empirical test and to give them predictive power, one must specify the conditions under which dissonance exists, the ways in which dissonance may be reduced, and the observable manifestations of attempts at dissonance reduction.

We cannot, in this chapter, take the space to spell these things out. A detailed and more formal account of the theory and related research may be found elsewhere (10). What we will concentrate on here is the explication of how this theory concerning individual psychological process has relevance for, and can help us make predictions about, social behavior and group behavior. The chapter will consist of three parts: (a) some introductory material to give the reader some impression of the scope of the theory and the kinds of behavior involved in dissonance

SOURCE: Festinger, L., & Aronson, E. In Cartwright & Zander, *Group dynamics.* New York: Row, Peterson, 1960, 214–231.

reduction; (b) consideration of the group as a source of dissonance arousal; and (c) as an aid in the reduction of dissonance.

Throughout the chapter we will attempt to discuss the theory in connection with empirical data concentrating, for the most part, on recent material, that is, data which have been collected since the publication of the theory (10).

Some Derivations from Dissonance Theory

Although the theory is, in essence, a very simple one, it can be used to predict a wide range of human behavior. A few of the ramifications of the theory will be discussed below. It should be stressed that in the majority of the experiments to be discussed only one avenue of dissonance reduction has been examined. This is not meant to imply, however, that only one means of dissonance reduction is possible in a particular situation. On the contrary, in uncontrolled situations many avenues for dissonance reduction are usually available.

Suppose, for example, that a person believes that the Democratic presidential candidate is the most qualified candidate for the position. For some reason, however, he votes for the Republican candidate. His cognition that the Democratic candidate is more qualified is dissonant with his cognition that he voted for the Republican candidate. This person might attempt to reduce dissonance by convincing himself that the Republican candidate is better than he had, at first, believed or that the Democratic candidate is less good. Such a change in his opinions would bring them more into line with his knowledge that he had voted for the Republican candidate.

His specific behaviors might involve: (a) subscribing to a Republican newspaper (where he'd be sure to read complimentary statements about the Republican candidate and derogatory statements about the Democratic candidate); (b) trying to associate with Republicans and trying to avoid Democrats; (c) trying to find subtle wisdom in the speeches of the Republican candidate which he hadn't noticed before, and the like. We have selected experiments for discussion below in an attempt to illustrate not only the variety of situations which produce dissonance but also the variety of ways in which dissonance reduction proceeds.

Dissonance as a Consequence of Decisions

If an individual chooses one from among several possible courses of action, he is almost certain to experience dissonance because the chosen alternative is seldom entirely positive and the unchosen alternatives are seldom entirely negative. His cognitions concerning any negative aspects of the chosen alternative are dissonant with his cognition that he chose it. Similarly, his cognitions concerning any positive aspects of the unchosen alternatives are dissonant with his cognition that he rejected these alternatives. Consequently, the greater the attractiveness of the rejected alternative relative to the chosen alternative, the greater will be the dissonance.

The theory of dissonance predicts that, following a decision, a person will attempt to convince himself that the chosen alternative is even more attractive (relative to the unchosen one) than he had previously thought.

Brehm (5) demonstrated that, following a decision between two alternatives, there was a general tendency for people to rate the chosen alternative as being slightly more attractive than they had previously rated it; and to rate the rejected alternative as being slightly less attractive than they had previously rated it. Furthermore, Brehm found that the more nearly equal the initial attractiveness of the alternatives had been, the stronger was the effect obtained. In other words, dissonance reduction did ensue following a decision and the amount of dissonance reduction was related to the magnitude of dissonance created by the decision.

A subsequent experiment by Brehm and Cohen (7) tested two more implications concerning post-decision dissonance:

1. The greater the number of alternatives among which a person must choose, the greater would be the dissonance following the choice. The more alternatives which were rejected, the more knowledge there would be concerning favorable characteristics of these rejected alternatives. These cognitions would all be dissonant with the cognition concerning the alternative which the person actually chose.

2. The greater the qualitative dissimilarity between the alternatives among which the person must choose the greater would be the post-decision dissonance (assuming that the relative attractiveness of the alternatives is held constant). This follows from the fact that similar alternatives have many characteristics in common. Thus, some of the favorable aspects of the rejected alternatives are also favorable aspects of the chosen alternative. Cognitions concerning these aspects of similarity would not, hence, contribute to dissonance following the choice.

Brehm and Cohen asked children to rate how much they liked various toys. The experimenters explained that they were employed by toy manufacturers to find out what kind of toys people like. One week later they returned and offered the children a choice of one of the toys as a gift for having participated in the research. The children were then asked once more to rate how much they liked each of the toys. In this experiment, two variables were manipulated: (a) The number of alternatives. Some children were allowed to choose from among four toys; some children were given a choice between two toys. (b) The qualitative similarity of the alternatives. Some children had to choose from among toys which were qualitatively similar; e.g., swimming fins vs. swimming masks. Other children had to choose from among toys where were qualitatively dissimilar; e.g., swimming fins vs. archery sets.

The results supported both hypotheses. Regardless of the qualitative similarity of the toys, the greater the number of alternatives, the more the liking for the chosen toy increased and the more the liking for the unchosen toy decreased. Likewise, regardless of the number of alternatives, the greater the qualitative dissimilarity among the alternatives, the greater was the observed change in the attractiveness of the toys in the direction of dissonance reduction.

Dissonance Arising from Temptation

If an individual commits an act which he regards as immoral in order to obtain a reward, his cognition that the act is immoral is dissonant with his cognition that he committed it. One way in which he could reduce this dissonance would be by changing his attitudes concerning the morality of the act, i.e., by convincing himself that the act is not very immoral. Thus, dissonance theory predicts that after a person has committed an immoral act, his attitudes concerning that act will be more lenient than they previously were.

On the other hand, if a person resists temptation and does not commit the act, his cognitions about the rewards he gave up are dissonant with his cognition concerning his behavior. Once again, he could reduce dissonance by changing his attitudes concerning the morality of the act. In this instance, the theory predicts that, after a person has resisted the temptation to commit an immoral act, his attitudes concerning the morality of the act will be more severe than they previously were. This would reduce dissonance by helping to justify the fact that he forsook the reward. The magnitude of the dissonance experienced by a person who commits an immoral act will, of course, be greater if the rewards he obtained by committing the act are small. Conversely, the magnitude of dissonance in the person who refrains from committing the immoral act will be greater if the reward he gave up by not engaging in the act is large.

These hypotheses were tested by Mills (16) in an experiment involving sixth-grade students. After measuring his subjects' attitudes toward cheating, the experimenter had them participate in a contest with prizes offered. In some classes a small prize was offered, in others a large prize. During the contest it was possible for the subjects to cheat. As may be expected, some of the students cheated while others did not.

One day later the subjects were again asked to indicate their attitudes toward cheating. The results confirmed the hypothesis. In general, those children who cheated became more lenient toward cheating, while those who did not cheat became more severe toward cheating. Again, the magnitude of this effect was a function of how much dissonance was introduced experimentally. Those children who cheated for a small prize changed more in feeling lenient about cheating than those who cheated for a large prize. Among those who did not cheat, the changes in the direction of greater severity toward cheating were larger for those who gave up a large prize by not cheating than for those who gave up only a small prize.

Dissonance Resulting from Effort

If an individual is in a situation in which he continues to expend effort in order to reach some goal, yet does not reach it, he will experience dissonance. His cognition that he is expending effort would be dissonant with his cognition that he is unrewarded. One way in which he could reduce dissonance would be by finding something about the situation to which he could attach value. Thus, an unsuccessful prospector might reduce dissonance by marveling at the magnificent beauty of the surrounding terrain; an unsuccessful fisherman might do so by boasting of the beautiful tan he received while wading through the streams or by becoming enamored of the skill involved in casting.

Aronson (2) tested these implications of the theory of dissonance in the laboratory. His subjects were given a task to perform in order to obtain rewards. Each subject was rewarded on about one-third of the trials. For some subjects the task was almost effortless while for others it involved considerable expenditures of effort and energy. For all subjects, the stimuli terminating a trial were different on rewarded trials from what they were on unrewarded trials. Specifically, on each trial the subject obtained a container. On rewarded trials the containers were red and contained money. On unrewarded trials the containers were green and empty. The subjects were asked to rate the relative attractiveness of the two colors both before and after the experiment.

The prediction was that, in the *Effortful* condition, the unrewarded color would become relatively more attractive than in the *Easy* condition. According to the theory, in the *Effortful* condition, each time the subject pulled out an unrewarded container, his cognition that the container was empty would be dissonant with his cognition that he exerted effort to obtain it. It was predicted that in order to reduce dissonance, the subject would attach value to the unrewarded color. In this way, he could justify the expenditure of effort by convincing himself that the sight of the color was worth working for even though it contained no money. In the *Easy* condition, since very little effort was expended, very little dissonance was created. Hence, one would expect no tendency to attach positive value to the unrewarded color.

The results are in line with the theoretical expectations. The *Easy* condition, where little or no dissonance was introduced on unrewarded trials, provides a baseline from which shifts in color preference may be evaluated. It happens that the *Easy* condition there is a marked shift of preference toward the *rewarded* color. In the *Effortful* condition, where dissonance was present on nonrewarded trials, the effects of dissonance reduction counterbalance this other effect. A large and clear difference is obtained between the Dissonance (Effortful) condition and the No Dissonance (Easy) condition in the relative preference of the two colors.

Dissonance Introduced by a Fait Accompli

Very often persons find themselves in a position where they must endure some unpleasant situation. The cognition a person has that the situation is or will be unpleasant is dissonant with his cognition that he must endure it. One way in which he can reduce this dissonance is by convincing himself that the situation is not as unpleasant as it first appeared. Brehm (6) induced eighth-grade children to eat a disliked vegetable (in school) by offering them a small reward. While eating, the children in the *experimental* condition were told that their parents would be informed which vegetable they had eaten; this strongly implied that they would be expected to eat more of this vegetable at home. The children in the *control* condition were told nothing. All of the subjects were asked to rate their liking for the vegetable both before and after the experiment. Those subjects who were led to anticipate that they would be eating more of the vegetable at home showed a significantly greater increase in their rated fondness for the vegetable than did the subjects in the *control* condition.

In the preceding several pages we have presented an extremely brief statement concerning the theory of dissonance and a few scattered illustrations of experimental studies on the reduction of dissonance in a variety of contexts. The theoretical statement is not intended as a complete, formal presentation nor are the studies discussed intended to be an adequate coverage of the relevant empirical data. The purpose was, rather, to present as briefly as possible some overall understanding of the theory of dissonance, the kinds of situations which arouse dissonance and the kinds of effects one may anticipate as a result of dissonance reduction.

It has been illustrated by our previous discussion that an individual can experience and reduce dissonance strictly as a result of his own actions. Other people need not be involved in the process. But an individual's interactions with other people may, in itself, be a source of dissonance. Moreover, an individual may utilize his interactions with other people as a means of reducing dissonance. In the following two sections we will discuss, and introduce more empirical data concerning the arousal and reduction of dissonance in situations which are primarily social. It should be emphasized, however, that the social context does not introduce anything qualitatively different into the processes of arousal and reduction of dissonance. Sometimes a social context introduces greater complexities; sometimes a social context makes it more difficult or even impossible for a person to avoid the introduction of dissonance into his cognitions; and sometimes a social context can make it spectacularly easy to reduce dissonance.

These latter aspects of dissonance arousal and reduction in social contexts are, of course, the ones that will be stressed in the following pages. The reader will, however, note the conceptual similarity between the experiments we have discussed in the preceding pages and the ones we will discuss in the remainder of this chapter.

Group Interaction as a Source of Dissonance

Dissonance Arising from Faulty Anticipation of Social Environment

An individual does not usually have good control over his social environment. One way in which this manifests itself is in his partial inability to predict the nature of the groups to which he exposes himself. For example, a person might go out on a blind date, join a club, or accept an invitation to a cocktail party, only to find the people to be less pleasant than he had anticipated. If he had not expended any time or effort in exposing himself to the group, he would experience little or no dissonance. But if he had invested a great deal in order to interact with these people—e.g., if he had driven fifty miles to pick up his date, or paid a huge admission fee to join the club, or neglected preparing for an exam to go to the cocktail party—he would experience dissonance. His cognitions concerning his investment of time and effort would be dissonant with his cognitions concerning the negative aspects of the group.

There are at least two ways that a person could reduce dissonance in such a situation: (a) He could undervalue the amount of his investment, that is, convince himself that the effort or expense was really negligible, or (b) he could overvalue the group by emphasizing its positive aspects and blinding himself to its negative aspects.

This kind of situation was simulated in a laboratory experiment by Aronson and Mills (3). In this experiment, college women volunteered to join a group for the purpose of participating in a series of discussions on the psychology of sex. The subjects were randomly assigned to one of three experimental conditions: a *severe initiation* condition, a *mild initiation* condition, and a *no initiation* condition. In the *severe* and *mild initiation* conditions each subject was told that, in order to gain admission to the group, she would be required to demonstrate that she was sophisticated enough to participate freely and frankly in a sexually oriented discussion. An "embarrassment test" was then administered in which the subject read aloud some sexually oriented material in the presence of the male experimenter. The experimenter explained that he would judge from her performance whether or not she qualified for admission to the group. In the *severe initiation* condition the "embarrassment test" consisted of the reciting of a number of obscene words plus some lurid sexual passages from contemporary novels. In the *mild initiation* condition the subjects were simply required to recite a short list of rather genteel sexually oriented words. In the *no initiation* condition the subject was allowed to enter the group without going through any initiation.

Each of the subjects then listened to the same tape recording of a group discussion which she believed was a live discussion being conducted by the group she had just joined. The recording was a rather dull, banal, and irrelevant discussion of the secondary sex behavior of lower animals. The participants spoke haltingly, inarticulately and unenthusiastically. Immediately after listening to the tape recording, each subject was asked to rate the discussion and the group members on several evaluative scales; e.g., dull-interesting, intelligent-unintelligent, etc.

The experimenters reasoned that, in the *severe initiation* condition, the subjects would experience dissonance; their cognition that they had undergone an extremely embarrassing experience to become a member of a group would be dissonant with their cognitions concerning the negative aspects of the group. They could reduce the dissonance by distorting their perceptions of the discussion in a positive direction. In the *no initiation* and *mild initiation* conditions, however, the subjects made relatively little investment in order to enter the group and hence, would not be expected to experience much dissonance. It was expected, then, that the subjects in the *severe initiation* condition would rate the group as being more attractive than the subjects in either the *mild* or *no initiation* conditions. The results strongly supported the prediction. The subjects in the *no initiation* and *mild initiation* conditions were generally unimpressed by the discussion. Those in the *severe initiation* condition, however, felt that the discussion was quite interesting and intelligent. They also liked the other group members better.

Dissonance Aroused by Disagreement with Others

When a person is confronted with an opinion contrary to his own which is held by people like himself, he experiences dissonance. The cognitions corresponding to his own opinions are dissonant with the cognition that these other persons hold differing opinions. It is almost impossible to avoid the introduction of such dissonance unless one altogether avoids any social interaction. One may be very attracted to a person or group of people because of shared interests and even shared opinions. But inevitably there will be some disagreement on matters of concern to the person.

There is considerable evidence from laboratory experimentation that the magnitude of the dissonance thus introduced will depend upon: (a) the importance of the person or group that voices the disagreement (4, 9); and (b) the importance and relevance to the individual of the issue concerning which the disagreement exists (17). There is also considerable evidence concerning the ways in which a person will attempt to reduce such dissonance. In general, he may attempt to convince himself that the content area in which the disagreement exists is relatively unimportant; he may attempt to derogate the person or group that disagrees with him; he may attempt to eliminate the disagreement either by changing his own opinion or attempting to influence the disagreeing persons to change theirs; or he may seek additional social support for the opinion he holds, thus, in essence, adding new cognitions which are consonant with his own opinions.

There are two major theoretical questions in this area about which there has not been much experimental evidence until recently. One question concerns the relation between the extent of disagreement and the magnitude of dissonance resulting from the disagreement. The other question concerns the conditions under which the dissonance will be reduced primarily by derogating the person who disagrees or primarily by attempting to lessen or eliminate the disagreement. We will discuss these two questions together, because, as will be seen, they are intertwined.

On purely theoretical grounds one would expect the magnitude of dissonance to increase as the extent of disagreement from someone else increases. Let us, for example, consider a person who believes that milk is very good for adults and everyone should drink at least one quart of milk a day. Let us suppose that he discovered that a friend of his believed that milk is poisonously harmful to adults and they should never drink milk. This would introduce more dissonance than if this friend only believed that one quart a day was too much and might be harmful and that, hence, adults should only drink one or two glasses of milk a day. If greater extent of disagreement implies greater magnitude of dissonance, then one should observe more attempts at dissonance reduction as extent of disagreement increases. Since opinion change is one means of reducing dissonance, one would expect that the more the extent of disagreement, the greater would be the ensuing opinion change.

Experimental work on the relation between extent of disagreement and amount of opinion change has not, however, yielded very consistent results (14, 15). Sometimes greater disagreement seems to result in more opinion change and sometimes in less opinion change. There are two possible explanations for these variable findings. It is possible that, if the disagreement is too extreme, that is, outside of the range that the present regards as a reasonable position, the dissonance introduced is rather negligible. Another possible explanation is that, as the extent of disagreement increases, the tendency to reduce dissonance primarily by derogating the disagreeing person also increases. If this were true, then an experiment which only measured opinion change and did not control the ease with which the disagreeing person could be derogated, might indeed be expected to show variable effects since these two are alternative methods of reducing dissonance.

Zimbardo (18) performed an experiment designed to yield results which would help choose between these two possible interpretations. In his study he attempted to minimize the possible use of derogation of the disagreeing person to reduce dissonance by always having the disagreement come from a very close friend. Eighty college women privately gave their opinion regarding the locus of blame in a hypothetical juvenile delinquency problem. Each of the subjects was then confronted

with the alleged opinion of a close friend with whom she had been simultaneously exposed to the problem. After a short lapse of time, each
subject was asked to state her opinion again.

Two variables were manipulated—the degree of involvement in the
problem and the degree of the discrepancy of opinion. One half of the
subjects were told that their opinion in the case was extremely important since it provided a good index of their personality, etc., . . . (high
involvement). The other half of the subjects were told that their opinion
in the case was inconsequential (low involvement). At the same time,
one half of the subjects were led to believe that the opinion of their
friend was extremely discrepant from their own while one half of the
subjects were led to believe that it was only slightly discrepant from
their own. "Extremely discrepant" in this study was defined as being in
a range which the subject had previously indicated was unreasonable
and indefensible.

On the assumption that derogation of a close friend would not occur,
change in opinion was used as an index of dissonance reduction. The
results showed that (a) the more involved a subject was, the more she
tended to shift her opinion in the direction of that of her friend; (b) the
greater the discrepancy between a subject's opinion and her friend's
opinion, the more she tended to shift her opinion in the direction of that
of her friend.

In short, the experiment by Zimbardo presents clear evidence that
the magnitude of dissonance introduced by disagreement from another
person does increase as the extent of the disagreement increases, even
where the disagreeing person voices an opinion outside of the range that
the person considers acceptable and reasonable. If alternative methods
of dissonance reduction such as derogating the source of the disagreement are ruled out, then the effects of the greater magnitude of dissonance can be measured by opinion change.

One more point remains to be demonstrated in order to strengthen
this interpretation. It is necessary to show that, if derogation of the
source of the disagreement is not ruled out as a possibility, then such
derogation becomes increasingly preferred as a means of dissonance reduction as the extent of disagreement increases. Unfortunately, no controlled experimental studies exist on this point. There is relevant evidence, however, from a field study by Adams, et al. (1) in which the
tendency to derogate the disagreer and the tendency to change one's
attitudes in the direction of the disagreer were studied simultaneously
as alternative manifestations of increased dissonance. In this study, married women were interviewed regarding their attitudes on the proper
time to begin toilet training. Two weeks later, the interviewers returned

and asked each subject to read a short and rather credible booklet which strongly advocated that training should not begin until the child is twenty-four months old. The subjects were then immediately reinterviewed regarding their attitudes toward toilet training and their opinion of the booklet. The experimenters compared the responses of subjects whose views were widely discrepant from those advocated in the pamphlet with the responses of subjects whose views were close to those advocated by the pamphlet.

The results show rather clearly the simultaneous operation of the two avenues of dissonance reduction. Those for whom the pamphlet did not introduce much dissonance tend not to derogate it. Only 19% of these people say that it was unfair, biased or the like. The comparable figure for those in whom the pamphlet introduced considerable dissonance is 59%. Certainly, the tendency to derogate the communication increased as the magnitude of dissonance increased. Furthermore, there are relatively few instances of opinion change among those who derogate the pamphlet. Among those who do not derogate the pamphlet, however, there is considerable opinion change and the amount of opinion change increases as the magnitude of dissonance increases. This latter point, of course, confirms the finding from the Zimbardo experiment.

Dissonance Resulting from Forced Public Compliance

There are many circumstances under which a group will force a person to behave overtly in a manner contrary to his beliefs. When this occurs, the person experiences dissonance. His cognition that he performed the overt act would be dissonant with his opinions and beliefs. One way in which a person could reduce dissonance would be by changing his beliefs to bring them more in line with his overt behavior.

Under what conditions will such dissonance be maximal? Suppose a great deal of force is brought to bear in order to induce a person to make a public statement which is contrary to his private opinion; e.g., suppose he is offered a great reward if he makes the statement. The size of the reward serves as a justification for making the statement. That is, recognition that he will receive a great reward for making the public statement is consonant with his cognition that he made the statement. The greater the reward the greater the consonance, and hence, the less over-all dissonance. Conversely, if a person makes a public statement which is dissonant with his beliefs in order to receive a small reward, there is little justification for having made the statement. Since there is little consonance between making the statement and receiving a small reward, the over-all dissonance will be greater. Thus, dissonance theory leads to the following prediction: If a person makes a public statement which he does not believe to be true, in order to receive a small reward, he will change his private belief in the direction of the public statement; increasing the size of the reward will decrease the degree to which he will change his private opinion.

This prediction was tested in a study of Festinger and Carlsmith (11). In this experiment, subjects performed a series of extremely boring and tedious tasks for one hour. After they had finished the tasks, the experimenter falsely "explained the purpose of the experiment." The subjects were told that the purpose of the experiment was to see whether people perform better if they are told beforehand that the tasks are interesting and enjoyable than if they are not told anything. Each subject was told that he was in the control condition; that is, he had not been told anything ahead of time about the tasks. The experimenter explained that in the experimental condition, an accomplice poses as a subject who has just finished the experiment, and tells the waiting subject that the task was a lot of fun. The experimenter then appeared very uncomfortable and explained to the subject that a girl was now waiting to be tested and the accomplice had not shown up yet. He then asked the subject if he would do him a favor and substitute for the accomplice and tell the waiting subject that the tasks are interesting and fun. He offered to pay the subject for doing this and for serving as a substitute accomplice in case of future emergencies.

The subjects were run in one of three conditions: (a) a $1 condition, in which the subjects were paid $1 for serving as an accomplice; (b) a $20 condition, in which the subjects were paid $20 for the same job; and (c) a control condition in which the subjects were not asked to lie to the waiting subject.

Each subject was then interviewed (by a different experimenter) and was asked to rate how enjoyable the tasks were. The results supported the predictions made from the theory. In the control condition and the $20 condition, the subjects felt the tasks were rather unenjoyable; there was no difference between the ratings made by the subjects in these two conditions. In the $1 condition, however, the subjects rated the tasks as rather enjoyable. The ratings of the tasks by the subjects in the $1 condition were significantly more positive than those in either the $20 condition or the control condition. In short, forcing a person to make a public statement which was contrary to his private belief introduced considerable dissonance when the reward offered for making the public statement was small. Under these circumstances the person reduces dissonance by changing his private opinion so as to lessen the discrepancy between what he privately believes and what he has publicly said. If too much force is applied to elicit the overt behavior, the dissonance aroused is correspondingly less and private change of opinion does not occur.

We have tried to illustrate in the preceding section some of the variety of ways in which groups and other persons arouse dissonance in an individual and the ways in which such dissonance tends to be reduced. We have given three examples; namely, (a) dissonance introduced by the behavior of others in providing or not providing satisfactions for the individual; (b) dissonance introduced by the expression of disagreement; and (c) dissonance introduced when others force an individual to behave in manners contrary to his private beliefs. Interaction with other people and membership in groups are not, however, only potentially dissonance arousing. There is also another side to the coin. Other people and groups can be and are used as a very effective means of reducing dissonance which has been introduced in some way. We will proceed, in the next section, to a discussion of this aspect of interaction with other people.

Group Interaction
as a Means of Reducing Dissonance

When a person experiences dissonance, he can use his interactions with other people as a means of reducing the dissonance. In general, there are two processes involved here:

1. He can reduce dissonance by obtaining support from people who already believe what he wants to persuade himself about.
2. He can reduce dissonance by persuading others that they too should believe what he wants to persuade himself about.

Individuals can and do employ both of these methods simultaneously. But something can also be said concerning the conditions under which one or the other will be used primarily. If a person's cognitions regarding an opinion are largely consonant before he is confronted with someone who disagrees with him, this disagreer is the main source of dissonance. In this situation, one would expect that an individual would attempt to reduce the dissonance by trying to convince the other person to change his opinion. On the other hand, if a person has been exposed to a great deal of evidence contrary to an opinion he holds and he is then confronted with someone who disagrees, his cognition that the

other person disagrees with him adds relatively little to his total dissonance. He might attempt to induce the disagreer to change his mind;
but since the disagreer is not the major source of dissonance, influencing
him would accomplish relatively little. This person is more likely to seek
social support from persons who hold the same opinion he does. Persons
who agree with him will very likely help reduce his dissonance by providing new information and new arguments consonant with his opinion
and by discrediting arguments which are dissonant with the opinion.

This distinction can be illustrated by comparing two experiments. In
an experiment by Festinger and Thibaut (13) small groups of college
students were presented with a problem to discuss. The problem was
especially selected so as to elicit a wide range of opinions. Each of the
members of the group was asked to state his opinion regarding the best
solution to the problem. This was done by marking a point on a seven-
point scale which represented the range of possible solutions. The scale
rating of each person's opinion was placed on a white card in front of
him in plain view of all of the other members of the group. The subjects
were then allowed to discuss the problem by writing notes to one another for twenty minutes. Each note that a subject wrote could be sent
to only one person.

What would one expect concerning the pattern of communication in
such a situation? After having formed an opinion, each person of course,
discovered that several people in the group disagreed with him. This
introduced dissonance regarding his opinion; the more extreme the disagreement the greater was the dissonance. One would expect that each
person should direct the majority of his communications to the group
members who disagree with him most. Furthermore, one would expect
these communications to be mainly attempts to persuade the other person to change his opinion. The results are quite consistent with this line
of reasoning. The notes that were written were almost exclusively attempts to persuade others and from 70% to 90% of all notes were addressed to members who held extreme opinions.

In contrast, let us examine the situation which was created in an experiment by Brodbeck (8). Groups of subjects were brought together
and each subject was asked to indicate his opinion, privately, regarding
the use of wire tapping by law enforcement officers. This issue was used
because there was considerable spread of opinion concerning it. They
were also asked to rate how confident they were of their opinion. The
subjects then listened to an authoritative speech on the issue. For one
half of the groups, the speech was a strong argument in favor of wire
tapping while for the other half of the groups the speech was a strong

argument against wire tapping. Thus, some subjects in each group were exposed to a persuasive communication which was in disagreement with their previously stated belief while other subjects in each group were exposed to a persuasive communication which supported their previously stated belief. After listening to the speech, each subject was asked, once again, to indicate whether he was for or against wire tapping and how confident he was of his opinion.

On the basis of the procedure thus far, the subjects could be divided into three classes: (a) *Consonant subjects;* those subjects whose initial opinions were supported by the communication. (b) *Strongly dissonant subjects;* those for whom the disagreeing speech had sufficient impact so that they lowered the confidence they had in their initial opinion. (c) *Mildly dissonant subjects;* those whose opinions disagreed with the communication but who did *not* lower the confidence they had in their initial opinions.

In the second session of the experiment, four *consonant* subjects and four *dissonant* subjects were selected from each group so that in each of these second session groups there were four persons in favor of and four opposed to wire tapping. They were placed in a room, each sitting behind a clearly visible placard which stated his opinion. The experimenter then informed them that the group was going to split up into pairs to discuss the issue and asked them to list the two persons with whom they would most like to discuss the issue. The *strongly dissonant* subjects more frequently wanted to discuss the matter with persons who agreed with them than did the *consonant* subjects. These results can be interpreted as indicating that the *consonant* subjects wanted to reduce what little dissonance they felt by converting those people who introduced the dissonance; i.e., those people who disagreed with them. They had little need to discuss the issue with individuals who held the same opinion. For the *strongly dissonant* subjects, however, the presence of people who disagreed with them was a relatively minor source of dissonance. Their primary source of dissonance was introduced by the communication. By discussing their opinions with persons who agreed with them they were more likely to gain the information and support needed to reduce this dissonance. The *mildly dissonant* subjects yielded results between the other two classes of subjects.

There are additional data from the Brodbeck experiment to support the interpretation offered above; namely, the *strongly dissonant* subjects wanted social support from those who agreed with them in order to reduce the dissonance introduced by the persuasive communication. The second session group of eight subjects did not split up into pairs but actually proceeded to discuss the issue in the total group. After this discussion they were once more asked to state their opinion on the issue and the confidence they had in this opinion.

It should be stressed again that in the group which carried on the discussion there were four persons on each side of the issue. It is interesting to note, therefore that, following this discussion, the *strongly dissonant* subjects had, on the average, completely regained the confidence in their initial opinion which they had before having listened to the dissonance introducing speech. In other words, these subjects indicated, by their choice of the persons with whom they wanted to discuss the issue, that they wanted support for their shaken opinions. They then proceeded to obtain such support and regained their confidence even in a situation where half the members of the group disagreed with them. Clearly, they either listened more carefully or gave more weight to the arguments advanced in the discussion by those that agreed with them.

This kind of phenomenon can be seen more clearly and dramatically, as one might expect, in real life situations. An example of this may be taken from a study by Festinger, Riecken, and Schachter (12). The study involved the systematic observation of the behavior of a group of people who firmly believed that the world would end by a cataclysm on a certain date and, in many ways, had committed themselves heavily to this belief.

The investigators were concerned with the effects on these people when their prophecy failed to be confirmed. The cognitions concerning the tremendous sacrifices they had made for their beliefs would be dissonant with their cognition that their beliefs were wrong. They could reduce this dissonance by convincing themselves that their beliefs were correct in spite of the fact that their specific prophecy was disconfirmed. They might accomplish this in at least two ways:

1. *By receiving social support from one another.* That is, by finding an explanation for the disconfirmation and convincing one another that it is a valid one.

2. *By proselyting other people.* By convincing outsiders that their beliefs are valid, they could add cognitions consonant with maintaining their beliefs and remaining in the movement.

On the night of the expected cataclysm, most of the believers gathered at a member's home where they were to await a flying saucer which was to rescue them at midnight. Several of the members, however, were instructed to wait by themselves at their own homes. When midnight came and passed, the group was overwhelmingly disappointed. They could not at first believe that their prophecy had not been fulfilled. When they finally grew to realize that the cataclysm would not be forthcoming they struggled to find a reason why. For several hours the believers kept assuring one another of the validity of their movement and they kept insisting to one another that an explanation would be forthcoming. Finally, they put forth the explanation that the earth was not destroyed precisely because of their belief and their faith. The group was able to accept and believe this explanation because they could support one another and convince each other that this was, in fact, a valid explanation. Although their belief was momentarily shaken by the disconfirmation, the members were able to maintain their membership in the movement because of the mutual social support which they received. Furthermore, the conviction of the members who had waited together did not show any signs of faltering several weeks after the disconfirmation (when the study was concluded). In fact, so powerful was the increased social support that two of the members who had occasionally expressed mild skepticism about a few tenets of the movement, now firmly believed all of them. The importance of the social support in reducing dissonance, moreover, is shown by the contrast provided by those members of the movement, who had waited for the fulfillment of the prophecy alone in their own homes. These persons did not maintain their beliefs. Without the continuous social support of their fellow members, the dissonance created by the disconfirmation was sufficient to cause them to renounce their belief in the movement in spite of their heavy commitment to it.

Perhaps even a more striking aspect of the effects of disconfirmation involved the proselyting behavior of the believers who remained believers. Prior to the disconfirmation, attempts on the part of the believers at convincing people of the validity of their movement were rather mild. For months before the disconfirmation they seemed to have little desire to attract new believers. They felt that those who had been chosen to be saved would join the group of their own accord. Hence, all visitors who expressed interest in the movement were treated casually; no attempt was made to sell the movement to them and very little information about the movement was given to them. There were even periods when the members were specifically instructed not to speak to outsiders. No attempt was made to attract publicity. On the contrary, all attempts on the part of the press to obtain interviews were rebuffed.

Immediately after the disconfirmation, the behavior of the believers changed dramatically. On four successive days they called press conferences, gave lengthy interviews and posed for pictures. They also attempted to attract new members. They invited the public and press to attend a meeting at which they sang songs while awaiting the appearance of a spaceman "who might come."

In summary, the believers, by engaging in mutual social support and proselyting new members, were able to reduce dissonance sufficiently to enable themselves to maintain their beliefs. Those members of the group who had been cut off from social support at the crucial time were unable to maintain these beliefs following the failure of the prophecy.

═══════

This chapter was prepared especially for *Group dynamics* by Leon Festinger and Elliot Aronson.

References

1. ADAMS, J. S., MACCOBY, N., ROMNEY, A. K., & MACCOBY, E. The effects of a persuasive communication on opinion change and rejection of the communication. Unpublished study, Stanford Univ.

2. ARONSON, E. The effect of effort on the intrinsic attractiveness of a stimulus. Unpublished doctoral dissertation, Stanford Univ., 1959.

3. ARONSON, E., & MILLS, J. The effect of severity of initiation on liking for a group. *J. abnorm. soc. Psychol.*, 1959, **59**, 177–181.

4. BACK, K. The exertion of influence through social communication. *J. abnorm. soc. Psychol.*, 1951, **46**, 9–24.

5. BREHM, J. Post-decision changes in desirability of alternatives. *J. abnorm. soc. Psychol.*, 1956, **52**, 384–389.

6. _____. Increasing cognitive dissonance by a *fait accompli. J. abnorm. soc. Psychol.*, 1959, **58**, 379–382.

7. BREHM, J., & COHEN, A. R. Re-evaluation of choice alternatives as a function of their number and qualitative similarity. *J. abnorm. soc. Psychol.*, 1959, **58**, 373–378.

8. BRODBECK, M. The role of small groups in mediating the effects of propaganda. *J. abnorm. soc. Psychol.*, 1956, **52**, 166–170.

9. FESTINGER, L. Informal social communication. *Psychol. Rev.*, 1950, **57**, 271–282.

10. _____. *Theory of cognitive dissonance.* Evanston: Row, Peterson, 1957.

11. FESTINGER, L., & CARLSMITH, J. Cognitive consequences of forced compliance. *J. abnorm. soc. Psychol.*, 1959, **58**, 203–210.

12. FESTINGER, L., RIECKEN, H., & SCHACHTER, S. *When prophecy fails.* Minneapolis: Univ. of Minnesota Press, 1956.

13. FESTINGER, L., & THIBAUT, J. Interpersonal communication in small groups. *J. abnorm. soc. Psychol.*, 1951, **46**, 92–100.

14. HOVLAND, C. Reconciling conflicting results derived from experimental and survey studies of attitude change. *The American Psychologist*, 1959, 14, 8–17.

15. HOVLAND, C., & PRITZKER, H. Extent of opinion change as a function of amount of change advocated. *J. abnorm. soc. Psychol.*, 1957, 54, 257–261.

16. MILLS, J. Changes in moral attitudes following temptation. *J. Personality*, 1958, 26, 517–531.

17. SCHACHTER, S. Deviation, rejection and communication. *J. abnorm. soc. Psychol.*, 1951, 46, 190–208.

18. ZIMBARDO, P. Involvement and communication discrepancy as determinants of opinion change. Unpublished doctoral dissertation, Yale Univ., 1959.

11

When Prophecy Fails

Seldom in the field of social psychology have the origins of important theories been so well explored in natural setting research as they have been for the theory of cognitive dissonance. The present paper reflects a classic study in which the social psychologist was alert to circumstances which fulfilled the requirements for a real-life test of an, as yet, unexplored theory. By using participant observers whose real identity (i.e., social psychologists) remained unknown to the people being studied, the authors obtained valuable, nonreactive data concerning a paradoxical attitude and behavioral change as a result of confronting an extreme dilemma or "cognitive dissonance." This real-life study was instrumental in generating a major area of research, both in the laboratory (where greater controls allow for a deeper probing of the theory), and in field settings, where extensions of this theory could be tested. As this paper illustrates, one great appeal of the theory of cognitive dissonance is its seemingly flexible application to a variety of situations and settings involving perplexing conflicts. Both behavior and verbal reports of attitudes are utilized in explaining such ambivalent reactions to conflicts. Even though different theories have been proposed to account for the same phenomena with which dissonance theory deals, it continues to be a major formulation in the field of behavior-attitude change and continues to stimulate research and debate in social psychology.

SOURCE: Adapted and condensed from Festinger, L., Riecken, H., & Schachter, S. *When prophecy fails.* Minneapolis: University of Minnesota Press, 1956.

A man with a conviction is a hard man to change. Tell him you disagree and he turns away. Show him facts or figures and he questions your sources. Appeal to logic and he fails to see your point. We are familiar with the variety of ingenious defenses with which people protect their convictions, managing to keep them unscathed through the most devastating attacks.

But man's resourcefulness goes beyond simply protecting a belief. Suppose an individual believes something with his whole heart; suppose further that he has a commitment to this belief and that he has taken irrevocable actions because of it; finally, suppose that he is presented with evidence, unequivocal and undeniable evidence, that his belief is wrong: what will happen? The individual will frequently emerge, not only unshaken, but even more convinced of the truth of his beliefs than ever before. Indeed, he may even show a new fervor for convincing and converting other people to his view.

How and why does such a response to contradictory evidence come about? Let us begin by stating the conditions under which we would expect to observe increased fervor following the disconfirmation of a belief. There are five such conditions.

1. A belief must be held with deep conviction and it must have some relevance to action, that is, to what the believer does or how he behaves.

2. The person 'holding the belief must have committed himself to it; that is, for the sake of his belief, he must have taken some important action that is difficult to undo. In general, the more important such actions and the more difficult they are to undo, the greater is the individual's commitment to the belief.

3. The belief must be sufficiently specific and sufficiently concerned with the real world so that events may unequivocally refute the belief.

4. Such undeniable disconfirmatory evidence must occur and must be recognized by the individual holding the belief.

The first two of these conditions specify the circumstances that will make the belief resistant to change. The third and fourth conditions, on the other hand, point to factors that would exert powerful pressure on a believer to discard his belief. It is, of course, possible that an individual, even though deeply convinced of a belief, may discard it in the face of unequivocal disconfirmation. We must, therefore, state a fifth condition specifying the circumstances under which it will be maintained with new fervor.

5. The individual believer must have social support. It is unlikely that one isolated believer could withstand the kind of disconfirming evidence we have specified. If, however, the believer is a member of a group of convinced persons who can support one another, we would expect the belief to be maintained and the believers to attempt to proselytize or to persuade nonmembers that the belief is correct.

These five conditions specify the circumstances under which increased proselytizing would be expected to follow disconfirmation. Given this set of hypotheses, our immediate concern is to locate data that will allow a test of the prediction of increased proselytizing. Fortunately, throughout history there have been recurring instances of social movements which satisfy the conditions adequately. These are the millennial or messianic movements, a contemporary instance of which forms the basis for the present study. Let us see just how such movements do satisfy the five conditions we have specified.

Typically, millennial or messianic movements are organized around the prediction of some future events. Our conditions are satisfied, however, only by those movements that specify a data or an interval of time within which the predicted events will occur as well as detailing exactly what is to happen. Sometimes the predicted event is the second coming of Christ and the beginning of Christ's reign on earth; sometimes it is the destruction of the world through a cataclysm (usually with some select group slated for rescue from the disaster); or sometimes the prediction is concerned with particular occurrences that the messiah or a miracle worker will bring about. Whatever the event predicted, the fact that its nature and the time of its happening are specified satisfies the third point on our list of conditions.

The second condition specifies strong behavioral commitment to the belief. This usually follows almost as a consequence of the situation. If one really believes a prediction (the first condition), for example, that on a given date the world will be destroyed by fire, that the sinners will die and the good be saved, he does things about it and makes certain preparations as a matter of course. These actions may range all the way from simple public declarations to the neglect of worldly things and the disposal of earthly possessions. Through such actions and through the mocking and scoffing of nonbelievers, the believers usually establish a heavy commitment. What they do by way of preparation is difficult to undo, and the jeering of nonbelievers simply makes it far more difficult for the adherents to withdraw from the movement and admit that they were wrong.

Our fourth specification has invariably been provided. The predicted events have not occurred. There is usually no mistaking the fact that they did not occur and the believers know that. In other words, the unequivocal disconfirmation does materialize and makes its impact on the believers.

Finally, our fifth condition is ordinarily satisfied—such movements do attract adherents and disciples, sometimes only a handful, occasionally hundreds of thousands. The reasons why people join such movements are outside the scope of our present discussion, but the fact remains that there are usually one or more groups of believers who can support one another.

History has recorded many such movements. Ever since the crucifixion of Jesus, many Christians have hoped for the second coming of Christ and movements predicting specific dates for this event have not been rare. However, most of the very early ones were not recorded in such a fashion that we can be sure of the reactions of believers to the disconfirmations they may have experienced. Occasionally historians make passing reference to such reactions as does Hughes in his description of the Montanists:

> Montanus, who appeared in the second half of the second century, does not appear as an innovator in matters of belief. His one personal contribution to the life of the time was the fixed conviction that the second coming of Our Lord was at hand. The event was to take place at Pepuza—near the modern Angora—and thither all true followers of Our Lord should make their way. His authority for the statement was an alleged private inspiration, and the new prophet's personality and eloquence won him a host of disciples, who flocked in such numbers to the appointed spot that a new town sprang up to house them. *Nor did the delay of the second advent put an end to the movement. On the contrary, it gave it new life and form* as a kind of Christianity of the elite, whom no other authority guided in their new life but the Holy Spirit working directly upon them. . . . [Italics ours.]

In this brief statement are all the essential elements of the typical messianic movement. There are convinced followers; they commit themselves by uprooting their lives and going to a new place where they build a new town; the Second Advent does not occur. And, we note, far from halting the movement, this disconfirmation gives it new life.

Why does increased proselytizing follow the disconfirmation of a prediction? How can we explain it, and what are the factors that will determine whether or not it will occur? For our explanation, we shall introduce the concepts of consonance and dissonance.

Dissonance and consonance are relations among cognitions—that is, among opinions, beliefs, knowledge of the environment, and knowledge of one's own actions and feelings. Two opinions, or beliefs, or items of knowledge are dissonant with each other if they do not fit together—that is, if they are inconsistent, or if, considering only the particular two items, one does not follow from the other. For example, a cigarette smoker who believes that smoking is bad for his health has an opinion that is dissonant with the knowledge that he is continuing to smoke.

Dissonance produces discomfort and, correspondingly, there will arise attempts to reduce dissonance. Such attempts may take any or all of three forms. The person may try to change one or more of the beliefs, opinions, or behaviors involved in the dissonance; to acquire new information or beliefs that will increase the existing consonance and thus cause the total dissonance to be reduced; or to forget or reduce the importance of those cognitions that are in a dissonant relationship.

If any of these attempts is to be successful, it must be met with support from either the physical or the social environment. In the absence of such support, the most determined efforts to reduce dissonance may be unsuccessful.

Theoretically, then, what is the situation of the individual believer at the predisconfirmation stage of a messianic movement? He has a strongly held belief in a prediction—for example, that Christ will return—a belief that is supported by the other members of the movement. By way of preparation for the predicted event, he has engaged in many activities that are entirely consistent with his belief. In other words, most of the relations among relevant cognitions are, at this point, consonant.

Now what is the effect of the disconfirmation, of the unequivocal fact that the prediction was wrong, upon the believer? The disconfirmation introduces an important and painful dissonance. The fact that the predicted events did not occur is dissonant with continuing to believe both the prediction and the remainder of the ideology of which the prediction was the central item. The failure of the prediction is also dissonant with all the actions that the believer took in preparation for its fulfillment. The magnitude of the dissonance will, of course, depend on the importance of the belief to the individual and on the magnitude of his preparatory activity.

In the type of movement we have discussed, the central belief and its accompanying ideology are usually of crucial importance in the believers' lives and hence the dissonance is very strong—and very painful to tolerate. Accordingly, we should expect to observe believers making determined efforts to eliminate the dissonance or, at least, to reduce its magnitude. How may they accomplish this end? The dissonance would be largely eliminated if they discarded the belief that had been disconfirmed, ceased the behavior which had been initiated in preparation for the fulfillment of the prediction, and returned to a more usual existence. Indeed, this pattern sometimes occurs. But frequently the behavioral commitment to the belief system is so strong that almost any other course of action is preferable. It may even be less painful to tolerate the dissonance than to discard the belief and admit one had been wrong. When that is the case, dissonance cannot be eliminated by abandoning the belief.

Alternatively, the dissonance would be reduced or eliminated if the members of a movement effectively blind themselves to the fact that the prediction has not been fulfilled. But most people, including members of such movements, are in touch with reality and simply cannot blot out of their cognition such an unequivocal and undeniable fact. They can try to ignore it, however, and they usually do try. They may convince themselves that the date was wrong but that the prediction will, after all, be shortly confirmed; or they may even set another date. Believers may try to find reasonable explanations, very often ingenious ones, for the failure of their prediction. Rationalization can reduce dissonance somewhat, but for rationalization to be fully effective, support from others is needed to make the explanation or the revision seem correct. Fortunately, the disappointed believer can usually turn to others in the same movement, who have the same dissonance and the same pressures to reduce it. Support for the new explanation is, hence, forthcoming and the members of the movement can recover somewhat from the shock of the disconfirmation.

Whatever the explanation, it is still by itself not sufficient. The dissonance is too important and though they may try to hide it, even from themselves, the believers still know that the prediction was false and all their preparations were in vain. The dissonance cannot be eliminated completely by denying or rationalizing the disconfirmation. There is, however, a way in which the remaining dissonance can be reduced. *If more and more people can be persuaded that the system of belief is correct, then clearly it must after all, be correct.* It is for this reason that we observe the increase in proselytizing following disconfirmation.

If the proselytizing proves successful, then by gathering more adherents and effectively surrounding himself with supporters the believer reduces dissonance to the point where he can live with it.

In the light of this explanation of the phenomenon that proselyting increases as a result of a disconfirmation, we sought a modern instance of disconfirmation, an instance which could be observed closely enough so that our explanation could be put to an empirical test.

One day at the end of September the Lake City *Herald* carried a two-column story, on a back page, headlined: PROPHECY FROM PLANET. CLARION CALL TO CITY: FLEE THAT FLOOD. IT'LL SWAMP US ON DEC. 21, OUTER SPACE TELLS SUBURBANITE. The body of the story expanded somewhat on these bare facts:

> Lake City will be destroyed by a flood from Great Lake just before dawn, Dec. 21, according to a suburban housewife. Mrs. Marian Keech, of 847 West School Street, says the prophecy is not her own. It is the purport of many messages she has received by automatic writing, she says. . . . The messages, according to Mrs. Keech, are sent to her by superior beings from a planet called "Clarion." These beings have been visiting the earth, she says, in what we call flying saucers. During their visits, she says, they have observed fault lines in the earth's crust that foretoken the deluge. Mrs. Keech reports she was told the flood will spread to form an inland sea stretching from the Arctic Circle to the Gulf of Mexico. At the same time, she says, a cataclysm will submerge the West Coast from Seattle, Wash., to Chile in South America.

Since Mrs. Keech's pronouncement made a specific prediction of a specific event, since she, at least, was publicly committed to belief in it, and since she was apparently interested to some extent in informing a wider public about it, this seemed to be an opportunity to conduct a "field" test of the theoretical ideas to which the reader has been introduced. Therefore, the authors joined Mrs. Keech's group in early October and remained in constant touch with it throughout the events to be narrated here.

About nine months before the newspaper story appeared, Marian Keech had begun to receive messages in "automatic writing" from beings who said they existed in outer space and were instructing her to act as their representative to warn the people of earth of the coming cataclysm. Mrs. Keech told many of her friends and acquaintances of her messages, and by September had attracted a small following of believers. Among them was Dr. Thomas Armstrong, a physician who lived in a college town in a nearby state. Dr. Armstrong spread the word among a group of students ("The Seekers") who met at his home regularly to discuss spiritual problems and cosmology. Dr. Armstrong and his wife also visited Lake City frequently to attend meetings of Mrs. Keech's group there.

Throughout the fall months the groups in Lake City and Collegeville held a series of meetings to discuss the lessons from outer space and to prepare themselves for salvation from cataclysm. As December 21 drew near some members gave up their jobs, others gave away their possessions, and nearly all made public declarations of their conviction. In September, Dr. Armstrong had prepared two "news releases" about the prediction of flood, although Mrs. Keech had not sought any publicity herself and had given only the one interview to the Lake City reporter who called on her after he had seen one of Dr. Armstrong's news releases. Except for that interview, Mrs. Keech had confined her proselyting to friends and acquaintances, and Dr. Armstrong had virtually limited his activities to "The Seekers." During October and November, a policy of increasingly strict secrecy about the beliefs and activities of the believers had been developing in both Collegeville and Lake City.

In December, Dr. Armstrong was dismissed from his hospital post, and the action brought him nation-wide publicity. Had the group been interested in carrying their message to the world and securing new converts, they would have been presented with a priceless opportunity on December 16 when representatives of the nation's major news-reporting services converged on the Keech home, hungry for a story to follow up the news break on Dr. Armstrong's dismissal from the college. But the press received a cold, almost hostile reception, and their most persistent efforts were resisted. In two days of constant vigil, the newspapermen succeeded in winning only one brief broadcast tape and one interview with Dr. Armstrong and Mrs. Keech—and that only after a reporter had virtually threatened to print his own version of their beliefs. A cameraman who surreptitiously violated the believers' prohibition against taking photographs was threatened with a lawsuit. Between December 16 and the early morning of December 21, the Keech home was the object of a barrage of telephone calls and a steady stream of visitors who came seeking enlightenment or even offering themselves for conversion. The telephone calls from reporters were answered by a flat, unqualified "No comment." The visitors, mostly potential converts, were paid the most casual attention and the believers made only sporadic attempts to explain their views to these inquirers.

By the late afternoon of December 20—the eve of the predicted cataclysm—the hullaballoo in the house had died down somewhat, and the believers began making their final preparations for salvation. Late that morning, Mrs. Keech had received a message instructing the group to be ready to receive a visitor who would arrive at midnight and escort them to a parked flying saucer that would whisk them away from the flood to a place of safety, presumably in outer space. Early in the evening, the ten believers from Lake City and Collegeville had begun rehearsing for their departure. First, they went through the ritual to be followed when their escort arrived at midnight. Dr. Armstrong was to act as sentry and, having made sure of the caller's identity, admit him. The group drilled carefully on the ritual responses they would make to the specific challenges of their unearthly visitor, and the passwords they would have to give in boarding the saucer. Next, the believers removed all metal from their persons. The messages from outer space left no doubt in anyone's mind that it would be extremely dangerous to travel in a saucer while wearing or carrying anything metallic, and all of the group complied painstakingly with this order—excepting only the fillings in their teeth.

The last ten minutes before midnight were tense ones for the group assembled in Mrs. Keech's living room. They had nothing to do but sit and wait, their coats in their laps. In the silence two clocks ticked loudly, one about ten minutes faster than the other. When the faster clock pointed to 12:05, someone remarked about the time aloud. A chorus of people replied that midnight had not yet come. One member affirmed that the slower clock was correct; he had set it himself only that afternoon. It showed only four minutes before midnight.

Those four minutes passed in complete silence except for a single utterance. When the (slower) clock on the mantel showed only one minute remaining before the guide to the saucer was due, Mrs. Keech exclaimed in a strained, high-pitched voice: "And not a plan has gone astray!" The clock chimed twelve, each stroke painfully clear in the expectant hush. The believers sat motionless.

One might have expected some visible reaction, as the minutes passed. Midnight had come and gone, and nothing had happened. The cataclysm itself was less than seven hours away. But there was little to see in the reactions of the people in that room. There was no talking, nor sound of any sort. People sat stock still, their faces seemingly frozen and expressionless.

Gradually, painfully, an atmosphere of despair and confusion settled over the group. They re-examined the prediction and the accompanying messages. Dr. Armstrong and Mrs. Keech reiterated their faith. The believers mulled over their predicament and discarded explanation after explanation as unsatisfactory. At one point, toward 4 A.M., Mrs. Keech broke down and cried bitterly. She knew, she sobbed, that there were some who were beginning to doubt but that the group must beam light to those who needed it most, and that the group must hold together. The rest of the believers were losing their composure, too. They were all visibly shaken and many were close to tears. It was now almost 4:30 A.M. and still no way of handling the disconfirmation had been found. By now, too, most of the group were talking openly about the failure of the escort to come at midnight. The group seemed near dissolution.

But this atmosphere did not continue long. At about 4:45 A.M. Mrs. Keech summoned everyone to attention, announcing that she had just received a message. She then read aloud these momentous words: "For this day it is established that there is but one God of Earth and He is in thy midst, and from his hand thou hast written these words. And mighty is the word of God—and by his word have ye been saved—for from the mouth of death have ye been delivered and at no time has there been such a force loosed upon the Earth. Not since the beginning of time upon this Earth has there been such a force of Good and light as now floods this room and that which has been loosed within this room now floods the entire Earth. As thy God has spoken through the two who sit within these walls has he manifested that which he has given thee to do."

This message was received with enthusiasm. It was an adequate, even an elegant, explanation of the disconfirmation. The cataclysm had been called off. The little group, sitting all night long, had spread so much light that God had saved the world from destruction.

The atmosphere in the group changed abruptly and so did their behavior. Within minutes after she had read the message explaining the disconfirmation, Mrs. Keech received another message instructing her to publicize the explanation. She reached for the telephone and began dialing the number of a newspaper. While she was waiting to be connected, someone asked: "Marian, is this the first time you have called the newspaper yourself?" Her reply was immediate: "Oh, yes, this is the first time I have ever called them. I have never had anything to tell them before, but now I feel it is urgent." The whole group could have echoed her feelings, for they all felt a sense of urgency. As soon as Marian had finished her call, the other members took turns telephoning newspapers, wire services, radio stations, and national magazines to spread the explanation of the failure of the flood. In their desire to spread the word quickly and resoundingly, the believers now opened for public attention matters that had been thus far utterly secret. Where only hours earlier they had shunned newspaper reporters and felt that the attention they were getting in the press was painful, they now became avid seekers of publicity. During the rest of December 21, the believers thrust themselves willingly before microphones, talked freely to reporters, and enthusiastically proselytized the visitors and inquirers who called at the house. In the ensuing days they made new bids for attention. Mrs. Keech made further predictions of visits by spacemen and invited newspapermen to witness the event. Like the millennial groups of history, this one, too, reacted to disconfirmation by standing firm in their beliefs and doubling their efforts to win converts. The believers in Lake City clearly displayed the reaction to disconfirmation that our theory predicted.

Among the members of the Collegeville group who had not gone to Lake City for the flood, matters took quite a different turn. Most of them were students who had gone to their homes for Christmas vacation. All but two of them spent December 20 and 21 in isolation from each other, surrounded by unbelievers. These isolates reacted to the disconfirmation in a very different fashion from their fellows in Lake City. Instead of recovering from the initial shock of disconfirmation, they either gave up their beliefs completely or found their conviction seriously weakened. There was no upsurge of proselytizing among the stay-at-homes in "The Seekers" even after they had been informed of the message rationalizing the disconfirmation. Indeed, the reverse seems to have occurred in two cases where the individuals attempted to conceal their membership in "The Seekers." Thus, most of the Collegeville group reduced the dissonance created by disconfirmation by giving up all their beliefs, whereas in Lake City the members held fast and tried to create a supportive circle of believers.

The comparison of the two situations—Lake City and Collegeville—permits at least a crude test of the importance of one element of theory proposed to explain the proselyting reaction to disconfirmation; namely, the element of social support. In Lake City, most of the members were in the constant presence of fellow believers during the period immediately following disconfirmation. They had social support; they were able to accept the rationalization; and they regained confidence in their beliefs. On the other hand, all of the members of the Collegeville group, with the exception of one pair, faced the morning of December 21 and the following days either with people who neither agreed nor disagreed or with people who were openly opposed to the views of "The Seekers." It would seem that the presence of supporting cobelievers is an indispensable requirement for recovery from disconfirmation.

At the beginning of this article, we specified the conditions under which disconfirmation would lead to increased proselytizing and, for most of the members of the Lake City group, these specifications were satisfied. Most of them believed in Mrs. Keech's prediction and were heavily committed to this belief. Disconfirmation was unequivocal, and the attempted rationalization by itself was never completely successful in dispelling dissonance. Finally, the members of the group faced disconfirmation and its aftermath together. The members responded with strong, persistent attempts at proselytizing. Among "The Seekers," all the conditions were the same except that the supportive group of co-believers was missing. Among these isolates there was no increase in proselyting, no attempt to seek publicity, but rather their characteristic response was to give up their belief and even to conceal their earlier membership.

The research reported here was supported by the Laboratory for Research in Social Relations at the University of Minnesota and by a grant-in-aid from the Ford Foundation. All the persons and places mentioned have been given fictitious names.

12

Cognitive Consequences of Forced Compliance

What happens to a person's private opinion if he is forced to do or say something contrary to that opinion? Only recently has there been any experimental work related to this question. Two studies reported by Janis and King (1954; 1956) clearly showed that, at least under some conditions, the private opinion changes so as to bring it into closer correspondence with the overt behavior the person was forced to perform. Specifically, they showed that if a person is forced to improvise a speech supporting a point of view with which he disagrees, his private opinion moves toward the position advocated in the speech. The observed opinion change is greater than for persons who only hear the speech or for persons who read a prepared speech with emphasis solely on elocution and manner of delivery. The authors of these two studies explain their results mainly in terms of mental rehearsal and thinking up new arguments. In this way, they propose, the person who is forced to improvise a speech convinces himself. They present some evidence, which is not altogether conclusive, in support of this explanation. We will have more to say concerning this explanation in discussing the results of our experiment.

Kelman (1953) tried to pursue the matter further. He reasoned that if the person is induced to make an overt statement contrary to his pri-

SOURCE: Festinger, L., & Carlsmith, J. M. *J. abnorm. soc. Psychol.*, 1959, **58**, 203–211. [Received November 18, 1957]

vate opinion by the offer of some reward, then, the greater the reward offered, the greater should be the subsequent opinion change. His data, however, did not support this idea. He found, rather, that a large reward produced less subsequent opinion change than did a smaller reward. Actually, this finding by Kelman is consistent with the theory we will outline below but, for a number of reasons, is not conclusive. One of the major weaknesses of the data is that not all subjects in the experiment made an overt statement contrary to their private opinion in order to obtain the offered reward. What is more, as one might expect, the percentage of subjects who complied increased as the size of the offered reward increased. Thus, with self-selection of who did and who did not make the required overt statement and with varying percentages of subjects in the different conditions who did make the required statement, no interpretation of the data can be unequivocal.

Recently, Festinger (1957) proposed a theory concerning cognitive dissonance from which come a number of derivations about opinion change following forced compliance. Since these derivations are stated in detail by Festinger (1957, Ch. 4), we will here give only a brief outline of the reasoning.

Let us consider a person who privately holds opinion "X" but has, as a result of pressure brought to bear on him, publicly stated that he believes "not X."

1. This person has two cognitions which, psychologically, do not fit together: one of these is the knowledge that he believes "X," the other the knowledge that he has publicly stated that he believes "not X." If no factors other than his private opinion are considered, it would follow, at least in our culture, that if he believes "X" he would publicly state "X." Hence, his cognition of his private belief is dissonant with his cognition concerning his actual public statement.

2. Similarly, the knowledge that he has said "not X" is consonant with (does fit together with) those cognitive elements corresponding to the reasons, pressures, promises of rewards and/or threats of punishment which induced him to say "not X."

3. In evaluating the total magnitude of dissonance, one must take account of both dissonances and consonances. Let us think of the sum of all the dissonances involving some particular cognition as "D" and the sum of all the consonances as "C." Then we might think of the total magnitude of dissonance as being a function of "D" divided by "D" plus "C."

Let us then see what can be said about the total magnitude of dissonance in a person created by the knowledge that he said "not X" and really believes "X." With everything else held constant, this total magnitude of dissonance would decrease as the number and importance of the pressures which induced him to say "not X" increased.

Thus, if the overt behavior was brought about by, say, offers of reward or threats of punishment, the magnitude of dissonance is maximal if these promised rewards or threatened punishments were just barely sufficient to induce the person to say "not X." From this point on, as the promised rewards or threatened punishment become larger, the magnitude of dissonance becomes smaller.

4. One way in which the dissonance can be reduced is for the person to change his private opinion so as to bring it into correspondence with what he has said. One would consequently expect to observe such opinion change after a person has been forced or induced to say something contrary to his private opinion. Furthermore, since the pressure to reduce dissonance will be a function of the magnitude of the dissonance, the observed opinion change should be greatest when the pressure used to elicit the overt behavior is just sufficient to do it.

The present experiment was designed to test this derivation under controlled, laboratory conditions. In the experiment we varied the amount of reward used to force persons to make a statement contrary to their private views. The prediction [from 3 and 4 above] is that the larger the reward given to the subject, the smaller will be the subsequent opinion change.

Procedure

Seventy-one male students in the introductory psychology course at Stanford University were used in the experiment. In this course, students are required to spend a certain number of hours as subjects (Ss) in experiments. They choose among the available experiments by signing their names on a sheet posted on the bulletin board which states the nature of the experiment. The present experiment was listed as a two-hour experiment dealing with "Measures of Performance."

During the first week of the course, when the requirement of serving in experiments was announced and explained to the students, the instructor also told them about a study that the psychology department was conducting. He explained that, since they were required to serve in experiments, the department was conducting a study to evaluate these experiments in order to be able to improve them in the future. They were told that a sample of students would be interviewed after having served as Ss. They were urged to cooperate in these interviews by being completely frank and honest. The importance of this announcement will become clear shortly. It enabled us to measure the opinions of our Ss in a context not directly connected with our experiment and in which we could reasonably expect frank and honest expressions of opinion.

When the S arrived for the experiment on "Measures of Performance" he had to wait for a few minutes in the secretary's office. The experimenter (E) then came in, introduced himself to the S and, together, they walked into the laboratory room where the E said:

> This experiment usually takes a little over an hour but, of course, we had to schedule it for two hours. Since we have that extra time, the introductory psychology people asked if they could interview some of our subjects. [Offhand and conversationally.] Did they announce that in class? I gather that they're interviewing some people who have been in experiments. I don't know much about it. Anyhow, they may want to interview you when you're through here.

With no further introduction or explanation the S was shown the first task, which involved putting 12 spools onto a tray, emptying the tray, refilling it with spools, and so on. He was told to use one hand and to work at his own speed. He did this for one-half hour. The E then removed the tray and spools and placed in front of the S a board containing 48 square pegs. His task was to turn each peg a quarter turn clockwise, then another quarter turn, and so on. He was told again to use one hand and to work at his own speed. The S worked at this task for another half hour.

While the S was working on these tasks, the E sat, with a stop watch in his hand, busily making notations on a sheet of paper. He did so in order to make it convincing that this was what the E was interested in and that these tasks, and how the S worked on them, was the total experiment. From our point of view the experiment had hardly started. The hour which the S spent working on the repetitive, monotonous tasks was intended to provide, for each S uniformly, an experience about which he would have a somewhat negative opinion.

After the half hour on the second task was over, the E conspicuously set the stop watch back to zero, put it away, pushed his chair back, lit a cigarette, and said:

> O.K. Well, that's all we have in the experiment itself. I'd like to explain what this has been all about so you'll have some idea of why you were doing this. [E pauses.] Well, the way the experiment is set up is this.

There are actually two groups in the experiment. In one, the group you were in, we bring the subject in and give him essentially no introduction to the experiment. That is, all we tell him is what he needs to know in order to do the tasks, and he has no idea of what the experiment is all about, or what it's going to be like, or anything like that. But in the other group, we have a student that we've hired that works for us regularly, and what I do is take him into the next room where the subject is waiting— the same room you were waiting in before—and I introduce him as if he had just finished being a subject in the experiment. That is, I say: "This is so-and-so, who's just finished the experiment, and I've asked him to tell you a little of what it's about before you start." The fellow who works for us then, in conversation with the next subject, makes these points: [The E then produced a sheet headed "For Group B" which had written on it: It was very enjoyable, I had a lot of fun, I enjoyed myself, it was very interesting, it was intriguing, it was exciting. The E showed this to the S and then proceeded with his false explanation of the purpose of the experiment.] Now, of course, we have this student do this, because if the experimenter does it, it doesn't look as realistic, and what we're interested in doing is comparing how these two groups do on the experiment—the one with this previous expectation about the experiment, and the other, like yourself, with essentially none.

Up to this point the procedure was identical for Ss in all conditions. From this point on they diverged somewhat. Three conditions were run, Control, One Dollar, and Twenty Dollars, as follows:

Control Condition

The E continued:

Is that fairly clear? [Pause.] Look, that fellow [looks at watch] I was telling you about from the introductory psychology class said he would get here a couple of minutes from now. Would you mind waiting to see if he wants to talk to you? Fine. Why don't we go into the other room to wait? [The E left the S in the secretary's office for four minutes. He then returned and said:] O.K. Let's check and see if he does want to talk to you.

One and Twenty Dollar Conditions

The E continued:

Is that fairly clear how it is set up and what we're trying to do? [Pause.] Now, I also have a sort of strange thing to ask you. The thing is this. [Long pause, some confusion and uncertainty in the following, with a degree of embarrassment on the part of the E. The manner of the E contrasted strongly with the preceding unhesitant and assured false explanation of the experiment. The point was to make it seem to the S that this was the first time the E had done this and that he felt unsure of himself.] The fellow who normally does this for us couldn't do it today—he just phoned in, and something or other came up for him—so we've been looking around for someone that we could hire to do it for us. You see, we've got another subject waiting [looks at watch] who is supposed to be in that other condition. Now Professor ———, who is in charge of this experiment, suggested that perhaps we could take a chance on your doing it for us. I'll tell you what we had in mind: the thing is, if you could do it for us now, then of course you would know how to do it, and if something like this should ever come up again, that is, the regular fellow couldn't make it, and we had a subject scheduled, it would be very reassuring to us to know that we had somebody else we could call on who knew how to do it. So, if you would be willing to do this for us, we'd like to hire you to do it now and then be on call in the future, if something like this should ever happen again. We can pay you a dollar (twenty dollars) for doing this for us, that is, for doing it now and then being on call. Do you think you could do that for us?

If the S hesitated, the E said things like, "It will only take a few minutes," "The regular person is pretty reliable; this is the first time he has missed," or "If we needed you we could phone you a day or two in advance; if you couldn't make it, of course, we wouldn't expect you to come." After the S agreed to do it, the E gave him the previously mentioned sheet of paper headed "For Group B" and asked him to read it through again. The E then paid the S one dollar (twenty dollars), made out a hand-written receipt form, and asked the S to sign it. He then said:

O.K., the way we'll do it is this. As I said, the next subject should be here by now. I think the next one is a girl. I'll take you into the next room and introduce you to her, saying that you've just finished the experiment and that we've asked you to tell her a little about it. And what we want you to do is just sit down and get into a conversation with her and try to get across the points on that sheet of paper. I'll leave you alone and come back after a couple of minutes. O.K.?

The E then took the S into the secretary's office where he had previously waited and where the next S was waiting. (The secretary had left the office.) He introduced the girl and the S to one another saying that the S had just finished the experiment and would tell her something about it. He then left saying he would return in a couple of minutes.

The girl, an undergraduate hired for this role, said little until the S made some positive remarks about the experiment and then said that she was surprised because a friend of hers had taken the experiment the week before and had told her that it was boring and that she ought to try to get out of it. Most Ss responded by saying something like "Oh, no, it's really very interesting. I'm sure you'll enjoy it." The girl, after this listened quietly, accepting and agreeing to everything the S told her. The discussion between the S and the girl was recorded on a hidden tape recorder.

After two minutes the E returned, asked the girl to go into the experimental room, thanked the S for talking to the girl, wrote down his phone number to continue the fiction that we might call on him again in the future and then said: "Look, could we check and see if that fellow from introductory psychology wants to talk to you?"

From this point on, the procedure for all three conditions was once more identical. As the E and the S started to walk to the office where the interviewer was, the E said: "Thanks very much for working on those tasks for us. I hope you did enjoy it. Most of our subjects tell us afterward that they found it quite interesting. You get a chance to see how you react to the tasks and so forth." This short persuasive communication was made in all conditions in exactly the same way. The reason for doing it, theoretically, was to make it easier for anyone who wanted to persuade himself that the tasks had been, indeed, enjoyable.

When they arrived at the interviewer's office, the E asked the interviewer whether or not he wanted to talk to the S. The interviewer said yes, the E shook hands with the S, said good-bye, and left. The interviewer, of course, was always kept in complete ignorance of which condition the S was in. The interview consisted of four questions, on each of which the S was first encouraged to talk about the matter and was then asked to rate his opinion or reaction on an 11-point scale. The questions are as follows:

1. Were the tasks interesting and enjoyable? In what way? In what way were they not? Would you rate how you feel about them on a scale from -5 to $+5$ where -5 means they were extremely dull and boring, $+5$ means they were extremely interesting and enjoyable, and zero means they were neutral, neither interesting nor uninteresting.

2. Did the experiment give you an opportunity to learn about your own ability to perform these tasks? In what way? In what way not? Would you rate how you feel about this on a scale from 0 to 10 where 0 means you learned nothing and 10 means you learned a great deal.

3. From what you know about the experiment and the tasks involved in it, would you say the experiment was measuring anything important? That is, do you think the results may have scientific value? In what way? In what way not? Would you rate your opinion on this matter on a scale from 0 to 10 where 0 means the results have no scientific value or importance and 10 means they have a great deal of value and importance.

4. Would you have any desire to participate in another similar experiment? Why? Why not? Would you rate your desire to participate in a similar experiment again on a scale from −5 to +5, where −5 means you would definitely dislike to participate, +5 means you would definitely like to participate, and 0 means you have no particular feeling about it one way or the other.

As may be seen, the questions varied in how directly relevant they were to what the S had told the girl. This point will be discussed further in connection with the results.

At the close of the interview the S was asked what he thought the experiment was about and, following this, was asked directly whether or not he was suspicious of anything and, if so, what he was suspicious of. When the interview was over, the interviewer brought the S back to the experimental room where the E was waiting together with the girl who had posed as the waiting S. (In the control condition, of course, the girl was not there.) The true purpose of the experiment was then explained to the S in detail, and the reasons for each of the various steps in the experiment were explained carefully in relation to the true purpose. All experimental Ss in both One Dollar and Twenty Dollar conditions were asked, after this explanation, to return the money they had been given. All Ss, without exception, were quite willing to return the money.

The data from 11 of the 71 Ss in the experiment had to be discarded for the following reasons:

1. Five Ss (three in the One Dollar and two in the Twenty Dollar condition) indicated in the interview that they were suspicious about having been paid to tell the girl the experiment was fun and suspected that that was the real purpose of the experiment.

2. Two Ss (both in the One Dollar condition) told the girl that they had been hired, that the experiment was really boring but they were supposed to say it was fun.

3. Three Ss (one in the One Dollar and two in the Twenty Dollar condition) refused to take the money and refused to be hired.

4. One S (in the One Dollar condition), immediately after having talked to the girl, demanded her phone number saying he would call her and explain things, and also told the E he wanted to wait until she was finished so he could tell her about it.

These 11 Ss were, of course, run through the total experiment anyhow and the experiment was explained to them afterwards. Their data, however, are not included in the analysis.

Summary of Design

There remain, for analysis, 20 Ss in each of the three conditions. Let us review these briefly: 1. *Control condition*. These Ss were treated identically in all respects to the Ss in the experimental conditions, except that they were never asked to, and never did, tell the waiting girl that the experimental tasks were enjoyable and lots of fun. 2. *One Dollar condition*. These Ss were hired for one dollar to tell a waiting S that tasks, which were really rather dull and boring, were interesting, enjoyable, and lots of fun. 3. *Twenty Dollar condition*. These Ss were hired for twenty dollars to do the same thing.

Results

The major results of the experiment are summarized in Table 12.1 which lists, separately for each of the three experimental conditions, the average rating which the Ss gave at the end of each question on the interview. We will discuss each of the questions on the interview separately, because they were intended to measure different things. One other point before we proceed to examine the data. In all the comparisons, the Control condition should be regarded as a baseline from which to evaluate the results in the other two conditions. The Control condition gives us, essentially, the reactions of Ss to the tasks and their opinions about the experiment as falsely explained to them, without the experimental introduction of dissonance. The data from the other conditions may be viewed, in a sense, as changes from this baseline.

How Enjoyable the Tasks Were

The average ratings on this question, presented in the first row of figures in Table 12.1, are the results most important to the experiment.

Table 12.1   Average Ratings on Interview Questions for Each Condition

Question on Interview	Experimental Condition		
	Control (N = 20)	One Dollar (N = 20)	Twenty Dollars (N = 20)
How enjoyable tasks were (rated from −5 to +5)	−.45	+1.35	−.05
How much they learned (rated from 0 to 10)	3.08	2.80	3.15
Scientific importance (rated from 0 to 10)	5.60	6.45	5.18
Participate in similar exp. (rated from −5 to +5)	−.62	+1.20	−.25

These results are the ones most directly relevant to the specific dissonance which was experimentally created. It will be recalled that the
tasks were purposely arranged to be rather boring and monotonous.
And, indeed, in the Control condition the average rating was −.45,
somewhat on the negative side of the neutral point.

In the other two conditions, however, the Ss told someone that these
tasks were interesting and enjoyable. The resulting dissonance could, of
course, most directly be reduced by persuading themselves that the
tasks were, indeed, interesting and enjoyable. In the One Dollar condition, since the magnitude of dissonance was high, the pressure to reduce this dissonance would also be high. In this condition, the average
rating was +1.35, considerably on the positive side and significantly
different from the Control condition at the .02 level[1] ($t = 2.48$).

In the Twenty Dollar condition, where less dissonance was created
experimentally because of the greater importance of the consonant relations, there is correspondingly less evidence of dissonance reduction.
The average rating in this condition is only −.05, slightly and not significantly higher than the Control condition. The difference between the
One Dollar and Twenty Dollar conditions is significant at the .03 level
($t = 2.22$). In short, when an S was induced, by offer of reward, to say
something contrary to his private opinion, this private opinion tended
to change so as to correspond more closely with what he had said. The

1. All statistical tests referred to in this paper are two-tailed.

greater the reward offered (beyond what was necessary to elicit the behavior) the smaller was the effect.

Desire to Participate in a Similar Experiment

The results from this question are shown in the last row of Table 12.1.
This question is less directly related to the dissonance that was experimentally created for the Ss. Certainly, the more interesting and enjoyable they felt the tasks were, the greater would be their desire to participate in a similar experiment. But other factors would enter also.
Hence, one would expect the results on this question to be very similar
to the results on "how enjoyable the tasks were" but weaker. Actually,
the result, as may be seen in the table, are in exactly the same direction,
and the magnitude of the mean differences is fully as large as on the
first question. The variability is greater, however, and the differences
do not yield high levels of statistical significance. The difference between the One Dollar condition ($+1.20$) and the Control condition
($-.62$) is significant at the .08 level ($t = 1.78$). The difference between
the One Dollar condition and the Twenty Dollar condition ($-.25$)
reaches only the .15 level of significance ($t = 1.46$).

The Scientific Importance of the Experiment

This question was included because there was a chance that differences
might emerge. There are, after all, other ways in which the experimentally created dissonance could be reduced. For example, one way would
be for the S to magnify for himself the value of the reward he obtained.
This, however, was unlikely in this experiment because money was used
for the reward and it is undoubtedly difficult to convince oneself that
one dollar is more than it really is. There is another possible way, however. The Ss were given a very good reason, in addition to being paid,
for saying what they did to the waiting girl. The Ss were told it was
necessary for the experiment. The dissonance could, consequently, be
reduced by magnifying the importance of this cognition. The more sci-
entifically important they considered the experiment to be, the less was
the total magnitude of dissonance. It is possible, then, that the results
on this question, shown in the third row of figures in Table 12.1, might
reflect dissonance reduction.

The results are weakly in line with what one would expect if the
dissonance were somewhat reduced in this manner. The One Dollar
condition is higher than the other two. The difference between the One
and Twenty Dollar conditions reaches the .08 level of significance on a

two-tailed test ($t = 1.79$). The difference between the One Dollar and Control conditions is not impressive at all ($t = 1.21$). The result that the Twenty Dollar condition is actually lower than the control condition is undoubtedly a matter of chance ($t = 0.58$).

How Much They Learned from the Experiment

The results on this question are shown in the second row of figures in Table 12.1. The question was included because, as far as we could see, it had nothing to do with the dissonance that was experimentally created and could not be used for dissonance reduction. One would then expect no differences at all among the three conditions. We felt it was important to show that the effect was not a completely general one but was specific to the content of the dissonance which was created. As can be readily seen in Table 12.1, there are only negligible differences among conditions. The highest t value for any of these differences is only 0.48.

Discussion of a Possible Alternative Explanation

We mentioned in the introduction that Janis and King (1954; 1956) in explaining their findings, proposed an explanation in terms of the self-convincing effect of mental rehearsal and thinking up new arguments by the person who had to improvise a speech. Kelman (1953), in the previously mentioned study, in attempting to explain the unexpected finding that the persons who complied in the moderate reward condition changed their opinion more than in the high reward condition, also proposed the same kind of explanation. If the results of our experiment are to be taken as strong corroboration of the theory of cognitive dissonance, this possible alternative explanation must be dealt with.

Specifically, as applied to our results, this alternative explanation would maintain that perhaps, for some reason, the Ss in the One Dollar condition worked harder at telling the waiting girl that the tasks were fun and enjoyable. That is, in the One Dollar condition they may have rehearsed it more mentally, thought up more ways of saying it, may have said it more convincingly, and so on. Why this might have been the case is, of course, not immediately apparent. One might expect that, in the Twenty Dollar condition, having been paid more, they would try to do a better job of it than in the One Dollar condition. But nevertheless, the possibility exists that the Ss in the One Dollar condition may have improvised more.

Because of the desirability of investigating this possible alternative explanation, we recorded on a tape recorder the conversation between each S and the girl. These recordings were transcribed and then rated, by two independent raters, on five dimensions. The ratings were, of course done in ignorance of which condition each S was in. The reliabilities of these ratings, that is, the correlations between the two independent raters, ranged from .61 to .88, with an average reliability of .71. The five ratings were:

1. The content of what the S said *before* the girl made the remark that her friend told her it was boring. The stronger the S's positive statements about the tasks, and the more ways in which he said they were interesting and enjoyable, the higher the rating.
2. The content of what the S said *after* the girl made the above-mentioned remark. This was rated in the same way as for the content before the remark.
3. A similar rating of the over-all content of what the S said.
4. A rating of how persuasive and convincing the S was in what he said and the way in which he said it.
5. A rating of the amount of time in the discussion that the S spent discussing the tasks as opposed to going off into irrelevant things.

Table 12.2   Average Ratings of Discussion Between Subject and Girl

Dimension Rated	Condition		
	One Dollar	Twenty Dollars	Value of t
Content before remark by girl (rated from 0 to 5)	2.26	2.62	1.08
Content after remark by girl (rated from 0 to 5)	1.63	1.75	0.11
Over-all content (rated from 0 to 5)	1.89	2.19	1.08
Persuasiveness and conviction (rated from 0 to 10)	4.79	5.50	0.99
Time spent on topic (rated from 0 to 10)	6.74	8.19	1.80

The mean ratings for the One Dollar and Twenty Dollar conditions, averaging the ratings of the two independent raters, are presented in Table 12.2. It is clear from examing the table that, in all cases, the Twenty Dollar condition is slightly higher. The differences are small, however, and only on the rating of "amount of time" does the difference between the two conditions even approach significance. We are certainly justified in concluding that the Ss in the One Dollar condition did not improvise more nor act more convincingly. Hence, the alternative explanation discussed above cannot account for the findings.

Summary

Recently, Festinger (1957) has proposed a theory concerning cognitive dissonance. Two derivations from this theory are tested here. These are:

1. If a person is induced to do or say something which is contrary to his private opinion, there will be a tendency for him to change his opinion so as to bring it into correspondence with what he has done or said.
2. The larger the pressure used to elicit the overt behavior (beyond the minimum needed to elicit it) the weaker will be the above-mentioned tendency.

A laboratory experiment was designed to test these derivations. Subjects were subjected to a boring experience and then paid to tell someone that the experience had been interesting and enjoyable. The amount of money paid the subject was varied. The private opinions of the subjects concerning the experiences were then determined.

The results strongly corroborate the theory that was tested.

When this article was written, Leon Festinger and James M. Carlsmith were at Stanford University.

The experiment reported here was done as part of a program of research supported by a grant from the National Science Foundation to Leon Festinger. The authors thanked Leonard Hommel, Judson Mills, and Robert Terwilliger for their help in designing and carrying out the experiment. They also acknowledged the help of Ruth Smith and Marilyn M. Miller.

References

FESTINGER, L. A *theory of cognitive dissonance*. Evanston, Ill: Row Peterson, 1957.

JANIS, I. L., & KING, B. T. The influence of role-playing on opinion change. *J. abnorm. soc. Psychol.*, 1954, **49**, 211–218.

KELMAN, H. Attitude change as a function of response restriction. *Hum. Relat.*, 1953, **6**, 185–214.

KING, B. T., & JANIS, I. L. Comparison of the effectiveness of improvised versus non-improvised role-playing in producing opinion changes. *Hum. Relat.*, 1956, **9**, 177–186.

13

The Psychological Effects of Insufficient Rewards

Some fields of Psychology have for many years been dominated by ideas concerning the importance of rewards in the establishment and maintenance of behavior patterns. So dominant has this notion become, that some of our most ingenious theoretical thinking has been devoted to imagining the existence of rewards in order to explain behavior in situations where, plausibly, no rewards exist. It has been observed, for example, that under some circumstances an organism will persist in voluntarily engaging in behavior which is frustrating or painful. To account for such behavior it has, on occasion, been seriously proposed that the cessation of the frustration or pain is rewarding and thus reinforces the tendency to engage in the behavior.

I want to maintain that this type of explanation is not only unnecessary but also misleading. I certainly do *not* wish to say that rewards are unimportant, but I propose to show that the absence of reward or the existence of inadequate reward produces certain specific consequences which can account for a variety of phenomena which are difficult to deal with if we use our usual conceptions of the role of reward.

Before I proceed, I would like to say that most of the thinking and most of the experimental work which I will present are the result of collaboration between Douglas H. Lawrence and myself. Indeed, whatever you find interesting in what I say you may safely attribute primarily to him.

SOURCE: Festinger, L. *Amer. Psychologist*, 1961, **16**, 1–2.

I will start my discussion in a rather roundabout manner with some remarks which concern themselves primarily with some aspects of the thinking processes of human beings. Human thinking is sometimes a strange mixture of "plausible" and "magical" processes. Let us examine more closely what I mean by this. For example, imagine that a person knows that some event is going to occur, and that the person can do something to prepare himself to cope more adequately with the impending event. Under such circumstances it is very reasonable (perhaps you might even want to use the word "rational") for the person to do whatever is necessary in preparation for the coming event. Human thinking, however, also works in reverse. Consider a person who goes to a lot of trouble to prepare himself for a future event which might possibly occur. Such a person will subsequently tend to persuade himself that the event is rather likely to occur. There is nothing very plausible or rational about this kind of mental process—rather, it has almost a magical quality about it. Let me illustrate this briefly by describing an experiment recently conducted by Ruby Yaryan.[1]

Under the pretext of investigating the manner in which students study for examinations, she asked subjects to study a list of arbitrary definitions of symbols in preparation for a possible test. Two conditions were experimentally created for the subjects. Half of the subjects were told that, if they actually took the test, this list of definitions of the symbols would be in their possession during the test, and so, all that was necessary in preparation was to familiarize themselves with the list. This was, essentially, an "easy preparation" condition. That is, not much effort was required of the subjects in advance preparation for the test.

The other half of the subjects were told that, if they actually took the test, they would *not* have the list of definitions with them and so it was necessary for them to memorize the symbols and their definitions in preparation for the test. It is clear that this constitutes a much more "effortful preparation" condition. Considerable effort was required of these subjects in advance preparation for the possible test.

It was carefully explained to each subject that not everyone would actually have to take the test. Specifically, they were told that only half of the people in the experiment *would* take the test. It was also carefully explained that the selection of who would, and who would not, have to take the test had already been made in consultation with their teachers (the subjects were all high school girls). Nothing that happened during

1. Yaryan, R. B., & Festinger, L. The effect of preparatory action on belief in the occurrence of possible future events. Unpublished paper.

the experiment would affect whether or not they took the test—this had already been decided in advance for each of them.

After they finished studying the list of definitions, they were asked a number of questions to preserve the fiction that the experiment was concerned with study habits. Each subject was also asked to indicate how likely she thought it was that she, personally, would have to actually take the test. The results show, quite clearly, that subjects in the effortful preparation condition, on the average, thought it was more likely that they would have to take the test than did subjects in the easy preparation condition. In other words, those who were experimentally induced to engage in a lot of preparatory effort, persuaded themselves that the thing they were preparing for would actually occur.

The relevance of this experiment to the problem of the effects of inadequate rewards will become clearer in the following example which illustrates the same psychological process. Consider some person who is strongly attracted to some goal. It is quite reasonable for this person to be willing to expend more effort, or to endure more pain, in order to reach the goal than he would be if he were less attracted. Once more, however, one finds the same process of reasoning in reverse. That is, if a person exerts a great deal of effort, or endures pain, in order to reach some ordinary objective, there is a strong tendency for him to persuade himself that the objective is especially valuable or especially desirable. An experiment conducted by Elliot Aronson and Judson Mills (1959) shows the effect quite nicely.

The subjects in the experiment by Aronson and Mills were college girls who volunteered to join small discussion groups. Each subject, when she appeared for the discussion group, was told that, instead of being put into a new group, she was being considered for inclusion in an ongoing group which had recently lost one of its members. However, the subject was told, because of the group's concern that the replacement be someone who would be able to discuss things freely and openly, the experimenter had agreed to test the replacement before admitting her to the group. Some subjects were then given a very brief and not painful test while others were given a rather extended and embarrassing test. The experimenter then, of course, told each subject that she had done well and was admitted to the group. Thus, there were some subjects who had attained membership in the group easily and some subjects who had endured a painful experience in order to be admitted to the group.

The experimenter then explained to the subject that the discussion was carried on by means of an intercommunication system, each girl being in a separate room. She was brought into her room which contained a microphone and earphones. The experimenter told her that the others had already started and perhaps it would be best for her not to participate in the discussion this time but just to listen. Next meeting, of course, she would participate fully. Speaking into the microphone the experimenter then went through the illusion of introducing her to the three other girls in the group. He then "disconnected" the microphone and gave the subject the earphones to wear. The subject then listened for about 25 minutes to a tape recording of a rather dull and halting discussion. All subjects, of course, heard exactly the same tape recording thinking they were listening to the actual live group discussion.

When the discussion was finished, the experimenter explained to the subject that, after each meeting, each of the girls filled out a "post-meeting reaction form." She was then given a questionnaire to complete which asked a variety of questions concerning how interesting she had found the discussion to be, how much she liked the other members of the group, and other similar questions. The results show, as anticipated, that those subjects who had gone through a painful procedure in order to be admitted to the group thought the discussion was more interesting and liked the other group members better than did those who had gained admission to the group easily. In other words, we see the same process operating here as we noted in the previous experiment. If someone is somehow induced to endure embarrassment in order to achieve something, she then persuades herself that what she has achieved is valuable.

In both of the examples which I have discussed (and one could present many more examples of similar nature) a situation has been produced where the organism has two pieces of information (or cognitions) which do not fit together. In the first example, these two pieces of information were: (a) I have worked hard in preparation for an event. (b) The event is not too likely to occur. In the second example, the two cognitions which did not fit together were: (a) I have endured pain to attain an objective. (b) The objective is not very attractive. This kind of "nonfitting" relationship between two pieces of information may be termed a dissonant relation (Festinger, 1957). The reason, of course, that dissonance exists between these cognitions is that, psychologically, the obverse of one follows from the other. Psychologically, if an objective *is* very attractive, it follows that one would be willing to endure pain to attain it; or if the objective is *not* attractive, it follows that one does *not* endure pain to attain it. This specification of why a given relation between cognitions is dissonant also provides the clues to predicting specifically how the organism will react to the existence of the dissonance. Assuming that the organism will attempt to reduce the dissonance between the cognitions, there are obviously two major classes of ways in which this can be done. He can attempt to persuade himself that the pain which he endured was not really painful or he can attempt to persuade himself that the objective *is* very attractive.

I will not spend any more time than this in general theoretical discussion of the theory of dissonance and the reduction of dissonance. I hope that this small amount of general theoretical discussion will be enough to give context to the specific analysis of the psychological effects of insufficient rewards.

Let us consider in more detail what is suggested by the example of the experiment by Aronson and Mills and by the theory of cognitive dissonance. In that experiment the dissonance which was created was reduced by enhancing the value of the goal. This suggests that organisms may come to like and value things for which they have worked very hard or for which they have suffered. Looking at it from another aspect, one might say that they may come to value activities for which they have been inadequately rewarded. At first glance this may seem to contradict a widely accepted notion in Psychology, namely, that organisms learn to like things for which they *have* been rewarded. In a sense it is contradictory, but not in the sense that it denies the operation of this widely assumed process. It does, however, state that another process also operates which is rather of an opposite character.

Let us analyze the situation with which we are concerned somewhat more carefully and more precisely. We are concerned with the dissonance between two possible cognitions. One of these is a cognition the organism has concerning his behavior, namely, I have voluntarily done something which, all other things being equal, I would avoid doing. The other is a cognition about the environment or about the result of his action, namely, the reward that has been obtained is inadequate. As we mentioned before, this dissonance can be reduced if the organism can persuade himself that he really likes the behavior in which he engaged or if he enhances for himself the value of what he has obtained as a result of his actions.

There is, of course, another way to reduce the dissonance, namely, for the organism to change his behavior. That is, having done something which resulted in an inadequate reward the organism can refuse to perform the action again. This means of reducing the dissonance is undoubtedly the one most frequently employed by organisms. If the organism obtains information which is dissonant with his behavior, he usually modifies his behavior so that it fits better what he knows concerning his environment. Here, however, I am going to consider only situations in which this means of reducing dissonance is not available to the organism. That is, I will consider only situations in which the organism is somehow tricked or seduced into continuing to engage in the activity in spite of the dissonance which is introduced. Under these circumstances we would expect one of the two previously mentioned dissonance reduction mechanisms to be used.

If one thinks for a while about the possible behavioral consequences of such a psychological process as we have described, an explanation suggests itself for the well known finding that resistance to extinction is greater after partial reward than after complete reward.

Before I explain this more adequately, I would like to digress for a moment. Since much of the research on the effects of partial reward has been done on rats, and since the experiments that Lawrence and I have done are also on rats, the question will inevitably arise as to whether or not I really think that rats have cognitions and that rats reduce dissonance the way humans do.

First for the matter of cognitions in rats: All that is meant by cognition is knowledge or information. It seems to me that one can assume that an organism has cognitions or information if one can observe some behavioral difference under different stimulus conditions. If the organism changes his behavior when the environment changes, then obviously he uses information about the environment and, equally obviously, can be said to have cognitions.

Now for the question of whether or not rats reduce dissonance as humans do: Although Lawrence keeps telling me that rats are smarter than humans, I suspect that the rat is a rather stupid organism and does not reduce dissonance nearly as effectively as the human being does. I suspect that the mechanisms available to the rat for dissonance reduction are very limited and that the amount of dissonance which gets effectively reduced is relatively small. Still, I suspect that they *do* reduce dissonance. At any rate, if we find that the theory of dissonance can make valid predictions for rat behavior, this will be evidence that they do, indeed, reduce dissonance.

Now to return to the matter of the increased resistance to extinction following partial reward. Let us examine what occurs, psychologically, during a series of trials on which the behavior of an organism is only occasionally rewarded. Imagine a hungry animal who dashes frantically down some runway and into some so-called "goal box" only to find that there is nothing there. The cognition that he has obtained nothing is dissonant with the cognition that he has expended effort to reach the goal box. If this state of affairs were continually repeated, as we all know, the animal would reduce the dissonance by refusing to go to the goal box, that is, he would change his behavior. But, in a partial reward situation, the animal is tricked into continuing to run to the goal box because an appreciable number of times that he goes there he does find food. But, on each nonrewarded trial dissonance is introduced when the animal finds the goal box empty. The assumed process of dissonance reduction would lead us to expect that, gradually, the animal develops some extra preference either for the activity or for the goal box itself. A comparable animal that was rewarded every time he ran to the goal box would not develop any such extra preference.

Consider the situation, then, when extinction trials begin. In addition to realizing that food is no longer present, the partially rewarded animal also has to overcome his extra preference before he stops going to the goal box. We would thus expect "extinction" to take longer for a partially rewarded animal than for an animal that was always rewarded. The magnitude of the difference should be far greater than just the slight effect which would exist if the 100% animal discovers more rapidly that the situation has changed.

If this explanation is correct, then the greater resistance to extinction following partial reward is a direct consequence of the process of dissonance reduction. This, of course, immediately suggests an extension of this line of reasoning to situations other than those involving partial reward. *Any* procedure which introduces dissonance during the training trials should similarly be expected to increase resistance to extinction since the same kind of dissonance reduction process should operate.

Let us, however, try to be precise about what kinds of procedures would introduce dissonance for an organism during training trials in an experiment. It is, fortunately, possible to define this operationally in a precise manner. Let us imagine that we test an organism in a single choice situation. In the case of a rat, for example, this might be simply an apparatus where, from the starting point the animal can turn either right or left. Let us further imagine that the organism we are testing is quite hungry and that, whichever alternative he chooses, he obtains food. We can, then, vary one at a time a variety of factors to discover what the organism will ordinarily avoid doing. One would, of course, find many such factors which would lead the organism not to choose the alternative with which that factor is associated. Dissonance will be created for the organism if he is somehow tricked into consistently engaging in an activity involving such a factor.

This may sound very involved so let me try to say it again, this time, a bit less abstractly. Imagine that we test rats in a simple left-right choice apparatus and, no matter whether the animal goes left or right, he obtains food. But, imagine that, if he goes left, the animal must swim through water to get to the food but, if he goes right, there is simply a short run down an alley to the food. Let us further imagine that, under such circumstances, the animal will consistently choose to go to the right, that is, he will avoid swimming through water. Armed with this knowledge concerning the behavior of the rat we can then assert the following: if one puts a rat in a situation where we somehow trick the rat into consistently swimming through water, dissonance will have been created.

Remembering what we have already said about the ways in which dissonance can be reduced in this kind of situation (provided that we are successful in tricking the organism into continuing to engage in the activity) we would then arrive at the following statement: any condition which the animal will avoid in the above mentioned test situation will increase resistance to extinction in a nonchoice situation.

Let us look at some of the data which exist which are relevant to this statement. We know that if a hungry rat is put in a situation where he has a choice between a goal box where he is rewarded 100% of the time and a goal box where he is rewarded only part of the time, he will fairly consistently go to the place where he is rewarded 100% of the time. And, of course, we also know that where no choice is involved, partial reward increases resistance to extinction. But there are other variables or conditions which should increase resistance to extinction in a similar manner if our theoretical analysis is correct.

Consider the question of delay of reinforcement. Once more, thinking of our hypothetical test situation, we can be reasonably certain that a rat, if faced with a choice where one alternative led to immediate reward while the other alternative involved an appreciable delay before the rat was allowed to continue to the goal box to obtain food, the rat would rather consistently choose the alternative that led to immediate reward. We should then expect that, in a nonchoice situation, delay of reward should lead to greater resistance to extinction. Existing data show that this is indeed correct. Appreciable delay of reward does lead to greater resistance to extinction. I will briefly review some of the data which exist on delay of reward to give you some idea of the effect which is obtained.

The usual experiment that has been done on extinction following delay of reinforcement compares one condition in which the rats encounter no enforced delay between starting down a runway and obtaining food in the goal box with other conditions in which, on some trials, the rats are detained in a delay chamber before being allowed to proceed to the food. The usual period of delay which has been used has been about 30 seconds. Crum, Brown, and Bitterman (1951) and Scott and Wike (1956) both find that a group of rats delayed on half the trials shows much greater resistance to extinction than a group which was never delayed. In another experiment, Wike and McNemara (1957) ran three groups which differed in the percentage (and of course, number) of trials on which they were delayed. They find that the larger the percentage or number of trials on which the animal experiences delay, the greater is the resistance to extinction. The same kind of result is obtained by Fehrer (1956) who compared rats who were delayed for 20 seconds on *every* trial with ones who were never delayed. She also finds that delay results in increased resistance to extinction.

Before we proceed to other matters, I would like to briefly raise a question concerning one kind of explanation that has frequently, in one form or another, been offered to account for increased resistance to extinction after partial reward. The basis of this kind of explanation, whether it be in terms of expectancy, or conditioning of cues, or any of a number of other varieties, rests in pointing out that there is more similarity between acquisition and extinction for partial reward conditions than for 100% reward conditions. I would like to point out that this type of explanation is clearly not very useful in explaining the increased resistance to extinction after delay of reward. From the point of view of the explanation I am here proposing, however, partial reward and delay of reward clearly involve the same psychological processes.

Let us go on now to examine the matter of work and effort. I am sure it is fairly obvious to all of you now what I want to say about work and effort. If we return to a consideration of our hypothetical test situation we know that, given a choice between an effortless path to food and a path requiring expenditure of effort, the hungry animal will choose the effortless path rather regularly. Hence, in accordance with our analysis concerning dissonance and dissonance reduction, we would expect the requirement of greater effort during acquisition to lead to increased resistance to extinction.

It is surprising that, in spite of the relative consistency of results among the studies which exist in the literature, the effect of effort during acquisition on resistance to extinction has not been generally noted. People have rather tended to note the finding that the greater the effort required during extinction, the faster does extinction occur. But the data are also clear with respect to the effect of effort during acquisition. They show quite clearly that, holding effort during extinction constant, the more effort required during acquisition, the more resistance there is to extinction. The data from one of the more adequately controlled experiments will suffice to illustrate the effect.

Aiken (1957) reports an experiment in which the animal was required to press a panel in order to gain access to food. Some rats were required to exert little effort while others were required to exert considerable effort during training. Half of the animals in each condition were extinguished with the low effort requirement and half with the high effort requirement. Holding effort during extinction constant, the results show clearly that the average number of trials to a criterion of extinction was considerably greater for the high effort acquisition condition than for the low effort acquisition condition. Other experiments in the literature also show this same effect if one examines the data carefully. It should once more be pointed out that any explanation of this effect which depends upon a notion of similarity between acquisition and extinction conditions is clearly inadequate.

One could list many other specific conditions which, analyzed in the same way, would be expected to increase resistance to extinction. I have chosen the three preceding ones to discuss because reasonably good data concerning them exist in the literature. Now, however, I would like to return to a more thorough consideration of the partial reward situation.

I have stated that, on nonrewarded trials in a partial reward situation, dissonance is introduced into the animal's cognition when he realizes that there is no food available. The amount of dissonance can, of course, vary in magnitude. It is important for us to consider the operational variables which will affect the total magnitude of dissonance which is introduced in this manner. This total magnitude of dissonance, of course, will determine how much dissonance reduction occurs through the development of extra preferences (always assuming that the animal does not change his behavior) and hence will determine the resistance to extinction.

In the past, it has generally been assumed that the major operational variable affecting resistance to extinction is the ratio of reward. That is, the smaller the proportion of rewarded trials, the greater the resistance to extinction. However, one might reason that since dissonance is created for the animal on every nonrewarded trial, it seems plausible to suppose that the major operational variable which will affect the resistance to extinction is, rather, the sheer total number of nonrewarded trials which the animal has experienced rather than the ratio of nonreward. From the data in published experiments it is impossible to assess whether or not this is correct since these two variables are completely confounded in the literature. Experiments on partial reward have always held constant either the number of rewarded trials or else the total number of trials that the animal experiences. It is clear, of course, that when either of these quantities is held constant, the number of nonrewarded trials is perfectly correlated with the ratio of nonreward and so the effects cannot be separated.

It is possible, perhaps, to get some hunch about this, however, from examining the results of experiments which have used rather few training trials. If we are correct, these experiments should show very weak effects of partial reward on resistance to extinction. Sheffield (1949), for example, using a total of 30 trials (only 15 nonrewarded trials) found very small differences between extinction after partial and complete reward. Wilson, Weiss, and Amsel (1955) and also Lewis (1956), replicating the Sheffield experiment almost exactly, also find such small differences that it requires an analysis of covariance to make them appear significant. However, Weinstock (1954), using a similar apparatus, but employing 75 training trials, finds huge and unmistakable differences.

It is unnecessary to belabor the matter by quoting many studies here since it is all a matter of hunch and impression. In general, when one goes through the literature one gets the impression that the experiments which show small effects after partial reward have tended to employ rather few trials. But comparison of this kind between different experiments done by different experimenters is a very shabby business at best since the variation from experimenter to experimenter can be quite large for unknown reasons. The question seemed important enough, however, so that Lawrence and I though it worthwhile to do a study which could answer the question. The study was carried out through the kind efforts of John Theios. I would like to describe it to you briefly.

The general design of the study is very simple and does not differ in any essential way from the usual study which has been done on the effects of partial reward. The major difference was that we were primarily concerned with seeing the effects of the absolute number of nonrewarded trials and with being able to separate these effects from the effects of ratio of reward. We employed four different conditions of "number of unrewarded trials." Some groups experienced 0 unrewarded trials; some groups of animals experienced a total of 16 unrewarded trials in the apparatus; still other groups experienced a moderate number of unrewarded trials, namely, 27; and finally some groups were run who experienced very many unrewarded trials, namely, 72.

Within these conditions, by varying the total number of trials, different conditions of ratio of reward were set up. Some animals were run with 33% reward, others with 50% reward, and still others with 67% reward. Of course, it was not possible to vary the ratio of reward for animals in the condition of 0 unrewarded trials but the animals were run for varying numbers of trials anyhow. Figure 13.1 shows the total design. The numbers in the cells indicate the total number of trials after preliminary training which the animals in that condition ran. During preliminary training, of course, all groups were rewarded 100% of the time. There were between 11 and 16 animals in each condition. It will

Reward Schedule	Number of Unrewarded Trials			
	0	16	27	72
33%		24	43	108
50%		31	54	144
67%		48		216
100%	0 54 216			

Figure 13.1   Total number of trials after preliminary training in partial reward experiment.

be noted that we did not run a condition of 67% reward and 27 unrewarded trials. The reason for this is simple. We ran out of patience and decided this condition was not essential.

It will also be noted that three groups of 0 unrewarded trials were run so that the total number of trials brackets the entire range for the other groups.

Figure 13.2 shows the results of the experiment. Along the horizontal axis of the figure are indicated the various values of number of unrewarded trials which we employed and along the ordinate are the average number of trials to reach a criterion of extinction. Each circle on the figure represents the results for one of our experimental conditions. The empty circles represent the data for those with the fewest total number of trials. Thus, except for the 0 unrewarded trials conditions, these empty circles represent the data for the 33% reward conditions. Similarly, the dark circles represent the longest number of total trials and hence, for the partial reward groups, represent the 67% reward conditions.

It is clear from an examination of the figure that, holding constant the number of unrewarded trials, there were only slight differences among the different conditions of ratio of reward. On the other hand, the variable of total number of unrewarded trials has a large and significant

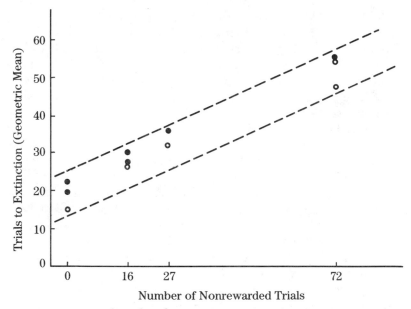

Figure 13.2 *Number of trials to extinction after partial reward.*

effect. It would, indeed, seem that in these data the only variable affecting resistance to extinction after partial reward is the number of unrewarded trials. The results of the experiment are, hence, quite consistent with the interpretations which we have made from the theory of dissonance.

These data are, of course, encouraging but certainly not conclusive. It would be nice to be able to have more direct evidence that nonreward tends to result in the development of extra preferences. From the point of view of obtaining such more direct evidence concerning the validity of our theoretical interpretation, the partial reward situation is not very adequate. For one thing, our theoretical analysis states that quite different processes occur, psychologically, on rewarded and on unrewarded trials. In a partial reward situation, however, the animal experiences both kinds of trials and, hence, an attempt to separate the effects of the two kinds of trials is bound to be indirect. And, of course, the possibility always exists that the increased resistance to extinction may depend upon some more or less complicated interaction between rewarded and unrewarded trials.

It would then be desirable to be able to compare pure conditions of reward and nonreward. That is, we could test the theory more adequately if we could compare the resistance to extinction of two groups of animals, one of which had always been rewarded in a given place, and the other of which had *never* been rewarded in that same place. This, of course, presents technical problems of how one manages to induce an animal to consistently go to a place where he never gets rewarded. This problem, however, can be solved by employing a variation of what is, essentially, a delay of reward experiment. With the very able assistance and hard work of Edward Uyeno we proceeded to do a series of such experiments in an attempt to get more direct validation of our theoretical derivations. I would like to describe some of these experiments for you.

The apparatus we used was a runway with two boxes in addition to the starting box. The two boxes were, of course, quite easily distinguishable. We will refer to one of them as the end-box and to the other as the mid-box. From the starting place, the animal was to run through a section of alley to the mid-box and then through another section of alley to the end-box. One group of rats was fed on every trial in the mid-box and also fed on every trial in the end-box. We will refer to this group as the 100% reward condition. Another group of rats was never fed in the mid-box but, instead, was delayed there for the same amount of time that it took the other to eat its food. These animals then continued to the end-box where they were also fed on every trial. We will refer to this group as the 0% reward condition. The designations of 100% and 0% reward refer, of course, to the reward in the mid-box. Both groups were rewarded on every trial in the end-box and this, of course, is what induced the animals in the 0% reward condition to run consistently to a place where they were never rewarded.

The procedure which was employed in extinction was also somewhat different from the usual procedure in a delay of reward experiment. Because we were interested in comparing the two groups of animals in their willingness to go to the mid-box where one group had always, and the other group had never, been fed, we ran extinction trials only from the starting position to the mid-box. During extinction, of course, no food was present for either condition and after a short period of time in the mid-box the animals were returned to their home cage. Thus, from this experiment we have a better comparison of the effects of reward and of nonreward. Figure 13.3 shows the average running times for the two groups during extinction.

The figure shows the data for the first 30 extinction trials averaged in groups of 3 trials each. It is clear from the figure that there is a very marked difference between the two groups of animals. Those who were always fed in the mid-box start off running quite fast (reflecting their

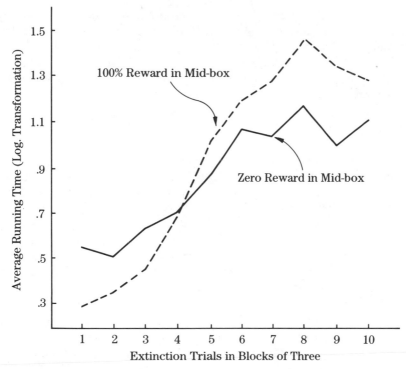

Figure 13.3   Running time during extinction in single mid-box experiment.

speed of running during acquisition) but slow down very rapidly. Those animals that were never fed in the mid-box start off more slowly (again reflecting their speed of running during acquisition) but they do not show as rapid a rate of extinction. Indeed, between the fourth and fifth blocks of trials the two curves cross over and thereafter the animals run considerably faster to a place where they have never been rewarded than they do to a place where they have always been rewarded.

One may certainly conclude from these data that increased resistance to extinction results from nonreward and that an explanation of the partial reward effect in terms of some interaction between reward and nonreward is not very tenable. Actually, in the experiment I have just described we ran a third group of animals which was rewarded 50% of the time in the mid-box and the results for these animals during extinction fall nicely midway between the two curves in Figure 13.3. The resistance to extinction of those who were never fed in the mid-box is greater than that of either of the other two groups of animals.

At the risk of being terribly repetitious, I would like to remind you at this point of the explanation I am offering for these data. Briefly, dissonance is introduced as a result of the insufficient reward or absence of reward. As long as the organism is prevented from changing his behavior, the dissonance tends to be reduced by developing some extra preference about something in the situation. The existence of this extra preference leads to the stronger inclination to continue running during extinction trials.

If this explanation is correct, however, one should be able to observe the effects of this extra preference even in a situation where all the motivation for food was removed. Indeed, it would seem that this would be a better test of this theoretical explanation. We consequently repeated the experiment I have just described to you with one modification. Three days were allowed to elapse between the end of acquisition and the beginning of extinction. During these 3 days food was always present in the cages so that by the time the extinction trials started the animals were quite well fed and not hungry. Food remained always available in their cages during the extinction period. In addition, during the 3 intervening days, each animal was placed for periods of time in the end-box without food being available there. In other words, there was an attempt to communicate to the animal that food was no longer available in the apparatus and anyhow the animals were not very motivated for food.

Extinction trials were, of course, run just from the starting box to the mid-box. Three trials were run each day and Figure 13.4 shows the results for the first 10 days of extinction. It is clear from an examination of the figure that the results are very similar to the previous results and are, in a sense, even stronger. Those animals who were always fed in the mid-box start off relatively fast and as extinction trials progress the curve shows steady and rather rapid increase in running time. In short, one obtains a familiar kind of extinction curve for these animals.

The group that was never fed in the mid-box, however, shows a very different pattern of behavior. They start off much more slowly than the other group but, for the first 4 days of extinction, they actually run faster than at the beginning. By the seventh day the two curves have crossed and thereafter the 0% reward group runs faster than the 100% reward group. It is also interesting to note that, for the 0% reward group, through the eighth day, one can see no evidence of any extinction having occurred at all. If one is inclined to do so, one can certainly see in these data some evidence that an extra preference of rather weak strength exists for the animals that were never rewarded in the mid-box.

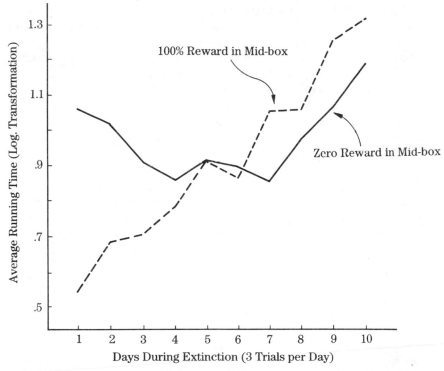

Figure 13.4   Running time while satiated during extinction in single mid-box experiment.

We were sufficiently encouraged by these results so that we proceeded to perform what I, at least, regarded as a rather ambitious experiment. Before I describe the experiment, let me briefly explain the reasoning which lay behind it. It is plausible to suppose that the extra preference which the organism develops in order to reduce dissonance may be focused on any of a variety of things. Let me explain this by using the experiment I have just described as an illustration. Those animals who were never fed in the mid-box, and thus experienced dissonance, could have developed a liking for the activity of running down the alley to the mid-box, they could have developed a preference for some aspect of the mid-box itself, or they could have developed a preference for any of the things they did or encountered subsequent to leaving the mid-box. Experimentally, of course, there was no control over this.

It occurred to us, in thinking about this, that if the dissonance were reduced, at least to some extent, by developing a preference for something about the *place* where the dissonance was introduced, then it would be possible to show the same effects in a very well controlled experiment. In other words, if the dissonance introduced by absence of reward were reduced, at least in part, by developing some liking for the place where they were not rewarded, then one could compare two groups of animals, both of which experienced the identical amount of dissonance, but who would be expected to develop preferences for different places.

To do this we used the same basic technique as in the previous two experiments I have described but with an important modification. Instead of one mid-box, two mid-boxes were used. From the starting box the animals went to Mid-box A, from there to Mid-box B, and from there to the end-box where all animals received food on every trial. Two groups of animals were run in this experiment. Group A was delayed in Mid-box A for a period of time and then was allowed to run directly through Mid-box B to the end-box. Group B was allowed to run directly through Mid-box A but was delayed for a period of time in Mid-box B before being allowed to go to the end-box. In other words, both groups of animals had identical experience. The only difference between the groups lay in the particular box in which they were delayed. (All three boxes were, of course, quite distinctive.) For the extinction trials the animals were satiated as in the preceding experiment. For the extinction trials, the animals were run only from Box A to Box B. That is, during extinction the animals were placed directly into Box A, the door was then opened, and when they ran to Box B were removed to their home cage.

Thus, Group A during extinction was running away from the place where they had been delayed, while Group B was running to the place where they had been delayed. If some extra preference had developed for the place where they had been delayed, we would expect Group B to show more resistance to extinction than Group A. In short, during extinction, Group B should behave like the 0% reward groups in the previous experiments. Group A, however, should behave during extinction more like the 100% reward animals in the preceding experiments.

Figure 13.5 shows the data for these two groups of animals for the first 10 days of extinction, three trials having been run on each day. The two curves in the figure must, by now, look very familiar to you. The same result is obtained as in the two previous experiments. The initial difference between the two groups again reflects their previous running speed in that section of the apparatus. During acquisition, Group B ran

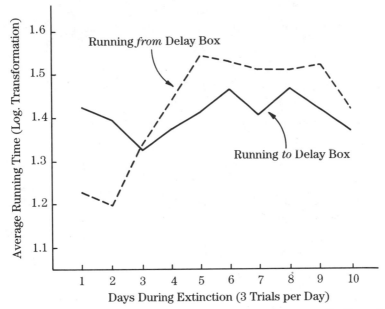

Figure 13.5 *Running time while satiated during extinction in double mid-box experiment.*

more hesitantly in the section between the two mid-boxes than did Group A. This difference, of course, still exists at the start of the extinction trials. Thereafter, however, Group A, which was running away from its delay box, rapidly increases its running time. Group B, which was running to its delay box, does not increase its time at all and shows no evidence of any extinction during 30 trials. By the fourth day of extinction, the two curves have crossed and thereafter Group B consistently runs faster than Group A.

If one looks carefully at all the data, I think one finds reasonable evidence that insufficient reward does lead to the development of extra preference. This extra preference, at least in the white rat, seems to be of a rather mild nature, but the magnitude of the effect is quite sufficient to account for the increased resistance to extinction after partial reward or after delay of reward.

Let us then briefly examine the implications of these findings and of the theory of dissonance for our traditional conception of how reward functions. It seems clear that the inclination to engage in behavior after extrinsic rewards are removed is not so much a function of past rewards themselves. Rather, and paradoxically, such persistence in behavior is increased by a history of nonrewards or inadequate rewards. I sometimes like to summarize all this by saying that rats and people come to love things for which they have suffered.

═══════════

At the time of this article, Leon Festinger was at Stanford University.

References

AIKEN, E. G. The effort variable in the acquisition, extinction, and spontaneous recovery of an instrumental response. *J. exp. Psychol.*, 1957, **53**, 47–51.

ARONSON, E., & MILLS, J. The effect of severity of initiation on liking for a group. *J. abnorm. soc. Psychol.*, 1959, **59**, 177–181.

CRUM, J., BROWN, W. L., & BITTERMAN, M. E. The effect of partial and delayed reinforcement on resistance to extinction. *Amer. J. Psychol.*, 1951, **64**, 228–237.

FEHRER, E. Effects of amount of reinforcement and of pre- and postreinforcement delays on learning and extinction. *J. exp. Psychol.*, 1956, **52**, 167–176.

FESTINGER, L. *A theory of cognitive dissonance*. Evanston, Ill.: Row, Peterson, 1957.

LEWIS, D. J. Acquisition, extinction, and spontaneous recovery as a function of percentage of reinforcement and intertrial intervals. *J. exp. Psychol.*, 1956, **51**, 45–53.

SCOTT, E. D., & WIKE, E. L. The effect of partially delayed reinforcement and trial distribution on the extinction of an instrumental response. *Amer. J. Psychol.*, 1956, **69**, 264–268.

SHEFFIELD, V. F. Extinction as a function of partial reinforcement and distribution of practice. *J. exp. Psychol.*, 1949, **39**, 511–526.

WEINSTOCK, S. Resistance to extinction of a running response following partial reinforcement under widely spaced trials. *J. comp. physiol. Psychol.*, 1954, **47**, 318–322.

WIKE, E. L., & MCNEMARA, H. J. The effects of percentage of partially delayed reinforcement on the acquisition and extinction of an instrumental response. *J. comp. physiol. Psychol.*, 1957, **50**, 348–351.

WILSON, W., WEISS, E. J., & AMSEL, A. Two tests of the Sheffield hypothesis concerning resistance to extinction, partial reinforcement, and distribution of practice. *J. exp. Psychol.*, 1955, **50**, 51–60.

PART
D

PERCEPTUAL PROCESSES

14

Efference and the Conscious Experience of Perception

A *historical review of past attempts at formulating theories in which efference plays a role in conscious perception is presented. A testable version of such a theory is formulated, and 4 experiments are presented testing implications from this theory. In all of these experiments, conditions in which Ss must learn a new afferent-efferent association are compared with Ss whose physical activity and perceptual experience are very similar but who need not learn a new association between afferent input and relevant efferent output. In all of the experiments significant change in the visual perception of curvature was obtained in the conditions in which the new associations had to be learned. Where no new associations had to be learned, significantly less visual change occurred. The results are consistent with the theoretical position that the efference and efferent readiness activated by visual input helps determine the visual perception of contour.*

Historical Introduction

Around the turn of the last century there were a few people who proposed that motor output was essential to the conscious experience of

SOURCE: Festinger, L., Burnham, C. A., Ono, H., & Bamber, D. *J. exp. Psychol. Monogr.*, 1967, **74** (4, part 2), 1–36. [Received June 6, 1966]

perception. Münsterberg (1899), for example, elaborated the view that incoming, afferent stimulation and outgoing motor innervation were a single, continuous nerve process with no point of separation between them. The motor discharge, he held, is necessary before any central activity corresponding to perception or consciousness takes place. Montague (1908) stated that "Perceptions are presumed to arise synchronously with the redirection in the central nervous system of afferent currents into efferent channels [p. 128]."

Ultimately, such views fell into disrepute for a variety of reasons. For one thing, these theories arose out of an attempt to understand consciousness and, with the rise of behaviorism, consciousness became less and less a proper subject for study. Thus, for example, Washburn (1916) devoted most of the introduction of her book to attacking Watson and behaviorism and to justifying that the study of consciousness is proper. But this book is one of the last attempts to state and elaborate a motor theory of consciousness.

Another reason for the decline of such theories was that they never were able to cope adequately with the facts. If the conscious experience of perception is occasioned by the motor discharge initiated by the afferent input, then one would expect all perception to be accompanied by motor movements. Münsterberg (1900) explained that we frequently do not perceive something if our attention is directed elsewhere because the appropriate motor responses are suppressed if attention is fixed on something else. He, consequently, stated that the vividness of conscious experience is a direct function of how free the motor pathway is to discharge. This view, however, seems to conflict with the fact that when a movement is well learned and occurs freely and easily, consciousness of the movement decreases. A skilled violin player, for example, is not conscious of all his movements. This led Montague (1908) to propose, contrary to Münsterberg, that consciousness is more vivid if the motor output is interfered with. Washburn (1916) attempted to reconcile all this is in the statement that "consciousness accompanies a certain ratio of excitation to inhibition in a motor discharge and if the amount of excitation either sinks below a certain minimum or rises above a certain maximum, consciousness is lessened [p. 25]."

Whichever of the above hypotheses one chooses, however, one must still search for movement correlates of perception. Even if the motor discharge is interfered with somewhat, there would still be some movement. The general absence of obvious movement accompanying conscious perception led to the necessity to postulate the existence of rudimentary or tentative movements. Thus Breese (1899), in discussing the perception of speech, stated:

The muscles of the vocal cords, throat, and respiratory organs are slightly innervated and adjusted, but the process goes no further. Sometimes, however, the enunciation is complete so far as the adjustment of the muscles of the vocal cords, throat and mouth cavities is concerned. There is a tendency to make these adjustments not only when we hear spoken words, but to make them in response to other stimuli. We are likely to utter the name of any object upon which the attention rests . . . . If, for any reason, the motor apparatus does not respond properly, there is an interruption in the conscious stream [p. 49].

The relationship between the conscious experience of perception and such motor movements, however, remained hypothetical and, to modern psychologists, implausible.

Another probable reason for the demise of these views concerning the importance of motor action for the conscious experience of perception is the unclarity concerning what explanatory power was added by the insistence that motor innervation had to exist for consciousness to exist. Up to the end of the nineteenth century there were many psychologists who accepted Helmholtz's (1962) view that there was a consciousness concerning innervation to the muscles and, as long as this view was held, motor theories of consciousness added something. James (1890), followed by Sherrington (1900), attacked this view successfully, however, and persuaded psychologists and physiologists alike that there was no conscious sense of innervation to the muscles and that afferent input via sense organs was the only input relevant to the conscious experience of perception. Thus, Münsterberg (1899) said:

The only theory which brings in a really new factor is the theory of innervation feelings. This well-known theory claims that one special group of conscious facts, namely the feelings of effort and impulse, are not sensations and, therefore, not parallel to the sensory excitements, but are activities of consciousness and parallel to the physiological innervation of a central motor path . . . . The psychologist can show (however) that this so-called feeling of effort is merely a group of sensations like other sensations, reproduced joint and muscle sensations which precede the action . . . . If the other sensations are accompaniments of sensory excitements in the brain the feelings of impulse cannot claim an exceptional position [p. 443].

If, as became widely accepted, there was no consciousness of innervation to the muscles and all perception depended upon afferent input, then it became unclear as to the value of a theory that states that innervation to the motor system is necessary for conscious experience.

More recently, however, evidence has accumulated that, in spite of having won the argument, James (1890) and Sherrington (1900) were wrong and that the organism *does* have usable conscious information about innervation to the motor system, that is, about efferent impulses issued from the central nervous system through the motor pathways. Reviews of the issue and of the evidence may be found in Merton (1964) and in Festinger and Canon (1965). Consequently, it may be worthwhile to examine once more the possible validity of some form of theory of the conscious experience of perception which depends in whole or in part on efference activated by afferent input and to see if there are any facts which would strongly argue in the direction of some such view.

Some Observation On Perception of Limb Movement

There are some observations reported in the literature, all of them made incidentally while investigating some other problem, which seem to point in the direction of a strong effect of efference on perception. Perhaps the most interesting of these was reported by Gibson (1933) in connection with an experiment on visual adaptation to curvature. Having noted previously that if S wore wedge prism spectacles that made vertical straight lines appear curved, after a while S adapted to the curvature so that the vertical lines looked less curved, he set out to explore the mechanism of this visual adaptation. His initial hypothesis was that the adaptation occurred as a result of "conflict between vision and kinesthesis [p. 4]." That is, since the vertical lines looked curved but, if felt would feel straight, this conflict might lead to the adaptation. His Ss, consequently, each spent about ½ hr. wearing the prism spectacles and looking at and running their fingers along vertical edges such as a meter rule.

The observation of relevance to us here is reported in the section on procedure as follows:

> It was discovered, however, that in actual fact the kinaesthetic perception, in so far as it was consciously represented, did *not* conflict with the visual perception. When a visually curved edge such as a meter stick was felt, it was felt as *curved*. This was true as long as the hand was watched while running up and down the edge. If the eyes were closed or turned away, the edge of course felt straight, as it in reality was. This dominance of the visual over the kinesthetic perception was so complete that when subjects were instructed to make a strong effort to dissociate the two, *i.e.* to "feel

it straight and see it curved," it was reported either difficult or impossible to do so [pp. 4–5].

This phenomenon reported by Gibson (1933) is clear and compelling and anyone who has a pair of prism spectacles can demonstrate it for himself. It has been tried in our laboratory, again and again. Wearing the spectacles and running one's hand up and down along, say, a door edge or door frame edge, the hand *feels* that it is moving in a curved path. It is not that one thinks the hand is moving in a curve because one sees a curve. The hand actually feels it is moving in a curve in spite of the fact that it actually is moving in a straight path. To say, as Gibson said, that visual perception dominates over kinesthetic perception does not explain the phenomenon. The question still remains as to how vision dominates proprioception so that the hand actually feels that the path of movement is curved.

If one thinks in terms of some theory in which efference affects perception, however, an explanation readily suggests itself. Let us imagine that the conscious perception of the path of movement of a limb is not the organization of informational input from the receptors in that limb, but is rather the organization of the efferent signals issued from the central nervous system *to* that limb. The arm would be felt to move in a curved path if the efferent signals issued through the motor pathways directed the arm to move in a curve. The fact that the arm and hand, because they are maintaining pressure on the straight edge, actually move in a straight line would then be irrelevant to the conscious experience of path of movement. The arm is felt to move as it has been directed to move.

From such a point of view one can understand the dominance of vision over proprioception in this instance. The dominance exists as it does because the visual input, perhaps because of years and years of prior learning, perhaps because of its greater precision, is heavily relied on to activate efferent instructions. If the visual input corresponds to a curve, then the efferent instructions activated by the input direct the arm to move in a curved path and the arm is felt to move that way. If this is true, one would expect to be able to observe some manifestation of the fact that the arm has been directed to move in a curved path and, indeed, one can observe indications of this. Typically, in this situation in which a person sees an actually straight edge as curved and runs his hand up and down along it, the wrist and hand twist somewhat in a manner consistent with directions to move in a curved path.

The view that the conscious perception of the movement of a limb is determined, or at least affected, by the efferent instructions issued from the central nervous system to that limb leads us to expect other observable phenomena. To take a very gross example, let us imagine that, using some drug, one paralyzed a person. We would expect that if this person tried to move, even though he actually did not move because of the paralysis, he would feel that he had moved. I know of no systematic data that have ever been collected in such a situation but an incidental observation by Campbell, Sanderson, and Laverty (1964) tends to support this expectation.

The authors report an experiment in which five Ss were injected with succinylcholine chloride dihydrate. This is what the authors said about the action of the drug:

> The drug acts so as to break the connection between the motor neurones and the skeletal musculature . . . . During the period in which the drug is active the skeletal musculature is very nearly completely paralyzed . . . . (The drug) has no anesthetic effect. Enquiries made of subjects following the paralysis indicate that they are aware of what is going on around them. . . . [p. 628].

The drug produced a very traumatic experience for Ss, largely because of the interruption of respiration. The average duration of this respiratory paralysis was about 100 sec. The incidental observation that is of interest to us here is the following:

> The subjects described their movements (during the paralysis) as part of a struggle to get away from the apparatus and to tear off the wires and electrodes. Though in fact their movements were small and poorly controlled the subjects were under the impression they had been making large movements [p. 632].

Surely, it seems difficult to imagine any basis for this phenomenon other than that their conscious experience of movement of their limbs was based on the efferent output to those limbs.

A similar instance, not involving paralysis, was reported by Merton (1964) in connection with experiments to demonstrate that joint receptors rather than muscle receptors carry information concerning the position of a limb. He stated:

> In some recent unpublished experiments, Dr. T. Davies, Mr. A. J. M. Butt and I have used the top joint of the thumb. The advantage of this joint is that the muscles that flex and extend it both lie in the forearm and have long tendons. Hence it is possible with a pneumatic tourniquet around the wrist to make the joint and the skin of the thumb anaesthetic without any effect on the muscles.

This experiment succeeds in making the top joint of the thumb show just the same properties as the eye as regards movements. After an hour to an hour and a half of aschaemia the subject becomes quite insensitive to passive movements of the joint of whatever range or rapidity. Nevertheless, active movements of the joint are made with much the same accuracy as before and, indeed, with much the same angular accuracy as eye movements in the dark. *If the movement is restrained by holding the thumb the subject believes he has moved it just the same* [pp. 393–394, italics ours].

Surely, it seems difficult to imagine any basis for these observations other than that the conscious experience of movement of the limbs, in one case, or the thumb, in the other instance, was based on the efferent output to the motor system.

The Problem
of a Motor Theory of Visual Perception

We have seen that there are instances in which the perception of a motor movement seems to be based on efferent output rather than on afferent input. If the discussion were to be confined to the perception of motor movements, there does not seem to be much difficulty in specifying and maintaining an "efference" theory of perception. If, however, we wish to broaden our considerations to include visual perception, we immediately encounter difficulties. Efferent instructions issued to the muscles associated with the eye do not seem to be integral in visual perception. It is difficult to imagine what specific eye movements would be relevant to the perception of brightness and color, in the first place. But even if we ignore brightness and color and think only of the visual perception of shape, pattern, and contour, there are still problems. We do not have to move our eyes along a contour in order to perceive that contour. Even if a steady point of fixation is maintained, we are able to perceive, and distinguish between, straight lines, curved lines, squares, circles, and the like. It is true that under ordinary conditions the eyes are always moving to a small extent, but these tremors, drifts, and small saccadic corrections do not seem to be at all associated with the contour that is perceived. If efference activated by visual input is important in visual perception, something other than actual efferent output from the central nervous system to the extraocular muscles must be involved.

The few who have suggested, or attempted to formulate, a theory of visual perception in terms of efference have, of course, recognized this and have maintained that "readiness" to issue efferent instructions is the basis for visual perception. Thus, Breese (1899), trying to explain the fluctuations obtained when there is binocular rivalry, states: "consciousness arises only when the cortical centers involved are *ready* to discharge toward the periphery [p. 60, italics ours]." He does not, however, attempt to specify what he meant by such a state of readiness.

More recently, Sperry (1952) has also suggested such a view:

> If there be any objectively demonstrable fact about perception that indicates the nature of the neural process involved, it is the following: Insofar as an organism perceives a given object, it is prepared to respond with reference to it. This preparation-to-respond is absent in an organism that has failed to perceive . . . . The presence or absence of adaptive reaction potentialities of this sort, ready to discharge into motor patterns, makes the difference between perceiving and not perceiving [p. 301].

Sperry, however, is no more specific than Breese (1899) about this suggestion. He simply made statements such as ". . . the preparation for response *is* the perception [p. 301]" and ". . . perception is basically an implicit preparation to respond [p. 302]" and urges the possible value of such a theoretical approach.

Very recently, Taylor (1962) proposed a more elaborated theory based on this same kind of idea. On the basis of his evaluation of existing data he came to the conclusion that all visual perception is learned. In facing the question of exactly what it is that the person learns, and how he learns it, Taylor stated that as a result of appropriately reinforced experience the person learns the appropriate motor responses to make to precisely given contellations of stimulus input.

So far, of course, this is not a very radical suggestion. He proceeded, however, to propose that the conscious experience of visual perception is nothing more or less than these learned responses. Specifically, Taylor developed a system in which, over a large number of repeated trials with appropriate reinforcement, the person learns to make a given response, say an eye movement or a hand movement, to a given visual input, taking account almost automatically of eye, head, and body position. The result of this learning is the formation of "engrams" that may be regarded as well-learned response tendencies that are triggered off by the visual input. These engrams, when they become well established, are automatically brought into play by the appropriate stimulus input. The totality of the engrams that are activated at any moment *is*, for Taylor, the conscious experience of visual perception. In short, Taylor said that what the person "sees" are the readinesses to respond that, over many years, he has learned.

Perhaps, to be complete, one should mention a few others, who in their theoretical considerations give some role to efferent output in affecting perception but not quite in the same way. Hebb (1949), for example, attributed considerable importance to eye movements in learning to perceive contour and shape and, hence, in establishing the cell assemblies that provide the perception of, say, a triangle. Thus, by implication, efference is important in perception for Hebb but he does not spell out any of these implications. Von Holst (1954) also stressed the importance of efference for one particular type of perception. He proposed that the organism is able to distinguish between self-produced movement and externally produced movement by matching a record of the efferent instructions issued to the musculature with the resulting afferent input. Von Holst, however, showed no intention of giving efference a role in perception generally.

Von Holst's theory of "reafference" has been pursued further by Held (1961). Held proposed that, as a result of experience, there is stored somewhere in the central nervous system a set of correlations between efferent output and reafferent input. Because of the wide variety of invariant relationships that provide redundancy through experience, this collection of correlations becomes well established. In a mature organism, following any issued efference, there is an expected reafferent input that should match with what is stored in this correlator. If in any situation the reafference does not fit the expected afferent input, that is, if there is unusual reafference, then there will be some kind of perceptual or behavioral change that occurs. Held was not very explicit about how this occurs except that such experience starts changing what is stored in the correlator. What Held would say about the conscious experience of visual perception is quite unclear.

Some Data About Visual Perception

The fact that a few people over a long period of time have suggested that efferent readiness activated by afferent input is responsible for the conscious experience of visual perception may have no more status than as a curiosity. Perhaps it is more important to note that only a very few have proposed such a view. In order to decide whether or not these suggestions should be taken seriously, we should look at the data that led these persons in this direction. If the data are compelling, that is, if they are difficult to explain in other ways, then these theories should seriously be examined.

Breese (1899) was led to this view by data he collected on binocular rivalry. He presented to one eye of his Ss a red square with five diagonal lines running from upper left to lower right. On the corresponding part of the retina of the other eye was presented a green square with five diagonal lines running from lower left to upper right. Under such circumstances, as is well known, there is fluctuation of what S sees—the red square and the green square alternate in conscious experience. Breese investigated some conditions that affected the length of time that one or another of the two squares was seen. He reported that an effort to pay attention to, say, the red square and keep it in consciousness was effective in increasing the amount of time it was seen only if eye movements occurred when the red field was seen and the eye was relatively still when the green field was seen. If S was trained not to make eye movements, effort of will had no effect on the fluctuations. Breese also found that if S was instructed to move his eyes along the lines of one of the squares or to count the lines of one of the squares, that square remained much longer in consciousness.

It is easy to understand why such data led Breese to adopt a theory involving efference in the conscious experience of perception. It is difficult to explain the efficacy of eye movements in other ways. If the eyes move when the red square is "seen," the same movement is occurring for both the red and green squares on their respective retinas; if the eyes are relatively still when the green square is "seen," the same relative stillness applies to each square on its respective retina. This suggested to Breese that an explanation should be sought in terms of readiness for motor activity.

Rather different considerations led Taylor (1962) to think in terms of an "efferent readiness" theory of visual perception. The reports of Kohler (1964), originally published in 1951, concerning dramatic changes in the visual perception of contour were of primary importance for Taylor. Kohler and Ss wear spectacles containing wedge prisms for prolonged periods of time. Such wedge prisms (with bases mounted laterally), among other things, make straight vertical lines appear curved. The dramatic nature of the visual changes that can occur is illustrated by the following quote from Kohler (1964) concerning one of his Ss:

> After ten days of continuously wearing the spectacles, all objects had straightened out and were no longer distorted. The subject then removed the spectacles. Immediately, impressions of curvature, distortions, and apparent movement set in. The subject complained: "What I experienced after I took off the spectacles was much worse than what I experienced when I first started wearing them. I felt as if I were drunk." Aftereffects continued for four days [p. 34].

In other words, after 10 days of wearing the spectacles S's visual perception had completely adapted and the distortions were eliminated. Curved retinal images were then seen as straight. On taking the spectacles off, distortion, of course, appeared since now straight retinal images were seen as curved. While Kohler did not report such complete adaptation for all of his Ss, the fact that some Ss largely, or completely, altered the visual perception of contour is important and requires understanding. How does it happen that the same pattern of retinal stimulation that at one time is "seen" as straight comes to be "seen" as curved?

The observations that Kohler made are not isolated observations. The same phenomenon was reported by Wundt (1898), by Gibson (1933), and more recently by Pick and Hay (1965). Gibson attempted to explain the change in perception of curvature by positing a tendency toward visual "normalization." He discovered that there was some small change toward perceiving less curvature in a contour after simply staring at that contour for 5–10 min. He erroneously assumed that this "Gibson effect" accounted for the entire phenomenon. It has since been shown by Held and Rekosh (1963) and by Cohen (1963) that there is adaptation to prismatically induced curvature over and above the small magnitude involved in the "Gibson effect" and that relevant motor movements are necessary to produce this visual adaptation.

Taylor (1962) felt that these facts forced him to the theory he proposes in which, in our own terms, the efferent readiness activated by the afferent visual input determines the conscious experience of perception. Thus, for him, the perception of contour changes because, while wearing the prism spectacles and engaging in normal activities, S learns to make, and then is ready to make, different motor movements in response to the visual input. It is also possible, of course, to think of the changed perception of contour as due to a recoding of the visual input on the central nervous system. But even if one thinks of it this way, one must say that this recoding was determined somehow by the motor activity of the person while he was wearing the spectacles. Perhaps Taylor's position is simpler and more adequate.

Taylor also attempted to derive additional testable propositions from his theoretical statement and to marshall data in support of it. The relationship between his theory and his data will leave many dissatisfied, however. For example, he reasons that, if his theory is correct, the specific visual changes occurring for a person should be unique, depending upon his previous learning and the specific motor adjustments he must make while he is wearing distorting lenses. He documents this by describing his own experiences with adaptation to prismatic distortion—a set of experiences which seem consistent with what he says but are not very compelling.

The most interesting, and most theoretically relevant, data that Taylor presented concern his experiences adapting to prismatically induced curvature when the prism was mounted on a scleral contact lens rather than in a spectacle frame. He realized that if the prism was mounted on a contact lens, the eye itself must move according to the objective contour when scanning that contour and not according to the retinal image. He reasoned that, under these circumstances, adaptation to the curvature distortion should occur as a result of eye movements alone. The S would learn quickly to make a different set of motor movements with his eye in response to a given visual input. Specifically, the input to the retina which used to activate "engrams" to move the eye over a curved path would, after some experience with the contact lens, activate engrams to move the eye over a straight path. Once this happened, the perception should have changed since it is based on the evoked "engram" and S would see the contour as straight in spite of the curved retinal image. Taylor reported that, indeed, with a prism mounted on a contact lens he adapted to the curvature quickly and completely by just looking back and forth along a contour.

Some data do exist, then, that encourage, even if they do not compel, a theory of visual perception in which the efferent readiness activated by the visual input determines the conscious experience of perception. These data that we have discussed were concerned with the question of "what a person sees." If, however, the conscious experience of visual perception is determined by efference and efferent readiness, we might expect to find some relevant data addressed to the question of "whether or not a person sees." The kind of theory we are discussing here would imply that if, somehow, a situation were created in which the person completely stopped being ready to react to visual input, there might be a cessation of the conscious experience of visual perception. There are two situations that have been used in experiments on visual perception that might produce such a state of affairs, namely, stabilized retinal images and ganzfelds. A close examination of the data reported from such experiments may be useful.

With suitable optical arrangements, a pattern of retinal stimulation can be maintained at a given location on the retina in spite of any eye movements that occur. These images have been called stopped or stabilized retinal images. The experimental findings are that when a retinal image is stopped, contours and shapes tend to disappear. The interpretation of these findings has been in terms of fatigue or satiation of neural mechanisms due to the constant stimulation of the same nerve endings on the retina. The conclusion has been that the ordinary small nystagmic eye movements are essential in maintaining visual perception.

One may also look at the situation produced by a stopped retinal image in another way. There has been a complete destruction of the usual correlation between eye movements and movement of the image across the retina—no matter what eye movements occur, the retinal position remains unchanged. We might well imagine that in such a situation, where movement of the eyes is completely irrelevant to position of retinal stimulation, the person might soon cease responding, or even being ready to respond, to the visual input. Why should the person continue to be ready to make motor movements when these motor movements are useless and irrelevant? From this point of view we might also expect the disappearance of contour and shape with a stopped retinal image as soon as the person stops being ready to react to the input. Furthermore, from this point of view one might expect to observe the same kinds of disappearance of contour even if the stabilized image were not *stopped* on the retina. That is, the stabilized image could be moved, by E, across the retina while maintaining the complete lack of correlation between position on the retina and eye movements. Since, from this viewpoint, the important factor would be the cessation of reactivity due to the total lack of correlation between eye movement and movement across the retina, we would still expect the disappearance.

Along these lines an interesting observation is reported by Campbell and Robson (1961). They studied stabilized images produced by making visible the shadows of the retinal capillaries, a very precise way of producing a stabilized image. They reported as follows:

> New findings are that a stabilized shadow of the retinal capillaries disappears in a few seconds and does not reappear even in flickering light. The capillary shadow can be seen for a much longer period if moved across the retina at certain amplitudes and frequencies but, even so, these moving shadows also ultimately disappear and never reappear again spontaneously. Similar observations have been made using the central details of the shadow of the macular pigment [p. 12P].

Clearly, these observations cannot be explained entirely in terms of fatigue or satiation of neural mechanisms. They do fit what we would expect from our conjectures about the importance of efferent readiness in visual perception.

There is another known situation in which persons experience the cessation of visual perception. This occurs sometimes if a person's total visual field is a "ganzfeld," that is a completely homogeneous, structureless field of vision. Typically, when viewing a "ganzfeld," O perceives a fog or mist of light and does not perceive any surface. Cohen (1960) reported that about one-third of Ss in his study also experience "blank out," that is, "complete disappearance of the sense of vision for short periods of time." It is conceivable that, in the absence of any structure in the visual field that the person can use for fixation, the person occasionally stops responding altogether to the visual input. We will not pursue the speculation further. We will leave it at this except for one piece of data that is interesting with respect to this speculation. Tepas (1962) found that there was a significant absence of saccadic eye movements just prior to the onset of a "blank out." The absence of saccadic eye movements continued during the blank out and the end of the blank-out period coincided with the resumption of such eye movements.

Some Theoretical Specifications

If one is to take seriously a theory proposing that the conscious experience of visual perception is determined by efferent readiness activated by afferent visual input, it is necessary to specify some of the characteristics that such a theory must have to fit the known data. It is also necessary to specify something about what "efferent readiness" is, how it is developed, how it is activated, and what particular efferent readinesses affect visual perception.

The published literature discussed above suggests that the visual perception of contour can be altered. If we wish to say that this visual perception is determined by efferent readiness, then we must postulate that the efferent readiness appropriate to a given visual input must, to at least some extent, be learned and modifiable. This would make it likely that visual perception of contour and shape must be learned, or at least in part. We might imagine that the visual experience of a newborn infant has no sharp contours or definite shapes but consists entirely of fuzzy blotches of brightness and color differentials. Perhaps more than this is innately built into the organism but we need not concern ourselves with the problem. Even if only this much is built in, mature visual perception based on efferent readiness can easily develop.

There is a precise and invariant relationship that always holds between the magnitude and direction of an eye movement and the magnitude and direction of movement across the retina of any point of stimulation on the retina. Thus, of course, the basis exists for being able to learn the appropriate efferent instructions to issue to move a point of stimulation from one part of the retina to any other part. To learn this, however, would mean to learn an almost countless number of efferent sets of instructions and the human organism almost certainly does not learn all of this. The part of the retina that is of the greatest interest is the fovea. We can imagine a tendency in our newborn infant to examine, in detail, parts of the visual field in which the brightness or the color changes. When such parts of the visual field fall on the fovea, the detail is best and so the organism learns to direct the eye so as to bring points of peripheral stimulation to the fovea. This, of course, is a much more restricted and manageable set of efferent instructions to learn. Most adult organisms have never learned to, and cannot, execute eye movements to bring a point of stimulation from 20 degrees to the right of the fovea, for example, to a point 10 degrees below the fovea. Thus, for example, Fender (1964) reported that "subjects find it almost impossible to track a moving target while maintaining fixation a few degrees away from it [p. 315]."

It is, then, a manageable set of efferent instructions that the organism learns to issue for eye movements. Considering that the saccadic fixating eye movement in the adult is not a completely accurate movement—errors up to half a degree are not unusual—the amount to be learned is manageable indeed. Thus, we can imagine the input to the retina coded as if the retina were calibrated in terms of distance and direction from the fovea. The organism learns the appropriate efferent instructions to be issued from the central nervous system to direct the eye to move so as to bring any point of stimulation on to the fovea. After a considerable amount of learning has gone on, these sets of efferent instructions can be viewed as becoming "preprogrammed" and as being automatically activated by brightness or color differentials stimulating the retina. We do not mean the term "activated" in the sense of efference actually being sent from the central nervous system through the motor neurones; we mean to use the term in the sense that these preprogrammed sets of efferent instructions are brought into a state of immediate readiness for use. Thus, those efferent instructions which if issued would bring areas of brightness differential onto the fovea, are ready for immediate use.

Although the idea of efferent instructions held in readiness for use is not a new one, as we have seen, it is still a rather vague one. Some attempt at clarification would perhaps to be helpful. Without trying to speculate about the exact physiological mechanisms and arrangements, it seems plausible to imagine that the physical system is limited in the number of sets of stored preprogrammed instructions that can be "immediately" sent out through the motor pathways. Thus, out of the very large number of sets of efferent instructions that the organism has learned, only some are held in readiness for immediate use. Without intending any precise analogy, we could imagine a jukebox which, at the push of the appropriate button, will immediately play any of a hundred different phonograph records. The owner of the jukebox could also have many thousands of other records available but, obviously, they cannot be played immediately. The owner could, however, with a little bit of work, change the entire set, or part of the set, of the hundred records that are immediately available for playing. One might think of these hundred records as being "ready for immediate use."

If we are to think of the conscious experience of visual perception as being determined by these preprogrammed sets of efferent instructions that are activated into readiness by the afferent input, then it is necessary to specify something about the level of generality or specificity of the efferent signals that are issued from the central nervous system. If, using an efference readiness theory of visual perception, we are to be able to have a person perceive a given shape or contour as the same no matter what the eye position is when viewing it, it seems necessary to specify that the efferent instructions issued from the central nervous system must be general in nature, that is, relatively far removed from the final signal that causes the exact muscle twitch. Thus, the efferent signal from the central nervous system could be concerned only with direction and magnitude of deviation from the fovea, and final computation to effectuate the actual muscle contractions could take account of afferent information at more peripheral levels. This is not an unlikely state of affairs. For example, Merton (1964) said: "Hughlings Jackson (no reference given) showed that, in the code used by the motor cortex, the orders sent out represent instructions to perform movements, not instructions to individual muscles to contract [p. 399]."

One might be tempted to say that the conscious experience of visual perception of contour and shape (and similar arguments could be made for perception of distance and depth) was determined by readiness to issue efferent instructions to the extraocular muscles. However, it is clear that this cannot be the whole story. The data show clearly that fairly large changes in the visual perception of curvature occur if wedge prism spectacles are worn for long periods of time. Pick and Hay (1964), for example, found an average of 30% adaptation to curvature in eight Ss who wore such spectacles all their waking hours for 42 days. But if S wears prism spectacles, no change in the efference or efferent readiness activated by the visual input should occur with respect to the extraocular muscles. The eye, under these conditions, must move with respect to the retinal contour, not with respect to the objective contour. However, head movements, arm movements, and all other body movements must, in order to be effective, correspond to the objective contour and so, efference and efferent readiness concerning these motor movements that are activated by the visual input must change. If we are to explain these adaptations to curvature in terms of an efferent readiness theory, then, it is necessary to say that the conscious experience of visual perception is determined by the total efferent readiness activated by the visual input, not just the efference relevant to the eyes.

Perhaps this represents sufficient specification of an "efference readiness theory" to permit submitting the theory to experimental test. Before proceeding to examine this question, however, it is necessary to consider an alternative interpretation of the data on which we have relied in the discussion. Harris (1965) proposed that the visual system and visual perception are probably not changeable and that the changes that occur when adapting to distorting spectacles are proprioceptive changes, that is, the end result of the adaptation is a change in the felt position of some part of the body. He stated,

> Vision seems to be largely inflexible, whereas the position sense is remarkably labile . . . proprioceptive perception of parts of the body (and therefore of the location of touched objects) develops with the help of *innate visual perception* . . . [italics ours, pp. 441–442].

Harris presented data to show that such changes in "felt position" do indeed occur as a result of adaptation to displacement of the visual field. He also presented a highly ingenious analysis in terms of changes in "felt position" to explain adaptation to spectacles that invert or reverse the visual field. With regard to curvature, Harris implied (although he retracted the implication partly in a footnote) that the same end result is achieved rather than any change in visual perception. He said,

> So perhaps adaptation to curvature also involves altered registration of eye movements without any change in scanning behavior. After adapting, the subject may feel that his eyes are moving in a straight line when they are actually tracing out a curve [p. 428].

On examination, however, this suggestion seems strange and even rather inconsistent with the position taken by Harris. First of all, if S is wearing prism spectacles, what could conceivably lead to a change in felt position of the eyes? The eye movements necessary to scan a contour would be precisely consistent with vision (retinal input) which is "largely inflexible" and "innate." After moving about in the environment an S might be expected to recalibrate the felt position of other parts of the body but *not* of the eyes. Second, Harris seemed to be making a very curious suggestion. He was apparently suggesting that the visual perception of a contour such as curvature is determined by how S feels his eyes are moving when he scans this contour. It becomes unclear what Harris meant by visual perception. Did he suggest that with steady fixation contours cannot be perceived, or did he suggest some notion of efferent readiness similar to ours?

Possible Experimental Tests

If the conscious experience of visual perception of contour is, indeed, determined by the efferent readiness activated by the visual input, there is a definite empirical implication that can be tested experimentally. If, without changing anything about the pattern of retinal stimulation, one could alter the particular preprogrammed sets of efferent instructions that were activated and held in readiness for immediate use, one would expect to produce a change in visual perception.

It is clear that, by using prism spectacles that produce a curved retinal input when looking at a straight line, one could induce a person to learn, say, to make a straight arm movement in response to a curved retinal image. It is also possible, as Taylor (1962) pointed out, that by using prisms mounted on contact lenses one could induce a person to make a straight eye movement in response to a curved retinal image. The problem is how to do these experiments with appropriate controls and appropriate comparison conditions so that alternative interpretations of the data can be ruled out. Since a major class of possible alternative interpretations of such changes in visual perception would be based on the idea that the change occurs because of conflicting information obtained from retinal input and from feedback from the muscles and joints, it would seem to be desirable to control for these factors. In other words, we would want different experimental conditions in which retinal input was identical and feedback from muscles and joints was identical but the efference issued from the central nervous system was different.

Theoretically, of course, it is possible to have quite different general efference issued ending in exactly the same muscle contractions. To use an analogy, instructions could be issued to a computer to divide 28 by 4 or to find the fifth prime number. As a result of these two very different instructions, the machine ends up doing the identical thing, namely, it prints the number 7. Operationally, it does not seem easy to do, but perhaps one may approach such a situation. For example, if an S wearing prism spectacles looks at a straight edge that appears curved and is instructed to run his finger along the edge, pressing on the edge, the finger will actually move in a straight line, of course, and feedback from the skeletal joint receptors will provide this information. There is no necessity, however, for efference from the central nervous system to concern itself with the exact contour involved. If, however, S had to learn to make an accurate sweeping motion with his finger that corresponded to the contour without any edge to press on, it seems more likely that the efference from the central nervous system would have to concern itself with contour. In both conditions, however, the feedback from the limb would be very similar. Only in the latter conditions would we expect S to develop the new efferent readiness to move his arm in a straight path when the retinal input is curved and, hence, only in that condition would we expect change in visual perception.

Four experiments have been designed to provide such tests of the theory that the conscious experience of visual perception is determined by efferent readiness activated by the visual input. They all used, for this purpose, the empirical vehicle of adaptation to prismatically induced curvature.

Experiment I

In this preliminary experiment an attempt was made to create two experimental conditions similar with respect to the active movements that occur and the proprioceptive feedback but different with respect to whether or not S learns a new afferent-efferent association. One-half of the Ss were required to learn to move a stylus in a continuous movement along a path between two brass rods. Since the path between the rods either was objectively straight and appeared curved or else was objectively curved and appeared straight, Ss needed to learn a new, unitary, afferent-efferent association in order to perform the continuous tracking motion without error, i.e., without striking one of the rods. The remaining Ss were not asked to learn a continuous tracking motion. Rather, they were asked to move the stylus, as slowly as they wished, between the rods with the paramount objective of never touching a rod. Thus, one-half the Ss were asked to learn a new, unitary, skilled movement; the remaining Ss were not.

Method

SUBJECTS. The Ss in this experiment were freshmen or sophomore female students at either Stanford University or Foothill College. All were right handed and did not wear spectacles. Each was paid $4.00 for participating in the experiment. Only females were used in the study because preliminary work had indicated that males tended to become more frustrated at the boring nature of the task and tended to lose interest and motivation. The Ss were run, assigned to experimental conditions at random, until 10 usable Ss in each condition were obtained. During the course of conducting the experiment, the data from 12 Ss were discarded for the following reasons: (a) Three Ss because of difficulties with the biteboard during the session; (b) Two Ss because of disregarding the instructions; (c) Seven Ss because of highly inaccurate or suspicious initial settings with the prisms.

APPARATUS.   The main piece of apparatus was a white formica board, 40 in. wide × 26 in. high. The board was held vertically in a wooden frame and rested on a table. Down the middle of the board ran two parallel vertical bass rods. The robs were slightly less than ⅛ in. in diameter and were mounted ½ in. apart between centers. The ends of the rods ran through holes at the top and bottom of the board. The ends of the rods were free to slip back and forth through these holes. The midpoints of the rods were rigidly attached to a horizontal center strip in the board which had an identical surface set flush with the surface of the rest of the board. A knob was mounted in the frame below the board and to the right of center. By turning this knob, S could move the center strip back and forth and thus adjust the rods to various desired degrees of curvature. On the back of the board was a pointer which ran along a centimeter scale. The pointer measured the horizontal deviation of the midpoints of the rods from true straight. A biteboard was mounted on the table directly in front of the center of the board so that the distance from S's eyes to the board was approximately 40 cm.

During most of the experimental session S wore goggles with 25-diopter prisms mounted with their bases left. While wearing the goggles and biting on the biteboard, the vertical extent of vision on the board was about 37 cm. For measurements involving the naked eye, Ss wore a similar pair of goggles with plate glass in them. For each S, the height of the chair and of the biteboard was adjusted so that her eyes were at the same height as the horizontal center strip on the board.

PROCEDURE.   Before any goggles were put on S, she was shown how, by turning the knob, the curvature of the lines could be changed. She was told that periodically she would be asked to adjust the lines so that they were straight. She was also told that she would spend part of the session moving a stylus down between the two rods using her right hand and was shown that if the stylus touched either rod a buzzer would sound. The type of stylus stroke was then explained to S, the specific instruction depending on the experimental condition.

In the condition designed to encourage learning a new afferent-efferent association (Learning condition) S was told to make a smooth, fast, sweeping motion with the stylus between the two rods. She was told to try to learn to avoid hitting the rods but not to be concerned about hitting them at the beginning. She was not to slow her motion down in order to avoid hitting the rods but to continue a smooth, rapid motion and gradually improve her performance. The smoothness and rapidity of the stylus stroke and the objective of learning to make the stroke better were emphasized.

In the condition designed to minimize the learning of a new afferent-efferent association (Accuracy condition) S was told to make a slow, very careful movement of the stylus between the rods so that she would not hit either rod. She was told to move slowly enough to be sure she was accurate. The importance of going slowly and never hitting the rods was stressed.

It was intended that, in the Learning condition, Ss would have to learn to make a straight arm movement when the retinal input was curved or a curved arm movement when the retinal input was straight. To the extent that they learned this, a new efferent readiness would be activated by the visual input. It was also intended that, in the Accuracy condition, Ss would respond primarily to the local deviation of the stylus from the rod and would never learn anything new about efferent instructions to the arm relevant to the contour. In order to keep the amount of experience constant for Ss in the different experimental conditions, each was instructed that a bell would sound very 12 sec. At this signal she was to insert the stylus between the two rods at the top of her visual field and make the downward stroke, ending near the bottom of her visual field. Thus, each S had exactly the same number of stylus strokes and the same time spent looking at the lines.

After telling S that, from this point on, she was to have her eyes open only while biting on the biteboard, she was asked to shut her eyes and E put the plain glass goggles on her.

The E then moved the rods a few centimeters to the left of where they would look approximately straight and S was asked to turn the knob so as to make the lines straight. The setting was recorded to the nearest ½ mm. He then moved the rods off in the opposite direction and another setting was made. This was continued until four measurements were obtained. The S then closed her eyes and the plain glass goggles were replaced by prism goggles. Initial settings of straight with the prism goggles were obtained in a similar manner.

The S closed her eyes again while E set the lines at the proper position. If S was in an "apparently straight" condition, the rods were positioned at the average of the settings of "straight" that S had just made wearing the prism goggles. If S was in an "apparently curved" condition, the rods were positioned at the average of the settings of straight that S had made wearing the plain glass goggles.

The S was then asked, with her eyes shut, to run her fingers up and down the two rods until she could tell whether they were straight or curved and, if they were curved, in which direction. The purpose of this was to provide some information to S that might help in the performance of the task. This aspect of the procedure was probably unnecessary. It was omitted in Exp. II reported below.

The S then opened her eyes, took the stylus in her hand, and after E quickly reviewed the stroking instructions and started the bell, began the actual practice. There were five stroking periods each intended to be 10 min. long. Some of the periods for S's in the Accuracy conditions were longer since, if they skipped some of the bell rings, the period was extended so that there would be 50 strokes in each period. The stroking periods were separated by rest periods of 3 min. during which S leaned back with eyes closed.

During the stroking periods, E observed the speed of S's strokes. If S in a Learning condition stroked too slowly (more than 1 sec. per stroke), she was reminded to go faster. The Ss in the Accuracy conditions were reminded to slow down if they went too fast (less than 4 sec. per stroke). The Ss in the Accuracy conditions were also reminded to be careful if they hit the rods, telling them to go slowly enough so that it would not happen.

Following the fifth 10-min. stroking period, while S rested, the board was washed to remove the slight traces left by the stylus. The S then spent 2 min. stroking and immediately afterwards the final settings of straight while wearing the prism goggles were made. The rods were then returned to the stroking position for that S and she stroked for another 2 min. With S's eyes shut, E removed the prism goggles and put the plain glass goggles in their place. He quickly washed the board off again and had S open her eyes and make the final settings looking through plain glass.

Results

INITIAL STRAIGHT SETTINGS.   Table 14.1 presents, for each of the four experimental conditions the average initial setting of straight with the naked eye (plain glass goggles) and with the prism goggles. It also presents the average change from the beginning to the end of the experimental session for each of these measures.

There are only minor variations among the four experimental condi-

Table 14.1 Initial Measurements and Changes (in Centimeters)
in the Perception of a Straight Line (Exp. I)

| | Experimental Cond. | | | |
| | Apparently Straight | | Apparently Curved | |
	Learning	Accuracy	Learning	Accuracy
Initial with prisms	4.55	4.34	4.29	4.39
Change with prisms	+.28	+.10	+1.59	+1.31
Initial with naked eye	9.92	9.96	9.90	9.96
Change with naked eye	+.18	+.02	+.86	+.65

tion on the initial measurements. The average setting of straight with the naked eye is very close to objectively straight (between 9.90 and 9.95 on our measurement scale). The average setting of straight with the prisms varies slightly around 4.40; in other words, the prisms produced a curvature of about 5.5 cm. displacement of the middle of the line. Analysis of variance on the initial measurements revealed that none of the differences among experimental conditions even approached statistical significance.

CHANGE FROM INITIAL TO FINAL MEASUREMENTS. These showed systematic differences in line with what one would expect on the basis of an efferent readiness theory. Although the effects were small, they were reasonably consistent. On both the measures of adaptation (changes measured with prisms in place) and aftereffects (changes measured with the naked eye) the Learning condition yielded more changes in visual perception than the comparable Accuracy condition. Neither of these quite reached conventional levels of acceptable significance.

We can increase the reliability of our measure of change of visual perception, however, by simply averaging for each S the adaptation and aftereffect measured. An analysis of variance on this combined index yielded $F (1, 36) = 6.46$, $p < .05$. Thus, we may conclude that the Learning conditions produced more change than the Accuracy conditions.

The differences between the apparently straight and apparently curved conditions were, of course, highly significant in all cases. This difference was due to the operation of the "Gibson effect" in the Apparently curved conditions and its absence in the Apparently straight conditions. It is clear, however, that the difference between the Learning and the Accuracy conditions existed independently of the Gibson effect.

Discussion

The data were consistent with the implications from an efferent readiness theory of visual perception of contour. In the condition intended to force S to learn a new afferent-efferent association significantly more change in the visual perception of curvature was obtained than in the condition intended to make such learning unlikely. Whether or not the Learning and Accuracy conditions really had their intended effect is, of course, not directly answerable from the data. All one can say is that the results obtained are in line with the predictions made from the theory and from intuitive notions as to the effects of the experimental manipulations.

The magnitude of the effect created by the experimental manipulation is, clearly, very small, being about 2 mm. between the Learning and Accuracy condition. It is, of course, unclear as to whether this magnitude of change of visual perception is, or is not, disappointing. Considering that visual perception is very likely heavily dependent upon efferent readiness concerning the extraocular muscles, and there was certainly no change in these afferent-efferent associations, and considering that the only other movement involved at all was that of the arm, one might not expect a very large change in visual perception.

The data have relevance to Held's (1961) theory concerning the importance of reafference. Both the Learning and the Accuracy conditions are, in Held's sense, active movement conditions. In both conditions the afference, and hence the reafference, would be unusual and from Held's theory one would expect perceptual change equally for both. It seems clear from the data, however, that Held's distinction between active and passive movement was too gross. Distinctions have to be made concerning the specific nature of the efference.

Experiment II

The attempt was made in the design of the previous experiment to keep the proprioceptive input from the arm the same in both Learning and Accuracy conditions so as to rule out possible interpretations of the visual changes as having been due to recoding of visual input based on information obtained from proprioceptive input. For this reason there were two rods spaced closely together so that, since the stylus was confined between the two rods in all conditions, the informational input from muscle and joint receptors would, of necessity, be similar for the two conditions. However, *E*s were obviously not successful in making the proprioceptive input identical in these experimental conditions since, at a minimum, the rate of input was systematically different. In the Learning conditions the hand moved quickly while in the Accuracy conditions the hand moved slowly. Perhaps the rate of informational input is important. In this experiment, consequently, a theoretical replication with quite different instructions to *S* was attempted so that the rate of input, as well as the specific proprioceptive information, would be held constant.

Method

SUBJECTS.   Sixty-two females, 22 freshmen or sophomores from Stanford University and 40 junior and senior high-school students, participated in the experiment. All *S*s were naive about the experiment and were paid $3.00 for participating. The *S*s were randomly assigned to one of four experimental conditions with the restriction that the ratio of college to high-school *S*s be kept nearly equal. The data from two *S*s were discarded—one because she did not follow the instructions and the other because the apparatus failed during the experiment.

APPARATUS.   The apparatus for the experiment was identical to that used in Exp. I except for a few minor changes. A sturdier biteboard was constructed; movable clips were attached to the rods at the top and bottom of *S*'s visual field so as to be sure that the stylus movement was always entirely within the visual field. The *S*s were seated so that the distance between their eyes and the rods was about 48 cm., approximately 8 cm. farther away than in Exp. I.

The experiment was conducted monocularly throughout so that we would also be able to measure interocular transfer. For this reason three sets of goggles instead of two were used. One set contained a 25-diopter prism mounted base left in front of the right eye, the left eye being occluded; the other two sets had plain glass, one in front of the right eye, the other in front of the left eye. The other eye was always occluded. There were two viewing conditions, one in which *S* viewed an objectively straight, apparently curved line; the other in which she viewed an objectively curved, apparently straight line. There were two movement conditions, one in which we attempted to maximize the learning of a new afferent-efferent association and one in which we attempted to minimize such learning while holding other variables constant. The instructions to *S*s in the Learning condition emphasized the learning of a smooth, fast, sweeping motion of the stylus between the rods. The *E* demonstrated the stroke and the buzzer sound resulting when a rod was touched by the stylus. The *S* was told that touching the rods was to be accepted at first, that the important aspect of the task was to learn the smooth stroking motion required to move the stylus between the rods. In the Contact condition *Ss* were instructed to learn a smooth, stroking motion while maintaining pressure on one rod. The *Ss* in both conditions were encouraged to rest when this was needed and proceed at the task at a self-determined pace.

Instructions were also given concerning how to set the line so that it was straight and to keep the eyes closed any time *S* was not biting on the biteboard. Measurements were made in the same way as in Exp. I with the addition that separate measurements were taken for each naked eye at the beginning and end of the experiment.

During the experimental period *E* recorded the number of strokes made and the cumulative time on and off the biteboard. He also recorded any verbal reports given by *S* while she was leaning back and resting. If *S* was not following instructions, she was corrected at once. When the time on the biteboard had accumulated to 10 min., 20 min., and 30 min., *E* reminded *S* of what she was supposed to be doing; e.g., "You're doing fine, but let me remind you that the important thing is that you make firm contact with one of the rods," or "You're doing fine, but let me remind you that you're supposed to be trying to learn to make a fast, smooth, sweeping stroke."

When *S* had been on the biteboard for 40 min., she was asked to close her eyes and to lean back. At this point *E* removed from the board any traces left by the stylus. The *S* was then asked to work for a little while longer. After *S* had stayed on the biteboard for 45 sec., she was instructed to remain on the biteboard but to close her eyes. Any traces of the stylus were again removed and the final measurements of straight were taken.

At this point *E* informed *S* that the experiment was over, but that he would like to ask a few questions. The *S* was asked how the board looked, whether she noticed any changes in the curvature of the rods, and how her eyes felt during the experiment.

Results

Table 14.2 presents the data for each experimental condition. As in Exp. I, the differences among the four conditions in the initial measurements were very small. In all four experimental conditions, the average settings of straight were slightly under 10.0 on the measurement scale with the right naked eye. With the left naked eye they were a shade over

Table 14.2 Initial Measurements and Changes (in Centimeters)
in the Perception of a Straight Line (Exp. II)

| | Experimental Cond. | | | |
| | Apparently Straight | | Apparently Curved | |
	Learning	Contact	Learning	Contact
Initial with prism (right eye)	5.02	4.86	4.94	5.01
Change	+.23	+.15	+1.20	+.88
Initial with right naked eye	9.77	9.72	9.74	9.88
Change	+.32	+.20	+.91	+.68
Initial with left naked eye	10.04	10.03	10.09	10.10
Change	+.14	+.05	+.35	+.20

10.0. This difference was significant; 52 Ss showed a higher mean setting
with the left naked eye than with the right naked eye; 7 Ss showed a
difference in the other direction; and for 1 S the average settings were
equal. This difference was undoubtedly due to the slightly different angle of view between the two eyes. The average setting of straight with
the prism spectacles was 4.96, a curvature represented by about 5 cm.
displacement of the rods from the middle of the board.

The data on changes from initial to final measurements were very
similar to those obtained in Exp. I. In the Learning conditions, where
one would expect some learning of new efferent instructions activated
by the visual input, greater change in visual perception was obtained
than in the Contact conditions. An analysis of variance on the changes
of the settings of straight with prisms yielded $F (1, 56) = 8.92$, $p < .01$,
for the difference between the Learning and Contact conditions. A similar analysis of variance on the changes from initial to final measurements for the right naked eye (the eye that wore the prism) showed the
Learning and Contact conditions to be significant also, $F (1, 56) = 5.47$,
$p < .05$. The combined index of adaptation and aftereffect that was used
in Exp. I was, of course, highly significant, $F = 15.57$.

The results for transfer from the right naked eye to the left naked eye
were less clear. In all of the experimental conditions there was some
transfer to the left naked eye and the amount of change in the left eye
was greater in the Learning conditions than in the comparable Contact
conditions. The difference between the Learning and Contact conditions
was not statistically significant, however, $F = 2.82$. The measurements

on the left eye were always taken after the measurements on the right eye in this study. It is impossible to assess the effect of the time delay on the results.

Similar to the results of Exp. I, there was a highly significant difference on all measurements between the conditions in which an apparently straight or apparently curved line was viewed. This Gibson effect clearly was independent of the changes of primary interest.

Discussion

The results of Exp. II completely supported the results, and the interpretation of the results, from Exp. I. In spite of the fact that quite different instructions were used to create conditions that would minimize the learning of new afferent-efferent associations, the results came out in the same way. In Exp. I Es depended on an instruction to go very slowly and to avoid ever hitting the rods. It was intended that this would force S to concentrate on the local deviation of the stylus from the rod and that she would, therefore, not learn new efference to issue in response to the visual input. In Exp. II Es depended, for the same purpose, on an instruction to maintain pressure and contact with one rod during the whole stroke. It was hoped that, since the movement of the arm would thus be guided by the actual rod, S need not, and would not, learn a new afferent-efferent association. The results of the two experiments support the interpretation that visual perceptual change occurs if one changes the efferent readiness activated by the visual input.

In both experiments the actual arm movement, and hence the actual proprioceptive feedback from the arm movement, was nearly identical for the Learning conditions and the comparable nonlearning conditions. In Exp. I it was possible to argue that, since the rate of proprioceptive input was different (fast vs. slow movements), perhaps this affected the results. In Exp. II this difference did not exist. The rate of movement was similar in all experimental conditions—if anything, the movement was faster in the Contact conditions. Table 14.3 shows the number of strokes made on the average by Ss in each experimental condition in the 40 min. of actual stroking. None of the differences are statistically significant but it is clear that the difference that does exist is in the direction of more strokes per unit time in the Contact conditions. Hence, it is no longer plausible to suppose that the rate of proprioceptive input affects the results.

It is worth pointing out that while the two different kinds of nonlearning conditions did probably reduce the extent to which Ss learned new afferent-efferent associations, we cannot be sure that these conditions

Table 14.3   Number of Strokes and Its Correlation
with the Combined Index of Perceptual Change

| | Experimental Cond. | | | |
| | Apparently Straight | | Apparently Curved | |
	Learning	Contact	Learning	Contact
Number of strokes	624.00	689.93	585.33	626.73
r between adapt + aftereffect and number of strokes	− .172	+ .525	+ .022	+ .500

prevented such learning altogether. The data from the Contact conditions in Exp. II provide some basis for assessing whether some learning did occur. One might expect that if learning occurred in these Contact conditions, it would probably depend on amount of experience to a greater extent that it would in the Learning conditions. In the Contact conditions those who made very many strokes might be more likely to have learned some new efference. To examine this possibility we computed the correlations, within each experimental condition, between the number of strokes made and the combined index of adaptation and aftereffect for the right naked eye. These correlations are presented in Table 14.3. There is no significant correlation at all for the two Learning conditions but significant (at the 5% level) correlation for each of the Contact conditions. It seems, then, that some Ss in the Contact conditions did learn. If such learning could have been entirely prevented, the difference between conditions would, presumably, have been larger.

Experiment III

Experiments I and II, while supportive of the theory, have in common a possible confounding factor. In the Learning conditions there were frequent error signals that were absent in the nonlearning conditions. The third experiment was designed to eliminate this possibly confounding factor while testing the theory again under very different empirical conditions.

Two general methodological changes were made in the third study: (a) Adaptation resulting from a change in efferent readiness and the adaptation resulting from the "Gibson normalization effect" were experimentally separated by allowing normalization to develop prior to the introduction of arm and hand movements; and (b) measurements of adaptation were made after short periods of activity to make it possible to study the course of adaptation throughout the experimental session.

Method

SUBJECTS.   All Ss were males, either high-school seniors or college students. All had good, uncorrected vision sufficient for an unrestricted driver's license or had vision fully corrected by contact lenses. A total of 73 Ss participated in the study but only data from 54 (9 in each condition) were used in the analysis. Sixteen of the discarded Ss made very inaccurate level settings during initial measures with prism goggles. One S was unable to make settings within time limits, and two Ss used background cues as a basis for their settings after the shooting period.

PROCEDURES.   The technique used in this study to provide Ss with an opportunity to make arm and hand movements discrepant with their visual input employed a shooting gallery. The Ss "shot" a pistol emitting a continuous light ray at a target that moved back and forth on a track. While engaging in this activity, they wore prism spectacles. When the light ray hit the center of the target, a photocell and relay mechanism activated a buzzer. In one experimental condition the light was visible; in the other an infrared filter was placed over the barrel of the pistol.

No adaptation to the prism induced curvature was expected in the visible light condition. The efference issued in this condition need not be made in response to the path of the target's movement or the contour of the track but rather to the discrepancy between the seen position of the light ray and the target's position, speed, and direction of movement. In essence, these Ss could act as servomechanisms as they performed a simple tracking task. Yet their arms and hands would move in a path consistent with the distal contour and be discrepant with the perceived proximal contour.

Ideally, Ss shooting with the invisible infrared light would have been forced to issue efference activated only by the perceived contour of the target's path. Guided by the information from the buzzer when on target, they would have to learn a new set of efferent responses to the distorted perception. Therefore, they would be expected to adapt to the prism induced curvature. Pretesting with this manipulation, however, rapidly led to the conclusion that it was almost impossible to hit the target; hitting occurred rarely and seemingly by chance. Consequently, Ss were permitted to aim while shooting with the infrared light. With aiming they were able to hit the target, although still with some difficulty, and make the required arm and hand movements. Although aiming was not necessary for Ss shooting with the visible light, they were also told to aim in order to equate this factor.

The two conditions involving infrared and visible light were combined with two conditions of viewing an apparently straight or apparently curved line, resulting in a 2 × 2 design. After these four initial groups were run, two supplementary groups of Ss were added to clarify the findings and interpretations of the results. The Ss in the Aim-only condition shot with the infrared light and were allowed to aim but received no information as to when they hit the target. The Ss in the other supplementary condition also shot with the infrared light and received no information. In addition, they were not allowed to view their arms, hands, or the barrel of the pistol. This No-information group was designed to determine whether there were any factors in the experimental situation which would result in a change in contour perception if Ss neither made discrepant efferent responses nor received any atypical visual reafference. The Ss in these two supplementary groups viewed only an apparently straight contour.

APPARATUS.   As indicated above, the experimental apparatus consisted of a prism to produce a curvature transformation of the visual world and a shooting gallery to give Ss a means of engaging in activity with the distorted world. In addition, there was a method for measuring adaptation to curvature.

A 30° wedge prism of optical plastic, 4 in. long and 1¾ in. in height, was used to produce curvature. It was mounted base upwards in welder's goggles with the front of the prism flush with the outside of the goggles. The field of view through the prism goggles was 86° wide and 48° high. Similar goggles with a plain piece of glass were used when Ss viewed the same size visual field without any distortion. The shooting-gallery component of the apparatus consisted of a 9-ft. horizontal track across which a target box moved at a rate of 1.5 ft/sec. The reversal and reacceleration of the target box were virtually instantaneous. The actual target was a 1 × 1 cm. photocell which was sensitive to both visible and infrared light. It was mounted in the middle of the target box; a series of concentric red and white rings surrounded the photocell and enhanced its target-like appearance. When the photocell was activated by light, a relay closed, starting a buzzer and clock. The buzzer signaled Ss that they were on target. The clock provided a record of the amount of time spent on the target.

The Ss shot at the photocell with a pistol emitting a continuous collimated ray of light approximately 1 in. in diameter. The infrared filter used in the invisible light conditions, inserted in front of the barrel of the pistol, effectively blocked visible light under the illumination conditions used in the study.

The track on which the target ran could be bent into a smooth curve. The track itself was attached to an aluminum bar 9 ft. long, 3 in. wide, and ¼ in. thick. The bar was held at a constant height at both ends by supports and forced up or down by pressure at the middle. A threaded rod affixed with a bracket to the center of the bar was raised or lowered by a motor and pulley arrangement. The position of the bar was measured by a cord running from the threaded rod along the length of a meter stick placed at the front of the table where E sat. The position of an indicator on this cord accurately reflected the position of the middle of the bar.

It was impossible to set the bar to appear perfectly straight with or without the prisms. Since it was supported only at the ends and middle, the bar sagged slightly at the ¼ and ¾ points, and curvature produced by bending the bar did not exactly compensate for the curvature induced by the prism. When set to appear approximately straight, the ¼ and ¾ points looked slightly elevated. Consequently, Ss were always told to set the bar to appear level, with the middle of the bar placed at the same height as the two ends. The Ss had no difficulty in doing this either with the naked eye or the prism goggles.

The Ss sat at a table directly in front of the middle of the track with their eyes 64 in. from the bar. From this position the target movement subtended a visual angle of 78°. While making settings, viewing the bar and target, or shooting, S's head was held fixed by a biteboard attached to this table. When Ss wore the nondistorting goggles, the biteboard was parallel to the surface of the table, and the bar appeared in the center of the field of view. When wearing the prism goggles, the biteboard was angled 15° downward to compensate for the prism displacement effect and make the bar still appear in the approximate center of the field of view.

Black cloth draped irregularly over, behind, and to the sides of the bar blocked S's view of the walls and ceilings of the experimental room and prevented him from realizing that the goggles produced curvature. The threaded rod and motor and pulley arrangement were also hidden by a piece of black cloth to prevent Ss from using the position of the bar relative to the motor and pulleys as a guide for their settings. In the no-information condition a shield prevented Ss from seeing their arms, hands, or the pistol.

The Ss were given first a demonstration of the use of the shooting gallery and the method of setting the bar to appear level. They were allowed to shoot briefly and thus became aware of the operation of the buzzer and time clock. At this time they were told how to hold the pistol and urged to do as well as they could when shooting. The Ss in the two supplementary groups were told that they would be unable to tell when they were on target since the buzzer would be disconnected and a "soundproof cover" placed over the relay and time clock to mask the clicking of these instruments. In actuality, these instruments were disconnected to insure that Ss would receive no indication when they were on target.

Initial measurements of straight with the plain glass goggles and then with the prism goggles were made. Each measurement consisted of six settings made by S from alternate displacements of the bar by E to positions approximately 8 cm. above and below an apparently level position.

The average of the initial setting made with the plain glass goggles indicated S's preexperimental perception of level. After the initial settings with the prism goggles were made, E either set the bar to the average of the initial measurements made with the plain glass goggles for Ss in the apparently curved viewing conditions or to the average of the measurements made with the prism goggles for Ss in the apparently straight viewing conditions.

All Ss then viewed the target moving back and forth across the track for a period of 8 min. to allow time for the Gibson effect to develop for Ss viewing the apparently curved bar. Following this viewing period all Ss made another series of settings. It was assumed that 8 min. was long enough to achieve complete adaptation due to "normalization" and that subsequent changes in the settings in the apparently curved viewing conditions would reflect adaptation resulting from a change in efference.

There followed five 8-min. shooting periods separated by rest periods of 5 min. Immediately after each shooting period Ss made a series of settings. A final setting with the plain glass goggles followed shortly after the last settings with prisms.

At the end of the experiment, which lasted for approximately 2 hr., Ss were questioned about their impression of the goggles they wore, and the method they used to set the bar to appear level. All were paid $3.00 for their time.

Results
The six experimental groups were approximately equal on the initial measurements. The average magnitude of the measured prism-induced curvature is about 20.5 cm. for all of them. The measurements made after the initial nonshooting viewing period may be expected to reflect

the Gibson effect for the apparently curved conditions. Those Ss who viewed the target moving back and forth along an apparently curved path changed an average of 1.42 cm. in the direction of adaptation. The change for Ss in the apparently straight viewing conditions was −.10 cm. The difference between the two viewing conditions was highly significant, $t(34) = 5.39$, $p < .001$.

The data used to test the major hypotheses were the differences between settings of apparently straight following the shooting periods and the settings which followed the initial nonshooting viewing period. This computation presumably removed the Gibson effect from the comparison between the apparently straight and apparently curved experimental conditions. The adaptation data for each shooting period are shown in Table 14.4. A negative sign indicates a change opposite to the adaptive direction, i.e., more perceived curvature.

Examination of the data in this table shows that the average amount of adaptation appears to vary nonsystematically from period to period. An analysis of variance of the increase in adaptation from the first two to the last two shooting periods produced no significant differences. The analysis of the data is, hence, presented using the most reliable single measure reflecting the effects of the experimental manipulations, namely, the average amount of adaptation for all five periods. The mean adaptation for the two infrared conditions was .27 cm.; for the two visible light conditions it was −.38 cm. These means were significantly different, $F(1, 32) = 14.19$, $p < .001$; and both were significantly different from zero by t test. There was no difference in the average magnitude of adaptation between the two apparently straight and the two

Table 14.4   Mean Adaptation After Each Shooting Period (in Centimeters)

| | Experimental Cond. | | | | | |
| Period | Apparently Curved | | Apparently Straight | | Supplementary Groups | |
	Infrared	Visible Light	Infrared	Visible Light	Aim Only	No Information
1	.32	−.59	.17	−.32	.36	−.20
2	.09	−.36	.25	−.07	.07	−.19
3	.03	−.59	.43	−.14	.05	−.62
4	.20	−.48	.49	−.45	.14	−.10
5	.28	−.29	.40	−.57	.07	−.07
Avg.	.19	−.46	.35	−.31	.14	−.24

apparently curved conditions. For the two apparently straight groups combined the adaptation was .02 cm.; for the two apparently curved groups combined it was − .14 cm. Apparently the initial nonshooting viewing period did eliminate the Gibson effect.

The Ss shooting with the visible light were on target an average of 49% of the total shooting time. Those shooting with the infrared light were on target only 18% of the time. This difference reflects the difficulty of hitting the target with the infrared light. The major question of interest concerning the performance data is the relative increase for the two shooting conditions. It was expected that Ss shooting with the infrared light would improve over periods as they learned the correct arm and hand movements. Those shooting with the visible light were expected to improve very little. Their task was one which could be mastered rapidly. An index of relative improvement, the difference between the average hit time for the last two periods and the average for the first two periods divided by the sum of these two averages, was computed for each S. The difference between indexes for the shooting conditions was significant, $F (1, 32) = 11.55$, $p < .01$. The Ss shooting with the infrared light showed more relative improvement. There was no significant difference between those who viewed apparently straight or apparently curved lines. There was, however, a significant interaction, $F (1, 32) = 5.39$, $p < .05$. In the apparently straight conditions there was a large difference between the shooting conditions; in the apparently curved conditions there was little difference.

It was expected that there would be significant positive correlations between the relative increase in performance and the amount of visual adaptation for Ss in the infrared conditions. As these Ss learned to issue appropriate efference they would be expected to both improve in performance and to visually adapt. The correlations between these two measures in the visible light conditions were expected to be negligible; improvement in performance was not expected to be associated with visual change since the efference issued in this condition was not associated with the perception of contour. None of these correlations, however, approaches statistical significance for any of the four groups.

The difference between the final and initial settings of straight with the plain glass goggles indicates the extent to which any visual adaptation persisted for "naked eye" measurements. As would be expected from the Gibson normalization phenomenon, there was a significantly larger aftereffect, $F (1, 32) = 5.55$, $p < .05$, for Ss who viewed an apparently curved line (.65 cm.) than for Ss who viewed an apparently straight line (− .02 cm.). The aftereffect data, unlike the adaptation data, include the normalization effect since they were computed from the initial settings of straight with the plain glass goggles that were made before the nonshooting viewing period. The difference between the shooting conditions, although in the expected direction, was not significant. The average aftereffect for Ss in the infrared condition is .50 cm.; for Ss in the visible light condition it was .13 cm. There was no interaction of the shooting and viewing conditions.

As was mentioned, two additional, apparently straight groups were run to clarify the findings and interpretations of the basic experiment. The Aim-only group was designed to test the conditions necessary for visual adaptation; the No-information group was designed to determine the changes resulting from prolonged viewing of the target and bar. The results of these two groups were analyzed by a one-way analysis of variance in conjunction with the results from the infrared and visible light apparently straight groups.

The average visual adaptation for each of these groups is also presented in Table 14.4. Using the average adaptation for all five periods, the four apparently straight groups differ significantly, $F (3, 32) = 3.54$, $p < .05$. The infrared group is significantly different from both the visible light group, $t(32) = 2.81$, $p < .01$, and the No-information group, $t(32) = 2.51$, $p < .02$. None of the other internal comparisons is significant. There is no significant difference in the aftereffect data between these four groups.

Discussion

The results continued to support a theory emphasizing the role of efferent readiness in determining the perception of contour. Those Ss who had to learn to issue a new set of efferent responses to the perceived contour of the target's movement adapted to the curvature transformation significantly more than those Ss who made approximately the same motor movements and had the same visual input but responded only to the discrepancy between the position of a visible spot of light and the target. Both the rate and path of the arm and hand movements were similar in these two conditions, but the responses of the Ss shooting with the visible light more closely approximated the actual contour. These Ss were on target almost three times as long as those shooting with the infrared light. The proprioceptive input from the hand and arm is, hence, clearly not the basis for visual adaptation.

The results further demonstrate that not all active or self-produced movement results in adaptation to curvature as Held's (1961) theory suggests. Instead, these results support the hypothesis that the important variable is whether or not the active movements are learned, so that the efferent readiness will be activated by a pattern of retinal stimulation.

Atypical visual reafference is assumed to have occurred in both the visible light and infrared conditions, yet visual adaptation was obtained in only one condition. It can be argued that the necessity to aim, and the consequent attention paid to the position of the arm and hand in the infrared condition, resulted in more salient or usable atypical visual reafference than that which occurred from merely seeing the arm and hand in the visible light condition. The Aim-only condition was designed to clarify the distinction between adaptation resulting from a change in efferent readiness and adaptation resulting from a change in the correlation between self-produced movement and visual reafference. Since there was no buzzer to guide the arm movements made by Ss in the Aim-only condition, more attention to the position of the hand would be expected in this condition than in the infrared condition with the buzzer feedback. Therefore, the Aim-only condition might result in maximum adaptation if this attention factor were critical. This group, however, showed no more visual adaptation than the apparently straight, infrared group, indicating that special attention to the hand and arm was not critical.

The negative adaptation found in the visible light condition was unexpected. The No-information group was run to test one obvious explanation. It was possible that continued viewing through prism spectacles resulted, in this situation, in increased perception of curvature. The average change for Ss in the No-information condition is $-.24$ cm.; for Ss in the visible light apparently straight group it is $-.31$ cm. These figures are very close and it appears that this shift does occur simply as a consequence of continued viewing in this situation.

Two of the findings were not in accord with the theoretical expectations, namely, the lack of significant differences between the shooting conditions in aftereffect and the lack of correlation between visual adaptation and performance improvement in the infrared conditions. Rapid decay of unstable adaptation may account for the lack of significant differences in aftereffect between the two shooting conditions, since about 5 min. elapsed between the end of the final shooting period and the beginning of the aftereffect measurements. The lack of expected correlation may be explained by the relative unreliability of the measurements and the fact that the correlations are each based on only nine Ss.

Experiment IV

If the efferent readiness that is activated by visual afferent input is important in determining the visual perception of contour, one might well expect that efferent readiness with respect to the extraocular muscles would be of particular importance. Considering the invariant relation that exists between eye movement and movement of stimulation across the retina, and considering the vast amount of experience that an individual has in establishing this relationship between input and output, it would not be surprising to find that efferent readiness relevant to eye movements was more intimately involved in visual perception than, for example, efferent readiness relevant to arm movements.

If this reasoning is correct, we would obtain, as we have obtained, only small amounts of change in visual perception of curvature when Ss wear prism spectacles. Such spectacles produce a complex situation in which there is inconsistency between eye movements and other body movements that are evoked by the contour. If S engages in normal activity while wearing such spectacles, head movements, arm movements, and other body movements relevant to contour must conform to the objective shape. Thus, to the extent that these movements are in response to retinal input, S must learn new efference to associate with the visual input. He learns that he must move his head or his arm in a curved path in response to a straight pattern of retinal stimulation. These new afferent-efferent associations would presumably account for the observed change in the visual perception of curvature in the preceding experiments. There is, however, one major hindrance to change of visual perception. During the entire experience with the prism spectacles, the relationship between retinal input and efferent output to the extraocular muscles remains unchanged. The eyes, in order to achieve or maintain fixation, must move in conformity to the retinal image and *not* to the objective contour. Hence, to the extent that efferent readiness relevant to eye movements is important, this would interfere with and retard any change of visual perception when prisms are worn in spectacles.

If a situation could be arranged in which the movements of the eye had to conform to the objective contour rather than the retinal contour while wearing prisms, change of visual perception might occur much more quickly and dramatically. This situation can, indeed, be achieved by putting the prism on a contact lens rather than in a spectacle frame, as was realized by Taylor (1962) who arranged to have a scleral contact lens manufactured for his own right eye with a prism on it. He reported that, after he found the proper procedure for scanning contours to make adaptation rate maximal, his adaptation to curvature distortion was complete after only a short period of scanning.

There are reasons for not placing complete reliance upon this report. Taylor reported no data concerning the amount of curvature distortion produced by the prism on his contact lens other than to say that ". . . the distortion was less than I had hoped for [p. 227]." However, it is likely that the curvature distortion produced by Taylor's contact lens was very small. Because a prism on a contact lens is curved to conform to the curvature of the cornea, there is much less curvature distortion obtained than from a prism with a plane surface. For example, in the experimental work presented here 30-diopter prisms were used on contact lenses. The amount of curvature distortion produced was about comparable to what one would obtain from a prism with a plane surface of 4–8 diopters. Taylor's prism of not quite 12 diopters probably produced very little curvature distortion.

Nonetheless, the theoretical issue raised by Taylor appears important. If the efferent readiness relevant to eye movements is especially important, we should be able to find large and rapid changes in visual perception from wearing a prism on a contact lens even if the only movement in which the person engages are eye movements. It was, consequently, decided to replicate Taylor's study under more controlled conditions, using several Ss who were completely naive as to what was happening and using prisms of large enough power to be sure that the curvature distortion would be clear and unmistakable.

Method

SUBJECTS.   Three Stanford University students, two male and one female, were paid to serve in the experiment. They were told that the study would involve wearing a scleral contact lens for which they would have to be individually fitted. None realized that the contact lens produced curvature distortion.

APPARATUS.   The lenses were manufactured by the Parsons Optical Laboratories of San Francisco, California. They succeeded in producing 30-diopter prisms on the contact lenses. The surfaces of the lenses were, of course, smoothed and rounded; none of the Ss complained of any pain, none of them had any difficulty blinking or closing their eyes during rest periods. The lens and prism were cast in one piece out of optical plastic and then ground. Each S wore the prism in the right eye, which was also the dominant eye, with the base of the prism down. None of the Ss had completely clear, sharp vision through the prism. There was some slight blurring.

The manufacture of the prisms was not easy and did not proceed without mishap. For the first S, it was thought that the contact lens would be stable with the prism base oriented laterally. It was manufactured in this way but, when the lens was first inserted into the eye, it immediately rotated so that the base of the prism was down. It was, however, stable in this position and that is how S wore it in the experiment. A serious error was made in the manufacture of the lens for the second S so that it did not fit at all. Fortunately, it was discovered that the lens manufactured for the first S fit the second one perfectly, also base downward, and so the first two Ss actually used the same lens. No problems were encountered in manufacturing or fitting the lens for the third S.

The experimental apparatus was the same one used in the first two experiments, except that it was positioned on its side so that the rods were horizontal rather than vertical. This was done because the prisms, mounted base down, produced curvature of horizontal straight lines.

PROCEDURE.   For the experimental sessions Ss were seated in front of the apparatus with the head in a biteboard so that the right eye was directly in front of the center of the lines. When in the experimental situation, S saw only the two bass rods, the white background, and a small portion of the side of the frame of the apparatus.

Several experimental sessions were conducted with each S, each session lasting for approximately 90 min. At the beginning of each session S, with the left eye occluded and head on the biteboard, was asked to turn the knob on the apparatus so as to see the horizontal lines straight with his naked right eye. Four such settings were taken. On two of these measurements E displaced the line upwards from apparently straight before asking S to make the setting. On the other two measurements the lines were displaced downward from apparently straight. For a few of the last sessions with the second S and for all of the sessions with the third S, such initial measurements were also taken for the naked left eye with the right eye occluded.

The S then inserted the contact lens into this right eye and, again with his head in the biteboard, was asked to make four settings of the lines using the same procedure. Care was taken by E, moving the lines back and forth before S opened his eyes, to prevent S from realizing that there was any curvature distortion. The subsequent procedure differed somewhat from S to S. The following aspects of the procedure were common to all three Ss.

After these measurements, the lines were set by E, while S's eyes were closed, either so that they were objectively straight, corresponding to the average of the settings S had made with his naked right eye, or apparently straight, corresponding to the average of the settings S had made with the contact lens in the eye. In each session S was then asked to simply look back and forth along the line. He did this usually for 5 min., was then once more asked to set the line so that it was straight, and was then given a 2-min. rest period during which he closed his eye and removed his head from the biteboard. The E reset the lines to the same position before the next period of looking back and forth along the lines. After a number of such periods, usually 8–10, the contact lens was removed and final measurements using the naked eye were taken.

The first few sessions for each S were conducted with the lines set so that they looked straight to S. Later sessions for each S were conducted with the line set objectively straight, so that they looked curved. The final session for each S was conducted with the line objectively straight, but with S looking monocularly through a prism in a spectacle rather than wearing the contact lens. This was done to get some information as to the magnitude of adaptation one might expect simply from the Gibson effect (Gibson, 1933) under these circumstances. The details of the procedure for each S follow.

S1

Session I. Lines set apparently straight. Ten periods of scanning the lines, periods ranging from 2 to 5 min. in length.

Session II. Lines set apparently straight. Ten periods of scanning the lines, periods ranging from 3 to 6 min. in length.

Session III. Lines set apparently straight. Five periods of scanning, each period 5 or 6 min. long. This was followed by two periods, one 3 min. and the other 6 min. long during which E moved a pointer along the line and S was asked to track the motion with his eye.

Session IV. Lines set apparently straight. Five periods ranging from 5 to 8½ min. in which S moved a stylus back and forth along the lines while looking. This was followed by two periods, each 6 min. long, in which S simply scanned back and forth.

Session V. Lines set objectively straight. Ten periods, 5 min. each, of scanning the lines.

Session VI. Lines set objectively straight. Six periods, ranging from 5 to 8 min., of scanning the lines.

Section VII. Lines set objectively straight. The S looking monocularly through prism in spectacle, 8 periods of 5 min. each of scanning the lines.

The procedure was more standardized for Ss 2 and 3. All sessions contained eight periods of 5 min. each. The following tabulation gives the exact schedule for each of them:

Sessions for

S2	S3	
I, II, & III	I, II, & III	Lines apparently straight, scanning
—	IV	Lines apparently straight, track pointer

IV & V	V, VI, & VII	Lines objectively straight, scanning
VI	VIII & IX	Lines objectively straight, track pointer
VII	X	Lines objectively straight, scan with prism in spectacle

Results and Discussion

In spite of the occasional procedural differences among the three Ss, it seems most sensible to present the data for all three together. In this way the uniformities among the three will most easily be seen.

COURSE OF ADAPTATION WITHIN A DAY. Table 14.5 presents the data for the average daily adaptation to the prismatic distortion for the first three sessions when Ss scanned an apparently straight line. There were no appreciable differences within any S in the course of adaptation among the different days and so the data are presented in terms of 3-day averages. The time point labeled "0" refers to the average settings made at the beginning of the session immediately after the contact lens was inserted in the eye. The time point labeled "10 min." refers to the averages of the setting made after the first 5 min. and after the second 5 min. of scanning the line. The row labeled "20 min." presents the average settings made after the third and the fourth periods of 5 min. of

Table 14.5 Course of Daily Adaptation to Prismatic Curvature Distortion While Viewing an Apparently Straight Line

Time of Setting with Prism	Subject		
	1	2	3
0 min.	12.00	12.17	10.88
10 min.	11.80	11.95	10.86
20 min.	11.65	11.94	10.71
30 min.	11.59	11.97	10.71
40 min.	—	11.95	10.69
Naked eye setting at start of session	10.10	10.10	9.99
Percentage of adaptation at end of session	21.6	10.6	21.3

Note.—Average readings (in centimeters) are of settings of apparently straight lines. Three-day averages for each S are presented.

scanning, and so on. For S 1 there were minor deviations from this because his scanning periods were not always 5 min. long.

The last row of the table presents the percentage of adaptation calculated as the percentage of the distance between objectively straight and apparently straight that S adapted during the day. Thus, S 1 set the lines as straight with the naked eye at 10.10; apparently straight at the beginning of the sessions with prism averaged to 12.00; the adaptation of .41 cm. divided by the initially perceived curvature of 1.90 cm. yielded the percentage of adaptation of 21.6. It is clear that all three Ss showed adaptation during the course of the day. For the second S the total adaptation was already present after 10 min. while the visual change seemed more gradual for the other two.

It has been well known since Gibson's (1933) article that some perceptual "adaptation" occurs simply by looking at a curved line. If one studies adaptation to prismatically induced curvature by exposing S to apparently curved lines, one cannot easily separate this Gibson effect from other possible adaptation processes. It is, hence, not inconsequential to show that, with all three Ss, definite and appreciable adaptation was observed to an apparently straight line—a situation in which the Gibson effect would not be contributing.

Each S also spent several sessions, one each day, exposed to an actually straight, and hence apparently curved, line. Each day the line was set according to S's own initial naked eye measurements at the beginning of that session. Table 14.6 presents the data for the course of daily adaptation for each S, averaged for all the days in which S scanned the apparently curved line. It is clear from these data that all three Ss showed large amounts of adaptation to the apparently curved line, over 40% after 40 min. of scanning. The rapidity and magnitude of these visual changes lend support to the idea that efferent signals to the extraocular muscles are heavily involved in determining perception.

In comparing the data in Tables 14.5 and 14.6, it is very clear that the adaptation to the apparently curved line was much larger than to the apparently straight line. In order to have a better basis for evaluating the magnitude of the adaptation effects obtained by scanning the apparently curved line, a measurement was made for each S of the Gibson effect on the last day on which S was run. The Ss 1 and 2 wore 25-diopter prism spectacles while S 3 wore a 10-diopter prism spectacle. Each S was seated farther from the apparatus in an attempt to roughly match the measurement of curvature obtained from the contact lens. The line was set in accordance with the initial naked eye setting of straight on the day and S spent the rest of the session scanning the line in 5-min. periods with his head fixed by a biteboard. The line was

Table 14.6   Daily Adaptation to Prismatic Curvature Distortion While Viewing an Apparently Curved Line

Time of Measurement with Prism	Subject		
	1[a]	2[a]	3[b]
0 min.	12.26	12.13	11.19
10 min.	11.73	11.44	10.79
20 min.	11.50	11.48	10.66
30 min.	11.24	11.38	10.55
40 min.	11.13	11.26	10.48
Naked eye setting at start of session	9.82	9.98	9.67
Percentage of adaptation at end of session	46.3	40.5	46.7

Note.—Averages of "apparently straight" settings on centimeter scale.
[a]2 days.
[b]3 days.

viewed monocularly with the same eye as was used with the contact lens. Table 14.7 presents the data on adaptation attributable to the Gibson effect and Figure 14.1 presents a comparison of the data from Tables 14.6 and 14.7, that is, a comparison of adaptation with spectacles attributable to the Gibson effect and adaptation with the prism on a contact lens. It is quite clear that the absolute magnitude of the Gibson effect was about the same for all three Ss. The large percentage figure for S 3 was due to the small magnitude of the initial curvature that was produced. The amount of adaptation with the contact lens was greater for all Ss than the magnitude that could be attributed to the Gibson effect.

EFFECT OF SACCADIC AND SMOOTH TRACKING EYE MOVEMENTS. There is some evidence that would lead us to expect that, if the efferent readiness activated by a given retinal input determines the visual perception of contour, then adaptation to curvature distortion with a prism on a contact lens would be greater if the eye engages in saccadic movements than if the eye follows the contour with smooth tracking movement. Rashbass (1961) reported that these two types of eye movements were controlled by different mechanisms in the central nervous system and that, while the saccadic movement was a fixation response, the

Table 14.7   Adaptation to Prismatic Curvature Distortion
While Viewing an Apparently Curved Line
Wearing Prism Spectacles

Time of Measurement with Prism	Subject		
	1	2	3
0 min.	12.52	12.78	10.84
10 min.	12.41	12.81	10.56
20 min.	12.26	12.40	10.46
30 min.	12.16	12.42	10.51
40 min.	12.18	12.31	10.39
Naked eye setting at start of session	10.05	9.93	9.68
Percentage of adaptation at end of session	13.8	16.5	38.8

Note.—Averages of "apparently straight" settings on centimeter scale.

smooth tracking movement was a response to direction and velocity of movement across the retina. This perhaps suggests that efference issued to produce the smooth tracking motion is not coded in terms relevant to contour while the efference to produce a saccadic movement, or a series of them, would be more concerned with contour, that is, with specific position in space of the point fixated relative to the point of fixation from which the eye moved. Festinger and Canon (1965) reported data which lend some support to this. They showed that after saccadic eye movements there is better localization of the fixated point in space than after a smooth tracking eye movement.

Some exploration was done to investigate this suggestion. During sessions in which S was to engage in smooth tracking eye movements E moved a pointer back and forth along the line and asked S to follow the pointer. The movement of the pointer in this way obviously did not provide a very uniform smooth motion for S to track and, over a 5-min. period there was, undoubtedly, many saccadic movements, but it was felt that this procedure might, at least, provide Es with some preliminary information.

The third session for S 1 began as a free scanning session with an apparently straight line. After 29 min. of such scanning, S spent 9 min. following the tip of the pointer as E moved it. The effect was interesting.

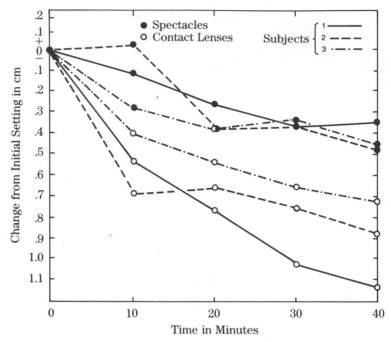

Figure 14.1   Adaptation to apparent curvature for prisms in spectacles and on contact lenses.

The initial straight setting on that day with the prism was 12.08; at the end of the 29 min. of scanning (saccadic eye movements) the settings of straight averaged 11.34, an adaptation of .74 cm. After an additional 9 min. of smooth tracking eye movements the settings of straight averaged 11.88, an adaptation of only .20 cm. Indeed, it seemed as though engaging in smooth tracking eye movements served to reduce adaptation that had already occurred during the session. No more "tracking" sessions were conducted with this S. This small bit of data was interesting enough, however, so that we explored it more systematically with the next two Ss.

The S 2 spent one session tracking the pointer while viewing an apparently curved line. At the end of this session there was .67 cm. (30.6%) adaptation to the curvature. This is to be compared with .87 cm. (40.5%) adaptation on the previous 2 days when scanning the apparently curved line. The S 3 spent one session tracking while viewing an apparently straight line. There was no adaptation whatsoever during this session. The measurement at the end of the session showed a change of −.27 actually in the opposite direction from adaptation. He also spent two sessions tracking while viewing an apparently curved line. The average adaptation for these two sessions was .65 cm. (38.0%). The comparable figure for the previous 3 days of scanning was .71 cm. (46.7%). Thus, in all instances, there was less adaptation when tracking with smooth eye movements than when scanning with saccadic eye movements. The difference was smallest for S 3 when viewing the apparently curved line and greatest for this same S when viewing the apparently straight line.

AFTEREFFECTS OF ADAPTATION.   At the beginning, and at the end, of every session S was asked to set the line so that it was straight with the naked eye. By comparing these two sets of measurements, one can see whether or not there were aftereffects for the naked eye of the adaptation occurring during the session while S wore the contact lens. Table 14.8 presents these data. Examination of the data shows that, except for the first day, there was an aftereffect on each day for each S. After the first session, all three Ss, on every day, showed a change from initial to final measurements with the naked eye in the same direction as the adaptation changes.

The data revealed another interesting result. There seems to be a cumulative effect over days in the settings made at the *beginning* of the session with the naked eye. Each of the three Ss shows the same pat-

**Table 14.8   Aftereffects of Adaptation for the Naked Eye
After Wearing Contact Lens**

	Subject 1		Subject 2		Subject 3	
	Pre	Post	Pre	Post	Pre	Post
Day 1	10.02	10.11s	9.99	9.78s	9.94	9.96s
Day 2	10.22	10.14s	10.22	9.75s	10.09	9.78s
Day 3	10.06	9.78s	10.10	9.74s	9.94	9.76s
Day 4	9.99	9.80sv	10.04	9.41c	9.93	9.64st
Day 5	9.93	9.51c	9.92	9.27c	9.81	9.41c
Day 6	9.71	9.43c	9.89	9.26ct	9.69	9.33c
Day 7					9.51	9.27c
Day 8					9.54	9.26ct
Day 9					9.57	9.28ct

Note.—Averages of "apparently straight" settings on centimeter scale, s = viewed apparently straight line, c = viewed apparently curved line, t = tracked pointer, v = on this day S 1 moved a stylus along lines himself.

tern. From the first to the second day the settings changed in a negative direction, that is, opposite to what would be expected on the basis of adaptation to the prism. From then on, however, each day showed a progressive effect, the naked eye settings at the beginning of the session becoming progressively more and more curved in the direction expected from adaptation.

There is no compelling reason to expect a carryover of adaptation to the prism from day to day. The S spent less than an hour each day looking through the prism and then had some 15 hr. of normal vision in which to readapt. It is, on the other hand, perfectly possible that a conditional adaptation and a conditional aftereffect might develop. That is, the stimulus conditions of the head in the biteboard in front of the apparatus could revive, or have become specifically associated with, the adaptation to the prism curvature and the progressive day to day cumulative effect could be due to the gradual development of this conditional learning.

This would be an attractive interpretation except for the fact that there exist data which make it implausible. If the progressive changes in initial settings with the naked eye at the beginning of each session are, indeed, due to conditional adaptation, then one would also expect to observe a similar cumulative effect on the first settings made on each day with the contact lens in the eye. No such trend for these settings was observed. Indeed, if anything, there was a tendency to perceive more and more curvature rather than less and less. It is difficult to believe that a conditional aftereffect had developed while, at the same time, a conditional adaptation had not developed.

INTEROCULAR TRANSFER OF AFTEREFFECTS.   About midway through the period of experimentation with S 2, it occurred to Es that it would be interesting and valuable to obtain data on interocular transfer. Taylor (1962) implied that the aftereffects of adaptation with a prism on a contact lens did not transfer. He wrote:

> The clearest evidence of adaptation came about half an hour after removal of the lens. Sitting in a stationary car I got the impression that the vertical lines of a tall building in front of me were not quite straight. I then inspected the lines monocularly, and found that with the right eye they were straight but with the left eye they were curved, the convexity being to the left, that is, the opposite of what I had seen through the lens [p. 225].

Theoretically, the issue is important. If the change in visual perception is actually due to a change in the efferent readiness activated by the retinal input, then there is every reason to believe there would be considerable, if not complete, interocular transfer.

The first time that initial and final measurements with each naked eye were taken was in Session V for S 2. The change from initial to final setting for the naked right eye (the one that wore the contact lens during the session) was +.65 cm.; for the left eye the change was +.33 cm., about 50% transfer of the aftereffect from one eye to the other. These measurements were repeated in Session VI in which S 2 visually tracked the pointer that E moved. This time the aftereffect for the right eye was .63 cm. but for the left eye was only .07 cm., indicating virtually no transfer at all.

Interocular transfer of the aftereffect was measured systematically for every session with S 3. With this S there is no question but that the aftereffect transferred completely from the right to the left eye. The simplest way to present the data is by showing, on the same figure, the initial and final naked eye measurements on each day for each eye. This is shown in Figure 14.2. It is clear that there was about 100% interocular transfer on every day except Day 8 when the transfer was not quite as large, only about 75%.

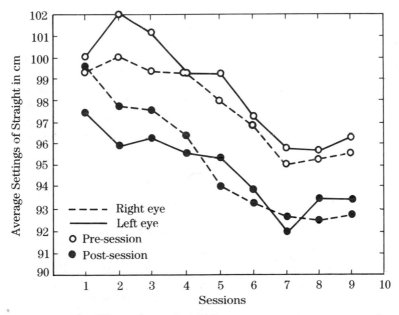

Figure 14.2   Aftereffect and transfer of adaptation to apparent curvature for S 3.

Discussion and Conclusions

Toward the end of the nineteenth century many psychologists held that the efferent system was importantly related to consciousness. Such theories fell into disrepute, however, and remained only as historical curiosities.

Recent evidence, both of a psychological and physiological nature, indicates the value of reexamining such theoretical positions. Several persons have also, recently, proposed new theories that afford efferent activity and readiness for efferent activity an important place in determining conscious perception.

We have reviewed the evidence relating to this question and have stated an experimentally testable theory of visual perception of contour. This theory, which seems to fit known facts, holds that visual perception of contour is determined by the particular sets of preprogrammed efferent instructions that are activated by the visual input into a state of readiness for immediate use.

Four experiments were done to test whether or not the conscious experience of visual perception is determined by the efferent readiness activated by the visual input. In three of these experiments Ss wore prism spectacles producing apparent curvature of straight lines and made arm movements corresponding to the objective contour of the lines while viewing them through the prisms. In each experiment one set of experimental conditions was designed to facilitate learning to issue new efference to the arm in response to the retinal contour and one set of conditions was designed to hinder such learning of a new afferent-efferent association. In all three experiments there was significantly more change in the visual perception of "straight" in the conditions that encouraged learning a new afferent-efferent association.

Theoretically the data support the view that visual input activates a whole set of learned efferent readinesses and that these latter determine the conscious experience of visual perception. In these three experiments Ss in the Learning conditions learned to issue efference to the arm appropriate to a curved path in response to visual input of a straight path. During the measurements of the perception of straight no relevant arm movements were involved. Consequently, it seems reasonable to conclude that, having learned such a new afferent-efferent association, the visual input of a straight line now activates efferent readiness relevant to arm movement corresponding to a curved path. There is a consequent change in the visual perception.

In a fourth experiment change in the visual perception of curvature was measured for three Ss who viewed a line monocularly through a wedge prism mounted on a contact lens. For each S the head was fixed by a biteboard and the only movement relevant to the contour was movement of the eyes. There is an important difference in the pattern of eye movements that S must make depending on whether the prism is mounted in spectacle frames or on a contact lens. In the former case, the eye in scanning the contour must move in accordance with the retinal image if fixation is to be maintained along the contour. However, if the prism is mounted on a contact lens so that the face of the prism moves as the eye moves, then the eye movements must conform to the objective contour in order to maintain fixation along the line. Under these circumstances the old, well-learned efference for an eye movement to fixate that is activated by visual input will result in a loss of fixation. To move the eye and maintain fixation along the contour, S wearing the contact lens must learn a new set of efferent instructions to issue in response to the visual input. If the conscious experience of visual perception of contour is, indeed, determined by efferent readiness activated by the visual input, then to the extent that S learns a new afferent-efferent association and, hence, a different efferent readiness is activated by the visual input, he will have a different visual perception of the contour.

In accordance with these theoretical expectations all three Ss showed appreciable change in the visual perception of curvature as a consequence of simply scanning the line while wearing the contact lens. This occurred whether S viewed an apparently straight line or an apparently curved line. Further evidence suggests that there is appreciable, perhaps complete, interocular transfer of this change in perception of contour. The data also provide a hint that, if the eye movement involved is a smooth tracking movement, there is less change in visual perception than if the eye movements are saccadic.

While the data are not conclusive with regard to an "efference readiness" theory of visual perception, they do support the theory. All four experiments taken together provide considerable evidence that such a theory has some validity and merits further consideration and exploration.

When this monograph was published, Leon Festinger and Donald Bamber were at Stanford University, Clarke A. Burnham was at the University of Texas, and Hiroshi Ono was at the University of Hawaii. The research reported in this monograph was conducted while all the authors were at Stanford University. Although they all worked together, different ones were involved in different experiments. Experiment III is a condensed version of a Ph.D. dissertation submitted at Stanford University by Clarke A. Burnham. Experiment I was conducted by Festinger, Burnham, and Bamber; Ono had primary responsibility for Experiment II; Festinger and Burnham were involved in Experiment IV.

The authors thanked Lance Kirkpatrick Canon and Stanley Coren for their help in the experimental work and Douglas H. Lawrence and Charles R. Hamilton for comments, criticisms, and general assistance.

All the research was supported by grants to Leon Festinger from the National Institute of Health, Grant MH–07835, and the National Science Foundation, Grant G–11255.

References

BREESE, B. B. On inhibition. *Psychol. Rev. Monogr. Suppl.*, 1899, **3** (1, Whole No. 11), 1–65.

CAMPBELL, F. S., & ROBSON, J. G. A fresh approach to stabilized retinal images. *Proc. Physiol. Soc.*, 1961, 11P–12P.

CAMPBELL, D., SANDERSON, R. E., & LAVERTY, S. G. Characteristics of a conditioned response in human subjects during extinction trials following a simple traumatic conditioning trial. *J. abnorm. soc. Psychol.*, 1964, **68**, 627–639.

COHEN, M. Visual curvature and feedback factors in the production of prismatically induced curved-line after-effects. Paper presented at the meeting of the Eastern Psychological Association, New York, April 1963.

COHEN, W. Form recognition, spatial orientation, perception of movement in the uniform visual field. In Marris, A. & Horne, E.P. (eds.). *Visual search techniques.* (Publication 712) Washington: National Academy of Science-National Research Council, 1960, pp. 119–123.

FENDER, D. H. The eye movement control system: Evolution of a model. In Reiss, R. R. (ed.). *Neural theory and modeling.* Stanford, Calif.: Stanford Univer. Press, 1964, pp. 306–324.

FESTINGER, L., & CANON, L. K. Information about spatial location based on knowledge about efference. *Psychol. Rev.*, 1965, **72**, 373–384.

GIBSON, J. J. Adaptation, after-effect and contrast in the perception of curved lines. *J. exp. Psychol.*, 1933, **16**, 1–31.

HARRIS, C. S. Perceptual adaptation to inverted, reversed, and displaced vision. *Psychol. Rev.*, 1965, **72**, 419–444.

HEBB, D. O. *Organization of behavior.* New York: Wiley, 1949.

HELD, R. Exposure-history as a factor in maintaining stability of perception and coordination. *J. nerv. ment. Dis.*, 1961, **132**, 26–32.

HELD, R., & REKOSH, J. Motor-sensory feedback and the geometry of visual space. *Science*, 1963, **141**, 722–723.

HELMHOLTZ, H. VON. *Physiological optics* (Trans. by J. P. C. Southall). New York: Dover, 1962.

JAMES, W. *The principles of psychology.* Vol. 2. London: Macmillan, 1890.

KOHLER, I. The formation and transformation of the perceptual world (Trans. by H. Fiss). *Psychol. Iss.*, 1964, 3(4), 173.

MERTON, P. A. Human position sense and sense of effort. Society of Experimental Biology Symposium XVIII, *Homeostasis and Feedback Mechanisms.* Cambridge: Cambridge Univer. Press, 1964, pp. 387–400.

MONTAGUE, W. P. Consciousness: A form of energy. *Essays, philosophical and psychological, in honor of William James.* New York: Longmans, Green, 1908, pp. 103–105.

MÜNSTERBERG, H. The physiological basis of mental life. *Science*, 1899, **9**, 442–447.

————. *Grundzuge der Psychologie.* Vol. I. Leipzig: J. A. Barth, 1900.

PICK, H., & HAY, J. Adaptation to prismatic distortion. *Psychon. Sci.*, 1964, **1**, 199–200.

RASHBASS, C. The relationship between saccadic and smooth tracking eye movements. *J. Physiol.*, 1961, **159**, 326–338.

SHERRINGTON, C. S. The muscular sense. In Schafer, E. A. (ed.). *A textbook of physiology.* Edinburgh & London: Pentland, 1900.

SPERRY, R. Neurology and the mind-brain problem. *Amer. Scient.*, 1952, **40**, 291–312.

TAYLOR, J. G. *The behavioral basis of perception.* New Haven: Yale Univer. Press, 1962.

TEPAS, D. I. The electrophysiological correlates of vision in a uniform field. In Whitcomb, M. A. (ed.). *Visual problems of the armed forces.* Washington: National Academy of Science-National Research Council, 1962, pp. 21–25.

VON HOLST, E. Relations between the central nervous system and the peripheral organs. *Brit. J. Anim. Behav.*, 1954, **2**, 89–94.

WASHBURN, M. F. *Movement and mental imagery.* Boston: Houghton Mifflin, 1916.

WUNDT, W. Zur Theorie der Raumlichen Gesichtswarnehmungen. *Philos. Stud.*, 1898, **14**, 11.

15

Inferences About the Efferent System Based on a Perceptual Illusion Produced by Eye Movements

Precise measurement of the position of the eye as it follows a moving target makes possible the exact computation of retinal information about the path of movement of that target. Comparing this retinal information with the reported visual perception of the path of movement enables inferences to be made concerning what information about eye position was used by the perceptual system. On the assumption that information available to the perceptual system about eye position comes only from monitoring efferent commands, these inferences are also about the content of those commands. Our data and analysis suggest that the efferent command for smooth pursuit eye movement, at the stage where it is monitored, contains good information about the direction of movement but only crude information about speed.

SOURCE: Festinger, L., & Easton, A. M. *Psychol. Rev.*, 1974, 81, 44–58. [Received May 29, 1973]

In the last decade neurophysiologists have increasingly emphasized the importance of understanding the organization and functioning of the efferent system. The general question is how, and in what form, motor commands are formulated and issued and how the nervous system controls motor activity. Some progress has been made on such questions at a neurophysiological level. For example, studies have been reported on the relationship between firing rates in motor neurons and force exerted by limb movements (Evarts, 1966, 1968, 1972); studies have identified cells in the central nervous system that regularly fire in connection with specific motor movement (Bizzi, 1968; Bizzi & Schiller, 1970); advances have been made in the understanding of how muscle spindles function in fine regulation of movement (Granit, 1970; Matthews, 1964). It is not our intention here to review this material but only to point out the nature of some of the questions that have been addressed. The problems, issues, and current state of the work is well presented by Evarts, Bizzi, Burke, DeLong, and Thach (1971).

However, there has been little or no work that addresses questions about the efferent system from a psychophysical point of view. There have been studies that have shown the importance of the efferent system in enabling adaptation to distorted visual input (Festinger, Burnham, Ono, & Bamber, 1967; Held, 1961) but this work only implicates the efferent system—it does not explicate it. We think that it is possible to make progress in understanding the nature and functioning of the efferent system through psychophysical methods. It is the purpose of this article to propose a paradigm for doing this, to present the results of a study following this paradigm, and to present the beginnings of a theoretical model, necessarily narrow in scope, that suggests itself as a result of these findings.

An Approach to the Study of the Efferent System

Some aspects of visual perception are particularly well suited for analyzing what happens in the efferent system. This suitability arises from the fact that the perceptual system does not have access to information about eye movements or eye position based on proprioceptive feedback from the extraocular muscles. Since there may be some who would dispute the preceding statement, it is worthwhile to briefly summarize the evidence.

The extraocular muscles in the human do contain muscle spindle receptors and tendon receptors. These are capable of transmitting information about length of the muscle or change of length (spindle receptors) and about tension or change of tension in the muscle (tendon receptors). Thus, it is possible that such information is transmitted in a way that might be used by the perceptual system. The psychophysical evidence, however, indicates that this is not the case. Brindley and Merton (1960), for example, anesthetized the surface of the eyeball and the eyelids, put an opaque cap over the cornea to eliminate retinal information, and moved the eyes of their subjects back and forth by seizing the tendon of the lateral or medial muscle with forceps. They reported that under these circumstances the subject completely lacks awareness that his eye is moving—an awareness that might be expected to exist if information from the extraocular muscles was available to the perceptual system. Brindley and Merton further reported that if the eye is held completely motionless, and the subject is told to move his eyes, the subject reports that his eye did move.

Recently Skavenski (1972) and Skavenski and Steinman (1970) have disputed this result. Among other things, they reported that if the eye is moved mechanically by large amounts (6° to 10°), the subject will correctly identify the direction of the eye movement 75% to 80% of the time. One cannot be certain in their study that some clues were not available from pressure on the eyeball or on eyelids. In another study, however, Skavenski, Haddad, and Steinman (1972), using the same technique, showed conclusively that, even if any proprioceptive information from the extraocular muscles exists, it is not used by the perceptual system for egocentric localization of visual direction. They find that the only extraretinal information that is used perceptually is "outflow" information, that is, information about the efferent commands to the muscles.

We can, then, conclude that, in the absence of retinal information, knowledge about eye movements or eye position that is available to the perceptual system is based on information about what the eye was commanded to do and *not* on information about what the eye actually did do. At some level of transmission of an efferent command from the central nervous system, this command is monitored and the information contained in that command at that level is available to the perceptual system.

How does this help us to study the efferent system? Let us imagine a situation in which an observer watches a target moving on a completely contourless background, his eyes more or less following the movement of the target. The observer's perception of the path of movement of the target must depend on a combination of two kinds of information: information about movement of the target on the retina and information about eye movements. Only if both these sets of information were accurate, and only if they were accurately combined, would the perception of the path of movement be veridical. If the eye is stationary, of course, perception could be based only on retinal information; but with a moving eye this is not possible.

Let us tentatively assume that position and movement on the retina are accurately transmitted to the perceptual system. It seems reasonable to assume this since, if it were not so, visual perception would rarely be veridical and we know it usually is. Let us further tentatively assume that the "calculations" that combine retinal information with information about eye position are accurate. We will examine this assumption further in connection with specific data, but let us proceed now accepting the assumption.

Under this set of assumptions it is realistically possible to collect data from which one can infer the informational content of the efferent commands for eye movements as they exist at the level of the output system at which they are monitored and are available to the perceptual system. If we had (a) precise measurement of the perception of the path of the target moving on a contourless field, (b) precise measurement of the position of the observer's eye at every moment in time while observing the target, and (c) precise information of the actual position in space of the target at every moment in time, we could then perform the following computations. From the information about the actual position of the target and the actual position of the eye, we could compute the actual path traveled by the target on the retina. By comparing this retinal information with the perception of the path of movement of the target, we could infer what information the perceptual system had about the movement of the eye. This inference would, according to our reasoning, also be an inference about the informational content of the monitored efferent commands.

If the observer's perception of the path of movement were veridical, the whole endeavor would, of course, be in vain. We would simply conclude that the perceptual system had complete and accurate information about the eye movements—a conclusion that would make this line of approach not very productive. There is evidence in the literature, however, that if the eye engages in smooth pursuit movements the observer's perception is, frequently, far from veridical. Johansson (1950), for example, reported various interesting misperceptions of the paths of movement when several luminous points move in a relatively contourless field at velocities that would be expected to elicit smooth pursuit eye movements. Johansson interpreted his data differently, however, rejecting the possibility that eye movements are important in the misperceptions. As another example, Stoper (1967) reported that during smooth pursuit movements of the eye, the perception of the location of a briefly flashed spot of light is determined almost entirely by its retinal location without much "compensation" for eye movement.

It is, then, possible that the monitored efferent command for smooth pursuit eye movements does not contain complete and accurate information. The data collection procedure we outlined above might enable us to infer what information is actually available. We consequently chose one such "illusion" for intensive study.

The Fujii Illusion

Fujii (1943) reported an extensive series of experiments that dealt primarily with the perception of the diameter of the circular path of a spot of light moving in an otherwise dark room. In the course of these experiments he also reported on the perceived path of motion of a spot that moved for one cycle, in a triangular path or in a square path. In his experiments each side of the triangular path subtended a visual angle of about 17° and each side of the square path subtended a visual angle of about 12.5°. He employed velocities of 6° to 22° per second. He reported a surprising difference between the actual and the perceived path of movement under these circumstances. Figure 15.1 (adapted from Figures 2 and 4 in Fujii, 1943) summarizes his report of these perceived paths. The solid lines indicate the physical paths, and the arrows indicate the direction of motion. The dashed lines describe the perceived paths. His report about this is very brief.

This misperception of the path of movement seemed to fit the conditions that would enable us to make inferences about the efferent output for smooth pursuit eye movements. We consequently engaged in a series of observations to see whether or not the Fujii illusion did fit the conditions and assumptions that we described above. These observations were all carried out with a spot repetitively cycling in a square path on a cathode ray tube display with a very fast phosphor so that there was no physical trace of the path of movement. A contrast screen in front of the cathode ray tube eliminated any general glow from the surface and the room was in total darkness. In short, for our observations the luminous spot moved on a contourless background.

The observations reported below are based primarily on verbal reports from many observers. All observers were asked to follow the spot with their eyes. In addition to the observations of the authors, colleagues, and graduate students in our laboratory, we also obtained reports from naive observers. Occasionally we encountered an observer

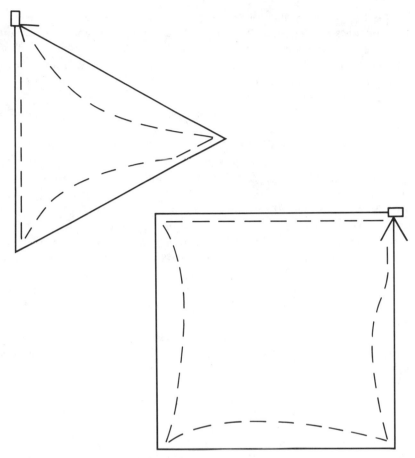

Figure 15.1   Perception of the path of a target moving in a square or triangular path. (Solid lines indicate the physical paths, and arrows indicate the direction of motion. Dashed lines describe the perceived paths.) (Adapted from an article by E. Fujii from the 1943 Japanese Journal of Psychology. *Copyrighted by the* Japanese Psychological Association, 1943.)

who simply did not perceive the illusion. We did not keep a record of how many since that was not our purpose at the time. Our memory is that this amounted to 2 or 3 persons out of more than 50 observers whom we used at one time or another. The results presented below were reported by all observers who perceived the illusion. We will present these results organized around major questions.

Does the misperception of the path of movement exist under conditions in which smooth pursuit movements are likely to occur? We explored the perception of the path of movement over a wide range of sizes of the square path (3° to 10° of visual angle per side) and a wide range of frequencies (.1 to 2.0 cycles per second) and velocities (2° to 60° per second). For these observations the spot always moved with uniform speed, turning corners instantaneously. The conclusions may be summarized as follows.

If the speed of the moving spot exceeded 40° to 45° per second, the misperception did not exist. Sometimes, at such high velocities the spot seemed to move erratically but the corners were perceived as right angles. At lower velocities, frequency was a critical variable. If the frequency exceeded 1.6 to 1.7 cycles per second, the illusion disappeared and the path was seen as square. Within the range of frequencies and velocities that produced the illusion, an additional observation is worth noting. At frequencies below .3 to .4 cycles per second, the perceived path of motion was usually of the form illustrated in Figure 15.2. At frequencies above .5 to .6 cycles per second, the perception was of the form shown in Figure 15.3.

In summary, we can answer the question positively. The velocities and frequencies that produce the misperception are ones that are likely to elicit some amount of smooth pursuit eye movement.

Is the retinal information accurate under these conditions? Since there are many visual illusions that do not depend on eye movements,

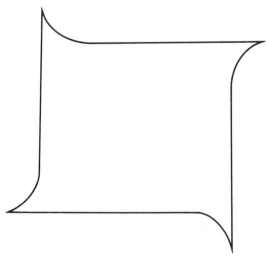

Figure 15.2 Perception of the path of a target moving in a square path at frequencies below .3 to .4 cycles per second.

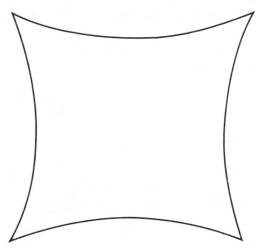

Figure 15.3   Perception of the path of a target moving in a square path at frequencies about .5 to .6 cycles per second.

it is important to know whether the Fujii illusion exists if the eye is stationary and all of the information about the path of movement is available from the retina. The answer to this question is clear. If a fixation point is provided, and the observer is asked to fixate that point and not follow the moving spot, the illusion disappears—the path is seen veridically as a square.

In addition, it may be pointed out that if a cathode ray tube display with a slow phosphor is used so that there is an extended physical trace of the path of movement of the spot, the path is seen as a square.

We still, however, do not have a complete answer to our question. One might suspect that even if the retinal information was accurate when the eye was relatively stationary, such information might be inaccurate while the eye was moving. Pursuing the hunch that the Fujii illusion might be due, at least in part, to the fact that the spot turned the corners instantaneously, a feat that the eye could not accomplish, we observed the path of movement with the eye following the spot while the spot moved with sinusoidally varying velocity along each side of the square. Under these conditions the velocity of the spot is fastest in the middle of each side, slowing up as it approaches each corner. The results are again clear. With sinusoidally varying velocity of the spot, the path of movement is seen as square. We can, then, assert that even while the eye is in motion the shape of the path of movement may be seen veridically. It may be noted that, under these conditions, the perceived square path is considerably smaller than the physical path. We will discuss this in detail later.

Is the computation that combines retinal information with information about eye position accurate? This question is, of course, least amenable to a direct answer. Since we do not know the exact information that the perceptual system has about eye position (that is what we hope to be able to infer), it is certainly difficult to show that computations involving that information are accurate. The best we can do is to show that under some circumstances, even with eye movements, perception is veridical. If the perception is veridical, it seems plausible to assume that the computation is accurate. We have already mentioned that when the spot moves with sinusoidally varying velocity, the path of movement is perceived correctly as a square. This lends weight to the assumption that the computation is accurate. Another piece of evidence can also be produced. If one provides two stationary points for fixation and asks the observer to move his eye from one to the other while the moving spot is cycling with uniform speed, one finds that again the perception is veridical. The path is seen as a square. Under these conditions, of course, the eye movements are saccades and not smooth pursuit movements; hence, we can at least assert that the computation for combining retinal information and information about saccadic eye movements seems to be accurate.

We may then say that, as far as we could determine, the Fujii illusion does fit the conditions that we would like to have for attempting to infer the content of the monitored efferent command for smooth pursuit eye movements. We proceeded to collect the relevant data.

Measurement of Eye Position

All observations during which eye movements were recorded were made with the observer's left eye occluded. The position of the right eye was recorded continuously, using a noncontacting eye tracker developed by Cornsweet and Crane (1972). Infrared light was projected onto the eyeball and the system measured the position of the reflection from the rear surface of the eye lens (fourth Purkinje reflection) in relation to the position of the corneal reflection (first Purkinje reflection). Two direct-current voltage outputs were obtained, one corresponding to the horizontal, the other to the vertical, component of eye position.

The output of the eye tracker has a noise level of about 2' of arc and is linear (except for possible local irregularities of the observer's eye) over a greater than 12° range both horizontally and vertically.

The data on eye movements were recorded in two ways. A record of the horizontal and vertical components was made, using an oscillograph, on chart paper moving at a rate of 100 millimeters per second. The two output voltages from the eye tracker were also put through two digital voltmeters used as analogue-digital converters, and the digital information was printed out once every 35 milliseconds by a high-speed printer. Event markers on both the chart paper and the digital printout indicated the time at which the moving spot in the visual display turned each corner of its square path so that the two records could be collated in time, and also, of course, to allow exact computation of the position of the eye in relation to the position of the moving target at each moment in time. The digital voltmeters used as analogue-digital converters took from 2 to 7 milliseconds from the time they received a command to sample to the time they completed the sampling: hence, there is that much uncertainty in the temporal resolution of our data. The commands to the analogue-digital converters to sample were synchronized with the movement of the spot in the visual display, so that a "sample command" always occurred at the moment the spot reached a corner of the square path.

Procedure for Data Collection
The moving spot was displayed on a Hewlett-Packard model 1310A display scope with a P15 phosphor. The movement of the spot was controlled by a Wavetek model 116 function generator and a Tektronix model 4701 eight-channel multiplexer. The visual display was located 100 centimeters in front of the observer's eye.

Data on eye movements while viewing the target that moved in a square path were collected from three observers. One of these (M.) was a highly experienced observer; another (T.) was inexperienced but had prior knowledge about the phenomenon; the third observer (C.) was inexperienced and totally ignorant about the phenomenon. After each observer was aligned in the apparatus, with head held steady using a biteboard, calibrations were made to determine the exact eye position measures that corresponded to positions fixated in the visual field. There is undoubtedly some error in these calibrations since the eye is not steady in fixation. We estimate this error to be no greater than 4' or 5' of arc.

The data were collected in total darkness. Each observer viewed four conditions of the visual display as follows: With the spot moving with uniform speed in a square path of 6° per side, the length of time for the spot to traverse each side was either 350, 700, or 1,015 milliseconds. In addition each observer viewed the spot moving in a smaller square path, 3° per side, the length of time to traverse each side being 350 milliseconds. The target velocities corresponding to these four conditions are, in order, approximately 18°, 9°, 6°, and 9° per second. For each of these conditions, the observer fixated a stationary spot which then started to move clockwise. After eight cycles of the square the spot stopped and the observer fixated the spot again. During this entire period eye movements were recorded.

For the analysis of the data we relied primarily on the digital printout at 35-millisecond intervals. The chart paper recordings were used for two purposes: easy identification of cycles during which eyeblinks occurred, which were excluded from analysis, and easy identification of the occurrence of saccades. Sometimes the digital sampling occurred during the course of a saccade and, when this happened, we used the chart paper record in an attempt to specify more exactly in time the beginning and end of the saccade.

Patterns of Eye Movements
Although the plotting of the exact pattern of eye movements that occur while the observer follows the moving spot is only the first step in the calculation we wish to make, it is nevertheless important to see what they look like. We selected four examples of such eye movements to illustrate each of the four conditions of observation that we employed and to represent each of the three observers. These examples are shown in Figures 15.4 through 15.7. They are quite representative of the typical kinds of eye movements.

Each figure shows the exact position of the eye in relation to the physical location of the moving spot for one complete cycle of the square path. The small squares indicate the physical location of the corners of the square path through which the spot travels. The filled circles in each figure indicate the position of the eye at one moment in time; successive circles are separated by 35 milliseconds. The position of the eye at the moment in time that the spot instantaneously turns each corner is indicated by an open circle around that particular data point. The cycle starts at the point labeled "S" and ends at the point labeled "E." If consecutive circles are not connected, that indicates that the eye was engaging in smooth pursuit movement. If the eye engaged in saccadic movements, the circles are connected by a solid line. The irregularities in the pattern of eye movements, most noticeable at the slower speed shown in Figure 15.4, are probably due to errors of measurement. The magnitude of these irregularities is well within the noise level and temporal resolution capability of our equipment.

It may be seen that all the eye movement patterns show a combination of smooth pursuit movements with interspersed saccades. As the velocity of the moving spot increases, the velocity of the smooth pursuit

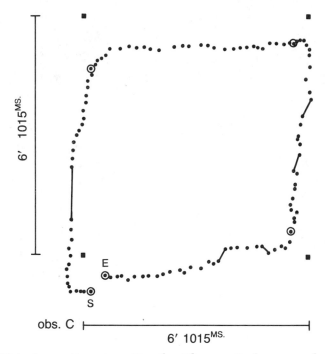

Figure 15.4 Successive eye position for Observer C. for one cycle of target moving at .25 cycles per second (6° path). (Small squares indicate the physical location of the corners of the square path. Filled circles indicate position of the eye at one moment in time; successive points are separated by 35 milliseconds. Open circles around filled circles indicate position of the eye at the moment the spot instantaneously turns the corner. The cycle starts at "S" and ends at "E." Unconnected consecutive circles indicate smooth pursuit movement. Circles connected by solid lines indicate saccadic movements. Abbreviations: Obs. = observer; ms. = millisecond.)

movement, of course, also increases. In addition, as the velocity increases, the interspersed saccades tend to become larger. There are no periods in which the eye is relatively stationary, as occurs in situations in which only saccadic eye movements are made. Here, the saccadic eye movement, when it occurs, seems to be superimposed on, and does not disturb or interrupt, the smooth pursuit movement. This is evident in all of the figures but can, perhaps, be seen most clearly in Figure 15.6. In this cycle, two saccades occurred while the eye was following the spot moving upward on the left side of the square path. In each case, at the end of the saccade, the eye immediately shows smooth pursuit move-

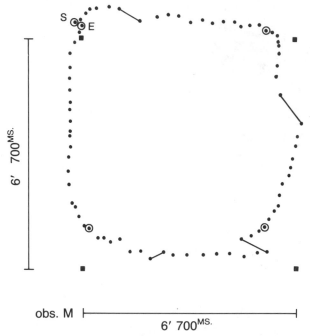

Figure 15.5 Successive eye positions for Observer M. for one cycle of target moving at .36 cycles per second (6° path). (Small squares indicate the physical location of the corners of the square path. Filled circles indicate position of the eye at one moment in time; successive points are separated by 35 milliseconds. Open circles around filled circles indicate position of the eye at the moment the spot instantaneously turns the corner. The cycle starts as "S" and ends at "E." Unconnected consecutive circles indicate smooth pursuit movement. Circles connected by solid lines indicate saccadic movements. Abbreviations: Obs. = observer; ms. = milliseconds.)

ment in essentially the same direction as the movement prior to the saccade. It is as if the smooth movement continued throughout with the saccade overlaid on it. It may be worth noting that Woodworth and Schlosberg (1956, p. 511) made this same point about such situations. It may also be worth noting, in passing, that there tend to be more vertically than horizontally oriented saccades. We do not find it mentioned in existing literature but, in our data, the strong suggestion exists that smooth pursuit movement in the horizontal direction is more adequate than in the vertical direction.

It is particularly relevant to our present purpose to examine, in Figures 15.4 through 15.7, the pattern of eye movements around the time

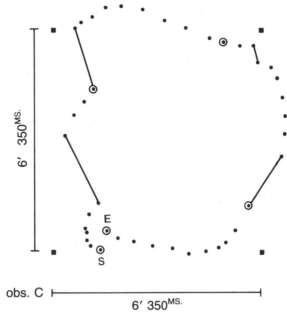

6' 350^{MS.}

obs. C

6' 350^{MS.}

Figure 15.6   Successive eye positions for Observer C. for one cycle of target moving at .71 cycles per second (6° path). (Small squares indicate the physical location of the corners of the square path. Filled circles indicate position of the eye at one moment in time; successive points are separated by 35 milliseconds. Open circles around filled circles indicate position of the eye at the moment the spot instantaneously turns the corner. The cycle starts at "S" and ends at "E." Unconnected consecutive circles indicate smooth pursuit movement. Circles connected by solid lines indicate saccadic movements. Abbreviations: Obs. = observer; ms. = milliseconds.)

that the moving spot actually turns a corner of the square, that is, near the encircled data points. It is clear, in all the eye movement records, that the eye does not turn corners instantaneously as does the spot. When the spot turns a corner the eye makes a rather gradual turn with a component of motion in the previous direction persisting for some time. At higher velocities particularly, the eye sometimes, probably in anticipation, begins its gradual turn even before the spot has reached the corner. While the eye is making these gradual turns, of course, the movement of the spot on the retina would show an indentation from the corner similar to what is reported perceptually. This gives us our first clue as to why the misperception of the path of movement takes its particular form, namely, the indentation from the corners.

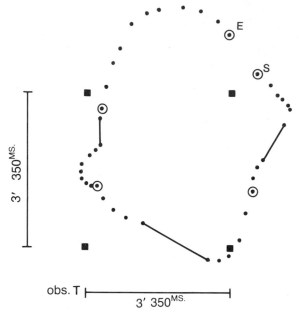

Figure 15.7   Successive eye positions for Observer T. for one cycle of target moving at .71 cycles per second (3° path). (Small squares indicate the physical location of the corners of the square path. Filled circles indicate position of the eye at one moment in time; successive points are separated by 35 milliseconds. Open circles around filled circles indicate position of the eye at the moment the spot instantaneously turns the corner. The cycle starts at "S" and ends at "E." Unconnected consecutive circles indicate smooth pursuit movement. Circles connected by solid lines indicate saccadic movements. Abbreviations: Obs. = observer; ms. = milliseconds.)

Calculation of "Corrected Retinal Information"

From the data on eye movements such as those shown in Figures 15.4 through 15.7, we could, of course, compute and plot on a graph the exact movement of the spot on the retina of the observer. This would tell us what retinal information existed concerning the path of movement of the spot. This would be an adequate procedure for our purposes if the eye movement patterns consisted entirely of smooth pursuit movements. We would then be able to make inferences about what information concerning these smooth pursuit movements is available to the perceptual system.

The eye movement patterns, however, do not contain only smooth pursuit movements but also show interspersed saccades. It is necessary then, for our purposes, to make some assumptions about what information the perceptual system has about saccadic eye movements and to correct the calculation of retinal information to take this into account. In other words, we want to calculate a combination of what is known about the path of movement of the spot from retinal information and from information about saccadic eye movements. Then the only missing information would be about the smooth pursuit eye movements, and we could proceed with our inferences about that information. It is clear, of course, that the validity of the inferences will depend, in part, on the validity of our assumptions concerning information about saccades.

It seems most plausible to make the assumption that the perceptual system does have good information about the extent and direction of a saccadic eye movement. Such eye movements are very rapid and are ballistic in nature. The efferent commands for such eye movements must, hence, be entirely preprogrammed. That is, the complete set of instructions for the movement has to be issued before the movement starts since, once the ballistic eye movement is under way, it is no longer controllable. It seems sensible to assume, then, that the monitored efferent command for such a movement contains all the information. In addition, our own informal observations indicate that if fixation points are provided, and only saccadic eye movements presumably occur, the perception is veridical. So in our calculations we will assume that, whenever a saccadic eye movement occurs, the perceptual system knows accurately and exactly the direction and magnitude of that movement.

Before we can proceed with these calculations one other decision has to be made. Do we assume that when a saccade occurs it has interrupted and replaced the smooth pursuit movement, or do we assume that the saccade is overlaid on, or added to, the smooth pursuit movement which persists? As mentioned above, particularly in reference to Figure 15.6 when we were discussing the patterns of eye movement, the records look as though the most plausible assumption is the latter—that the smooth pursuit component of the motion of the eye persists and the saccadic movement is added on to that. In our calculations we have attributed a speed and direction of smooth pursuit movement during the interval occupied by a saccade by interpolation from the smooth pursuit movements immediately preceding and immediately following the saccade.

"Corrected Retinal Paths" of the Moving Spot
Given these assumptions we can calculate what the perception of the path of motion of the spot would be if it were based solely on information about movement on the retina and correct information about sac-

cades that were superimposed over an ongoing smooth pursuit motion. Representative examples of the results of these calculations are presented in Figures 15.8 through 15.11. They are chosen, again, to show one example from each of our four observation conditions and at least one example from each of our three observers. These figures are quite typical of all of the data.

Each of the figures shows the "corrected retinal path" for a single cycle of the eye following the spot. Each filled circle again represents successive relative positions (35-millisecond intervals) of the moving spot on the retina (plotted in terms of visual field rather than the reversed retinal field) corrected for saccadic eye movements. The encircled data points again indicate retinal position of the spot at the moment that it turns a corner. For the sake of visual clarity, the retinal path for each side of the square is separated from the others. It may be remembered that the direction of target movement is always clockwise. On each figure is indicated the scale equivalent of 1° of visual angle. At the lowest frequency, illustrated in Figure 15.8, many of the data points cluster so closely that the path on the retina is not readily apparent. Where this is the case we have indicated, with a dashed line, the general path on the retina.

Let us first point to the most salient features of Figures 15.8 through 15.11. It is clear that in many instances they conform to the general features of the reported perceptions of the path of movement of the spot. At the lower frequencies, illustrated in Figures 15.8 and 15.9, the typical pattern along one side of the path is a rapid inward indentation from the corner point, followed either by a slow stretching out of the path until the next corner, as in Figure 15.9, or by a close clustering of points, as in Figure 15.8. The best illustrations of this are, perhaps, the path on the left-hand side of Figure 15.8 and on the lower side of Figure 15.9.

At the higher frequencies, illustrated in Figures 15.10 and 15.11, the corrected retinal paths look much more symmetrically indented, conforming to the general form of the perception shown in Figure 15.3. The best examples of this are the right-hand side of Figure 15.10 and several sides in Figure 15.11. It may be of interest to note that Observer T., whose data are shown in Figure 15.10, often reported the perception of asymmetrical sides even at higher frequencies.

It is clear from an examination of Figures 15.8 through 15.11 that the information contained in these corrected retinal paths provides a major basis for the Fujii illusion. One can readily come to the conclusion that the information available to the perceptual system about the position of the eye during smooth pursuit movement is not very great. Our pur-

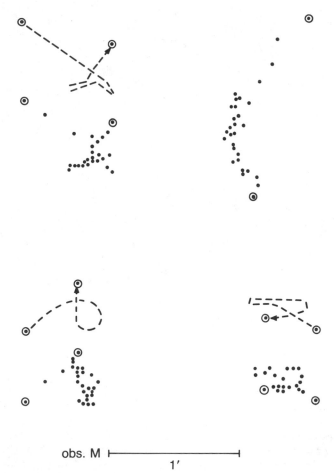

obs. M ⊢——————————⊣
1′

Figure 15.8   Corrected retinal path for Observer M. for one cycle of target moving at .25 cycles per second (6° path). (Each filled circle represents successive relative postions at 35-millisecond intervals of the moving spot on the retina, plotted in terms of visual field rather than the reversed retinal field, corrected for saccadic eye movements. Encircled circles indicate retinal postion of the spot at the moment it turns a corner. For visual clarity, the retinal path for each side of the square is separated from the others. Dashed line indicates general path on retina where data points were clustered very closely. Abbreviation: Obs. = observer.)

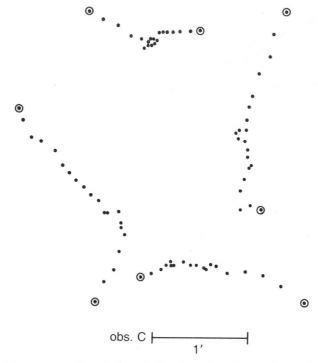

Figure 15.9 Corrected retinal path for Observer C. for one cycle of target moving at .36 cycles per second (6° path). (Each filled circle represents successive relative positions at 35-millisecond intervals of the moving spot on the retina, plotted in terms of visual field rather than the reversed retinal field, corrected for saccadic eye movements. Encircled circles indicate retinal position of the spot at the moment it turns a corner. For visual clarity, the retinal path for each side of the square is separated from the others. Abbreviations: Obs. = observer.)

pose, however, is to try to infer as much as we can about exactly what information is available about smooth pursuit movements; hence, our next step should be to examine the major ways in which these patterns of corrected retinal path differ from the reported perceptions. There are two major differences that are important to point out.

Let us consider the corrected retinal paths shown in Figure 15.8. It is clear that they all differ considerably from the perception of the path of movement of the spot. Never did this observer, or any other observer, report seeing the moving spot circle back or reverse direction along any one side. These data points must, obviously, be stretched out in space in a temporal sequence if they are to conform more closely to

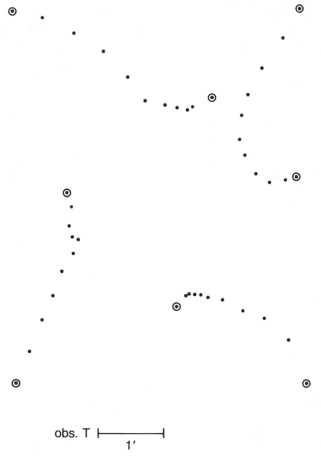

obs. T ├————————┤
1'

Figure 15.10 Corrected retinal path for Observer T. for one cycle of target moving at .71 cycles per second (6° path). (Each filled circle represents successive relative positions at 35-millisecond intervals of the moving spot on the retina, plotted in terms of visual field rather than the reversed retinal field, corrected for saccadic eye movements. Encircled circles indicate retinal position of the spot at the moment it turns a corner. For visual clarity, the retinal path for each side of the square is separated from the others. Abbreviations: Obs. = observer.)

the actual perception. In other words, the perceptual system does add something about velocity of smooth pursuit eye movement into the perception.

The same point can be made again, on a slightly different basis, con-

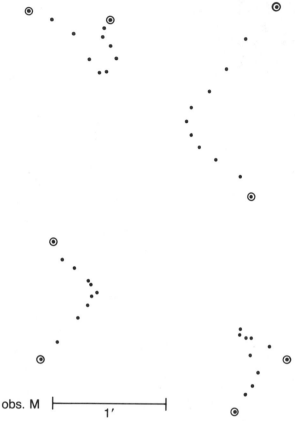

obs. M

1′

Figure 15.11   Corrected retinal path for Observer M. for one cycle of target moving at .71 cycles per second (3° path). (Each filled circle represents successive relative positions at 35-millisecond intervals of the moving spot on the retina, plotted in terms of visual field rather than the reversed retinal field, corrected for saccadic eye movements. Encircled circles indicate retinal position of the spot at the moment it turns a corner. For visual clarity, the retinal path for each side of the square is separated from the others. Abbreviations: Obs. = observer.)

sidering any of the figures showing the corrected retinal paths (Figures 15.8 through 15.11). For example, these paths in Figure 15.9 would indicate that the perceived path would have an apparent extent of about 2° of visual angle per side on the average. This, again, does not correspond to the perception. Although we tried, we were not successful in obtaining precise estimates of the perceived extent from our observers. It was a very difficult thing for them to report on.

The most successful procedure was to have the observer follow the moving spot for a number of cycles and then to suddenly paint the entire square on the cathode ray tube display. One could then obtain gross comparisons of the perceived size and the actual size. What can be said from such reports is that at lower frequencies the extent of the perceived path usually looked smaller than at higher frequencies; that the perceived extent of motion was always less than the actual physical extent; and that rarely did the perceived extent seem less than about half of the physical extent. The corrected retinal paths shown in Figures 15.8 through 15.11 are almost all too short. Again we must come to the conclusion that the perception has had something added in about the position of the eye during smooth pursuit movements.

The second major difference between the corrected retinal paths and the perceptions of the observers concerns the directional orientation of the paths. This can be illustrated by examining the paths in Figure 15.11. For this observer, as well as for all others, the perceptions are oriented correctly as they are shown in Figures 15.2 and 15.3. But the corrected retinal paths are frequently tilted. This orientation difference does not always appear, but as can be seen in Figures 15.8 through 15.11, it frequently does exist. We are consequently led to the conclusion that the perceptual system knows something about the direction in which the eye was commanded to move during smooth pursuit.

Content of the Efferent Command for Smooth Pursuit Eye Movement
We previously stated, with support from the research literature, that whatever information the perceptual system has about the smooth pursuit movement of the eye must represent the information contained in the efferent commands for those movements at the level at which those commands are monitored. Our task now is to infer, as precisely as we can, what this exact information is. We have already said that the information cannot be very exact and specific—the corrected retinal paths are too similar to the perceptions for this to be the case. We have also said that some information about movement of the eye must be present—the corrected retinal paths need to be stretched out in temporal order; and that information about the commanded direction of the eye movement must be present—the perceived orientation of the paths was not tilted as are many of the corrected retinal paths.

If we had been successful in obtaining very precise measurement of the perception of the path of the moving spot, we would have an easier task at this point. However, we were not successful at this. We were not able to get adequate measures of the magnitude of perceived indentation from the corners, or of the perceived extent of movement of the spot. On the basis of the general reports of perception that we obtained it seems reasonable, however, to make the following inferences:

1. The efferent command for a smooth pursuit eye movement contains specification of the direction for the eye to move. Any instance in which the corrected retinal path does not correspond to the physical path, but the perception is veridical, must indicate that the efferent command contained correct information about the relevant aspect of the eye movement. The correctly perceived orientation of the path indicates that there must be some information about direction in which the eye is commanded to move. This does not, of course, mean that the perceptual system knows the direction in which the eye is actually moving. It only knows the direction in which the eye was commanded to move. In the particular instance of the Fujii illusion, since the eye cannot turn corners suddenly, the actual directions of eye movements probably differ from what the eye was commanded to do in the neighborhood of the corners of the path. This accounts for the perceived indentations from the corners that are reflected in the corrected retinal paths. The perceptual system only knows the direction contained in the efferent command.

2. The efferent command for a smooth pursuit eye movement contains very inadequate information about the speed of the eye movement. Since the extent of the perceived path was always considerably less than the physical extent of movement, we know that the efferent command does not contain accurate information about speed of eye movement. On the other hand, as we discussed in the previous section, some information about this is present. It must be that the actual speed of the eye movement is controlled by some more peripheral loop in the efferent output system so that the speed of the eye can be approximately matched to the speed of the target even though the command, at the monitored level, does not contain this information.

We cannot say more about this with great confidence at this point but, in speculation, we would propose the following. The efferent command for smooth pursuit movement, in addition to specifying the direction for that movement, contains only the command to move. Hence, the perceptual system knows that the eye is moving and will attribute at least some minimal velocity to that movement. When the target changes direction suddenly a new command will be issued which, in addition to ordering a direction change, may contain instructions to move faster or slower. Thus, the perceptual system could know that, at different parts of the path, the speed of the eye differed as instructed. This is our guess. Further explorations are needed in situations in which the perception can be measured more exactly.

Possibility of an Alternative Interpretation
The validity of our conclusions about the efferent output for smooth pursuit eye movements rests, obviously, on a chain of reasoning that includes a number of assumptions. It is important, consequently, to consider other possible interpretations of the Fujii illusion and the data we have collected concerning it. A successful alternative interpretation would cast serious doubt on our analysis.

There is a major possible alternative that has been suggested to us many times. This alternative would hold that the perceptual system does have accurate information about eye position during smooth pursuit movements, but that there is some time mismatch between retinal information and information about eye position. Perhaps the retinal information arrives at some central processing stage sometime later (or earlier) than the eye position information. Then the retinal information might be matched to the later (or earlier) eye position, and this temporal mismatch might produce the misperception of path of movement rather than inadequate information about eye position, as we have argued.

We can, of course, take our records of eye movements, from which we know the exact position of the eye and the position of the target on the retina at each point in time, and compute what the predicted perception would be for various assumed differences of arrival times of the two pieces of information. We have done this and in no instance does the perception predicted in this manner at all resemble the Fujii illusion. Figure 15.12 shows examples of the results of these computations to illustrate the outcome. In this figure the upper set of circles, labeled A, shows the result of our computation of corrected retinal path for Observer C. along the upper side of the 6° square path, the spot taking 350 milliseconds to traverse each side. The next two sets of circles, B and C, show the results of calculations that assume eye position is accurately known, and assume that the retinal information arrives 70 milliseconds earlier (B) and 70 milliseconds later (C) than the information about eye position. The fourth set of circles (D) represents the eye and target positions from which the above calculations were made. These examples are quite typical of these computations. They do not resemble the per-

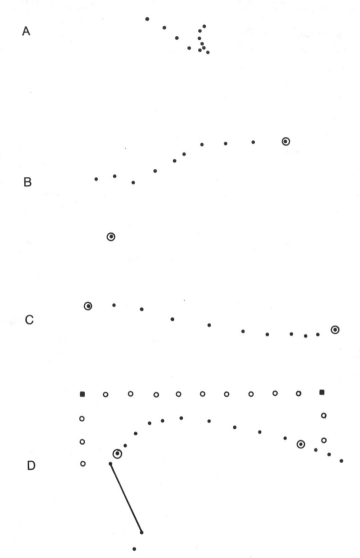

Figure 15.12 *Comparison with computations based on differential latencies of retinal and eye-position information. (Section A shows corrected retinal path; Section B, eye-position information delayed 70 milliseconds; Section C, retinal information delayed 70 milliseconds; Section D, eye and target positions used in computations. Small squares indicate physical location of the corners of the path. Open circles indicate target positions, filled circles eye positions when the spot turns the corner. Solid line indicates saccadic eye movements.)*

ceived Fujii illusion. This particular alternative interpretation does not seem viable.

Summary

When an observer's eyes follow a target moving on a contourless background, his perception of the path through which the target moved has to be based on a combination of retinal information and information about eye position. Precise measurement of the eye position as it follows the target can provide exact computation of what information was available on the retina. A comparison of this retinal information with the reported visual perception of the path of movement enables inferences to be made concerning what information about eye position was used by the perceptual system.

Such observations and computations were made using a situation in which the path of the moving target is known to be misperceived. On the assumption that the perceptual system does have accurate information about saccadic eye movements, some conclusions could be reached about what the perceptual system knows about smooth pursuit eye movements.

Since existing data point to the fact that the perceptual system does not have information about eye position based on feedback from the extraocular muscles, it seems that whatever information about eye position is known is based on monitoring the efferent commands issued to those muscles. Thus, inferences and conclusions about what the perceptual system knows about smooth pursuit eye movements may also be regarded as inferences about the content of the efferent commands for such movements at that point in the efferent system at which those commands are monitored.

Our data and analysis suggest that the efferent command for a smooth pursuit eye movement, where it is monitored, contains information about the direction of movement but does not contain precise information about the velocity of the movement.

Leon Festinger and A. Montague Easton were at the New School for Social Research when this article was written.

The research on which this article is based was supported by Grant MH-16327 from the National Institute of Mental Health to

Leon Festinger. The authors acknowledged the help, during the course of experimentation and interpretation, of Saulo Sirigatti, Melvin K. Komoda, and Harold A. Sedgwick.

References

BIZZI, E. Discharge of frontal eye field neurons during saccadic and following eye movements in unanesthetized monkeys. *Experimental Brain Research,* 1968, **6,** 69–80.

BIZZI, E., & SCHILLER, P. H. Single unit activity in the frontal eye fields of unanesthetized monkeys during eye and head movement. *Experimental Brain Research,* 1970, **10,** 151–158.

BRINDLEY, G. S., & MERTON, P. A. The absence of position sense in the human eye. *J. Physiol.,* 1960, **153,** 127–130.

CORNSWEET, T. N., & CRANE, H. D. *An accurate two dimensional eye tracker using first and fourth Purkinje images.* Menlo Park, Calif.: Stanford Research Institute, 1972.

EVARTS, E. V. Pyramidal tract activity associated with a conditioned hand movement in the monkey. *J. Neurophysiol.,* 1966, **29,** 1011–1027.

————. Relation of pyramidal tract activity to force exerted during voluntary movement. *J. Neurophysiol.,* 1968, **31,** 14–27.

————. Activity of motor cortex neurons in association with learned movement. *International Journal of Neuroscience,* 1972, **3,** 113–124.

EVARTS, E. V., BIZZI, E., BURKE, R. E., DeLONG, M., & THACH, W. T., Jr. Central control of movement. *Neurosciences Research Program Bulletin,* 1971, No. 9.

FESTINGER, L., BURNHAM, C. A., ONO, H., & BAMBER, D. Efference and the conscious experience of perception. *J. exp. Psychol. Monogr.,* 1967, **74,** (4, Pt. 2).

FUJII, E. Forming a figure by movement of a luminous point. *Japanese Journal of Psychology,* 1943, **18,** 196–232.

GRANIT, R. *The basis of motor control.* New York: Academic Press, 1970.

HELD, R. Exposure-history as a factor in maintaining stability of perception and coordination. *J. nerv. ment. Dis.,* 132, 26–32.

JOHANSSON, G. *Configurations in event perception.* Uppsala, Sweden: Almquist & Wicksell, 1950.

MATTHEWS, P. B. C. Muscle spindles and their motor control. *Physiol. Rev.,* 1964, **44,** 219–288.

SKAVENSKI, A. A. Inflow as a source of extraretinal eye position information. *Vision Res.,* 1972, **12,** 221–229.

SKAVENSKI, A. A., HADDAD, G., & STEINMAN, R. M. The extraretinal signal for the visual perception of direction. *Perception & Psychophysics*, 1972, **11**, 287–290.

SKAVENSKI, A. A., & STEINMAN, R. M. Control of eye position in the dark. *Vision Res.*, 1970, **10**, 193–203.

STOPER, A. E. Vision during pursuit movement: The role of oculomotor information. Unpublished doctoral dissertation, Brandeis University, 1967.

WOODWORTH, R. S., & SCHLOSBERG, H. *Experimental psychology.* New York: Holt, 1956.

16

Visual Perception During Smooth Pursuit Eye Movements

With accurate measurement of eye position during smooth tracking, comparison of the retinal and perceived paths of spots of light moving in harmonic motion indicates little compensation for smooth pursuit eye movements by the perceptual system. The data suggest that during smooth pursuit, the perceptual system has access to information about direction of tracking, and assumes a relatively low speed, almost irrespective of the actual speed of the eye. It appears, then, that the specification of innervation to the extraocular muscles for smooth tracking is predominantly peripheral, i.e., it occurs beyond the stage in the efferent command process monitored by perception.

There are many reports in the literature that indicate inaccurate perception of the paths, extents and velocities of movement of targets that move with reasonably slow velocities on a homogeneous background. The earliest study that bears directly on the issues addressed in this paper is reported by Dodge (1904). Observers were instructed to track a spot of light moving with simple harmonic motion in a darkened room.

SOURCE: Festinger, L., Sedgwick, H. A., & Holtzman, J. D. *Vision Res.*, 1976, **16**, 1377–86. [Received January 19, 1976; in revised form April 23, 1976]

The eyes engaged in predominantly smooth pursuit eye movements. Dodge reports that the perceived extent of movement of this tracked target was about one third of the perceived extent of motion of another untracked spot that moved simultaneously through an identical physical extent but 180 degrees out of phase with the tracked spot. From examination of the photographic records of the eye movements of his observers, Dodge concluded that the perceptual system had no information at all about smooth pursuit eye movements and that the perceived extent of motion was entirely determined by retinal slip.

This interpretation was disputed by Carr (1907) and the controversy never seems to have been clearly resolved (Dodge, 1910; Carr, 1935). The issue of the extent to which the visual perceptual system compensates for smooth pursuit eye movements was not clearly and directly addressed again until Stoper (1967) investigated the problem. He briefly flashed, in succession, two lines while the observer's eye was engaged in more or less accurate smooth pursuit of a target on a homogeneous ground. The observer's judgments of the relative spatial location of these successive flashes indicate the extent to which this perception takes into account the actual movement of the eye. In his Experiment II, he used interflash intervals of up to 306 msec. His data show that the perception is almost completely determined by retinal location of the flashes, i.e. there is almost no compensation for smooth pursuit eye movements. He states: "Expressed in terms of 'percentage of compensation,' there is never more than 16% compensation for the time intervals used here" (p. 112).

In a further experiment, Stoper explored longer interflash intervals and reports that the compensation for the smooth pursuit eye movements increases as the interval increases. However, even at his longest interval of 1734 msec, the average % of compensation for eye movement is only 64%. Moreover, at these longer time intervals the author reports that the perceptions were very ambiguous.

From the Stoper report one would come to the conclusion that the perceptual system takes relatively little account of the actual eye movement when it is engaged in smooth pursuit. A similar conclusion was reached by Festinger and Easton (1974) in a more indirect manner. Following up an observation by Fujii (1943), they found that, when a target is moved on a homogeneous ground with uniform speed in a square path at a frequency of, say, 0.5 Hz with target speeds of 10°–15°/sec, an observer who follows the target motion with his eyes (head restrained) perceives the path of the target as resembling a pincushion rather than a square. By recording the actual eye movements of observers while following such a target, they were able to compute the exact movement of the target on the retina and showed that the perception closely resembled the form of actual retinal path. This again implies that the perceptual system takes rather little account of actual smooth pursuit eye movements.

There are other related reports in the literature that have been interpreted differently, usually in terms of principles of perceptual organization. Duncker (1929) mounted a light near the rim of a wheel and reports that moving the wheel in a dark room produces the expected perception of cycloid motion of the light. However, if a second light is also mounted at the hub of the wheel, the outer light is then seen to move in a circular path around the center light as the wheel moves. This kind of finding has been interpreted in terms of the dissociation of a common group motion from the total motion, resulting in the perception of the relative motions of the individual lights. Johansson (1950) reports an excellent series of studies guided by this principle of the organization of perception. These authors have, understandably, been less concerned about the observer's eye movements and have not measured them. It is likely, as Stoper (1973) points out, that many of these "organizational" phenomena are attributable to the lack of information the perceptual system has concerning smooth pursuit eye movements.

Johansson (1950), for example, reports that if an observer follows a target moving horizontally in simple harmonic motion, a vertically moving spot, which is 90° out of phase with the tracked spot, is perceived to move in a nearly circular path. This vertically moving spot would, of course, sweep out a circular path on the retina if the eye tracked the horizontally moving spot perfectly. The close resemblance of the perception to the likely retinal path might simply indicate the lack of compensation for smooth pursuit eye movements. This is not to say that organizational principles do not at all affect perception. Indeed, the demonstration by Johansson (1971) of the vivid perception of, say, a man walking when the observer only sees the movement of lights attached to limbs and body, argues strongly for the operation of such organizational principles in some circumstances.

In a somewhat different vein, Sumi (1964a, b, 1971) and Gogel (1974) report studies concerning distortion in the perception of the paths of motion of spots moving toward and away from each other at right angles. Again in these studies eye movements are not measured. Gogel did instruct his subjects not to move their eyes but it is not at all certain that such an instruction could be followed in the absence of any fixation point. It is our guess that the reported perceptions in these studies are probably attributable to the lack of compensation for smooth pursuit eye movements by the perceptual system.

There are some studies in the literature that seem to dispute our conclusions about compensation for smooth pursuit eye movement. Dichgans, Körner and Voigt (1969) report that the perceived speed of a smoothly tracked target is 63% of the speed perceived when the eye is stationary. Mack and Herman (1972) report only a 10% reduction in perceived extent of motion of a tracked target, which would imply 90% compensation for smooth pursuit eye motion. In both studies, however, the target starts to move instantaneously at a uniform speed. The eye is thus stationary for probably about 150 msec or so while the target is moving at its full speed. The retinal information obtained during this period is undoubtedly excellent and the perceptual system may be capable of integrating such information over time. The situation is, of course, very different if the target moves in simple harmonic motion since little relevant retinal information is obtained during the initial stationary eye period.

Coren, Bradley, Hoenig and Girgus (1975) present data on the perceived diameter of a target moving in a circular path in darkness while the observer is instructed to follow the target with his eyes. The reported results would lead to a conclusion of very high compensation for eye movements. Again, however, the target starts moving instantaneously at its full uniform speed. Thus considerable retinal information may be obtained which can be used by the perceptual system. In addition, except for the lowest frequency, this study uses target speeds that the human eye is not capable of following adequately with smooth pursuit motion (Young, 1971).

The issue of whether or not the perceptual system takes smooth pursuit eye movements into account has considerable theoretical importance. It seems likely (Brindley and Merton, 1960; Skavenski, Haddad and Steinman, 1972) that the perceptual system does not have access to inflow information about eye position from the extraocular muscles but only has access to outflow information. In other words, the perceptual system gets information about eye position by monitoring the outflow commands to the oculomotor system. This information would only be complete to the extent that the information contained in that central outflow command is complete. The existing literature indicates that the perceptual system can be grossly inaccurate in its compensation for changes in eye position brought about by smooth pursuit motion and this raises the possibility that the central commands for such movements may be quite general in nature, lacking specific information. By exploring this, we may be able to open a window on the functioning of the oculomotor control system for smooth pursuit eye motion.

The experiments to be reported below are an attempt to collect data that would enable accurate, quantitative assessments about what the perceptual system "knows" about actual smooth pursuit eye movements.

Procedure

In order the assess the amount of information available to the perceptual system concerning smooth pursuit eye movements, the following general procedure was used.

1. Observers were asked to track a luminous target moving in simple harmonic motion. This kind of motion was chosen since, at appropriate frequencies and velocities, good smooth pursuit motion of the eyes can be sustained.
2. Measures were obtained concerning (a) the perceived extent of motion of the target, and (b) the perceived direction of motion of another luminous spot moving in phase with the target.
3. Accurate measures of eye position were recorded throughout so that we could compute the retinal information available to the observer.
4. Comparing the retinal information available with the measured perception of the observer could provide answers to our basic question, i.e. how much information about the change in eye position over time is available to perception.

The Visual Display

The visual display contained spots of light moving in the dark. The spots always moved back and forth along linear paths in simple harmonic motion and in phase with each other. The two basic spatial configurations of spot motion which we used are diagrammed in Figures 16.1(a) and (b), where the open circles labeled A, B and C represent the spots at the midpoints of their paths, and the lines represent typical extents, positions, and orientations of these paths. Spots A and B always moved along horizontal paths and through equal extents, but the orientation of the linear path of motion of Spot C in Figure 16.1(b) was variable, Spot A was always the tracked spot. Part of the observer's task on each trial was to visually track Spot A as accurately as he could at all times.

Spot B was the adjustment spot, whose offset from the tracked spot was under the control of the observer. The two-spot display, exemplified in Figure 16.1(a), was used when measurements were to be made of the

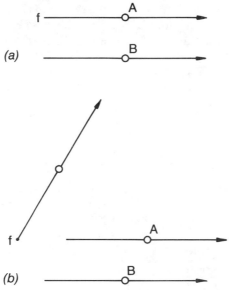

Figure 16.1   Scheme of visual displays. (a) Visual display for trials in which the perceived extent of Spot A was measured. Spots A and B represent spots at the midpoints of their paths, always moving horizontally through equal extents. Spot B is the adjustment spot, its vertical offset adjustable to indicate the perceived horizontal extent of Spot A. For control trials, Spot "f " was also present to be fixated while the adjustment was made. Spots A and B remained aligned vertically throughout a trial. (b) Visual display for trials in which the perceived orientation of Spot C was measured. The linear orientation of Spot C varied from trial to trial. Subjects tracked Spot A and adjusted the horizontal offset of Spot B so that the orientation of an imaginary line connecting Spots A and B would be parallel to the perceived orientation of Spot C. For control trials, Spot "f " was also present to be fixated while the adjustment was made.

perceived extent of motion of the tracked spot. The adjustment Spot B was always directly beneath that tracked spot but its vertical position was variable. The observer's task was to adjust this vertical distance until it appeared equal to the horizontal distance through which the two spots appeared to move on each half cycle.

The three-spot display, exemplified in Figure 16.1(b), was used when measurements were to be made of the perceived direction of motion of the vertically moving Spot C. The path of the adjustment spot was always 1° below the path of the tracked spot, and the horizontal offset of the adjustment spot from the tracked spot was variable. The observer's task with these displays was to adjust this horizontal offset until the orientation of the imaginary line connecting the tracked Spot A and the adjustment Spot B appeared to parallel the orientation of the path of motion of Spot C.

To obtain control measures of perception of extent or direction of motion while the eye was stationary, the identical displays were used with the addition that in each case a stationary fixation spot was added at the point labeled "f" in Figure 16.1.

The visual displays were generated digitally by a Nova 2 computer linked, through an oscilloscope control containing two 13 bit digital to analogue converters, to a Hewlitt Packard 1310 oscilloscope, equipped with a p15 phosphor. The decay time of this phosphor is less than 3 μsec so that the moving spots left essentially no physical trace behind them. A contrast screen served to effectively remove any general glow from the oscilloscope face. The observers viewed the display in total darkness from a distance of 1 m with head held in place with a biteboard and forehead rest.

Measurements of Eye Position

The position of the observer's right eye (left eye always occluded) was monitored by a double Purkinje image eye tracker, which has been described in detail elsewhere (Cornsweet and Crane, 1973). Briefly, the eye tracker operates by measuring the relative position of the two images created by reflecting a beam of i.r. light off of the front surface of the cornea and the rear surface of the lens. When appropriately calibrated, the eye tracker output provides two continuous analog voltage signals proportional to horizontal and vertical eye position over an approx. 16 by 16° field with a noise level less than 4' of arc.

Because the measurement involves a comparison of two reflections from the eye which do not change relative to each other for translational movements of the eye, one major source of inaccuracy is eliminated. The raw output of the eye tracker, however, is not linear with respect to direction of gaze and these non-linearities vary somewhat from observer to observer. In addition, different observers required different scale factor adjustments, probably due to differences in the radius of curvature of the cornea, of the rear of the lens, and the size of the eyeball. The accuracy of the eye position data is hence primarily determined by the accuracy of calibration and the correction for nonlinearities. Accordingly, the first 2-hr session with each observer was devoted to gathering calibration data. The observer fixated a spot of light that jumped in a quasi-random path through 81 positions forming a 9 × 9 square matrix. At each spot position the median eye position was computed and recorded. The data from eight such trials were used to empirically construct a two dimensional matrix of correction vectors and to compute a scale factor for the observer.

The voltage outputs from the eye tracker corresponding to the horizontal and vertical components of eye position were sampled every 2 msec, converted to digital form with 12 bit resolution, corrected for linearity and scale factor and stored in the computer. Every 2 sec the accumulated data were written out on magnetic tape for permanent storage.

Measures of Perception

The observers' adjustments of Spot B in Figure 16.1 were also under the control of the computer. The observer had access to a two way switch which was monitored every 2 msec by the computer through a general purpose digital interface. Depending on the position of the switch, the computer gradually moved Spot B to the left or the right (or up or down). When the observer was satisfied with the adjustment, pushing a second switch, also monitored by the computer, caused the trial to end. The computer then printed out the exact position of Spot B in relation to Spot A.

Experimental Design

Data were collected from observers in three different conditions designed to answer somewhat different questions.

Condition 1

The purpose here was to assess whether the information concerning smooth pursuit eye movements that was available to perception varied as the speed of the actual eye movements varied. Three observers with no previous relevant experience, who knew nothing about the purposes of the experiment, were used. They were all paid volunteers.

In this condition, the extent of motion of the tracked spot was always 4°. Four different frequencies of simple harmonic motion were used, namely 0.125, 0.25, 0.50 and 1.00 Hz. The corresponding maximum speeds of the tracked spot at the center of its excursion were about 1.6, 3.1, 6.3 and 12.6 deg/sec. At each frequency there were six experimental trials using the two-spot display [Figure 16.1(a)] to obtain measures of the perceived extent of motion of the tracked spot. On three of these trials the initial separation between the tracked spot and the adjustment spot was 0.25° and on the other three it was 4.18°. Six fixation control trials for extent settings were also run at each frequency at each of three extents, namely 1°, 2° and 3°, chosen from pilot work to bracket the settings made on the experimental trials.

In the experimental trials using the 3 spot display [Figure 16.1(b)] in which the perceived orientation of the path of the untracked spot was measured, that spot always had a vertical component of motion of 4° of visual angle, but the horizontal component of its motion was varied from trial to trial in order to obtain different orientations of its path of motion. For each frequency eight different orientations were chosen so that the retinal paths, if the eye were to track the target (Spot A) perfectly, would cluster in 5° steps between 60° and 75° and between 105° and 120°, measured counter-clockwise from the horizontal. The avoidance of the 90° area and the variation in orientation was intended to prevent the development of habitual responses. Two trials were run at each orientation, the adjustment spot having an initial horizontal offset of 3° to the left or to the right of the tracked spot. Fourteen fixation control trials were run at each frequency, two at each of seven physical orientations, ranging in 15° steps from 30° to 120°. These values were also chosen from pilot work to bracket the perceptions on the experimental trials.

The experiment was run in four, approx. 2-hr sessions with all of the 42 trials for a given frequency contained within a single session. Each session was run on a separate day. Within each session all four kinds of trials (experimental and control, extent and orientation) were mixed together in a random, counter-balanced order.

Condition 2
Results obtained in Condition 1 could be affected by the fact that, on any one day, an observer experienced only one frequency of spot motion. The question may be asked whether more, or different, information would be available to the perceptual system if frequencies were mixed within each day. Two additional naive observers were run to answer this question.

This condition was identical to Condition 1 except that all four frequencies were mixed on each day. In order to maximize the mixing of frequencies within each session, the number of trials per session was increased and we did not mix measurements of extent with measurements of orientation on the same day. All of the orientation measurements were presented on two successive days and all of the extent measurements were made on a third day. Each session contained an equal number of trials at each of the four frequencies of spot motion, the trials being arranged in a random counterbalanced order with the restriction that the same frequency never occurred on two successive trials.

Condition 3

To separate the variables of frequency and velocity two more naive observers were run in a series of trials similar to the previous ones. Now, however, the frequency of harmonic motion of the spots was held constant at 0.5 Hz while the velocity of motion was varied by varying the extents through which they moved. Three extents of motion of the tracked spot were chosen, namely 2°, 4° and 8°. The horizontal components of motion of the untracked spot in the orientation trials were adjusted to give the same retinal angles, with perfect tracking, as were used in Conditions 1 and 2. The same range of orientation controls was also used.

For each of the three physical extents, six experimental trials were run on which perceived extent was measured. On three of these the initial vertical separation of the tracked and adjustment spots was 0.25°, and on the other three was 6.25°. Six extent measurement control trials were also run at 0.5°, 1° and 1.5° for the 2° extent controls; 1°, 2° and 3° for the 4° extent controls; and 2°, 4° and 6° for the 8° extent controls.

The experiment was run in three sessions, and analogously to Condition 1, all the trials for a given extent of motion of the tracked spot were run within the same session.

Analysis of Data

The linearized data from the eye tracker specify rather precisely the angular orientation of the observer's right eye at 2 msec intervals. By subtracting this eye position information from the known positions, in terms of visual angle, of each of the spots in the display at each time interval, we can calculate the motion of each of these spots relative to the moving eye. These calculations tell us what retinal information exists and our subsequent analysis is based on the assumption that this retinal information is available, in some fairly accurate form, to the perceptual system.

If the eye movements of the observers contained no saccades the analysis of our data would be straightforward. Our data show, however, that at all speeds of the tracked spot, even the slowest, saccadic eye movements do occur. To ignore the many half-cycles in which saccades occurred would seriously bias the data. Since our purpose is to assess the amount of information the perceptual system has about smooth pursuit eye movements, certain decisions had to be made about how to treat these saccadic eye movements.

It seems plausible to assume that the perceptual system has sufficient information to be able to discount retinal motions produced by saccades.

This does not involve the assumption that the perceptual system has accurate extraretinal information about the saccadic eye movement itself. To the extent that the saccadic eye movement is executed in order to bring the target from some relatively peripheral point on the retina onto the fovea, the perceptual system has retinal information, before the saccade, concerning the distance of the target from the fovea, and also has information, after the saccade, about the extent to which that distance was reduced.

Since we want to calculate a combination of everything the perceptual system knows except for possible information about smooth pursuit movements, we must also make some assumptions about how the saccadic and smooth pursuit systems interact. There are two somewhat different assumptions that could be made. It is possible that the saccadic eye movement, when it occurs, replaces the smooth pursuit motion of the eye. That is, the smooth pursuit system might be turned off for the duration of the saccade and then turned on again at its conclusion. On the other hand, it is possible that the saccade, when it occurs, is superimposed on the ongoing smooth pursuit motion which continues unabated as a component of the total eye movement.

Close examination of our eye movement data persuades us that the second possibility is more likely to be correct. There are two main reasons for this. First of all, there are never any pauses of the eye following a saccade. At the completion of the saccade the eye immediately moves in smooth pursuit. Secondly, there are never any marked modifications of the velocity of smooth pursuit motion from before to after a saccade. Following a saccade the eye movement appears to be a smooth continuation of the pursuit movement preceding the saccade. We have, consequently, assumed in our calculations, that the saccades are superimposed onto continuing smooth pursuit motion.

To be precise, the velocities of the eye over 20 msec periods before and after the saccade are averaged and this average velocity is assumed to have been maintained by the smooth pursuit system for the duration of the saccade. The magnitude of the saccade is calculated as being the total change if eye position from before to after the saccade minus the distance the eye is calculated to have moved in smooth pursuit during that period. The eye movement records are then corrected to remove this calculated magnitude of saccade. When these corrected eye positions are subtracted from the known spot positions in our visual displays, the result is a combination of information available from the retina and from saccades. We will call this "retinal information."

To summarize the relevant "retinal information" for trials on which we measured the perceived orientation of the non-tracked, vertically moving spot, we calculated a best fitting straight line to the "retinal path" swept out by that vertically moving spot for each half cycle of spot motion. For trials on which we measured the perceived extent of movement of the tracked spot we calculated, for each half cycle, the extent of "retinal motion" swept out by the tracked spot. In both kinds of trials, we obtained a single estimate by averaging the last ten half cycles up to the final one prior to the completion of the observer's setting. At low frequencies of spot motion the observer frequently completed the setting in less than 10 half cycles. In such cases all but the first and the final half cycles were averaged. All of the eye movement data were visually examined on a computer controlled display. Half cycles during which the observer blinked or during which the tracker lost the eye (both relatively infrequent occurrences) were excluded from the analysis.

Results

Our data concern the perception of paths and extents of motion of moving luminous spots on a totally contourless ground while the eye, itself, is engaged in smooth pursuit motion. In the absence of stationary contours in the visual field, these perceptions can be based on two sources of information only. There is potential information available from the paths swept out on the retina, paths which are a joint function of the spot motion and the eye motion. There is also potential extraretinal information available about saccadic and about smooth pursuit eye movements. The data enable us to examine the extent to which information about smooth pursuit eye movements contributes to the visual perception. We will examine the data on this point separately for the perception of the path of the nontracked spot and the perception of the extent of motion of the tracked spot.

Perception of the Path of the Nontracked Spot

The measures of the perception of the path of Spot C can be expressed as the perceived angle (measuring counter-clockwise from the horizontal). The slopes of the best straight lines fitted to the "retinal information" were also converted to "retinal angles" for comparison with the perception.

The smooth pursuit motion of the eye is, of course, never perfect. How adequate it is depends on the frequency (and velocity) of the motion of the tracked spot. In our data, the tracking is least adequate at 1 Hz and improves steadily up to 0.25 Hz. At 0.125 Hz the eye frequently moves faster than the spot and many of the interspersed saccades are counter to the direction of smooth pursuit motion.

Because of the differing adequacy of the smooth pursuit motion, the computed "retinal angle" of Spot C differs for different frequencies of the same physical constellation of spot motions. Figure 16.2 presents these average "retinal angles" for each frequency and each physical constellation of spots. The data represent the averages of five subjects, three run with only one frequency on each day and two run with the four frequencies mixed together each day (Conditions 1 and 2). These two conditions are combined because there are no discernable differences between them on these measures. The solid curve indicates the "retinal angle" that would correspond to perfect smooth pursuit motion

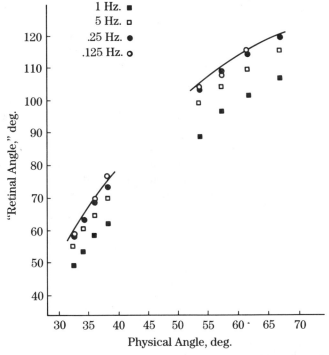

Figure 16.2   Relationship between "retinal angle" and physical angle for Spot C at each frequency employed. Each point represents the average setting of five subjects for a given frequency and physical angle. Spot C's "retinal angle" (measured counterclockwise from the horizontal) is computed from the best straight line fitted to the "retinal information." The solid curve indicates the "retinal angle" that would correspond to perfect smooth pursuit of the eye.

of the eye. With these differences among frequencies in mind, the remainder of the presentation of data will be with respect to these "retinal angles."

The main result is easily stated. The perception of the direction of motion of the nontracked spot is much closer to the "retinal angle" than to the physical angle. Figure 16.3 shows the relation between perceived

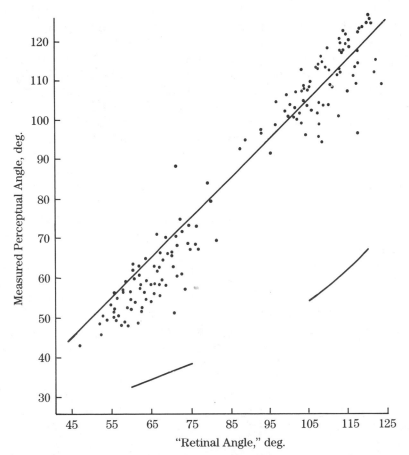

Figure 16.3   Relationship between "retinal angle" and perceived angle for Spot C. Each point is the average of two measurements at a given physical angle. Each subject is represented by 32 points—eight physical angles at four frequencies. The straight line represents exact correspondence between perceived angle and "retinal angle." The curved lines represent exact correspondence between perceived angle and physical angle.

angle and retinal angle. Each point on the figure is the average of two measurements at a given physical angle for each of the five subjects mentioned above. Each subject is represented by 32 points, eight physical angles each at four different frequencies. The straight line that runs through the plotted points is the line of exact correspondence between perceptual angle and "retinal angle." The curved lines in the lower part of the figure indicate exact correspondence of perceptual angle and physical angle.

From the data in Figure 16.3 we cannot be certain about the exact extent to which the perception is dominated by the "retinal angle" since any psychophysical measurement may be affected by constant errors. It was for this reason that control measurements were obtained while observers fixated the stationary point labeled "f" in Figure 16.1. Examination of these control measurements reveals, however, that this choice of a control situation was very unfortunate. With Spots A, B and C all in the periphery, the distance between the spots had a large effect on the measures, thus particularly distorting the control data for oblique angles. Our control data seem quite useless.

There is also another consideration that limits what we can say about absolute magnitudes of effects in Figure 16.3. There is a possible question that might be raised as to whether our method of measurement itself might not have encouraged reliance on retinal information. We can say, however, that perceptions that are close to "retinal angles" are obtained with other methods of measurement also. In preliminary work we asked observers to estimate the angle of the perceived path or to draw it. Our basic results seem quite independent of the method of measurement. It is still possible, nonetheless, that the exact absolute quantities of difference between "retinal angle" and perception might be, to some extent, influenced by our method.

We can, however, compare different frequencies since, whatever the constant errors, they should be roughly the same. With these problems in mind we may examine the data more carefully to see if there are differences in the extent to which the smooth pursuit eye motion is taken into account perceptually in the various frequency conditions. Since the frequencies varied over an eight-fold range, and hence the smooth pursuit eye velocities also varied over a considerable range, we may look to see whether the perceptual system takes account of these differences.

Figure 16.4 illustrates the computations on which the rest of our analysis of the data is based. Since we know the "retinal angle" and the perceived angle, we can calculate the distance that the perceptual system assumed the eye to have moved in smooth pursuit. In the figure

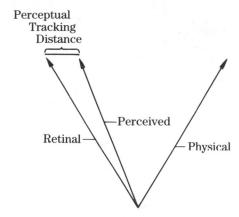

Figure 16.4 Computation of "perceptual tracking distance." Arrows (from right to left) indicate typical physical, perceived, and retinal paths of motion of a spot of light while the eye smoothly tracks another spot of light (not shown) which is moving horizontally. The "perceptual tracking distance," which is the distance that the perceptual system assumes the eye to have moved in smooth pursuit, is the horizontal component of the difference between the perceived and retinal paths of motion.

we have labeled this "perceptual tracking distance." We can also compute the average distance per half cycle that the eye actually did move in smooth pursuit. These data are presented in the upper half of Table 16.1.

It can be seen that, while the extent of the actual smooth pursuit eye movement varies from 3.2° at 1.0 Hz to a full 4° at 0.125 Hz, the amount of eye movement that the perceptual system seems to know about is small. There is, however, a systematic tendency for the "perceptual tracking distance" to increase somewhat for lower frequencies at which the eye actually moves in smooth pursuit over a larger extent. To interpret this trend it is helpful to examine the comparable data from the two additional subjects for whom the frequency was held constant at 0.5 Hz while the actual extent of movement of the tracked spot was either 2°, 4° or 8° (Condition 3). The range of actual horizontal eye movement for these two subjects is, of course, much greater. These data are presented in the lower half of Table 16.1.

These two observers both show negative values for "perceptual tracking distance." To take this at face value would mean that the perceptual system acts as if the eye were moving in a direction opposite to its actual motion. Since this is not sensible, we must interpret these negative val-

**Table 16.1   Calculations Based on Perceived Angle: Average "Perceptual"
and Actual Distance of Smooth Pursuit Eye Movement
(deg. of visual angle)**

	Tracked spot extent $=$ 4°			
Hz $=$	1.0	0.5	0.25	0.125
"Perceptual"	0.04	-0.01	0.21	0.49
Actual	3.22	3.71	3.94	4.01
	Frequency $=$ 0.5 Hz			
Extent $=$		8°	4°	2°
"Perceptual"		-0.61	-0.56	-0.29
Actual		7.45	3.72	1.88

ues as reflecting constant errors of measurement, emphasizing again the caution that must be exercised in interpreting absolute magnitudes in the data.

Again, however, if we compare these values across the different extents of motion of the tracked spot, it seems clear that the perceptual system does not take into account much about the distance that the eye actually moves in smooth pursuit. Here we have an appreciable range of distance the eye travels, from about 7.5° down to about 1.9°. Nevertheless the differences in "perceptual tracking distance" remain very small. It seems clear that there is not much correspondence between the "perceptual tracking distance" and the actual distance the eye moves.

Perception of Extent of Movement of the Tracked Spot

If the perceptual system knows little about the distance over which the eye moves in smooth pursuit, then we should also expect to obtain evidence of this in the perception of the extent of movement of the tracked spot. These measurements were much more difficult for the subjects to make, and are more variable. Again, unfortunately, we cannot apply any proper correction for possible constant errors of measurement because the control measures that we did obtain are quite inappropriate. Again, they seem inappropriately distorted because of the distance in the visual periphery at which the measurement had to be made.

Table 16.2 presents the data on the perceived extent of movement of the tracked spot. The means are presented separately here for the three subjects who experienced only one frequency per day and the two for

Table 16.2.   Perceived Extent of Tracked Spot (deg. of visual angle)

	Tracked spot extent = 4°			
Hz =	1.0	0.5	0.25	0.125
One frequency per day		1.34	1.29	1.28	1.31
Mixed in same day		2.33	2.35	2.61	2.76
	Frequency = 0.5 Hz			
Extent =		8°	4°	2°
One extent per day		2.05	1.26	1.04

whom frequencies were mixed because their results on this measure are different. It can readily be seen that in the one frequency per day situation the perceived extent is just a bit more than 30% of the true extent of spot movement. In the mixed frequency situation it is almost two-thirds of the true extent. We will comment below on the possible reasons for this difference.

When frequency was held constant at 0.5 Hz and the actual extent of movement of the tracked spot was varied there is a relationship, clearly, between the true extent and the perceived extent. When the true extent was 2°, the perceived extent was 1°; when the true extent was 8°, the perceived extent was 2°. Clearly the perceived extent is not, here, a constant percentage of the true extent of movement.

The data in Table 16.2 do not tell us much, however, since these numbers reflect the combination of "retinal information" about movement of the tracked spot and information about smooth pursuit eye movements. We want to subtract the "retinal information" from the perceived extent in order to estimate the "perceptual tracking distance." Table 16.3 presents these data together with the means of the actual extent of smooth pursuit eye movements. The rather large values for extent of eye movement at 0.25 and 0.125 Hz in the second row of the table are entirely attributable to one subject. It can readily be seen that when the true extent was constant at 4° and frequency varied, the "perceptual tracking distance" is considerably smaller than the actual distance of smooth pursuit eye movement.

One thing that emerges here, however, is the fact that as the frequency decreases the "perceptual tracking distance" increases. We noted this as a suggestion in the data on the perceived angle of move-

Table 16.3. Calculations from Perceived Extent of the Tracked Spot: Average "Perceptual" and Actual Distances of Smooth Pursuit Eye Movement (deg. of visual angle)

		Tracked spot extent = 4°			
	Hz =	1.0	0.5	0.25	0.125
One frequency per day	"Perceptual"	0.30	0.97	1.46	1.77
	Actual	2.93	3.67	4.19	4.45
Mixed in same day	"Perceptual"	1.58	2.07	2.66	2.86
	Actual	3.25	3.72	4.05	4.10
		Frequency = 0.5 Hz			
	Extent =		8°	4°	2°
One extent per day	"Perceptual"		1.34	1.10	0.88
	Actual		7.28	3.73	1.85

ment of the nontracked spot, but here it is a very clear and pronounced effect. On the other hand, for the subjects for whom frequency was held constant while the actual extent was varied, there is only a very small increase in "perceptual tracking distance" for an almost fourfold increase in the actual distance that the eye moved in smooth pursuit. These data suggest that the "perceptual tracking distance" is primarily dependent, not upon the distance the eye moves, but upon the time it takes the spot to move through a half cycle. When this time is held constant at 0.5 Hz, the calculated "perceptual tracking distance" does not change much in spite of large changes in the extent of actual smooth pursuit eye movements. When this time per half cycle varies over an eight-fold range (from 1.0 to 0.125 Hz) the "perceptual tracking distance" changes considerably even though there are only small changes in the actual extent of smooth pursuit eye movements.

This would suggest that the perceptual system does not have direct information, however imperfect, about the distance the eye travels in smooth pursuit. Rather it would seem that there is some information about the speed with which the eye moves and that this information is integrated over time. If this were the case then the relevant thing to ask would be what the perceptual system knows about the speed of the smooth pursuit eye movement. We can look at the data from this point of view by dividing the calculated "perceptual tracking distance" by the time for one half cycle of spot movement yielding a measure of "perceptual tracking speed" averaged over the half cycle. The results of these computations are presented in Table 16.4 both for the measurements of

Table 16.4.   Average "Perceptual" and Actual Speed of Smooth Pursuit
Eye Movement (deg. of visual angle/sec)

Computation based on		Hz = 1.0	0.5	0.25	0.125
Perceived angle	"Perceptual"	0.08	−0.01	0.10	0.12
	Actual	6.44	3.71	1.97	1.00
Perceived extent	"Perceptual"	0.60	0.97	0.73	0.44
(1 Hz/day)	Actual	5.86	3.67	2.09	1.11
Perceived extent	"Perceptual"	3.16	2.07	1.38	0.72
(mixed Hz)	Actual	6.50	3.72	2.02	1.10

angle of the spot moving with a vertical component and for the measurements of extent of the tracked spot. The values are not repeated for
the variable distance condition since at 0.5 Hz the time per half cycle is
1 sec and, consequently, the numbers in Tables 16.1 and 16.3 already
represent the "perceptual tracking speed."

We may see, in Table 16.4, that when this computation is based on
the perceived angle of the nontracked spot, the "perceptual tracking
speed" is rather constant, about 0.1°/sec over a wide range of actual
average smooth pursuit eye speeds. The same is true for the computations based on perceived extent of motion of the tracked spot in the "one
frequency per day" condition. Although the "perceptual tracking speed"
seems to increase somewhat from 0.125 to 0.5 Hz it falls again at 1 Hz.
The differences in absolute magnitude between the above two computations might well be due to constant errors associated with the specific
measurement procedures.

The data are strikingly different, however, for the subjects in the
situation in which all frequencies were mixed in each day. For these
subjects there is a clear, and almost constant, relationship between "perceptual tracking speed" and actual speed of the eye. The reason for this
probably lies in the different procedure used. In this condition, not only
were all frequencies mixed together on each day but all the measurements of perceived extent of motion of the tracked spot were done on
one and the same day. It is possible that the mixture somehow enabled
the perceptual system to obtain better information about eye velocity.
If this were the case it is puzzling that the same information was not
available, or at least not used, in connection with the perception of the
path of the non-tracked spot. After all, the various frequencies were
mixed together for those measurements as well. It is also possible, how-

ever, that a measurement artifact exists because the repeated trials of the same 4° spot movement may have introduced extraneous cues and enabled the subjects to make certain assumptions. Such a factor would not have affected the perception of the path of movement of the non-tracked spot since the physical angles were being varied.

A word should be said about the control data that we have not used. If the data had been presented with respect to the controls the following effects would exist:

1. Calculations based on perceived extent of motion of the tracked spot become more variable. Values of "perceptual distance" in Table 16.3 change by amounts ranging from −0.08 to +0.68. The trends, or absence of trends, in Tables 16.3 and 16.4 remain substantially unaffected.

2. Calculations based on perceived path of motion of the nontracked spot are affected. About 0.5 (range of 0.39 − 0.59) gets added to each of the "perceptual distances" in Table 16.1. This is entirely due to the distorted control values for oblique angles. Consequently, if we had used the control data, the "perceptual speed" values in the first row of Table 16.4 would also increase and would show a slight but steady decrease from left to right.

Discussion

The data presented above were collected under conditions in which any information about smooth pursuit eye movement must be derived from some possible extraretinal signal. It is clear that, under these conditions, the perceptual system takes into account very little about smooth pursuit eye movements. Some information seems to exist, however, and it is important to ask where this information comes from.

In principle, it is possible that such information could be based on afferent (inflow) signals from muscle spindles in the extraocular muscles or from Golgi tendon organs associated with these muscles. In a muscle system in which the load on the muscles never varies, as is true of the ocular system, information from these receptors concerning change of length and tension of the muscles might provide position information. There is, however, a fair body of evidence that they do not provide such information to the perceptual system. This evidence has been reviewed frequently (Merton, 1964; Skavenski et al., 1972; Festinger and Easton, 1974).

The same evidence also indicates that the perceptual system does obtain information about eye position and eye movement by somehow monitoring the central nervous system's efferent commands (outflow) to the oculomotor system. To state it briefly, the perceptual system knows where the eye is insofar as it knows where the eye was told to go. This fact has important implications for the interpretation of the data we have presented. It means that where the perceptual system knows, apart from retinal information, about eye movement is an indication of the informational content of the efferent command at the point at which it is monitored.

Let us then look at the data from this point of view. We know from our data that precise instructions about speed are not monitored centrally. Let us, tentatively, accept the guess that, for the experimental condition in which measurements for all frequencies were collected on the same day, the perception of extent of movement of the tracked spot was influenced by cues extraneous to the issue with which we are concerned. The remainder of our data indicate that, over a wide range of actual speeds of smooth pursuit eye motion, the perceptual system assumes nearly the same speed. Just what this assumed speed is is open to question. Probably the estimate of $0.1°/sec$ derived from the perception of the angle of the non-tracked spot is too low. From the data on extent of movement of the tracked spot, the estimate would be that this assumed speed is one degree per second or less. In any event, we can guess that the perceptual system knows that the eye is moving, does not know much about the speed of that movement, and assumes some low value for this speed of movement.

It is, hence, consistent with the data to imagine that the central command that is monitored contains merely an instruction for the eye to move. For example, the central command may simply activate the smooth pursuit system. If the more peripheral smooth pursuit system cannot function effectively over a very wide range of speeds without adjustment of some parameters of the system, then the central command might also occasionally contain further instructions to reset some parameters. Thus the perceptual system might sometimes have information that the eye was moving faster, or more slowly, than previously. When the eye is engaged in repetitive tracking of simple harmonic motion the perceptual results of such a system would be consistent with what we have found.

It also seems clear that the perceptual system knows the direction in which the eye moves in smooth pursuit. The tracked spot, for example, always was perceived to move horizontally. Therefore, the central command that is monitored must also contain information about the direction of movement.

This implies that the central command for smooth pursuit eye movements is rather general, containing only information about direction and starting movement. Yet, we must remember that the eye does execute rather accurate smooth pursuit movements. If the necessary information is not all contained in the central command, the actual calculation of the innervation to the extraocular muscles must be accomplished more peripherally, i.e. somewhere in the efferent transmission system past the point at which the central command is monitored.

If we are correct about this system, some difficult questions arise: What information does the peripheral sub-system use to execute the accurate smooth pursuit eye movements? It seems plausible to imagine that the peripheral sub-system does get information from muscle spindles and uses this, together with informaiton about retinal slip of the target.

This, then, raises another question. How does the peripheral sub-system know which of the several possible moving points is the "target" and what retinal slip to use in its computations? We would conjecture that the designation of "target" is accomplished simply by a central command to the saccadic system that brings that "target" to the fovea. If, during smooth pursuit motion, the "target" got too far from the fovea, the central system would have to intervene to bring it back to the foveal area in order for the peripheral sub-system to be able to function adequately.

The peripheral sub-system would have to be more sensitive to retinal slip in the neighborhood of the fovea than in the periphery. The direction of appropriate retinal slip for the target would also have to be specified. It is relevant here that Miles (1975) reports that the flocculus, an area involved in smooth pursuit movement, contains cells that are sensitive to retinal movement in specific directions primarily near the fovea. Much more evidence is needed before these questions can be settled.

At the time of this article, Leon Festinger and Jeffrey D. Holtzman were at the New School for Social Research; Harold A. Sedgwick was at the State College of Optometry, State University of New York.

The research on which this article is based was supported by Grant MH-16327 from the National Institute of Mental Health to Leon Festinger.

References

BRINDLEY, G. S., & MERTON, P. A. (1960) The absence of position sense in the human eye. *J. Physiol., Lond.*, **153**, 127–130.

CARR, H. A. (1907) The pendular whiplash illusion of motion. *Psychol. Rev.*, **14**, 169–180.

———. (1935) *An introduction to space perception.* New York: Longmans, Green and Co.

COREN, S., BRADLEY, D. R., HOENIG, P., & GIRGUS, J. S. (1975) The effect of smooth tracking and saccadic eye movements on the perception of size: the shrinking circle illusion. *Vision Res.*, **15**, 49–55.

CORNSWEET, T. N., & CRANE, H. D. (1973) Accurate two-dimensional eye tracker using first and fourth Purkinje images. *J. Opt. Soc. Am.*, **63**, 921–928.

DICHGANS, J., KÖRNER, F., & VOIGT, K. (1969) Vergleichende Skalierung des afferenten und efferenten Bewegungsschens beim Menschen: Lineare Funktionen mit verschiedener Anstiegssteilheit. *Psychol. Forsch.*, **32**, 277–295.

DODGE, R. (1904) The participation of the eye movements in the visual perception of motion. *Psychol. Rev.*, **11**, 1–14.

———. (1910) The "pendular whiplash illusion." *Psychol. Bull.*, **7**, 390–394.

DUNCKER K. (1929) Über induzierte Bewegung (Ein Beitrag zur Theorie Optisch wahrgenommer Bewegung). *Psychol. Forsch.*, **12**, 180–259. Translated and summarized in Ellis, W. D. *A source book of Gestalt psychology*, 1938. London: Routledge & Kegan Paul.

FESTINGER, L., & EASTON, A. M. (1974) Inferences about the efferent system based on a perceptual illusion produced by eye movements. *Psychol. Rev.*, **81**, 44–58.

FUJII, E. (1943) Forming a figure by movement of a luminous point. *Jap. J. Psychol.*, **18**, 196–232.

GOGEL, W. C. (1974) Relative motion and the adjacency principle. *Q. J. exp. Psychol.*, **26**, 425–437.

JOHANSSON, G. (1950) *Configurations in event perception: an experimental study.* Uppsala: Almquist & Wiksells.

———. (1971) Visual perception of biological motion and a model for its analysis. Report from Psychological Laboratories, University of Uppsala, No. 100.

MACK, A., & HERMAN, E. (1972) A new illusion: the underestimation of distance during pursuit eye movements. *Percept. Psychophys.*, **12**, 471–473.

MERTON, P. A. (1964) Absence of conscious position sense in the human eyes. In Bender, M. B. (ed.). *The oculomotor system.* New York: Harper & Row.

MILES, F. A., & FULLER, J. H. (1975) Visual tracking and the primate flocculus. *Science*, **189**, 1000–1002.

SKAVENSKI, A. A., HADDAD, G., & STEINMAN, R. M. (1972) The extraretinal signal for the visual perception of direction. *Percept. Psychophys.*, 11, 287–290.

STOPER, A. E. (1967) Vision during pursuit movement: the role of oculomotor information. Unpublished doctoral dissertation. Brandeis University.

————. (1973) Apparent motion of stimuli presented stroboscopically during pursuit movement of the eye. *Percept. Psychophys.*, 13, 201–211.

SUMI, S. (1964) Path of seen motion of two small light spots. *Percept. Mot. Skills*, 19, 226.

————. (1964) Further observations on the path of seen motion of two small light spots. *Percept. Mot. Skills*, 19, 254.

————. (1971) The apparent displacement of a moving light spot. *Psychol. Forsch.*, 34, 349–360.

PART
E

THE HUMAN LEGACY

17

The Human Legacy

Introduction

Four years ago I closed my laboratory which, over time, had become devoted to studying ever narrowing aspects of how the human eye moves. It is natural for me to talk as if the laboratory was at fault, but a laboratory is only a collection of rooms and equipment. It was I who conceived of, and worked on narrower and narrower technical problems.

That is not a proper occupation for an aging man who resents that adjective. Young men and women should work on narrow problems. Young people become enthusiastic easily: any new finding is an exciting thing. Older people have too much perspective on the past and, perhaps, too little patience with the future. Very few small discoveries turn out to be important over the years; things that would have sent me jumping and shouting in my youth now left me calm and judgmental. And my lack of enthusiasm kept reminding me of that despised adjective, aging.

Having a critical perspective on the recent past is debilitating in other ways also. I have been actively engaged in research in the field of psychology for more than forty years and during that time have worked on statistics, studied the behavior of animals, worked on decision processes and motivation, proposed theories about social behavior, and explored visual perception. Along with me, many other talented and active people have done research and filled the journals with technical articles in these fields and more. Indeed, these forty years have covered an extraordinarily active period in psychology generally.

Forty years in my own life seems like a long time to me, and while

SOURCE: Festinger, L. *The human legacy*. New York: Columbia University Press, 1983.

some things have been learned about human beings and human behavior during this time, progress has not been rapid enough; nor has the new knowledge been impressive enough. And even worse, from a broader point of view, we do not seem to have been working on many of the important problems.

Let us take a look at this curious animal, the modern human being, to ask if we really know much about him or are we simply accustomed to, and adapted to, his peculiarities. Just superficial reflection reveals many facets of human activity that seem very strange. One striking thing about us is that we have no natural habitat. Other animals live and prosper best under relatively specific climatic conditions, but we do not seem to care. We flourish all over this planet. If we once had a natural habitat, has its loss affected our thoughts, emotions, and patterns of behavior, or doesn't it matter?

Another strange thing is the amount of energy, work, and time we devote to aesthetic activities: decoration, color, visual art, music, dance, poetry. Yet there is no major body of knowledge or theory that we could call a Psychology of Aesthetics. We seem to have almost totally ignored an area of important human concern.

Equally strange is our general addiction to games, both physical and mental. The profusion of games is truly startling: card games, board games, word games, ball games, electronic games. Some games are entirely dominated by chance, others mix chance and skill, while still others are games of complete knowledge in which only skill matters. Some games are competitive; others are played alone. We even assemble in huge crowds to watch others playing games. What does all this mean? Do we simply get easily bored and cannot tolerate inactivity? I can find nothing in the literature of scientific psychology that helps me to understand such bizarre behavior.

Looked at from a purely evolutionary point of view, that is, the capacities, characteristics, and proclivities that enhance the survival possibilities of the species, the human carries quite a bit of useless excess baggage. Moreover, he cherishes this excess baggage—to him it is not a burden but a source of pleasure. If anyone wants to pursue the unedifying quest for differences between humans and other animals, the human activities connected with this cherished baggage is the place to look. It is not difficult to imagine why issues such as this have been shunned by the science of psychology. Wedded to quantitative measurement and experimental methodology, more or less in the image of the natural sciences, such issues are difficult to approach.

So I closed my laboratory, deserted experimental methodology, and decided that I wanted to learn whatever I could about humans by searching for origins in prehistory. How did humans evolve? What were the beginnings of our present way of life? What were the origins of human societies that today face so many problems? In short, I embarked upon a thoroughly unfocused, almost unbounded, pursuit. I cannot even try to specify what I was pursuing. If this endeavor seems crazy, I want to assure you that it was highly pleasurable insanity.

In the last few years I have learned many things that I did not know before: about humans who lived two million years ago; about the techniques of making stone tools; about the earliest beginnings of art; about the circumstances in which humans settled down to live in one place all year round; about the origins of agriculture and the development of organized societies. I have learned by reading indiscriminately and by talking with many people who were experts and were discriminating.

Coming to such a task with my background, it is natural that the questions I asked myself and the facts that I found interesting were ones that bordered on the social and psychological. Most of the data, however, did not lend themselves easily to inferences about such questions. Reading long, detailed accounts of the shape, size, and style of the stone tools uncovered at some site, for example, benefited me little. Although I tried to learn about and understand the data and the techniques, I have certainly not succeeded very well. There is too much to learn. If I visited a site that was being excavated, it remained largely meaningless to me until the excavator told me what to look at and what it meant. I can only hope that I have not made too many errors of fact and interpretation.

The developments over a period of more than three million years from the first fully bipedal primates until the appearance of modern man about forty thousand years ago are revealed primarily in fossil bones and stone tools. The prehistory of modern man left a much more varied record—art, houses, pottery, and more. The strands that might weave it together are multiple and tangled, many of them still hidden. Possibly, because of the sparseness of the data, no totally coherent pattern of evolution, change, and development will ever appear.

What I have tried to do, while stuffing my head with facts and data, was to pick up a thread here and a thread there, threads that seemed to me to show some continuity over that huge period of time, threads that could help me understand how we arrived where we are today. The chapters in this book contain the variety of ideas that I managed to pick up and hold onto.

I have grappled, I fear unsuccessfully, with one persistent problem. I cannot, and do not want to, rid myself of the conviction that ideas, hypotheses, and guesses must maintain a close relationship to empirical data. I do not talk here about proof or disproof—this is almost never attainable. But at least the data should constrain the interpretations and the interpretations should carry implications about new data. Otherwise, one may be concocting fascinating tales, tales which may suit our predispositions, but, nevertheless, are only tales. And imaginative humans can easily make up stories and yarns.

The paleontological and archaeological record is rather unfriendly to the kind of thinking I like to do. There is almost nothing that cannot, with seemingly equal plausibility, be viewed in a variety of ways, some diametrically opposed to others. The scarcity and incompleteness of data, and the lurking fact that what we do know is limited by where someone decided to dig, makes for an ambiguity that frequently remains unresolved.

I have tried to keep interpretations, those borrowed from others as well as those emerging from my own ideas, in touch with and constrained by the known facts. But I realize that in many instances alternative interpretations are not only possible, but easily supplied. I have, of course, explicated the facts and the contexts that led me to the explanations that I offer. I must admit, however, that not only do I present an unintegrated set of causes and continuities, but what I present is, in the end, what seems most plausible to me.

I have purposely avoided, wherever possible, using anthropological data about modern groups to support interpretations about the past. There are many who do this, but it seems risky and unwarranted to me. Modern groups, no matter how simple or "primitive" their social organization, their life style, or their belief systems, are not equivalent to human groups that lived twenty thousand, or even ten thousand years ago. Biologically they are the same, and if one wants to make biological inferences, one can exploit the anthropological data. But psychologically and socially there is no reason in the world to believe modern groups can be equated with groups of very long ago. An additional ten or twenty thousand years has elapsed during which societal forms and life styles may have changed; groups such as these are highly selected either because they have been isolated or because, for some reason, they have resisted the dominant trends in human societies; such groups also, generally, live in marginal locations into which they have been pushed by the "more developed" societies.

So if modern groups that live by hunting and gathering, rather than agriculture, usually have a division of labor between the sexes in which the men hunt and the women gather, this does not mean that it was that way 20,000 years ago. At best it indicates that this is one possible means of organization of work that humans may employ. If modern pastoral, nomadic groups resist efforts to induce them to settle down, this does not mean that 10,000 years ago humans resisted sedentary existence. Magical and religious beliefs held by simple modern groups are no indication of what beliefs were held by humans in the very remote past.

I do not want to be misinterpreted; I certainly do not think that the study of modern groups is without value. At a minimum they have enriched the variety of speculations about the past by pointing to the great cultural diversity that is possible. However, interpretations of the past must be based primarily on data about the past, sometimes with an eye on the sequence of events; that is, understanding of occurrences 10,000 years ago can be profitably guided by knowledge of what had evolved by 9,000 years ago. But the best we can do with knowledge about modern groups is to view it as indicating a *possible* means of adaptation by humans.

I cannot pretend that this book* is exhaustive—it is not. It covers neither the entirety of human evolution and development, nor does it deal with all the available data. The selectivity in what I do cover stems from a variety of considerations. First of all, I have ignored or dealt only tangentially with data from many parts of the world. In describing developments, and trying to explain them, I have usually limited myself to data from those areas where those developments started. For example, agriculture spread to Europe between one and two thousand years after it had started in western Asia. To understand how and why it started, one must, then, look at western Asia, not Europe. The consequence is that at different times and for different topics I talk about different parts of the inhabited world. I have tried not to allow this to distort the accounts; I hope I have succeeded. I think that I am talking not just about humans in this place or that place but about humans generally.

There is a major omission that exists for a different reason. I have ignored the wealth of archaeological data on the American Indian. In the course of trying to absorb what is known and what is conjectured about the last three and a half million years, I have periodically been forced to set some boundaries so as to make my task possible. Where I have explored, I have tried to learn enough to be able to make my own evaluations of interpretations in the existing literature. That's a lot of information to acquire. The most severe restriction I enforced on myself was to stay away from data on the American Indian. They appear late in prehistory and nothing is known about continuity into the past; they

*See SOURCE.

lived in different circumstances and in isolation from the developments in the rest of the world. This omission may be a big mistake. If data from American Indians can produce additional insights into some of the problems I discuss, or cast doubt on some of my interpretations, I trust someone will tell me.

The book is also limited by the ideas in the literature that I found convincing and by the ideas that occurred to me that survived my self-criticism. I did not want to write chapters in which I merely said that little was known, some say this, some say that, and I myself do not know what to say. Fragmentary as it is, I hope that the book* introduces some better understanding of what kind of an organism the human is and how we developed the way of life we now "enjoy."

I have organized the remaining chapters* into two parts which have different objectives. The first part is an attempt to infer something about the "nature of the beast" from the evolutionary record. Every animal has innate characteristics that are genetically determined and it seems to me that we should be able to learn something about such human characteristics by examining the directions of biological evolution and the conditions under which it took place. I have certainly not tried to describe the totality of "human nature," that nasty phrase, but to speculate wherever I could about some characteristics that I felt one was almost forced to assume if one were to understand anything at all.

The second part of the book* deals mainly with the last twenty or thirty thousand years before the present, a period in which there are no discernible evolutionary changes. Modern man, the species of human being that now exists, did not always live the way we do. The patterns of life style and social organization have gone through enormous changes in the last fifteen thousand years. I have tried to examine, in the hope that it may add to our understanding of human beings and human society today, how and why this species, with the innate characteristics that I think it possesses, initiated these changes. How did it come about that human groups settled down to live in one place and changed from depending on wild plants and animals to agriculture? What are the origins of some of the belief systems that are so widely held today? Where are the beginnings of large, highly stratified, societies?

Needless to say, it is impossible for any person to examine and interpret the past, without being inordinately influenced by the belief system and the values that he has grown up with and lived with. I think it is also necessary, in order to interpret the past adequately, to separate oneself from precisely those things that it is impossible to discard. And

*See Source.

so, obviously, the endeavor here is not successful. Archimedes is reputed to have declared that if he had a lever long enough, a fulcrum strong enough, and presumably a place far enough away to stand, he could move the world. I would only wish for the third of these requirements: a place far enough away to stand so that I could see human society clearly.

18

The Social Organization of Early Human Groups

There is evidence for the existence of groups that, by some definitions, we might call human—at least they were fully bipedal primate animals—going back to between 3 and 3½ million years ago. We will not, however, go back that far in this chapter. The farther back in time one goes, of course, the smaller is the similarity between them and the current species of human being. In addition, the farther back in time, the less available evidence there is about how they lived and what they did.

Our own current species has been around for only the last 35,000 to 40,000 years. About 11,000 years ago, major changes began to occur in the way human groups lived, so I want to begin earlier than that. I will then start arbitrarily about 20,000 years ago and try to describe something of the way of life of human groups and to speculate about how and why some patterns of their existence changed in the course of time. I will attempt to do this to the extent to which archeological data permit it. It is clear that inferences about social existence can be difficult to make from stones, bones, and bits of artifacts, so my account will not be very complete.

I will avoid the use of anthropological data about modern groups to support interpretations about the past. There are many who do this, but it seems risky and unwarranted to me. Modern groups, no matter how simple or "primitive" their social organization, their life-style, or their

SOURCE: Festinger, L. In Graumann, C. F., & Moscovici, S. (eds.). *Changing conceptions of crowd mind and behavior*. New York: Springer-Verlag, 1986.

belief systems, are not equivalent to human groups that lived 20,000, or even 10,000 years ago. Biologically they are the same, and if one wants to make biological inferences, one can exploit the anthropological data. But psychologically and socially there is no reason in the world to believe modern groups can be equated with groups of very long ago. An additional 10,000 or 20,000 years has elapsed during which societal forms and life-styles may have changed; groups such as these are highly selected either because they have been isolated or because, for some reason, they have resisted the dominant trends in human societies; such groups also, generally, live in marginal locations into which they have been pushed by the "more developed" societies. If modern pastoral, nomadic groups resist efforts to induce them to settle down, this does not mean that 10,000 years ago humans resisted sedentary existence. Magical and religious beliefs held by simple modern groups are no indication of what beliefs were held by humans in the very remote past.

I do not want to be misinterpreted; I certainly do not think that the study of modern groups is without value. At a minimum they have enriched the variety of speculations about the past by pointing to the great cultural diversity that is possible. However, interpretations of the past must be based primarily on data about the past, sometimes with an eye on the sequence of events; that is, understanding of occurrences 10,000 years ago can be profitably guided by knowledge of what had evolved by 9,000 years ago. But the best we can do with knowledge about modern groups is to view it as indicating a *possible* means of adaptation by humans.

To imagine the style of life of humans 20,000 years ago, think of a small group of, perhaps, about 25 persons, usually rather well-fed, who spent part of the year, spring and summer perhaps, in one suitable camp and the rest of the year in a different one. Each of their camps, one of which may have been more "permanent" than the other, would have been chosen to be in the midst of plentiful food supplies and for ease of living in the climate of the appropriate season. It would have been somewhat of a burden to pack up tools, equipment, and other belongings, walk for 2 or 3 days (or perhaps even weeks) to the new site, which would usually be at a different altitude, and to erect the temporary shelters and facilities needed by the group. But, by doing this twice a year, perhaps even three times a year, they otherwise could have the best of all possible worlds, availability of plant and animal food, easy and pleasant living conditions, and all without excessively hard work.

These people had become very effective exploiters of their environment. They hunted and trapped animals for meat and also gathered varieties of plant food. In addition, about 20,000 years ago, two major new food sources started to become important. Food from the sea and from lakes, ordinary fish and shell fish, which had previously only been occasionally available in small quantities, began to appear as major items of the human diet. In addition, on the basis of the prevalence of mortars in the Near East, one can infer the growing use of cereal grains, a food source that assumed more and more importance as time went on. Considering the low population densities and the rather high state of technological development, these new food sources, in addition to the foods relied on previously, presented a plentiful supply in most years in most of the areas of the world in which humans lived.

Human population was not very large and the inhabited areas were sparsely populated. A seasonally mobile way of life was not difficult. In addition to the work of providing food and shelter, they had to manufacture the sharp stone tools that were used for a variety of purposes and, the evidence indicates, must have spent a fair amount of time on aesthetic activities. Ornaments and coloring matter existed in profusion.

It seems to have been a very acceptable and stable pattern of existence. Perhaps we can illustrate this by summarizing Bar-Yosef's (in press) description of the Kebaran cultural complex in the Near East that lasted from about 19,000 to, perhaps, 12,000 years ago. The number of people in a group that lived and moved together is quite small during this entire period of 6 or 7 millennia. The size of such a group has to be inferred, of course, from the size of the sites that have been discovered and there is, of course, considerable variability—not all campsites cover the same extent. A site that was returned to again and again would be larger, while some very temporary hunting camp might be confined to a quite small area of only 25 to 50 m^2. Bar-Yosef examined the reports on about 30 sites dating to between 17,000 B.C. and 12,500 B.C., together with about 35 later sites covering the period up to about 11,000 B.C.; this later period, with a slightly different style of stone tool, is referred to as "Geometric Kebaran." His conclusion is that the largest of these Kebaran living groups contained, perhaps, "four nuclear families." He characterized this as a cautious estimate, but even if one does not want to be cautious, the group size is small.

Where they chose to live is, naturally, an easier inference to make. The larger sites, 450 m^2 at most, are exclusively in lowland areas, either in the Mediterranean climate of the coastal plain or in the Jordan valley on the other side of the hills, with a predilection for the former. These larger, lowland sites probably represent the base camps that were occupied for the major part of the year and were returned to every year. The sites in the inland hilly areas are smaller and were probably seasonal summer camps. Such was the distribution of campsites for the entire Levant, with no differences between the early and later Kebaran periods, except for the most southern areas. No Kebaran sites at all have been found south of the Beer Sheva valley dating earlier than 12,500 B.C., in other words, the most arid regions were unoccupied during this drier period of climate. A period of climatic amelioration with higher humidity enabled human groups to move into the Negev, and even into the Sinai deserts in the later "Geometric Kebaran" period. None of these desert campsites were large: the maximum found is about 150 m^2. These desert sites probably represent quite temporary wintertime locations.

The Kebaran was not a particularly innovative period. The stone tool industry was, of course, highly developed with its roots in the preceding millennia. Bone tools were not yet in very general use; very few such tools are found in Kebaran sites and the ones that do exist are in the pattern of the preceding 10,000 years. Ground stone implements, bowls, mortars, pestles, tools for grinding and for pounding, do exist but they are very few in number. It is generally assumed that in addition to pounding red ocher, these tools were used to pound or grind roasted wild cereal grains that were part of the diet. We do not know this for certain, however, because the sites where these grinding tools have been found were located in areas in which conditions for the preservation of plant remains were very poor and, so, direct evidence for the use of cereal grains does not exist. The animal bones uncovered indicate clearly they had few special preferences; they hunted and ate whichever ungulates were most available in the general area of the camp in that season. Remains of birds (an occasional pigeon or buzzard or goose) are scanty.

The picture is reasonably clear and consistent. They had evolved a rather stable mode of existence. For 6,000 or 7,000 years this same technical and cultural complex persisted; stability is the dominant theme. The size of group did not change; except for the desert areas the preferences in location of campsites remained the same; the same basic tools, with small variations and minor stylistic differences, continued throughout the period. To the archeologist, the Kebaran campsite is easily and immediately recognizable; they were so similar for so many thousands of years that they became, as Bar-Yosef said, somewhat boring.

The functioning of these groups, the nature of the relations among members of a group, the distribution among them of the work of getting food are matters that are, however, not at all clear. Fossil bones, unfortunately, do not provide clues about social organization. One can only speculate, make inferences from seemingly rational arguments, or extrapolate backward from what we know about contemporary human groups, and, of course, writers have done all of these things.

It has been proposed, for example, that there has always been a division of labor between males and females. On the basis of a reasonably uniform pattern that exists in contemporary groups that still live by hunting and gathering wild foods, it is suggested that in human groups males always did the hunting of wild animals while women gathered plant food (Lee and DeVore, 1968). Perhaps this was the case—arguments can be made for it. Certainly, only the woman could feed the infant at her breast and so would frequently have been somewhat more limited in her mobility. In addition, sexual dimorphism has existed in all human species: The males were larger than the females and, presumably, also stronger and swifter as they are today. All these factors may have made it easier and surer for the males to do the hunting.

But such arguments are weak. It is difficult to imagine that the small incremental strength and swiftness that the male possessed was an important factor in hunting. Surely, the male hunter did not outrun animals that were twice or three times as swift as he. And if the woman did go hunting, she might have left the infant in the temporary care, for a day or two, of someone else in the group. It is possible, however, that such a division of labor between males and females did indeed exist. We do not and will not know. If it did always exist, then one might be tempted to speculate that it is because of a genetically relevant difference rather than a purely cultural difference that men enjoy hunting as a sport more than do women.

In spite of the tenuous nature of speculation about prehistoric forms of social organization, the issues are important enough to lure almost anyone into trying. While fossil bones may not provide any grounds for such speculation, the artifacts created by humans may provide a basis for inference about some aspects of social life, particularly about division of labor, not between males and females, but within the group as a whole. If we come forward in time sufficiently, to periods in which humans produced many artifacts that have survived and have been unearthed, one can, I think, make some statements that can be somewhat constrained and supported by data, concerning specialization of labor or the lack of it.

The specific issue on which we might make headway is this: We know that, say, 20,000 years ago, humans manufactured from stone a variety of tools with sharp edges and points. The *technology* of making such tools is, in principle, simple enough so that with instruction we can be sure it was available to virtually anyone and, given the importance of these tools in the life of those people, we can well imagine that children started to learn how to make tools at quite early ages. At the same time that the technology is simple, its effective *execution* requires practice and considerable coordination and skill. While everyone did, undoubtedly, learn how to make such tools, there must have been considerable variation in the level of skill and competence achieved by different people. How, then, did the group choose to organize their work? Did they rely on the most skillful members of the group to make the tools while the less skillful toolmakers did other things? Or did each person make all his tools for himself, regardless of the level of skill he had attained? The issue applies, of course, not only to stone tool technology but to all the activities that were necessary or important in these people's lives.

If we regard the human being as a rational creature, one might expect that there would have been at least partial specialization of function in accordance with level of skill. If human groups organized their work so as to exploit their environment more efficiently and to make things easier for themselves, certainly the more skillful stone knapper would make the stone tools and the more skillful hunter would do the hunting. It would seem foolish for a skillful hunter to spend much of his time making his own inferior tools. To find consistent evidence of specialization by skill would, consequently, not be at all surprising. It is surprising, however, that one does not find such evidence. Although the indications are far from overwhelming, they mostly point to a social organization without even partial specialization of function by level of skill, each person doing everything himself, each one making his own stone tools, for example. It is only much later, perhaps about 6,000 B.C. that one begins to find the kind of specialization of function that is so prevalent today.

What kind of archeological evidence are we talking about from which we can infer anything about social organization? The only kind of archaeological evidence that I can think of that would be at all convincing with regard to specialization of function by skill in such very early communities is the uniformity, or lack thereof, in the quality of the artifacts uncovered. Assuming that there would be considerable variation in any particular skill among humans, an assumption that seems highly warranted, there would be considerable variation in the quality of manufactured items within any community that did not practice specialization. Only if a particular craft was exclusively in the hands of those who were highly skilled would we expect to find uniformity of quality—at a high level, of course.

Unfortunately for us, the archaeological reports of excavations rarely make statements about the uniformity of quality of the manufactured goods. The evidence is there but it exists in the minds of the archaeologists, not in print. Discussing the issue, for example, with Professor Bar-Yosef and his colleagues, and looking at a large collection of stone tools from Natufian and Kebaran sites, it was apparent that there was great variation in the quality of the tools and in the skill with which they had been made. Perhaps the reason that this kind of variation is not mentioned often in published accounts is that it is the usual, expected thing and causes no particular notice.

One does, here and there, find occasional statements in the literature about this issue, almost always when the excavator is surprised to discover uniform, excellent quality. One of these is especially valuable. Mellaart, who excavated Çatal Hüyük—an unusual place in Anatolia which existed from about 6,500 B.C. to perhaps 5,800 B.C.—reported as follows: "The amount of technological specialization at Çatal Hüyük is one of the most striking features. . . . The result of this specialization is equally apparent, for the quality and refinement of nearly everything made here is *without parallel in the contemporary Near East*" (1967, p. 211; emphasis added).

Clearly, there was specialization by skill in Çatal Hüyük. Equally clearly, according to the knowledge possessed by Mellaart, such specialization was unusual, if not unique, for western Asia in the seventh millennium before the Christian era.

The evidence is scanty enough, and indirect enough, so that we may wonder whether there is any unequivocal evidence that such an inefficient form of organization of work in a group has ever existed; is it even a possible form of social organization? We can try to answer this last question by looking at anthropological data concerning modern groups.

It is rather strange that most of the published reports about modern hunter-gatherer groups do not mention anything about this issue. In a book entirely devoted to such groups (Lee and DeVore, 1968), there was not a single statement of relevance to specialization by skill although there are many mentions of specialization by sex. Here and there, fortunately, we do find an occasional statement. Lee, in his book about the !Kung, people who live by hunting and gathering in the Kalahari desert of southern Africa, provided a detailed description of each tool they use, how it is made, and whether it is a tool made by men or by women. In one instance he said, "Ironworking skill is generally distributed throughout the !Kung population, although a few men are acknowledged to be better at it than others" (Lee, 1979, p. 137). Another somewhat less direct comment may be found when he discussed a list of tools and said: "Column 1 shows the time in minutes required to make the item and indicates whether *the maker is the man or woman of the household*" (p. 272; emphasis added). The implication seems clear that among the !Kung there is no specialization, even partial, based on differences in skill.

A graphic description of this same kind of situation was provided by Vial concerning stone tool manufacture by Jimi natives of New Guinea:

> It took one man fifty or sixty blows before he got a suitable slab from the original block. He was sitting cross-legged with the block in front of him and soon his shins were bleeding from cuts by the flying fragments. The other operator, a much younger man, got a good slab quickly and, holding it in his left hand, began chipping it with a smaller round sphere of stone in his right hand, hitting it on the edges and chipping little pieces off. He had quite a good blade, seven inches long, chipped ready for polishing half an hour after arriving at the quarry. The process looked easy, as if anyone could do it. The older man was not successful, taking longer to get a suitable slab, and having more difficulty in reducing it to the shape for polishing. (1940, p. 159)

Vial went on to say:

> According to my informants, all men of the villages in the area are able to make stone axes; the craft is not confined to a few men. All the processes of manufacture are also carried through by the one man, and there is no specialization. (p. 160)

Such total absence of specialization is not universal, however. Among the Australian aborigines there are some clear references to specialization by skill. Berndt and Berndt reported:

> A few men here and there may have a reputation for being particularly expert in some task: building a canoe, making feathered string, preparing a dugong or turtle harpoon, and so on. They will expect some "payment" for their extra help in such matters, even if this is only a share of the meat caught with the harpoon or the fish carried in the canoe. This could almost be called craft specialization, but of a rather elementary kind. (1964, p. 111)

Another example is mentioned by Allchin, discussing the manufacture of ground stone axes in central Australia. She wrote that "the manufacture of such an axe was a specialist's task and the man who made it was recognized as an expert craftsman" (1956, p. 119).

It is quite clear that not all modern groups that live by hunting and gathering abhor specialization or work on the basis of skill. On the other hand, it is clear that some do, that some human groups find it congenial to have everyone manufacture his own tools—it is a *possible* form of social organization. It seems most consistent with the available evidence to conclude that before the seventh or eighth millennium B.C. there was a general absence of specialization in human groups.

If this conclusion is correct, there is a very important new question that must be answered. If the usual, natural, and preferable inclination of humans was to preserve a certain independence of function in which everyone did everything, then why did this pattern of social organization change? Why, from about 4000 B.C. on is specialization of function increasingly the usual pattern to be found?

My guess is that specialization was gradually forced upon human groups by two processes. One of these was the increasing growth of long-distance trade, which made high-quality products necessary in order to sell or barter them. The other was the rapid proliferation of new technologies, so that by about 4500 B.C. it was no longer possible for one person, no matter how talented, within one lifetime to acquire all of the knowledge and skills necessary to manufacture all the things that humans had come to depend on for survival. There is no way to communicate this state of affairs except the painful one of enumerating the large variety of technologies that came into existence. To spare the reader I will not be exhaustive. I will mention only enough of the major technological developments to make the point. What we all know is true today—no one can know and do but a small fraction of the things we depend on in our lives—was already true more than 6000 years ago. The fraction has simply become smaller and smaller.

By 6500 B.C. ceramic pottery is found in many areas of western Asia, and by 4500 B.C. it was a major industry. Pottery requires knowing about and finding proper clay, knowing how to prepare the clay, how to fashion the pot and, what is very important, the ability to produce very high temperatures to fire the clay-finished pot into a serviceable, durable container. By 4500 B.C., the potters wheel had been invented.

The earliest known use of copper to my knowledge dates to about 7000 B.C. in Çayönü Tepesi, southeastern Turkey (Braidwood, Cambel, Redman, & Watson, 1971). Here they made some simple metal tools by cold-hammering native copper. By 4500 B.C., the use of copper had become so widespread in western Asia that this is generally thought of as the beginning of the "Chalcolithic Period," meaning the age of copper and bronze. This use of metal did not just add one new isolated technology. In addition to working and fashioning the metal, there were also the technologies of mining and smelting the ore. The introduction of bronze, which required mixing of copper and tin, made the process even more complex.

The spinning of thread and the weaving of cloth, which may have started as early as 7500 B.C., developed into a widespread textile industry. Together with this, domestication of sheep introduced the new material of wool with its attendant technology; needles were made of bone for sewing; serviceable hand looms had to be invented and manufactured.

The evidence for boats that made long voyages dates back to 7000 B.C. The technology of boat construction continued to develop and was far along by 4500 B.C. The earliest drawings of boats, Egyptian and Sumerian, date back no further than about 3500 B.C., but they represent already highly developed vessels.

We know that the earliest construction of permanent houses dates back to the first sedentary communities about 9000 B.C. Here, too, the technology became more complex. While the earliest houses were oval-shaped or round, by 7000 B.C. they were square, and by 6500 B.C. multichambered structures existed. Plaster had been invented and plastered walls and floors become more and more common. By 5500 B.C. multistoried buildings were constructed in some places.

Food production required knowledge concerning planting in the proper season, storing food, breeding animals, and, by 4500 B.C., in Mesopotamia there were already the definite beginnings of extensive artificial irrigation. And the old skills were still needed—humans still quarried and flaked stone for tools, leather was still worked, wild animals were still hunted, mats and baskets still woven, and so on.

Man's ingenuity, imagination, and inventiveness—a dominant characteristic for millions of years—had accumulated a body of knowledge and techniques that surpassed the capacity of any single human. Specialization of function was certainly forced on human groups. It is easy to view this accumulation of knowledge, this proliferation of technologies, as a marvelous accomplishment, which it is—one must marvel at it. More and more, the environment had been controlled, and more and more the human lived in a world made by himself.

The implications of the absence of specialization of function in prior millennia should be examined. Why did humans, fully as intelligent as we are, choose such an irrational, outlandishly inefficient system? Again, of course, we can only guess, but it seems plausible to imagine that it fulfilled an important human preference—it preserved a large measure of independence for the individual. Cooperation existed, of course. It was necessary for hunting, for building shelters and other activities, but it was cooperation among independent individuals. Once specialization existed, such independence was lost. Eventually, with trade, people even became dependent on others whom they did not know and had never seen—as we are today.

Another aspect of the absence of specialization and of the independence it provided is perhaps more important.

A social system in which each person carried out every needed function would have preserved a certain equality of status and power among members of a group. It is difficult to imagine the existence of strong hierarchical structures in such circumstances. Once specialization of function existed, however, whether or not that in and of itself led to power and status differentials, the basis for such differentials existed. There was, however, a major exception to the argument that prior to general specialization of function, status, and power differences would not have existed, an exception probably dating to very early times.

My image of man convinces me that he must have tried to control just about everything—and he still does. He undoubtedly tried to make it rain when it was too dry. (We are still trying, and perhaps cloud seeding may one day be more effective.) He probably tried to make it locally cool if the weather was too hot. (It is only recently that he succeeded in producing effective air conditioners.) He certainly tried to ensure an adequate supply of game and plant food and, later, did bring these supplies more under his control through agriculture. It would be surprising if he had not tried to find ways to prevent floods (we now build levees and dams), to prevent earthquakes, to prevent volcanic eruptions, and the like.

Certainly, there is no essential difference between an attempt to make warmth when the climate is too cold (which the use of fire accomplished) and an attempt to produce rain when the climate is too arid. The thought processes are the same and are, in their essence, peculiarly human: the idea that it is possible to control the environment in which you live; the imaginative invention of ways in which it might be done; the ingenuity and persistence to put an idea into practice. To us, with hindsight, knowing the natural technologies that were available at the time, it is clear that 20,000 or 10,000 years ago man was unable to produce rain, prevent earthquakes, or to control any events of that nature. That does not mean, however, that he did not try and did not, at times, convince himself that he had succeeded. In whatever way he did it, it was all the same kind of technological endeavor—inventing ways to control the world in which he lived.

There were, indeed, differences in the reliability with which warmth and rain could be produced at will. In retrospect we can conceptualize a difference between these two technologies, making fire and making rain, but to him they were both technologies, uncertain at times, very effective at other times. Thus, in the same way that we recognize the discovery of how to make, use, and control fire as a highly important technological event, we must also recognize that the invention of a god who controlled rain, together with the invention of ways to influence that god, was an equally or, perhaps, even more important technological innovation.

The technology that involved "gods," let us call it religious technology, had broad, powerful implications. The natural technologies were relatively narrow in their application. Fire had specific uses but did not help point the way to the invention of more effective hunting techniques. The invention of a god that controlled rain, however, suggests the possibility of a god that controlled the sun, or of a god that controlled human fertility. Indeed, so general were the implications of this means of environmental control that natural and religious technology were thoroughly mixed together. Humans realized that gods could also help make the natural technologies considerably safer and more effective.

Actually, however, there are two essential differences between natural technology and religious technology that ultimately forced them further and further apart. For natural technologies there are a limited number of ways in which an objective can be achieved, some ways easier or more reliable than others. The more effective techniques spread and took over, and there was a convergence of practice over very wide areas. For religious technologies, however, there was a wide variety of possible gods to invent and an almost unlimited number of ways to propitiate and influence those gods, no particular practice being more effective than any other. Religious technological practices, consequently, diversify, and large differences are found within even small areas.

The other difference between the religious and the natural technologies had broad social and societal implications. As we have said, in early times, say before 7000 or 8000 B.C., the natural technologies were all available to each person, and as we have discussed, were practiced by each person. Even those who were relatively untalented could still make fire, flake stone, gather food, and hunt; it may have taken such untalented persons longer, the end result may have been less adequate, but each one could and did do all these things. It seems highly likely, however, that the effective use of religious technology would not have been available to everyone. Not everyone would prove to be successful in influencing the appropriate god to produce rain or to make the next hunt very bountiful. During a time of food scarcity, for example, one can well imagine a number of people failing to influence one or another god to produce more food. One individual who, after his own appeals to some god, found the location of some game to hunt would have acquired a well-deserved reputation for expertise, perhaps the reputation of having a special relationship with that god. The lack of personal relationship between most people and the formalized god would be consistent with such wide differences in effectiveness. It was no longer a situation where some were more, and some less, talented. Rather, the facts were that some could, while others simply could not. In this kind of situation specialization of function was forced. To again make a hazardous comparison with modern simple groups, the practice of religious technology or the making of religious ceremonial objects is usually a specialized craft even when no other functions are specialized.

One cannot help but imagine that the status of expert in any aspect of religious technology would have been somewhat insecure in the early stages of the development of this technology. Someone who had demonstrated effective influence over the god that controlled fertility might very well fail the next time that he was called on to influence this same god. One can also imagine the explanations and modifications of procedure that would follow such failure. Later on, the status and qualifications of the experts would have become more adequately protected. The effective propitiation of a god by the expert may have come to require proper exercise of rites by many others; the elaboration of the pantheon of gods produced considerable overlapping of power and function within the pantheon. One failure by the expert might be inconclusive since the god one sought to influence might be temporarily in conflict with some other god. The gods in a pantheon were rarely always in harmony with each other. The specialist in religious technology was eventually, of course, seen to be stably possessed of his ability, an ability others relied heavily on and that conferred status and power on the expert. Religious technology probably presented the earliest basis for the beginning of social stratification.

It is no accident that from the first evidence of the existence of rulers and ruled, the rulers are regarded as having divine powers. From the earliest written records, which come from Sumer, it is clear that there was a close relationship between the gods and the rulers and, furthermore, an identity of the ruler and the priest. The person who could divine the wishes of the gods, who knew how to keep them friendly, who could propitiate and influence them, was the ruler of the city-state. The title of *en* was first used for both priest and city governor. The relation that developed later between the governor, the *ensi*, and the priest is well summarized by Gadd:

> It may be inferred that originally the *ensi* himself was the priest and that, even when the functions began to be distinguished, perhaps through delegation of religious duties, the priest was still the relative and sometimes the destined successor of the *ensi*. (1970, p. 137)

Authority and power were closely linked to the ability to maintain good relationships with and to influence the gods. This ability was, undoubtedly, the source of power and once the positions of governor and priest-technician were not held by the same person, the potentiality for conflict naturally existed. By about 2400 B.C. one finds evidence of this in the records, scant as they are. Written records exist for this period from the city of Lagash (Safar, 1949). During the years that Lagash was ruled by Entemena, the high priest of the main deity, Ningirsu, was named Dudu. Dudu dedicated objects to himself and had monuments inscribed to himself, something only rulers should have done. He even got his name inserted in some of the royal texts.

Another, somewhat later ruler of Lagash, named Urukagina, instituted changes that are generally called reforms, but which principally reasserted his own direct, close connection with the god Ningirsu. The changes directed a return to the practices that Ningirsu had originally ordained, Urukagina proclaiming that he had a covenant with Ningirsu. Throughout the document there hovers the problem of potential conflict between the ruler and the priesthood.

The effectiveness of the priests in propitiating a god was, as for any technology, an empirical question and the outcome of wars among cities was a major piece of relevant evidence. Certainly, being defeated in war could only mean one of two things—either our own god was no longer friendly, a failure of the priesthood, or the other god was simply much more powerful than our god, at least temporarily. Accordingly, the characteristics of the gods, the relative power of the gods, and the appropriate religious practices did not remain constant over time. Things were frequently changing in minor or major ways and the explanations of defeat in wars, the changing relations between humans and gods, and the shifting power structure within the pantheon are documented in many poems, myths, and laments.

As with all technologies, the practical results justify the theory behind the technology. The outcome of a military campaign frequently provided clear-cut, practical results. Success in war established whose god was superior or whose techniques for influencing the gods were better. Thus, with conquest came the vindication of a principal god. When empires developed, as larger and larger areas of land were brought under a single domination by military conquest, there were large regions in which one principal god was accepted as obviously the most important and the most powerful among the many gods.

Although the specific content of religion in Egypt was radically different from that in western Asia, the dynamics of religious practices and of change in such practices were similar. The Egyptian pantheon bore no similarities to the Sumerian and later Babylonian pantheons, the division of functions and power were different, the practices for propitiating gods were different; but again one observes the close relation between ruler and priest. The kings of ancient Egypt were themselves descendants from gods, the divine line of descent carried through the female. The instability of power relations within the pantheon was also similar. With each new Egyptian dynasty there was a radical change in which gods were the most powerful. As with Sumer, it is not that new gods were adopted and others discarded. It was rather a very eclectic process in which power relations among gods might alter, new gods might be merged into the existing pantheon, or even whole pantheons might merge.

Polytheism was very successful and quite functional for a religious technology: It enabled the technology to remain empirically rooted. If one god failed to accomplish what was sought, one could try to influence some other god. There could be differences of opinion about which god was more appropriate to influence for a particular personal desire, and different people, with the aid of different priests, could pursue their own best means of controlling events. If one region suffered drought while another had sufficient rain, the former could, and undoubtedly did, adopt some of the gods and practices of the more favorably treated region. If the technology worked, that was fine; if it did not, one could try new things until one found a procedure that did, again, work. Perhaps it was a bit like trying to find an effective physician to treat an elusive illness—one tries one after another until the illness goes away.

Editors' Note

This chapter is based on, and contains many excerpts, from Chapters 9 and 10 of *The human legacy* by Leon Festinger published by Columbia University Press (1983). Reprinted by permission.

References

ALLCHIN, G. (1956). Australian stone industries, past and present. *R. Anthrop. Insti. J.*, **87**, 115–136.

BAR-YOSEF, O. (in press). The Mediterranean Levantine epi-paleolithic as the background of the "neolithic revolution." In Sorenson, P. & Mortenson, P., (eds.). *The origins of agriculture and technology.*

BERNDT, R. M., & BERNDT, C. (1964). *The world of the first Australians.* Chicago: University of Chicago Press.

BRAIDWOOD, R. J., CAMBEL, H., REDMAN, C. L., & WATSON, P. J. (1971). Beginnings of village-farming communities in southeastern Turkey. *Proc. Nat. Acad. Sci.*, **68**, 1236–1240.

FESTINGER, L. (1983). *The human legacy.* New York: Columbia Univer. Press.

GADD, C. J. (1970). The cities of Babylonia. In *The Cambridge ancient history* (Vols. 1 & 2). Cambridge: Cambridge Univer. Press.

LEE, R. B. (1979). *The !Kung San.* Cambridge: Cambridge Univer. Press.

LEE, R. B., & DeVORE, I. (1968). *Man the hunter.* Chicago: Aldine.

MELLAART, J. (1967). *Çatal Hüyük.* New York: McGraw-Hill.

SAFAR, F. (1949). The identification of Dudu. *Sumer*, **5**, 133–135.

VIAL, L. G. (1940). Stone axes of Mount Hagen. *Oceania*, **11**, 158–163.

PART
F

A MISCELLANY

19

Development of Differential Appetite in the Rat

That organisms prefer one thing to another is a common observation. We have little knowledge, however, of the psychological dynamics behind such preferential behavior. This experiment is an attempt to study one factor which might bring about such "differential taste"; namely, differences in previous experience. More specifically, the question is: if an animal is given more of one food than of another, will it eventually come to prefer that food on which it has experienced relative deprivation?

Procedure

Rats were used as subjects so that feeding habits and general hunger drive could be controlled.

The apparatus used is shown in Figure 19.1. "S" is the starting box; movable doors are indicated by "d." Three groups of animals were run in this apparatus under the following conditions:

1. Experimental Group: (N = 10).
The two experimental foods chosen were powdered whole wheat

SOURCE: Festinger, L. *J. exp. Psychol.*, 1943, **32**, 411–423. [Manuscript received October 19, 1942]

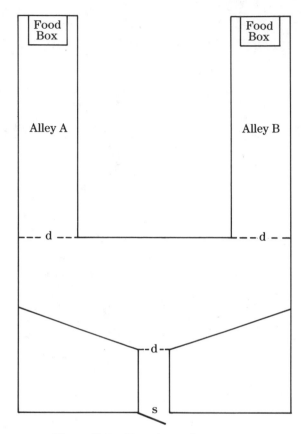

Figure 19.1   Experimental apparatus.

grain and dry milk.[1] The former was placed in the food box of Alley A, the latter in the food box of Alley B.

The subjects were hooded rats of the Western Reserve "non-emotional" strain. The animals, under 12 hours' deprivation of food, were given 4 runs per day for 24 consecutive days. Every fourth day they were allowed to choose; that is, doors to both alleys were open. On all the other days, the runs were forced (only one door would be open) so that the animal ran twice to each alley each day. These forced runs were given in an ABBA order on one day, BAAB order the next, and so on. Thus in the 24 days, the animals had 6 days of free runs to food. Five

1. P. T. Young (5) found that rats in a free-choice situation liked these two foods equally well, that is, ate them both equally often.

of the rats were allowed to feed for one minute upon going to Alley A, but only for 10 seconds when they ran to Alley B. The other 5 rats were given the one-minute feeding in Alley B, and the ten-second feeding in Alley A.

After the 24 days described above, each animal was given free runs in the apparatus under 0, 6, 18, 24, and 36 hours of deprivation of food.

2.   Control Group A: (N = 6).

These rats were Albinos from the stock of the Department of Psychology of the University of Iowa. They were run in the same manner as the experimental group except for one difference. For this group, the powdered whole wheat grain was placed in both alleys. The purpose of this group was to establish whether rats could discriminate between ten-second and one-minute feeding.

3.   Control Group H: (N = 9).

These rats were bred from the animals in the experimental group and were treated exactly as control group A. The purpose here was to be able to compare rats of the same stock.

All groups were fed regularly in their cages on the usual laboratory food employed. The experimental foods were encountered only in the experimental apparatus.

Results and Discussion

The results are presented in terms of the mean number of runs made to the food on which one minute of feeding was allowed. Since 4 runs were made on each day, a mean of 2.00 represents running equally often to both alleys, and a mean of 4.00 represents running every time to the "one-minute food."

The results are shown in Figure 19.2. The experimental group, on the first day of free runs, has an average of 2.6 runs to the "one-minute food." (It should be remembered that the first day of free runs was the fourth day of running in the apparatus.) On the second and third day of free runs, the runs to the "one-minute food" drop. They rise again on the fourth day, and on the fifth and sixth days of free runs, both show an average of 2.5 runs to the "one-minute food." On both the fifth and sixth days there was only one subject that ran all 4 times to one side. The low number of runs to the "one-minute food" is not, then, the result of some animals running always one way and others running always the other way.

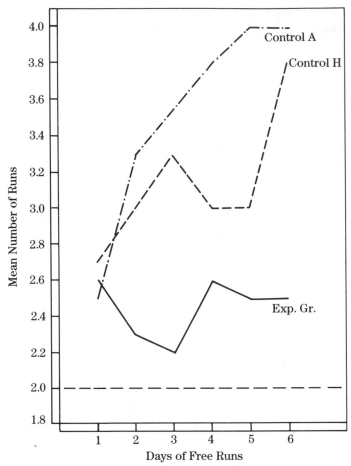

Figure 19.2   Mean number of runs to "one-minute food" on days of free runs.

One would ordinarily expect that if the animal wants food, and if the animal has learned where food is to be obtained, then it will run to the place where it can obtain a greater quantity. The experimental group does not do this. Is it because the tendency to go to a greater amount of food is counterbalanced by a tendency to go to "less food" because it has become more desirable? Or is it simply that the animals have not learned to discriminate between one minute and 10 seconds of feeding?

The question of whether rats can discriminate between one-minute and ten-second feeding can be answered directly by means of the control groups.

From Figure 19.2 it can immediately be seen that both control groups learn to run to the "one-minute food." On the first day of free runs, the differences between the experimental and the two control groups are not significant. The *t*-values for differences between the means of the experimental group and control A and control H are .23 and .20, respectively. From then on, however, the control groups run consistently more often to the "more food" than the experimental group.

The statistical significance of this difference between the experimental group and the control groups can easily be demonstrated with the use of the binomial expansion. If there is really no difference between the experimental group and the control groups, then the chances of having the control groups superior on five consecutive test days are one out of thirty-two. The difference between the experimental group and either of the control groups is significant at the 3.1 percent level of confidence.

The control groups demonstrate two interesting things. In addition to showing that rats can discriminate between one-minute feeding and ten-second feeding, they also show that when presented with a choice between a greater and a lesser amount of food, the animal will run to the greater amount. The effect of the amount of food offered upon the behavior of the organism has been demonstrated by Grindley (3), Gagne (2), and Fletcher (1). In all of these experiments, however, no choice was involved, and the measure taken was the time of running to the food, which in all experiments was found to decrease as the amount of food offered was increased. The data of the two control groups in this experiment demonstrate that the effect of offering a greater amount of food also holds for choice or discrimination situations.

If we then accept the fact that the rat will run to the greater amount of food when given a choice, and if we also accept the fact that the rats are able to discriminate between the one-minute and the ten-second feeding in our experimental situation, we must come to the following conclusion. Some factor, acting opposite to the tendency to run to the greater amount, is operating with respect to the experimental group so as to produce the observed result (to reduce the number of runs to the greater amount of food).

The only difference between the experimental and control groups is the fact that the control groups had the same food in both alleys and the experimental group had different foods in the two alleys. For the experimental group, there exists a food of which they have been relatively deprived. If this food has become more desirable relative to the other experimental food, then the results obtained should be expected. The increased desirability of the "less food" would act counter to the tendency to run to the greater amount.

If this interpretation is correct, the following should be correct. The more intense the general hunger drive becomes, the smaller role should the differential appetite play in the choice; that is, quantity should become a more important factor. The less intense the general hunger drive becomes, the more important should the differential taste become. If the explanation offered is correct, we may then make the prediction that for the experimental group the number of runs to the "one-minute food" should increase as the intensity of the hunger drive increases.

Figure 19.3 presents the data for the runs under different numbers

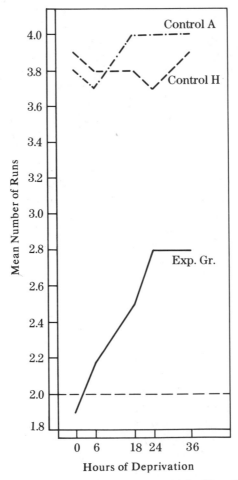

Figure 19.3   Mean number of runs to "one-minute food" under different hours of deprivation of laboratory food.

of hours of deprivation of food and shows this prediction to be correct. Under zero hours of deprivation of food, the animals run 1.9 times to the "more food" on the average. This is less than they have ever run before. The number of runs to "more food" increases steadily with increase in the number of hours of deprivation until it reaches a value of 2.8 at both 24 and 36 hours of deprivation. This last is more than these animals had ever run in the past.

The control groups, on the other hand, maintain essentially the same level of performance under different hours of deprivation. The difference between the experimental and control groups is even more striking here than before. We are then left with the plausible interpretation that during a period of relative deprivation one food has become more desirable than another, whereas previously they were both equally desirable.

Not directly pertinent to the main question involved, but worthy of mention, is the question of whether the "habit pattern" acquired by the control group was exhibited under zero motivation. It can hardly be said that zero hours of deprivation indicates zero motivation. The feeding occurred in the cages on the usual laboratory food and it cannot be said that the need for the experimental food was satisfied completely by the other food.

In fact, the whole experiment tends to show that needs for food can exist other than that of general hunger need. Corroborative of this point of view is the fact that all the animals, experimental and control groups both, ate the experimental foods under zero hours of deprivation of the laboratory food. The decrease in motivation, which undoubtedly was present, is shown by the fact that all the rats ran more slowly under zero hours of deprivation than under other conditions.

Theoretical Interpretation

Although the results can be made meaningful in common-sense terms, a formal theoretical explanation presents certain difficulties. There are two major findings which are in need of explanation. The first is the fact that the rats did not run always to the "more food" when a different food in lesser quantity was available. The second fact is that increasing the general hunger drive increased the number of times the rats did run to the "more food."

In common-sense terms, we may say plausibly enough that the animals acquired a relatively greater liking for one food because they got less of it, and we may make is more plausible by drawing analogies to people who like things which they are unable to get. This, however, offers no clue to the dynamic relationships behind the development of this differential preference. With respect to the second result, we may say that the more intense the general need for food becomes, the greater role quantity should play, and the less influential taste becomes in determining a choice; therefore, the rats would choose the greater quantity more often when the hunger need gets stronger. This again amounts merely to a restatement of the observed fact.

It seems desirable to be able to explain the obtained results in terms of the constructs of some theoretical system. Although this may present difficulties, an attempt in this direction should prove of value. It may at least be possible to indicate the direction which such theories must take in the formulation of their empirical laws to handle data of this nature.

Some constructs from the theoretical system of Lewin (4) seem to be of such nature as to be able to handle the results of this experiment. The principal reference is made here to the construct of tension system. The individual possesses various needs. We may speak of these needs as representing separate regions in the person. These regions may be more or less differentiated or subdivided. As an example, we may point to the hunger need which may be subdivided into a need for meat, a need for vegetables, etc. A system such as this, when unsatisfied, is said to be in tension. The construct of tension has another property, namely that of spreading. As time progresses, the tension in a system tends to spread in such a way as to become equal to that of the surrounding regions. One of the factors influencing the rate of spread is the strength of the boundaries separating the regions involved. The weaker the boundary, the more rapid will be the spread of tension. The question of strength of boundary can, in many cases, be looked at as a matter of discrimination. The more clear the discrimination, the more clear will be the separation between the regions, or the stronger the boundary between them.

When a system is in tension, a given realm of objects or activities becomes attractive in consequence of the tension. This can be illustrated by another example of hunger. When a person is not hungry (system not in tension), food may not seem particularly attractive to him. As the person becomes more and more hungry (system in tension), not only do foods become more attractive to him, but a greater number of foods become attractive. In a more formal manner, we may say that coordinate to the existence of a system in tension is the existence of regions of positive valence which will satisfy this tension, and furthermore, the magnitude of valence is a monotonic function of strength of the tension.

Our experimental situation and procedure can be stated in terms of the constructs outlined above. Because of the experience with the two experimental foods and as a consequence of discriminating between them, the general hunger drive becomes differentiated so that specific tension systems exist for each of the two experimental foods. Since the animals' appetites for these two foods are equal at the start of the experiment, we may say that these two tensions, if differentiated, would be equal to begin with.

It is probably necessary to state here that the needs for the two experimental foods have two components. One of these is due to hunger (a nutrient need); the other must be regarded as a non-nutrient need (due to taste and many other factors). At this point we are confronted with the problem of the interaction between these two components. We shall, for the purpose of the present discussion, make the simple assumption that the fluctuations in general hunger add or subtract equally from the total tension in all sub-systems.

When one states that the amount of tension reduction in these sub-systems is proportional to the amount of the corresponding food consumed, one can immediately see the effect of the experimental procedure. Starting with the two systems equal in tension, we continually reduce one by a greater amount than the other. The tension reduction in the sub-system corresponding to the "one-minute food" is greater than the tension reduction in the sub-system corresponding to the "ten-second food." As a result, at the end of one day's runs, the sub-system corresponding to the "ten-second food" is in a higher state of tension than the "one-minute food" sub-system. After repeated trials, the difference in tension between the two sub-systems will fluctuate within a stable range, depending upon the strength of the boundary separating the two regions. Of course, if the animal has not discriminated between the two foods, the boundary is nonexistent, and there will be no difference in tension.

Co-existent with the difference in tension, a *unit* of that food corresponding to the sub-system with the greater tension will be more attractive (have a greater positive valence) for the animal. Since the less attractive food exists in greater quantity, there will be a conflict of forces resulting in fewer runs to the "one-minute food" than would be the case if both were equally attractive.

This analysis may also be used to derive the increase of runs to the greater amount of food with increase in the general hunger need. If an increase in the general hunger need increases the tension in both of the sub-systems under consideration, then we may regard it as increasing the forces acting on the boundaries of the sub-regions. Thus, by increasing the hunger need, we increase the probability that these forces acting on the boundary will be stronger than the maximum boundary forces. If such a situation obtains, then the general hunger need obscures the discrimination and the animal should run to the greater quantity of food. Therefore, as we increase the hunger drive we should, as we do, observe an increase in the number of runs to more food.

An explanation of the obtained results is also feasible in S-R terms.[2] Through the training process we eventually come to a state of affairs such that S_1, S_D, and $S_{r_{g1}}$ are associated with R_1 (eating the "one-minute food") while S_2, S_D, and $S_{r_{g2}}$ were associated with R_2 (eating the "ten-second food"). The habit strength is stronger in the former due to the greater amount of reinforcement. One must here assume that the relative deprivation or frustration of R_2 makes the anticipatory goal responses for the "ten-second food" stronger than in the case of the "one-minute food." Therefore, because of the stronger stimulus complex, the animal will run less often to the "one-minute food" than if $S_{r_{g1}}$ and $S_{r_{g2}}$ were equal in strength.

The increase in the number of runs to the "one-minute food" with increasing hunger drive is also taken care of, since that means an increase in S_D which is common to both R_1 and R_2, therefore making the total difference in response tendency more in favor of the "one-minute food."

Summary and Conclusions

A group of rats were run in a single discrimination point apparatus. The choice involved was between a ten-second feeding on one food and a one-minute feeding on a different food. The appetites for the two foods used were equal at the start of the experiment. After 24 days, the animals ran only slightly more than 50 percent of the time to the greater amount of food. A control group showed that if only one food were involved, the animals would learn to run to the greater amount of food almost 100 percent of the time.

It was further found that the number of runs made by the experimen-

---

2. This explanation was suggested by Dr. R. R. Sears, Director, Iowa Child Welfare Research Station, State University of Iowa. In what follows, S_1 will refer to the stimuli of turning at the choice point in the direction of the "one-minute food"; S_2 will refer to similar stimuli in the direction of the "ten-second food"; S_D will refer to the hunger drive stimuli; R_1 and R_2 will refer to the responses of eating the one-minute food and eating the ten-second food respectively; $S_{r_{g1}}$ and $S_{r_{g2}}$ (one-minute food and ten-second food, respectively) will refer to the stimuli aroused by the anticipatory goal responses made by the subject before the goal is reached.

tal group to the greater amount of food was increased by increasing the strength of the hunger drive.

An interpretation was made in terms of the one food's becoming more attractive to the animal because of the relative deprivation.

———————

At the time of this article, Leon Festinger was at the Child Welfare Research Station of the State University of Iowa.

He acknowledged his indebtedness to Dr. K.W. Spence, Head, Department of Psychology, State University of Iowa, for his aid and suggestions, and Mrs. Nancy Phillips Perkins for gathering the data for the control group H.

References

1. FLETCHER, F. M. Effects of quantitative variation of food incentive on the performance of physical work by chimpanzees. *Comp. Psychol. Monogr.*, 1940, **16**, (3), 46.

2. GAGNE, R. M. The effect of spacing of trials on the acquisition and extinction of a conditioned operant response. *J. exp. Psychol.*, 1941, **29**, 201–216.

3. GRINDLEY, G. C. Experiments on the influence of the amount of reward on learning in young chickens. *Brit. J. Psychol.*, 1929, **20**, 173–180.

4. LEWIN, K. *Principles of topological psychology.* New York: McGraw-Hill, 1936.

5. YOUNG, P. T. Preferences and demands of the white rat for food. *J. comp. Psychol.*, **26**, 545–588.

20

Some Consequences of De-Individuation in a Group

Anyone who observes persons in groups and the same persons individually is forced to conclude that they often behave differently in these two general kinds of situations. Casual observation would seem to indicate that one kind of behavior difference stems from the fact that people obtain release in groups, that is, are sometimes more free from restraints, less inhibited, and able to indulge in forms of behavior in which, when alone, they would not indulge.

The most often noted instance of such freedom from restraint is the behavior of persons in crowds. In a crowd, persons will frequently do things which they would not allow themselves to do under other circumstances. In fact, they may even feel very much ashamed later on. Such behavior is not, however, limited to crowds. It occurs regularly in groups of all sizes and of many different types. For example, a group of boys walking down the street will often be wilder and less restrained than any of them individually would be; at an evening party persons who are usually very self-conscious and formal will sometimes behave quite freely; the delegates to an American Legion convention, all dressed in the same uniform manner, will sometimes exhibit an almost alarming lack of restraint. The question with which we will concern ourselves is: *when does this kind of behavior occur and why does it occur?*

There occurs sometimes in groups a state of affairs in which the individuals act as if they were "submerged in the group." Such a state of affairs may be described as one of de-individuation; that is, individuals are not seen or paid attention to as individuals. The members do not

SOURCE: Festinger, L., Pepitone, A., & Newcomb, T. *J. abnorm. soc. Psychol.*, 1952, **47**, 382–389. [Received July 7, 1951]

feel that they stand out as individuals. Others are not singling a person out for attention nor is the person singling out others.

We would like to advance the theory that, under conditions where the member is not individuated in the group, there is likely to occur for the member a reduction of inner restraints against doing various things. In other words, many of the behaviors which the individual wants to perform but which are otherwise impossible to do because of the existence, within himself, of restraints, become possible under conditions of de-individuation in a group.

If individuals, then, have needs which they are generally unable to satisfy because of the existence of inner restraints against doing certain things, a state of de-individuation in a group makes it possible for them to obtain satisfaction of these needs. A group situation where de-individuation does occur will consequently be more satisfying, other things being equal, than one where de-individuation never takes place. We would expect groups which do occasionally provide conditions of de-individuation to be more attractive to their members.

The satisfaction obtained during states of de-individuation is only one of many kinds of satisfactions which persons obtain in groups. Groups help people achieve goals which require joint or cooperative action, they provide support for opinions and behavior patterns, they sometimes satisfy persons' needs for approval and status, and the like. Many kinds of satisfactions which groups provide and which, consequently, make groups attractive to members may be put into two incompatible classes:

1. *Those which necessitate individuation in the group.* Prestige and status in a group, for example, require singling out an individual and behaving toward him in a special manner. Helping members achieve certain of their goals requires paying attention to the individual and to his particular needs.

2. *Those which necessitate de-individuation in the group.* These are the satisfactions which result from the lessening of inner restraints which we have discussed above.

It is clear that these two classes are incompatible in the sense that groups cannot provide both individuation and de-individuation at the same time. Groups can, however, provide both on different occasions.

Groups which can provide only states of de-individuation are probably not very stable. Crowds are a good example of this kind of group. The momentary and evanescent existence of crowds is probably due to the inability of this type of group to satisfy needs requiring individuation. On the other hand, groups which can provide only conditions of individuation are probably not very satisfying to their members. A group, for example, in which members were constantly being singled out for praise, approval and attention would most likely prove frustrating in the long run. Groups which succeed in being very attractive to their members probably provide both types of situations on different occasions.

As a beginning toward support of this theory concerning the consequences of de-individuation we set out, in the present study, to demonstrate:

1. That the phenomenon of de-individuation in the group occurs and is accompanied by a reduction in inner restraint for the members.
2. That groups in which inner restraints are reduced are more attractive to their members than groups in which this does not occur.

The attempt was made, in a laboratory situation, to provide conditions which would facilitate de-individuation in the group and would also provide adequate opportunities for measurement. To do this, we wanted to create a situation in which there would be a strong force acting on the members to engage in some behavior against which there were strong inner restraints. Under such conditions some groups would be better able to create de-individuation situations than others. If de-individuation in the group did occur it would seem, from our theory regarding the phenomenon, that during such periods of de-individuation individuals in the group would not be paying particular attention to other individuals *qua* individuals. If this were true then, while being attentive to, and consequently well able to remember, what was done in the group, they should be less attentive to and less well able to remember which particular member had done what.

The extent to which inner restraints against engaging in the particular behavior were reduced should be reflected in the extent to which the members showed the behavior in question. This measure would undoubtedly be subject to error because of variation from group to group in the strength of the force acting on the members to engage in the behavior. If, however, we find a positive correlation between the extent to which the behavior in question was produced and the extent to which they were unable to identify who did what, this would be evidence supporting our theory of de-individuation in the group.

In those groups in which the restraints against engaging in the particular behavior were reduced the members would have obtained more satisfaction from the group situation. From our theoretical considerations we would consequently expect that the groups which did provide the conditions for de-individuation would be more attractive to their members.

Procedure

The subjects (Ss) for the study were males who volunteered in various undergraduate classes at the University of Michigan to participate in a group experiment. Seven volunteers were scheduled for each session, but for various reasons (study pressures, forgetfulness, etc.) all seven rarely appeared for the discussion meeting. Our sample consists of 23 groups, ranging in size from 4 to 7.[1]

When they arrived at the discussion room, Ss were seated around a conference table and were engaged by the observer in mildly cheerful small talk. This procedure was adopted to prevent excessive prediscussion interaction among Ss which we felt might introduce additional factors.

When all Ss had arrived, the experimenter (E) directed them to print their first names on cards so that each could be identified by the others in the discussion, and then proceeded to read aloud the following statement. The alleged survey and its findings are, needless to say, entirely fictitious.

The following statement represents a summary of an important research project that has recently come to the attention of psychiatrists and social scientists concerned with problems of personal adjustment among students. Although the results are demonstrably reliable, it is believed that additional implications can be brought to light by having small groups of students discuss their personal views relating to these results.

A highly representative sample of 2365 students (1133 female and 1232 male) on 14 campuses, from all social-economic classes and several nationality backgrounds, was subjected to an intensive three-week psychiatric analysis consisting of repeated depth interviews and a battery of sensitive diagnostic tests. The results show unequivocally that 87 per cent of the sample possessed a strong, deep-seated hatred of one or both parents, ranging from generalized feelings of hostility to consistent fantasies of violence and murder. A finding of further significance was that those individuals who at first vehemently denied having such hostile impulses or

---

1. Eight female discussion groups were also conducted. These are not included with our experimental sample of male groups because of their considerably poorer memory with respect to who said what during the discussion. The results for these female groups, however, are in the same direction as those herein reported for the males.

who were unwilling to discuss their personal feelings in the matter were subsequently diagnosed as possessing the most violent forms of hostility. In other words, conscious denial, silence, or embarrassment were found to be almost sure signs of the strongest kind of hatred. Of the 13 per cent in whom no trace of hostility was found, the great majority thought they probably hated their parents and were willing to discuss every aspect of their feelings with the investigator.

In summary, 87 percent were found by modern psychiatric techniques to possess deep-seated resentments and hostilities toward one or both parents. Individuals in this category who most vigorously denied that they had such feelings revealed, at the conclusion of analysis, the strongest degree of hatred. Thirteen per cent were found to be free of such aggressive impulses. Most of these individuals at first thought they were basically hostile and were interested in discussing their feelings toward their parents freely.

Discuss in detail your own personal feelings toward your parents in the light of these results. Try to analyze yourself in such a way as to get at the basic factors involved.

The Ss were each given a copy of the above statement and were asked to start discussing the matter. The discussion lasted 40 minutes.

The discussion material was designed to create conditions in which the phenomenon of de-individuation might occur. The particular topic was chosen because it was felt that most people would have inner restraints against expressing hatred of their parents and, in fact, many would not even want to admit it to themselves. In preliminary experiments, the statement given to Ss did *not* include the part which indicated that those who initially denied it later turned out to be the ones with the strongest hatred toward their parents. In these preliminary experiments the most frequent occurrence was complete avoidance of the topic they had been asked to discuss. Including this statement provided a force on Ss to talk about it. In other words, to the degree that Ss accept the statement, they experience a more or less strong pressure to reveal negative feelings toward their parents. This, together with the inner restraints against saying such things, provided the conditions that we wished to create.

Observation Methods

During the 40-minute discussion an observer categorized statements in terms of whether they reflected positive or negative attitudes toward parents in the present or the past; positive or negative attitudes of others toward their parents; impersonal theories about parent-child relationships; and whether they expressed concern with the interaction of group members and the discussion procedure. Each contribution to the discussion was categorized and recorded next to the name of the person who made it together with the length of the contribution in seconds. Pauses which lasted for 20 seconds or longer were also recorded. In order to permit a detailed analysis of the discussion, the observations were divided into 3-minute sequential frames.

Of particular relevance to the hypothesis being tested are those contributions which expressed existing negative or positive attitudes that the group members have toward their own parents, since from these we can infer the degree to which there was a reduction in the inner restraint against expressing negative feelings.

Experience in our preliminary experiments indicated that each contribution would have to be categorized as an entity. Frequently a statement would begin with the implication that the person loved his parents deeply and end with an explicit denunciation of them. The reverse also appeared quite often—the group member would begin to describe various hostilities he feels toward his parents, only to end with a highly favorable over-all estimate of them. Such examples made it clear that expressions of attitudes toward parents could be coded meaningfully only in terms of the contribution as a whole rather than in terms of specific and often contradictory statements within the contribution. When the observer could not make a judgment of the total unit, that is, whether the basic feeling revealed toward parents was positive or negative, she categorized it as "questionable."

To represent the degree to which inner restraint against expressing "hatred of parents" was reduced in the group, we calculated the difference between the number of contributions which expressed negative attitudes (categorized as N) and the number of contributions which expressed positive attitudes (categorized as P). The number of P contributions was subtracted from the number of N contributions because it was felt that P contributions were indications of the nonreduction of restraint. The larger the difference, the more successful the group had been in reducing restraint against the expression of negative attitudes toward their parents. Statements categorized as "questionable" were omitted from this calculation. Examples of statements falling into the two major observation categories follow:

Negative Attitudes (N)

"Frequently I get very angry at my mother and seemingly there's a good reason; but I don't get angry that way with others."

"There are times when my parents are so stubborn and bull-headed; they think they know best. Sometimes I don't think so."

"No matter how much I try to think that my folks are good to me, the fact remains that they've done me wrong."

Positive Attitudes (P)

"I respect my father because he's got a head on his shoulders; he's more of a leader and a man."

"I feel toward my father that if I could be half the man he is, I'd be a great success."

"I respect my parents for understanding how important independence is for the person."

The observer[2] was trained intensively in preliminary experiments and in informal practice sessions. To check reliability, the experimenter independently observed one of the discussion groups. Calculating reliability by correlating the number of seconds of N in each of the 3-minute observation frames for the two observers yields a coefficient of .91. A correlation could not be computed for P because, in that group, it occurred too infrequently. One would expect it to be of comparable magnitude.

The Recording of Statements

To obtain a measure of Ss ability to identify who had said what in the discussion, the experimenter recorded, as nearly verbatim as possible, 10^3 statements made by the group members during the discussion. The following criteria were employed in selecting these statements from the discussion:

1. The content of the statement should be distinct enough to permit identification of the person who made it, i.e., the statement should be as dissimilar as possible from those made by other group members.
2. The statement should be about a sentence in length.
3. The statement should be grammatically coherent.

2. Miss Dorothy Peterson, a graduate student in the Department of Sociology.
3. In 7 of the groups only 8 or 9 statements were recorded. This was occasioned by a lack of statements which fitted the criteria employed.

4. The 10 statements should come from as many group members as possible.
5. The 10 statements should be distributed over the entire 40-minute discussion period.

At the conclusion of the discussion, E made sure that the name cards were visible, and separated Ss to prevent copying. He then distributed a form and gave the following instructions:

> I am going to read off some statements that were made in the discussion and some that were not made. If you do not remember the statement having been made, place a check in the first column next to the appropriate number. If you remember the statement, but offhand you do not recall who made it, place a check in the second column next to the appropriate number. Finally, if you recall who made the statement write the first name of that person in the third column. This is not a memory test of any kind, and there is no need to guess.

The statements were then read off in the same temporal order in which they were made in the discussion. Interspersed among the 10 statements, in constant order for all groups, were 5 statements that were not made in the discussion. These were included so as to provide a basis for comparing "Identification Errors," i.e., errors in recalling who said what, with "Memory Errors," i.e., errors in remembering the content of the discussion.

The Ss' responses to the statements were scored in the following way. If, on any of the 10 statements actually made in the discussion, the person failed to recall who had made it or if he attributed the statement to the wrong person, he was given an error. The average number per person of these "Identification Errors" was calculated for each group. Errors of general memory were calculated similarly: Whenever an S thought that a given statement had been made which actually had not or whenever an S thought that a given statement had not been made which actually had, he was given an error. As with "Identification Errors" these "Memory Errors" were averaged for the group.

The E, in recording the statements, frequently had trouble meeting the criteria mentioned above. The statements recorded varied greatly in their identifiability. Sometimes a statement would be recorded and later on others would make very similar statements, thus making the identification ambiguous and difficult for Ss. Sometimes, when the discussion was proceeding rapidly the experimenter would not be able to record the statement accurately and consequently the recorded statement would be quite different from what was actually said. To cope with these difficulties some of the statements were eliminated from the analysis when there were good grounds for believing they were poor statements.

The specific criteria used to eliminate the statement were as follows: In groups of five persons or more a statement was eliminated if: (a) all or all but one S made errors on it, or (b) all but two made errors and the S who made the statement erred himself.

In groups of four Ss a statement was eliminated if all or all but one, including the S who made the statement, made errors on it.

When statements had been eliminated the average number of "Identification" (I) and "Memory" (M) errors was corrected so as to make all groups comparable with respect to number of statements. The correction consisted of multiplying the number of I and M errors, respectively, by 10 and 15 and dividing by the number of statements actually used in the counting of errors, i.e., the number of statements recorded and not eliminated.

The measure used to represent the ability of the group to identify who said what was the average number of "I-errors" minus the average number of "M-errors." The average number of "M-errors" is subtracted in order to correct the general memory level of the group.

The Measurement of Attraction to the Group

A postsession questionnaire included an item designed to measure the attractiveness of the group for the members. The question and the possible responses are as follows:

> Frankly, how much would you like to return for further discussions of similar topics with this same group (assuming your schedule to be free)?
> _____definitely want to return
> _____fairly strong desire to return
> _____feel neutral about it
> _____fairly strong desire not to return
> _____definitely do not want to return

Numerical values were assigned to each alternative (1 for "definitely do not want to return"; 5 for "definitely want to return") and an average attraction score was computed for each group.

Explanation to the Subjects

In each group, after the questionnaire had been administered, E explained the purposes of the study in details to Ss. They were told that the data presented for the discussion topic were entirely fictitious and the reasons for using it, together with the reasons for the rest of the procedure, were discussed with them. Sufficient time was spent in this manner with each group for them to leave with a good understanding of the experiment. They were also asked not to tell others about the experiment since we did not want future Ss to know what was going to happen in the group. As far as the experimenters know, Ss faithfully kept silent about it.

Results

There are two relationships with which we will be primarily concerned in examining the results of this experiment: (a) the relation between the frequency of negative attitudes toward parents revealed in the discussion and the ability to identify who said what, and (b) the relation between the frequency of negative attitudes revealed in the discussion and the attractiveness of the group for its members. After examining the evidence on these two points we will look at possible alternative explanations of the data and evidence for or against such alternatives.

De-Individuation and Reduction of Inner Restraint

It will be recalled that our measure of de-individuation in a group was the extent to which the members of the group were unable to identify who said what during the discussion (I-errors—M-errors). The measure of the extent to which inner restraints were reduced is the frequency of negative attitudes toward parents revealed in the discussion ($N - P$). Figure 20.1 shows the scatter diagram of the obtained relation between these two measures. From the theory we elaborated above we would expect to find them positively correlated.

Figure 20.1 shows the scatter diagram of the obtained positive correlation between these two variables. The correlation, including all of the groups, is only .22. One of the groups, however, indicated on the figure by an arrow, is considerably off the scale on poorness of identification of who said what. There are grounds for believing that this group was affected by a very different factor, namely, disinterest in the experiment and in the discussion.

The major grounds for asserting this are the great number of pauses in the discussion for this group. Observing pauses only of 20-second duration or longer, this group had a total of over 5 minutes of complete pauses during the 40-minute discussion. No other group had pauses to-

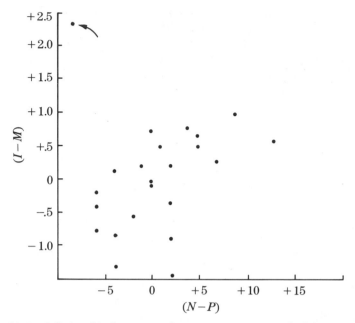

Figure 20.1   Relationship between reduction in restraint and ability to identify who said what.

taling more than one and a half minutes. Most of the groups had no pauses at all lasting as long as 20 seconds.

If we can take this as indicative of disinterest and, consequently, attribute the poor memory in this group to disinterested inattentiveness to people, then, considering how far off the scale of the other groups it is, it may be legitimate to omit this group from the calculations. Omitting this group, the correlation between the two variables in Figure 20.1 is .57. This correlation is significant at the .01 level of confidence. Our further presentation and discussion of the data will omit this deviant group.

It is also instructive to examine the relations between the measure of reduction in restraint and the I-errors and M-errors separately. We would expect the reduction in restraint to be positively correlated with the average number of I-errors alone, although this correlation should be lower because of the uncontrolled general memory factor which enters. The correlation obtained between $N - P$ and I-errors is .31.

Perhaps a more accurate way to eliminate the general memory factor from this correlation would be to calculate the partial correlation of $N - P$ with I-errors, holding M-errors constant. Table 20.1 shows the

Table 20.1 Intercorrelations Among *I*-Errors, *M*-Errors and $N-P$

	M-Errors	$N-P$
I-errors	.24	.31
M-errors		$-.39$

intercorrelations among the three variables involved in this partial correlation. The partial correlation of $N-P$ with *I*-errors, holding *M*-errors constant, is .45.

It is interesting to understand why the measure of reduction in restraint $(N-P)$ correlates negatively with the number of *M*-errors. This is probably due to the fact that the less the members of a group revealed negative attitudes and the more they tended to skirt the real discussion topic, the less distinctive were the statements which *E* was able to record verbatim during the discussion. Consequently, the greater the number of negative contributions, the better were they able to recall what was said. It is also possible that the greater the extent to which negative attitudes were revealed in the discussion, the more attentive were the members to what was being said and, consequently, the more adequate their memory. It then appears that an increase in the expression of negative attitudes toward parents is accompanied by an increase in the inability to identify who said what, *in spite of* a general improvement in memory.

Reduction of Inner Restraint and Attraction to the Group

Since the reduction of inner restraints allows the group member to behave more freely and to satisfy needs which would otherwise be difficult to satisfy, groups in which reduction of restraint occurs should be more attractive to their members. We should then expect to find a positive correlation between the measure of the reduction of restraint $(N-P)$ and the average attraction to the group as measured on the postsession questionnaire. This correlation turns out to be .36, which is significant at almost the 10 percent level of confidence considering both tails of the probability distribution.

There is evidence, then, supporting the two major derivations stemming from the theory about de-individuation in a group, namely, that it does tend to result in the reduction of inner restraints and that its occurence does tend to increase the attractiveness of the group for its members.

Possible Alternative Explanations

In connection with any set of data for which a specific theoretical explanation is given the question arises: are there alternative and perhaps simpler explanations of the data? This question is especially pertinent in connection with a study such as the present one since a relatively new theory is being presented. We will consequently present possible alternative explanations which various persons have suggested to the authors and discuss whether or not these explanations are compatible with the data.

1.   Can the results be explained in terms of theories of repression or selective forgetting? The Ss have been put in a situation where they were virtually forced to reveal attitudes which they perhaps considered shameful. It is plausible to expect that under these conditions they would tend to repress the shameful material and, consequently, the more shameful material is expressed in a group, the poorer is their ability to identify who said what.

It seems to the authors that any theory of repression would predict that the content of what was said would be forgotten as well as, or even sooner than, who said it. The data, however, indicate that the more "shameful material" expressed in the group the *better* is the members' memory for what was said. It is *only* the ability to identify who said what which is worse. It would seem further that if something like "shame" were the determining variable, those groups which produced more shameful content would be *least* attractive to their members. The data show exactly the opposite result. One may conclude that a theory of repression cannot adequately explain the results.

2.   Can the results be explained in terms of the Ebbinghaus laws of forgetting? Those groups which followed the experimental instructions best stated more instances of negative attitudes toward their parents and said more things of a personal nature. This means they produced more statements of the kind that E recorded verbatim and tested them on. From experiments on forgetting we know that the more statements there are to be remembered, the poorer will the memory be.

This type of explanation again would predict poorer memory for what was said in those groups who revealed a lot of negative attitudes toward their parents. This is contrary to the facts. It would also seem that this explanation cannot handle the obtained positive relation with the attractiveness of the group.

3.   Can the results be explained in terms of division of attention? It is plausible to suppose that in those groups where more negative atti-

tudes were revealed, the members became correspondingly more interested and engrossed in the content of the discussion. Since they were
paying so much attention to what was said they could not pay attention
to who was saying it. This theory would account for the fact that there
is a negative correlation between the frequency of negative attitudes
revealed and number of M-errors while a positive correlation exists between the former variable and number of I-errors. This theory would
also explain the relation with attraction to the group. Those groups in
which more interesting discussions took place were more attractive to
their members.

This theory has one additional implication. It would imply that one
should obtain a sizeable negative correlation between the number of I-
errors and the number of M-errors. This should certainly be the case if
it is a matter of division of attention and the more one pays attention to
content the less attention is it possible to pay to who is saying what. The
actual result is that there is a correlation of .24 between these two kinds
of errors. This would seem definitely to refute the division of attention
explanation.

4.   Can the results be explained simply in terms of individual reactions rather than as a group phenomenon? Perhaps those individuals
who revealed negative attitudes toward their parents tended to ignore
who was speaking because of the shameful nature of the content.

This possible explanation can be refuted by an analysis of the data in
terms of individuals within each group. If it is a matter of individual
reaction, then, within each group, the same relationship should hold
that we find when we use the group as the unit of analysis. Accordingly,
we ranked the members of each group on the basis of the extent to
which each member made contributions to the discussion which revealed negative attitudes toward their parents $(N-P)$. We then examined the measure of ability to identify who said what (I-errors $- M$-er-
rors) in relation to these ranks.

If we split each group in half on the basis of the $N-P$ measure there
is no consistent difference between the upper and lower halves on the
ability to identify who said what. In 10 of the groups those who contributed more negative statements made more identification errors and in
the other 12 groups the relationship is reversed.[4] In other words, the
analysis on an individual basis reveals no relationship at all between the
two measures.

---

4. This analysis continues to exclude the extremely deviant group. If this group were
included it would make 13 groups where the relationship was reversed.

It might be argued that dividing each group into two parts is a rather gross analysis and might obscure an existing relationship. We consequently also analyzed the data dividing each group into four parts. This required some arbitrary decisions as to the division when there were actually more than four $N-P$ scores in a group, but these decisions could be made fairly easily. When there were only three different $N-P$ scores in a group, they were analyzed as belonging to the top three quartiles when groups were combined. When there were only two different $N-P$ scores in a group they were analyzed as belonging to the middle two quartiles. In this manner all groups could be combined and the average calculated for each quartile of I-errors minus M-errors. The following tabulation shows these data:

Quartile division on $N-P$	N	Average I-errors $-$ M-errors
Highest quartile	25	.32
Second quartile	32	$-.42$
Third quartile	34	.44
Fourth quartile	23	.37

It is clear that there is no relationship between the two measures when analyzed in this manner. The variation within any quartile is quite large and none of the differences even approach statistical significance.

It might also be argued that this analysis does not dispose of the notion that it may be individual reaction rather than a group phenomenon because this analysis obscures the absolute magnitude of the $N-P$ measure which may be important. The data were accordingly also analyzed by individuals simply on the basis of absolute amount of $N-P$. The following tabulation presents the results of this analysis:

Absolute score on $N-P$	N	Average I-errors $-$ M-errors
Greater than zero	42	.27
Zero	28	.04
Less than zero	43	.25

None of these differences are appreciable or statistically significant. Once more it is clear that analyzing the data by individuals does not show the same relationship which was found when the data were analyzed by groups. This certainly lends support to the theory which explains the results as a group phenomenon.

Summary

A group phenomenon which we have called de-individuation has been described and defined as a state of affairs in a group where members do not pay attention to other individuals *qua* individuals, and, correspondingly, the members do not feel they are being singled out by others. The theory was advanced that such a state of affairs results in a reduction of inner restraints in the members and that, consequently, the members will be more free to indulge in behavior from which they are usually restrained. It was further hypothesized that this is a satisfying state of affairs and its occurence would tend to increase the attactiveness of the group.

A laboratory study was conducted to test this theory and the data from this study tend to support it. Other possible explanations of the obtained results have been considered and found inadequate.

When this article was prepared, Leon Festinger was at the University of Minnesota; A. Pepitone and T. Newcomb were at the University of Michigan.

The study was done at the Research Center for Group Dynamics at the University of Michigan.

21

The Effectiveness of Unanticipated Persuasive Communications

It seems plausible to suppose that an attempt to persuade a person to change his opinion on some issue would be more effective if the persuasive communication were unexpected than if the person anticipated the influence attempt. At least many people find this to be plausible. Lazarsfeld, Berelson, and Gaudet, for example, state:

> If we read or tune in a speech, we usually do so purposefully, and in doing so we have a definite mental set that tinges our receptiveness . . . . This mental set is armor against influence. The extent to which people, and particularly those with strong partisan views, listen to speakers and read articles with which they agree in advance is evidence on this point. (1948, p. 152)

and Festinger says:

> It seems clear that the avoidance and evasion of material which might produce or increase dissonance depends on anticipations (probably unverbalized ones) about the material or on preliminary assessments of the material. (1957, p. 158).

SOURCE: Festinger, L., & Allyn, J. *J. abnorm. soc. Psychol.*, 1961, **62**, 35 – 40. [Received November 12, 1959]

There are, however, virtually no data either to challenge or to support such statements. A study by Ewing (1942) comes closest to being pertinent. Ewing exposed two groups of subjects to a persuasive communication that supported a very extreme point of view. The only difference in treatment between the two groups was in the introduction to the persuasive communication. This introduction led one group to expect that the communication would support the extreme view which it actually espoused. For the other group, the introduction led the subjects to expect that the communication would agree with their existing views. The results indicated that those subjects who expected the communication to disagree with their opinions were actually less influenced by it. In other words, the persuasive communication was more effective if the audience falsely anticipated that it would support their existing views. This study does not deal with the effectiveness of a communication to an entirely unprepared audience, but it does point to the operation of some anticipatory resistance by an audience which expects to hear a disagreeing speech.

One may, of course, raise the further question as to the exact nature of the process by means of which the prepared audience is able to resist the effects of the attempted persuasion.

Some understanding of this process may be obtained from Festinger's theory of cognitive dissonance (1957). We may say that a persuasive communication which argues for an opinion different from that held by the audience creates dissonance in the listeners. Specifically, dissonance is created between the opinion the listener holds and his knowledge of the arguments favoring a contrary view. Since a person who reads a persuasive communication, or is a listener in an audience, cannot attempt to influence the source of the communication, there are only two immediate ways in which he can reduce this dissonance. He can change his opinion to a position closer to that advocated by the communication or he can reject and derogate the communication and the communicator.

What, then, are the effects of being prepared or unprepared to hear a persuasive communication? If the conditions of exposure to a communication are such as to guarantee attentiveness, it seems plausible to assume that, hearing the same speech, the same amount of dissonance is introduced whether or not the person is prepared for it. In such a case, the effect of preparedness, if any, would be on the particular mechanism used to reduce the dissonance, namely, whether the person more readily changes his opinion or rather rejects the source of communication.

There is no rigorous derivation to be made here but one may argue that, if a person anticipates hearing a communication that will disagree with an opinion he holds strongly, he will approach the situation with hesitancy, suspicion, and perhaps some hostility. If he does approach the situation in this way, then it seems natural to expect that his first and easiest reaction will be to reject the communicator.

Thus, being prepared for the communication would not, in a sense, make the communication less effective. It would simply alter the way in which the dissonance is reduced. Those prepared for the communication would tend less to change their opinion and tend more to reject the commmunicator. The study by Ewing (1942) gives some support to this analysis of the situation. He found that the discrepancy between the subjects' initial opinion and the position they expected the communication to espouse was the major determinant of how biased they felt the communication to be. In other words, irrespective of what the communication actually said, if they expected disagreement, they later felt the communication to be more biased. Anticipation of disagreement seems to have led to more rejection of the communication.

The present experiment was designed to throw more light on this process by comparing two groups exposed to the same persuasive communication, one group expecting a disagreeing persuasive communication and the other group not expecting a persuasive communication at all.

Procedure

A questionnaire was given to 128 students of the Palo Alto High School in order to discover a topic that was important to these students and on which their opinions were relatively extreme and homogeneous. This questionnaire was administered in the classrooms by the teachers who described it as a "Youth Survey." The subjects were assured that their replies would be confidential. The questionnaire included questions about the control of teenage drivers, teenage curfew regulations, and the treatment of communists in this country. All questions had four alternative answers: "agree strongly, agree slightly, disagree slightly, disagree strongly." The subjects were also asked to rank the three topics according to how important they were. On the basis of these rankings of importance and the clustering of their opinions toward one extreme, the issue of controlling teenage automobile driving was chosen for use in the actual experiment. The four questions concerning this topic on this questionnaire also served as our first measure of opinion.

Only 91 of these subjects were present at the experimental session 2 weeks later. The data from four of these were not analyzed; two arrived too late, and two were discarded because their responses were mainly attempts at humor. Of the remaining 87 subjects, 53 were females and 34 were males. The mean age was 15.7 years, with a range from 14–18.

The experimental session was conducted in the high school auditorium. As each student entered, he was given a questionnaire booklet. The students were asked to sit apart from each other and not to open the booklets until instructed to do so. The experimenter then explained to them that they were participating in an experiment conducted by the Stanford Psychology Department and assured them that their answers would be confidential and would have no effect on the grades they would receive in their classes. The subjects were then asked to open their booklets to the first page and read the printed instructions. There were two different sets of instructions and the booklets had been randomized in this regard when they were passed out. In one condition, "Opinion Orientation," subjects read the following:

> We are very much interested in studying the opinions and attitudes of high school students on the teenage driving problem. We particularly want to get your reactions to a talk by an expert on the subject. We have asked Mr. Nathan Maccoby, who is very well known for his reports and articles on this problem, to come here today and talk to you. In his articles, Mr. Maccoby has stated his very strong opinion that teenagers are a menace on the roads and should be strictly controlled by effective new laws. It is important that you pay close attention to him and to what he has to say, as you will be asked to give your opinions on the problem after he has finished his talk.

In the other condition, "Personality Orientation," subjects read the following:

> We are very much interested in studying how members of an audience form impressions of the personality of a speaker. We particularly want to see how high school students will "size up" the personality of an adult who is speaking to them on a serious subject. We have asked Mr. Nathan Maccoby, who is considered to be an expert in his field, to come here today and talk to you. We have asked him to speak on the topic that he knows the best, so as to put him more at his ease. It is important that you pay close attention to him and to what he has to say, as you will be asked to give your impressions of his personality after he has finished his talk.

When they had finished reading the instructions, the speaker was introduced. He delivered a speech that stressed the teenager's lack of a mature sense of responsibility and advocated stricter legal measures for the prevention and control of teenage driving. The communication was more extreme in the direction of control than the opinions of any of the students. After the speech, the experimenter thanked the speaker and instructed the students to answer the questions in their booklets. The booklets contained the same four questions on control of teenage driving which had been used previously together with other questions designed to measure rejection of the speaker, importance of the topic, and other items. These will be discussed in more detail under "Results." At the conclusion of the session the experiment was explained in simplified terms and any questions the students had were answered. The session took approximately 45 minutes.

Results

Effectiveness of the Experimental Manipulation

The purpose of one of the sets of instructions was to create an orientation toward the personality of the speaker so that the actual persuasive communication would be unanticipated. The other set of instructions was intended to create an orientation toward the opinion of the speaker together with the expectation that the speaker would disagree with their own opinion. To check on whether or not the two different orientations were successfully created, the following question was asked:

> The psychologists who are doing this experiment are mainly interested in
> (1) what kinds of opinions people have
> (2) how people judge other people's personalities.

If our manipulation was successful, we would expect the majority of Opinion Orientation subjects to check the first alternative and the majority of Personality Orientation subjects to check the second. Out of a total of 41 subjects who received the Opinion Orientation instructions, 80% said the experiment was concerned with opinions. Out of the total of 46 subjects who received the Personality Orientation instructions, 63% said the experiment was concerned with judgment of personality. The difference between the two conditions is, of course, highly significant statistically. Thus it appears that our experimental manipulation was effective in creating different orientations toward the speaker in the two groups.[1]

1. There were no significant differences in the responses given by boys and girls on any of the measures in the study. Therefore, the data were analyzed for the group as a whole.

It should be noted in the instructions to the subjects that in each of the two conditions an effort was made to introduce the speaker as equally expert. This was done because we wanted to keep constant the magnitude of dissonance occasioned by the persuasive communication. The following question was asked to check on this point:

> When we introduced Mr. Maccoby, we said that he is considered to be an expert in his field. How much do you think he really knows about the problem he discussed?
> (1) He is a real expert, who is very familiar with the problem.
> (2) He knows quite a lot about the problem.
> (3) He knows about as much as most people do about the problem.
> (4) He knows less than most people about it.
> (5) He knows very little, and a lot of his information is wrong.

The results show that we were successful in keeping the expertness of the speaker constant between the two conditions. In the Opinion Orientation condition 78% said the speaker was a real expert or knew quite a lot about the problem. In the Personality Orientation condition the comparable figure is 80%. Clearly, there are no appreciable differences between the two conditions.

Since the purpose of the experimental manipulation was to affect the orientation of the subjects but to keep constant the magnitude of dissonance, it is also important to know whether or not the subjects in the two conditions paid equal attention to what the speaker said. For this purpose a number of factual recall questions were asked. The results show no difference between the conditions in amount of material recalled. Since the two conditions were the same with respect to both attention paid to what the speaker said and degree of expertness attributed to him, we may regard the experimental manipulation as having created a difference in orientation or preparedness on the part of the subjects while holding constant the magnitude of dissonance introduced by the persuasive communication.

Comparison of the Two Experimental Conditions

We expected subjects in the Opinion Orientation condition to reduce dissonance mainly by rejecting the communicator and expected those in the Personality Orientation condition to reduce dissonance mainly by changing their opinion in the direction advocated by the communication. Change scores were calculated as follows: If a subject changed his answer to an adjacent category, e.g., from "agree strongly" to "agree slightly," he received a score of 1; if he changed to an answer two steps away, e.g., from "disagree strongly" to "agree slightly," he received a score of 2; since we used a four-point scale, the maximum possible change was 3. Changes in the direction of the position advocated by the communication were given a plus sign, and the changes were summed algebraically for the four questions to obtain a single score. Thus, if a subject changed from "disagree strongly" to "agree slightly" on one question in the direction advocated by the communication (a change of +2); changed from "agree strongly" to "agree slightly" on another question in the direction opposite to that advocated by the communication (a change of −1); and did not change at all on the other two questions, his opinion change score would be +1.

Rejection of the communicator was measured by the following question:

Do you think Mr. Maccoby covered all the facts pretty well, or do you think he was unfair or biased in some way?
(1) He was very unfair and biased.
(2) He was somewhat unfair; he didn't give all the facts.
(3) He was very fair; he covered all the facts pretty well.

Table 21.1 presents the data for opinion change and rejection. Two indices of opinion change are presented in the table: the average change

Table 21.1 **Opinion Change and Rejection of Communicator for the Two Experimental Conditions**

	Experimental Condition	
	Opinion Orientation (N = 41)	Personality Orientation (N = 46)
Average change of opinion	+.40	+.63
Percentage changing appreciably[a]	20%	43%
Percentage saying communication was very or somewhat biased	80%	61%

[a] An appreciable change is defined as a change of two or more points in the direction of the communication.

and the percentage of subjects changing appreciably (two or more points) in the direction advocated by the communication. Both of these measures show differences between the two experimental conditions in the predicted direction. Subjects in the Personality Orientation condition change their opinion more in the direction advocated by the communication than do subjects in the Opinion Orientation condition. While the difference in average change of opinion is not at all significant, the percentage who change appreciably is significant statistically (chi square $= 5.71$, $p = .02$).[2] The difference between the two experimental conditions on rejection of the communicator is also in the expected direction. Subjects in the Opinion Orientation condition are more likely to reject the communicator. The difference is statistically significant (chi square $= 4.06$, $p = .05$).

In other words, our expectations were borne out. If the subjects are led to expect that a persuasive communication will disagree with them, they reject the communicator more and are less influenced than subjects who are, so to speak, caught unprepared. The obtained differences, however, while significant statistically, are rather small. Let us, therefore, examine the data further to see what additional light can be shed on the process with which we are dealing.

Initial Opinion and Importance of Issue

The topic of teenage driving was chosen for the experiment because the initial opinions of the high school students were more extreme on this issue than on either of the other issues that we pretested. Theoretically, of course, we would expect that the differences between our two experimental conditions would be greater for people who held opinions very divergent from the position advocated by the communication since more dissonance is introduced for them. Although opinions on the issue of teenage driving were relatively extreme, still, only a minority of the subjects held entirely one-sided opinions on the issue.

The four questions used as the measure of opinions about teenage driving on both questionnaires were as follows:

1. Since most accidents involving teenagers happen at night, people between the ages of 16 and 20 should only be allowed to drive during the daytime.
2. Tests for obtaining a license to drive should be made much harder for teenagers and should also test for judgment and knowledge of the traffic laws.

2. All p values reported are two-tailed.

3. I think that the minimum age for obtaining a driver's license in California should be raised to 18. [Note: present age is 16.]
4. If a person between 16 and 20 years of age receives a ticket for speeding or reckless driving, his license should be revoked until he is 21.

If we define an extreme opinion as disagreement (either strong or slight) on all four questions, we find that only 16 of the 41 subjects in the Opinion Orientation condition and 16 of the 46 subjects in the Personality Orientation condition initially held such extreme opinions.

Another variable that should affect the results of the experiment is the importance of the issue to the subjecct. The more important the issue of teenage driving is to a particular person, the greater should be the magnitude of dissonance created in him by the persuasive communication. In order to obtain a measure of the importance of the issue to each subject, we asked the following question:

How important is it to you to be able to have a license to drive a car?
(1) very important
(2) quite important
(3) not too important
(4) not at all important

Ideally we would have wanted to analyze the data from the experiment separately for the effect of extremeness of opinion and the effect of importance of the issue. Unfortunately, it turns out that there is a very appreciable correlation between these two variables. In both experimental conditions equally, those who hold extreme opinions also overwhelmingly state that the issue is important to them. Hence, we cannot look at the effect of each of these variables separately. Consequently the data were analyzed for those with extreme opinions versus those with moderate opinions on the issue, ignoring the specific responses on importance. It should be remembered, however, that these two go hand-in-hand in this sample. Since, theoretically, both of these variables should affect the data in the same manner, the interpretation will be, of necessity, slightly ambiguous. That is, the greater the difference between initial opinion and the position advocated by the communication, and the greater the importance of the issue, the greater will be the magnitude of dissonance introduced by the communication. Hence, we cannot separate the effects of these two variables in our data.

Let us, then, examine the data to see the effect of the combined action of both variables. Table 21.2 presents the data on opinion change

Table 21.2   Opinion Change in Relation to Initial Opinion

	Experimental Condition	
	Opinion Orientation	Personality Orientation
Extreme initial opinion		
Average change	+.81	+2.31
Percentage changing appreciably	19%	60%
	(N = 16)	(N = 16)
Moderate initial opinion		
Average change	+.28	−.27
Percentage changing appreciably	20%	30%
	(N = 25)	(N = 30)

separately for those who initially held extreme opinions and those who initially held moderate opinions for each experimental condition. It should be remembered that a subject was labeled as holding a moderate opinion if he initially agreed with the position advocated by the communication on one or more of the questions.

It is clear from Table 21.2 that the difference between initial opinion and position advocated by the communication is a major variable. For those who held extreme opinions initially (and for whom the issue was more important) there is an average change of + 2.31 in the Personality Orientation condition as compared to an average change of only +.81 in the Opinion Orientation condition. The difference on the measure of percentage who change appreciably is also similarly large. Both differences are significant at better than the 2% level. For those whose initial opinion was moderate (and the issue was less important) there is practically no difference between conditions and, indeed, practically no impact of the communication at all. The average change for the Opinion Orientation group is only +.28 and the average for the Personality Orientation group is even slightly in the opposite direction from that advocated by the communication. In other words, the entire difference that we found between the experimental conditions is attributable to those subjects for whom the persuasive communication introduced considerable dissonance.

We would also expect the difference between the two experimental conditions on the measure of rejection to be greater for those with initially extreme opinions. Surprisingly, however, this does not turn out to be the case. There are simply no differences between those holding extreme opinions and those holding moderate opinions in the percentage who feel the communicator was biased. In the Personality Orientation condition these figures are 62.5% and 60%, respectively, and the comparable figures for the Opinion Orientation condition are 81% and 80%. There is, of course, no reason to expect a difference in the Personality Orientation condition where dissonance was reduced mainly by changing opinion. There is reason, however, to have expected a difference in the Opinion Orientation condition. It is conceivable, however, that the overall level of rejection was already so high in this condition (80%) that a virtual ceiling had been reached as far as our relatively crude measure is concerned. This cannot, of course, be settled with the present data. The only thing that can be said is that, if there is not a ceiling phenomenon here, there is a theoretical difficulty involved in interpreting the rejection data.

Summary

Eighty-seven high school students who were in favor of allowing teenagers to drive with few restrictions were presented with a communication advocating strict control of young drivers. One group was given an orientation to attend to the speaker's opinions and was informed of his topic and his point of view in advance; the other group was given an orientation to evaluate the speaker's personality and was not told the topic of the speech or the speaker's point of view. It was found that subjects who were forewarned of the nature of the communication changed their opinions less and rejected the communicator as biased to a greater degree than unprepared subjects. Differences in amount of opinion change between prepared and unprepared subjects were greater among those holding extreme opinions initially.

Jane Allyn and Leon Festinger were at Stanford University when this article was written.

The authors expressed their thanks to Nathan Maccoby for his help in writing the persuasive communication and in the conduct of the experimental sessions. They were also indebted to John G. Caffrey and Curt R. Demele for their help and cooperation in obtaining subjects.

References

EWING, T. A study of certain factors involved in changes of opinion. J. *soc. Psychol.*, 1942, **16,** 63–88.

FESTINGER, L. *A theory of cognitive dissonance.* Evanston, Illinois: Row, Peterson, 1957.

LAZARSFELD, P., BERELSON, B., & GAUDET, H. *The people's choice.* (2nd ed.) New York: Columbia Univer. Press, 1948.

22

The Effectiveness of "Overheard" Persuasive Communications

It is widely believed that a communication, if inadvertently overheard, is more likely to be effective in changing the opinion of the listener than if it had been deliberately addressed to him. Intuitively, the advantages of an overhearing situation for effective influence seem so obvious that it is accepted as virtually proven. Berelson (1950), for example, gives two reasons for the presumed extraordinary effectiveness of overheard communications. He states that,

> in such exposure defenses against new ideas are presumably weaker because preconceptions are not so pervasively present. Finally, there may be other psychological advantages centering around the gratification of "overhearing" something "not meant for you," a consideration that also weakens the resistance to "propaganda" (since "it would not be propaganda if it wasn't intended for you") (p. 458).

This last parenthetical remark is amplified by Hovland, Janis, and Kelley (1953) as follows:

> Remarks such as those overheard in subways and other crowded public places would be especially effective in this respect because under such

SOURCE: Walster, E., & Festinger, L. *J. abnorm. soc. Psychol.*, 1962, **65**, 395–402. [Received September 18, 1961]

circumstances it is quite apparent that the speaker has no intention to persuade the bystanders (p. 23).

In short, on an intuitive level, there seem to be three factors which increase the effectiveness of overheard persuasive communications.

1. Because of the accidental nature of the communication the listener is caught, so to speak, with his defenses down.
2. It is more powerful because the listener is not supposed to hear it.
3. The speaker cannot possibly be seen as intending to influence the listener.

Let us see to what extent there is experimental evidence to support these intuitively plausible assertions. On the first factor, namely, lack of defenses when the communication is unanticipated, there are some supporting experimental data. It has been shown (for example, Allyn & Festinger, 1961; Ewing, 1942) that if a person expects a communication to disagree with the opinion he holds, he does erect defenses, tends to reject the communicator, and is less influenced than if he hears the same communication without having been led to expect disagreement. It should be pointed out, however, that these studies did not involve accidental communications. There is no evidence in the literature that there would be fewer defenses to an accidental communication than to a purposeful one, provided the listener did not expect disagreement.

On the second factor, the gratification of hearing something one is not supposed to hear, there is no evidence at all. To our knowledge no studies which bear on this have been done.

On the third factor, however, there is some evidence. There are studies in the literature which have investigated the effectiveness of communications from biased and unbiased sources. A biased source may be seen as having some ulterior or personal motive for wanting to influence the listener. Hence, the difference in effectiveness of communications from biased and unbiased sources may be seen as relevant to the factor of whether or not the speaker is seen as "intending" to influence the listener. The evidence on this point, however, is ambiguous. Kelman and Hovland (1953), for example, find that when a communication is ascribed to a selfishly motivated communicator there is less influence. Hovland and Mandell (1952), however, find no difference in the amount of opinion change when the communication is ascribed to a partial or impartial person. This latter finding is of particular interest since the lack of difference in effectiveness existed in spite of the fact that the listeners rated the impartial source as having done a better job and having been more fair and honest.

Clearly, the evidence for the assertion that overheard communications are especially effective in changing opinions is less than adequate. The first of the two studies to be reported in this paper was designed to provide some better evidence on this point. In order to narrow the field of possible interpretations, the study was designed to avoid entirely any differences which might be due to direct versus indirect persuasive communications. Thus, two conditions were set up in the experiment. In both conditions a subject listened to two persons carrying on a conversation. The only difference between the two conditions was that in one the subject thought that the speakers knew that some people were listening, while in the other the subject thought that the speakers were unaware that anyone at all was listening. The exact details of the experiment follow.

Experiment I

Procedure

During a lecture in the introductory psychology course at Stanford University, students were informed that, as part of the course, they were required to sign up for a 15-minute tour of the social psychology laboratory's observation room. The next day, in one-half of the recitation sections, arrangements were made with students to tour in groups of 2–4. Students in the other sections were told arrangements would be made with them later in the term—these students were then utilized as a control group. One hundred subjects actually took the tour; 84 subjects comprised the control group.

When subjects reported for the tour, the mechanics and common uses of the observation room (a small booth from which one could look into a larger room through a one-way mirror and could listen through earphones) were explained. Subjects were told that a common technique for analyzing group behavior was "blind listening." The experimenter explained that they would be told more about, and given a chance to try, this technique later. After these instructions the experimenter took the subjects to the observation room.

As the groups began walking down the corridor toward the observation room, the experimenter remarked casually,

Since the large observation room is rarely in use for experiments, graduate students usually use it as a lounge. There's almost always someone in there.

One-half of the groups were given instructions to convince them the graduate students would know they were listening; the other subjects were led to believe the graduate students would be unaware of their presence.

For the Regular condition, subjects were told that,

A couple of graduate students are in there now. I'll tell them we're coming through.

Upon reaching the end of the corridor, the experimenter stuck her head into the large room to the right of the small observation booth, and said to the two graduate students within,

Hi. Some Psych I people are coming through. Would you mind just continuing your conversation so we can try a little blind listening?

For the Overheard condition, the experimenter said instead,

I think a couple of graduate students are in there now. If we're quiet, we can probably get into the observation booth without their hearing us.

The experimenter then led the subjects quietly past the large room into the booth, shut the door of the booth, and looking through the one-way mirrror at the graduate students, who had not looked up, said,

Well, I guess we made it.

In both conditions, as subjects watched the graduate students talking, the experimenter described some of the techniques of blind listening. (Noticing incomplete sentences, pauses, etc.) Subjects were then told to try a little blind listening. Curtains were drawn over the one-way mirror, and earphones passed out. (Instruction in this "technique" had been so sketchy and uninformative that subjects really had nothing to do but listen casually.)

The "conversation" all subjects heard through the earphones was actually a taped 6-minute persuasive communication. On this tape, two speakers discussed the common "misconception" that smoking causes lung cancer. A series of (nonexistent) studies were described which showed there was no relationship between smoking and cancer when all confounding factors were eliminated. In fact, the data were said to suggest that smoking might even be beneficial since it released tension.

The degree to which the subjects agreed with the communication was assessed a week later. A mimeographed questionnaire purporting to be from the National Institutes of Health was given to the 100 experimental and the 84 control subjects during the regular class recitation sections by a second experimenter. The "medical survey" included four questions concerning students' opinions about the causal relationship between smoking and cancer.

About 10 minutes after this health questionnaire was completed, the first experimenter entered the classroom and passed out a second questionnaire asking students to evaluate the tour she had conducted. These data were presumably "to be used in planning next quarter's demonstrations."

Fourteen of the 100 subjects in the experimental conditions indicated on this second questionnaire that they thought the conversation they heard from the observation booth was a prepared recorded conversation. The data from these 14 subjects were discarded.

Following the collection of data, the true purposes of the experiment were explained to all subjects.

Results

The answers to the four questions on the Health Questionnaire which concerned their opinions about the link between smoking and lung cancer provided a measure of the relative extent to which the persons in our various conditions were influenced by the persuasive communication they listened to in the guise of a conversation. Since all the questions yielded comparable results, we summed the responses to all four questions to provide one measure of agreement with the communication. On each question an answer was given a higher score the more it agreed with the position that the link between smoking and lung cancer was *not* proven—the position advocated by the communication. Table 22.1 presents these data for the three conditions.

It is clear from an examination of Table 22.1 that the conversation between the two graduate students was an effective persuasive communication. While the control group (who did not hear the conversation) shows an opinion score of 11.4, those in the Regular condition have a score of 13.6, and those in the Overheard condition have a score of 14.5. The differences between the Control condition and each of the experimental groups are both highly significant. We are, however, more con-

**Table 22.1   Opinions Concerning the Link
Between Smoking and Lung Cancer**

Condition	Smokers	Nonsmokers	Total
Students not participating in the demonstration (Controls)	11.8 (24)[a]	11.2 (60)	11.4 (84)
Regular	13.6 (12)	13.6 (36)	13.6 (48)
Overheard	15.3 (9)	14.2 (29)	14.5 (38)

[a]Number in parentheses is the number of cases on which the cell mean is based.

cerned with the difference between the two experimental groups. As seemed plausible and as most persons would have expected, the Overheard condition produces more opinion change than the Regular condition. The difference is significant at the .08 level of significance $(t = 1.76)$. In other words, if a person feels that the speaker does not know that anyone is listening he is influenced more than if he thinks the speaker knows someone is listening.

A difference which is of such borderline significance statistically, however, is not entirely satisfactory. We, hence, attempted to gain further insight into the data by doing some further analyses. Because of the content of the persuasive communication, the first variable which suggested itself for internal analysis was, of course, the smoking behavior of the subjects in the study. It seemed possible to us that, since smokers might be very desirous of believing the content of the persuasive communication, they might have changed a great deal, and equally, in both experimental conditions thus, perhaps, attenuating the difference. The analysis of the data, however, revealed a very perplexing finding. Not only was this suggestion not true, but the opposite was true. Table 22.1 presents the data separately for smokers and nonsmokers for the three conditions.

It is clear in this table that the differential effectiveness of the Regular and Overheard conditions is due almost entirely to the small group of smokers. For the nonsmokers there is a very small difference between these two conditions which is not significant. For the smokers, however, the difference is significant at better than the .10 level $(t = 1.88)$ even though the number of cases is very small. It is also clear that the smokers are not more influenced than are the nonsmokers in the Regular condition. These means are almost identical. It is only in the Overheard condition that the smokers, who presumably would like to believe the content of the communication, are actually more influenced than the nonsmokers.

In an attempt to understand the reasons for this surprising finding we looked at the data from the second questionnaire where the subjects were asked how sincere and honest they thought the speakers had been. Perhaps the smokers, for some reason or other, attributed greater sincerity to the speakers in the Overheard condition than did the non-smokers. The data show, however, that this cannot account for the obtained result. Everyone, it turns out, rates the speakers as more honest and sincere in the Overheard than in the Regular condition. In the Overheard condition the mean ratings are 6.4 and 6.1 for the smokers and nonsmokers, respectively. The comparable figures for the Regular condition are 5.6 and 4.8. Thus, actually, the nonsmokers are the ones with the bigger differential between the two conditions in the rating of the speakers' sincerity but it is the smokers who show a differential in how influenced they were. None of the other questions that were asked on this second questionnaire revealed any differences at all in reactions to the two conditions.

The remaining alternative is that the obtained result may be a chance difference. After all, it seems somewhat implausible that the Overheard condition should only be more effective for persons who are behaviorally involved in the issue. We, consequently, carried out a second experiment which was more adequately controlled and which was specifically designed to see if this implausible finding was or was not correct.

Experiment II

Procedure

Two groups of persons, wives of college students living in an on-campus housing development, and Junior and Senior women students living in dormitories, were used as subjects in the experiment. Two persuasive communications were employed. One of them, "Student husbands should spend a great deal more time at home," was expected to be an involving issue primarily for the married women. The other, "Junior and Senior women should be allowed to live off campus if they desire," was relevant only for the unmarried students living in dormitories.

Two weeks before the experimental sessions, prospective subjects were sent letters from the National Institutes of Mental Research, informing them that a nationwide study of the therapy process was being conducted, and inviting them to observe and evaluate a regular therapy session. Final appointments were made with 41 married women and 40 single students in follow-up telephone calls. Groups of one to four subjects were scheduled at a time. One-half of these groups were randomly assigned to the Regular condition; the remaining groups were placed in the Overheard condition.

After all the women in any group had arrived, the supposed "purposes" of our study were discussed at greater length. Subjects were told they were to evaluate two therapists, the patient's regular therapist and a visiting psychiatrist who was consulting with the patient's regular therapist. Subjects were instructed just to listen casually to the therapy session in order to give us some very general impressions at the end. It was explained to the subjects that they were to listen to the sessions from individual listening rooms connected to the therapy room by a one-way speaker. Separate listening rooms were used "since we wanted independent judgments" and since they "obviously could not sit *in* the therapy room."

At this point Regular condition subjects were told,

Of course both the therapists and the patient know you'll be listening in today.

Those in the Overheard condition were told,

Of course, the therapists don't know you're listening in today.

As they were led to their individual rooms, the experimenter commented to Regular condition subjects,

Now I'll run downstairs and tell the therapists you're here and turn on the main speaker.

Overheard condition subjects were merely told,

You'll be able to hear as soon as I turn on the main speaker.

Instead of "turning on the main speaker," the experimenter actually turned on a tape recorder which began playing a casual conversation between the two "therapists," through the subjects' speakers. The ex-

perimenter then returned to the subjects' rooms, identified the therapists' voices, and remarked to the subjects in the Regular condition,

When I looked in downstairs, Bill [the patient] hadn't arrived yet.

Subjects in the Overheard condition were told,

Bill apparently isn't there yet.

The experimenter then left the subjects alone to hear the remainder
of the tape. The "conversation" between the two waiting therapists continued for 14 minutes. During his discussion of student problems, the
visiting therapist spent 6 minutes delivering the first persuasive communication, "Women should be allowed to live off campus." The regular
therapist only commented in order to clarify and agree with the arguments of the visitor. The regular therapist then began discussing a problem "common to his patients." During the next 6 minutes, he presented
the second persuasive communication, "Husbands should spend more
time at home."

At the end of this discussion, the patient arrived, his therapy session
began, and for the next 35 minutes both therapists limited their remarks
to "Yes," "No," and extremely obvious interpretations. At the end of the
50-minute taped "session," subjects were asked for their evaluations of
the therapists' competence—supposedly the focus of our study. The experimenter then gave them a questionnaire asking for their opinions on
several problems of concern to Standford students and student-wives.
From a few of the questions in this attitude survey, an Index of Agreement with each of the communications presented by the therapists was
computed.

Control Group

In order to get some indication of the attitudes of subjects who did not
hear the tape, the questionnaire was also mailed to 21 married women
and 20 single students selected in the same way as our experimental
subjects. Seventeen married women and 17 students returned the completed forms. Since Control subjects answered the questionnaire at
home with unlimited time to complete it, their responses may not be
completely comparable to those of our experimental groups.

Results

Each subject in the experiment heard two persuasive communications,
one of which was supposed to be personally involving and the other not.

It is important to assess the extent to which we were successful in accomplishing our purpose in the design. On the questionnaire, subjects were asked how intensely they felt about each of the issues and also how often they discussed each of them. The results show that the appropriate conditions were, indeed, created. The dormitory women report feeling more intensely about the "off-campus living" issue than do married women ($t = 3.98$) and report having discussed it much more often ($t = 8.32$). On the "husbands at home" issue, on the other hand, the married women feel more intensely than do the dormitory women (although not significantly so) and report discussing the issue much more often ($t = 8.05$).

We may then look at the results to see if the findings from the first experiment do or do not hold up. In order to present one measure, for each issue, of extent of agreement with the persuasive communication, the answers to the relevant questions on the questionnaire were summed. In all cases higher scores were assigned to those responses which indicated more agreement with the position advocated in the communication. Table 22.2 presents these data.

An examination of the data makes it clear that we obtained precisely the same kinds of results in this experiment as were obtained in the first experiment. When the issue is one which is immediately involving for the subject ("husbands at home" for married women and "living off cam-

Table 22.2   **Index of Agreement on Relevant and Irrelevant Issues for Married Women and Single Students**

Issue	Married Women		Single Students	
	N	Mean Index Score	N	Mean Index Score
Involving				
Control subjects	18	7.11[a]	18	7.57[b]
Regular condition	20	6.17	20	8.85
		8.48	20	9.69
Overheard condition	21			
Noninvolving				
Control subjects	18	7.20[b]	18	8.58[a]
Regular condition	20	8.47	20	8.17
Overheard condition	21	8.75	20	8.49

Involving: Married Women — $p = .01, t = 5.18$; Single Students — $p = .02, t = 2.45$
Noninvolving: Married Women — ns; Single Students — ns

[a] Husband issue.
[b] Dormitory issue.

pus" for dormitory students) there are large and significant differences in the persuasive effectiveness of the communication between the Regular and Overheard conditions. When the issue is not immediately involving, the differences between the Regular and Overheard conditions are negligible and not significant.

For the dormitory issue, the interaction between listening condition (Overheard or Regular) and degree of subjects' involvement was significant at $p < .05$ ($F = 5.44$, $df = 1/77$). The interaction was not significant for the "Husbands at home issue."

It is worth emphasizing at this point that the design used in this experiment is rather well controlled. The types of subjects and content of issues were chosen for the specific purpose of testing the suggestion from the first experiment and each subject is, in a sense, her own control. The same subjects who are more affected by the "overheard" conversation when the issue involves them actively are *not* more affected by the "overheard" communication when the issue does not involve them. The consistency of the results we have obtained warrants rather high confidence in the effect. The degree to which the results are consistent may be seen by looking simultaneously at the results of both experiments. We have presented these results graphically in Figure 22.1.

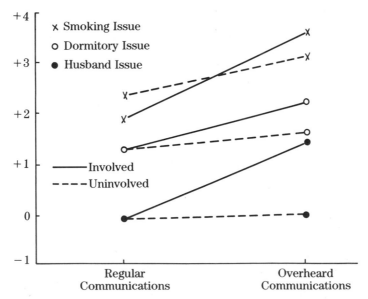

Figure 22.1 *Opinion change with "regular" and "overheard" communications.*

The data in Figure 22.1 are plotted, for all three issues used in the two experiments, in terms of presumed change of opinion as a result of hearing the persuasive communication. In other words, the data are plotted in terms of differences from the control groups who never heard the communication. The solid lines indicate data from subjects for whom the particular issue was an actively involving one. The dashed lines represent the data when the issue was not involving for the subjects. The consistency of the data is so immediately apparent in the figure that it hardly needs comment. We may certainly conclude that, at least when the position advocated by the persuasive communication is one which the involved subjects would like to accept, overheard communications are more effective for involved subjects and not particularly more effective for subjects not directly involved in the issue.

Discussion

There is clearly a problem involved in explaining these results. Let us say right now that we have no explanation to propose in any true sense of a theoretical explanation. There are, however, some specific directions into which one seems to be forced by the data, and these are worth discussing.

We will begin this discussion by examining what our results have to say about the three "plausible" factors which have been generally presumed to make overheard communications more effective. It will be recalled that we listed these and discussed them somewhat in the introduction to this article. We will examine them in relation to our data in turn.

1. Because of the accidental nature of the communication the listeners' defenses are not prepared. This factor, whether or not it is relevant to other situations, cannot conceivably account for our data. After all, we were not comparing a "direct attempt to influence" with an "overheard communication." Neither of our experimental conditions represented direct attempts to influence the subject. In neither case were they prepared for the communication. There is also another interesting point that should be made about the meaning of the term "defenses," a term widely used in discussing resistance to persuasive communications. If one does a study in which one attempts to persuade persons of something which they do not want to believe, it is intuitively plausible to think of the person defending himself. But in our study we were not doing this. Why would a smoker defend himself against the opinion that smoking is not harmful; why would a student living in a dormitory de-

fend herself against the opinion that, if she wanted to, she should be allowed to live off campus?

2. Because the listener is not supposed to hear it, an overheard communication is more powerful. This factor, at least as specified, also cannot account for our results. In the overheard conditions neither the subjects who were or who were not involved in the issue were "supposed to hear the communication." Nevertheless, we obtain a difference favoring the Overheard condition only when the issue is one which is involving for the subjects. One might argue that perhaps the psychological interest aroused by hearing something one is not intended to hear is greater if the content is immediately relevant. This, of course, is possible. But, if this is true, it would seem equally plausible that psychological interest would be heightened equally in the Regular condition if the content is immediately relevant. Consequently, it is difficult to see why this factor alone would make for a differential between our two conditions.

3. Because the speaker does not know the listener is there, the speaker cannot be seen as intending to influence the listener. This factor seems to be the one to which we are driven in our search for an explanation of our findings. It seems reasonable that if a speaker is seen as intending to influence one, then suspicions concerning possible ulterior motives may serve to nullify the possible effectiveness of the communication. But how does this apply to our data? Let us look at our experimental conditions and examine to what extent it would be possible, in any of them, to impute "intention to influence" to the speaker. First of all, let us dispose of the overheard conditions. Clearly, since the speaker does not know anyone is listening, it is not conceivable that the listener, knowing this, could imagine that the speaker intends to influence him. In the Regular condition, however, the situation is a little different. Here the speaker knows that someone is listening but does not know who. Since the listener in the Regular condition knows he has not been personally identified by the speaker, if the content of the communication is not personally relevant, it would also seem quite difficult to imagine that the speaker was intending to influence him. If, however, the content of the communication in the Regular condition is of direct personal relevance, then it is possible for the listener to feel that the speaker is, indeed, attempting to influence him and has ulterior motives.

If this is correct, then one comes to the conclusion that the difference between the two conditions for those who were involved in the issue exists because the effectiveness of the communication in the Regular condition was partially nullified by the possibility of imputing ulterior motives to the speaker. When this possibility is eliminated, as in the Overheard condition, those involved in the issue change more in the direction of the communication. This is, of course, to be expected since the communication urges them in a direction they would like to move.

There is, of course, still the interesting question, to which we have no answer, as to why, when the involved subjects hear a communication *which advocates a position they would like to accept,* they still tend to impute ulterior motives to the speaker when this is at all possible.

Clearly, these are suggestions for explanation and for further exploration rather than actual theoretical explanation of the findings. The results certainly indicate that the effectiveness of overheard communications is a more complicated matter than has been generally assumed. If imputation of ulterior motives to the speaker only comes into play, or comes primarily into play, when the content of the communication is personally involving, this may indeed account for the inconsistency of previous experimental results on this topic. And it may also be, of course, that if the communication urges the listeners in a direction in which they do not want to move, quite different results might be obtained.

Summary

Two experiments were conducted to assess the effectiveness of overheard communications:

1. When subjects touring an observation room "overheard" a persuasive communication, they changed their attitudes more than when they were told speakers knew they were listening. Quite unexpectedly, those subjects for whom the communication (smoking is not harmful) was especially relevant and involving (smokers) accounted almost entirely for the difference between the two conditions.

2. A second study was done to verify this finding. Two groups, married women and women in dormitories, were each given two communications, one concerning husbands and one dormitory living. It was expected that when the issue was an involving one for the group, the overheard communication would be especially effective. When the issue was not involving, the difference between the overheard and regular conditions was expected to be small. The results completely confirmed those expectations.

At the time of this article, Elaine Walster and Leon Festinger were at Stanford University.

They expressed their appreciation to the Ford Foundation for its support of this research.

References

ALLYN, J., & FESTINGER, L. The effectiveness of unanticipated persuasive communications. *J. abnorm. soc. Psychol.*, 1961, **62,** 35 – 40.

BERELSON, B. Communication and public opinion. In Berelson, B., & Janowitz, M. (eds.). *Reader in public opinion and communication.* Glencoe, Ill.: Free Press, 1950, p. 458.

EWING, T. A study of certain factors involved in changes of opinion. *J. soc. Psychol.*, 1942, **16,** 63 – 88.

HOVLAND, C. I., JANIS, I. L., & KELLEY, H. H. *Communication and persuasion.* New Haven: Yale Univer. Press, 1953.

HOVLAND, C. I., & MANDELL, W. An experimental comparison of conclusion drawing by the communicator and by the audience. *J. abnorm. soc. Psychol.*, 1952, **47,** 581 – 588.

KELMAN, H. C., & HOVLAND, C. I. "Reinstatement" of the communicator in delayed measurement of opinion change. *J. abnorm. soc. Psychol.*, 1953, **48,** 327 – 335.

23

On Resistance to Persuasive Communications

Three separate experiments were done at different universities to test the hypothesis that a persuasive communication that argues strongly against an opinion to which the audience is committed will be more effective if the audience is somewhat distracted from the communication so that they cannot adequately counterargue while listening. Two films were prepared, each containing the same communication arguing strongly against fraternities. One was a normal film of the speaker making a speech. The other film, with the same track, had an utterly irrelevant and highly distracting visual presentation. Fraternity men were more influenced by the distracting presentation of the persuasive communication than by the ordinary version. There was no difference between the 2 for nonfraternity men. In general, the hypothesis concerning the effect of distraction was supported.

Some time ago Allyn and Festinger (1961) reported an experiment which showed that if subjects were forewarned concerning the content of a communication arguing against an opinion they hold strongly, they

SOURCE: Festinger, L., & Maccoby, N. *J. abnorm. soc. Psychol.*, 1964, **68**, 359 – 366. [Received January 15, 1963]

tend to reject the speaker more and are influenced less than if they are not forewarned. Since the ideas which form the basis for the present article emerge in part from that experiment, it is necessary to examine it in some detail.

Allyn and Festinger, in their experiment, used high school students as subjects on the assumption that high school students, at or approaching the age at which they could obtain licenses to drive automobiles (age 16 in California), would be rather strongly committed to opinions that teen-agers were good and capable drivers. This assumption was, of course, largely correct. For the experiment a sizable number of these high school students were assembled in the high school auditorium where they heard a person, announced to them as an authority on the subject, deliver a speech denouncing teen-age drivers and arguing that the only thing to do was to keep teen-agers off the road for as long as possible. The subjects were then asked several questions to measure their opinions about driving by teen-agers.

Two conditions were run in this experiment. As each subject entered the auditorium, he was given a booklet. For half of the subjects, the cover page on this booklet told them that they were to hear a speech against teen-age driving and that they should listen carefully since they would be asked questions about the speaker's opinions. This was the "forewarned" condition. For the other half of the subjects, the cover page told them that they would hear a person make a speech (nothing about the content of the speech) and that they should listen carefully because, afterwards, they would be asked questions about the speaker's personality.

The results of the experiment showed that in the "forewarned" condition, the students were relatively uninfluenced by the speaker and rejected him more than in the "personality" condition where the speaker successfully influenced their attitudes. The authors of the experiment interpret this result as implying that, if persons who are rather committed to a given opinion are forewarned that their opinion will be attacked, they are better able to marshal their defenses and, hence, are more successful in rejecting the speaker and in resisting his persuasions.

At first glance, this seems like a plausible interpretation of the result and fits many common-sense conceptions such as "forewarned is forearmed" and the like. Further consideration of the matter, however, produces some concern about the adequacy of this interpretation. The difference between the "forewarned" and the "personality-orientation" conditions was created by what they read on the face sheet of the booklet. After having read this, the speech commenced. Virtually the first words out of the speaker's mouth were a vigorous denunciation of teenagers in automobiles. In other words, after the first few sentences of the speech, the personality-orientation subjects were *also* forewarned. Indeed, in terms of being forewarned, the only difference between conditions seems to have been a matter of when the forewarning took place, at the beginning of the speech or 2 to 3 minutes earlier. It does seem somewhat implausible for such a small time difference to have produced the result reported in the experiment.

But if we do not like the explanation offered by Allyn and Festinger, the problem is then created as to how one would, plausibly, explain the results they obtained. In order to arrive at such an explanation, let us first try to understand the cognitive behavior of a person who, strongly committed to an opinion, listens to a vigorous, persuasive communication that attacks that opinion. Certainly, such a listener is not passive. He does not sit there listening and absorbing what is said without any counteraction on his part. Indeed, it is most likely that under such circumstances, while he is listening to the persuasive communication, he is very actively, inside his own mind, counterarguing, derogating the points the communicator makes, and derogating the communicator himself. In other words, we can imagine that there is really an argument going on, one side being vocal and the other subvocal.

Let us imagine that one could somehow prevent the listener from arguing back while listening to the persuasive communication. If one created such a passive listener, it seems reasonable to expect that the persuasive communication would then have more of an impact. The listener, not able to counterargue, would be more influenced and would be less likely to reject the communication. And perhaps this is exactly what was really done in the experiment reported by Allyn and Festinger. The group that was not forewarned was also told to pay attention to the speaker's personality. In other words, a good deal of their attention was focused on a task which had little to do with the persuasive communication itself. It may be that, under such circumstances, they still listen to, and hear, the content of the speech that is being delivered but, with a good deal of their attention focused on something irrelevant, they are less able to counterargue while they are listening.

If this interpretation is correct, then the forewarning variable is irrelevant, at least in this particular experiment. The critical variable would be the extent to which the attention of the person was distracted from the persuasive communication while listening to it. If the attention of the listener were distracted sufficiently to make it quite difficult for him to counterargue, but not so much as to interfere with his hearing of the speech, this would represent a maximally effective influence situation.

How can we test the validity of this interpretation? The simplest procedure which suggested itself to us was to choose an issue such that we could easily identify a group of people strongly committed to a given position on that issue, devise a persuasive communication strongly attacking this committed position, and present this persuasive communication to these people under two different conditions, one where their attention was focused on the communication and one where they were distracted on a completely irrelevant basis. We decided to use attitudes toward college fraternities as the issue since fraternity members were likely to be strongly committed to a favorable opinion on this matter. We also decided to use as pure a form of distraction as we could think of so as to reduce the plausibility of alternative interpretations. We settled on a procedure whereby the subjects were visually distracted while listening to a speech.

Method

Experimental Materials and Procedure

A persuasive communication arguing strongly against college fraternities was prepared in the form of a color, 16-millimeter sound film. The film was about 12 minutes long. The first 2 minutes told the audience that this film was Part 4 of a series on university life, this part dealing with college fraternities. The visual showed various scenes of campus buildings and students walking on college campuses. These scenes then dissolved to a scene of a young college professor[1] who, after stating that he himself had been a member of a fraternity in college, proceeded to argue for almost 10 minutes that fraternities encouraged cheating and dishonesty, encouraged social snobbishness and racial discrimination, were antithetical to the purposes of a university and should be abolished. This film was used to present the persuasive communication to subjects in those experimental conditions in which the attention of the audience was to be focused on the communication.

A second film was prepared to present the same persuasive communication under distraction conditions. We chose to use, as the basic vehicle, an existing short color film *Day of the Painter* produced by Little

---

1. We wish to express our thanks to William McCord for preparing and delivering the persuasive communication in the film.

Movies, Incorporated, which had sound effects and music but no dialogue or narration and which was very amusing and rather absorbing to watch. This film was edited somewhat to shorten it to match the length of the other film. It opened with the identical titles and preliminary visuals used in the original film, and the identical sound track from the persuasive-communication film superimposed over it. Thus, this film for the distraction conditions of the experiment was identical visually for the first 2 minutes with the nondistracting film. Instead of the scene shifting to the young college professor making a speech, however, the visual of this distracting film dissolved to the amusing and absorbing short film. The sound tracks on the two films were identical throughout. In short, in the distraction conditions, the subjects heard the same persuasive communication while watching a completely irrelevant and highly interesting movie.

Experiments using these film materials were conducted at three different academic institutions: the University of Minnesota, San Jose State College, and the University of Southern California. In all three institutions the procedure employed was similar. Subjects were assigned at random to a particular room. In each room the subjects were given the identical verbal introduction which told them they were to see a film about fraternities, that the presentation was a rather unusual one, and that we would appreciate their paying close attention since we would want to ask them some questions about it later. In one room they were then shown the straight film version of the persuasive communication while in the other room the subjects saw the distracting version. Following the showing of the film, the subjects were asked to answer a number of questions designed to measure their attitudes toward fraternities and their perception of the expertness and fairness of the speaker. When the questionnaires had been completed and collected, the total procedure, its purposes and our hypotheses were explained in detail to all subjects.

After having prepared the film materials, our first step was to try them out on a preliminary basis with students at Stanford University. The results were very encouraging. We then ran the experiment at the University of Minnesota using two groups, fraternity men who saw the straight version and fraternity men who saw the distracting version of the film. The identical design was next used at San Jose State College. Finally we ran a more complete design at the University of Southern California which involved six conditions: Fraternity men and nonfraternity men, one-third of each seeing the straight version, one-third the distraction version, and one-third answering the questionnaire before seeing any film.

Results

We will present the data and discuss the results separately and in the sequence in which the experiments were actually conducted for the three different academic institutions.

University of Minnesota Experiment

At the University of Minnesota[2] 65 fraternity men participated in the experiment. Thirty-three of them saw the straight film version of the persuasive communication and 32 saw the distracting version. The questionnaire which they answered after having seen the film had six questions oriented toward measuring their attitude toward fraternities. These questions were:

1. In your opinion, what should be done with American college fraternities (5-point scale from "definitely should be abolished" to "their power in university life should be increased")?

2. On the whole, how do you feel about the ways in which fraternities influence university life (5-point scale from "excellent influence" to "very poor influence")?

3. How do you personally feel about fraternities (8-point scale from "dislike fraternities strongly" to "like fraternities very much")?

4. As far as you know, how do fraternity men's grades compare with comparable independent men's grades in most universities and colleges (5-point scale from "fraternity men do much better" to "independent men do much better")?

5. How do you feel about the nature of the contribution to American college life that fraternities make (4-point scale from "fraternities contribute nothing" to "fraternities contribute considerably")?

6. What effect, if any, do fraternities have on those students who are not chosen by them (4-point scale from "very harmful effect" to "no harmful effect")?

All answers to these questions were scored so that the larger number represented a more favorable attitude toward fraternities. The maximum profraternity score possible was 31. The more influenced they were by the persuasive communication, the lower should their score be.

2. We would like to thank Ben Willerman and Elliot Aronson for their help and cooperation in arranging for the conduct of the experiment at the University of Minnesota.

The questionnaire also contained two questions to obtain a measure of the extent to which they rejected the speaker. These questions were:

1. In your opinion, how well qualified to discuss fraternities was the lecturer in this film (3-point scale from "very well qualified" to "not well qualified")?

2. In your opinion, how fair was the presentation about fraternities (4-point scale from "quite fair" to "quite biased")?

These two questions were summed to provide a rejection measure. Maximum rejection of the speaker would be represented by a score of 7.

Table 23.1 presents the data on attitude toward fraternities and rejection of the speaker for each of the two conditions at the University of Minnesota. It is clear from the table that the differences between conditions were negligible. The slight difference that does exist is in the direction of having been more influenced in the distraction condition and rejecting the speaker less in that condition, but the difference is disappointingly small.

One reason for continuing our investigation was an explanation offered by those familiar with the situation at the University of Minnesota for the failure to obtain any difference. It was suggested that the fraternity system at Minnesota is very weak and, for many years now, has been under constant attack and pressure from the University. It was suggested that the fraternity men at the University of Minnesota have already heard all the antifraternity arguments many, many times and, consequently, their counterarguments are all formed and ready. Hence, distraction may not have had the effect which we anticipated.

True or not, we proceeded to do our experiment again, this time in an institution where the fraternity system was strong and prestigeful and was *not* under attack and pressure.

Table 23.1 Average Ratings for Fraternity Men at University of Minnesota

Condition	Attitude Toward Fraternities	Rejection of Speaker
Ordinary (N = 33)	26.2	6.0
Distraction (N = 32)	26.0	5.8

San Jose State College Experiment

At San Jose State College[3] 99 fraternity men participated in the experiment. Fifty-one of them saw the straight film version and 48 saw the distracting version of the persuasive communication. The procedure and the questionnaire were identical in all respects to the experiment done at the University of Minnesota. Table 23.2 presents the data collected at San Jose.

An examination of the data in Table 23.2 shows that they clearly support our theoretical expectations. The subjects who heard the persuasive communication under distracting conditions are significantly less favorable to fraternities ($t = 3.63$, $p < .01$) and reject the speaker less ($t = 2.80$, $p < .01$).

These results are, of course, consistent with the notion that, if distracted while listening to the persuasive communication, the subject is less able to counterargue against the communication and against the speaker. As a result, under these circumstances he is less likely to reject the speaker and is more influenced by the communication than subjects who focused all their attention on the persuasive communication. However, this interpretation of the data is not quite unambiguous in the absence of a control group. It is quite conceivable, for example, that the ordinary presentation of the persuasive communication aroused so much resentment and anger in the fraternity men who were listening that a boomerang effect could have ensued. That is, in the ordinary condition they may have moved away from the position advocated by the speaker. For our interpretation to be strongly supported, it would be well to show that the distraction presentation results in effective influence which is not only significantly greater than the ordinary presentation

Table 23.2   Average Ratings for Fraternity Men at San Jose State College

Condition	Attitude Toward Fraternities	Rejection of Speaker
Ordinary (N = 51)	25.7	6.0
Distraction (N = 48)	24.0	5.5

3. We would like to thank Robert Martin, Dean, for his help and cooperation in arranging for the conduct of the experiment at San Jose State College.

condition but also represents significant change from a control group whose attitudes were measured before seeing any film. We thus decided to repeat the experiment once more using a more complete experimental design.

University of Southern California Experiment

The University of Southern California[4] was selected as the site for the experiment because, among other things, the fraternity system there was important on the campus, fraternities were prestigeful and had not been too much under attack in recent years. In short, we attempted to select a situation which would be comparable to San Jose State College rather than like the University of Minnesota.

The plan at the University of Southern California was to have three conditions: those who saw the straight presentation, those who saw the distracting version, and those who saw no film at all—these latter constituting a control group to give us an indication of attitudes prior to exposure to the persuasive communication. We also decided to do the experiment here using both fraternity and nonfraternity men in order to provide further clarification of the theoretical interpretation of the results. It will be recalled that the idea behind the experiment was that people will actively counterargue while listening to a persuasive communication which attacks an opinion to which they are committed. The distraction condition is intended to interfere with this activity of counterarguing while listening. If this is the correct interpretation, one should find that the distracting presentation is indeed more effective in influencing fraternity men but one should not find it any more effective in influencing nonfraternity men. After all, many, if not most, of the nonfraternity men will already tend to agree with the speaker and, although their opinions may not be as extreme as those represented in the persuasive communication, there is little reason to expect nonfraternity men to be motivated to counterargue while listening. Thus, the distraction version of the film should not provide any advantage in effectiveness over the straight version.

The experiment was carried out as planned with 179 fraternity men and 114 independents. In order to have the two samples as comparable as possible, the samples were restricted to sophomores, juniors, and seniors, since relatively few freshmen already belong to fraternities. Subjects were randomly assigned to one of three rooms, fraternity and

4. We wish to thank James Finn, Harold Gluth, Robert Heinick, Francis Joyce, and Bernard Kanter at the University of Southern California.

nonfraternity men being mixed in each room. In one room, after the same introduction as in the previous studies, they saw the straight version of the persuasive communication; in another they saw the distracting version; and in the third room they were asked to answer the questionnaire before seeing the film.

The questionnaire was changed somewhat for this experiment. Questions 1 and 2 were extended to 6-point scales; Question 3 was contracted to a 7-point scale; Questions 5 and 6 were omitted and in their place they were asked to indicate on a 7-point scale their "overall reaction to college fraternities"; Question 4 on the original questionnaire was retained unchanged. The two questions measuring rejection of the speaker had the scales extended to 5- and 6-point scales in place of the original 3- and 4-point scales. Thus, on this revised questionnaire, the maximum profraternity attitude would be represented again by a score of 31. Maximum rejection of the speaker and the communication would be represented by a score of 11. Table 23.3 presents the results of the experiment at the University of Southern California.

Let us first examine the data from the fraternity men to see how they compare with the data collected at San Jose. It is clear that, once more, the distracting persuasive communication has resulted in a less favorable attitude toward fraternities and less rejection of the speaker than the ordinary, nondistracting version. Although the differences are not quite as significant as they were at San Jose, they are quite adequate considering the fact of replication. The difference between the two experimental conditions on attitude toward fraternities is significant at the 6% level ($t = 1.88$), and the difference in rejection of the speaker is significant at

Table 23.3   **Averages for Fraternity Men and Independents at the University of Southern California**

Condition	Fraternity Men		Independents	
	Attitude to Fraternities	Rejection of Speaker	Attitude to Fraternities	Rejection of Speaker
Control	24.8	—	17.4	—
	($N = 59$)		($N = 37$)	
Ordinary film version	24.6	8.6	16.3	7.4
	($N = 59$)		($N = 34$)	
Distracting film	23.5	8.0	16.1	7.5
	($N = 61$)		($N = 43$)	

the 5% level ($t = 1.97$). In other words, we have replicated and confirmed the San Jose result.

It is also clear in Table 23.3 that the straight film version does not produce a boomerang effect. Rather, it produces virtually no effect at all. The difference between the control condition and the ordinary film version is negligible. On the other hand, those who saw the distracting version of the persuasive communication have indeed been influenced significantly ($t = 1.94$).

Let us now turn our attention to the results on the nonfraternity men. First of all, it is clear and not surprising that there is a huge initial difference between their attitude toward fraternities and the attitudes of fraternity men. In other words, the independents do agree more initially with the speaker in the film and should not be expected to counterargue while listening. And, indeed, it may be seen that there are only negligible differences either in attitude toward fraternities or in rejection of the speaker between those who saw the ordinary version and those who saw the distracting version of the persuasive communication. Both of these conditions seem to have been somewhat influenced although the differences from the control condition are not significant ($t = 1.17$ and $t = 1.08$).

Relation Between the Attitude and Rejection Measures

It is of interest to examine the relation which exists between attitude toward fraternities after seeing the persuasive-communication film and the extent to which the speaker is rejected. It is generally accepted that the extent to which a person is influenced by a persuasive communication is related to the extent to which he accepts the speaker as trustworthy, expert, unbiased, and the like. There is, for example, a fair amount of research which shows that if the source of a communication is regarded as untrustworthy, the communication is less effective in influencing people. And in the data we have presented above, we also find that in the distraction condition, where we find more effective influence, we also find less rejection of the speaker.

In terms of the reaction of one individual to a persuasive communication, however, the direction of the empirical relation we would expect is less clear. On the one hand, we would still expect that if a person, listening to a persuasive communication, succeeds in utterly derogating and rejecting the communicator and his arguments, he would not have been influenced. On the other hand, since changing one's opinion and derogating the communicator are both modes of coping with the impact of the persuasive communication, one might expect that a person on whom the communication has a strong impact might do both of them to some extent rather than one to the exclusion of the other. Thus, if within any experimental condition one correlated the amount of change of opinion with the amount of rejection of the speaker, the size and direction of the correlation would depend on whether or not these two reactions were alternate forms of coping with the situation or whether they were both simultaneously available to the same person.

The data from our three experiments are rather interesting in this respect. Table 23.4 presents the correlations between attitude toward fraternities and rejection of the speaker for fraternity men in each of our two conditions in the three universities. It will be recalled that a larger number indicated greater profraternity sentiment and indicated greater rejection of the speaker. Hence, a positive correlation between these two variables indicates that the less the person was influenced by the persuasive communication, the more he rejects the speaker.

An examination of the figures in the table makes it clear that there is a consistent difference in the magnitude of the correlations between the two conditions. While all of the correlations are positive, none of them is significantly different from zero for those subjects who saw the ordinary, straight version of the film and had their attention focused on the persuasive communication. On the other hand, all of the correlations for those subjects who saw the distracting film are significantly different from zero at the 5% level or better. While none of the differences between the correlations is significant for any one of the experiments, the consistency of the result lends considerable weight to the conclusion that they are different.

We did not anticipate this finding and we must regard it as tentative but suggestive. It may be that in the distraction condition, not being

Table 23.4   Correlations Between Attitude and Rejection of Speaker for Fraternity Men

Academic Institution	Experimental Condition	
	Ordinary Film	Distracting Film
University of Minnesota	+.04	+.36
San Jose State College	+.18	+.37
University of Southern California	+.16	+.39

able to effectively counterargue, subjects are influenced by the communication unless they are able to derogate and reject the speaker. In the condition where they are able to counterargue, the result suggests that they are able to resist influence by other means even if they do not reject the speaker. If this tentative interpretation of the magnitudes of these correlations is correct, one could perhaps summarize it by saying that, to the extent one does not counterargue while listening to a persuasive communication, there will be a positive correlation between rejecting the speaker and being able to resist influence. Such a hypothesis would, of course, suggest that one should also find such positive correlations for the nonfraternity men in the experiment at the University of Southern California. After all, there is little reason for the nonfraternity men to be motivated to counterargue even when seeing the straight, ordinary version of the film. The correlation between attitude and rejection for the independents who saw the ordinary version is, indeed, + .45, a significant correlation. Things are not, however, as clear-cut as one might like to have them. The comparable correlation for the independents who saw the distracting film is − .02, certainly not consistent with what we might expect from our tentative hypothesis. Perhaps the distracting film introduces other variables for the independent men who would not counterargue anyhow, or perhaps our suggested hypothesis to account for the correlations is not quite correct. We will leave it at this, a suggestion which may be worthwhile to explore more adequately in the future.

Possible Alternative Interpretations

An experiment can never rule out all possible alternative explanations of the findings and, perhaps, the best support for one particular interpretation is to say that the experiment was designed with that interpretation in mind and, indeed, it came out as predicted. Nevertheless, it is useful to look briefly at the plausibility of some other explanations. Two such possible explanations readily come to mind and we will examine them each.

1. It is conceivable that the so-called "distracting" version of the communication was actually not distracting. In fact, it may have produced the reverse effect, namely, because of the attempt to distract, the subjects may have concentrated harder on listening to the speech. If this did occur, it could explain the results for the fraternity men—the more closely they listened, the more they were influenced. There are two sources of data relevant to this possible explanation. In the experiment done at the University of Southern California the questionnaire con-

tained one page on which the subjects were asked to "list the main criticisms of fraternities which the speaker made." If the greater influence among fraternity men in the distracting condition was due to *more* careful attention on their part to the verbal content, we might expect this to reveal itself on this question. Analysis of the answers to this question, however, reveals no superior retention of arguments for those viewing the distracting film. In fact, the mean number of arguments repeated by those viewing the ordinary version was slightly higher (3.9) than for those exposed to the distracting version (3.7).

Another relevant source of data comes from comments written by subjects in a space provided for "general comments." The following are some rather typical comments obtained from subjects who had seen the distracting version of the persuasive communication:

> The presentation was interesting because, although I had already seen that film, and was interested in the monologue which was against something I am in favor of, I would still find myself watching the film instead of listening fully.

> It was extremely difficult to pay close attention to both the audio and visual parts of of the film. It would seem that attention would be determined by whether you wanted to defend fraternities or enjoy the visual part.

> I could see only a slight correlation between the acting and the commentary. Trying to understand the action detracted from the commentary.

> I could not see any tie in between what was being said and what was being shown. It was very hard to concentrate on what was being said without completely looking away from the movie.

There seems to be little question but that the distracting film was really distracting.

2. It is possible that the effect obtained for the fraternity men is simply the result of reward and reinforcement. The visual portion of the distracting film was a highly amusing thing and, consequently, those in the distracting condition heard the message while they were being rewarded or entertained and, hence, were more influenced. It is difficult, of course, to marshal data relevant to such a possible explanation. There are two things which can be said, however, to indicate a lack of plausibility. No spontaneous comments were obtained which indicated that they actually enjoyed the film. Comments that dealt with the issue almost always indicated some irritation with the difficulty of both watching and listening. This is clear to anyone who has seen the film used in the

distracting condition. The visual portion commands attention but the experience is not as entertaining as it would have been with its original sound track. The other point that can be made in reference to this possible interpretation is that, if it is true, it is difficult to understand why the independents at the University of Southern California do not respond in the same way to the same reinforcing mechanism. It seems difficult to believe that the distracting film would be reinforcing for fraternity men but not for independents.

We, ourselves, have not been able to think of other possible explanations which even superficially promise plausibility. For example, the experience of those subjects who see the distracting film must certainly constitute an unusual, and rather strange experience for them. There does not seem to be, however, any plausible reason for assuming that simply the unusual and strange would be more effective in influencing people in this context. The data strongly suggest that our own explanation has validity.

Leon Festinger and Nathan Maccoby were at Stanford University when this article was written.

The studies reported in this paper were supported by funds from Grant G-11255 from the National Science Foundation to Leon Festinger and by funds from Stanford University Institute for Communication Research to Nathan Maccoby.

The authors expressed their thanks and appreciation to Ernest W. Rose and Henry Breitrose for their help in planning the experiments, devising and preparing the experimental materials, and in conducting the actual experiments.

References

ALLYN, J., & FESTINGER, L. The effectiveness of unanticipated persuasive communications. *J. abnorm. soc. Psychol.*, 1961, **62**, 35 – 40.

24

Laboratory
Experiments

Empirical science in general has as its major objective the understanding or control of phenomena as they occur in the real world. Nevertheless, laboratory experimentation generally plays a significant part in the development of a science. It is important to have some understanding of why this should be true and of the exact function which laboratory experimentation should have in relation to the science as a whole.

We shall, consequently, attempt to clarify two aspects of laboratory experimentation—namely, what a laboratory experiment is and how the results of such experiments can be applied to the "real world." It would be relatively easy to discuss the role of laboratory experimentation by means of examples from the physical sciences, but we shall attempt, rather, to illustrate the points to be made by examples from the problem area of social psychology. Although by doing this we may not be able to make our point as clearly as would otherwise be the case, we hope that the discussion will be more meaningful and carry more weight if it is entirely oriented toward the field which is now under consideration.

The Nature of Laboratory Experimentation

What Constitutes a Laboratory Experiment in Social Psychology?

A laboratory experiment may be defined as one in which the investigator creates a situation with the exact conditions he wants to have and in which he controls some, and manipulates other, variables. He is then

SOURCE: Festinger, L. In Festinger, L., & Katz, D. (eds.). *Research methods in the behavioral sciences.* New York: Dryden, 1953.

able to observe and measure the effect of the manipulation of the independent variables on the dependent variables in a situation in which the operation of other relevant factors is held to a minimum. Such a definition is, however, a great over-simplification. Given the techniques of experimentation today available, an investigator can at best achieve only a rough approximation of the degree of precision implied by the definition. As better techniques are developed, more control over laboratory experiments will, of course, be possible. At present, however, we must include under the term "laboratory experiment" a wide range of studies with varying degrees of control and precision.

We shall attempt, largely by means of examples, to distinguish between what might properly be called "field experiments" and "laboratory experiments." In many cases, of course, the distinction is clear and easy to make; in other cases it is difficult to maintain. In general, we shall be guided by the two parts of our definition: whether or not there was an attempt to create a specially suited situation, and the degree of precision in the control and manipulation of variables.

It would seem clear that experiments in industry such as have been described in the preceding chapter should not be called laboratory experiments. There is little or no attempt to set up special conditions. Typically, the situation is accepted as it is found and some manipulation is imposed. The manipulation of the independent variable is usually a simultaneous manipulation of a set of factors. The degree of control obtained in these experiments is usually not sufficient to guarantee that the effects observed are unequivocally related to the manipulation of the independent variable.

Let us compare such field experiments with the Lewin, Lippitt, and White study (21) on autocratic and democratic atmospheres. This was a relatively early experiment in social psychology and is perhaps close to the boundary between laboratory and field experiments. In this study a number of boys' clubs were set up for the express purpose of performing the experiment. There was no real-life situation which was taken as given. Rather, a special set of circumstances was created because it was felt that the situation thus achieved would be an appropriate one for the study of the variables in which the experimenters were interested. In this sense it should properly be called a laboratory experiment, although its precision is perhaps not very much greater than the precision of an experiment in industry, such as the one reported by Coch and French (7).

In the Lewin, Lippitt, and White experiment, the manipulation of the independent variables consisted in having one leader of a boys' club behave in a certain prescribed manner as compared to another leader of another club who behaved quite differently. These two sets of behavior, which produced measurable differences in the behavior of the club members, were complex and differed in many dimensions. The experimenters were undoubtedly not clear about all aspects of the differences created. Thus, rather than isolating and precisely manipulating a single variable or small set of variables, the experimenters attempted a large and complex manipulation. There was also little attempt at control in setting up the clubs. In terms of the control achieved and the degree of refinement in manipulation of the independent variables, this study is probably indistinguishable from most field experiments.

We shall now consider, as an example of a laboratory experiment with a relatively high degree of control and precision, an experiment by Festinger (10) on voting behavior. In this experiment an attempt was made to vary a single factor—namely, whether or not the subjects knew the religious affiliation of the other members of the group. Groups were set up for the express purpose of the experiment, with care taken to ensure that every member of the group was initially a stranger to every other member. Exactly comparable conditions were created for each group. The nominees for whom subjects voted were always paid participants whose behavior was standardized. These same paid participants identified themselves as having different religions in the different experimental groups, thus controlling for a wide variety of personality factors and first impressions.

In such an experiment, we can be more certain than we can in a field experiment that the results obtained are due directly to the variable manipulated by the experimenter. It is probable that a variable such as "whether or not the subjects know the religious affiliation of the other members" is still not a fine or precise factor; it is probably, once more, a cluster of factors. A laboratory experiment should, however, attempt to refine the manipulations as much as the present state of knowledge permits. One of the marks of progress in a science is the extent to which such laboratory manipulation can be refined and specified.

There is frequently a tendency in social psychology to criticize laboratory experiments because of their "artificiality." A word must be said about this criticism, because it probably stems from an inaccurate understanding of the purposes of a laboratory experiment. A laboratory experiment need not, and should not, be an attempt to duplicate a real-life situation. If one wanted to study something in a real-life situation, it would be rather foolish to go to the trouble of setting up a laboratory experiment duplicating the real-life condition. Why not simply go directly to the real-life situation and study it? The laboratory experiment should be an attempt to create a situation in which the operation of variables will be clearly seen under special identified and defined conditions. It matters not whether such a situation would ever be encountered in real life. In most laboratory experiments such a situation would certainly *never* be encountered in real life. In the laboratory, however, we can find out exactly hòw a certain variable affects behavior or attitudes under special, or "pure," conditions.

This is certainly not the end of the task. One must also find out how these variables interact with other variables. The possibility of application to a real-life situation arises when one knows enough about these relationships to be able to make predictions concerning a real-life situation after measurement and diagnosis of the state of affairs there.

The Relationship Between Laboratory Experimentation and the Study of Real-Life Situations

In the conducting of research, there should be an active interrelation between laboratory experimentation and the study of real-life situations. It is relatively rare in social psychology that hypotheses, hunches, and recognition of important variables emerge initially from the laboratory; most often they arise in either the formal or the informal study of real-life situations. In studying real-life situations, we are forced to deal with the factors and variables as they exist in all their complexity. Because of this complexity and lack of control, it is rather rare that definitive conclusions and unequivocal interpretations are reached in such studies, but frequently new variables and new hypotheses are brought to our attention. One can take these suggestions, hypotheses, and hunches and use laboratory experimentation to verify, elaborate, and make more secure the theoretical basis for the empirical results which have been obtained.

In the laboratory experiment, sufficient control can be achieved to obtain definitive answers, and systematic variation of different factors is possible. As a result of this greater control, precision, and manipulability, conclusive answers can be obtained and relatively precise and subtle theoretical points can be tested. For example, in a study of the spread of a rumor in a community (11), it was found that the more friends people had, the more likely they were to have heard the rumor. This finding may suggest the hypothesis that friendship reduces restraints against communication of various types of content; or it may suggest the hypothesis that the existence of a friendship makes for an active pressure to communicate; or it may suggest the hypothesis that those who have more friends see more people and spend more time with these people and consequently are more likely to have an opportunity to hear the rumor. In a laboratory experiment it would be possible to set up a situation in which one could, with a high degree of rigor, collect data which would enable one to choose among these possible interpretations. One could, for example, form groups of strangers and friends mixed together in which the amount of contact among members and the opportunity for communication among them were experimentally held constant. The results would enable one to say whether the effect of friendship existed in the absence of differential amounts of contact. It would enable one to accept or reject the third hypothesis stated above. In other groups one could experimentally vary the accessibility of other members for communication to obtain evidence as to whether the friendship represented a decrement in restraint against communication or whether there were actual pressures to communicate in the specific direction of friends.

Such an experiment would undoubtedly be difficult to set up, but, since the major body of this chapter will be devoted to the discussion of how to perform such experiments and how to produce the desired conditions, we shall not, at the moment, go into the details of how it might be done. Let it suffice now to say that in the laboratory, by setting up an artificial situation, we should be able to verify, elaborate, and refine our knowledge so as to increase our understanding of important processes in social life. It should be stressed again, however, that the problem of application of the results of such laboratory experiments to the real-life situation is not solved by a simple extension of the result. Such application requires additional experimentation and study. It is undoubtedly important that the results of laboratory experiments be tested out in real-life situations. Unless this is done the danger of "running dry" or "hitting a dead end" is always present. A continuous interplay between laboratory experiments and studies of real-life situations should provide proper perspective, for the results obtained should continually supply new hypotheses for building the theoretical structure and should represent progress in the solution of the problems of application and generalization.

Difficulties of Performing Laboratory Experiments

Laboratory experiments, however, do not represent an easy road to the collection of data for the resolution of theoretical problems. In social psychology they are typically difficult to do, and many dangers are present in their execution. It is extremely difficult to create in the laboratory forces strong enough for results to be measurable. In the most excellently done laboratory experiment, the strength to which different variables can be produced is extremely weak compared to the strength with which these variables exist and operate in real-life situations. One is able to obtain results and to see clearly how these variables operate, in spite of this weakness, because of the increased control one has in the laboratory situation. But it is always possible, even probable, that the factors will be so weak that no differences between conditions experimentally created are apparent in spite of the increased control. Thus, in the setting up of a laboratory experiment, especial care must be taken to make the variables as strong as one possibly can. Unfortunately, one can determine whether or not one has succeeded only after the experiment is over. An exception to this generalization about the weakness of laboratory manipulation can be seen in Asch's use of the announced perceptions of group members (2). This involved, however, the use of seven confederates for a single experimental subject.

Related to the problem of the strength of forces in the laboratory situation is the difficulty of manipulating several variables simultaneously. In the complex field of research with which we are here concerned, it is frequently theoretically important to see the effect of the simultaneous operation of two or more variables. Unfortunately, however, the more variables the experimenter attempts to manipulate, the lower will be the strength of each variable. This is especially true if the manipulation of the variable is to be done by means of verbal instructions to the subjects. The result of this is, at least at the present stage of technical development, that the number of variables which it is possible to manipulate simultaneously in the laboratory is relatively restricted. This will undoubtedly become less true as more powerful techniques of manipulating variables in the laboratory are developed.

These difficulties have an important implication for the conclusions one can draw from the results of laboratory experiments. As in any study, it is possible that the experimenter is dealing with entirely irrelevant variables—that is, there may actually be no relationship among the variables that are being studied. Such a condition would result in negative results—that is, no differences between experimental and control groups. However, we should also find a lack of differences between experimental and control conditions if our experimental manipulations were not sufficiently strong to reveal measurable differences even though such differences really exist. Thus, negative results from a laboratory experiment can mean very little indeed. If we obtain positive results—that is, demonstrably significant differences among conditions—we can be relatively certain concerning our interpretation and conclusion from the experiment. If, however, no differences emerge, we can generally reach no definitive conclusion unless we are quite certain that the manipulation of variables in the experiment was done successfully and adequately. At the present stage of technical development, it is seldom that we can be certain, in the absence of positive results, that our manipulations were adequate. Undoubtedly, as more and more experiments are done, good evidence will become available for believing that a certain manipulation is an adequate one, and then negative results can be interpreted as demonstrating no relationship. At the present time, however, it is all too easy to set up a laboratory experiment which, because of the ineffective manipulation of variables, will show no differences among conditions. It should be stressed again that, at the present stage of technical development, negative results perhaps reveal only the fact that the experiment was not set up carefully and that the experimenter's attempted manipulation of the variables was ineffective.

Keeping in mind these difficulties and the relationship which must exist between laboratory and field investigation, we shall now proceed to a more detailed examination of how laboratory experiments can be performed.

The Design of Laboratory Experiments

The first and foremost requirement for a successful laboratory experiment is that the problem be stated in experimental terms. This means, essentially, that there must be a high degree of specificity and clarity in the statement of the problem and in the definition of the variables involved. The foregoing implies that before one can successfully do a laboratory experiment, one must already know quite a bit about the phenomena one is investigating.

The process of specifying and clarifying the statement of a problem so that it is amenable to experimental treatment is by no means a simple or easy one. Let us take an example to illustrate the kinds of problems which confront the experimenter at this stage. In a field study of transmission of a rumor in an organization (4), it was observed that communication tended to be directed upward in the organizational hierarchy. This result was explained as depending upon forces acting on members to move upward in the organization; i.e., the upward communication represented substitute movement on the part of the members.

Kelley (19) set out to perform a laboratory experiment to test this hypothesis more thoroughly. At this point the statement of his problem might have been "What direction does communication tend to take in a structured hierarchy?" This statement, however, is still much too general and vague for the purposes of an experiment. An attempt to think in terms of setting up an experiment makes it immediately clear that one must answer questions such as "What exactly is a hierarchy?" and "Exactly what kinds of communication are we talking about?" There are many aspects to what is customarily thought of as a hierarchical structure. Do superior levels in the hierarchy have power over subordinate levels and, if so, what kinds of power? Is each successive level upward in the hierarchy characterized by increased attractiveness of the work, or increased freedom of choice of what work to do, or increased importance of the work? For the purpose of setting up a laboratory experiment, the theory involved and the definition of hierarchy must be made more specific. Kelley chose to establish a hierarchy in the laboratory on the basis of the perceived importance of the job to the subjects, holding the actual attractiveness of the job and the exact work that was done constant for both levels in the hierarchy.

Let us now consider the question of what kind of communication would be expected to go upward in such a hierarchy. It was clear that a distinction had to be made between work-oriented communication, communication of criticism, communication of information, and communication which was irrelevant to the task. It was largely in the last category of communication content that the effect of substitute movement would be expected to appear. Consequently, the experiment was set up to allow and, in fact, to encourage communication of irrelevant content. The final problem in Kelley's experiment was phrased as "What is the direction of irrelevant communication content in a hierarchy based upon perceived differential importance of the task?" This statement was specific enough to permit the design of the actual experiment. This process of clarifying the objectives of the experiment takes considerable time, although it may not take long to describe after it has once been done.

The difficulties of designing a laboratory experiment are by no means overcome when the problem has been specifically defined. There remain the major tasks of inventing measurement devices and techniques for manipulation of variables which will clearly measure and manipulate the variables which have been defined in the statement of the problem. No matter how specifically and clearly the concepts are defined in the statement of the problem, the laboratory experiment cannot be successful unless the measurement and the manipulation of variables actually relate to these defined concepts.

Thus, for example, in the Kelley (19) experiment mentioned above, it was necessary to develop techniques for producing a hierarchy as defined, while other variables, such as the type of work done, power, and attractiveness, would be controlled. The situation created had to be one in which irrelevant communication would occur. Adequate techniques for measuring the amount and direction of communication had to be developed. In the experiment, a two-level hierarchy was established. Each level did exactly the same kind of work, although each was under the impression that the other level was doing something different. High and low hierarchic perceptions were encouraged by the instructions to the subjects: one subgroup was told that its own job was the important one; the other subgroup was told that the job of the other level was the more important. Communication of irrelevant material was encouraged by having all communication carried on in writing and by injecting into the communication stream prepared fictitious notes which were irrelevant in their content, thus encouraging subjects to do such writing themselves. All notes were collected and kept, and thus analysis of the content of the communication, its direction, and amount was possible.

It is rarely safe to assume beforehand that the operations used to manipulate variables will be successful and will tie in directly with the concept the experimenter has in mind. It is a worth-while precaution to check on the success of the experimental manipulations. In the experiment by Kelley, the subjects were asked a number of questions after the session was over to determine whether or not the manipulation of status in the hierarchy had been successful. It was found that, in terms of their reported perception of status and their desire to be in the other role, the manipulation had created a difference between two levels. This difference was a relatively small one, however. Small differences in the results could be directly attributed to the small difference in perceived status. When the difference in perceived status was made larger by selecting out those subjects for whom the experimental manipulations were clearly successful, the results become much clearer and more conclusive. If there had been no check on the success of the experimental manipulation, such analysis would have been impossible. It would also have been impossible to attribute unequivocally the inconclusiveness in the results to the relative inadequacy of the experimental manipulation.

The problem of the adequacy of the manipulation of variables may be dealt with in part by preliminary studies. In almost any laboratory experiment, the initial design will have certain inadequacies which will become clear after a few trial experiments. Such preliminary runs are also important to provide practice for the investigator so that his behavior and his instructions become standardized by the time the regular experiments start.

The Execution of Laboratory Experiments

Techniques of measurement, manipulation, or control of variables can be introduced at almost any stage in the process of a laboratory experiment. We shall attempt, in the following pages, to cover in detail most of the techniques which have been used fruitfully and to give examples of their successful use.

Decisions About Subjects for the Experiment

Decisions about the kinds of persons to be used as subjects, how they are to be recruited, and what they are to be led to expect before they come to the experiment provide important opportunities for the manipulation of variables.

Controlling the Composition of the Group

It is possible to arrange the composition of the group so as to control the number of friends in each group or to select subjects to ensure that all of the members of a group are strangers to one another at the beginning of the experiment. The decision concerning the composition of the group depends, of course, upon the purpose of the experiment and on the variables upon which the experimenter desires to focus his investigation. We shall give some examples of the introduction of an experimental control or manipulation at this stage of the procedure.

The experiment by Festinger (10) previously referred to had as its objective the determination of whether knowledge of religious affiliation in a mixed Catholic-Jewish group would affect the attitudes of members toward one another. It was assumed that these attitudes would be reflected by their votes in elections for officers of a club. It was decided to have groups meet in the laboratory and elect officers of a club into which they formed themselves. Half of the elections were to take place while no one in the group knew the religious affiliation of any one else; the other half of the elections were to take place after the religious affiliation of each member was publicly announced. It was obviously essential, for this procedure to be successful, that none of the six members of any group know one another. Contact was made with nine colleges in the Boston area and permission to recruit volunteers in each college was obtained. Experimental sessions were then scheduled so that in each group only one person from any one college was present. Thus, when the group met, the six members each came from a different college in the area and the chances of their knowing each other were quite low. In spite of all these precautions, however, one out of 13 groups had to be eliminated because two of the members did know each other, having gone to high school together. In the other 12 groups, all the members were complete strangers to one another.

Schachter (26), in an experiment designed to investigate the relationships between difference of opinion and rejection, also wanted his groups composed of strangers to minimize the effects of past history, such as established preferences or aversions, among members. Having strangers was important because he was particularly concerned with the effect of the experimental condition upon acceptance and rejection. He recruited volunteers from courses which were divided into small recitation sections. By scheduling, in any one group, only one person from any one recitation section, he was fairly successful in eliminating acquaintanceship.

In both the examples above, having strangers compose the group was a technique used to exercise additional control over the experimental situation. In experiments on the effects of discussion on opinions about matters of fact, Jenness (18) controlled the range of difference of opinion in the group by the assignment of subjects to given groups on the basis of their original estimates of the facts in question. French (16), in an experiment on the effects of frustration and fear, used the composition of the group as a means of manipulating a variable. He was concerned with the differential effects of frustration and fear upon organized and unorganized groups. For his unorganized groups he used subjects recruited at Harvard University who met together as a group for the first time in his laboratory. For his organized groups he used club members who had a long history of working together and engaging in activities as a group. The members of each organized group came to the laboratory together. This type of manipulation is, of course, a gross one, since an organized group is different in many ways from an unorganized one. The same type of manipulation of the composition of a group can, however, be used in any number of ways to produce fine or gross differences among conditions. Some of the earliest experiments with groups, for example, employed as their major variable the presence of absence of other persons (1). Whether the person worked alone or in a group of people or before an audience was found to affect his performance (8).

Duration of the Group's Existence

Before recruiting subjects, it is necessary to decide whether the experiment will be conducted in one meeting or whether the group will be required to continue for several sessions. Each of these procedures has advantages and disadvantages. If the experiment is to be performed in only one meeting, it is generally easier to obtain volunteers. If the experimenter is restricted to one session, however, it may be more difficult to manipulate variables adequately. On the other hand, if the experimenter plans on more than one meeting per group, he must expect that a certain percentage of subjects will not return after the first meeting.

Designs which require the group to meet several times encounter another difficulty. Many uncontrolled factors may be introduced, since the subjects may contact one another outside the experiment and, in this way, materially change the situation between experimental meetings. The decision as to which of these two types of experimental designs to employ depends, again, upon the objectives of the experiment and on how these objectives can best be accomplished. A number of examples of each kind of experiment will be given to illustrate the advantages and difficulties.

Deutsch (9), in his study of the effects of competitive and cooperative situations on group problem-solving, felt that the full effects of the experimental variables would reveal themselves only if the group would have considerable experience working together under the prescribed conditions. He decided on six successive meetings of each group and, to accomplish this, persuaded the instructor of a course to give students credit for participating in his experiment. Under these conditions most subjects attended all six sessions. Such an arrangement is not usually possible, but it is generally necessary to have some means of ensuring that subjects will return when the group is to meet several times.

Schachter's (26) experiment on rejection of deviates used one meeting of each group. It was necessary, however, for the subjects to be under the impression that they were to continue to meet once a week for a considerable period of time. The experimenter recruited subjects by telling them about clubs that were being formed and giving them the opportunity to join one of the clubs. Subjects were told that by joining they were committing themselves to attend the first meeting. After the first meeting they would be able to decide for themselves whether or not they wanted to continue.

In an experiment on strength of attraction to groups, Libo (22) used the number of meetings which subjects attended as one of the major measures of the strength of their attraction to the group. He, too, gave subjects an opportunity to volunteer to join clubs which were to continue to meet every week. Subjects could decide, after the first meeting, whether they wanted to continue their membership. Little pressure was applied to the subjects to return to subsequent meetings. The number of meetings actually attended was assumed to reflect their attraction to the group.

Starting the Manipulation of a Variable

It is possible, and sometimes necessary, to start the manipulation of an experimental variable at the time the subjects are recruited for the experiment. This can be done by providing various expectations for the subjects which will affect the attitudes with which they come to the experimental situation, or by collecting information which will later be used to manipulate a certain desired variable. We shall give some examples of the experimental manipulation of a variable which begins at the time of recruitment.

Several experiments (3, 14, 28) have varied attraction to the group experimentally by manipulating the degree to which the subjects expected they would like, and be congenial with, the other members of the group. At the time of recruiting, those who volunteered to be subjects were asked to answer a number of questions which concerned characteristics of themselves, characteristics which they liked in other people, and characteristics which they disliked in other people. No attention was actually paid to these data in setting up a group, but, because the subjects had provided such information, the experimenters were plausibly able to tell some groups that the members would like one another and be congenial and to tell others that they would not be very congenial. The results of such experiments showed that the manipulations were successful.

Schachter (26), in his experiment on the rejection of deviates, wanted to manipulate attraction to the group on the basis of interest in the activity in which the group was to engage. When the subjects were asked to join one of the clubs, each club was described in detail. Those who desired to join filled out an information sheet on which they were asked to give ratings of how interested they were in joining each of the available clubs. Some groups were composed of subjects who were highly interested in joining that specific club (high attraction to the group), whereas other groups were composed of persons who had indicated relatively low interest in joining that specific club (low attraction to the group).[1] This manipulation of attraction to the group was also shown to

---

1. This is not strictly an experimental manipulation of a variable. Rather, it represents selection of subjects on the basis of some measure in order to create contrasting conditions.

be successful by the results and by answers which subjects made to questionnaires after the experiment.

Size of the Experimental Groups

No matter what techniques the experimenter employs, there will always be some subjects who, after having agreed to be at the laboratory at a certain time, will not appear. They may have forgotten, they may have changed their minds, or something may have happened which made it impossible for them to attend. In any event, the problem for the experimenter is the same. In designing a laboratory experiment in which human subjects are to be used, it is well either to design the experiment so that it may be conducted with a variable number of subjects or to make some provision to ensure the proper number of persons in each group. It is generally most desirable to allow for variation in the number of subjects. Thus, for example, an experiment may be designed so that it can be conducted with either five, six, or seven members in the group. If seven persons are then scheduled for each meeting, and if sufficient precautions are taken,[2] very few groups will be lost.

When a design requires a constant number of subjects in each group, there are a number of techniques to ensure the presence of the proper number. Festinger (10), in his experiment on the effects of knowledge of religious affiliation, felt it necessary to keep the size of the groups exactly constant at six subjects per group. Three of these were to be Jewish and three Catholic. This was essential because of the desire to have the group evenly divided between the two religions. Leeway in the number of subjects in each group would have produced deviations from an even division which might have introduced additional complexities. Before each experiment each subject was written a letter stressing the importance of her coming to the experiment. On the day before the meeting, each subject was spoken to by telephone to make sure that she would be present. In spite of these efforts, only five subjects appeared in a number of groups. In most of these instances the subjects who had arrived agreed to wait while others who had volunteered were telephoned until an appropriate person was reached who agreed to come down immediately. By this procedure very few groups had to be discarded. In Pepitone's (25) experiment on group productivity, the situation was designed so that it was essential to have three subjects present

2. There are many factors which will affect the proportion of subjects who, having volunteered, actually come to the experiment. If, for example, volunteers are recruited from university classes, the more pressure applied upon them to participate, the lower the proportion of subjects who appear when scheduled (27).

in each group. The group was to work on a task which was divided into three parts, each of which had to be performed by one subject. The experimenter scheduled four subjects for each group. Occasionally only two subjects appeared and the group had to be canceled; most frequently three subjects appeared. When all four came, the last one was taken aside, the situation was explained to him, and he was allowed to observe the experiment in progress.

The Content and Form
of the Experimental Situation

The investigator must make a number of decisions concerning how the situation is to be structured cognitively for the subjects, in what kinds of activities they will engage, and with what attitudes they come to the experiment.

"Real" or "Experimental" Situations

The experimental situation can vary from one which is frankly experimental to a situation which, for the subjects, is a "real" one. The pros and cons for the various possibilities within this range are by no means all clear. Good evidence is lacking concerning which types of experimental situations are superior for which purposes. We shall, however, discuss some of the considerations which might lead an experimenter to set up his groups in one or another manner.

To discuss these advantages and disadvantages we must explain somewhat further the distinction between a situation which is "real" for the subject and a situation which is "experimental" for him. All of the situations are, in a sense, "real" for the subject, and all of them, likewise, are experiments from the point of view of the investigator. Some examples from other fields of investigation may illustrate our point more clearly. If a psychologist does an experiment in discrimination learning, using rats as subjects, the situation is obviously an experimental one for the investigator. For the rat, however, it is undoubtedly a very real situation. The maze or discrimination box is placed where he works and gets fed. The basis of the "reality" of the experimental situation for the subject is somewhat less clear when humans are used as subjects. Thus, for example, in an experiment on level of aspiration the subject may come to the laboratory knowing he is to help in an experiment. He is given a series of tasks to perform and is asked, before each task, what he is going to try to score on the subsequent task. One may well ask,

"In what sense is this situation a real one for the subject?" Certainly it is not "real" in the sense that it is a situation similar to those which the subject encounters in the ordinary course of events; on the other hand, it is certainly "real" in the sense that powerful motives are brought into play and strong forces are set up which act on the subject and determine his behavior in lawful ways. Thus, the situation in which one places the subject can be "real" for him in that it brings into play powerful forces, regardless of whether or not it is cognitively an experimental situation for him.

If the situation is cognitively a real one for the subject, it is probably easier to bring powerful forces into play. It may be more difficult to produce equally strong forces if the situation is cognitively experimental. In the latter case, the strength of the forces which can be brought into play depends largely upon the relations between the subject and the experimenter, the motivations which made the subject decide to volunteer for the experiment, and his desire to cooperate. These forces can, in the proper circumstances, be quite strong. It is much easier to create a laboratory situation which is cognitively experimental for the subjects. To create a cognitively "real" situation and still be able to control and manipulate variables successfully may require a great deal of subterfuge and much attention to technical details. If the subject sees through the subterfuge, the whole experiment may be invalidated.

We have, then, these relative advantages and disadvantages which the experimenter must consider when deciding whether to make the experimental situation cognitively experimental or cognitively real for the subject. If the experiment is cognitively real, it will be easier to make it motivationally strong. On the other hand, if the situation is cognitively experimental, it will be easier to set up with an adequate amount of control and precision. These examples below illustrate the kinds of decisions which have been made on this question.

Lippitt (23), in his experiment on the effects of the behavior of autocratic and democratic leaders, chose to make their experimental situation cognitively real for the subjects. To do this he organized school-age children into clubs which had their club rooms in the investigator's laboratory. The experimenter functioned as the adult leader of these clubs. In this role he was able to manipulate the desired variables. Because of the desire to maintain a cognitively real situation, the possible variations in the leader's behavior were also limited. The differences between conditions that were produced were rather gross. It is possible that the lack of control and precision in this experiment offset the advantages gained by having a cognitively real situation.

Schachter (26), in his experiment on rejection of deviates, also chose to have a cognitively real situation for the subjects because the major measures of rejection were to be obtained from verbal responses to questions. The investigator felt that these responses would have more validity if they were commitments to action on the part of the subject rather than answers to hypothetical questions. To obtain a cognitively real situation, he organized clubs of college students.

Once more a major difficulty was the restriction on the manipulation of variables. Manipulations had to be devised which were consistent with the notion of a bona fide club. To create groups with high and low cohesiveness, the investigator first ascertained the degree of interest of the subjects in each of two kinds of clubs and then manipulated the attraction to the group by composing some groups of persons who were all highly interested in the activity and other groups of persons who were only mildly interested. This type of manipulation of a variable by selection is probably not so satisfactory as other techniques would be. Because of the cognitively real aspects of the situation, it was also not possible for the experimenter to engage in any further manipulation of variables while the meeting of the group was in progress. These problems, in this experiment, were satisfactorily solved by the use of paid participants, a technique which will be described later.

In an experiment on the effects of knowledge of religious affiliation Festinger (10) decided to use a cognitively experimental situation. This decision was made because it was obviously of importance to control the group session firmly and to carry on manipulations of variables while the session was in progress. The group consequently met with the knowledge that it was helping in an experiment. They were told to "imagine" that they were a club. There is no doubt that the forces in this situation were weaker than the forces which would have operated had the subjects actually been members of a club engaged in the same procedure. By virtue of the cognitively experimental aspects of the situation, however, this disadvantage of weaker motivation was counterbalanced by the precision of measurement and the control of extraneous variables.

The Choice of Activity for the Group

The choice of the activity in which the group, once assembled in the laboratory, is to engage is somewhat dependent upon the decision concerning the cognitive reality of the experiment. There is, of course, much leeway in the choice of activity, although it must be one which is consistent with the purposes of the experiments and does not conflict with the other experimental decisions which have been made. If the experimental situation is to be cognitively real, there are restrictions on the type of activity which can be employed. If the situation is to be cognitively experimental, there is much less limitation and the selection of an activity which is well suited to the experimental purposes is easier. The activity must be chosen to allow for the manipulation of the variables, the collection of the measures in which the investigator is interested, and the arousal of sufficiently strong forces so that the effects will be measurable. It is impossible, of course, to list all of the various activities in which the laboratory groups may engage. We shall present a few examples of different kinds of activities which have been used and the reasons for their use.

Perhaps the most frequently employed group activity is discussion. Such an activity may be chosen when the purpose of the experiment is either to study the involvement of people in an activity, the amount of participation in an activity, or the communication or influence process that goes on in groups, or to provide a relatively interesting activity which will involve the subjects in order for the experiment to accomplish some other purpose in the meantime. Any topic which will be interesting to the subjects is suitable. The discussion may concern differences in opinion, as in the experiment by Back (3), it may be directed toward solving a problem, as in the experiment by Deutsch (9) or it may involve a sharing of experiences, as in the study of Festinger, Pepitone, and Newcomb (15).

When children are used as subjects, a play activity may frequently be appropriate. Thus, Thibaut (30), when he endeavored to create privileged and underprivileged subgroups, had one subgroup play an interesting and enjoyable game while the other subgroup took the role of helpers and servants to those who were actively engaged in having fun. Lippitt (23), in his experiment on autocratic and democratic leader behavior, used various games and craft activities which were appealing to school-age children.

It is also possible to use work situations as the activity for the group. Kelley (19) felt that a work situation would be more conducive to the establishment of a status hierarchy, so in order to create a two-level status hierarchy he used a work task in which the subjects had to arrange bricks according to a certain pattern. Pepitone (25), in an experiment on group productivity, used a work task which was constructed so that measures of production would be relatively easy to obtain.

These are but a few of the many possible examples of activities that can be prepared for a group. There is almost limitless room for the experimenter's ingenuity to create a situation which will be best for his experimental purpose.

The Orientation of the Subjects

Related to both the cognitive nature of the situation and the activity in which the group is to engage is the problem of what orientation to give the subjects in the experiment. It is highly desirable to have some plausible and understandable purpose for the experiment which the investigator can communicate to the subjects and which they will accept. If this is not done, the subjects usually conjecture about it and make guesses as to the true purpose. If a plausible orientation is not given, this important aspect remains uncontrolled.

The orientation which the experimenter gives the subject at the beginning should be plausible and should remain plausible as the experiment progresses. It is usually important that this plausible orientation *not* reveal to the subject the true focus of the experiment. The true purpose of the experiment and the true focus of the investigator's interest can, and should, be revealed to the subjects at the conclusion of the experiment.

Techniques for the Control
and Manipulation of Variables

Since the basic purpose of a laboratory experiment is to achieve a simple situation in which certain variables can be well controlled while others can be varied at will, we shall attempt, in the present section, to be as detailed as possible. We shall illustrate not only the various techniques which have been developed for controlling and manipulating variables but also the kinds of variables which have been successfully controlled and manipulated in the laboratory.

Use of Pre-experimental Instructions

The most obvious technique for controlling or manipulating variables is the use of pre-experimental instructions to the subject. Such pre-experimental instructions vary greatly in their effectiveness. It is probably safe to say that instructions to the subjects will be successful in manipulating variables when these instructions are kept simple, are given emphatically, and are plausible in the sense of being integrally related to the experimental activity in which the subjects are to engage. The major dangers in the use of instructions as a device for manipulating variables are (1) the possible inattention of the subjects when the instructions are given and (2) the possible variability from subject to subject in interpretation of the instructions. Because of these difficulties, it is probably undesirable to manipulate more than one variable at a time through the use of pre-experimental instructions. Instructions which attempt to manipulate several variables simultaneously are likely to become so complex and so long that they render the manipulation ineffective. We shall illustrate the problems involved in the use of instructions by giving examples of successful and unsuccessful attempts at manipulating variables in this manner.

Deutsch (9), in his experiment on competitive and cooperative groups, produced competitive or cooperative situations by differential instructions to the groups. In the competitive groups he told the subjects that all the members would be ranked according to their contributions in solving the problems given to the group and that their grades in the course would depend in part upon these rankings. It was explained that, thus, the one in the group who contributed most, irrespective of how the group as a whole performed, would get the highest grade and the one who contributed least would get the lowest grade. In the cooperative groups the experimenter told the subjects that their group was going to be compared with other groups, that everyone in the group would receive the same grade, and that this grade would be determined by how well the group as a whole did. These instructions were successful in creating the required conditions, and they provide a good example of how instructions can be integrated into the experiment. They were successful because they provided essential explanation of the situation to the subjects—they defined the goals for the subject and defined the manner in which these goals were to be reached.

Back (3), in his experiment comparing groups of high and low cohesiveness, wanted to vary the attraction to the group by using several kinds of motivation. In some groups he wanted to create in the members high or low attraction on the basis of personal liking for the other group members. To create high attraction, he told the subjects that, on the basis of the information they had written down when they volunteered, he had matched people in this group so that he was quite sure they would be congenial and like one another. To create low attraction he told subjects that, because of time-scheduling difficulties, he had been unable to match them very well but that he did not think they would dislike each other. In other groups, attraction to the group was made dependent upon the personal goals that could be achieved through membership. This was done by informing the subjects that there was (or was not) a reward that would be given as a prize to each of the members in the best group.

These instructions were probably moderately successful. On the one hand, they were not integral to the experimental task. That is, the subjects could have done everything the experimenter required of them without these instructions ever having been given. The possibility of winning a reward or the likelihood that members would get along well with others in the group was, however, relevant to fairly important motives in the subjects. They probably were concerned about whether or not they would like the other persons and be liked by them. The possibility of a reward probably added to the motivation to do well in the eyes of the experimenter. The results of the experiment show that a difference between high and low attraction was created by means of these instructions.

In an experiment on the direction of communication in a group, Festinger and Thibaut (12) wanted to manipulate the subject's perception of the homogeneity or heterogeneity of the group. To create the perception of homogeneity, groups were told that the members had been carefully selected so that they were all in the same year in college and had equal interest in, and knowledge about, the problem they were to discuss. To create the perception of a heterogeneous group, they were told that great differences existed among them in their knowledge about, and interest in, the problem under discussion. The manipulation of the variable by these instructions was only mildly successful. Probably few of the subjects were much concerned with whether the group was homogeneous or heterogeneous. Although differences between these conditions were obtained in the results, these differences were by no means strong. It might be expected that a more adequate manipulation of these variables would have produced much larger differences between the conditions.

In an experiment by Festinger et al. (14), an attempt was made to manipulate three variables simultaneously, all by means of verbal instructions at the beginning of the experiment. The investigators were interested in the interaction among the variables of attraction to the group, perception of whether or not there were experts in the group, and perception of whether or not there was a correct answer to the discussion problem. This attempt to manipulate all three variables by pre-experimental instruction was not very successful. The amount of instruction which had to be given to the subject and the complexity of the instructions rendered them rather ineffective. It probably would have been better to manipulate one of these variables by instructions and to have devised techniques for manipulating the other two in other ways. We shall discuss below such other techniques of manipulating and controlling variables.

Use of False Reporting

False reporting to the subjects of the results of votes or of sociometric choices and the like is another technique for control and manipulation of variables. Such false reporting must always be done in a manner which will make the report appear plausible. If sufficient care is used to ensure the acceptance of the report as true, this can be an effective means of manipulating some kinds of variables.

Festinger (10), in his experiment on the voting behavior of Catholics and Jews in mixed groups, used the technique of false reporting to the subjects to keep the situation identical for all groups. The members of the group voted for officers of the club in the following manner. There was first a nomination ballot to select two candidates for the election. The members of the group who received the most votes were to be the candidates in the final election. This nomination ballot was tabulated by the experimenter and, since the ballots were secret, it was simple for him to report falsely which two members had won the nominations. In this manner the experimenter was able to control which two persons were the candidates in each election. This experiment also employed paid participants (the use of which will be elaborated below) who were members of every group. By means of the false reporting of the results of the nomination ballot, the two candidates for each election in every group were two of the paid participants. One of the two candidates in each election identified herself as Jewish and the other identified herself as Catholic. Each election in each group was, thus, a standard situation.

In the experiment by Festinger et al. (14) in which an attempt was made to manipulate simultaneously three variables by verbal instructions to the subjects, a fourth variable was manipulated successfully by means of false reporting to the subjects. The subjects were to have a discussion among themselves concerning an issue about which each of them had already formed an opinion. Before the discussion some subjects were given the impression that the group overwhelmingly *agreed* with their own opinion on the issue, whereas other subjects were given the impression that the group overwhelmingly *disagreed* with them. This was done in the following manner. Each subject wrote, on a slip of paper, his opinion on the issue which was to be discussed. Subjects were told that the experimenter would tabulate these and then give each person a tally which would show the opinion of each person in the group. Thus, knowing everyone's opinion, they would be able to proceed sensibly with their discussion. The tally which was handed to each of the subjects was entirely fictitious. Each of the subjects in whom the perception of group agreement was to be created was given a tally which showed all but one of the subjects agreeing very closely with him. Each of those in whom the perception of disagreement with the group was to be created was handed a tally sheet which showed everyone in the group at least two opinion steps removed from his own opinion. This false reporting proved successful in varying the degree of perceived agreement with the group.

We shall conclude the discussion of the technique of false reporting to subjects with an illustration of an unsuccessful attempt. Festinger and Hymovitch (13) attempted to create in subjects a feeling of rejection by the group. Four subjects, strangers to one another, met in the laboratory and were told that they were to work on a task which required cooperative effort, although the various parts of the task would be divided among them. They were first to have a brief discussion among themselves and get to know one another so that they could decide how they wanted to organize the task. They were told that people who liked one another worked more productively together. Consequently, if there was any one in the group that they disliked, it would be better to exclude that person from the group. After the discussion, the subjects were given ballots on which each could indicate whether he wanted to work together with all the others or wanted to eliminate a member from the group. If subjects chose the latter alternative, they wrote down the name of the member they wanted to reject. Each subject was then taken to a separate room and was told that the experimenter would tell him the results of the ballot as soon as possible. Each subject was then privately told that the others had unanimously voted to reject him.

This false report to the subject was rarely successful. The overwhelming majority of the subjects refused to accept it and immediately suspected that the experimenter was not telling the truth. The reason for the failure was probably twofold. The experience with the others in the preliminary discussion did not provide grounds on the basis of which they could accept the reported rejection. Also, the false report was unpleasant enough so that the subjects did not want to accept it. Many subjects refused to accept the report even though they could not verbalize any reason for suspicion or disbelief. This technique had to be abandoned in this experiment.

Use of Paid Participants

The use of paid participants who are part of the experimental group and are accepted as such by the subjects is a powerful technique for the control and manipulation of variables. It is, however, a relatively expensive and tedious procedure. When paid participants are used, the details of their behavior must be exactly planned in advance and much time must be spent training and rehearsing them. We shall give some examples to illustrate the great variety of uses to which such paid participants may be put.

A relatively simple and effective use of paid participants to manipulate a variable is found in an experiment by Sherif (29). The same technique has been used by others for the same specific purpose (6). These experiments brought two persons together in the laboratory so that the degree to which the judgments of one would influence the judgments of the other might be investigated. The subjects were asked to judge the amount of movement of a point of light. This autokinetic effect (the light does not actually move) provided a rather ambiguous stimulus. These experiments used as one of the group members a paid participant who, by making a standard, prearranged series of judgments, was able to produce a standard situation for all subjects with specified differences between his judgments and the subjects' initial judgments.

Pepitone (24) reports an experiment in which he investigated the determinants of the perception of authority and approval in people. He was faced with the problem of how to provide a standard social situation for his subjects in which it would be meaningful to ask them for their perceptions of authority and approval. Using school-age children as his subjects, he let it be known in the school that, as part of a survey on interest in athletics, a three-man board would arrive in a few days to interview many of the students. Those who successfully answered the questions asked by the three-man board would win tickets to a college basketball game. The three-man board which came to the school and interviewed students individually consisted actually of three paid participants who had been trained by the experimenter. Scripts for each of the three had been carefully written so that each boy who was interviewed was asked exactly the same questions. The responses to the boys' answers were also standard for each of the conditions. In different conditions, however, the experimenter created authority differentials among the three board members and also differences among them in the extent to which they openly voiced approval of the boy who was being interviewed. The boy's perception of the relative authority and approval among the board members could be ascertained in an interview with each boy directly after his appearance before the three-man board. Thus, the experimental situation was effectively standardized.

Schachter (26), in his study of rejection of deviates, had three paid participants in each group. The topic for discussion was chosen so that all of the subjects would have opinions which very nearly agree with one another. Paid participants were used to create various conditions of deviation from this group norm. One paid participant voiced an extremely deviant opinion and held to it throughout the discussion. Another paid participant voiced a deviate opinion at the outset but allowed himself to be influenced so that, in the end, he agreed with the other subjects. The third paid participant agreed at the beginning and continued to agree with the modal opinion in the group. Thus, standard conditions of deviation from the group norm were achieved and, by rotating the paid participants among the various roles from group to group, it was also possible to equate for personality factors. We must emphasize that these paid participants had been very carefully trained in how to behave in the group and in what kinds of things they could and could not say.

In the study by Festinger (10) of the effect of knowledge of religious affiliation, four paid participants were members of every group which met. These paid participants were relied upon to control many variables and to create a standard situation. In the middle of the experiment, when everyone was identified according to her name and religious affiliation, two of these paid participants announced that they were Catholic and two announced that they were Jewish. The ones who said they were Jewish or Catholic were rotated from group to group so that actual religious affiliation and personality differences were equated among all the conditions. In this manner, many powerful variables, which would affect preferences for people, were controlled and the effects of knowledge of religious affiliation were permitted to emerge quite clearly.

The three foregoing examples of the use of paid participants in laboratory experiments hardly demonstrate adequately the possible range of uses to which this technique may be put. With sufficient ingenuity on the part of the experimenter and sufficient time in planning the behavior of the paid participants and in adequately training and rehearsing them, very powerful effects can be produced. There is ample evidence of the success of the control and manipulation of variables with the aid of paid participants.

Restriction of Behavior Possibilities

It is possible to exercise control over a situation and to manipulate variables by creating a situation which restricts the possibilities of behavior.

Festinger and Thibaut (12), in their experiment on the determinants of direction of communication, restricted the group to the use of written notes in carrying on their discussion. This decision was made for a number of reasons. If the discussion had been an oral one, the direction of communication (who spoke to whom) would have had to be recorded by observation of the group while the discussion was in progress. Such observation in fairly large groups is difficult and sometimes quite unreliable (see Chap. 9). By the use of written notes, a permanent record was immediately available. The exact time each note was written was recorded on it before it was delivered to another group member, so that the whole communication process could be reconstructed in the analysis. Aside from these measurement problems, there were other reasons for restricting the discussion to written notes. In an oral discussion, the person who is talking may be primarily addressing one or two others in the group, but, whether he likes it or not, what he is saying is simultaneously heard by everyone. This introduces additional complexities. By limiting the communication process to written notes, with the further restriction that each note could be sent to only one person, the situation was kept simple and manageable. A further difficulty in using an oral discussion for the purposes of this experiment is the marked tendency for people to answer when remarks are addressed to them. This is fully demonstrated by the usually high correlation obtained between the number of times a person communicates to others and the number of times he is the recipient of communication (17). Since the experimenters were concerned primarily with other determinants of the direction of communication, this would have been a complicating factor. The further restriction that the written notes could not be signed avoided this complication. The recipient of a note did not know from whom it came. The pads of paper on which the subjects wrote their notes were marked so that later, in analysis, the experimenter could tell who had written each note as well as to whom each note was addressed.

In his experiment on communication in a status hierarchy, Kelley (19) also restricted communication to written notes. Again there were a number of functions served by this restriction on the communication process. First, the experimenter intercepted all the notes written and thus had a detailed record of the communication process. Secondly, since all communication was by written notes, the experimenter could easily manipulate the communication process. Actually, none of the notes which the subjects wrote to one another was delivered. The notes which they received were fictitious ones designed to produce certain effects. In this manner a standard pattern of receiving communications from others was established for every group in all of the experimenter's conditions.

Restrictions on the behavior of the group can also be produced by an appropriate activity in which the group must engage. An activity can be chosen to eliminate certain complications, restrict the range of behavior, or produce certain reactions in the subject.

French (16), in his experiment on the effects of frustration and fear on organized and unorganized groups, produced frustration in his groups by means of the activity in which they engaged. The groups were put to work on a task which was impossible to complete. The frustration engendered in this manner was unmistakable.

In his experiment on the relationship between influence and group cohesiveness, Back (3) wanted to produce a situation in which two subjects, meeting together, have different interpretations of, or opinions about, the same set of facts. Before they came together, each subject was given a set of three pictures and asked to write a story about them. Each of the subjects was actually given different pictures, which would force different interpretations. The differences between the sets of pictures, however, were so slight that none of the subjects ever suspected that he had seen different pictures. In this manner, by appropriate choice of activity, Back was able to ensure that, in every group, there would be a difference of opinion between the two subjects at the beginning of their discussion.

In experiments by Bavelas (5) and his colleagues (20) on the effectiveness of different patterns of communication in groups, a technique has been employed which is perhaps the most extreme example of restriction in a situation. In this studies the experimenters were concerned with determining which of a number of patterns of communication among members of a group would result in more effective problemsolving. To produce the different patterns of communication, the experimenters allowed some members· to communicate to one another and prevented others from doing so. By this simple restriction, on which channels of communication were or were not available, various communication patterns were established. In these experiments the purposes of the investigators and the artificiality of the manipulation device were not hidden from the subjects. The restriction of the situation, however, was such that the subjects had to behave within it as well as they could. The results of these experiments show that the manipulation was successful. Such extreme and frank restriction of the situation would be appropriate, of course, only for a relatively selected range of problems.

In the foregoing discussion, we have by no means covered exhaustively the various kinds of techniques for the control and the manipulation of variables. Those described are no more than a few examples of the wide variety of which an experimenter can avail himself. Many more possible techniques are likely to be developed in the near future. It should again be stressed that when one employs new techniques for manipulation of variables, or even some of those already developed, it is important to conduct preliminary experimentation to make sure that the manipulation is actually working.

Opportunities for Measurement
in Laboratory Experimentation

Opportunities for collecting data in a laboratory experiment are present at all phases, from the recruiting of subjects until the end of the experimental sessions. There are, of course, some restrictions on what kinds of measurement can be employed at various phases in this process. These depend upon the design of the experiment and the way in which it is cognitively structured for the subjects. We shall point out some of the measurement possibilities at each of the stages of a laboratory experiment.

The first opportunity for measurement occurs before the experimental session takes place. Such measurement may be made at the time of recruiting subjects or when the subjects have assembled in the laboratory but before the experiment has begun. The exact time at which the measurement is done is immaterial and is generally selected for convenience. Such measurements, using a questionnaire or an interview, can have the following purposes: (1) to obtain some measure which will be compared to a similar one taken during or after the experiment; and (2) to enable the experimenter to control a variable by manipulating the composition of the group according to these measures.

In some experiments, it is essential for data to be collected before the experiment began. Thibaut (30), in his experiment on the cohesiveness of privileged and underprivileged subgroups, employed pre-experimental measurements to equate groups in the experiment and also to have a comparison between a pre-experimental and a postexperimental measure. The subjects were members of already existing clubs. The investigator met the group at some designated place, usually their Y.M.C.A. or their club. He provided transportation for them to the experimental rooms. Before setting out for the laboratory, he asked them to answer a questionnaire concerning who their friends were among the other boys. He then brought them to the experimental rooms and was able to divide them into two subgroups so that each person had about as many of his friends within his own subgroup as in the other subgroup. After the experiment was concluded, the boys were again asked to answer the same sociometric questions. In this manner the investigator was able not only to equate his subgroups for amount of friendship within them but also to provide a basis for determining the effect of the experimental procedure on this variable.

Most of the possibilities for measurement occur, of course, during the actual progress of the experiment. One of the most frequently used measurement devices is observation of the group as it carries on its activities (dealt with in detail in Chapter 9*). We shall discuss here some of the other kinds of data collection which are possible during the experiment.

The product of the activity in which the group engages is a major source of data. This product may take any of a variety of forms and may be analyzed in various ways by the investigator.

Kelley (19), in his experiment on communication in a status hierarchy, had his subjects arrange bricks in a certain pattern on the floor in accordance with instructions communicated to them. The actual product—that is, the exact pattern of bricks with which the group finished—was recorded by the experimenter and was used to obtain a measure of adequacy of production.

In his experiment on competitive and cooperative groups, Deutsch (9) had the subjects discuss, and write solutions to, various human-relations problems. He then analyzed these written products of the group discussion to obtain measures of the adequacy of the solution to the problem.

Closely related to such products are various records which the subject makes in the process of doing the required activity. Thus, in the Kelley (19) experiment and in the Festinger and Thibaut (12) experiment on direction of communication, the actual notes which the subjects wrote while carrying on the discussion were the main source of data.

Questionnaires and interviews may also be used during the course of the experiment. These may take the artificial form of questions interpolated into, and momentarily interrupting, the experiment or they may be disguised as election votes or expressions of opinion necessary to the conduct of the experiment.

Schachter (26), in his experiment on rejection of deviates, created a situation which was cognitively real to the subject. The groups were clubs which the subject had joined and which the subject expected would continue meeting periodically. It was fitting, consequently, to ask the subjects to elect committees to carry on various of the club functions and to vote on when and how often the club should meet. In this experiment, the data collection was seen by the subjects not as such but rather as part of their functioning as members of a club.

In the Festinger (10) experiment on mixed Catholic and Jewish groups, the major data were collected by holding elections for officers of a club. Here the situation was cognitively experimental for the subjects and the voting was undoubtedly seen as part of the experimental pro-

*See SOURCE.

cedure. The results indicate it to have been an adequate method of data collection.

One can also collect a wide variety of data by questionnaires, interviews, or tests at the conclusion of the experimental session. The techniques of such data collection are discussed in Chapters 8 and 9.*

Summary

Laboratory experiments constitute a powerful technique for investigating relationships among variables. The essence of such experiments may be described as observing the effect on a dependent variable of the manipulation of an independent variable under controlled conditions. Such experiments, if well designed, can produce clear and unambiguous results which may add to a theoretical body of knowledge.

It is important to remember, however, that laboratory experimentation, as a technique for the development of an empirical body of knowledge, cannot exist by itself. Experiments in the laboratory must derive their direction from studies of real-life situations, and results must continually be checked by studies of real-life situations. The laboratory experiment is a technique for basic and theoretical research and is not the goal of an empirical science.

We have, in this chapter, enumerated in some detail many techniques for designing laboratory experiments and for manipulating different kinds of variables in a variety of ways. Many of these techniques for the manipulation of variables involve deception, prevarication, misdirection of subject, and the like. As long as an investigator works with human subjects, it is impossible to over-emphasize the necessity for keeping in mind the responsibilities to the subject and the ethics which the experimenter must follow. It is important, if such experimentation is to continue and is to be tolerated by the people who help in it, that the experimenter perform a service to the subjects in exchange for their help. In all laboratory experiments it should be a firm policy to give the subjects a full explanation at the conclusion of each experiment. This sometimes requires spending more time explaining and discussing matters with the group than it took to do the experiment. If it is done well, the subjects leave feeling that they have learned something and have not wasted their time. The subjects do not resent having been misdirected and deceived if they can see the reasons for the deceptions and understand the purposes.

*See SOURCE.

References

1. ALLPORT, F. H. The influence of the group upon association and thought. *J. exp. Psychol.*, 1920, **3**, 159–182.

2. ASCH, S. E. Effects of group pressure upon the modification and distortion of judgments. In Guetzkow, H. (ed.). *Groups, leadership and men*. Pittsburgh: Carnegie Press, 1951, pp. 177–190.

3. BACK, K. Influence through social communication. *J. abnorm. soc. Psychol.*, 1951, **46**, 9–23.

4. ———, FESTINGER, L., HYMOVITCH, B., KELLEY, H., SCHACHTER, S., & THIBAUT, J. The methodology of studying rumor transmission. *Hum. Relat.*, 1950, **3**, 307–312.

5. BAVELAS, A. Communication patterns in task-oriented groups. In Lerner, D., and Lasswell, H. D. (eds.). *The policy sciences*. Stanford, Calif.: Stanford Univer. Press, 1951, pp. 193–202.

6. BRAY, D. W. The prediction of behavior from two attitude scales. *J. abnorm. soc. Psychol.*, 1950, **45**, 64–84.

7. COCH, L., & FRENCH, J. R. P., JR. Overcoming resistance to change. *Hum. Relat.*, 1948, **1**, 512–532.

8. DASHIELL, J. F. An experimental analysis of some group effects. *J. abnorm. soc. Psychol.*, 1930, **25**, 190–199.

9. DEUTSCH, M. An experimental study of the effects of cooperation and competition upon group process. *Hum. Relat.*, 1949, **2**, 199–232.

10. FESTINGER, L. The role of group belongingness in a voting situation. *Hum. Relat.*, 1947, **1**, 154–181.

11. ———, CARTWRIGHT, D., BARBER, K., FLEISCHL, J., GOTTSDANKER, J., KEYSEN, A., & LEAVITT, G. A study of rumor: its origin and spread. *Hum. Relat.*, 1948, **1**, 464–486.

12. ———, & THIBAUT, J. Interpersonal communication in small groups. *J. abnorm. soc. Psychol.*, 1951, **46**, 92–99.

13. ———, & HYMOVITCH, B. *Communication as a consummatory activity*. Unpublished manuscript.

14. ———, GERARD, H. B., et al. *The influence process in the presence of extreme deviates*. In press.

15. ———, PEPITONE, A., & NEWCOMB, T. Some consequences of deindividuation in a group. *J. abnorm. soc. Psychol.*, 1952, **47**, 382–389.

16. FRENCH, J. R. P., Jr. Organized and unorganized groups under fear and frustration. Univ. of Iowa Studies: Studies in Child Welfare, Volume 20. *Studies in Topological and Vector Psychology III*, 1944, pp. 229–308.

17. ———, & BRADFORD, L. (eds.). The dynamics of the discussion group. *J. Soc. Issues*, 1948, **4**, 65.

18. JENNESS, A. Social influences in the change of opinion: the role of discussion in changing opinion regarding a matter of fact. *J. abnorm. soc. Psychol.*, 1932, **27**, 29–34, 279–296.

19. KELLEY, H. H. Communication in experimentally created hierarchies. *Hum. Relat.*, 1951, **4**, 39–56.

20. LEAVITT, H. J. Some effects of certain communication patterns on group performance. *J. abnorm. soc. Psychol.*, 1954, **46**, 38–50.

21. LEWIN, K., LIPPITT, R., & WHITE, R. Patterns of aggressive behavior in experimentally created "social climates." *J. soc. Psychol.*, 1939, **10**, 271–299.

22. LIBO, L. *The use of a projective device to measure attraction to a group.* Ph.D. thesis, Stanford University, 1951.

23. LIPPITT, R. An experimental study of the effect of democratic and authoritarian group atmospheres. Univ. of Iowa Studies: Studies in Child Welfare, *Studies in Topological and Vector Psychology I*, 1940, pp. 45–195.

24. PEPITONE, A. Motivational effects in social perception. *Hum. Relat.*, 1950, **3**, 57–76.

25. PEPITONE, E. *The productivity of groups.* Ph.D. thesis, Univ. of Michigan, 1952.

26. SCHACHTER, S. Deviation, rejection and communication. *J. abnorm. soc. Psychol.*, 1951, **46**, 190–207.

27. _____. *Group-derived restraints and audience persuasion.* In press.

28. _____, ELLERSTON, N., McBRIDE, D., & GREGORY, D. An experimental study of cohesiveness and productivity. *Hum. Relat.*, 1951, **4**, 229–238.

29. SHERIF, M. An experimental approach to the study of attitudes. *Sociometry*, 1937, **1**, 90–98.

30. THIBAUT, J. An experimental study of the cohesiveness of underprivileged groups. *Hum. Relat.*, 1950, **3**, 251–278.

PART
G
BIOGRAPHICAL NOTES

Since Festinger steadfastly refused all invitations to publish autobiographical notes or memoirs in such series as "Psychology in Biography," we have, in order to give the reader some notion of the bare bones of his career, reproduced the Festinger entry in "Who's Who in America."

FESTINGER, LEON, educator, psychologist; b. N.Y.C. May 8, 1919; s. Alex and Sarah (Solomon) F.; B.S., Coll, City N.Y., 1939; M.A., State U. Iowa, 1940, Ph.D., 1942; m. Mary Oliver Ballou, Oct. 23, 1943; children—Catherine, Richard, Kurt; m. 2d, Trudy Bradley, Sept. 7, 1968. Research asso. State U. Iowa, 1941–43; instr. U. Rochester, 1943–45; asso. prof. Mass. Inst. Tech., 1945-48; asso. prof. U. Mich, 1948–51; prof. psychology U. Minn., 1951–55, Stanford U., 1955–68; Else and Hans Staudinger prof. psychology, grad. faculty New Sch. for Social Research, 1968 —. Fellow Am. Psychol. Assn. (pres. div. 8, 1963; Distinguished Scientist award 1959), Am. Acad. Arts and Scis., Nat. Acad. Scis. Author: Conflict, Decision and Dissonance, 1964. Home: 37 W 12th St New York City NY 10011

This entry appeared unchanged in all annual issues of "Who's Who" from 1972 to 1981. After 1981, he appears to have been flung out of "Who's Who," undoubtedly because he flung out all requests to update his entry. We do so by adding the following facts. The major additional honors of which we know are these: In 1978 he received an Honorary Doctorate from the University of Mannheim; in 1980 he was named Einstein Visiting Fellow of the Israel Academy of Sciences and Humanities; and in 1980 he received the Distinguished Senior Scientist Award of the Society of Experimental Social Psychology. As for publications, in addition to the single book which is listed in his "Who's Who" entry, he was author, coauthor, and editor of seven other books and monographs all listed in the bibliography at the end of this volume.

Festinger just once wrote a semiautobiographical, somewhat personal, memoir. He did so by falling into a trap of his own devising. He had agreed to edit a book dedicated to the memory of Alfred Marrow and concerned with the impact of Kurt Lewin and the Research Center for Group Dynamics on social psychology. The book called "Retrospections on Social Psychology" consisted of contributions from students of

Kurt Lewin, their students, and their students' students. It was, in effect, a festschrift for the Research Center for Group Dynamics.

As editor, Festinger took on himself the job of integrating the various contributions into a summary statement—a job that proved impossibly difficult. In his words:

> My various lines of thought about how to summarize, organize, or interrelate these different personal statements . . . kept ending in blind alleys. After a number of approaches, I decided that there was only one way to avoid being pedantic, uninteresting, and trivial—namely, to write a personal statement of my own. So this chapter is, indeed, a personal view— actually, an extremely personal one—of some aspects of the history of the trend begun by the Research Center for Group Dynamics and its relationship to social psychology. (Festinger, L. 1980, p. 236)

His statement, adapted for the current collection, follows.

Looking Backward

This book does not, nor was it intended to, paint a comprehensive picture of the growth of social psychology. It was intended to be selective, reflecting primarily the personal interests and views of each individual author. And the various chapters in the book are just that—personal views and personal interpretations of where we were, where we are, how we got here, and where we ought to be going. Each of them has, to me, a delightfully different flavor that identifies the writer.

The original plan for this chapter was to present an integration of all the contributions to this book as a summary statement. My various lines of thought about how to summarize, organize, or interrelate these different personal statements, however, kept ending in blind alleys. After a number of approaches, I decided that there was only one way to avoid being pedantic, uninteresting, and trivial—namely, to write a personal statement of my own. So this chapter is, indeed, a personal view—actually, an extremely personal one—of some aspects of the history of the trend begun by the Research Center for Group Dynamics and its relationship to social psychology.

A few friends of mine who read and criticized an early draft of this chapter persuaded me that it should be read in conjunction with the Preface, where the genesis and purpose of the book are stated. They also persuaded me that very few persons read prefaces to books. So, for self-protection, I urge you to read the Preface before reading this concluding chapter. It won't take long; the Preface is very brief.

A Small Bit of Personal History

In September 1939, some forty years ago, I arrived in Iowa City as a new graduate student at the University of Iowa. I had gone there to study with Kurt Lewin, whose writings I had read while an undergraduate. I worked and studied with, and learned from, Lewin until his death in 1947.

When I came to Iowa, I was not interested in social psychology. Indeed, I had never had a course in social psychology. My graduate education did nothing to cure that. I never had a course at Iowa in social psychology either. As an undergraduate, I had done a study on level of aspiration (Hertzman & Festinger, 1940) and had become interested in the concepts that Lewin had developed in connection with the work of his group in Berlin—tension systems and the remembering and completion of interrupted tasks; boundaries and psychological satiation; force fields and *Umweg* situations. There was creativity, newness, and a sense of importance in these ideas of Lewin. Also, the closeness between theory and data was particularly appealing to me. I arrived in Iowa with great enthusiasm.

Unfortunately for me, by the time I arrived, the things that fascinated me were no longer on center stage. True, we talked about life spaces and forces and regions and tension systems, but the main interest of Kurt Lewin was now in the area of social psychology; he wanted to understand the behavior of groups. The work of Ronald Lippitt and Ralph White (1943) on groups operating in "autocratic" and "democratic" atmospheres had been the beginning of this new direction. Kurt Lewin already spoke of his dream to create a new, independent Institute for Group Dynamics.

Undeterred, and enjoying the tolerance of the others, I did research on level of aspiration, on a mathematical model of decision making, on statistics, and even strayed to doing a study using laboratory rats. The looser methodology of the social psychology studies, and the vagueness of relation of the data to the Lewinian concepts and theories, all seemed unappealing to me in my youthful penchant for rigor.

In 1945 I joined Kurt Lewin, Ronald Lippitt, Dorwin Cartwright, and Marian Radke (now Yarrow) as an Assistant Professor at the Research Center for Group Dynamics at the Massachusetts Institute of Technology. It was a research center rather than an institute simply because one couldn't have an institute within an institute. At this time I became, by fiat, a social psychologist and immersed myself in the field with all its difficulties, vaguenesses, and challenges. Just as Elliot Aronson recalls his days at Stanford University as a time of excitement, the years at M.I.T. seemed to us all to be momentous, ground breaking, the new beginning of something important.

The Impact of Lewin on Social Psychology

Of course, social psychology had been developing for many years. It flourished long before Lewin became interested in it. People like All-port, both Gordon and Floyd, Sherif, Newcomb, Katz, and many others had done, and were doing, very significant work. This work has endured and is still important. For example, Richard Nisbett, in his chapter, goes back to Hartshorne and May (1928) and to Newcomb (1929) to find some of the best data about "trait consistency." Singer, in his chapter, properly points out that the beginnings of theory about interpersonal social influence and social comparison processes go back to Newcomb (1943) and to Sherif (1935).

But Kurt Lewin and his co-workers had changed something, had brought something new and original into the field. In retrospect, it is perhaps possible to specify what some of these new things were.

In part, the originality of Lewin's early contribution to social psychology lay in the choice of problems to investigate—in the judgment of what was, or was not, an interesting or important problem. I would like to be able to explain how such judgments are made and why some persons seem to do it so well. Unfortunately, the way in which one makes a priori judgments about "interesting" and "important" are, to me, still in the realm of unverbalizable art. But Kurt Lewin had a fine talent for it, and somehow that talent rubbed off a little on those around him. In his paper "Formalization and Progress in Psychology," Lewin (1940) describes how, from "three years of experimentation with hundreds of series of nonsense syllables and after thousands of measurements of reaction times," he decided that he had to discard the classic law of association. Convinced that it was necessary to distinguish between habits (associations) that did or did not involve needs or quasi-needs, he emerged with his ideas about the importance of "tension systems." This idea led to a long series of very fruitful experiments on goal-directed activities and the effects of interrupting them. From the classic law of association to Lewin's concept of tension system is quite a long leap, however, and how he got there remains mysterious.

Similarly, when Lewin turned to social psychology, together with all his other concepts, he emphasized the idea that the small face-to-face group was a powerful factor in people's lives and in the transmission of social forces. So group atmospheres, group decision, group cohesiveness, group goals, and the like became important problems to theorize about and to investigate.

Another aspect of "important," however, is more easily verbalizable. It was important if it made a difference with respect to actual problems in the world, real events and processes. It is no accident that so many of the chapters in this book, chapters by Kurt Back, Al Zander, Mort Deutsch and Stan Schachter, deal, in a major sense, with practical problems.

Out of such an orientation in which a priori "importance of problem" reigned supreme there emerged a methodological approach that was distinctive. It arose from the insistence on trying to create, in the laboratory, powerful social situations that make big differences. This seemed necessary in a field so new, where so many things were probably multiply determined. So experiments were done with all these things in mind, plus a large dose of bravura and enthusiasm. Who would have imagined doing a "scientific experiment" in which the independent variable to be manipulated was autocratic versus democratic atmospheres? Certainly no one can describe, with reasonable precision, all the facets that were experimentally varied in those studies. When one experimenter (group leader) seemed unable to run a group democratically, a third group atmosphere came into being—namely, laissez-faire. Who would have imagined doing experiments in real world situations—comparing lectures and group decisions for their effectiveness in getting women to buy glandular meats during World War II? I still have no clear conceptual understanding of what all the differences were between these procedures. I have always admired the fantastic skill of Alex Bavelas, a grand master in dealing with groups, that enabled him always to produce a unanimous group decision in the desired direction.

But big changes were produced, we did learn things from these studies, and the spirit of them had a lasting impact (Bavelas, 1942; Lewin, 1943; Lewin, Lippitt and White, 1939; Lippitt, 1940). We learned that one could, indeed one must, do studies both in the real world and in the laboratory. And when one was in the laboratory, it was vital not to lose sight of the substance in the quest for greater precision. Precision is highly desirable but only if one has retained the reality and essence of the question. Thus, a tradition grew of bringing very complicated problems into the laboratory. That tradition also included maintaining, always, a mixture of laboratory and field work. And how did one manipulate complicated variables in the laboratory? Well, that too is an art form. As Bob Zajonc points out in his chapter, Back's (1951) experiment employed a manipulation that was based solely on intuition. Not until ten years later was it shown to be valid, As Mort Deutsch so vividly describes in his chapter, it was wonderful to find a tool, such as the Prisoners Dilemma game, that enabled more precise control of important variables. But precision had to take its place in the context of the primary question.

As a small aside, I would like to quote some things that Kurt Lewin wrote on these issues in 1944 (Lewin, 1951). The reader may want to compare these statements with the chapter by Kurt Back and with his own impressions of social psychology today.

> The relation between scientific psychology and life shows a peculiar ambivalence. In its first steps as an experimental science, psychology was dominated by the desire of exactness. . . . Experimentation was devoted mainly to problems of sensory perception and memory, partly because they could be investigated through setups where the experimental control and precision could be secured with the accepted tools of the physical laboratory. (p. 168)

> The term "applied psychology" became—correctly or incorrectly—identified with a procedure that was scientifically blind even if it happened to be of practical value. As the result, "scientific" psychology that was interested in theory tried increasingly to stay away from a too close relation to life.

> It would be most unfortunate if the trend toward theoretical psychology were weakened by the necessity of dealing with natural groups when studying certain problems of social psychology . . . close cooperation between theoretical and applied psychology . . . can be accomplished . . . if the theorist does not look toward applied problems with highbrow aversion or with a fear of social problems. (p. 169)

What was the theoretical aspect of Lewin's contribution that was new and different? I have always felt that Kurt Lewin had an exquisite sense of the relation of theory to data. If you deal with highly formalized, specific theoretical statements, then perhaps you don't need this sense. You simply write down your statements in mathematical form, do your mathematical manipulations, a theorem falls out that is testable, and you then test it. But that was not, and is not, the situation in social psychology—nor do I think it is ever the situation at the forefront of knowledge in any science. When theory is not fully formulated, when much of the content of the theory is carried by the connotations of somewhat vague words, then the problem of the relation between theory and data is a difficult one.

Was there a relationship between the theoretical concepts that Lewin and his colleagues and students used and the empirical work they did? What did "life space," "region," "force field," "tension system," and the like have to do with group functioning, group decision, or social influence, for example? It is easy to say, and it is partly correct, that the whole Lewinian system served as a heuristic device. It provided a framework within which to think, and for some it was more useful, as such, than for others. To the extent that it served this function there was, of course, no clearly explainable relation between theory and data. The experiments and field studies did not test theoretical predictions in that strict sense.

There was more to it than that, however, and it is still difficult to verbalize precisely what it was. It is surprising to me that so many of the contributors to this book find that the roots of their topic go back to some aspect of Lewinian theory. Perhaps this should not be surprising in view of the basis for choosing the authors—namely, their close connection to the Research Center for Group Dynamics. But, nevertheless, it seems to stand in rather sharp contrast to the fact that for at least two decades the social psychology literature has been virtually devoid of mention of those old Lewinian concepts and terms.

From an historical viewpoint, however, we see Al Zander making connections between group goals and the early work on tension systems and on level of aspiration. We see Dick Nisbett resting some of his current conception of trait generality on Lewin's early conceptions of field theory and of behavior as an interactive function of the person and the environment. Hal Kelley traces the roots of attribution theory to the concept of force fields. Elliot Aronson sees dissonance theory as having emerged from views that were intrinsically inherent in the Lewinian approach. Jerry Singer finds the theories about social influence and comparison processes stemming from the concepts of life space, region, and tension. Even more explicit and direct influences from Lewin's concepts are spelled out by Mort Deutsch. The clarification of different kinds of conflict situations came directly from Lewin's analyses of force fields, driving forces, and restraining forces.

There is a kind of greatness that provides new ideas, new directions, and new frameworks for thinking. Just as Franz Boaz, who is rarely referred to today, transformed the face of anthropology, Kurt Lewin had a general but profound influence on social psychology. His ideas, their meanings and connotations, heavily directed the research and were taken over, modified, and embodied in the newer, somewhat more specific theoretical formulations.

The Postwar Surge in Social Psychology

The immediate post–World War II period was, in my view, the most seminal period in the history and development of social psychology. Four distinctly new influences were brought to bear on the field. All these influences had their roots in the war itself, either methodologically or ideologically:

1. During the war the techniques of surveying attitudes and opinions of persons, randomly sampled from specified populations, had developed markedly. It became a practical tool that was available to social psychology. It could be used, for example, to study such diverse matters as voting patterns (Lazarsfeld, Berelson, and Gaudet, 1944), reactions to real or imagined crises (Cantril, 1940), and political attitudes (Campbell, Eberhart, and Woodward, 1947). It made it more feasible to investigate many questions in social psychology outside the laboratory or the classroom. It has remained a powerful though expensive tool.

2. After the war, Carl Hovland started a research program at Yale University that stemmed from work he and others had done in the armed forces (Hovland, Lumsdaine, and Sheffield, 1949). Before the war, Hovland had worked in the area of human learning, and he brought his experimental psychology background with him to his new interest in social influence, social persuasion, and social communication. Together with his colleagues at Yale, particularly Irving Janis, Hovland did controlled experiments on communicator credibility, retention of effects of persuasion, primacy and recency effects in persuasion, and the like. In addition to the substantive contributions to the field, this group brought a different theoretical and methodological orientation to laboratory experiments in social psychology.

3. At the University of California, a group of people who had come to the United States to escape from the dangers of Nazi Germany brought a personality approach more strongly into social psychology. Adorno, Frenkel-Brunswik, and others were convinced that at least part of the explanation of what has happened in Europe lay in personality characteristics. Their book *The Authoritarian Personality* (1950) had a very large impact at the time.

4. At the Research Center for Group Dynamics, over and above what I have already described, there was new emphasis on what was called "action research." The phrase did not have an exact meaning. It somehow connoted research oriented toward social problems and social action, research together with social action, or research as a part of social action. One of the more direct outgrowths of this emphasis was the growth of workshops to train people in social sensitivity and in how to deal effectively with social groups (Lippitt, 1949). These activities eventually led to the formation of the National Training Laboratory, which ran annual workshops in Bethel, Maine.

Doing research in an action context was a difficult endeavor, but it was very seriously pursued. I remember very well the massive research effort that was undertaken at the first workshop in Bethel in the summer of 1947. Almost every graduate student from the Research Center for Group Dynamics, and many from the Social Relations Department at Harvard, were there to observe, record, and take notes on the processes of leadership, interaction, and change. The urgencies of social action, however, tended to take priority and seriously interfered with the perhaps too massive research effort. Subsequently Jack French worked hard for many years to get whatever he could out of the data. These workshops led gradually to a wide proliferation of training groups, sensitivity groups, and the like. But emphasis on research soon disappeared. The research that did go on for a while seems to me to have been little more than the gathering of testimonials.

Together with these new trends and new influences there also existed an active, more traditional center of social psychology at Harvard University, the newly formed Department of Social Relations. For historical reasons, and simple geographical proximity, there was considerable interaction between that department and the Research Center for Group Dynamics. In 1938, and again in 1939, Kurt Lewin had spent one semester at Harvard. Doc Cartwright, who came to Iowa in a postdoctoral position and later helped start the Research Center for Group Dynamics, was a graduate student at Harvard during those two years. Jack French, who joined the Research Center slightly later, was similarly attracted to Kurt Lewin during these two semesters at Harvard.

Thus, while we were at M.I.T. there was easy contact with Gordon Allport, Jerome Bruner, and others because of already existing personal relations. Also at that time (I don't know whether the arrangement still exists), students at either of these neighboring institutions could take courses at the other freely. It was in this way that we and Henry Riecken, who later worked with me and Stan Schachter at Minnesota, first came to know each other. That was also our first contact with Gardner Lindzey, who has never forgiven me for giving him a B in a seminar, thus spoiling an otherwise spotless transcript.

The Harvard Department of Social Relations added a healthy current to the field. Because of the inclusion of social psychology, sociology, and cultural anthropology in one department, the people there had a broader, and different, perspective. And our contacts with them helped keep us in touch with other points of view.

It seems clear to me in retrospect that the postwar surge had its roots deeply embedded in vital social problems. It also seems clear to me that these roots, together with daring to deal with difficult issues in novel and ingenious ways, gave a vitality to social psychology at that time.

The Strands Through the Fifties

For many reasons there was considerable interaction among all of these centers of social psychology. When Kurt Lewin died in 1947, the young Research Center for Group Dynamics found itself without a secure home. The Research Center had, from its beginning, been quite peripheral to the activities, interests, and goals of M.I.T. Without the leadership, the persuasiveness, and the prestige of Kurt Lewin, that institution was not very receptive to the idea of the Research Center remaining there.

With the help of Rensis Likert, director of the Survey Research Center, and Donald Marquis, head of the Psychology Department, we moved the Research Center for Group Dynamics in 1948, faculty, students and all, to the University of Michigan, where we, together with the Survey Research Center, constituted a newly created Institute for Social Research. Thus, Michigan, which already had Theodore Newcomb and Daniel Katz on its faculty, became a huge institution with regard to social psychology. There ensued a natural interchange of ideas among all of these people. For example, the book *Research Methods in the Behavioral Sciences,* edited by myself and Katz (1953), was undertaken there as a truly cooperative venture involving all of us.

Hal Kelley, after completing his doctoral work, went to Yale to work with Carl Hovland and Irving Janis. Thus, there was mutual influence on ideas and methodology between Yale and Michigan. The book by Hovland, Janis, and Kelley (1953), in addition to its substantive value, shows, I think, some of the beneficial effects of this mutual influence. The early death of Carl Hovland meant the end of that particular coordinated research program at Yale but did not end the interactions.

Social psychology was growing rapidly during this period, and movement of people among universities contributed much to maintaining active contact and interaction. In 1951, for example, I left the Research Center for Group Dynamics for the University of Minnesota, where Stan Schachter and Ben Willerman already worked. Later, Henry Riecken came there and we formed a very active research group. The new Ph.D.'s from the various centers added to the expansion and interaction. To give a few examples: Bob Cohen, from the Research Center for Group Dynamics, and Jack Brehm, who worked with me at Minnesota, were both on the faculty at Yale; William McGuire, who worked with Carl Hovland, did postdoctoral work at Minnesota; Elliot Aronson was, for a time, on the faculty at Harvard.

Perhaps the least active interaction took place with those who carried on the work stemming from the book *The Authoritarian Personality.*

Although the Berkeley group stimulated a very large amount of research, it seems to have remained more separate from the rest of social psychology. This was not because of lack of contact, however. The field had not yet come to the point where almost every department of psychology had to have a program in social psychology. There were still relatively few active research workers in the area, and we all knew each other.

However, despite the active interaction and the easy contact, mutual influence among the various trends was slow to develop and remained incomplete. I think there were deep philosophical and methodological differences that could not be totally bridged because they were never fully and openly addressed. Let us examine a few of them.

There was in American psychology, and in social psychology also, a tradition of emphasis on individual differences, on the measurement of the characteristics of the person. Intelligence testing and testing for vocational guidance were well established. In social psychology, techniques were devised and scales constructed to measure social attitudes, social stereotypes, and relevant personality traits. Dick Nisbett presents, in his chapter, an excellent analysis of this tradition and where it went. The work on the authoritarian personality already mentioned, the work by McLelland et al. (1953) on need for achievement and need for affiliation, the developments stemming from the authoritarian personality work that led to measuring rigidity, tolerance for ambiguity, and the like were all in this tradition. On a conceptual level, Gordon Allport (1937) was, perhaps, the major proponent of such an approach. The idea that each individual is unique and that social psychology should focus on that uniqueness appealed to many. Recently, as Nisbett points out, Bem and Funder (1978) have revived this view as a way out of the problem of low generality across situations of measured traits. One can perhaps describe the bottom line of this approach as the study of individual differences about individual differences.

In contrast, it appears strange that those connected with, and influenced by, Kurt Lewin virtually ignored the entire question of individual differences. It seems strange because, if there was serious acceptance of the simple statement that behavior is a joint function of the person and the environment, how could one ignore measurement of the person? The philosophical ideas that explain this are easy to locate. They are perhaps best expressed in the paper by Lewin on Aristotelian and Gallilean conceptions of science (1935). Too much concern with individual differences could create a mask that hid the underlying dynamic processes. These underlying processes had to be discovered. The kind of analogy that existed in our minds was something like the following. It would be hopeless to have tried to discover the laws concerning free-falling objects by concentrating on measuring the different rates of descent of stones, feathers, pieces of paper, and the like. It is only after the basic dynamic laws are known that one can make sense of the individual differences.

The way I have always thought about it is that if the empirical world looks complicated, if people seem to react in bewilderingly different ways to similar forces, and if I cannot see the operation of universal underlying dynamics—then that is my fault. I have asked the wrong questions; I have, at the theoretical level, sliced the world up incorrectly. The underlying dynamics are there, and I have to find the theoretical apparatus that will enable me to reveal these uniformities.

We tend, too much, to ignore the impact of philosophical underpinnings on how scientists approach their task. These varying approaches to individual differences came from deep philosophical disagreements that, I think, were partly responsible for an incomplete meeting of minds and of less than optimal mutual influence among social psychologists.

The tradition of behaviorism that dominated much of American psychology also had its impact on social psychology. One consequence of this impact was avoidance of concern with "inner" experience, such as cognition and affect, and a taboo on theorizing about matters that were not directly measurable. When I was a young student, the phrase "dust bowl empiricism" was used by many in a self-congratulatory manner. Another far-reaching consequence of behaviorism was the specification of what things were legitimate for study. One could describe the characteristics of a physical stimulus and one could observe the behavioral response of the organism—that was all. Hence, the task of the science was to find the laws relating stimulus to response. Starting with Thorndike's (1927) work on the "law of effect," there was major emphasis on the variables of reward and punishment. Hull (1943) and Spence (1948) brought theoretical thinking along these lines to their peak.

The problems with which social psychology dealt were a bit too complex for the straightforward application of stimulus-response theorizing. Yet, at a more general level, this orientation affected the kinds of problems studied and how they were approached. The orientation of the group at Yale around Carl Hovland perhaps best illustrates the behaviorist approach in social psychology. The problem of social persuasion was seen as elucidating the relations between stimulus characteristics (e.g., stating the conclusion or not, order of material in the communication) and the response magnitude (degree of measured opinion change).

The orientation of Kurt Lewin and those around him was drastically at odds with behaviorism. The theoretical ideas were primarily about internal states. Many of the chapters in this book illustrate this: goals and aspirations that people and groups have (Zander); how people evaluate themselves (Singer); cognitions about others (Zajonc); processes of self-persuasion (Aronson). There was a basic incompatibility between such different orientations as behaviorism and the Lewinian approach. This can be seen in their impact on formulations of problems and theory in social psychology. Elliot Aronson, in his chapter, gives some good examples of difficulties produced by this incompatibility which interfered with mutual influence and a coherent approach to problems in social psychology.

In spite of these difficulties, or perhaps because of them, great progress was made in social psychology through the fifties and sixties. In addition to the small number of topics covered by the chapters of this book, there was research on social perception, leadership, the relation between personality and social behavior, group productivity and effectiveness, affiliation, and much more. The approaches to the field of social psychology were diverse and fruitful.

But the negative aspects of the philosophical divergences were there also. Much of the field seemed to me to be fragmented. Unfruitful disagreements and controversies arose all too easily. New work that appeared could be quite ignored by others. For example, Stan Schachter's early work on emotion and affiliation (1951, 1959) was ignored for much too long. I still remember my own reaction to the review in *Contemporary Psychology* of my book on dissonance theory (1957) by Professor Solomon Asch (1958). He summarized his view of the book by declaring: "This reviewer is compelled to return a verdict of *not proven*" (italics in the original, p. 195). And I said to myself, "What an interesting choice—the other two possible verdicts in Scottish law being 'guilty' and 'not guilty.' "

Too often the notion of originality lay in finding an alternative interpretation to someone's work. At one point there must have been at least three different models of opinion change, each supported by one carefully constructed study. Although this kind of thing did not dominate the field, it was in the atmosphere and somewhat of a hindrance. Too often the approach to data was such as to make apt a recent quip by a representative of the tobacco industry, commenting on a new report about the harms and evils of cigarette smoking. The authors of that report, he said, use data and statistics the way a drunk uses a lamppost— more for support than for illumination.

As I said, this is an extremely personal view of recent history and is undoubtedly distorted. It is not bad to have independent trends, disagreements, and controversies. It lends spirit and excitement. One would not desire a monolithic approach to a subject matter. Anyone who reads the chapters in this book will readily see the cumulative progress made in a number of areas in social psychology. And it must be emphasized again that these chapters do not, in any way, represent a total statement of that progress.

The "Malaise" as Seen from Outside

I left the field of social psychology in 1964. This had nothing to do with the importance of the problems—they are very important—or with the vitality of the field—it was, and remains, vigorous. It had to do only with a conviction that had been growing in me at the time that I, personally, was in a rut and needed an injection of intellectual stimulation from new sources to continue to be productive. But the fact is that for the last fifteen years I have been pretty completely out of touch with social psychology. My friends kept telling me that social psychology was in the doldrums, was ill, was devoid of new developments. At least two of the chapters in this book, those by Zajonc and Nisbett, are in part related to understanding that period of real or imagined malaise.

Two things happened in the latter part of the sixties that had unfortunate consequences for social psychology. One of these was the particular direction that the general increase in concern with ethics took; the other was the impact of student activism and the general questioning of social values on an area of study which was substantively so close to those troubling issues.

No one would want to minimize the importance of ethical considerations. It is rather shocking to learn, for example, that persons were given large doses of a potentially dangerous substance like LSD, without their knowledge or consent, in order to explore possible military uses of such drugs. One need not even discuss such an example. But what about the well-publicized, and criticized, study on syphilis? A sample of persons who had syphilis, living in very poor rural areas with no medical attention, were randomly divided into two groups. One group was treated; the other was also followed in time but not treated. Was this an ethical violation? Is it "harming" someone, who would have had no medical attention anyway, to withhold an experimental treatment for the purpose of having a comparison group? I am not so sure about this. These persons were not harmed by the research in the sense that they were no worse off than if the research had not been done at all. But the judgment of society was that it did violate our ethics.

I don't want to dwell too long on such difficult problems, however.

In social psychology the ethical issues were much simpler. Was it ethically justifiable to require students, as part of a course, to be subjects in experiments? (This used to be, perhaps still is, a widespread and easy way to get subjects.) Was it justifiable to deceive subjects, to lie to them, in order to create desired laboratory conditions, even if, following the experiment, all was explained and discussed? Was it all right to join a public group and pretend to be ordinary members in order to observe that group? This is the kind of question that arose.

These ethical issues never seemed extraordinarily difficult to me. Students should not be required or coerced to participate in experiments only to provide the investigator with an easy way to get subjects. The investigator can expend some energy to obtain subjects who are volunteers in a true sense. On the other hand, I do not see the harm in temporarily deceiving persons in order to study some important question. Clearly one cannot investigate something like the effect of threat on social interaction without creating a real, believable threat. That's hard enough to do in the laboratory, and one certainly cannot tell the volunteer, ahead of time, that he will be deceived and lied to. On the contrary, one wants to convince him that dreadful things will indeed happen. Of course, the dreadful things do not happen and the investigator has to take seriously the responsibility for explaining what was done, why it was important to do it, and for discussing it adequately.

But enough. In none of these issues do questions of harm to the subject arise in any real form. In many years of doing experiments involving elaborate deceptions, I have never encountered an instance in which a subject felt harmed or ill used. On the contrary, with good explanation and discussion, most subjects felt that they had learned something about how and why experiments are done. Others whom I know confirm this. There is also no real issue of invasion of privacy or maintaining confidentiality that cannot be adequately and easily dealt with.

It has frequently seemed to me that the continued concern of some individuals with these issues was really an attack on empirical work in social psychology in principle. Many researchers, however, were affected by it. Why involve oneself in such problems? Instead of creating powerful and real conditions in the laboratory, it is easier and safer to present hypothetical situations on questionnaires. I think the attack on ethical matters has had a long-run impact on the field. I think that the great emphasis today on cognitive information processing in social psychology is, in part, the result of these pressures on the field. One can stay far away from ethical questions and at the same time be quantitative and precise. But it seems to me that steering clear of these difficulties keeps the field away from problems that are important and distinctive to social psychology. The chapters by Bob Zajonc and Dick Nisbett are illuminating on this issue.

Let us move on to the other development that left its mark on social psychology—the social turmoils of the late sixties. The issues that produced these upheavals and the problems addressed by them were too close to the core of social psychology for that science to remain unscathed. In the United States it seemed that at the core of the trouble was the war in Vietnam, but this cannot have been the single or even the central issue. The unpopular war provided the substance by means of which deeper, more universal concerns were manifested. After all, the same turmoil, the same dissent, the same protest movements were prevalent at the same time, perhaps even earlier, in France, Germany, Japan, Holland, and many other countries which were not involved in the Vietnam war.

The deeper issues more likely centered on basic values concerning the individual in his social milieu. Why were some groups socially, educationally, and economically disadvantaged? Why were women treated differently from men? Whence came the dicta that alcohol was okay but other drugs were not, that short hair and ties were the proper attire for men, and the like?

The cry that research should be "relevant" could not be ignored totally by researchers in a field that presumably dealt with such questions. The cries for relevance were urgent, but they were ill defined. Was research on conflict, on social comparison processes, on social perception and causal attribution relevant to these large, major issues? Distantly, I am certain the answer is yes. But "distantly" was not satisfactory. Even research that dealt more directly with practical problems was not acceptably relevant in the mood of the time. That mood demanded instant solutions to the most difficult social problems.

There were two major ways in which researchers reacted to these pressures. If one were going to continue to "play around" in the laboratory, it was more comfortable to work on problems far away from these urgent social questions. If one moved far enough away, the issue of relevance was no more severe than it would be to a biochemist working in his laboratory. The other reaction was to plunge into the real world and deal with the real issues.

However, without a backlog of scientific knowledge, scientists are no better at solving social problems than anyone else. They are only more troubled because they do not know the "truth" as securely as do others who engage in social action. And research on such global questions often ends up with disappointingly few findings. Some excellent long-term effects did grow out of this research, however. New areas such as environmental psychology and community psychology were established and developed. They are productive but difficult areas and should be more closely intertwined with the rest of social psychology.

Other, less productive, trends also grew from the headlong dash into the relevant world, however. From my biased point of view, there was some confusion between "relevant" and "newsworthy." Certainly, if some finding was picked up by the mass media, that was clear evidence that it was relevant. One can improvise a jail and have subjects volunteer (with full, informed consent, of course) to be "prisoners." One can then report some interesting reactions of certain individuals. It's an important topic and clearly newsworthy. But it's not research, does not seriously attempt to look at relations among variables, and yields no new knowledge. It's just staging a "happening."

One could insert a questionnaire on an interesting topic such as "sex," "loneliness," "shyness," "happiness" or "preposterousness" in some nationally distributed magazine and ask readers to fill it out and return it. It turns out that one can get very large numbers of replies. The data can be analyzed and reported—usually in the magazine that carried the questionnaire. But who knows how seriously the questionnaires were answered or who chose to return them and who didn't? One doesn't even know the characteristics of the population from which the highly distorted sample was drawn. But I suppose it makes no difference anyway.

Also about this time, the field had to bear the assaults of Rosenthal (1966), who questioned the trustworthiness of the results of any experiments in social psychology. Rosenthal showed that, in various kinds of experiments, the hypotheses of the experimenter influenced the results. I've always wondered why, if these spurious experimenter effects were so strong, so many of my own experiments did not show the expected results. I've also wondered how Rosenthal protected his own experiments from these pernicious effects. But others didn't seem to have these worries. If the experimenter's expectations could affect the results, even in rat studies, then what must be the impact on much more complicated experiments in social psychology? For those social psychologists who chose to work on theoretical problems in the laboratory, the "experimenter bias" attack exerted additional pressure toward simpler problems that could be handled with doubly buffered precision.

But precision of measurement and precision of experimental control are means to an end—the discovery of new knowledge. Too much emphasis on precision can lead to research which is barren. There is, in my opinion, such a thing as "premature precision"—that is, insisting on precision at the empirical level while, at the theoretical level, concepts are still somewhat vague. It is crucial to accept the notion of vagueness in discovering new knowledge. How can one insist on empirical precision at the beginning of an idea that seems important and promising? If one does, the idea will be killed; it cannot at birth live up to such demands.

The results of such pressures on, and strains within, a scientific field can have serious consequences. The questions that are posed can become very narrow and technical; research can increasingly address itself to minor unclarities in prior research rather than to larger issues; people can lose sight of the basic problems because the field becomes defined by the ongoing research. I am reminded of a luncheon conversation I had recently with a colleague. He was questioning me, persistently, about why I was currently spending so much time reading books and articles in archeology and ancient history (which I am doing). After many attempts to answer, none of which satisfied him, I tried to summarize by saying: "Well, I guess I want to see what can be inferred from different vantage points, from different data realms, about the nature, the characteristics, of this species that we call human." Whereupon he asked his last question: "But is it going to have anything to do with psychology?"

Conclusions About Social Psychology Today

In spite of the disturbances and pressures and the feelings of malaise, one can look at the period from a different perspective. In part, the later sixties and the seventies represented a period of consolidation of knowledge in social psychology, a necessary activity in any field of study. By now, controversy has receded and there is more general agreement about an established body of knowledge. I feel that in the last five years new formulations have begun to emerge as a result of the consolidation process. This is, I think, reflected in many chapters of this book, particularly the ones by Mort Deutsch and Hal Kelley. The malaise is probably over.

How does one assess the overall progress in a field as complicated as social psychology? There are, of course, some very clear examples of significant accumulation of new knowledge. We can see such instances in the chapters by Al Zander (a data base, albeit spotty, has replaced sheer "wisdom"); by Jerry Singer (the progression from "reference groups" to "social comparison processes"); by Elliot Aronson (better understanding of the durability of attitude and opinion changes); and, to some extent, in most of the other chapters. There are also, as mentioned above, some clear instances of the attainment of greater conceptual clarity.

Other kinds of developments are less clearly seen as progress—although they may be. The return to the examination of questions that had, for a period of time, been neglected (trait consistency, for example), or the questioning of the adequacy of some current approaches (as cognitive information processing) may not reflect much progress. On the other hand, however, the returns and the questioning are done with new perspectives and increased understanding of the problems involved.

The most difficult assessment of progress is the kind reflected in the chapter by Stan Schachter. Problems which once seemed appropriate to psychological inquiry turn out not to be. A long sequence of studies leads an investigator toward physiological variables and to the judgment that social psychological factors are much less important, for a given problem, than he had previously imagined. To me, this does represent progress of a very significant kind. Others may disagree, however.

How can I present my own overall evaluation of the progress of social psychology over this forty-year period and my own sense of this book? Perhaps the best way is by analogy and there is one, probably distorted by my own memory, that keeps intruding into my mind. It is a scene from the movie *The Horse's Mouth*. I have checked the book itself and that scene does not exist there, but I will describe my memory of the movie.

The main character, a rather self-willed and eccentric artist, has just finished painting a mural, unauthorized, on the wall of an apartment whose owners are away on vacation. In the process he has pawned furniture, fixtures—everything pawnable from the apartment—to pay for his oils, brushes, and models, scrupulously putting every pawn ticket in a jar. He is now about to leave. The apartment is a chaotic mess, but he has finished the mural. He opens the door to depart, looks back at the mural, which is later to be considered a masterpiece, and says: "It's not exactly what I had in mind."

References

Adorno, T. W., Frenkel-Brunswik, E., Levinson, D. J., & Sanford, R. N. *The authoritarian personality.* New York: Harper & Row, 1950.

Allport, G. W. *Personality: A psychological interpretation.* New York: Holt, 1937.

ASCH, S. E. Review of "A theory of cognitive dissonance." *Contemp. Psychol.*, 1958, **3**, 194–195.

BACK, K. Influence through social communication. *J. abnorm. soc. Psychol.*, 1951, **8**, 251–274.

BAVELAS, A. Morale and the training of leaders. In Watson, G. (ed.). *Civilian morale*. Boston: Houghton-Mifflin, 1942.

BEM , D. J. & FUNDER, D. C. Predicting more of the people more of the time. *Psychol. Rev.*, 1978, **85**, 485–501.

CAMPBELL, A., EBERHART, S., & WOODWARD, P. *Public reactions to the atomic bomb and world affairs. Part II: Findings of the intensive surveys*. Ithaca: Cornell University Press, 1947, pp. 80–310.

CANTRIL, H. *Invasion from Mars*. Princeton: Princeton University Press, 1940.

FESTINGER, L. *A theory of cognitive dissonance*. Stanford, Calif.: Stanford University Press, 1957.

FESTINGER , L. & KATZ, D. *Research methods in the behavioral sciences*. New York: Dryden, 1953.

HARTSHORNE, H. & MAY, M. *Studies in deceit*. New York: Macmillan, 1928.

HERTZMAN, M. & FESTINGER, L. Shifts in explicit goals in a level of aspiration experiment. *J. exp. Psychol.*, 1490, **27**, 439–452.

HOVLAND, C. I., JANIS, I. L., & KELLEY, H. H. *Communication and persuasion*. New Haven: Yale University Press, 1953.

HOVLAND, C. I., LUMSDAINE, A. A., & SHEFFIELD, F. D. *Experiments on mass communication*. Princeton: Princeton University Press, 1949.

HULL, C. L. *Principles of behavior*. New York: Appleton-Century-Crofts, 1943.

LAZARSFELD, P. F., BERELSON, B., & GAUDET, H. *The people's choice*. New York: Duell, Sloan and Pearce, 1944.

LEWIN, K. *Dynamic theory of personality*. New York: McGraw-Hill, 1935, pp. 1–42.

———. Formalization and progress in psychology. *University of Iowa Studies in Child Welfare*, 1940, **16**, 3, 9–42.

———. Forces behind food habits and methods of change. *Bull. Nat. Res. Council*, 1943, **108**, 35–65.

———. *Field theory in social science*. New York: Harper, 1951.

LEWIN, K., LIPPIT, R., & WHITE, R. Patterns of aggressive behavior in experimentally created "social climates." *J. soc. Psychol.*, 1939, **10**, 271–299.

LIPPITT, R. An experimental study of authoritarian and democratic group atmospheres. *University of Iowa Studies in Child Welfare*, 1940, **16**, 45–195.

———. *Training in community relations*. New York: Harper, 1949.

LIPPITT, R. & WHITE, R. The "social climate" of children's groups. In Barker, R., Kounin, J., & Wright, H. (eds.). *Child behavior and development*. New York: McGraw-Hill, 1943.

McClelland, D. C., Atkinson, J. W., Clark, R. A., & Lowell, E. L. *The achievement motive.* New York: Appleton-Century-Crofts, 1953.

Newcomb, T. M. *Consistency of certain extrovert-introvert behavior patterns in 51 problem boys.* New York: Columbia University, Teachers College, Bureau of Publications, 1929.

————. *Personality and social change.* New York: Dryden, 1943.

Rosenthal, R. *Experimenter effects in behavioral research.* New York: Appleton-Century-Crofts, 1966.

Schachter, S. Deviation, rejection and communication. *J. abnorm. soc. Psychol.*, 1951, **46**, 190–207.

————. *The psychology of affiliation.* Stanford: Stanford University Press, 1959.

Sherif, M. A study of some social factors in perception. *Arch. Psychol.* 1935, No. 187.

Spence, K. W. The postulates and methods of behaviorism. *Psychol. Rev.*, 1948, **55**, 67–78.

Thorndike, E. L. The law of effect. *Amer. J. Psychol.*, 1927, **39**, 212–222.

PART
H
BIBLIOGRAPHY

Published Works
of Leon Festinger

In Chronological Order

HERTZMAN, M., & FESTINGER, L. Shifts in explicit goals in a level of aspiration experiment. *J. exp. Psychol.*, 1940. **27,** 439–452.

FESTINGER, L. Wish, expectation, and group standards as factors influencing level of aspiration. *J. abnorm. soc. Psychol.*, 1942, **37,** 184–200.

FESTINGER, L. A theoretical interpretation of shifts in level of aspiration. *Psychol. Rev.*, 1942, **49,** 235–250.

FESTINGER, L. Development of differential appetite in the rat. *J. exp. Psychol.*, 1943, **32,** 266–234.

FESTINGER, L. Studies in decision: I. Decision-time, relative frequency of judgment, and subjective confidence as related to physical stimulus difference. *J. exp. Psychol.*, 1943, **32,** 291–306.

FESTINGER, L. Studies in decision: II. An empirical test of quantitative theory of decision. *J. exp. Psychol.*, 1943, **32,** 411–423.

FESTINGER, L. An exact test of significance for means of samples drawn from populations with an exponential frequency distribution. *Psychometrika,* 1943, **8,** 153–160.

CARTWRIGHT, D., & FESTINGER, L. A quantitative theory of decision. *Psychol. Rev.*, 1943, **50,** 595–621.

FESTINGER, L. A statistical test for means of samples from skew populations. *Psychometrika*, 1943, **8,** 205–210.

LEWIN, K., DEMBO, T., FESTINGER, L., & SEARS, P. Level of aspiration. In Hunt, J. McV. (ed.). *Personality and the behavior disorders.* New York: Ronald Press, 1944.

FESTINGER, L. The significance of difference between means without reference to the frequency distribution function. *Psychometrika,* 1946, **11** (2).

FESTINGER, L. The treatment of qualitative data by "scale analysis." *Psychol. Bull.*, 1947, **44,** 149–161.

FESTINGER, L. The role of group belongingness in a voting situation. *Hum. Relat.*, 1947, **1,** 154–180.

FESTINGER, L., CARTWRIGHT, D., et al. A study of a rumor: its origin and spread. *Hum. Relat.*, 1948, **1,** 464–486.

FESTINGER, L. The analysis of sociograms using matrix algebra. *Hum. Relat.*, 1949, **2,** 153–158.

FESTINGER, L. Laboratory experiments: The role of group belongingness. In *Experiments in social process.* New York: McGraw-Hill, 1950, pp. 31–48.

FESTINGER, L. Informal social communication. *Psychol. Rev.*, 1950, **57,** 271–282.

FESTINGER, L., SCHACHTER, S., & BACK, K. *Social pressures in informal groups: A study of human factors in housing.* New York: Harper & Bros., 1950.

BACK, K., FESTINGER, L., HYMOVITCH, B., KELLEY, H., SCHACHTER, S., & THIBAUT, J. The methodology of studying rumor transmission. *Hum. Relat.*, 1950, **3,** 307–312.

FESTINGER, L. Current developments in group dynamics. *Social work in the current scene.* New York: Columbia University Press, 1950, pp. 253–265.

FESTINGER, L., et al. *Theory and experiment in social communications: Collected papers.* Ann Arbor: Institute for Social Research, 1950.

FESTINGER, L., & THIBAUT, J. Interpersonal communication in small groups. *J. abnorm. soc. Psychol.*, 1951, **46,** 92–99.

FESTINGER, L. Informal communications in small groups. In Guetzkow, H. (ed.). *Groups, leadership and men.* Pittsburgh: Carnegie Press, 1951.

FESTINGER, L. Assumptions underlying the use of statistical techniques. Jahoda, M., Deutsch, M., & Cook, S. W. (eds). *Research methods in social relations,* Part II. New York: Dryden Press, 1951.

FESTINGER, L. Architecture and group membership. *J. soc. Issues,* 1951, **7,** 152–163.

FESTINGER, L., & KELLEY, H. *Changing attitudes through social contact.* Ann Arbor: Institute for Social Research, University of Michigan, 1951.

FESTINGER, L., PEPITONE, A., & NEWCOMB, T. Some consequences of de-individuation in a group. *J. abnorm. soc. Psychol.*, 1952, **47,** 382–389.

FESTINGER, L., GERARD, H. B., HYMOVITCH, B., KELLEY, H. H., & RAVEN, B. H. The influence process in the presence of extreme deviates. *Hum. Relat.*, 1952, **5,** 327–346.

FESTINGER, L., & KATZ, D. (eds.). *Research methods in the behavioral sciences.* New York: Dryden Press, 1953.

FESTINGER, L., & KATZ, D. (eds.). Laboratory experiments. *Research methods in the behavioral sciences.* New York: Dryden Press, 1953.

FESTINGER, L. An analysis of compliant behavior. In Sherif M., & Wilson, M. O. (eds.). *Group relations at the crossroads.* New York: Harper and Bros., 1953.

FESTINGER, L. A theory of social comparison processes. *Hum. Relat.,* 1954, **7,** 117–140.

HOFFMAN, P. J., FESTINGER, L., & LAWRENCE, D. H. Tendencies toward group comparability in competitive bargaining. *Hum. Relat.,* 1954, **7,** 141–160.

FESTINGER, L., TORREY, J., & WILLERMAN, B. Self-evaluation as a function of attraction to the group. *Hum. Relat.,* 1954, **7,** 161–174.

FESTINGER, L. Motivations leading to social behavior. In Jones, M. R. (ed.). *Nebraska Symposium on Motivation.* University of Nebraska Press, 1954, pp. 191–218.

FESTINGER, L., & HUTTE, H. An experimental investigation of the effect of unstable interpersonal relations in a group. *J. abnorm. soc. Psychol.,* 1954, **49,** 513–522.

FESTINGER, L. Social psychology and group processes. *Ann. Rev. Psychol.,* 1955, **6,** 187–216.

FESTINGER, L., RIECKEN, H., & SCHACHTER, S. *When prophecy fails.* Minneapolis: University of Minnesota Press, 1956.

FESTINGER, L., & BREHM, J. Pressures toward uniformity of performance in groups. *Hum. Relat.,* 1957, **10,** 85–91.

FESTINGER, L. The relation between behavior and cognition. In *Contemporary approaches to cognition.* Cambridge: Harvard University Press, 1957.

FESTINGER, L. *A theory of cognitive dissonance.* Evanston, Ill.: Row, Peterson, 1957.

FESTINGER, L. The motivating effect of cognitive dissonance. In Lindzey, G. (ed.). *Assessment of human motives.* New York: Rinehart & Co., 1958.

FESTINGER, L., & CARLSMITH, J. M. Cognitive consequences of forced compliance. *J. abnorm. soc. Psychol.,* 1959, **58,** 203–211.

FESTINGER, L., & ARONSON, E. Arousal and reduction of dissonance in social contexts. In Cartwright, D., & Zander, A. (eds.). *Group Dynamics.* Evanston, Ill.: Row, Peterson, 1960, pp. 214–231.

FESTINGER, L., & ALLYN, J. The effectiveness of unanticipated persuasive communications. *J. abnorm. soc. Psychol.,* 1961, **62,** 35–40.

FESTINGER, L., SCHACHTER, S., WILLERMAN, B., & HYMAN, R. Emotional disruption and industrial productivity. *J. applied Psychol.,* 1961, **45,** 201–213.

YARYAN, R. B., & FESTINGER, L. Preparatory action and belief in the probable occurrence of future events. *J. abnorm. soc. Psychol.*, 1961, **63,** 603–606.

FESTINGER, L. The psychological effects of insufficient reward. *Amer. Psychologist,* 1961, **16,** 1–12.

FESTINGER, L. Cognitive dissonance. *Scientific American,* 1962, **207,** 93–102.

WALSTER, E., & FESTINGER, L. The effectiveness of "overheard" persuasive communication. *J. abnorm. soc. Psychol.*, 1962, **65,** 395–402.

FESTINGER, L., & LAWRENCE, D. H. *Deterrents and reinforcement: The psychology of insufficient reward.* Stanford: Stanford Univ. Press, 1962.

FESTINGER, L., & BRAMEL, D. The reactions of humans to cognitive dissonance. In Bachrach, A. (ed.). *Experimental foundations of clinical psychology.* New York: Basic Books, 1962, 255–279.

FESTINGER, L., & MACCOBY, N. On resistance of persuasive communications. *J. abnorm. soc. Psychol.*, 1964, **68,** 359–366.

FESTINGER, L. Behavioral support for opinion change. *Public Opinion Quarterly,* 1964, **28,** 404–417.

FESTINGER, L. *Conflict, decision and dissonance.* Stanford: Stanford University Press, 1964.

FESTINGER, L. & FREEDMAN, J. L. Dissonance reduction and moral values. In Worchel, P., & Byrne, D. (eds.). Personality change. New York: Wiley, 1964, 220–243.

FESTINGER, L., & CANON, L. K. Information about spatial location based on knowledge about efference. *Psychol. Rev.,* 165, **72,** 373–384.

FESTINGER, L., BURNHAM, C. A., ONO, H., & BAMBER, D. Efference and the conscious experience of perception. *J. exp. Psychol.,* 1967, **74,** no. 4, part 2, 1–36.

COREN, S., & FESTINGER, L. An alternative view of the "Gibson normalization effect." *Perception & Psychophysics,* 1967, **2,** 621–626.

FESTINGER, L., WHITE, C. W., & ALLYN, M. R. Eye movements and decrement in the Müller-Lyer illusion. *Perception & Psychophysics,* 1968, **3,** 376–82.

FESTINGER, L. Neurophysiological coding for the perception of color. In *Perception and its disorders.* Res. publ. A.R.N.M.D. vol. XLVIII, 1970, The Association for Research in Nervous & Mental Disease, 26–34.

FESTINGER, L., COREN, S., & RIVERS, G. The effect of attention on brightness contrast and assimilation. *Amer. J. Psychol.,* 1970, **83,** 189–207.

FESTINGER, L. Eye movements and perception. In Bach-Y-Rita, P., Collins, C. C., & Hyde, J. E. (eds.). *The control of eye movements.* New York: Academic Press, 1971, pp. 259–273.

FESTINGER, L., ALLYN, M. R., & WHITE, C. W. The perception of color with achromatic stimulation. *Vision Res.*, 1971, **11,** 591–612.

KOMODA, M. K., FESTINGER, L., PHILLIPS, L. J., DUCKMAN, R. H., & YOUNG, R. A. Some observations concerning saccadic eye movements. *Vision Res.*, 1973, **13,** 1009–1020.

BRUSSEL, E. M., & FESTINGER, L. The Gelb effect; brightness contrast plus attention. *Amer. J. Psychol.*, 1973, **86,** 225–235.

FESTINGER, L., & EASTON, A. M. Inferences about the efferent system based on a perceptual illusion produced by eye movements. *Psychol. Rev.*, 1974, **81,** 44–58.

FESTINGER, L. Perceiving the path of a moving object. In *Proceedings of XXth International Congress of Psychology,* 1972, Tokyo, Japan. Science Council of Japan, University of Tokyo Press, 1974, pp. 126–134.

SEDGWICK, H. A., & FESTINGER, L. Eye movements, efference, and visual perception. In Monty, R. A., & Senders, J. W. (eds.). *Eye movement and psychological processes.* New York: Wiley, 1976, pp. 221–230.

FESTINGER, L., SEDGWICK, H. A., & HOLTZMAN, J. D. Visual perception during smooth pursuit eye movements. *Vision Res.*, 1976, **16,** 1377–1386.

MILLER, J., & FESTINGER, L. Impact of oculomotor retraining on the visual perception of curvature. *J. exp. Psychol.*, 1977, **3,** 187–200.

KOMODA, M. K., FESTINGER, L., & SHERRY, J. The accuracy of two-dimensional saccades in the absence of continuing retinal stimulation. *Vision Res.*, 1977, **17,** 1231–1232.

HOLTZMAN, J., SEDGWICK, H., & FESTINGER, L. Interaction of perceptually monitored and unmonitored efferent commands for smooth pursuit eye movements. *Vision Res.*, 1978, **18,** 1545–1555.

FESTINGER, L., & HOLTZMAN, J. Retinal image smear as a source of information about magnitude of eye movement. *J. exp. Psychol.*, 1978, **4,** 573–585.

FESTINGER, L. Sozialpsychologie: Bindeglied zwischen Verhaltens- und Sozial-wissenschaften. *Z. Sozialpsychologie,* 1979, **10,** 214–219.

FESTINGER, L. (ed.). *Retrospections on social psychology.* New York: Oxford University Press, 1980.

FESTINGER, L. Looking backward. In *Retrospections on social psychology.* New York: Oxford University Press, 1980.

FESTINGER, L. Human nature and human competence. *Soc. Res.*, summer, 1981, **48,** 2, 306–321.

FESTINGER, L. *The human legacy.* New York: Columbia University Press, 1983.

Name Index

Subject Index

A

abilities: discrepancies of, in groups, 144–149, 150–153, 156, 157–158; drive to evaluate, 134–135, 148, 149–150; evaluation of, by comparison, 135–136, 138–142; and group formation, 155–157; non-social constraints on, 143–144; unidirectional drive upward, 142–143
achievement: academic, and discrepancy scores, 57; following pattern, 55, 58; past, 78
action: and belief, 259; goal, 37–38, 39; goal, and reality, 48–49, 80; level, 67; research, 553
activity structure, 74
aesthetic activities, 416
affect, 557
affective judgments, 107
affiliation, 558
alternatives: attractiveness of, 233, 234–235; qualitative dissimilarity of, 240
ambiguity, 556
ambition, 56
American Indian, 419–420
anthropology, 418–419, 422
"anxiety provoking" vs. "anxiety justifying" rumors, 202
applied psychology, 551
area of no-decision, 96
aspiration, 558; first study on, 548; group, 46; influence of wish, expectation and group standards on, 3–20; personality traits and, 56–60; rudimentary, 60–61; secondary measures of, 51; theoretical considerations, 62–85; theoretical interpretation of shifts in level of, 21–34. See also level of aspiration

association, laws of, 549
attainment: discrepancy, 36, 38, 39; transfer of, 41–43
attention, divided, 464–465
attitude: measurement of, 556; and rejection measures, 505–507
attraction to group, 150–151, 161
"atypical" cases, 41
Australian aborigines, 429
Authoritarian Personality, The (Adorno et al.), 553, 555–556
authority, 533, 553
autocratic and democratic atmospheres, 511–512, 525, 527, 548, 550

B

Babylonians, 435
bargaining, 176–197
behavior(al): -attitude change, 258; cognitive elements, 215, 217, 221–222; possiblities restricted in experiments, 534–536
behaviorism, 308, 557–558
beliefs, disconfirmation of, 259–260
bias, 470, 481; experimenter, 562
binocular rivalry, 316
blank-out, 320
boat construction, 431
boundaries, 548; of group, redefining, 163, 171; and zone of ability, 78
bronze, 430

C

California, University of, 553
Cartesian theory, 111
case study problem, 171, 172